Applied Structural Equation Modeling Using AMOS

This is an essential how-to guide on the application of structural equation modeling (SEM) techniques with the AMOS software, focusing on the practical applications of both simple and advanced topics.

Written in an easy-to-understand conversational style, the book covers everything from data collection and screening to confirmatory factor analysis, structural model analysis, mediation, moderation, and more advanced topics such as mixture modeling, censored data, and non-recursive models. Through step-by-step instructions, screen shots, and suggested guidelines for reporting, Collier cuts through abstract definitional perspectives to give insight on how to actually run analysis. Unlike other SEM books, the examples used will often start in SPSS and then transition to AMOS so that the reader can have full confidence in running the analysis from beginning to end. Best practices are also included on topics like how to determine if your SEM model is formative or reflective, making it not just an explanation of SEM topics, but a guide for researchers on how to develop a strong methodology while studying their respective phenomenon of interest.

With a focus on practical applications of both basic and advanced topics, and with detailed work-through examples throughout, this book is ideal for experienced researchers and beginners across the behavioral and social sciences.

Joel E. Collier, Ph.D., is the Tommy and Terri Nusz Professor of Marketing at Mississippi State University, USA. He is also Ph.D. Director for doctoral studies in the Department of Marketing. Dr. Collier teaches structural equation modeling on the doctoral level and has published numerous articles in the top journals of his field using this technique. He has also worked as a consultant for the following firms: Time Warner, Muvico, Reeds Jewelers, Cashman Photo, and the Carolina Hurricanes professional hockey team.

Applied Structural Equation Modeling Using AMOS

Basic to Advanced Techniques

Joel E. Collier

NEW YORK AND LONDON

First published 2020
by Routledge
52 Vanderbilt Avenue, New York, NY 10017

and by Routledge
2 Park Square, Milton Park, Abingdon, Oxon, OX14 4RN

Routledge is an imprint of the Taylor & Francis Group, an informa business

Library of Congress Cataloging-in-Publication Data
A catalog record for this book has been requested

ISBN: 978-0-367-86329-6 (hbk)
ISBN: 978-0-367-43526-4 (pbk)
ISBN: 978-1-003-01841-4 (ebk)

Typeset in Perpetua
by Apex CoVantage, LLC

Contents

Preface ix
Acknowledgments xi

1 **Introduction to Structural Equation Modeling** 1
What Is Structural Equation Modeling? 1
Basics of SEM Input: The Covariance Matrix 2
Correlations Between Constructs 4
Is SEM Causal Modeling? 6
A Confirmatory Approach to SEM 7
Theory Should Lead Conceptualization 8
Assumptions of SEM 8
SEM Software 9
Understanding Diagram Symbols 9
Independent vs. Dependent Latent Variables 11
How to Measure an Unobserved Construct 11
Greek Notation and SEM 13

2 **Data Screening, Assessing Reliability, Validity, and Identification** 17
Data Screening 17
Screening for Impermissible Values in the Data 19
How Do I Assess If I Have Missing Data? 21
How Do I Address Missing Data? 23
Assessing Reliability 25
Identification With SEM Models 29
How Do I Calculate the Degrees of Freedom? 30
What Do I Do if My Model Is Under-Identified? 32
Sample Size: How Much Is Enough? 33
Understanding the Validity of Measures 33

3 **Understanding the AMOS Program** 36
Overview of the AMOS Graphics Window 36
AMOS Functions Listed as Icons in Pinned Ribbon 38

Tips to Using AMOS More Efficiently 53
Quick Reference to AMOS Functions 59

4 Measurement Model Analysis 62
Introduction to Confirmatory Factor Analysis 62
How Is a CFA Different From an EFA? 63
Interpretation of Factor Loadings 64
Setting the Metric 65
Model Fit and Fit Statistics 65
Modification Indices 68
CFA Example in AMOS 71
Assessing Convergent and Discriminant Validity of Your Measures 83
If I Have a Weak Factor Loading, Should I Drop It? 87
How to Calculate Composite Reliability 87
What If I Have a Standardized Factor Loading Greater Than 1? 88
How Do I Report My CFA Results? 89
Measurement Model Invariance Across Groups 90
Full vs. Partial Metric Invariance 98
How Do I Know Which Parameter to Free in a Partial Invariance Test? 98
Common Method Bias 102
What If My Test for Common Method Bias Is Significant? 108
What if My Common Method Bias Test Is Non-Significant? 109
What Is a Second Order Confirmatory Factor Analysis Model? 109
Reflective vs. Formative Indicators 110
Potential Identification Problems With Formative Indicators 113
Dependent Relationships With Formative Constructs 115
Higher Order Formative Construct Example 116
How Do I Present the Result of My Higher Order Formative Model? 122
Error Messages in AMOS 122

5 Path and Full Structural Models 128
Path Analysis 128
Can I Use a Correlation Matrix as My Data Input? 133
Full Structural Model Analysis 137
How Do I Report My Full Structural Model Results? 142
Using Specification Search to Aid in Model Trimming and Fit 143
What Are Alternative Models, and Why Should I Be Concerned With Them? 146
How Do I Add a Control Variable to My Structural Model? 147
Two Group Analysis 149
What if I Have More Than Two Groups in My Analysis? 161
When I Try to Run My Structural Analysis, I Get an Error Message About My Matrix Not Being Positive Definite 161
Can I Correlate the Error Terms of Two Unobservable Constructs in a Full Structural Model? 162

How Do I Present the Results of My Two Group Analysis? 162
How Do I Search for Multivariate Outliers? 162
How Do I Determine if My Data Is Not *Normally Distributed (Non-Normal)?* 165
What if I Get an Error Message in the Analysis That Says "Iteration Limit Reached"? 166

6 Mediation 170
Introduction to Mediation 170
How to Test for Mediation 172
How Do I Report the Results of My Mediation Test? 180
Can I Use a Correlation Matrix or Summary Data to Test Mediation in AMOS? 181
What if I Have Multiple Mediators in My Model? 182
How Do I Test Serial Mediation? 188
Setting the Seed in Bootstrapping 194

7 Moderation 197
Introduction to Moderation 197
Probing the Interaction 202
Testing Moderation in a Full Structural Model 207
How Do I Present My Moderation Results? 219
Mean Center vs. Z Score in Moderation Testing 221
Moderation Testing With a Categorical Moderator 223
Calculating Categorical Moderation via Pairwise Parameter Comparison 227
Moderated Mediation With a Continuous Moderator 229
How Do I Report the Results of My Moderated Mediation Test? 234
Moderated Mediation With a Categorical Moderator 234

8 Using Categorical Independent Variables in SEM 240
Binary Categorical Variables in SEM 240
Mediation with Binary Categorical Independent Variables 242
Multicategorical Independent Variables in SEM 244
Mediation With Multicategorical Independent Variables 247
Moderated Mediation With a Multicategorical Independent Variable 251
How Do I Report the Results of My Multicategorical Moderated Mediation Test? 256

9 Latent Growth Curve Models 260
Introduction to Latent Growth Curve Models 260
Including Predictors Into a Latent Growth Curve Model 269
How Do I Present My Latent Growth Curve Results? 273
Latent Growth Curves With Nonlinear Patterns 274
Latent Growth Curves Across Two Domains 277

10 Advanced Topics in SEM 282
Using Weighted Scores in AMOS 282
How to Use Bootstrapping to Account for Non-Normal Data 287

Mixture Modeling 293
Analyzing Censored Data 302
Non-Recursive Models (Feedback Loops) 310
Post-Hoc Power Analysis 317
Using Specification Search to Perform Exploratory Factor Analysis 317
How to Use Plugins to Create a Model Instead of Drawing a Model in AMOS 323
How to Use the Program Editor to Conceptualize Your Model and Run the Analysis 338

Appendix: Table of Chi-Square Statistics 347
Index 348

Preface

I remember my first exposure to structural equation modeling (SEM) as a doctoral student thinking, "Who in their right mind would want to use this?". I was using a software program that was all coding, and it seemed like I spent more time looking for that missing apostrophe in the code than I did trying to conceptualize the model. My overall thoughts were initially that SEM was unnecessarily complicated and the coding for many advanced functions was a mystery. Fast forward a couple of years and I decided to write a dissertation that was going to require structural equation modeling. Thankfully, my mentor introduced me to a SEM software called AMOS that allowed the user to have the option of using syntax code or a graphical interface to conceptualize a SEM model. I was surprised at how easy it was to conceptualize and test a model in AMOS. The graphical interface of AMOS was intuitive, and I could conceptualize and even alter a model in a third of the time using other SEM programs. From that point, I started to really love the topic of structural equation modeling. I was a researcher on fire to know more and more about SEM and specifically how to run basic and complex analyses in AMOS.

When I decided to write this book, I wanted to take a very different approach than existing books on the topic. A lot of books dig into the theoretical details of SEM, but very few explain how to apply the different techniques of SEM to your research. I wrote this book as a guide for researchers to use SEM to further their work. I believe in providing a detailed but concise explanation of a SEM topic and then focusing on the step-by-step instructions on how to run the analysis, highlight where the important results are in the output, and ultimately, provide guidelines on how to present the final results. If you are looking to get into the mathematical minutiae of SEM, then you are better off seeking other resources on the topic. This book is going to focus on the practical application of how to use AMOS to better understand your phenomenon of interest. For simplicity and clarity, I am going to primarily use a consumer behavior example throughout the book. Though we may be in many different research fields, we are all consumers, and the example I consistently use is a consumer in a retail/service environment. These easy-to-understand examples should aid in understanding issues of measurement and relationship testing throughout the book. Lastly, this book is purposely written in a conversational style to make complex concepts easy to grasp. I am not going to display statistical gymnastics just to prove how much I know, but I focus on the easiest and simplest method to explain a concept and how to perform a SEM technique in AMOS. I have always been a fan of finding simple ways to describe complex issues. My ultimate goal is for you to easily grasp the concept and how to independently run an analysis in your area of interest.

The book is organized in five sections. The first section can be classified as an introduction to SEM and the AMOS software. In Chapter 1, I initially discuss what SEM is and what advantages it has over other statistical techniques. I will also introduce the different terminology used in SEM along with diagramming symbols. The chapter will introduce the basic concepts of SEM along with assumptions of using this statistical technique. In Chapter 2, I talk about the importance of data screening before using the AMOS software. The old saying of "garbage in, garbage out" is so true in statistical analysis techniques like AMOS. Hence, I talk about how to screen your data, assessing reliability of measures, how to handle missing data, and understanding the different types of validity with your measurement items. The last chapter in this section (Chapter 3) is an introduction to the AMOS software. I provide detail examples of how to use the software and also include a section on tips to being more efficient using AMOS.

The second section of the book (Chapter 4) is concerned with measurement model analysis. In this section, I detail how to run a confirmatory factory analysis, understanding measurement model invariance, how to handle potential bias like common method bias, and how to address more complex measurement concerns like higher order models with reflective and formative indicators.

The third section (Chapter 5) focuses on the relationships between constructs. Structural relationships are explained through both path and full structural modeling. Model trimming and addressing alternative models is presented along with a discussion on how to include control variables. Lastly, the chapter explains how to run a two group analysis along with determining if you have multivariate outliers or non-normal data.

The fourth section examines mediation and moderation in a SEM model. In Chapter 6, the topic of mediation is introduced. I discuss how to assess mediation using a bootstrapping method and discuss how to run different types of mediation like parallel and serial mediation. In Chapter 7, I introduce the topic of moderation and discuss how to perform moderation testing with continuous and categorical variables. The chapter progresses to more advanced topics such as probing a moderated influence along with moderated mediation testing. In Chapter 8, I address how to test a SEM model using categorical independent variables. This discussion starts with binary categories and progresses to multiple categorical fields that have three or more categories.

The fifth and final section addresses more advanced topics in SEM. In Chapter 9, latent growth curves are addressed as well as how to assess linear and curvilinear growth curves. The last chapter (Chapter 10) will cover a wide range of advanced topics such as how to use weighted scores, how to run a SEM analysis with non-normal data, mixture modeling, using censored data, and non-recursive modeling. The end of this chapter is dedicated to those researchers that would like to code their SEM model. Instructions and examples are given on how to use coding to conceptualize and run an analysis in AMOS.

Acknowledgments

I have numerous people to thank for making this book a reality. The encouragement of my family is immeasurable. My wife, Heather, has always been my biggest supporter and has a knack of spurring me to do more than I think I can. To her credit, she never complained when I would constantly ask her to read a paragraph and tell me if it makes sense. I'm thankful for two understanding sons, Luke and Thomas. They had to sacrifice a lot of "Daddy time" at nights and weekends while I was writing this book.

I don't think this book gets written if it was not for the constant encouragement of my current and former doctoral students asking me to write this book. When I first started teaching structural equation modeling, I initially wrote the first version of this book. It was really more like a 95-page manual that I thought would be a good aide for students to understand the subject. Each year, I would get students asking me if I was going to turn this into a book and each year I would say no, that is a huge undertaking. Every time I taught the class, I added a little more to the document and each time the students kept telling me this needs to be turned into a book because it would really help researchers figure out how to run their unique analysis. I did not seriously consider writing the book until someone I did not know approached me at a conference and said she had got a copy of my SEM manual used in class and could not thank me enough for giving her a tool to finally understand structural equation modeling. That day, I decided that I was going to start writing a full book on the subject. Without the encouragement of my current and former doctoral students, I don't think that initial 95-page document ever gets turned into a full book.

I think inspiration comes in many ways, but it seems to come with more frequency when I am around my fellow colleagues. I have a group of friends affectionately called the "Dirt People" who have been a great resource through this whole process. One of my colleagues, Adam Farmer, is a straight shooter and that is what we love about him. I told him over lunch that I was going to write this book and he asked what is the title going to be? I told him and he said that is a weird title for a book. Why don't you just call it Applied Structural Equation Modeling. After a brief discussion, I agreed, and the title of the book was settled on over lunch. Other colleagues who have supported me in countless ways include Mike Breazeale, Carol Esmark Jones, Kevin Shanahan, Frank Adams, Rob Moore, Jason Lueg, Nicole Ponder and many more.

A debt of gratitude goes to Mississippi State University and, specifically, to Melissa Moore who encouraged me to write this book and also supported me in getting a sabbatical. This book would have taken me twice as long to write without her giving me dedicated time focus on the book. She was incredible through the whole process and has always tried to help me in any professional capacity. She believed in me from the very beginning that I could make this book a reality. A special thanks also needs to be extended to my Dean, Sharon Oswald, for also supporting me in the writing process and encouraging me to write this book.

I would also like to thank my current and former coauthors. Many of our research projects spurred me to learn new and different SEM techniques that were often out of my comfort zone. Those coauthors include Donald Barnes, Alex Krallman, Mark Pelletier, Allyn Cascio, Sherly Kimes, Bob Barnwell, Jennifer Stevens, Stacie Waites, Tyler Hancock, Christian Barney, Brett Kazandjian, and numerous others. A special thanks needs to be given to Shannon Westlake. She was instrumental in the early drafts and was a great resource to producing a strong final product.

Finally, I would like to thank Lucy McClune at Taylor and Francis. From the very beginning, Lucy could see the value of this book and how it could help researchers in various fields. I am sure it was not an easy task convincing her boss why a marketing professor, who is not a formal statistician, should be the next author to publish a structural equation modeling book at Taylor and Francis. Lucy fought for me and the vision of the book I wanted to write. She has been great through the whole process and I owe her special debt of gratitude. Similarly, I would like to thank Kate Fornadel and the team of associates at Apex CoVantage. This book was a nightmare in regards to the layout and I was quite particular in the details throughout the book. Kate was especially accommodating and ultimately kept revising the book until I was happy with the final output. I am grateful for her and everyone who helped in this process along the way.

Chapter 1

Introduction to Structural Equation Modeling

What Is Structural Equation Modeling?

Structural equation modeling, or SEM, is a statistical method that examines the relationships among numerous variables in a simultaneous way. SEM is not considered a single procedure but rather a family of related statistical techniques. This family of analysis techniques examines the measurement properties of a variable along with the interrelationships between variables and is often seen as a combination of regression and factor analysis. The use of SEM will often take a confirmatory approach in which the researcher has proposed a "model" of relationships between variables of interest and examines whether the observed data will provide evidence of directionality and significance of the relationships. SEM is very similar to multiple regression but is much more robust and has greater flexibility in the analysis. SEM allows you to model multiple independent and dependent variables, error terms, interactions, and correlations. Using a SEM model will also let you denote which independent variables will influence dependent variables, and subsequently, let dependent variables be independent variables in other relationships.

Structural equation modeling is fundamentally built around the idea of modeling, or drawing a model that represents relationships between variables. This model will use symbols to represent variables, relationships between variables, and even error in your model. While drawing a model is easy to do and can help a researcher conceptualize and understand a phenomenon of interest, what we are really doing with this modeling approach is specifying mathematical equations between variables. The use of symbols makes an extremely complicated set of simultaneous mathematical equations easy for the researcher to understand. Later in this chapter, I will introduce and explain in detail the various symbols used in SEM.

The main advantages of structural equation modeling compared to other techniques are (1) it lets you analyze the influence of predictor variables on numerous dependent variables simultaneously, (2) it allows you to account for measurement error and even addresses error in predicting relationships, and (3) it is capable of testing an entire model instead of just focusing on individual relationships. This is in direct contrast to similar techniques like regression that can test only one dependent variable at a time, does not account for measurement error, and focuses on singular relationships instead of the collective whole.

Basics of SEM Input: The Covariance Matrix

For the purposes of this book, I will strictly use a covariance-based approach to structural equation modeling. This method is the most robust for theory testing and assessing the "structure" of a specified model along with its relationships. Before we move forward, a discussion is warranted on concepts such as variance, covariance, and correlation so we are all clear on the fundamental foundation that SEM operates in the analysis.

Variance of a construct—The term variance describes how spread out the values (responses/observations) are in a concept you are measuring. You can calculate this by finding the mean of all your observations and then taking the distance from the mean to a record (response/observation) and squaring that value. You then take the average of all squared differences from the mean to get the variance. This is usually a large number and has little interpretation; but if you take the square root of this number, you get the standard deviation from the mean, and this is useful. The standard deviation is typically what is used to discuss the amount of dispersion or variation in trying to measure a concept.

Covariance between constructs—Covariance is the measure of how much two variables change together. If greater values of one variable correspond to greater values in another variable, you have a positive covariance. If greater values in one variable correspond to lower values in another variable, then you have a negative covariance value. The main function of a covariance analysis is to determine directionality of two variables. If the covariance is positive, then the two variables will move in the same direction. If the covariance is negative, the two variables will move in opposite directions. One of the primary assumptions in SEM is that the relationship between constructs follows a linear pattern. Put another way, if you ran a scatter plot of the values of two variables, the data would be in a line pattern that was increasing upward or decreasing downward. The function of a covariance analysis is simply to assess if the relationship between two variables is positive, thus having an increasing relationship, or negative and a decreasing relationship. While it is extremely unlikely that you will ever have to hand calculate a covariance value, it does provide us with a better understanding of the concept to see how the value is derived.

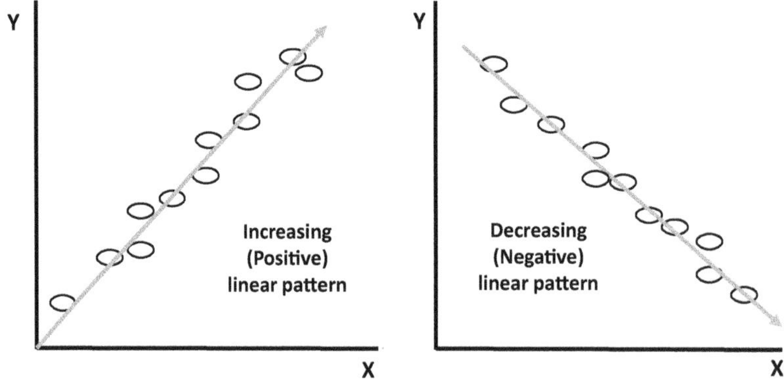

Figure 1.1 Linear Patterns

The covariance formula is:

For a population: $Cov(X,Y) = \frac{\sum(X_i - \bar{X})(Y_j - \bar{Y})}{n}$

For a sample of the population: $Cov(X,Y) = \frac{\sum(X_i - \bar{X})(Y_j - \bar{Y})}{n-1}$
(The most frequently used)

I know this might look like an intimidating formula initially, but it is really not once you break down what all the symbols mean. In this formula, we are looking at the covariance value across two variables. Let's call one of the variables "X" and the other variable "Y". In our formula,

X_i = represents the values of the X variable
Y_j = represents the values of the Y variable
$\bar{X}$ = represents the mean (average) of the X variable
$\bar{Y}$ = represents the mean (average) of the Y variable
n = represents the total number of our sample
$\sum$ = represents the symbol for summation

Let's look at a quick example to clarify things. In this example, let's say I wanted to test if the number of advertisements over a month increased a business's sales. Each week I would need to get the number of advertisements the business placed, and the total sales at the end of the week. I would do this for four weeks. Thus, I would have four data points for this analysis. See the example in Table 1.1.

The $X-\bar{X}$ value for week 1 is the number of ads (10) minus the mean (8.5) over the week = 1.50. You would need to get this value for each week. The $Y-\bar{Y}$ for week 1 is 7,000 minus the mean 6,150 = 850. Again, you would need to get the value for each week. The next step is to multiply the $X-\bar{X}$ value by the $Y-\bar{Y}$ value. If you sum up all these products, you get the numerator for our equation (16,700). The denominator of our equation is the total number of samples subtracted by the value of 1. Thus,

$$\text{Cov (Ads, Total Sales)} = \frac{16{,}700}{4-1} = 5{,}566.67$$

Table 1.1 Example for Calculating Covariance

	Number of Ads (X)	*Total Sales (Y)*	*X–X̄*	*Y–Ȳ*	*(X–X̄) (Y–Ȳ)*
Week 1	10	7,000	1.5	850	1,275
Week 2	5	3,700	−3.5	−2,450	8,575
Week 3	7	5,900	−1.5	−250	375
Week 4	12	8,000	3.5	1,850	6,475
Mean	8.5	6,150			*SUM* 16,700

Our covariance value is 5,566.67. This positive value lets us know that the relationship between the two variables is positive and increasing. Outside of that, the value of 5,566.67 does not give us any more information other than directionality. To determine the strength of the relationship, we will need to assess the correlation between the constructs.

Correlations Between Constructs

While directionality is calculated with a covariance analysis, the strength of the relationships is determined through a correlation analysis. A correlation between two concepts is essentially derived from the covariance. With a covariance analysis, the calculated values do not have a definable range or limit. If you have two variables that are measured on completely different scales, such as our previous example with number of ads and total sales, then the covariance can be a very large (or small) number that is difficult to interpret. A correlation will take that covariance value and standardize it by converting the score on to a −1 to a +1 scale. By limiting the values to a −1 to a +1 scale, you can now compare the strength of relationships that have all been put on a similar scale. If a correlation has a −1 value, this means that the two variables have a strong inverse (negative) relationship, whereas when one variable increases, the other variable decreases. A correlation of +1 means two variables have a positive relationship where both variables are moving in the same direction at roughly the same rate. If you have a correlation value of zero, this means that the two variables are independent of one another and have no pattern of movement across the variables.

Following our same example from the covariance discussion, let's now determine the correlation of number of ads placed in a week and a business's total sales. The formula for calculating a correlation coefficient is a little more straightforward than the covariance formula. To calculate a correlation, you use the following formula:

$$\textit{Correlation}\ (\mathrm{X},\ \mathrm{Y}) = \frac{\textit{Covariance of}\ \mathrm{X}\ \textit{and}\ \mathrm{Y}}{\textit{Standard Deviation of}\ \mathrm{X} * \textit{Standard Deviation of}\ \mathrm{Y}}$$

You will also see this formula represented as:

$$\mathrm{r} = \frac{\textit{Cov}(\mathrm{X},\mathrm{Y})}{\mathrm{S}_x \mathrm{S}_y}$$

The lowercase "r" represents the correlation coefficient and the uppercase "S" represents the standard deviation of the variable. Using our previous example, if we assume the standard deviation for X (# of Ads) is 3.11 and the standard deviation for Y (total sales) is 1,844.81, then we can calculate the correlation between the two variables.

$$\mathrm{r} = \frac{5566.67}{(3.11)\ (1844.81)}$$

$$\frac{5566.67}{5737.35} = .97$$

The correlation between number of ads and totals sales is .97, which shows a strong positive relationship between the two variables. Again, you will probably never hand calculate these values because we have software programs that can do the work for you in seconds. Saying that, understanding how the values are calculated can help in understanding how a SEM analysis is accomplished.

With SEM, you are initially going to get an "observed" sample covariance from the raw data, where you are getting a covariance across all possible combinations of variables. This observed covariance matrix will then be compared to an "estimated" covariance matrix based on your denoted model. The estimated model does not look at all possible variable combinations but solely focuses on combinations that you denote as having a relationship. For example, let's look at a simple four variable model. In this model, the variables of Trust and Satisfaction are proposed to positively influence a consumer's attitude toward a store. This attitude evaluation is then proposed to positively influence a consumer's intention to shop at that store. Notice that we are proposing only three relationships across the variables. See Figure 1.2.

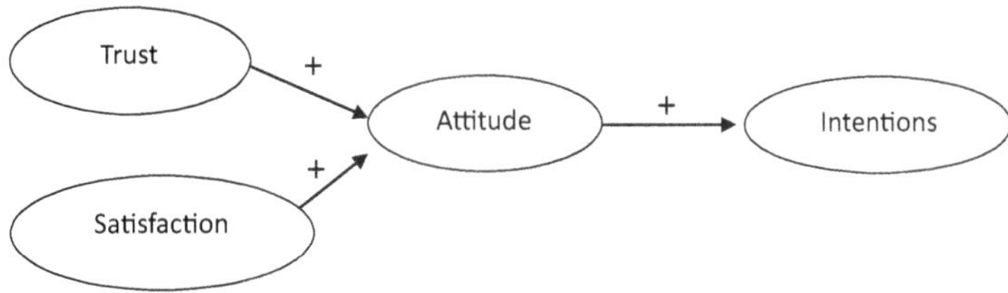

Figure 1.2 Simple Structural Model

To calculate the observed covariance matrix, you would assess the variance for each variable and then determine the covariance for each possible variable combination. Here is an example of how the observed covariance matrix would be calculated with our four variable model.

	Trust	*Satisfaction*	*Attitude*	*Intentions*
Trust	Var (Trust)			
Satisfaction	Cov (Trust-Sat)	Var (Sat)		
Attitude	Cov (Trust-Att)	Cov (Sat-Att)	Var (Att)	
Intentions	Cov (Trust-Int)	Cov (Sat-Int)	Cov (Att-Int)	Var (Int)

Note: Var = Variance; Cov = Covariance

After you have conceptualized your model, you are now going to "estimate" those specific relationships in your model to determine how well your estimated covariance matrix compares to the observed covariance matrix. The estimation of proposed relationships is done through a series of bivariate correlations, and the estimates will determine the strength of each relationship. These estimates are interpreted just like regression coefficients. Unlike other techniques, SEM does not treat each calculation separately. With SEM, all relationships are calculated simultaneously, thus providing a more accurate picture of the relationships denoted.

You will also see the term "model fit" used in SEM to determine how well your "estimated" covariance matrix (based on the denoted model) compares or fits the observed covariance matrix. If the estimated covariance matrix is within a sampling variation of the observed covariance matrix, then it is generally thought to be a good model that "fits the data".

Is SEM Causal Modeling?

You will often hear SEM referred to as a causal modeling approach. SEM does not determine causation between two variables. This is a misnomer that is used quite often with SEM. As stated earlier, SEM uses a covariance matrix as its input, so you are essentially looking at correlations between variables to determine how one influences the other, but it will not determine causation. Just because two things are highly correlated does not mean one causes the other. For instance, let's look at an example about Divorces in the U.S. and how it relates to Organic food sales. If you look at the data from 2010 to 2017, the correlation between those two concepts is −.98, which means that when consumers started eating more organic foods, the divorce rate in the U.S. went down at almost the same rate. So, does this mean that the key to a good marriage is eating fewer preservatives in your food? Of course not; just because a correlation is highly significant does not mean that one thing is "causing" the other. In this case, we have what is called a spurious relationship. The constructs appear to be interconnected, but in reality, they have no association with each other. There are numerous examples of spurious relationships, one of the most popular being that the length of women's skirts can determine the direction of the stock market. While those two things may have a strong correlation historically, it does not show evidence that one is causing the other.

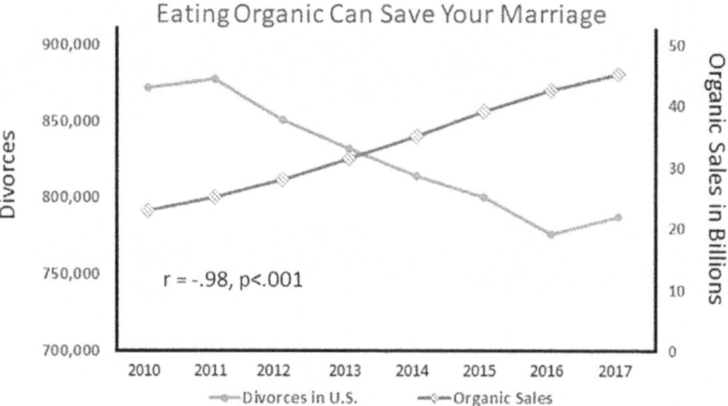

Figure 1.3 Example of Spurious Correlation

SEM is a great technique to determine how variables influence one another, but to determine causation you would really need to use an experimental design. While the majority of SEM research has been performed with non-experimental data, SEM is more than capable of analyzing experimental data. SEM can examine the differences of a control and a manipulation group while exploring their influence on multiple dependent variables, which can overcome many of the limitations of other statistical techniques. Though SEM requires a large sample, this statistical technique can provide you with flexibility in the conceptualization and analysis of an experimental design. So, while a SEM analysis itself will not determine causation, you can use SEM to analyze an experimental design study to aid in understanding causation between constructs. Later in this book (Chapter 8), I will talk more about how to use SEM to analyze experimental data and provide a detailed example of how to analyze data with numerous experimental groups.

A Confirmatory Approach to SEM

Testing a SEM model is said to take a confirmatory approach. Put another way, a conceptual model is determined *a priori* and then data is collected to test how well the model fits the data, thus trying to "confirm" the researcher's hypotheses about how constructs influence one another. Joreskog (1993) outlines how SEM testing usually follows one of the following approaches in confirmatory model testing.

1. *Strictly Confirmatory Approach*—the researcher has a single model that is accepted or rejected based on its correspondence to the data. This could be considered an "all or nothing" approach where either all of the model is accepted, or it is fully rejected. This is a very narrow approach and is rarely used.

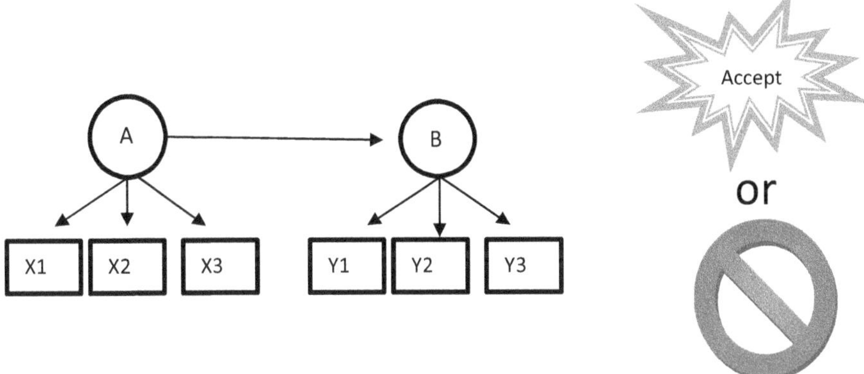

Figure 1.4 Strictly Confirmatory Approach

2. *Alternative Models Approach*—more than one theoretical model is suggested, and you test to see which one has a superior fit (Figure 1.5). Most of the time, researchers are hard pressed to find two alternative models supported by the literature.

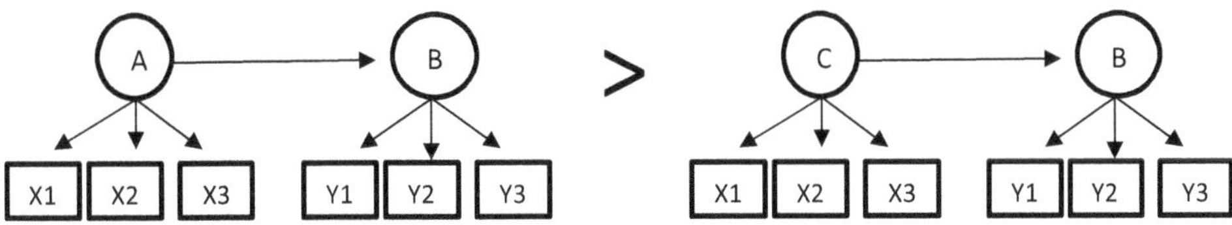

Figure 1.5 Alternative Models Approach

3. *Model Development Approach*—a model is initially tested using SEM and any area of the model that is non-significant or ill-fitting is changed based on the data. Hence, an alternative model is suggested based on the data analysis. These suggestions are often based on modification indices or analysis properties that point out where stronger relationships exist. This is by far the most common method. There is a drawback to this approach because these "developed" or modified models can be hard to replicate. The suggested changes to a model may just be an artifact of a specific data set. Thus, you are often capitalizing on chance if your data set is determining your model conceptualization. Once a "developed" model is found to be acceptable, it is a good idea to achieve another data set to verify the structure of the revised model.

Theory Should Lead Conceptualization

A problem you will see with many SEM studies is when a model is conceptualized apart from any theory. A theory should be a guide to understanding a phenomenon of interest and ultimately help to explain why two variables are influencing each other. Sadly, it seems like many SEM models are conceptualized first and then retrofitted to a theory. What typically takes place is that only part of a theory is actually tested, or SEM results are found but are weakly tied to theory that is supposed to explain the relationships. Without understanding the theory first, you are relying solely on the findings of your data, which could lead to erroneous results. As shown earlier with spurious relationships, sometimes examining the data alone can lead to wrong conclusions. Theory should be your guidepost to the conceptualization of a model along with the explanation between concepts. As a researcher, SEM should be used to confirm theory or expand our knowledge by revising theory, and in some instances to develop new theories. Trying to conceptualize a SEM model before understanding the theory that is going to drive the results is similar to the analogy of putting the cart in front of the horse. A theory should be the foundation of the research that everything else is subsequently built upon to understand a relationship or series of relationships.

Assumptions of SEM

With any statistical technique, assumptions are made. Here are a few of the assumptions with SEM that you need to be aware of going forward:

1. Multivariate Normal Distribution of the Indicators—there is an assumption that the data has a normal distribution.
2. Dependent variables need to be continuous in SEM—while the independent variables do not have this assumption, dependent variables need to be continuous.
3. SEM assumes linear relationships between variables.
4. Maximum likelihood estimation is the default method—maximum likelihood estimation is a technique known to provide accurate and stable results (Hair et al. 2009). You can use other estimations, but maximum likelihood is the default unless otherwise specified.
5. SEM assumes a complete data set—more to come on this topic later if you have missing data.
6. Multicollinearity is not present—multicollinearity makes it difficult to determine the influence of a concept if it is highly correlated with another variable in the model.

7. Adequate sample size—this is one of the challenging assumptions with SEM because this technique does require a large sample size compared to other techniques.
8. Unidimensionality of a construct—the idea that you are solely capturing a construct of interest.

SEM Software

This book will detail how to use SEM techniques using the AMOS software. AMOS stands for "Analysis of Moment Structures". Moment structures refer to means, variance, and covariance. AMOS is a program tied to SPSS that uses a graphical interface for input. Saying that, I will provide some examples using the SPSS program when the data needs to be altered or calculated before using the AMOS program. There are other data input programs that you can use, but SPSS has the most seamless transition to AMOS of the statistical programs. Ultimately, I find AMOS to be the most user friendly of all the SEM software programs, especially for new users. There are other SEM software programs that are comparable to AMOS, such as LISREL, EQS, and MPLUS. The big difference between these programs is that AMOS is designed to conceptualize and analyze models in a graphical interface format whereas the other programs focus on inputting code to analyze a model.

There is also a SEM program that uses a variance-based matrix as its input. This software is called PLS or SMARTPLS. The PLS stands for partial least squares. I find this type of SEM analysis to be especially problematic and do not recommend the use of variance-based SEM. For a full discussion on why covariance-based SEM is more advisable to variance-based SEM, see Chapter 5.

Understanding Diagram Symbols

SEM uses diagrams to denote relationships to be tested. It is important that you understand what these diagram symbols mean because AMOS is going to make you draw out your conceptual model. One of the frustrating aspects of SEM is that there are often multiple terms that mean the exact same thing. You can read three different books, and all three can use different terms to mean the same thing. Hence, I have consolidated all the overlapping terms here to add greater clarity to the different nomenclature.

1. **Latent Variable/Construct**—A latent variable is also referred to as an "unobservable". This is a concept that cannot be directly observed. It would be nice to just look at someone and tell his/her level of anxiety, but the fact is some people are great at hiding their true feelings. In these instances, we cannot simply observe a person and determine levels of anxiety. Thus, concepts such as anxiety are an "unobservable" and require the researcher to find a way to capture the concept by other means, such as asking survey questions. You will also see the term "Factors" used when referring to latent/unobservable constructs. Examples of unobservable constructs in psychology are Anxiety, Motivation, and Trust. In sociology, examples are Perceived Stress and Disconnectedness. Other areas, such as business, have constructs like Brand Attitude, Intentions to Purchase, Employee Burnout, and Satisfaction. Examples of education constructs are Frustration, Self-Efficacy, and

Engagement. Examining unobserved constructs has even expanded into diverse areas such as wildlife and fisheries, with constructs like Attitudes toward wildlife/pollinators and Intentions for conservation practices. These unobservable constructs are often measured by "indicators", or "measurement items", which often take the form of survey questions. For example, you might ask survey questions (indicators) to measure a consumer's level of trust with a company (unobservable).

The diagram shape represented for latent/unobservable variables is a circle or oval.

2. **Observed Variable/Indicator**—As the name denotes, measures are taken to capture an unobservable concept through observable means. This can be done through survey questions, manipulations, or behavioral tracking. This concept is also referred to as Manifest Variables or Reference Variables. You will often see the term "items" and "indicators" used to represent observed variables. In essence, observed variables/indicators are the raw data captured that will be used to explain concepts in a SEM model. These observed variables/indicators can be categorical, ordinal, or continuous.

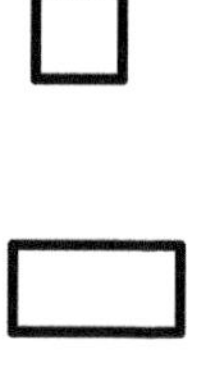

The diagram shape represented for observed variables is a square or rectangle.

3. **Measurement Error/Residual Term**—Measurement error represents the unexplained variance by an indicator measuring its respective latent construct. In trying to capture an unobservable construct with a measurement indicator, the unexplained variance in the measurement is error, or "measurement error". Along with the indicator, an error term is also present on a dependent latent construct. This is the unexplained variance on the construct level as a result of the relationships from the independent variables. Error terms for latent variables are also called residual terms or disturbance terms. Since measurement error and residual terms represent unexplained variance, AMOS treats these terms like unobserved variables. Thus, the symbol for these error terms are a circle and a one-way arrow.

The diagram shape represented for error terms is a circle and one-way arrow.

4. **Direct Path Effect**—Hypothesized directional effects of one variable on another.

The diagram shape is represented by a line and a single arrowhead.

5. **Covariances**—the amount of change in one variable that is consistently related to the change in another variable (the degree to which the two variables change together on a reliable and consistent basis).

The diagram shape for a covariance is a curved line with two arrowheads.

Independent vs. Dependent Latent Variables

Independent variables (also called exogenous variables) are the constructs that influence another variable. Dependent variables (called endogenous variables) are constructs influenced by independent variables.

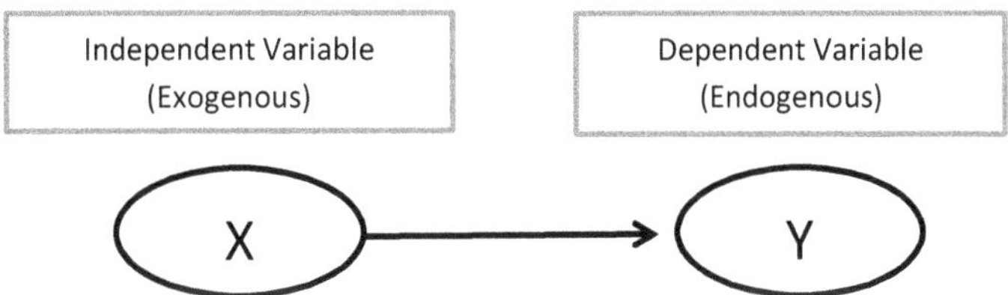

Figure 1.6

How to Measure an Unobserved Construct

With an unobservable construct, we are trying to use indicators to measure the concept. With any unobservable analysis, you will rarely be able to say you are capturing the "true" or actual score without some degree of error. Thus, an indicator is a function of the "true" score plus error:

Construct Indicator = True or Actual Score of Concept + Error in Measuring the Concept
Or, put in mathematical form: $X = A + e$

With this formula, the construct indicator (X) is the measured item which is going to capture the "true" value of the concept (A) while also accounting for any error in the measurement (e). You will often see unobservable constructs using a single measured indicator to measure the concept. This can be problematic for a number of reasons. With a single measure, you are making the claim that a single item can capture the "true" value of an unobservable construct. Referring back to our formula of X = A + e, you cannot determine the error of a single indicator measure. You have two unknowns (A and e) with only one known (X). The formula is unsolvable. Thus, with a single indicator, the error is ignored, and the formula is converted to X = A. Obviously, this is a big leap of faith that a single observed indicator can perfectly measure an unobservable construct. For this reason, you will often see unobservable constructs measured with multiple indicators, which have a higher likelihood of capturing the "true" or actual score of the unobservable. Additionally, multiple indicators allow us enough information to determine the error of each indicator. Thus, we are using more indicators to capture a potentially complex concept and at the same time accounting for error in the measurement. Let's look at how single and multiple indicators of an unobservable construct are represented in SEM.

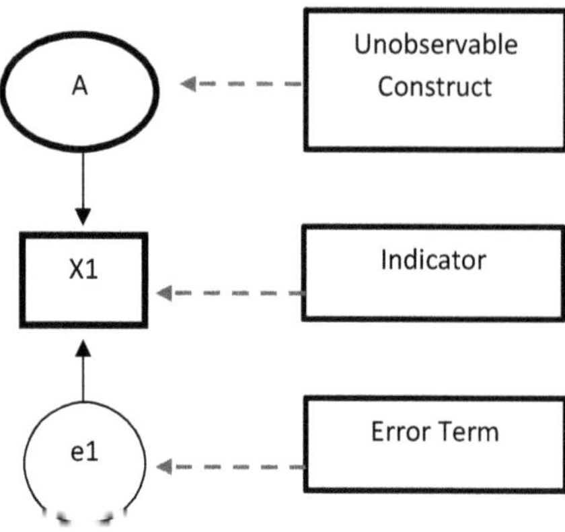

Figure 1.7 Single Indicator Construct

Single Indicators—one observed item/indicator is used to capture the entire unobservable construct. In the representation shown in Figure 1.7, the unobserved construct of "A" is going to represent the "true" or actual score of the unobserved concept. The single indicator of "X1" is a measure of the concept and "e1" represents the error in measuring the unobserved construct in the single indicator. Again, if you use a single item to measure an unobservable construct, you cannot account for error. You are saying this indicator is a perfect measure and has no unexplained variance.

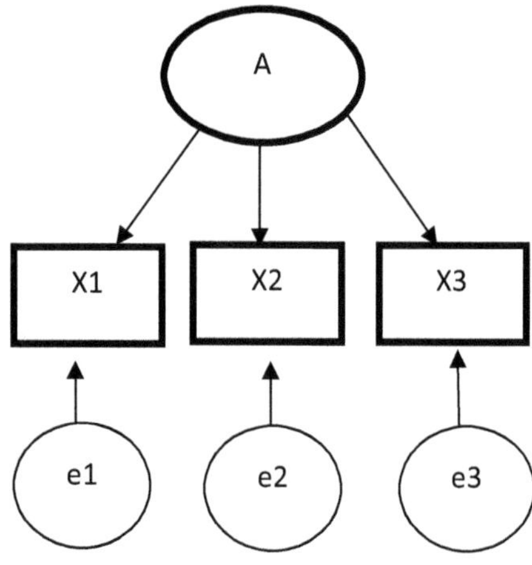

Figure 1.8 Multiple Indicator Construct

Multiple Indicators—more than one observed item is used to capture the construct. In the example shown in Figure 1.8, the unobservable construct "A" is being captured or measured by three indicators (X1–X3). The rationale is that complex constructs cannot be fully captured without multiple indicators. As well, multiple indicators aid the researcher in understanding the reliability and validity of the captured unobserved variable. Lastly, you can determine the measurement error of each indicator, giving you a better understanding of whether your indicators/items are capturing the unobservable concept.

Measurement Model vs. Structural Model—the measurement model in SEM is where the researcher is going to assess the validity of the indicators for each construct. After showing the validity of the measurement model, the researcher can proceed to the structural model. The structural model is concerned

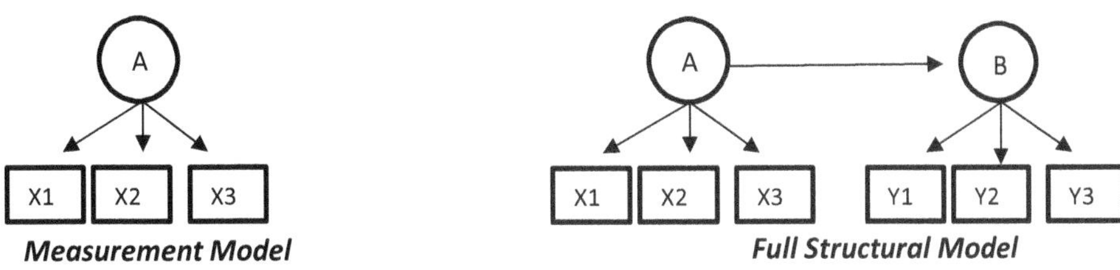

Figure 1.9

with the influence and significance between constructs. The term "full structural model" means that the measurement and structural relationships of each construct are included in the model testing.

Parameters—the term "parameter" indicates the size and nature of the relationship between two objects in a model. Parameters can be fixed to a constant or can be estimated freely from the data. A parameter estimate will take place on the measurement level with indicators and error terms as well as on the structural level between constructs.

Greek Notation and SEM

Many SEM programs produce their results using Greek notations. They use Greek letters to represent different constructs and relationships. AMOS does not produce output using Greek notations, but you need to be familiar with them so you can understand the results from other SEM programs.

What Do All These Greek Symbols Mean?

Latent Constructs

ξ (Ksi) Represents an independent latent variable
η (Eta) Represents a dependent latent variable

Item Measures

X Indicator measures associated with independent latent constructs
Y Indicator measures associated with dependent latent constructs

Structural Relationships

γ (Gamma) Parameters representing regression relationships from independent latent constructs to dependent latent constructs
β (Beta) Parameters representing regression relationships from dependent latent constructs to dependent latent constructs

Error Terms

ζ (Zeta)	Error term for a latent dependent construct
ε (Epsilon)	Measurement error terms associated with Y item measures
δ (Delta)	Measurement error terms associated with X item measures

Measurement Relationships

λ (Lambda)	Is the relationship from the latent construct to its indicators. Lambda represents the relationship to X and Y indicators from a latent construct.

Covariances

φ (Phi)	Represents covariances between latent constructs

Table 1.2 contains a list of English and Greek letter symbols for your reference.

Table 1.2 English and Greek Letter Symbols

English Letter	*Greek Letter*	*Lower Case*	*Upper Case*
a	alpha	α	A
b	beta	β	B
c	chi	χ	X
d	delta	δ	Δ
e	epsilon	ε	E
f	phi	φ	Φ
g	gamma	γ	Γ
h	eta	η	H
i	iota	ι	I
k	kappa	κ	K
l	lambda	λ	Λ
m	mu	μ	M
n	nu	ν	N
o	omicron	ο	O
p	pi	π	Π
q	theta	θ	Θ
r	rho	ρ	P
s	sigma	σ	Σ
t	tau	τ	T
u	upsilon	υ	Y
w	omega	ω	Ω
x	ksi	ξ	Ξ
y	psi	ψ	Ψ
z	zeta	ζ	Z

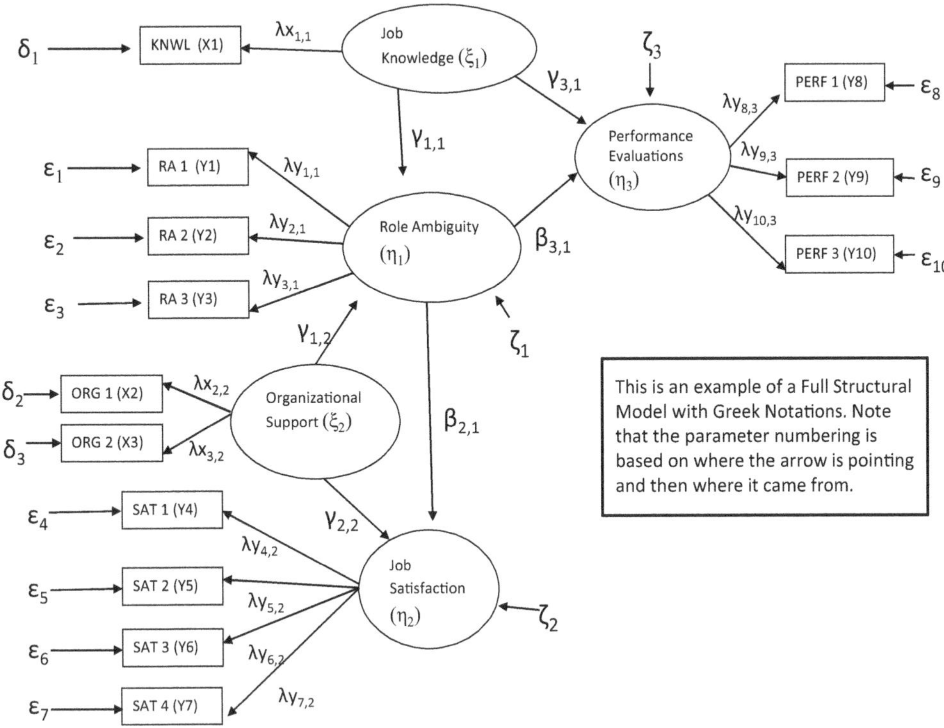

Figure 1.10 Full Structural Model with Greek Notation

Highlights of the Chapter

1. Structural equation modeling (SEM) is a family of statistical techniques that examine the measurement properties of a variable along with the interrelationships between variables.
2. The advantage of SEM over other techniques is that it can assess multiple dependent variables at once and also account for measurement error in each variable.
3. The covariance matrix is the primary input for SEM in AMOS, though the correlation matrix can be used. The covariance matrix will primarily determine directionality where correlations determine strength.
4. SEM is often called "causal" modeling, but correlations alone do not determine causation. Causation is often determined through a manipulation group and control group to see if differences exist.
5. With any SEM model, theory should lead model conceptualization and justification for proposed relationships.

6. SEM uses diagrams to denote relationships. The symbols used in these diagrams are:
    a. Unobserved variables are circles
    b. Observed variables are boxes
    c. Path relationships are single headed arrows
    d. Error terms are represented by a circle and a one way arrow
    e. Covariances between variables are double headed arrows
7. Independent variables, also known as exogenous variables, will influence dependent variables, also known as endogenous variables.
8. It is preferred to measure unobservable constructs with multiple indicators. Measuring an unobservable construct with a single indicator is problematic because you cannot determine measurement error in the indicator.
9. A measurement model examines the relationships from the constructs to their indicators. A structural model examines the relationships between constructs. A full structural model examines the relationships between constructs while also including the measurement model properties of each construct.

References

Hair, Joseph F., William C. Black, Barry J. Babin, and Rolph E. Anderson. (2009), *Multivariate Data Analysis* (7th ed.). Upper Saddle River, NJ: Prentice Hall.

Jöreskog, Karl G. (1993), "Testing Structural Equation Models", in K.A. Bollen and J.S. Long (eds) *Testing Structural Equation Models*. Newbury Park, CA: Sage.

Chapter 2

Data Screening, Assessing Reliability, Validity, and Identification

Before you can assess if one construct is influencing another, you need to make sure you are actually capturing the construct of interest via your observed variables/indicators. In Chapter 2, I will go over how to initially screen your data for problems before you even start the analysis. After addressing any issues with the data, the next step is to assess the reliability of a construct's indicators. Following this analysis, I will discuss degrees of freedom in a model and why that is important in assessing viability of a model's structure. The chapter will conclude with a discussion of sample size in SEM models along with an initial discussion on types of validity that need to be addressed in order to have confidence in your findings.

Data Screening

The first step before analyzing your SEM model is to examine your data to make sure there are no errors, outliers, or respondent misconduct. We also need to assess if you have any missing data. Once your data has been keyed into a data software program like Excel, SAS, or SPSS, the first thing you need to do is set up an "ID" column. I usually do this on the first column of the data, and it is simply an increasing number from 1 (on the first row) to the last row of the data. This is done to make it easier to find a specific case, especially if you have sorted on different columns. After forming an ID column, it is a good idea to initially examine if you have any respondent abandonment or misconduct. The quickest and easiest way to see if respondent abandonment has occurred is simply to sort the last few columns of the data in an ascending order. Hence, you can see if the respondent dropped out of the survey and stopped answering questions. These incomplete rows are then subject to deletion. If a respondent failed to answer the last few questions, you need to determine if this amount of missing data is sufficiently acceptable to retain the respondent's other answers. If the respondent has an excessive amount of missing data, then you are better off just deleting that respondent from the overall data. Later in this chapter, I will discuss how much missing data is acceptable in order to proceed with an analysis.

After making a determination if respondents who failed to complete the survey should be deleted, the next thing you need to assess is respondent misconduct. Let's say you have a survey asking Likert scale questions (1 to 7 scale). You want to assess if a respondent simply marked the same answer for every question. The likelihood that the respondent feels the exact same way for every question is small and is subject to deletion because of respondent misconduct. Sometimes you will also hear this called "yea-saying", where the respondent is not reading the questions and just marks agreement at the same level for the rest of the survey. An additional step you can take to assess if respondent misconduct is taking place is to add attention check measures to your survey. These questions are added simply to make sure the respondent is paying attention to the questions, and they may ask the respondent to specifically select a number on the 1 to 7 scale.

To see if you have a problem in your data set, examining the standard deviation of answers for each specific respondent is a good way to assess if respondent misconduct is present. While SPSS is great at analyzing data, accomplishing this task in SPSS is quite laborious. If your data is in SPSS, a better (and quicker) option is to use Microsoft Excel; you copy the "ID" column and the Likert scale indicator questions from SPSS and paste this data into Excel. Go to the last column that is blank and simply input the standard deviation function =STDEV.P(selected columns) and highlight "only" the Likert Scale items in the row (do not include the ID column). This will allow you to see the standard deviation for each row (respondent). Anything with a standard deviation that is less than .25 is subject to deletion because there is little to no variance among the responses across the survey. Saying that, it does not mean that if a standard deviation is under .25, you need to automatically delete the record. As the researcher, you need to determine what is an acceptable level of agreement (or disagreement) within the questions, and this can be a matter of how large or small the survey is as well. You may have an extremely hard to get sample with a short survey, and in that instance, you might want to lower the value before deleting records. There are no golden rules that apply to every situation, but if you have a standard deviation of a respondent that is under .25, then you need to strongly consider if this respondent's answers are valid moving forward. See Figure 2.1 for assessing the standard deviation of a respondent's answers in Excel.

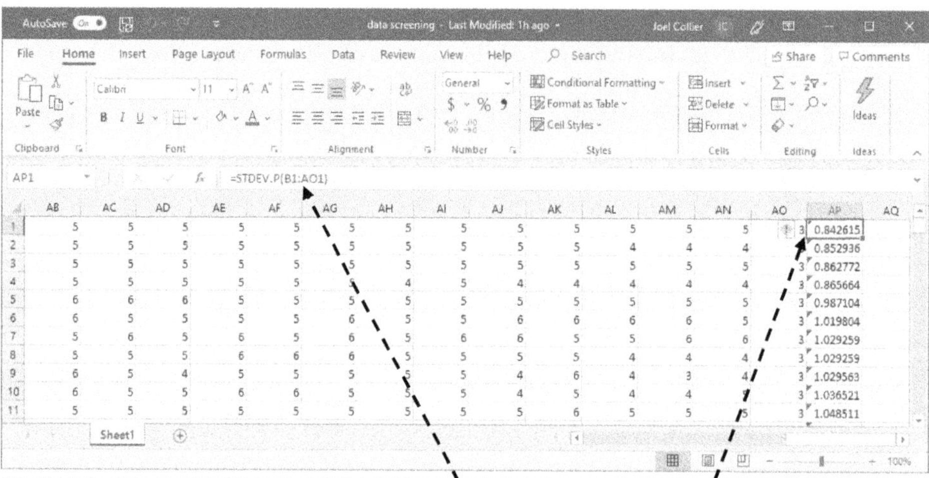

Here is the function in Excel along with the row highlighted (excluding the first column which is the ID column). You can see that the standard deviation for each row is greater than .25, which means no column is subject for deletion because of "yeah saying" or respondent misconduct.

Figure 2.1 Data Screening Standard Deviation of Respondent's Answers

Another type of respondent misconduct is the time/duration the respondent takes to complete the survey. Many online surveys will tell you the start time and stop time of each respondent. An extremely short period of time may be indictive of respondent misconduct. If you have a 50-question survey and it takes a respondent only 57 seconds to take the full survey, then most likely that respondent is not reading the questions and is not answering in a valid manner. This type of respondent misconduct needs to be considered for deletion as well.

After assessing if there is a problem with a particular respondent, it is a good idea to screen your indicators for issues. For instance, let's say I am asking customers if they were delighted about a restaurant experience and, specifically, if the restaurant server produced these feelings of delight. To capture customers' perceptions of delight, I will ask customers three separate survey questions. The questions are asked on a 7-point scale, and I want to make sure that no answers are outside of the 7-point scale range. The first step in data screening of an indicator is to see if you have any impermissible values.

Screening for Impermissible Values in the Data

There are times when respondents simply key in a value wrong or list an invalid response to an inquiry. To test if an answer is outside of an acceptable range, you need to go to your SPSS file, select the "Analyze" option at the top, and then select "Descriptive Statistics". Next, you will select the "Descriptives" option.

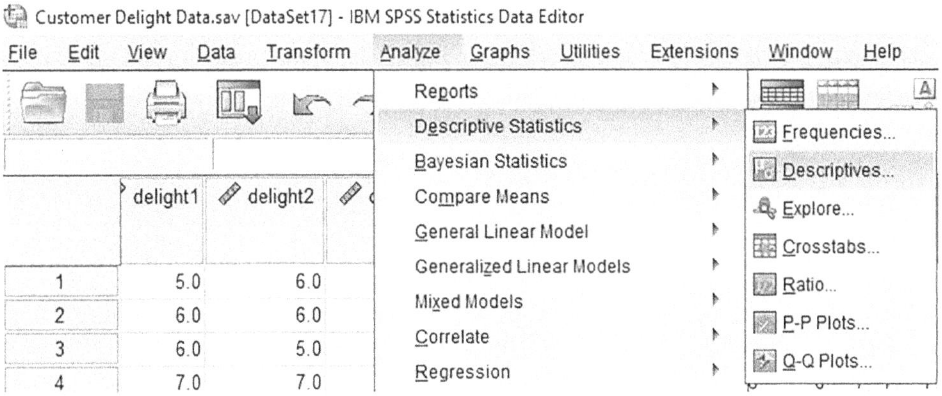

Figure 2.2 Descriptives in SPSS

After selecting "Descriptives", a pop-up window will appear. Let's say I want to see if any of my customer delight indicators have an impermissible value. I select all three indicators for analysis and move them into the "Variable(s)" field. I also want to select the "Options" button in order to see all the necessary fields. The "Options" window will give you lots of analysis choices. I like to see the Mean, Standard Deviation, and, most importantly, the Minimum and Maximum values to determine if a value is outside of an acceptable range. You can also examine if an indicator has a high degree of kurtosis or skewness on this options page. Once

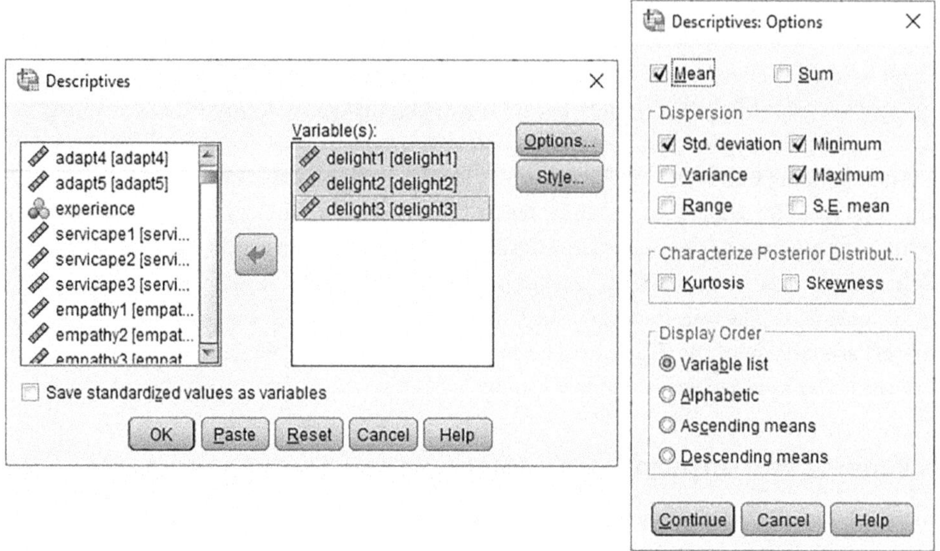

Figure 2.3 Descriptives Window With Options

I have selected all my options. I hit the continue button and then hit the "OK." button on the main descriptives page.

The descriptives output (listed below) lets you see the minimum and maximum value for each indicator. With all three indicators on a 7-point scale, the maximum value should not be below 1 or higher than 7. With some online survey companies, I have actually seen where data from the company is converted to other numbers. Instead of a 1 to 7 scale, the software changes the scale to a 14 to 20 scale. This is rare, but in the event something like this does happen, you will know what analysis to use to catch this impermissible response.

Table 2.1 Descriptive Statistics of Customer Delight Indicators

	N	Minimum	Maximum	Mean	Std. Deviation
delight1	500	4.0	7.0	6.316	.8182
delight2	500	2.0	7.0	6.135	.9349
delight3	500	1.0	7.0	6.045	.9922
Valid N (listwise)	500				

With closed-ended questions where the respondent is making a choice (via Likert or Semantic Differential), you will rarely find that your responses are out of an appropriate range. The area you see this most frequently is with open-ended questions where the respondent inputs the data directly. For instance, lets say we perform the exact same analysis again but examine the "Age" of the respondents this time.

Table 2.2 Descriptive Statistics of Respondents' Age

	N	Minimum	Maximum	Mean	Std. Deviation
Age	500	18	270	34.48	14.965
Valid N (listwise)	500				

The results of the analysis show us the minimum age was 18 and maximum age was 270. Unless Dorian Gray was one of the respondents, the 270 record is most likely respondent error. Based on the mean, the respondent was probably 27 but could be 70. In this instance, it is better to delete the record and then impute the missing data. As stated earlier, this analysis will let you see if any of your values are outside of an accepted range. Failing to address this issue could significantly skew your data depending on the sample size.

How Do I Assess If I Have Missing Data?

We have already addressed how to find respondent abandonment, but finding missing data that takes place in a random manner can be more challenging. To initially see if any data is missing, let's start in the SPSS data file. In SPSS, go to the "Analyze" option at the top, then select "Descriptive Statistics", and then the "Frequencies" option.

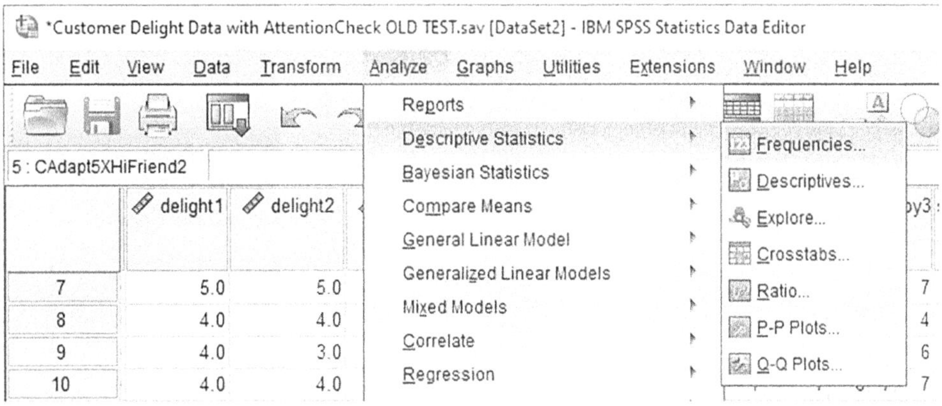

Figure 2.4 Frequencies Function in SPSS

After choosing the "Frequencies" option, a screen will appear (Figure 2.5) where you will select the three delight indicators and move them into the Variable(s) input section. I also like to choose the "Statistics" option on the right-hand side of the screen in order to select all the information I want presented. After selecting all the needed options, I hit the "Continue" button and then the "OK" button in the initial "Frequencies" window.

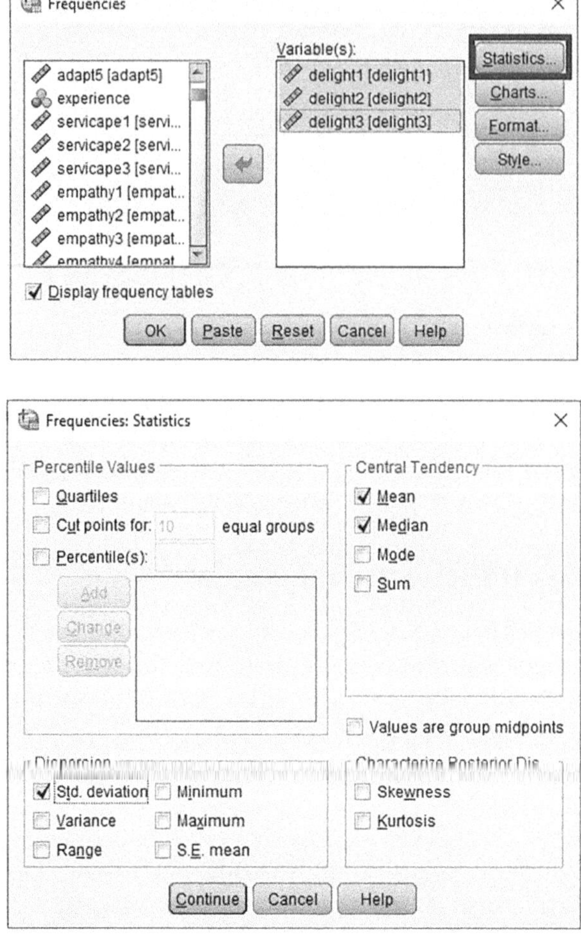

Figure 2.5 Frequencies–Statistics Options

Table 2.3 Output of Frequencies Function to Determine if Missing Data Is Present

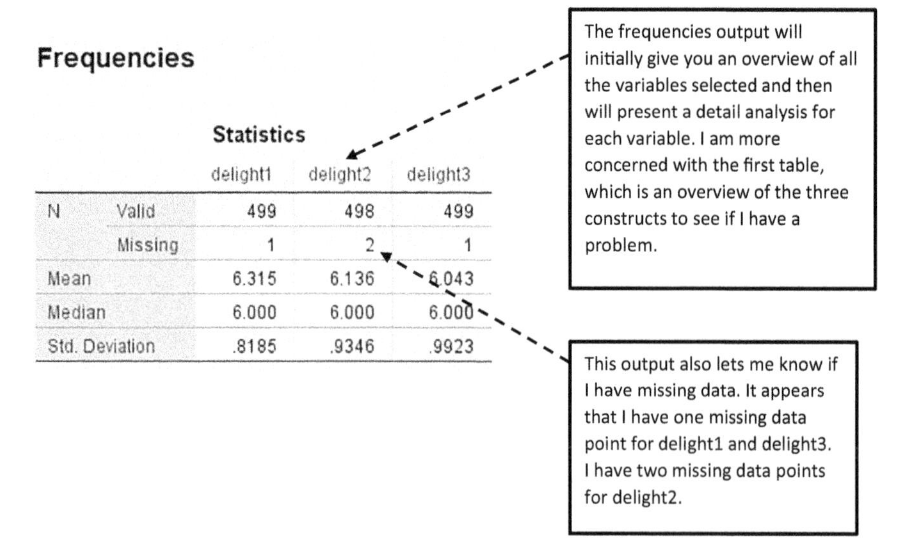

Frequencies

Statistics

		delight1	delight2	delight3
N	Valid	499	498	499
	Missing	1	2	1
Mean		6.315	6.136	6.043
Median		6.000	6.000	6.000
Std. Deviation		.8185	.9346	.9923

The frequencies output will initially give you an overview of all the variables selected and then will present a detail analysis for each variable. I am more concerned with the first table, which is an overview of the three constructs to see if I have a problem.
This output also lets me know if I have missing data. It appears that I have one missing data point for delight1 and delight3. I have two missing data points for delight2.

How Do I Address Missing Data?

Before we address what to do with missing data, we need to understand why data goes missing. Missing data is typically classified in three ways: (1) missing completely at random, (2) missing at random, and (3) missing not at random. The first category, missing completely at random, is where the missing data is unrelated to the other variables in a study. An example of this would be where a respondent simply skipped a question by accident. The missing data took place randomly and was not due to any other observed variables in the study. The second category, missing at random, is where the missing data can be explained by other variables in the study. For instance, if you have a survey where younger consumers have more missing data than older consumers, then the age of the respondent is a factor in explaining why missing data is taking place. Note that the data may still be randomly missing in the younger and older respondents, but the variable of age is providing insights on why the data is missing. The last category, missing not at random, is where missing data takes place often because of the values of a given variable. For example, individuals with a high income will often skip the income question on a survey, or older females may skip the age question. In each of those examples, the missing data is not random because the respondent simply does not want to give the value or score to that question. In that instance, the missing value is directly related to the values given on the variable.

There are two prominent ways to handle missing data: (1) listwise/pairwise deletion, and (2) imputation. I do not encourage deletion because you throw away a lot of data by doing this. If a respondent misses one question, the whole survey is dropped from the analysis. Previous research has shown that you can remedy up to 20%–30% of missing data with an imputation technique and still have good parameter estimates (Hair et al. 2009; Eekhout et al. 2013). Thus, imputation is often a better option if you do not have an excessive amount of missing data. Imputation is where your software program will replace each missing value with a numeric guess. The most popular imputation method is replacing a missing value with a series mean of the indicator. This is usually done for its ease of use, but it has the drawback of reducing the variance of the variables involved (Schafer and Graham 2002). Not to mention, this fails to account for the individual differences of the specific respondent. A second way to impute data is to use a linear interpolation option. This method examines the last valid value before the missing data and then examines the next valid value after the missing data and imputes a value that is between those two values. The linear interpolation imputes based on the idea that your data is in a line, or is linear. You can also use regression imputation, which replaces missing values with an estimated score from a regression equation. This imputation method has disadvantages as well in that it often leads to overestimation of model fit and can inflate correlation estimates (Little and Rubin 2002).

Another prominent way to address missing data is through the full information maximum likelihood approach. This method is not an imputation but uses a likelihood function that is based on all variables of the study to estimate a parameter. This approach takes into account complete and incomplete data when estimating parameters. I would love to tell you that there is one preferred way that missing data should be addressed. An ample number of papers discuss the merits of each method. I will say there is a strong consensus that series mean imputation is the least favorable option.

For clarity, I will show you how to perform all four approaches discussed in order to address missing data. To use a series mean imputation and linear interpolation imputation, this can be easily accomplished in SPSS (Figure 2.6). To replace missing values in SPSS, you need to go to the "Transform" option at the top and then select "Replace Missing Values". Once you click "Replace Missing Values", a pop-up window will appear where you will need to select which indicators have missing values and need to be imputed. When you select the indicators to impute, the default imputation is "series mean", labeled as "SMEAN". SPSS will impute the series mean for these indicators and create a new variable with an underscore and "1" as the new variable name. For instance, delight1 is renamed delight1_1 where all the missing values in this indicator are replaced with the series mean.

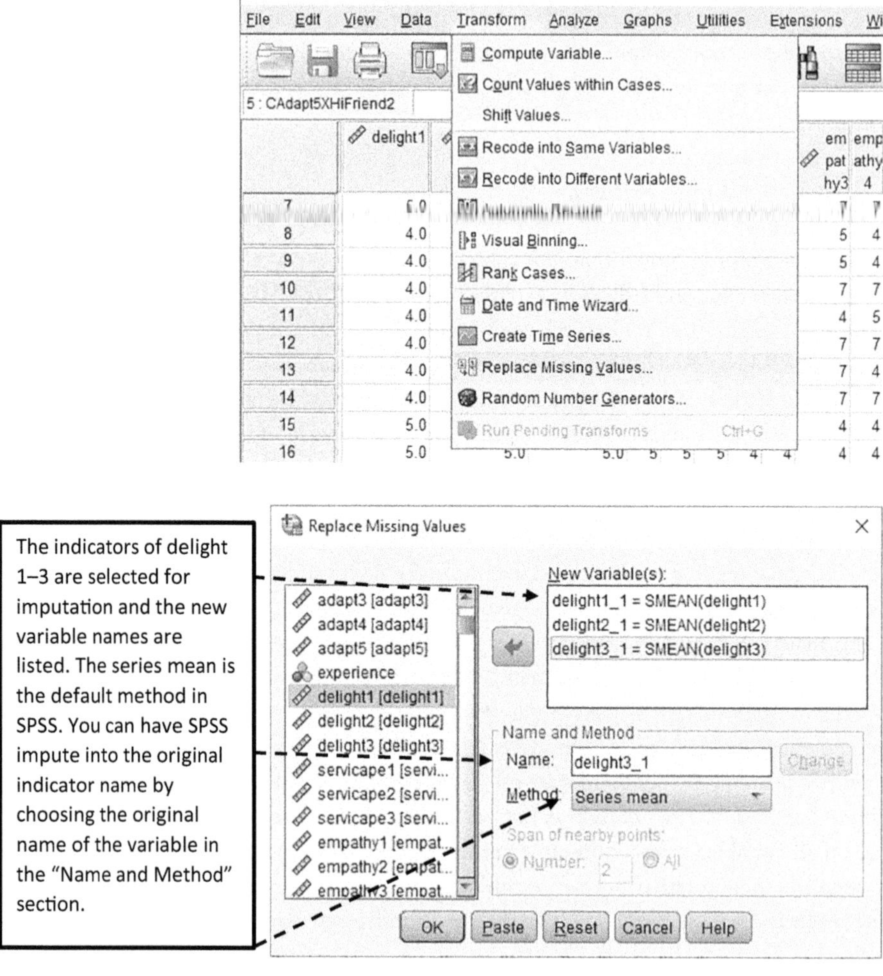

Figure 2.6 Replacing Missing Values in SPSS

It is a very similar method to impute using the linear interpolation method. After selecting the "Transform" and "Replace Missing Values" options again, you need to select each indicator for imputation. As stated earlier, the default method is series mean, but another option under the "Name and Method" section is linear interpolation. You will need to highlight each indicator (individually), change the method to "Linear interpolation", and then hit the "Change" button. Make sure to hit the "Change" button for each indicator. You will also see that SPSS will try to create a new column for the imputed indicator. In the example below, you will see that the indicator delight2 is (by default) being changed to delight2_1. If you do not want another column for the imputed data and simply want to keep your existing labels, you just need to change the name back to the original. In the example in Figure 2.7, delight1 is being imputed with a linear interpolation (listed as LINT), and I am keeping the same name which tells AMOS to impute the missing values in the existing column.

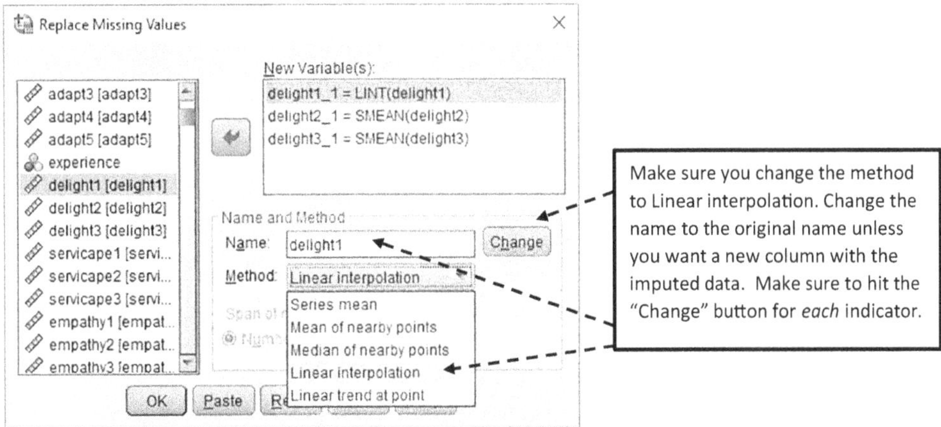

Figure 2.7 Replacing Missing Values With Linear Interpolation

Once you have made your changes and hit the "OK" button at the bottom, SPSS will impute the missing data and will give you an output of how many values were imputed. Take note in the SPSS data file that all the imputed columns (even if you kept the same name) will now be moved to the very last set of columns.

The last two imputation methods of regression imputation and full information maximum likelihood will be addressed using the AMOS program. It is much easier to address these methods in AMOS than in SPSS. In Chapter 10, I go into detail on how to address regression imputation and full information maximum likelihood with the AMOS program (page 314).

Assessing Reliability

After you have screened your data on both the respondent and variable levels, the next step is to assess the reliability of your indicators to predict the construct of interest. While having a single indicator for a construct might be easy, it does not provide us a lot of confidence in the validity of the response. What if the respondent did not understand the question? Asking multiple questions allows us to see the consistency of response to a construct's indicators. A good rule of thumb is that having at least three indicators for each construct will allow you to determine the reliability of your items. One of the most popular techniques for assessing reliability with indicators is to calculate Cronbach's alpha (also called coefficient alpha α). Cronbach's alpha ranges from 0 to 1, where higher numbers denote a more reliable scale. This analysis measures the degree to which responses are consistent across the items within a construct (internal consistency). Nunnally and Bernstein (1994) state that an acceptable level of reliability is a Cronbach's alpha that is greater than .70. Cronbach's alpha does have some drawbacks that need to be addressed. First, Cronbach's alpha is inflated when a construct has a large number of indicators, and second, Cronbach's alpha assumes that all indicators have an equal influence. Even with those drawbacks, it is still the most widely used technique to assess the reliability of a construct's indicators.

Let's go back to our example with the three indicators measuring customer delight, and let's determine the reliability of those indicators to capture delight. To calculate Cronbach's alpha, you need to go to the SPSS file where your data is located. Next, go to the Menu function "Analyze", then go to "Scale", then to "Reliability Analysis".

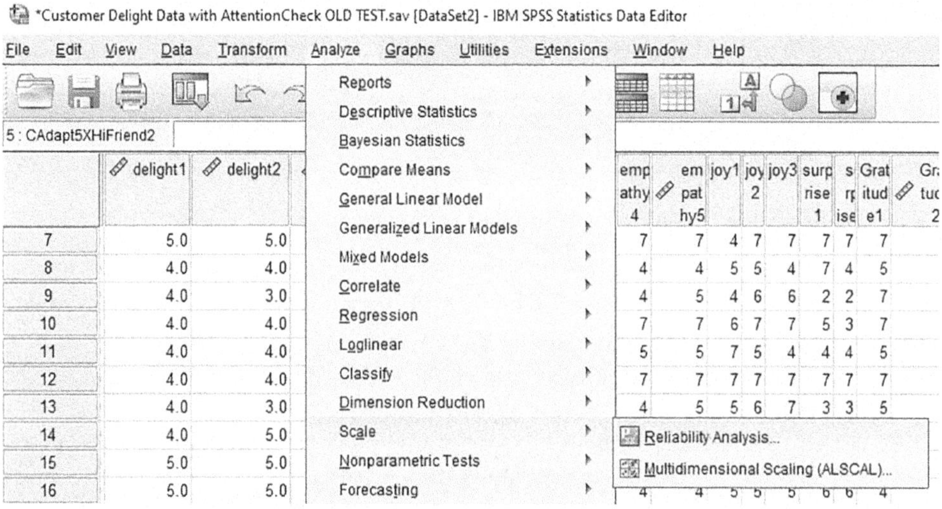

Figure 2.8 Reliability Analysis in SPSS

A pop-up window will appear where you will select your construct's indicators of interest. In this case, we are going to select all three delight indicators. Make sure the model selection is listed as "Alpha".

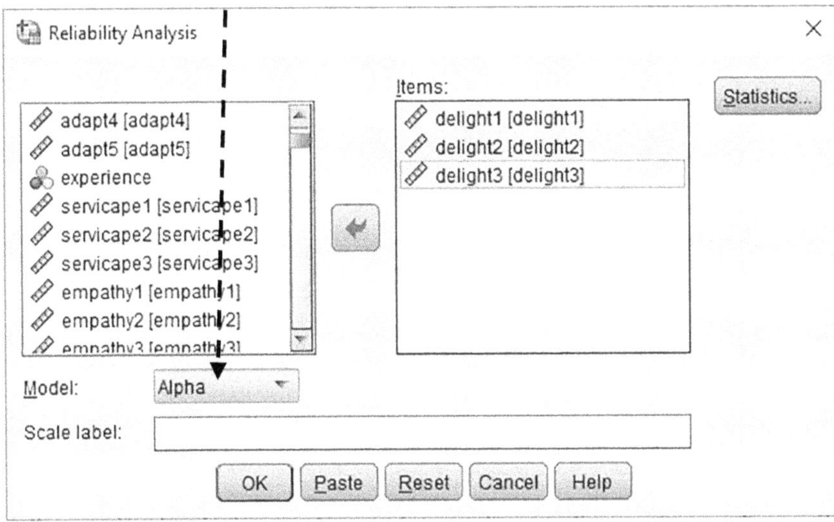

Figure 2.9 Reliability Analysis Pop-Up Window

Next, select the "Statistics" button in the upper right-hand corner. This will let you see numerous details about each indicator. When simply calculating reliability, I usually select only "Item", "Scale", and "Scale if item deleted". The "Scale if item deleted" lets you know how Cronbach's alpha changes if a specific indicator was deleted from the analysis. After making your selections, select "Continue", then "OK" on the main reliability analysis screen.

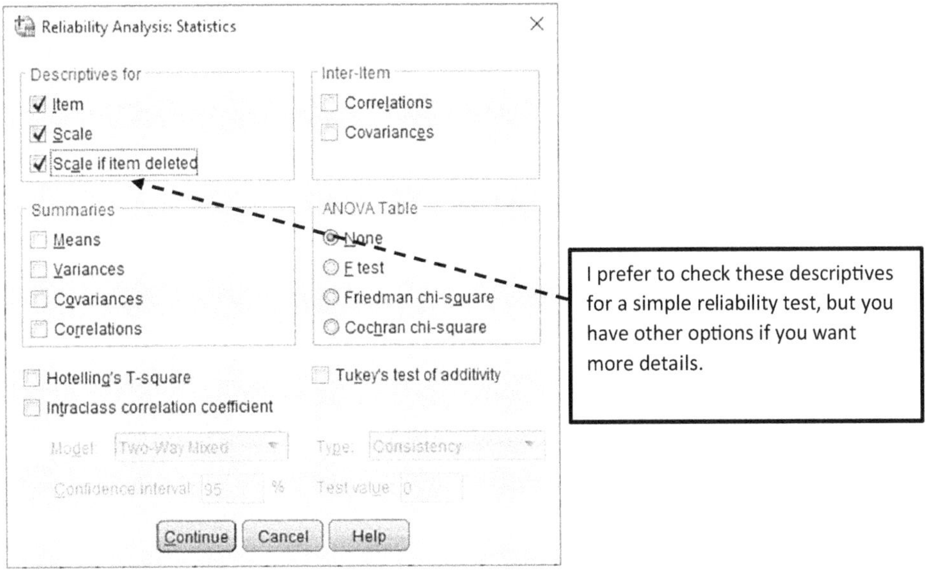

Figure 2.10 Reliability Analysis—Statistics Options

In the output (see Figure 2.11), the Cronbach's alpha value is .900, which is well above the .70 criteria of acceptable reliability. By including the "Item" statistics in the output, you can see if one indicator has a large standard deviation, which could contribute to unreliability if this is present. Lastly, the "Scale if item deleted" presents the change in Cronbach's alpha if an item was removed.

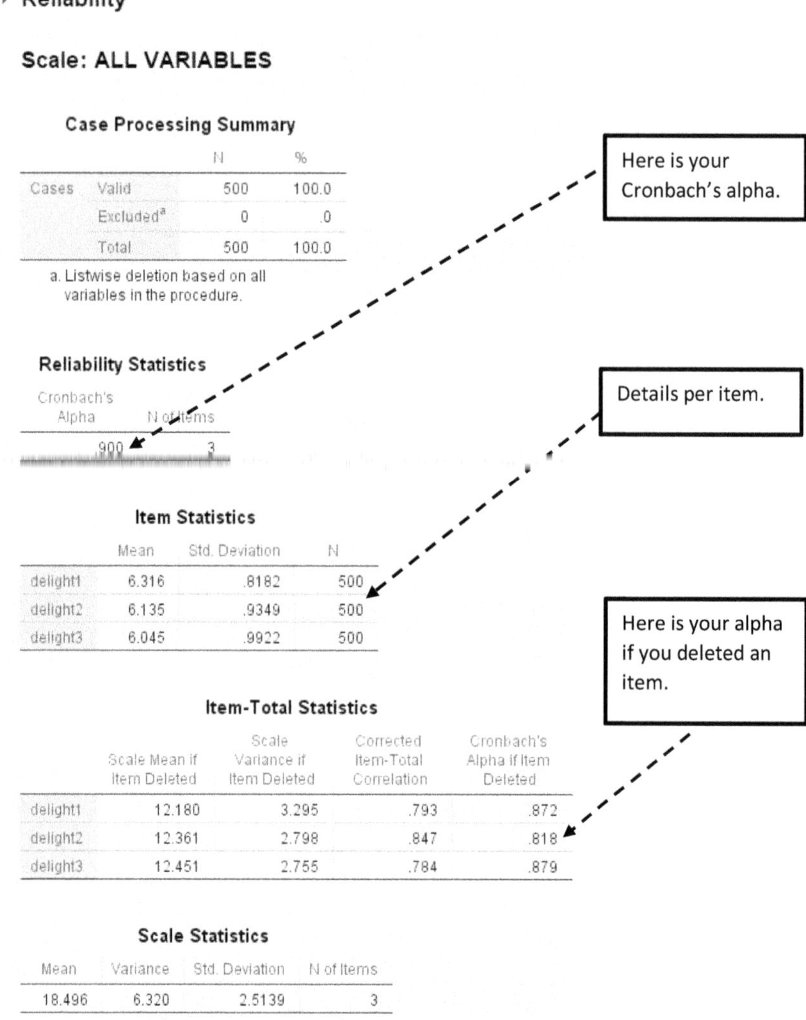

Reliability

Scale: ALL VARIABLES

Case Processing Summary

		N	%
Cases	Valid	500	100.0
	Excluded[a]	0	.0
	Total	500	100.0

a. Listwise deletion based on all variables in the procedure.

Reliability Statistics

Cronbach's Alpha	N of Items
.900	3

Item Statistics

	Mean	Std. Deviation	N
delight1	6.316	.8182	500
delight2	6.135	.9349	500
delight3	6.045	.9922	500

Item-Total Statistics

	Scale Mean if Item Deleted	Scale Variance if Item Deleted	Corrected Item-Total Correlation	Cronbach's Alpha if Item Deleted
delight1	12.180	3.295	.793	.872
delight2	12.361	2.798	.847	.818
delight3	12.451	2.755	.784	.879

Scale Statistics

Mean	Variance	Std. Deviation	N of Items
18.496	6.320	2.5139	3

Here is your Cronbach's alpha.
Details per item.
Here is your alpha if you deleted an item.

Figure 2.11 Example of Output in SPSS for the Reliability Analysis

Composite Reliability—Another popular reliability analysis is composite reliability, also called Raykov's Rho (ρ). This reliability calculation is based on factor loadings from a confirmatory factor analysis. More details on how to calculate this reliability is presented in Chapter 4 in the confirmatory factor analysis section (page 87). Composite reliability has the same range and cutoff criteria as Cronbach's alpha for acceptable level of reliability >.70.

In My Opinion: Choosing and Deleting Indicators

I do not like to delete indicators unless there is an obvious problem. Yes, deleting an indicator could raise Cronbach's alpha levels, but as long as alpha is greater than .70, I am often hesitant to delete an item. Later in the book, I will discuss how validity issues with items can lead to deletion, but having multiple items gives the reader assurance that you have captured the construct from multiple perspectives. In theory, the more items you have, the better your chances of capturing the construct. Saying that, I think some researchers go overboard with the number of items to capture a construct. I have seen some constructs that have more than 20 indicators. This seems like overkill and ultimately leads one to believe that this scale could be refined to still have a comparable level of accuracy with a far smaller number of indicators. I think brand new concepts obviously need a higher number of indicators. Well-established constructs that have been refined can have a much smaller number. At a minimum, you need at least three indicators to calculate Cronbach's alpha, but the choice on number of indicators should be based on the complexity of the construct.

Identification With SEM Models

Identification in regards to a SEM model deals with whether there is enough information to identify a solution (or in this instance, estimate a parameter). A model that is "under-identified" means that it contains more parameters to be estimated than there are elements in the covariance matrix. For instance, let's say we are trying to solve the following problem:

$$X + Y = 10$$

In this example, you have more parameters to estimate (X and Y) than observations (10). It is impossible to find a unique solution. The same principle applies in SEM. If you have more parameters to estimate than observations in the covariance matrix, SEM will not produce an answer because your model is considered under-identified.

Extending the example, let's say now it is the following:

$$X + Y = 10$$
$$2X + Y = 16$$

Now we have two observations and two parameters to estimate. In this instance, we can figure out that X = 6 and Y = 4. Having a model with the exact same number of observations and parameters is called a "just-identified" (or saturated) model. When a model is saturated, you cannot determine how well your model fits the data (fit statistics are invalid). Just-identified models often do not test a theory because the model fit is determined by the circumstances. These models often have very little interest to researchers.

The desired position in a SEM model is to be "over-identified". This means you have more observations than parameters that need to be estimated. When researchers talk about identification, they will often discuss them in terms of "degrees of freedom". The degrees of freedom (df) in a model is the difference between the total number of observations in a covariance matrix and the number of parameters to be estimated in your model. For instance:

Just-Identified (Saturated) Model: df = 0
Under-Identified Model: df < 0
Over-Identified Model: df > 0

AMOS does a lot of the work for you in regards to identification. AMOS will give you a breakdown of proposed estimated parameters and elements in the covariance matrix. All of this information is in the output AMOS provides under a tab titled "Parameter Summary". If you have an under-identified model, AMOS will indicate the specific constructs or errors terms where the problem is originating. Other SEM programs are not as helpful and just state your model is under-identified (good luck finding out where). Though AMOS provides this information to you, it is beneficial to understand how to calculate degrees of freedom. I do this sometimes when I am reviewing for a journal and I think the ultimate analysis is inaccurate.

How Do I Calculate the Degrees of Freedom?

As stated earlier, AMOS will calculate your degrees of freedom, but if you have a problem or want to verify another researcher's work, you need to know how to calculate degrees of freedom. To determine your degrees of freedom, you can use this simple formula outlined by Rigdon (1994) for your measurement model:

df = m * (m + 1)/2 − 2*m − X * (X − 1)/2 (Don't freak out; it looks worse than it is.)

M = number of indicators
X = number of exogeneous (independent) latent constructs

- The first term, m * (m + 1)/2, represents the total number of elements in the variance-covariance matrix (maximum df).
- The second term, 2*m, represents the number of parameters to be estimated.
- The third term, X * (X − 1)/2, represents the free off-diagonal covariances of the constructs.

For instance, let's say we have a simple measurement model that has two latent (unobserved) constructs that have three indicators each.

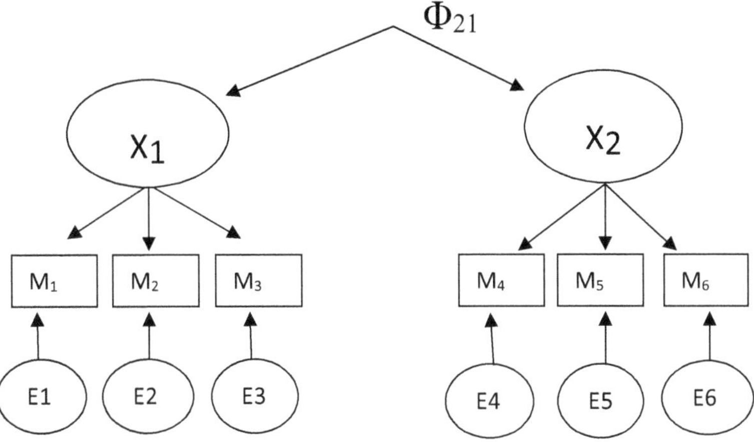

Figure 2.12 Degrees of Freedom Identification in a Measurement Model

In our example, we have 6 indicators (M) and 2 constructs (X):

$$6*(7)/2 - 2*6 - 2(1)/2 = 21 - 12 - 1 = 8$$

The measurement model has 8 degrees of freedom.

The formula used is only for the measurement model, because all constructs are treated as independent variables. Let's say you want to calculate a structural model. It is the same formula, except you are going to subtract the structural relationships: the independent to dependent relationships (γ—gamma) and the dependent to dependent relationships (β—beta).

Here is the formula:

$$df = m * (m + 1)/2 - 2*m - X * (X - 1)/2 - g - b$$

g (gamma relationships) = structural relationships from independent constructs to dependent constructs
b (beta relationships) = structural relationships from dependent constructs to dependent constructs

Let's look at an example of a structural model. This simple model tests how an individual's levels of Social Anxiety and Shyness influence Loneliness perceptions. These Loneliness perceptions will then directly influence evaluations of Depression. Let's try to calculate the degrees of freedom. You have 12 indicators, 4 constructs, 2 gamma relationships, and 1 beta relationship.

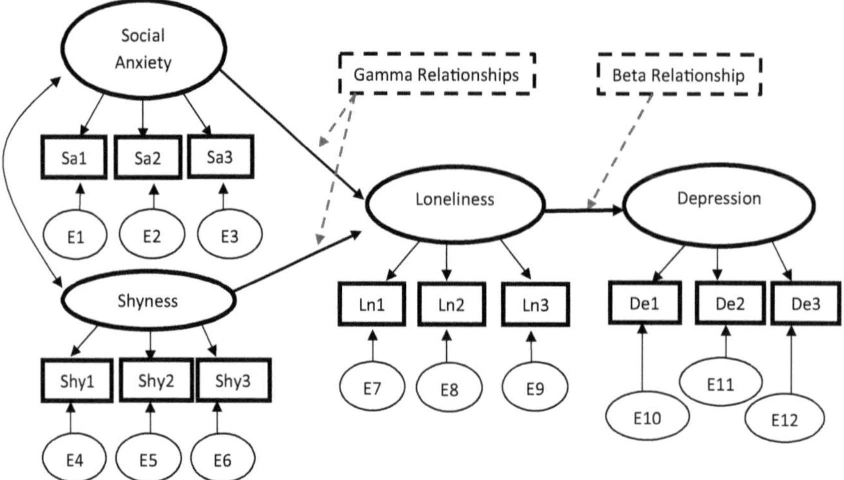

Figure 2.13 Degrees of Freedom Identification in a Structural Model

$$\text{df} = 12 * (13)/2 - 2 * 12 - 2(1)\ /\ 2 - 2 - 1 = \\ 78 - 24 - 1 - 2 - 1 = 50$$

We have 50 degrees of freedom in this structural model. Again, AMOS will calculate the degrees of freedom for you, but it is still handy to know how to calculate degrees of freedom if you are verifying another researcher's work.

What Do I Do if My Model Is Under-Identified?

If your model is under-identified, you have two primary solutions to fix this problem. First, you can reduce the number of proposed parameter estimates. This means that you can delete a covariance or structural relationship. Second, you can add more exogenous (independent) variables. By adding more exogenous variables, you increase the number of observations which could rectify your identification problem.

In My Opinion: Just-Identified or Near Identified Models

The closer you are to a just-identified model, the more skepticism reviewers have about your model unless you have a very simplistic model with few unobserved constructs. As stated earlier, a just-identified model will not allow you to assess how well your proposed model fits the data. Similarly, when you start approaching a just-identified model (df < 3), model fit indices start to bias upward. The bigger issue is a just-identified model or nearly just-identified model is often conceptualized where every construct is influencing every other construct in the proposed model. These types of models have unflatteringly been called "Big TOE" models, where the "TOE" represents "Theory of Everything". A Big Toe model infers that everything is affecting everything else. Ultimately, that type of model is not discriminatory and just lets every construct have a relationship with every other construct in the model. These models are often met with skepticism, mostly because the theory underlining your proposed model is not going to justify that every construct in a model is interconnected and has a relationship. Having an over-identified model is a better option, as you can truly assess if the proposed model fits the data.

Sample Size: How Much Is Enough?

With covariance-based SEM, one of the major assumptions is that this technique requires a larger sample size than other statistical techniques. SEM relies on tests which are sensitive to sample size as well as to the magnitude of differences in covariance matrices. There are a litany of suggestions in regards to necessary sample size using SEM. One of the most common suggestions for sample size is Nunnally and Bernstein's (1994) rule of 10. The rule of 10 states that you should have 10 observations for each indicator in your model. Another rule of thumb, based on Stevens (1996), is to have at least 15 cases per indicator. Bentler and Chou (1987) argue that a more accurate calculation should be based on free parameters of your model where you should have at least 5 cases for each parameter estimate (including error terms as well as path coefficients). Schreiber et al. (2006) made the argument that it should be 10 participants for every parameter estimated. There is no shortage of cites and methods for suggesting how large a sample is needed. More recently, a simple rule of thumb is that a "critical sample size" of 200 (Garver and Mentzer 1999; Hoelter 1983) provides stable parameter estimates and has sufficient power to test a model. While this critical sample size of 200 simplifies things, it fails to address the idea of power. Your sample should be determined by the effect size you desire to capture, or put another way, the ability to capture the smallest correlation between latent variables that you wish to detect. Your sample size should be based on the complexity of your model rather than on the bare minimum sample necessary to run the analysis. If you want to understand how to calculate the specific sample size for a desired level of power, see Kim (2005) or McQuitty (2004).

Understanding the Validity of Measures

After screening your data and assessing if the measures are reliable, you need to examine the validity of your constructs and indicators. There are numerous validity tests that a researcher needs to be aware of to support the legitimacy of their findings. Before moving on, I want to initially introduce what validity means, and specifically the idea of construct validity, or the assessment of a construct and its measures that include content, predictive, convergent, and discriminant validity. I will talk more in detail about how to assess these validities in a confirmatory factor analysis (Chapter 4), but here is a quick overview of the topics.

Content Validity—also known as face validity, this validity assesses if the indicators represent the construct of interest. Are you capturing the unobserved variable? With a sufficient number of indicators, a researcher can make this argument. If it is a new construct and the researcher includes a small number of indicators (like two), you set yourself up for criticism that you may not have achieved content validity. Content validity is often an "eyeball" test by simply assessing if these indicators even attempt to measure the unobserved construct on face value. This type of validity is focused on appearance. Do the indicators asked in a survey appear to measure the specified construct? One could argue that this is a superficial assessment, but it is only one of many steps to determine the validity of a construct.

Convergent Validity—this type of validity determines if the indicators for a construct are all measuring the "same" thing. Do all indicators "converge" in measuring this construct? A lack of convergent validity notes that your indicators are weakly measuring your construct or that your indicators are actually a better measure for a separate and maybe similar construct.

Discriminant Validity—this involves a set of indicators presumed to measure a construct and that differentiate from other constructs. This can be problematic with constructs that have multicollinearity or a high correlation between constructs. For instance, if the constructs of Speed and Efficiency were trying to be measured and the final analysis showed that these two constructs had a correlation of .90, you could make the argument that you are not actually measuring two different things (very few distinguishing characteristics between the measurements). In essence, discriminant validity assesses if your construct is distinct and different from other potential constructs of interest.

Predictive Validity—does the construct actually predict what it is supposed to be predicting?

Highlights of the Chapter:

1. Data screening is important before analyzing your data in AMOS. Problematic data will lead to problematic (or even inaccurate) results.
2. Data screening concerns are: respondent abandonment, respondent misconduct, and impermissible values.
3. Missing data usually takes three forms: missing complete at random, missing at random, and missing not at random.
4. Addressing missing data can be accomplished by deletion or imputation.
5. Imputation often takes place with series mean, linear interpolation, and regression methods.
6. The reliability, or the consistency of responses to indicators, needs to be assessed. The most popular way is to calculate Cronbach's alpha. A Cronbach's alpha value that is greater than .70 denotes an acceptable amount of reliability.
7. Identification in a SEM model is the difference of observations in the covariance matrix and the number of parameters to be estimated. Identification is often discussed in "degrees of freedom".
8. Under-identified models have a degrees of freedom less than zero. Just-identified models have a degrees of freedom that equals zero. An Over-Identified model has a degrees of freedom greater than 0.
9. SEM requires a larger sample size than other statistical techniques. The sample size needed depends on the complexity of the model and the desired level of power.

10. Understanding the validity of your measures is important. Four important validity concerns are content validity, convergent validity, discriminant validity, and predictive validity.

References

Bentler, P.M. and Chih-ping Chou. (1987), "Practical Issues in Structural Equation Modeling", *Sociological Methods Research*, 16 (1), 78–117.

Eekhout, Iris, Henrica De Vet, Jos Twisk, Jaap P.L. Brand, Michiel de Boer, and Martijn W. Heymans. (2013), "Missing Data in Multi-Item Instrument Were Best Handled by Multiple Imputation at the Item Score Level", *Journal of Clinical Epidemiology*, 67 (3), 40–55.

Garver, Michael S. and John T. Mentzer. (1999), "Logistics Research Methods: Employing Structural Equation Modeling to Test for Construct Validity", *Journal of Business Logistics*, 20 (1), 33–57.

Hair, Joseph F., William C. Black, Barry J. Babin, and Rolph E. Anderson. (2009), *Multivariate Data Analysis* (7th ed.). Upper Saddle River, NJ: Prentice Hall.

Hoelter, Jon W. (1983), "The Analysis of Covariance Structures Goodness of Fit Indices", *Sociological Methods Research*, 11 (3), 325–344.

Kim, Kevin H. (2005), "The Relation Among Fit Indexes, Power and Sample Size in Structural Equation Modeling", *Structural Equation Modeling*, 12 (3), 368–390.

Little, Roderick J.A. and Donald B. Rubin. (2002), *Statistical Analysis With Missing Data* (2nd ed.). New York, NY: Wiley.

McQuitty, Shaun. (2004), "Statistical Power and Structural Equation Models in Business Research", *Journal of Business Research*, 57 (2), 175–183.

Nunnally, Jum C. and Ira H. Bernstein. (1994), *Psychometric Theory* (3rd ed.). New York, NY: McGraw-Hill.

Rigdon, Edward E. (1994), "Calculating Degrees of Freedom for a Structural Equation Model", *Structural Equation Modeling*, 1 (3), 274–278.

Schafer, Joseph L. and John W. Graham. (2002), "Missing Data: Our View of the State of the Art", *Psychological Methods*, 7 (2), 147–177.

Schreiber, James B., Frances K. Stage, Jamie King, Amaury Nora, and Elizabeth A. Barlow. (2006), "Reporting Structural Equation Modeling and Confirmatory Factor Analysis Results: A Review", *The Journal of Educational Research*, 99 (6), 323–337.

Stevens, James P. (1996), *Applied Multivariate Statistics for Social Sciences*. New York, NY: Routledge and Taylor & Francis.

Chapter 3

Understanding the AMOS Program

The AMOS software is nicely designed for you to use a graphic interface to draw your structural equation models. Unlike other SEM programs that are all coding, AMOS allows you to quickly draw a model and visually see the paths and relationships between constructs. The software is flexible in that it allows you to use icons to select options or to even use hot keys if you feel more comfortable that way. I will initially explain the basic functions of setting up a structural equation model in AMOS, and then I will present tips on how to be more efficient using the program.

Overview of the AMOS Graphics Window

When you open the AMOS graphics program, the software will display a window that looks like it has a white page in the middle of the screen. This is your working area in AMOS. You need to try to keep your model within the confines of the white page because the software program can have issues trying to evaluate a model that is off the white page. One of the many nice functions in AMOS is it has a drag and drop function with your data. Once you tell AMOS what data file to use, you will be able to see a list of all variables in the data file. From there, you can find the variable you want, drag it from the list, and drop it in your white page area. All variables dragged in will be recognized as an observable variable and will be represented by a square from a graphical perspective. If you have drawn an unobservable construct along with its indicators, you can drag a variable right into an existing box (indicator).

On the left-hand side of the graphic window, you will see a series of blocks. These blocks will provide information about your model while you are still in the graphics window. Next, I provide a breakdown of the information each block presents in the graphics window.

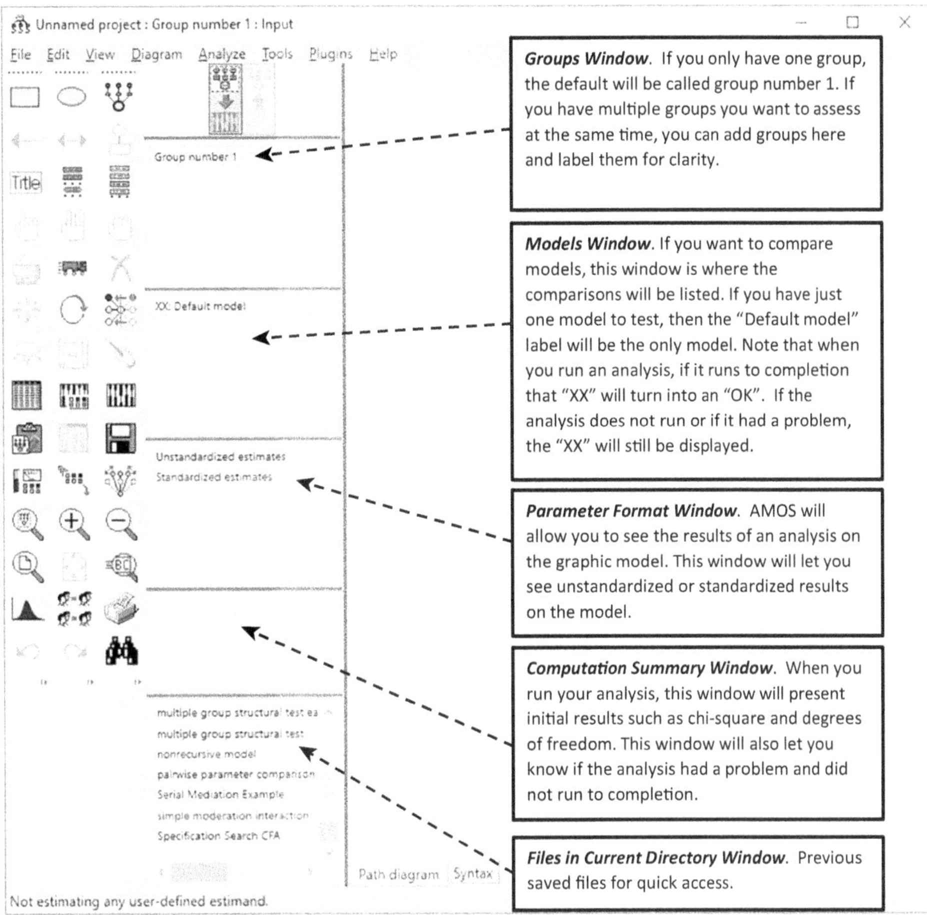

Figure 3.1 Explanation of blocks in AMOS Graphics Window

Along with the boxes on the left-hand side, AMOS will pin a ribbon of icons to the screen. These icons represent the most frequently used functions in AMOS. All of these same functions are also offered in the menu bar at the top of the screen. You can move these icons to either side of the screen and customize what icons are seen. There are many more functions and options in AMOS that are not listed in the pinned icon ribbon. Most of those are located at the menu bar at the top of the screen as well.

You do have the option to use a coding format as the input of your structural equation model and I cover how to do this in the advanced topics chapter (Chapter 10). While some will make the argument that you really don't understand SEM if you are not using a coding (syntax) format (i.e., you are just pushing buttons), I find this argument outdated. Typing out the names of the variables and functions needed does not provide any more insight than using the graphical interface. If anything, I find many researchers using syntax-only programs are so dependent on existing scripts used in previous research that they just cut and paste the syntax code into the program without thinking about whether this script is the most appropriate one to use. With the software AMOS, the strength of the program is the graphical interface, and I will focus on those options going forward. Saying that, there are some functions that can be accessed only through a coding (syntax) option. Those specific functions will be discussed on how to access and run them via a coding (syntax) method. All other functions will be presented and explained using the graphical interface.

Next, a detailed explanation of all the icons in the pinned ribbon will be presented. An example is provided for each icon to aid in the understanding of each function. All other functions not in the pinned ribbon will initially be discussed in an abbreviated manner. Throughout this book, these other functions will be discussed in more detail when they become relevant to the analysis discussed.

Figure 3.2 AMOS Icon Ribbon

AMOS Functions Listed as Icons in Pinned Ribbon

This function allows you to draw an observable variable. You can drag the square in the graphics window to the size of the box you want.

Example 3.1:

Drag to the size you want

=

This function allows you to draw an unobservable variable. You can drag the circle in the graphics window to the size of the circle you want. Note: you will rarely need to use this function. AMOS provides a better option for drawing unobservable variables.

Example 3.2:

Drag to the size you want

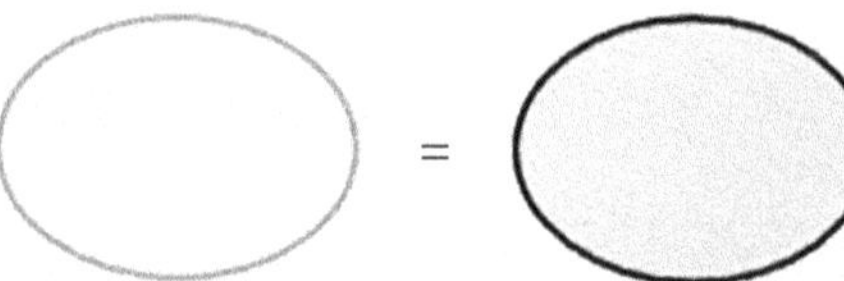

This function allows you draw an unobservable variable that includes indicators and error terms. This is the primary function you are going to use for drawing unobservable variables because it will include the indicators. You will initially draw/drag a circle to the size you want and then left-click on this circle to include an indicator. If you click twice on the unobservable (circle), AMOS will include two indicators. You can choose the number of indicators. If you have drawn the unobservable construct and indicators but forgot to add an indicator, just select this function and click on the unobservable, and it will add another indicator.

Example 3.3:

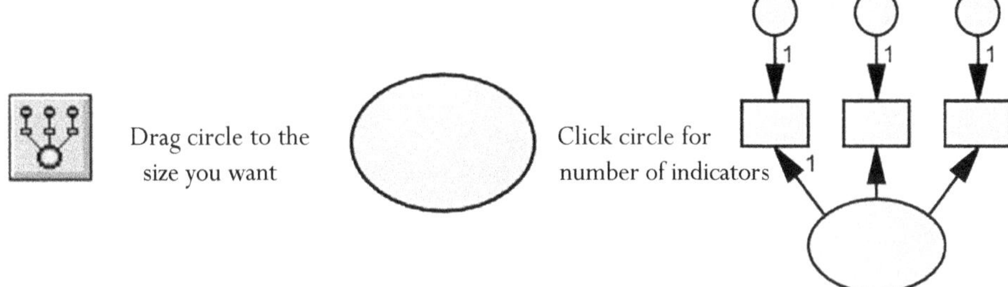

Example 3.4:

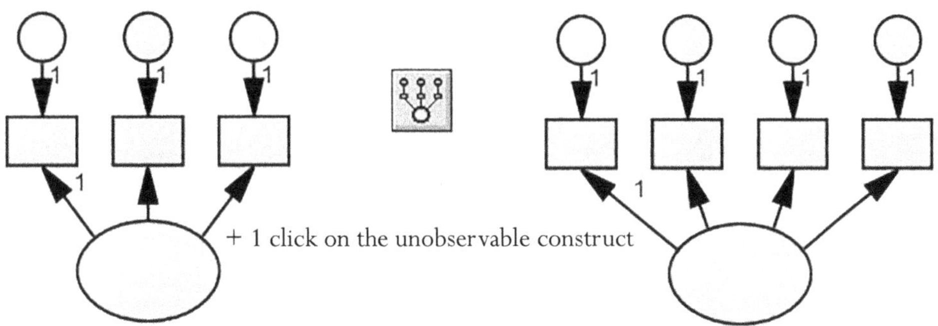

This function lets you draw a path (parameter) between two objects in the graphics window.

Example 3.5:

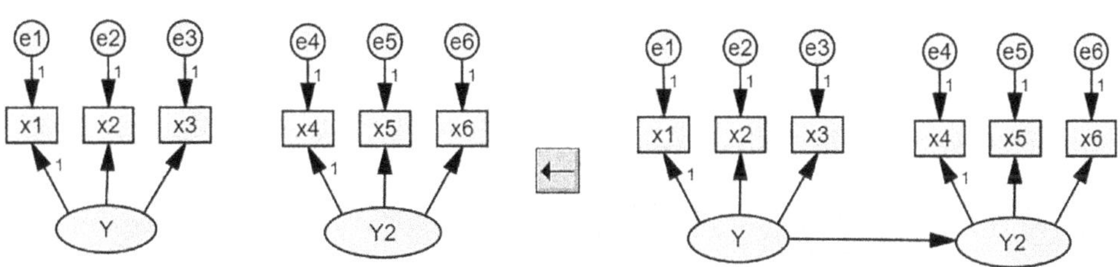

This function lets you draw a covariance. Note, if you drag this double headed arrow left to right, the arc of the line will be at the top. If you drag it right to left, the arc will be at the bottom. If you drag it top to bottom, the arc will be on the right. If you drag it from bottom to top, the arc of the line will be on the left.

Example 3.6:

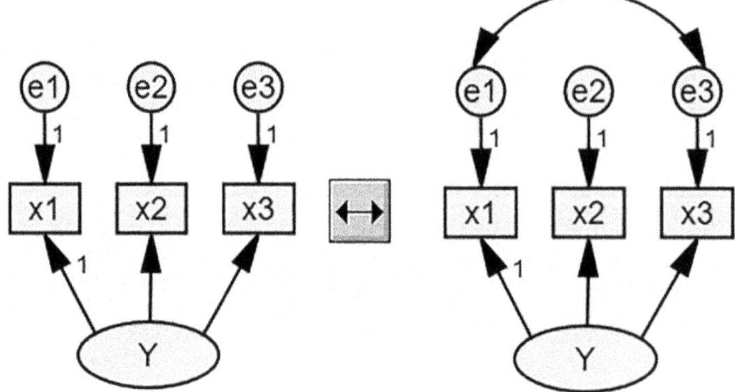

This function lets you add an error term to a variable. If a variable already has an error term added, then selecting this function and clicking on the variable again will rotate the error term. You can select the position you want the error term to be located.

Example 3.7:

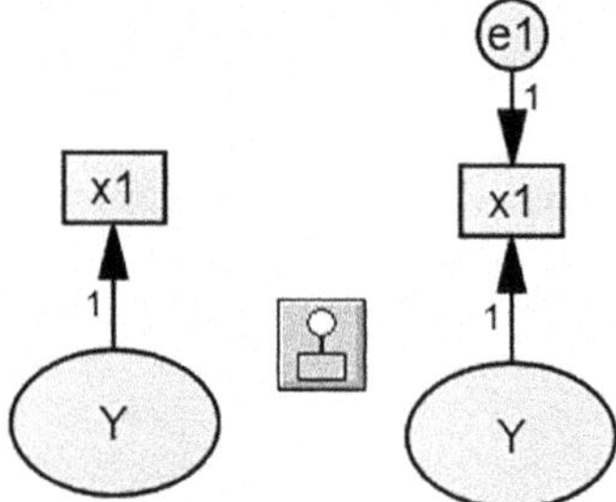

Example 3.8:

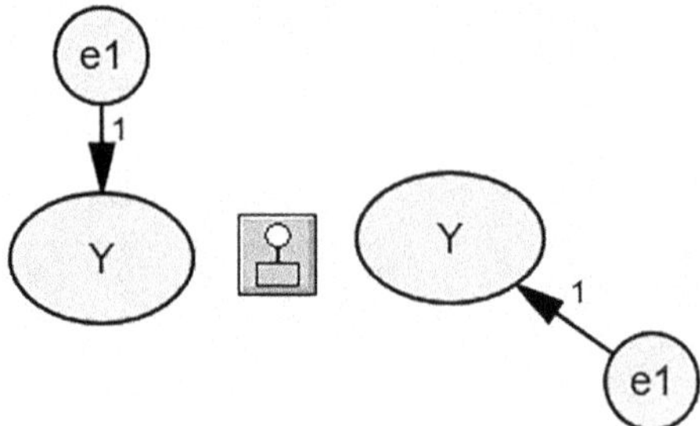

This function will let you add a title to the graphics window. There is no real need for this unless you are printing your model or trying to share it with another person.

Example 3.9:

After clicking this function, you will get a pop-up window to enter a title along with position.

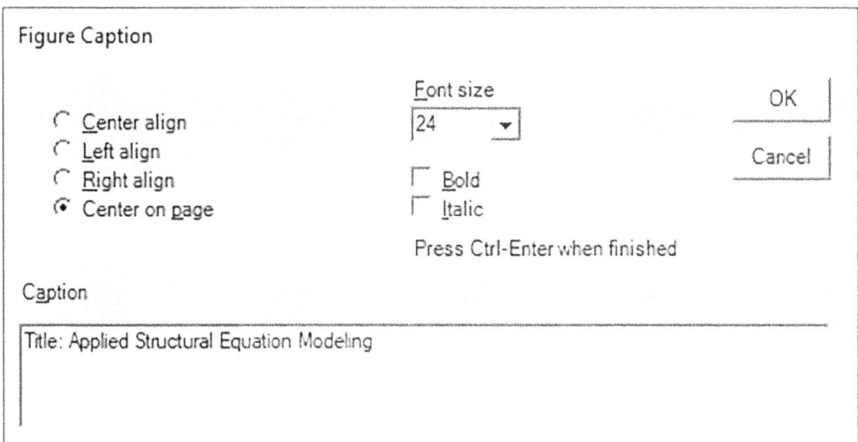

This function will allow you see all the variables that have been labeled in the drawn model.

Example 3.10:

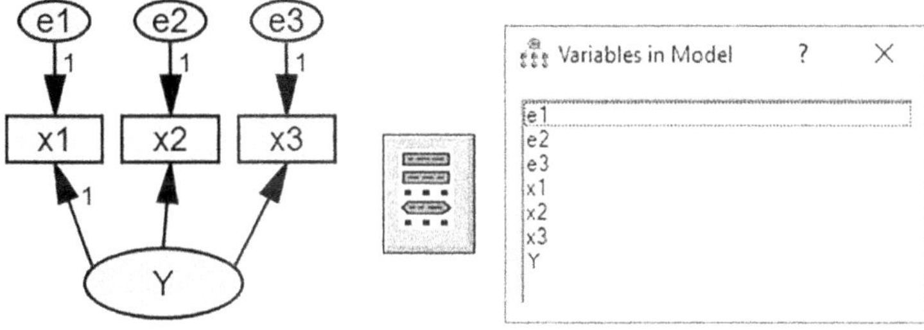

This function will show you all the variables that are listed in your data set. It will show the variable's name, label, and the column number.

Example 3.11:

Variables in Dataset ? ×

Name	Label	#.
satisfaction1	To what extent did you feel ________ because of your purchase at (Retailer) - Dissatisfied:Satisfied	1
satisfaction2	To what extent did you feel ________ because of your purchase at (Retailer) - Unpleasant:Pleasant	2
satisfaction3	To what extent did you feel ________ because of your purchase at (Retailer) - Not Content:Content	3

This function will allow you to select one object at a time. When you select an object, it will highlight it in blue.

Example 3.12:

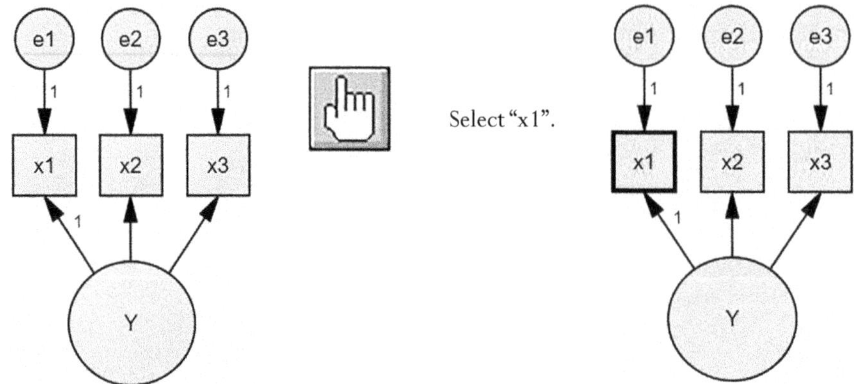

This function will allow you to select every object that is on the graphics window.

Example 3.13:

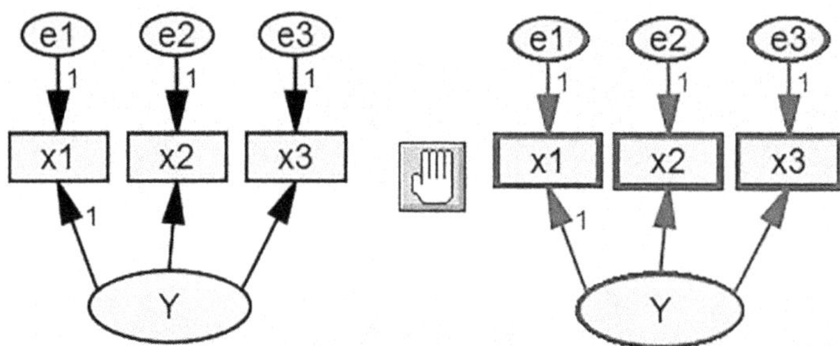

This function will allow you to deselect all objects that are selected/highlighted.

Example 3.14:

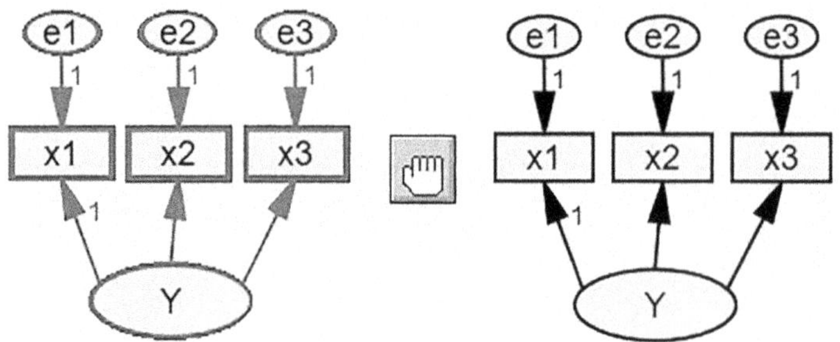

This function will allow you to delete an object that is in the graphics window.

Example 3.15:

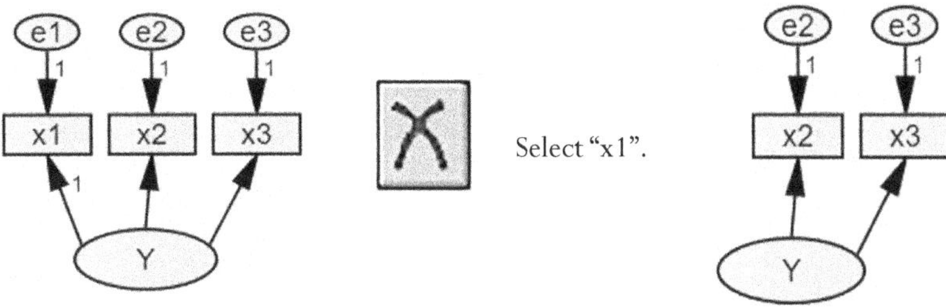

This function will allow you to move an object around the graphics window. If you select just this icon, you can move one object at time. If you want to move more than one object at a time, see the "preserve symmetries" function.

Example 3.16:

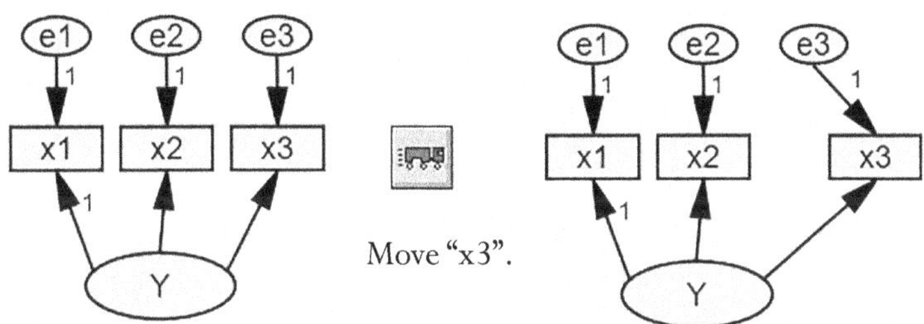

Example 3.17:

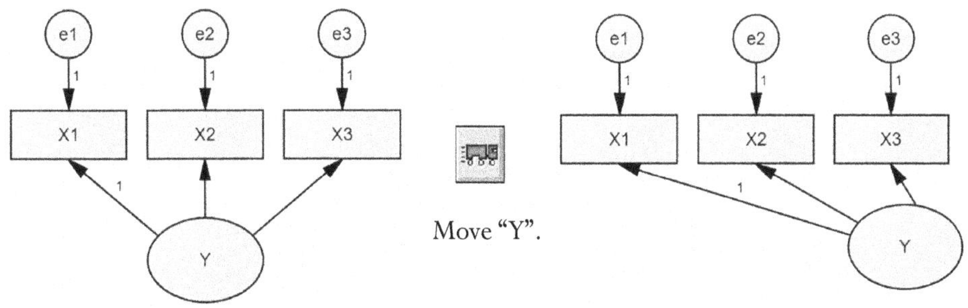

This function will create a duplicate of an object. If you choose this function and then select an object and drag, you will see a duplicate. This function will duplicate only one item at time unless the "preserve symmetries" button is selected, too. Note, the duplicate will have the same label, so this will need to be changed if it remains in the graphics window.

Example 3.18:

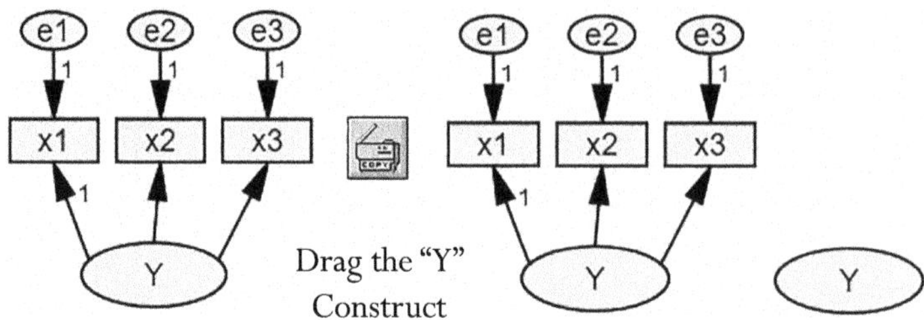

This function will allow you to change the shape of an object. You can change the height and width of an object. This is a handy function in order to see full variable names if they are bigger than the original object size. This function will let you resize only one object at time unless the "preserve symmetries" button is selected.

Example 3.19:

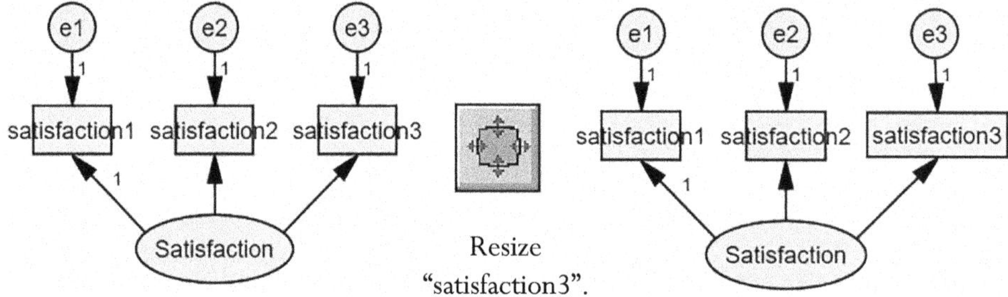

This is the preserve symmetries button which will allow you to change or move multiple objects within an unobservable construct that has indicators and error terms. This function is especially handy with the "move", "resize", and "copy" functions.

Example 3.20:

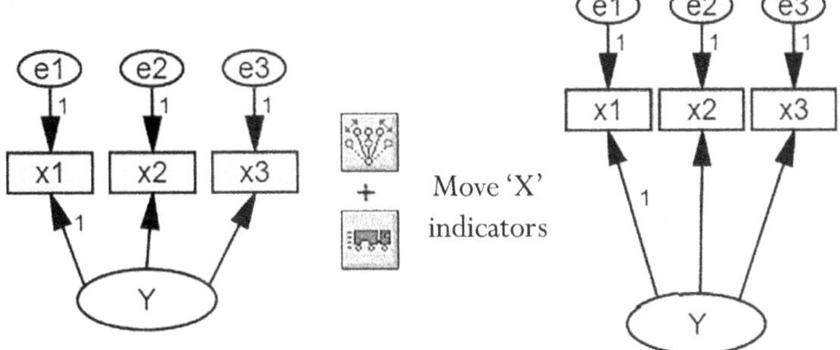

This will allow you to move all the "x" indicators at once instead of one at a time. You can space them out or move them in or out from the unobservable construct.

Example 3.21:

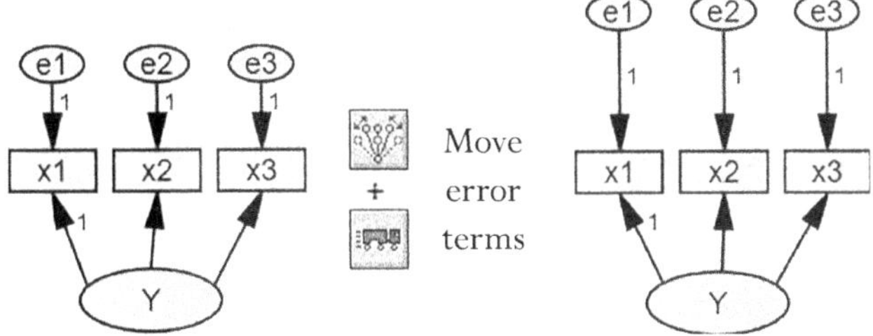

This will allow you to move all the error terms at once instead of one at a time. You can space them out or move them in or out from the indicators.

Example 3.22:

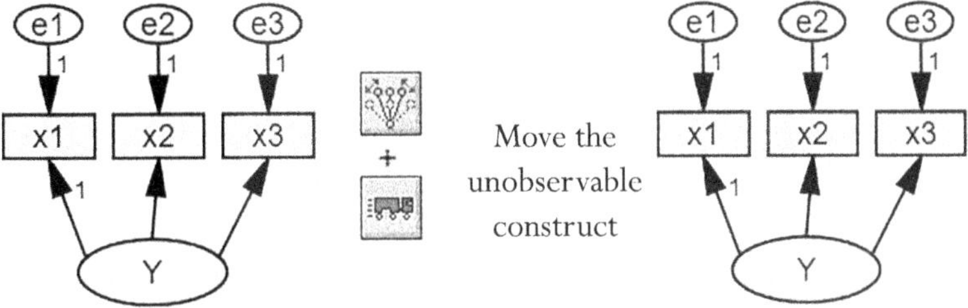

This will allow you to move the unobservable construct and all objects attached to it. In essence, this will move everything associated with the construct.

Example 3.23:

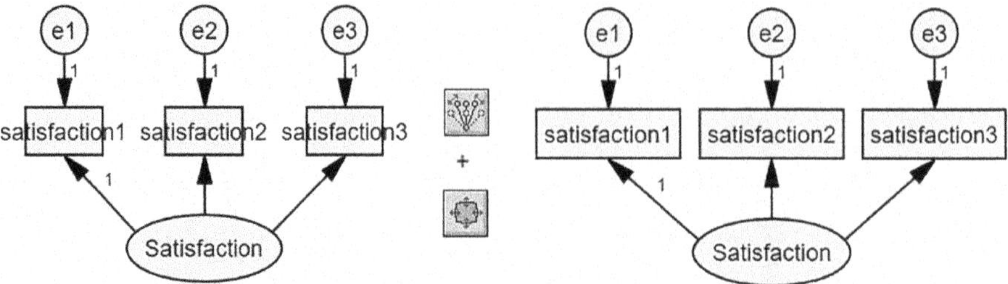

With the preserve symmetries icon selected, you can resize numerous objects at once. If we were trying to resize the indicators, the boxes for all the indicators would resize to the desired size.

Example 3.24:

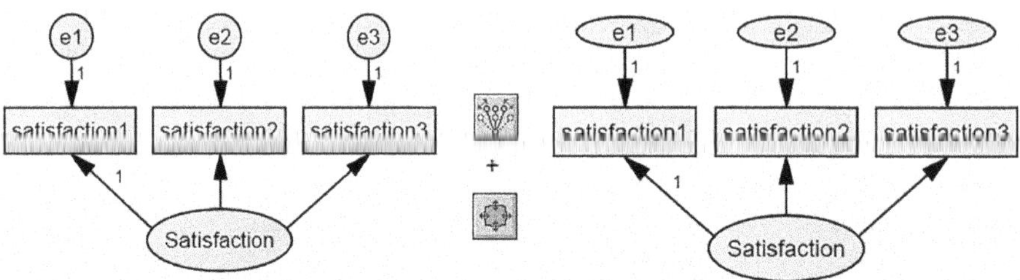

With the preserve symmetries icon selected, you can resize all the error terms at once instead of one at a time.

Example 3.25:

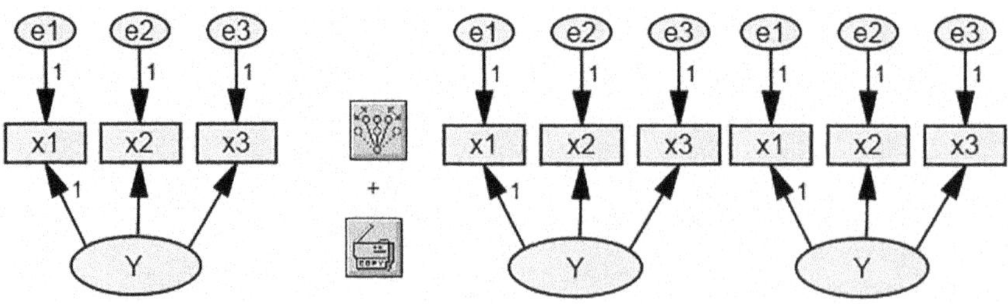

With the preserve symmetries icon selected, you can copy an unobservable and all its indicators. It makes a duplicate of the unobservable and all objects attached to it. Again, the labels are exactly the same in the duplicate, so you will need to change those if it is going to stay in the graphics window. This function is handy to use before the constructs have been labeled and you need another construct with the exact same number of indicators and error terms.

This function will allow you to rotate the indicators around the unobservable construct.

Example 3.26:

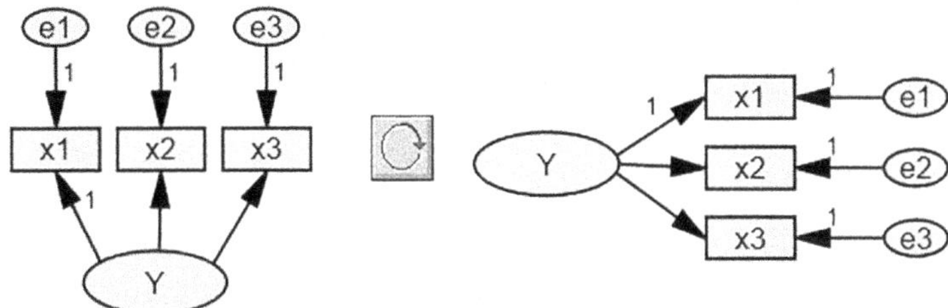

This function will reflect the indicators of an unobserved construct. It is like a mirror function.

Example 3.27:

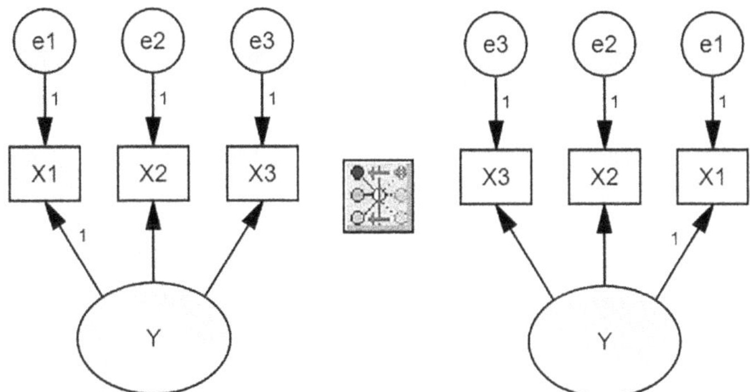

This function will allow you to move parameter labels so that you can see them clearly.

Example 3.28:

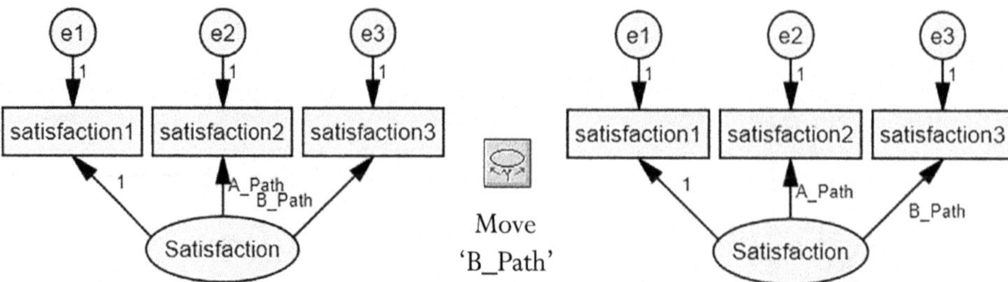

This is the touch up icon. It will rearrange paths and covariances to make them easier to see. It makes the paths and covariances pleasing to the eye from a graphical standpoint. Click the areas you want to clean up.

Example 3.29:

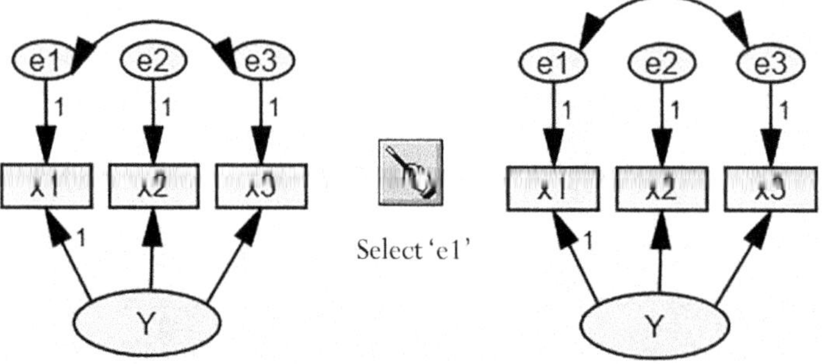

This is the select data file function. This is where you will link the raw data to AMOS.

Example 3.30:

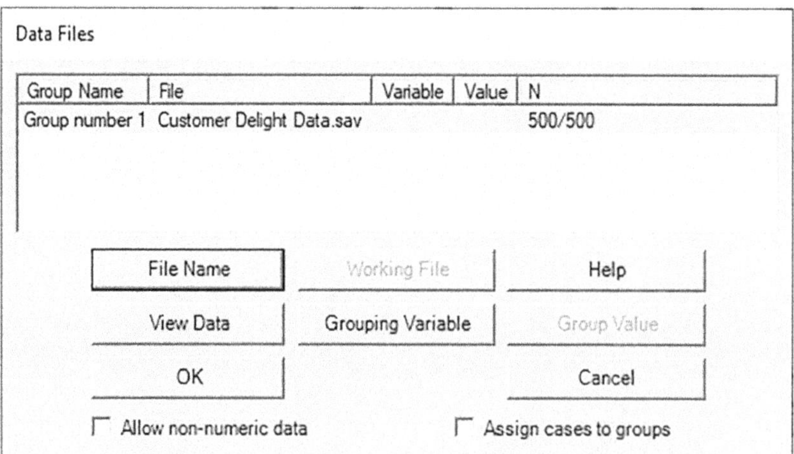

This is the Analysis Properties icon. This function will allow you to see numerous options for the output you want displayed after running the analysis. After clicking this icon, a pop-up window will appear. There are eight tabs at the top of the pop-up window that will allow you to choose different output options.

Example 3.31:

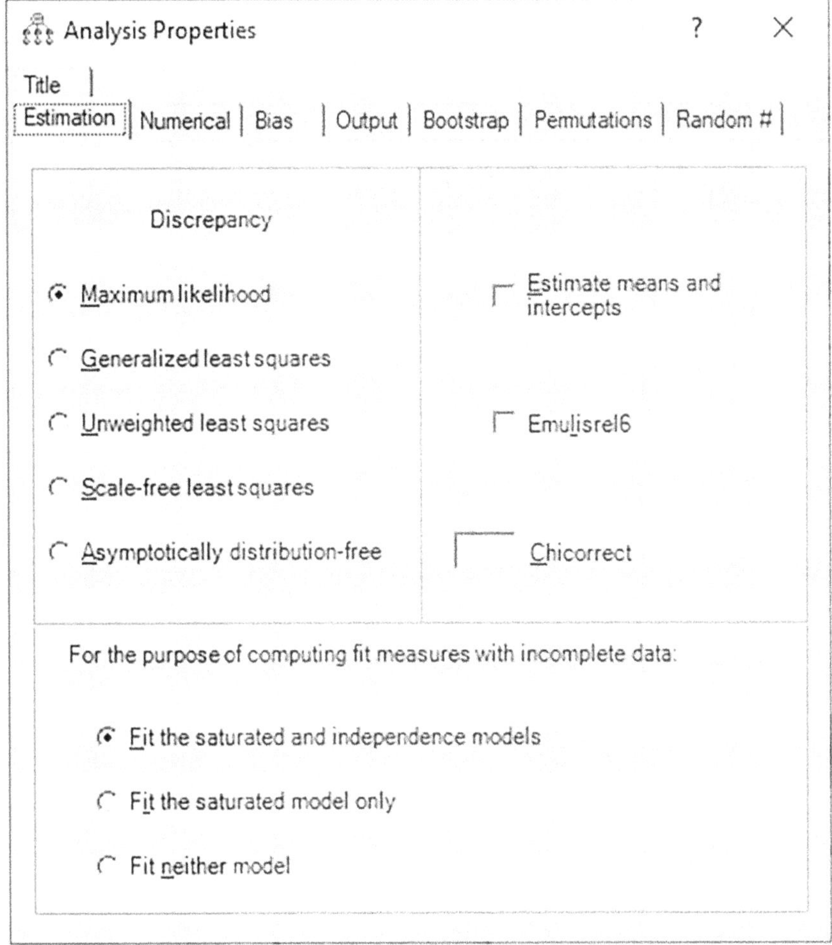

This is the calculate results icon. This is the icon you will select when you are ready to run your analysis.

This is the view output icon. Selecting this icon will take you to the text output after an analysis has been run.

This is the copy model to the clipboard icon. This will copy the model drawn on the graphics window to the clipboard for you to paste in another area or document.

This is the save current model icon. This will let you save your work.

This is the zoom on a specific area function. After selecting this icon, you can drag a box around a specific area and that selection will be zoomed in.

Example 3.32:

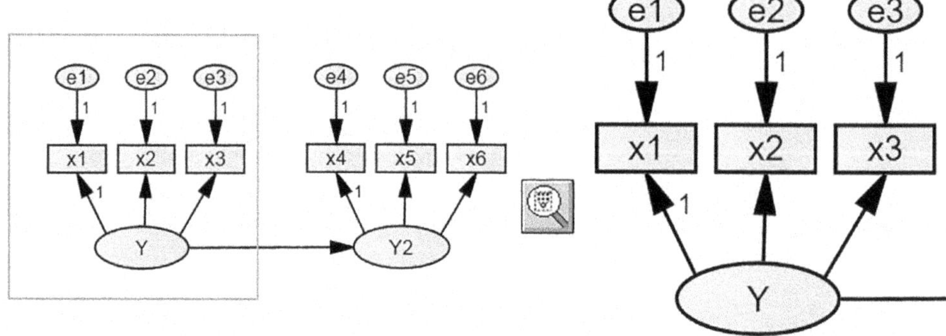

This is the zoom in function. It will zoom the whole page on the graphics window in order for everything to become larger.

This is the zoom-out function. It will zoom out the whole page on the graphics window in order to see more of the page.

This is the Object Properties function. This is where you can change the properties of an object such as changing a variable name or label. You can also name and fix parameters. Another option available in this function is to change text size, style, and color scheme. There are five tabs at the top that will change different properties of an object.

Example 3.33:

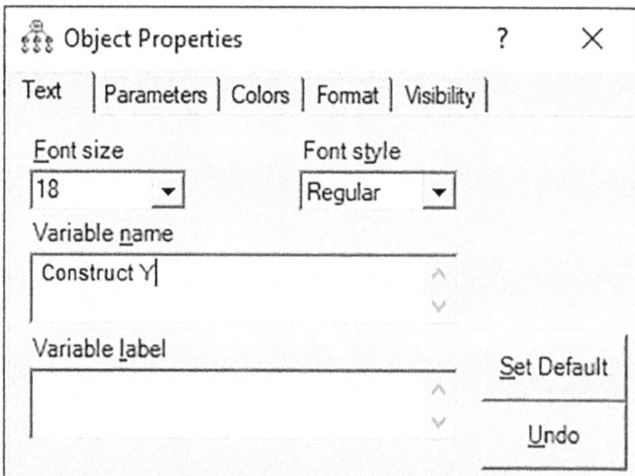

This is the drag properties function. This function will let you drag object properties to other objects in the graphics window. Note that the drag properties pop-up window has to be active for the "dragging" function to work across properties. You can drag an object's properties to numerous objects if they are selected/highlighted first.

Example 3.34:

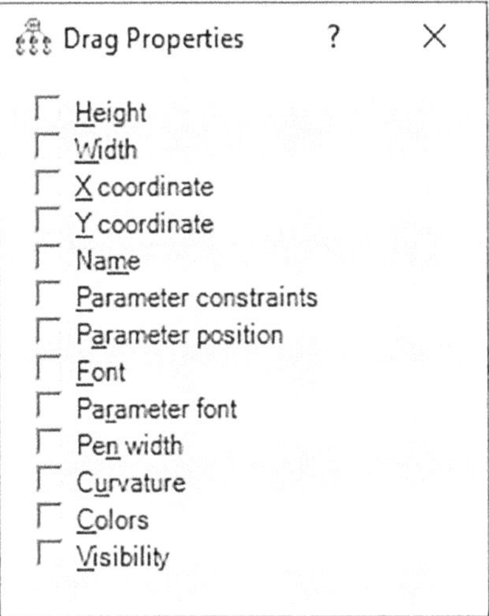

This is the reposition model function. This where you can scroll your model to the left and right and see more of what is on the graphics window. This is usually needed only if you have zoomed in on an area and need to see a subsequent area that is off the screen.

This is the examine diagram with loupe icon. This is just a big magnifying glass that lets you see in a desired area without zooming in.

Example 3.35:

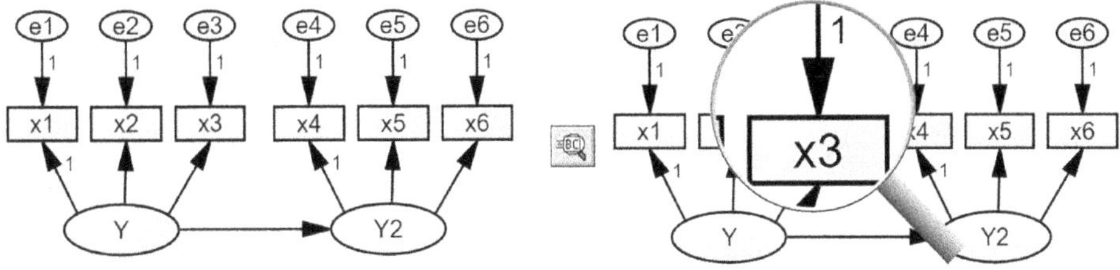

This is the "zoom page" function. This function will magnify to view the whole page. Selecting this icon will either zoom in or out to let you see the whole page AMOS graphics is using.

This is the resize whole model to fit the page icon. This is where AMOS will resize the entire model to fit on the page. I would caution you not to use this option. It will force the model to the page in often weird and cramped ways.

This is the Bayesian Analysis function. Selecting this icon will take you to a pop-up window that will perform Bayesian analysis.

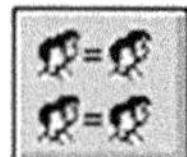

This is the multi-group analysis function. Choosing this icon will label parameters across groups and also suggest models to compare across groups.

This is the print function. This icon will allow you to print the model on the graphics window. It will also allow you to print unstandardized and standardized estimates on the model. You can also choose between groups on the model you choose to print.

Example 3.36:

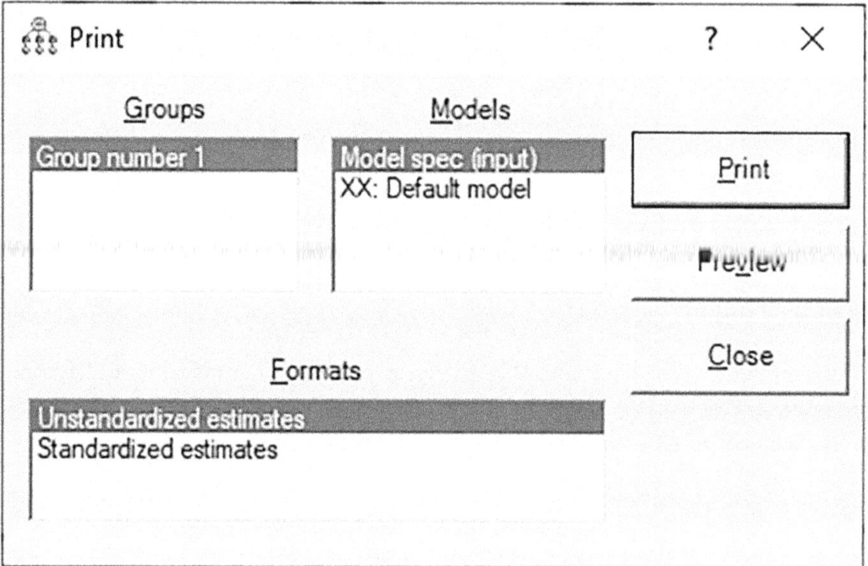

This is the undo change function.

This is the redo change function.

This is the specification search function. This function lets you explore what the fit of a model is if you remove paths from the initial model.

Tips to Using AMOS More Efficiently

Tip 1: Change the AMOS graphics page from portrait to landscape. In the AMOS graphic window, the program will default with the page in a portrait format. Most models take more space from left to right than from top to bottom. If you change the format of the page to landscape, you have potentially more space to create complex models. To make this change, go to the "View" menu option at the top and then select the "Interface Properties" option. (Here is what the icon for that function looks like .) After selecting this option, a pop-up window will appear. There are seven tabs at the top of this window that let you change numerous visual options in AMOS. Go to the "Page Layout" tab at the top and then select the paper size option from "Portrait-Letter" to "Landscape-Letter". This will now rotate your page into a landscape format.

Example 3.37:

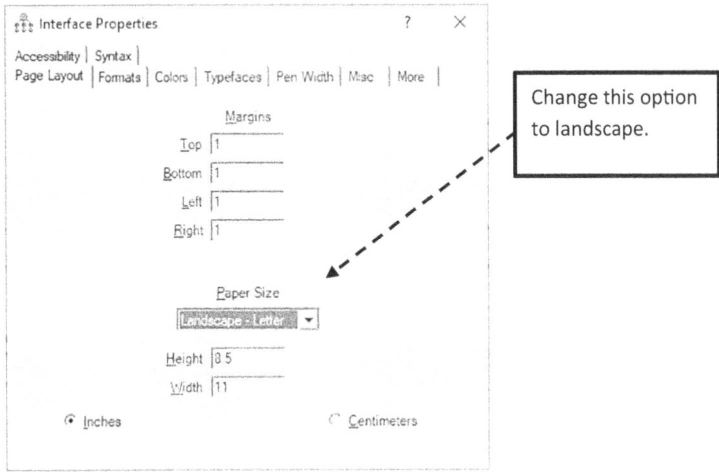

Tip 2: Display Variable Names Instead of Labels. When you drag a variable from the variable list into the AMOS graphics window, the variable will be displayed as its label in AMOS. The label is often where you will see the actual question asked in a survey. Hence, instead of just listing a short name for each variable, you have a huge variable label that lists the whole question asked. To have AMOS change from displaying variable labels in the graphics window to displaying the variable name, you need to go to the interface properties window. In the tab at the top called "Misc", you will see a series of checkboxes that are already checked. One of those checkboxes is "Display Variable Labels". You want to uncheck this box. By doing this, the variable name will now be displayed instead of the label.

Example 3.38:

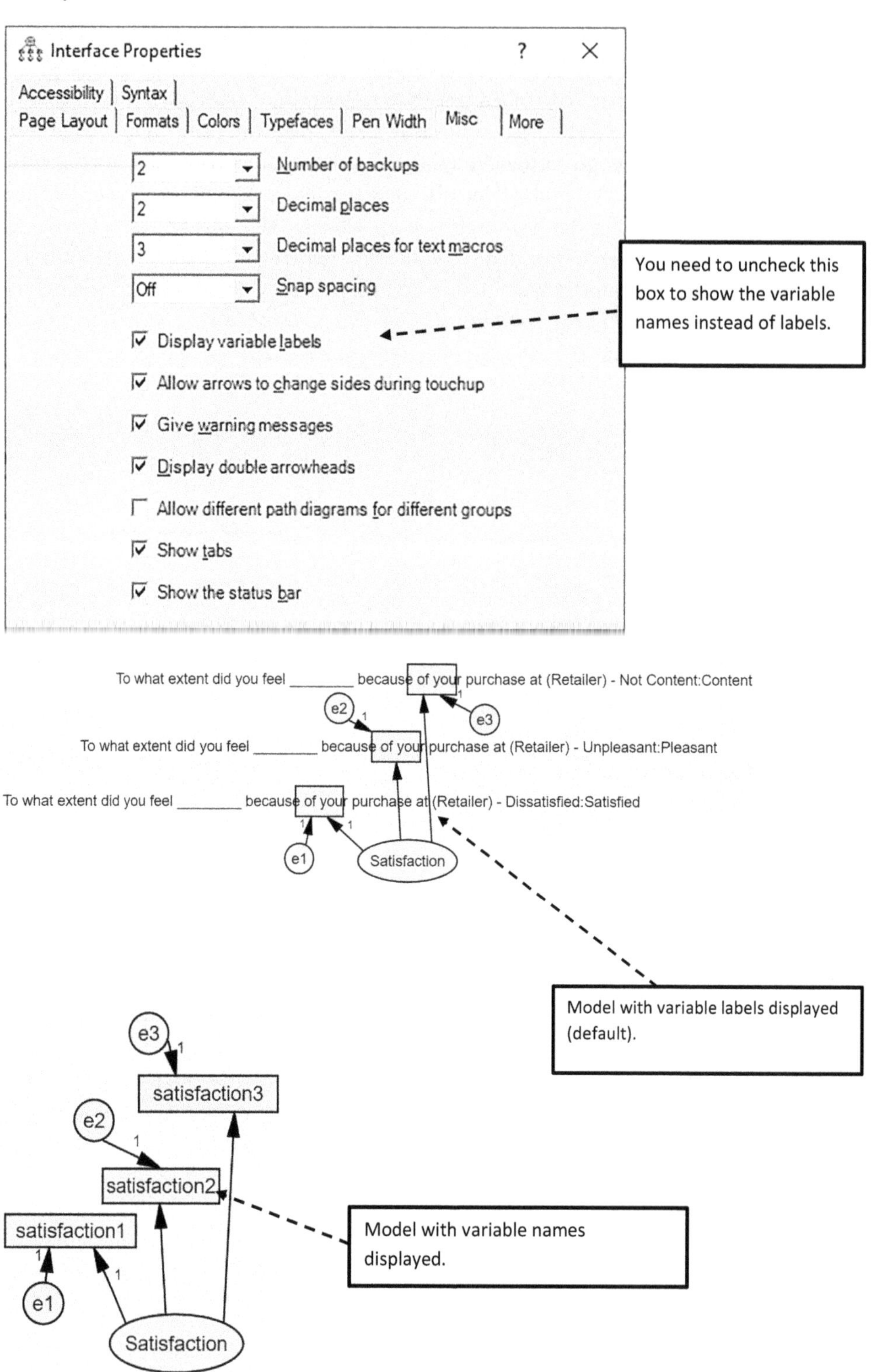
Interface Properties
Accessibility | Syntax |
Page Layout | Formats | Colors | Typefaces | Pen Width | Misc | More
2 Number of backups
2 Decimal places
3 Decimal places for text macros
Off Snap spacing
Display variable labels
Allow arrows to change sides during touchup
Give warning messages
Display double arrowheads
Allow different path diagrams for different groups
Show tabs
Show the status bar
You need to uncheck this box to show the variable names instead of labels.
To what extent did you feel ________ because of your purchase at (Retailer) - Not Content:Content
To what extent did you feel ________ because of your purchase at (Retailer) - Unpleasant:Pleasant
To what extent did you feel ________ because of your purchase at (Retailer) - Dissatisfied:Satisfied
e1
e2
e3
Satisfaction
Model with variable labels displayed (default).
satisfaction1
satisfaction2
satisfaction3
Model with variable names displayed.

Tip 3: Have AMOS label all your error terms. If you have a model with numerous constructs and indicators, you will find that it can be quite laborious to label all the error terms for every indicator. AMOS has a function that will label all error terms for you. In the "Plugins" menu option at the top, you need to select "Name Unobserved Variables". This will label all error terms with a letter "e" and a number. AMOS will start numbering error terms based on the order of creation. The first unobservable construct and error terms created in AMOS will be where the error numbering will start.

A word of caution: this function will try to label unobserved constructs, too, if you have not labeled them already. The unobserved constructs will be labeled a letter "F" and a number. I would not recommend letting AMOS label your unobservable constructs, but I do find this function quite handy in labeling all the error terms in your model.

Example 3.39:

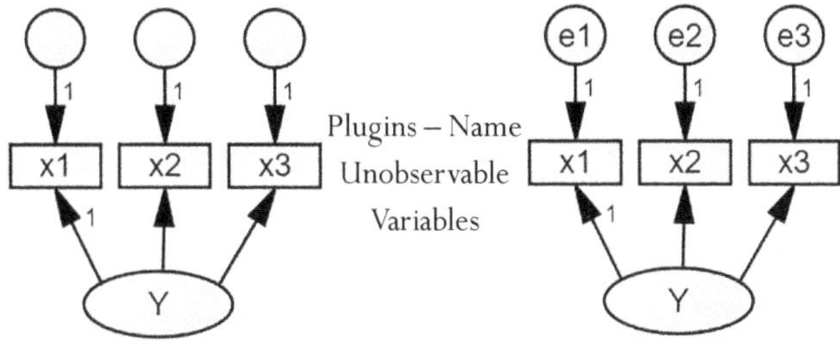

Tip 4: Browse Path Diagrams to find previously saved models. If you are like me, you may have numerous versions of a model you are working on and sometimes the name of the saved file does not help me find a specific version of a model. The browse path diagrams function lets you preview previously saved files to find the specific model you desire. To use this function, go to the "File" menu option at the top and then to the "Browse Path Diagram" option.

Example 3.40:

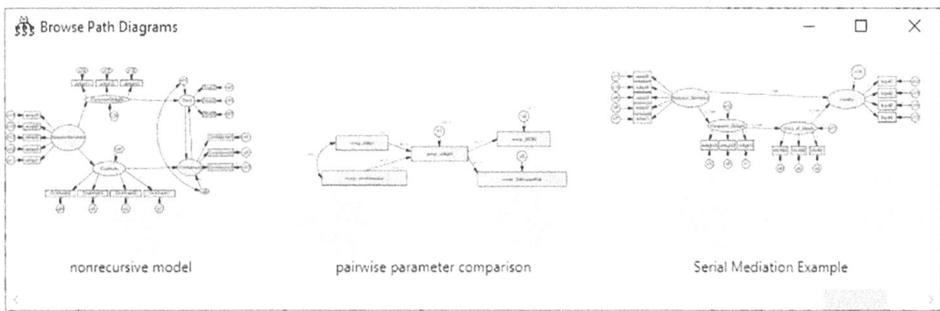

Tip 5: Let AMOS draw covariances between independent variables. All independent variables should have a covariance between them. If you have a large model, this can be quite a few covariances to add. If you select/highlight all the independent unobservable constructs

(circles), then go to the "Plugins" menu option at the top and select "Draw Covariances". This option will draw a covariance between all variables selected/highlighted. It is a good idea to hit the "deselect" button when you are done.

Example 3.41:

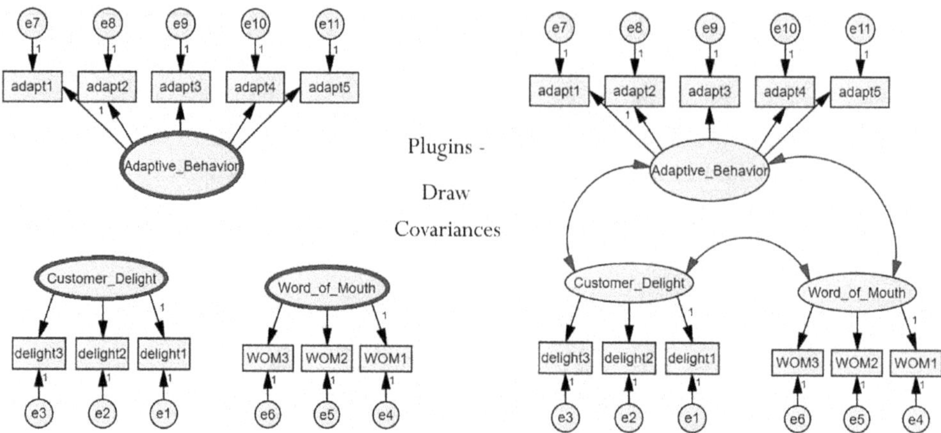

Tip 6: AMOS can resize all observables/indicators to fully show a variable name. The variable names for your indicators can vary wildly in length, and AMOS can help with the resizing of the boxes to fully show the variable names. In the "Plugins" menu at the top, select the "Resize Observed Variables". This will change the size of all observable variables in the model to fully contain the variable name within the box. Instead of resizing observables/indicators after every construct that is added to the model, you can wait until all constructs are included in the model and use this function to resize all the boxes to fit the variable names.

Example 3.42:

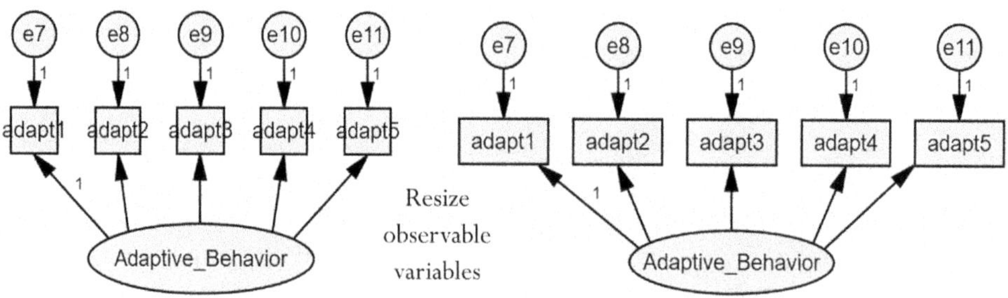

Tip 7: Save the middle of the page for paths/relationships. With full structural models, you can have a lot of indicators and error terms that can really make it hard to see the relationships between constructs. Try to keep indicators and error terms near the edge of the

page and leave the middle of the page for structural relationships. You will need to rotate indicators around the unobservable constructs to accomplish this.

Example 3.43:

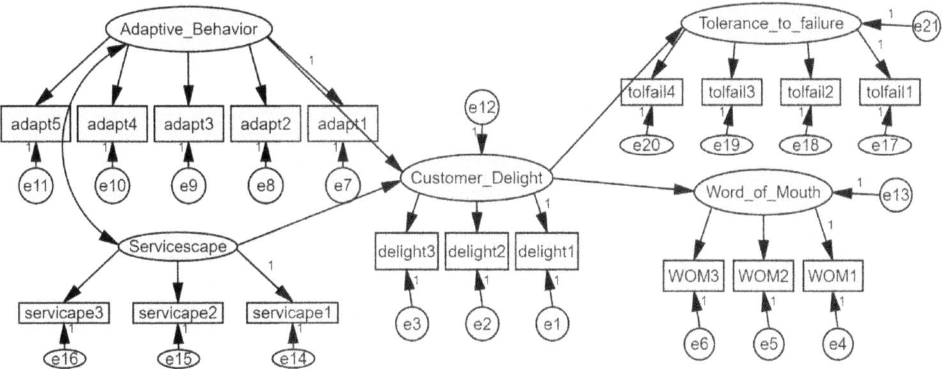

The top model is very busy and hard to see the structural paths because of all the indicators. The bottom model has moved the indicators to the edges of the page so that the structural paths are easier to see.

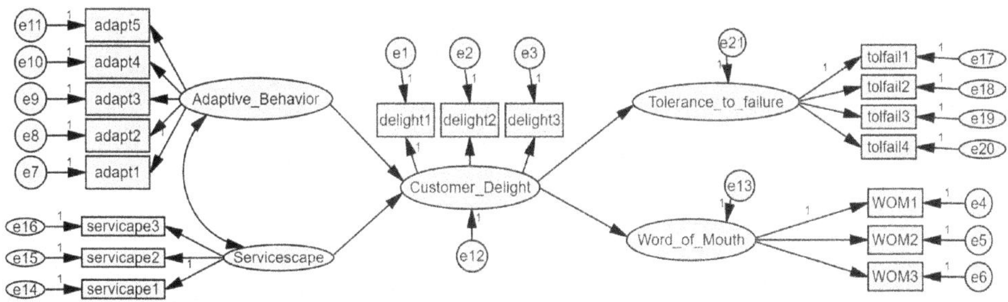

Tip 8: Standardize the look of your observable and unobservable constructs. One way to standardize the look of your observables is to use the "square" function [ ]. If you select the square function and then draw an observable on the graphics window, it will draw every box as a square. Similarly, if the "square" function is selected, ever drawn unobservable will be a perfect circle. There is a subsequent function called "Golden" [ ] which will create rectangles with observables and ovals with unobservables.

Example 3.44:

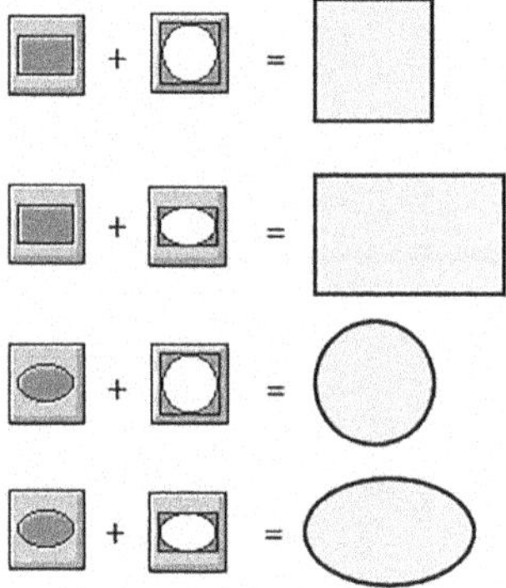

Tip 9: Force Objects in the Graphics Window to line up on a grid line. If you would like for all of your boxes or circles to be in a straight line down the graphics window, you need to use the option called "Snap Spacing". In the Interface Properties window, you want to go to the "Misc" tab and then change the Snap Spacing option from "off" to a number. When snap spacing is turned on, AMOS will include (invisible) grid lines in the graphics window and will space the gridlines out based on your preference. If you choose a snap spacing of 24, then AMOS will separate the grid lines by 24/96 = .25 inches apart. If you select a snap spacing of 12, then the separation is 12/96 = .125 inches apart. To turn the grid lines back off, just change Snap Spacing to "off". If you are researcher that likes to have your objects in the graphics window in an orderly pattern, then Snap Spacing will save you some time from trying to eyeball objects to be in line with one another.

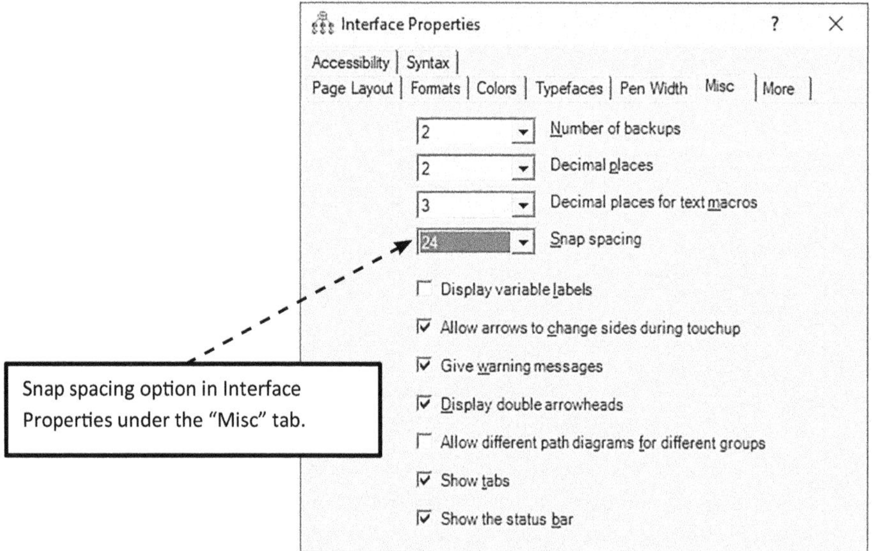

Tip 10: Automatically show text output after running an analysis. After running an analysis, AMOS will require you to select the "View Output" icon [icon] to see your results. The newer

version of AMOS will allow the text output to automatically appear after running an analysis. In the Interface Properties option [icon], there is a tab at the top of the pop-up window called "More". Clicking on this tab, you will see an option titled "Automatically show text output". Clicking this option will allow you to automatically see the output of an analysis without having to select the "View Output" icon.

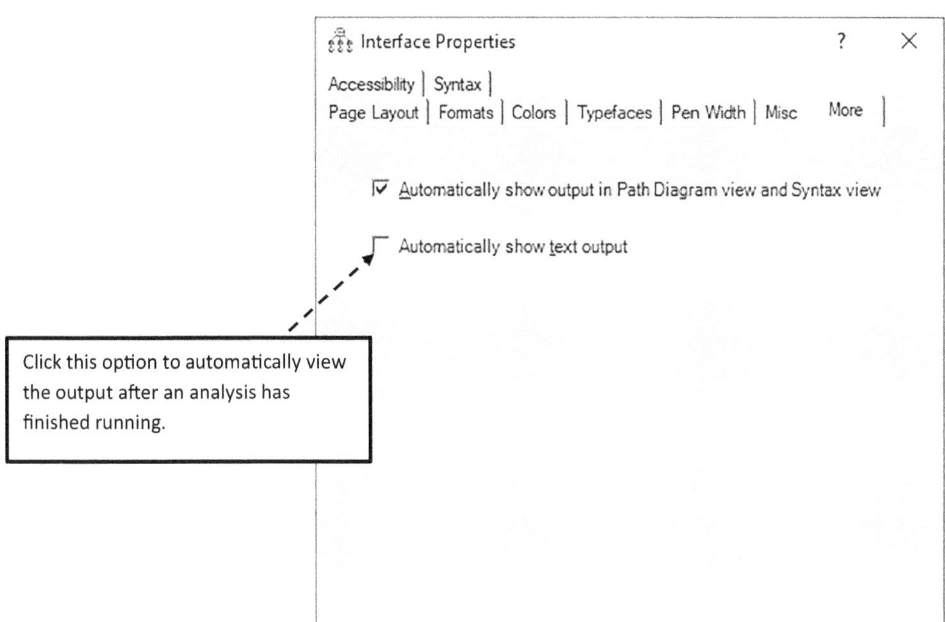

Quick Reference to AMOS Functions

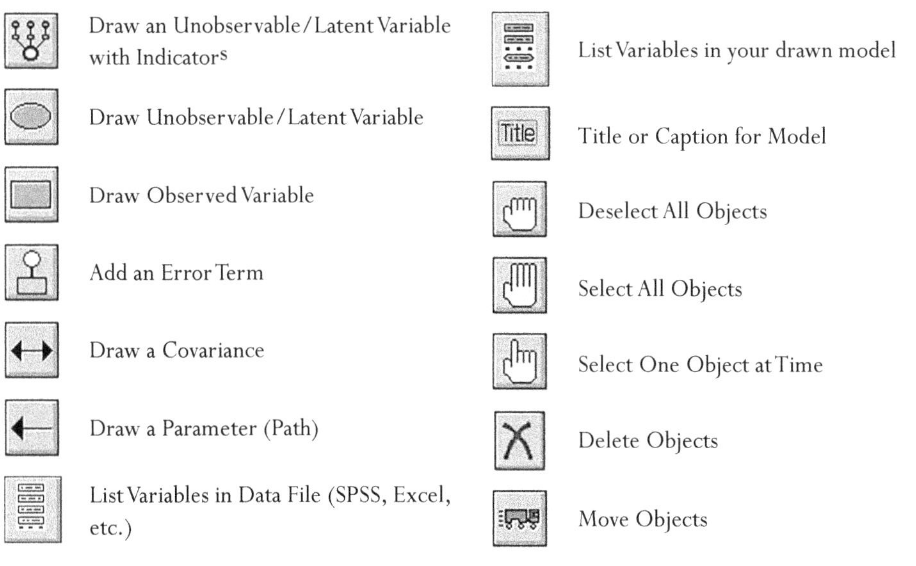

Duplicate Objects

Reflect Indicators of a Latent Construct (mirror function)

Rotate Indicators of an Unobservable/ Latent Construct

Change the Shape of an Object (height and width)

Touch Up (cleans up parameters on a construct—makes it easier to see)

Reposition your model on the screen (scroll across the model)

Move Parameter Values (so you can see the parameter values easier)

Calculate Estimates (run your analysis)

Analysis Properties (select different output options)

Interface Properties (page layout, margins, colors)

Select a Data File

Save the Current Model

View Output (view results)

Copy Model to the Clipboard

Preserve Symmetries (allows you to move a latent construct and indicators together)

Drag Properties (drag the property of one object to another)

Object Properties (properties of an individual object selected)

View a larger area of the model

View a smaller area of the model

Zoom in on an area you have selected

Examine the Path Diagram with a Loupe (just a big magnifying glass to look a specific area)

Resize the Model to fit on a page

Undo the previous change

Redo Change

Show the whole page on the screen

Print the selected model (will print what is on the page)

Multiple Group Analysis

Bayesian Analysis

Specification Search (exploratory analysis of paths and covariances)

Manage Models (show comparison of parameters across models or groups)

Manage Groups (create groups and label them)

Modeling Lab (allows you to enter parameter values and see how the covariance matrix is impacted with changes)

Toggle an object from a latent to an observable (and vice versa)

Degrees of Freedom (shows total parameters as well)

Any rectangle you draw will be square and any oval will be a circle.

Creates standard rectangles and ovals

Data Recode function (lets you recode categorical data into numerical data)

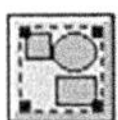 Link objects together (for printing, copying, resizing, moving)

 Space Objects Horizontally (select dependent variables first—this will evenly space them vertically from the independent variable)

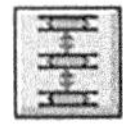 Space Objects Vertically (select dependent variables first—this will evenly space them vertically from the independent variable)

 List all parameters

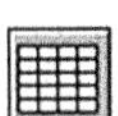 Matrix Representation

 Stop Calculating Estimate (stop the analysis in the middle of analyzing the data)

 Plugins–Multiple Functions

 Data Imputation (missing values)

 Font, Text Color, Size

 This button erases a path diagram and redraws it:

 This button lets you see your model in full screen mode:

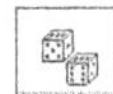 Seed Manager (used to produce the same results in a Bayesian Analysis)

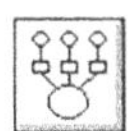 Show the outline of model (text removed—hit the button again to get text back)

 Write a Program (this icon will convert a graphic model in AMOS to Visual Basic code)

 D-Separation Preview (lets you perform a D-separation analysis)

Shortcut Keys for AMOS Functions:

F1 = Search Content Directory
F2 = "Select one object at a time" button
F3 = "Draw Observed Variable" button
F4 = "Draw Unobserved Variable" button
F5 = "Draw Path (single head)" button
F6 = "Draw Covariance" button
F7 = "Zoom in" button
F8 = "Zoom out" button
F9 = "Zoom page" button
F10 = "View Output" button
F11 = "Full Screen viewing" button
F12 = "Examine diagram with Loupe" button—magnifying glass

Ctrl + B = Bayesian Analysis function
Ctrl + C = Copy model to clipboard
Ctrl + D = Select Data file function
Ctrl + E = View Interface Properties
Ctrl + F = Fit the model to the page
Ctrl + G = Drag properties function
Ctrl + H = Use the touch up function
Ctrl + M = Move one object at a time
Ctrl + O = Object Properties function
Ctrl + P = Print the model
Ctrl + R = View Analysis Properties
Ctrl + S = Save function
Ctrl + V = Paste model from clipboard
Ctrl + Y = Redo function
Ctrl + Z = Undo function
Ctrl + F9 = Calculate Estimates function
Alt + F8 = Plugins Menu

*Note: These are the shortcut keys as of AMOS 26

Chapter 4

Measurement Model Analysis

Introduction to Confirmatory Factor Analysis

Confirmatory factor analysis (CFA) is a statistical technique that analyzes how well your indicators measure your unobserved constructs and if your unobserved constructs are uniquely different from one another. In a CFA, an unobservable construct is often referred to as a "factor". So, when I use the term "factor", it represents an unobservable construct we are trying to measure. In a diagram format, an unobserved variable is represented by a circle or oval. The indicators that measure the unobserved variable will have single headed arrows coming from the unobserved construct to each of the indicators. Each indicator is represented by a square or a rectangle. The single arrow line directly from the factor, or unobservable construct, to the indicator represents the influence that is reflected from the unobservable construct to its indicators. Statistical estimates of these direct effects are called "factor loadings" and are interpreted as regression coefficients that may be in unstandardized or standardized form. Indicators that "reflect" an unobservable construct or factor are called simply reflective indicators. In special instances, some indicators are classified as "formative", and they will be discussed later in the chapter (page 110).

With most indicators, a level of error is present. Each measurement error of an indicator represents "unique variance", or variance not explained by the factor level. Measurement errors are represented by two types of unique variance: random error and systematic error. Random error occurs when the measurement of a concept is unpredictably fluctuating due to unforeseen or random influences. This type of error is considered "noise" because there is often no consistency to the measurement error. Systematic error is different in that the error is systematic in nature. The results of a measurement can be consistently high or low due to a systematic influence in the measurement of a concept. For instance, taking a survey online as compared to a paper and pencil survey may systematically influence the way respondents answer questions about a construct. With systematic error, this is often classified as a "bias" compared to the "noise" of random error. Note that if an unobserved variable has only one indicator, then the error term for the single indicator variable is constrained to have a mean of 0 and a variance of 0. (You must assume the indicator has no measurement error—which is often a very flawed assumption.)

In a CFA, you also want to account for "unmeasured covariance". To do this, a two-headed arrow is drawn between all independent unobservable variables. In a CFA, the analysis will treat all unobserved variables as exogenous or independent variables. Thus, you will draw a covariance double headed arrow between each unobservable construct in a CFA. If you don't do this, AMOS will give you an error message stating that a covariance should be drawn between all unobserved constructs in your CFA.

As an example, let's use our Customer Delight construct mentioned earlier, and now let's include another construct of how likely a consumer is to spread positive word of mouth about an experience. The diagram of this simple CFA would look like this:

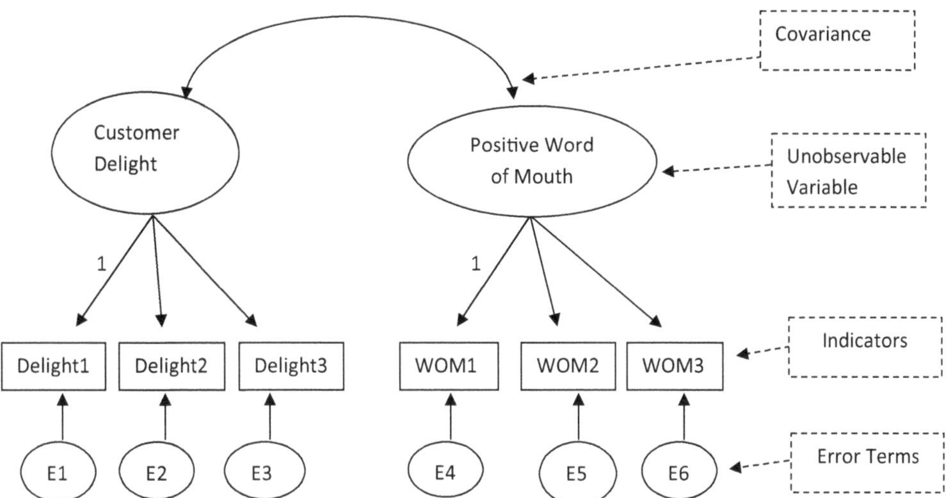

Figure 4.1 Two Construct CFA Analysis

A word of caution: do not use "E" and a number for an unobserved or observed variable name. The letter "E" is reserved for an error term.

How Is a CFA Different From an EFA?

An exploratory factor analysis (EFA) is useful in data reduction of a large number of indicators and can be quite helpful in seeing if indicators are measuring more than one construct. EFAs are typically the first step in determining if an indicator is measuring a construct. In an EFA, the researcher is not denoting which indicators are measuring a construct. The analysis simply tries to let every indicator load on every construct. This is where "cross loading" can occur, where an indicator is actually loading strongly on more than one construct. This is a concern that your indicator is not a strong measure of the specified construct. In contrast, a CFA does not allow an indicator to load on more than one construct. The researcher prior to the analysis will specify what the indicators are for each construct, and those indicators can load only on that specific construct. Other ways that an EFA and CFA are different is an EFA is typically conducted with correlation matrices, which can be problematic in comparing parameters across samples. CFA uses a covariance matrix and is more adept at handling comparisons across samples. An EFA will also consider data rotation that is often done to achieve a better loading of indicators on a construct or sometimes a reduction of cross loading with other constructs. A CFA does not worry about rotation because you are denoting the specific items that are loading on a construct. For a graphic representation of EFA versus CFA, see Figure 4.2.

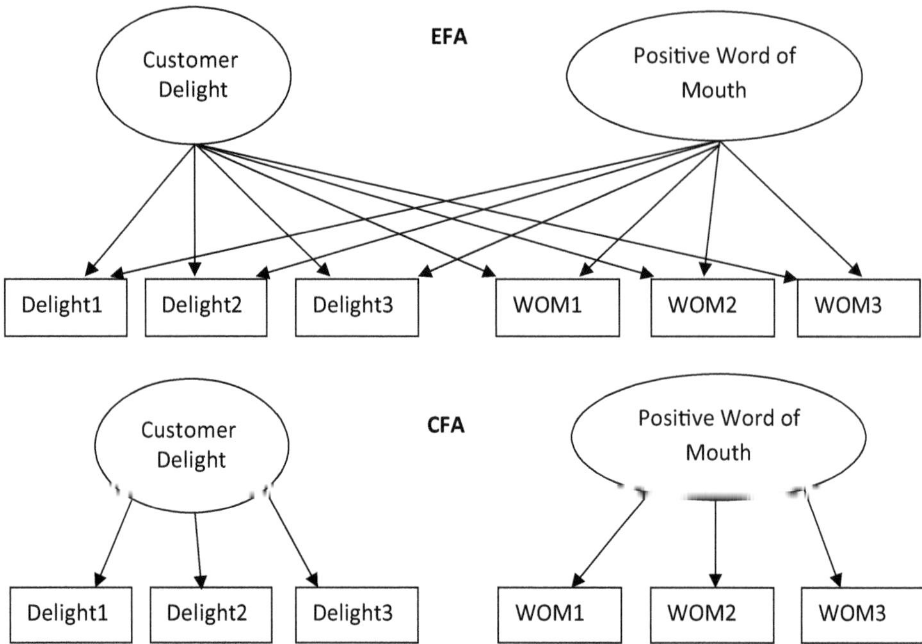

Figure 4.2 Difference between EFA and CFA

Interpretation of Factor Loadings

The factor loadings in a CFA estimate the direct effects of unobservable constructs on their indicators. If an unstandardized factor loading is 2.0 for the direct effect of Customer Delight→Delight1, then we expect a two-point difference in the indicator Delight1 given a difference of 1 point on the factor of Customer Delight. While unstandardized estimates can be insightful, they are rarely reported in the results of a CFA. Standardized estimates are most frequently reported because they allow you to compare the weights of indicators across a CFA. Standardizing an estimate converts your factor loading to a 0 to 1 scale, which allows for an easier comparison of indicators. Additionally, squaring the standardized factor loading will give the proportion of explained variance (R^2) with each indicator. This lets you know how much of the variance in the indicator is explained by the unobserved construct. For instance, if a standardized factor loading is .80, then the unobserved variable explains $.80^2 = .64$, or 64% of the variance of the indicator.

How do I know if I have an acceptable indicator? If you have a standardized factor loading that is greater than .70 or explains at least half of the variance in the indicator ($.70^2 = .50$), then your indicator is providing value in explaining the unobserved construct. If you are not explaining at least half of the variance, that indicator is contributing little to the understanding of the unobservable construct. Once we have determined the standardized value for each factor loading, we can also determine the measurement error for each indicator. The measurement error for each indicator is simply $1 - R^2$. Thus, the lower the explained variance is in an indicator, the higher the measurement error.

Setting the Metric

In SEM, each unobserved variable must be assigned a metric, which is a measurement range. This is done by constraining one of the factor loadings from the unobservable variable by assigning it a value of 1.0. The remaining loadings are then free to be estimated. The factor loading that is set to 1.0 is acting as a reference point (or range) for the other indicators to be estimated. This process is called "setting the metric", and the indicator constrained to 1.0 is often referred to as a "reference item".

So, which indicator should I constrain to 1.0? Typically, I have seen no rhyme or reason on how the metric is set. I think many researchers simply constrain the first indicator of each construct to be set to 1.0. If you fail to set the metric or constrain one of your indicators to 1.0, the analysis of your SEM model will not run and will give you an "under-identified" error message. Lastly, if you are analyzing and comparing multiple samples, make sure that the same indicator is constrain to 1.0 for each sample.

Model Fit and Fit Statistics

One of the advantages of SEM is that you can assess if your model is "fitting" the data or, specifically, the observed covariance matrix. The term "model fit" denotes that your specified model (estimated covariance matrix) is a close representation of the data (observed covariance matrix). A bad fit, on the other hand, indicates that the data is contrary to the specified model. The model fit test is to understand how the total structure of the model fits the data. A good model fit does not mean that every particular part of the model fits well. Again, the test of model fit is looking at the overall model compared to the data. One caution with assessing model fit is that a model with fewer indicators per factor will have a higher apparent fit than a model with more indicators per factor. Model fit coefficients reward parsimony. Thus, if you have a complex model, you will find it more difficult to achieve a "good model fit" compared to a more simplistic model.

The AMOS software will give you a plethora of model fit statistics. There are more than 20 different model fit tests, but I will discuss only the prominent ones seen in most research.

Model Chi-Square Test: the chi-square test is also called the chi-square goodness of fit test, but in reality, chi-square is a "badness of fit" measure. The chi-square value should **not** be significant if there is a good model fit. A significance means your model's covariance structure is significantly different from the observed covariance matrix of the data. If chi-square is $<.05$, then your model is considered to be ill-fitting. Saying that, a simple chi-square test is problematic for a number of reasons. First, the closer you are to a just-identified model, the better the model fit. You are penalized for having a complex model. Second, chi-square is very sensitive to sample size. In very large samples, even tiny differences between the observed model and the perfect fit model may be found. A better option with chi-square is to use a "relative chi-square" test, which is the chi-square value divided by the degrees of freedom, thus making it less dependent on sample size. Kline (2011) states that a relative chi-square test with a value under 3 is considered acceptable fit. I have seen some researchers say that values as high as 5 are okay (Schumacker and Lomax 2004). Conversely, some researchers state that a value less than 1 is considered "overfitting" and a sign of poor fit (Byrne 1989). Ultimately, reporting chi-square and the degrees of freedom is always advisable when presenting model fit statistics.

Comparative Statistics: these type of model fit statistics (also called an incremental fit statistics) compare competing models to determine which provides a better fit.

Null Model: many of the fit indices require a test (comparison) to be done against a "null model". The default "null model" in AMOS allows the correlations among observed variables to be constrained to 0 (implying that the latent variables are also uncorrelated). The means and variances of the measured variables are also unconstrained.

Comparative Fit Index (CFI): this test compares the covariance matrix predicted by your model to the observed covariance matrix of the null model. CFI varies from 0 to 1. A CFI value close to 1 indicates a good fit. The cutoff for an acceptable fit for a CFI value is $\geq$.90 (Bentler and Bonett 1980)—indicating that 90% of the covariation in the data can be reproduced by your model. CFI is not affected by sample size and is a recommend fit statistic to report.

Incremental Fit Index (IFI): this is calculated by (chi-square for the null model − chi-square for your model)/(chi-square for the null model − degrees of freedom for your model). IFI should be .90 or higher to have an acceptable fit. IFI is relatively independent to sample size and is one that is frequently reported.

Normed Fit Index (NFI): this is calculated by (chi-square for the null model − chi-square for your model)/(chi-square for the null model). An NFI statistic equal to .50 means your model improves fit by 50% compared to the null model. An acceptable fit is above .90 or above. Note that NFI may underestimate fit for small samples and does not reflect parsimony (the more parameters in the model, the larger the NFI).

Tucker Lewis Index (TLI): this fit index is also called the Non-Normed Fit Index. It is calculated by (chi-square for the null model − chi-square for your model)/(chi-square for the null model/degrees of freedom for your model − 1). As with the other fit indices, above .90 equals an acceptable fit.

Relative Fit Index (RFI): this is calculated by (chi-square for your model/degrees of freedom for your model)/(chi-square for the null model/degrees of freedom for your model). RFI close to 1 indicates a good fit. Acceptable fit is .90 and above.

Root Mean Square Error of Approximation (RMSEA): This is a "badness of fit" test where values close to "0" equal the best fit. A good model fit is present if RMSEA is below .05. There is an adequate fit if it is .08 and below—values over .10 denote a poor fit (MacCallum et al. 1996). AMOS will also give you a 90% confidence interval of the RMSEA value. Instead of just examining a single estimate, examining confidence intervals will provide more information on the acceptability of the model to the data. If your RMSEA value is .06, this value initially appears to be an adequate fitting model. If you examine the confidence intervals and see that the lower bound is .04 and the upper bound is .16, then you can see that the fit is not as good as you once thought when simply viewing only the RMSEA value. This wide range in the confidence interval lets you know that the initial estimate may not be a very accurate determination of model fit. Conversely, if the confidence interval is small around your initial estimate, then you can conclude that the RMSEA value is quite precise in regard to model fit.

Unlike some of the other model fit assessments, the RMSEA test does not compare against the null model but is calculated by:

$$\sqrt{\frac{X^2 - df}{df\,(N-1)}}$$

Standardized Root Mean Square Residual (SRMR): this is the average difference between the predicted and observed covariances in the model based on standardized residuals. Like RMSEA, this is a badness of fit test in which the bigger the value, the worse the fit. A SRMR of .05 and below is considered a good fit and a fit of .05 to .09 is considered an adequate fit (MacCallum et al. 1996). This fit statistic has to be specially requested in AMOS compared to other fit statistics that are presented in the analysis. To request this in AMOS, you need to select the "Plugin" tab at the top menu screen and then select "Standard RMR".

Goodness-of-Fit Index and Adjusted Goodness-of-Fit Index (GFI/AGFI): not to be confused with the other indices that examine the "goodness of fit" of a model to the data, this index with the name of goodness-of-fit index and adjusted goodness-of-fit index were initially created as another option to understand the proportion of variance being captured in the estimated covariance matrix. While this index was quite popular in its infancy, it was shown to be problematic because of its sensitivity to sample size (Sharma et al. 2005). As well, these indices were not very responsive to identifying misspecified models. Thus, the growing consensus was that these specific indices needed to be avoided (Hu and Bentler 1999).

What Value Means the Model Is a Good Fit?

There is no shortage of controversy on what should be the cutoff criteria for these fit indices discussed. Bentler and Bonett (1980) is the most widely cited research encouraging researchers to pursue model fit statistics (CFI, TLI, NFI, IFI) that are greater than .90. This rule of thumb became widely accepted even though researchers such as Hu and Bentler (1999) argued that a .90 criteria was too liberal and that fit indices needed to be greater than .95 to be considered a good-fitting model. Subsequently, Marsh et al. (2004) have argued against the rigorous Hu and Bentler criteria in favor of using multiple indices based on the sample size, estimators or distributions. Hence, there are no golden rules that universally hold as it pertains to model fit. The criteria outlined in this section is based on the existing literature and provides guidance on what is an "acceptable" model fit to the data. Even if a researcher exceeds the .90 threshold for a model fit index, one should use caution in stating a model is a "good" fit. Kline (2011) notes that even if a model is deemed to have a passable model fit, it does not mean that it is correctly specified. A so-called "good-fitting" model can still poorly explain the relationships in a model.

Let me be clear: model fit indices have value, and it is still an important step in the analysis. If you can pass the initial step of assessing if the observed covariance matrix and estimated covariance matrix are similar, then you have initial evidence that the model is appropriately specified. Again, it should be a first step in making that determination based on not only model fit but also the parameters and relationships that need to be estimated.

Modification Indices

Modification indices are part of the analysis that suggest model alterations to achieve a better fit to the data. Making changes via modification indices should be done very carefully and have justification. Blindly using the modification indices to achieve a better model fit can capitalize on chance and result in model adjustments that make no sense. With a large sample size, even a small discrepancy can trigger a modification indices flag. With modification indices, improvement in fit is measured by the reduction of chi-square. In AMOS, modification indices are concerned with adding additional covariances within a construct's indicators or relationship paths between constructs. Note that the modification indices option in AMOS will not run if you have missing data.

In the output of the modification indices, AMOS will list potential changes by adding covariances between error terms and also presenting possible relationships between constructs (listed as regression weights). In a CFA, we are concerned only with covariances between error terms. All other modification indices for a CFA are inappropriate. The modification indices will have an initial column that simply says "MI", which stands for modification indices threshold. This value presented under the MI heading is the reduction of the chi-square value by adding an additional covariance. A modification indices threshold value needs to be at least be 3.84 to show a significant difference. If you look at a chi-square difference table (see the Appendix), a reduction of one degree of freedom by adding a covariance will require a change in a chi-square value of 3.84 to be significant on the .05 level. In AMOS, the default threshold is a value of 4 where any potential modification below this value is not presented. The next column in the modification indices output is "Par change". This column is the estimated change in the new parameter added when the model is altered.

As stated, with a CFA, you are concerned only with modification indices related to the covariances, but to clarify this, *covariances of indicators within a construct*. It is inappropriate to covary indicators across constructs even though the modification indices will suggest it. Below are some suggestions of "dos and don'ts" with modification indices using our previous example of Customer Delight and Positive Word of Mouth.

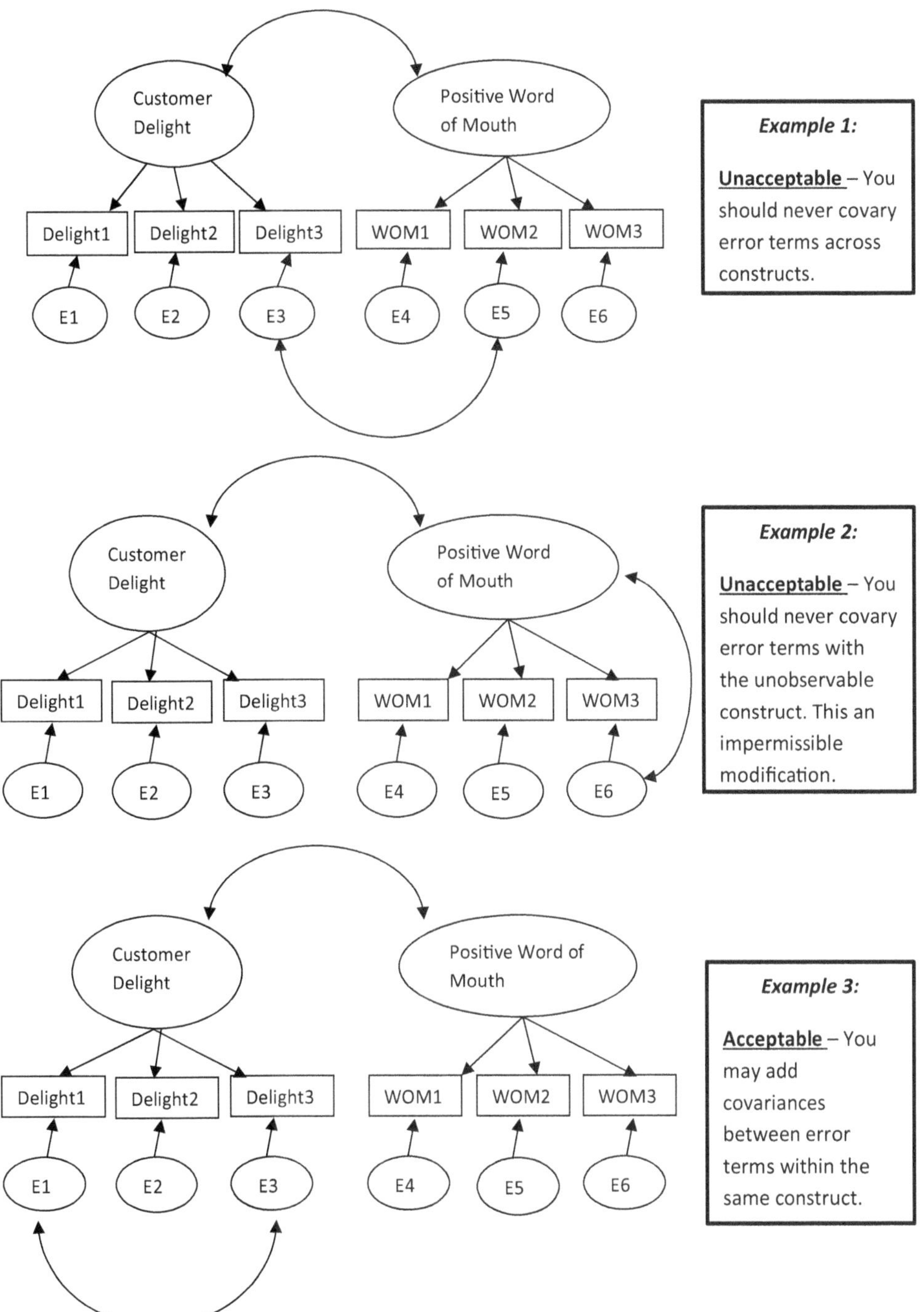

Figure 4.3 Modifications With a CFA

In My Opinion: Correlating Error Terms Within a Construct

In instances where an unobserved variable has multiple indicators, you might want to correlate the error terms if it is theoretically justifiable and helps to explain the variance within the construct. This is often done when the error of one indicator helps in knowing the error associated with another indicator. Frequently, indicators within a construct are very similar to one another and there is redundancy between the indicators.

How big does the modification indices value need to be to add another covariance? I rarely consider any valid modification suggestion if the chi-square value is not changing by at least 10. A chi-square value of 10 at the expense of one degree of freedom is almost significant at a .001 level. Saying that, I do not always covary error terms even when a modification suggestion is over 10. I look for instances where the change is extreme. It is not uncommon to have a modification suggestion greater than 20 in large models. You want to explore what modifications will actually make an impact in regards to your model. A modification suggestion with a chi-square change of 7 will probably show relatively little influence or change in the model itself. Correlating error terms can strengthen factor loadings within a construct, and in rare cases I have seen it actually lower factor loadings. Ultimately, correlating an error term is about explaining common variance across indicators instead of treating them as independents which could hurt your overall model fit.

If you have multiple error terms within a construct that are showing high modification indices levels, then you have cause for concern. This is a sign that you are not capturing different parts of the unobservable construct. The unexplained error in the construct is very similar across the indicators. This could be a sign that your indicators are extremely redundant and you are not really asking different questions. You may find that model fit is substantially increased when you correlate multiple error terms within a construct, but you are also raising other concerns that your indicators are lacking in regards to capturing the unobservable. An equal concern for multiple high modification indices within a construct is the possibility that this shared unexplained error is the result of a method bias in how the data was collected.

Some researchers from a traditional perspective think that you should not correlate error terms even within the construct (Gerbing and Anderson 1984). The rationale is that the need for a covariance between error terms suggests there is an unknown common source or construct that is the result of this common unexplained variance. Potential remedies instead of correlating error terms were to include an "unknown" factor into the model, which ultimately was equally problematic. In my opinion, the idea that you should never correlate error terms is too restrictive. Complex models and constructs with numerous indicators are inevitably going to have error terms that are eligible to be correlated. Before correlating an error term, you need to assess if this high modification index is a result of redundancy in your indicators or if you have a potentially larger problem of a missing influence or a method bias.

CFA Example in AMOS

Let's say I want to test a simple model that has three unobserved variables. The first variable is a concept called "Adaptive Behavior", which explores customer's perceptions that an employee adapted their behavior to the customer during an experience. This adaptation could be through verbal interaction or through their direct actions. The perceived Adaptive Behavior construct is hypothesized to positively influence feelings of Customer Delight, which is going to influence intentions to spread positive word of mouth about the experience (Positive WOM).

The construct of Adaptive Behavior has 5 indicators, and the other two constructs have 3 indicators each. Once I have collected and screened my data, I am ready to perform a CFA. The first thing you need to do is to read in your data file to AMOS (I have listed the data file as Customer Delight Data). You need to select the "Data Files" icon. The following window will appear:

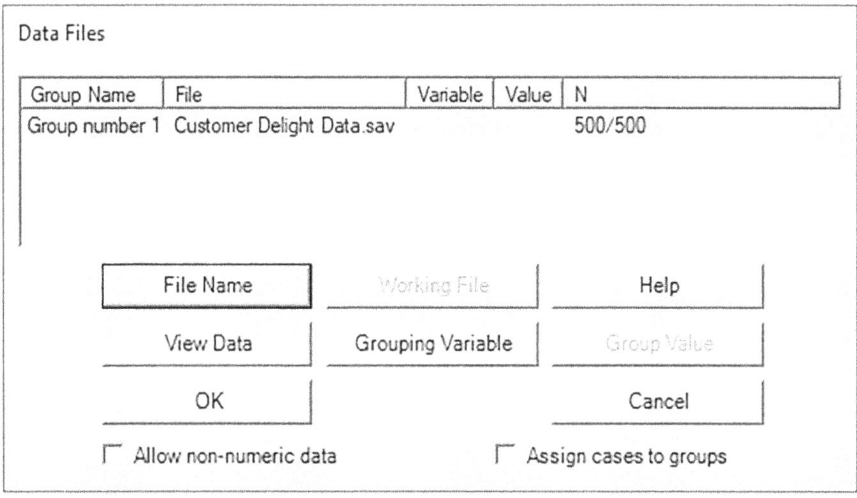

Figure 4.4 Data Files Pop-Up Window

Click on "File Name", find your data file, and then hit OK. You should also see the number of responses in the data file (N). Next, you need to click the variable icon:

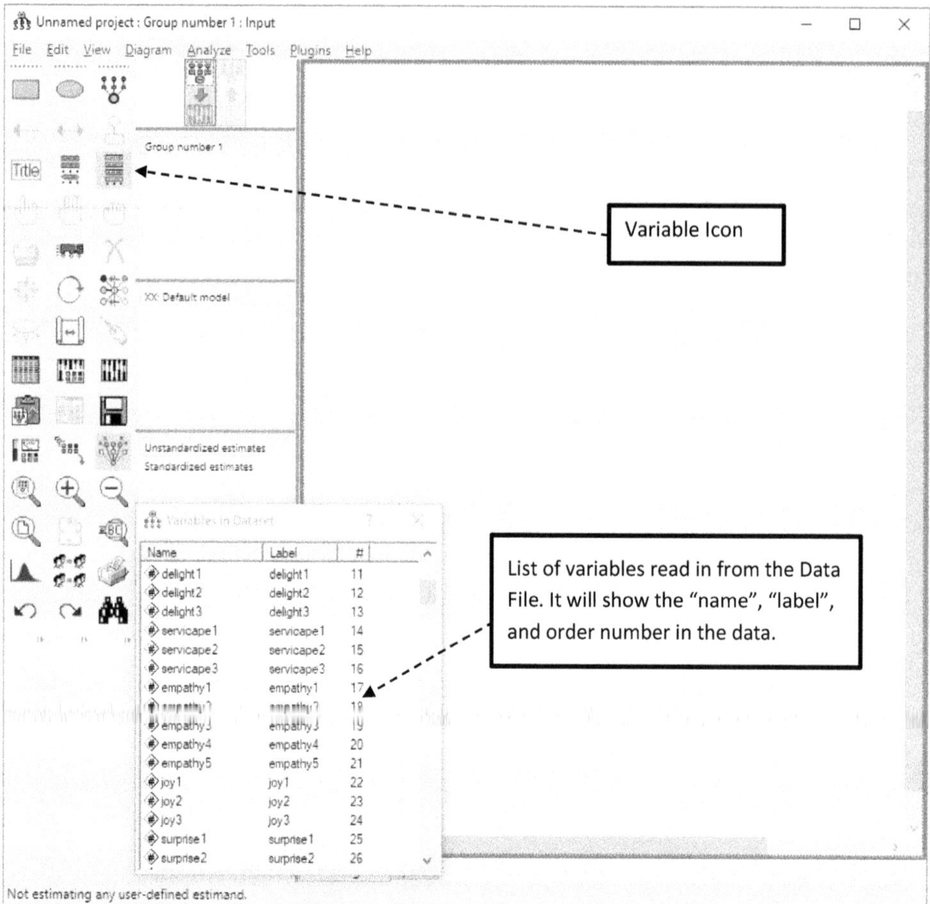

Figure 4.5 List of Variables AMOS Window

You will then draw out your unobservable variables along with denoting the indicators for each construct. Remember, the "Draw Latent Variable" icon is the easiest way to do this . After selecting this icon, drag your circle (indicating the unobservable) to the desired size, then click in the circle to add the number of indicators. If you click in the circle three times, it will add three indicators. If you forget to add enough indicators, no problem; just make sure the "Draw Latent Variable" icon is selected and then click in the circle again to add another indicator. Once you form the unobserved variable and indicators, you will then drag in from the variable window your measured items to the indicator boxes for the specific construct. You will also need to label your unobserved constructs. You can let AMOS do it for you, but I do not suggest this. To label the unobserved construct, you need to right-click on the unobserved variable you want to label. Next, you need to select "Object Properties" (you can also double click into a variable and it will bring up object properties). In the variable name section, you will label your construct. Please note that all variable names for your constructs and indicators must be unique. You cannot have the same name for multiple things in your model, or AMOS will not be able to clearly run the analysis and will ultimately give you an error message. You cannot have spaces between words in a variable name; AMOS will recognize the space as an illegal character and stop the analysis. I typically use the underscore character to denote a space between words. After dragging in your indicators from the variable view and labeling your unobserved constructs, you might need to select the "Change Shape" icon . This will let you change the size of your circles or squares of your variables to see the full name of each one listed. You will also notice that with each indicator added, AMOS will automatically include an error term for that indicator. Every error term has to be labeled as well. This can be a painstaking process if you have a lot of indicators. As noted in the "Tips" section in Chapter 3, AMOS has a function that will label all the error terms for you.

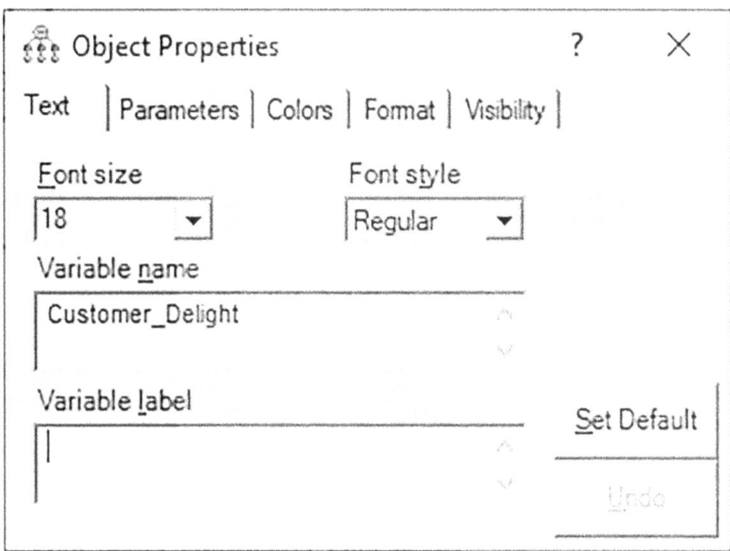

Figure 4.6 Object Properties Pop-Up Window

A few things need to be addressed about AMOS before we move on. First, you will notice that AMOS automatically sets the metric with one of your indicators (constrained to 1.0), so that you do not have to do that. If you decide for whatever reason to delete that indicator, you will need to set the metric on another indicator. This can be done by double clicking on another indicator arrow which will bring up the "Object Properties window". You will then need to select the "Parameters" tab at the top of the pop-up window, and then place a "1" in the "Regression Weight" field. Second, all unobserved constructs in a CFA are considered independent constructs, which means a covariance needs to be added between every construct. In small models with a few constructs, it is just easier to select the "Draw Covariance" button and connect the constructs one at a time. If you have a very large number of constructs, then see the "Tips" section in Chapter 3 on how to covary multiple independent constructs at once. Lastly, AMOS will require you to save and label the project you are working on before an analysis will take place. You would be well served to save your file names that list the specific analysis and subject of the project.

To see the completed graphical diagram of the CFA for our three construct model, see Figure 4.7.

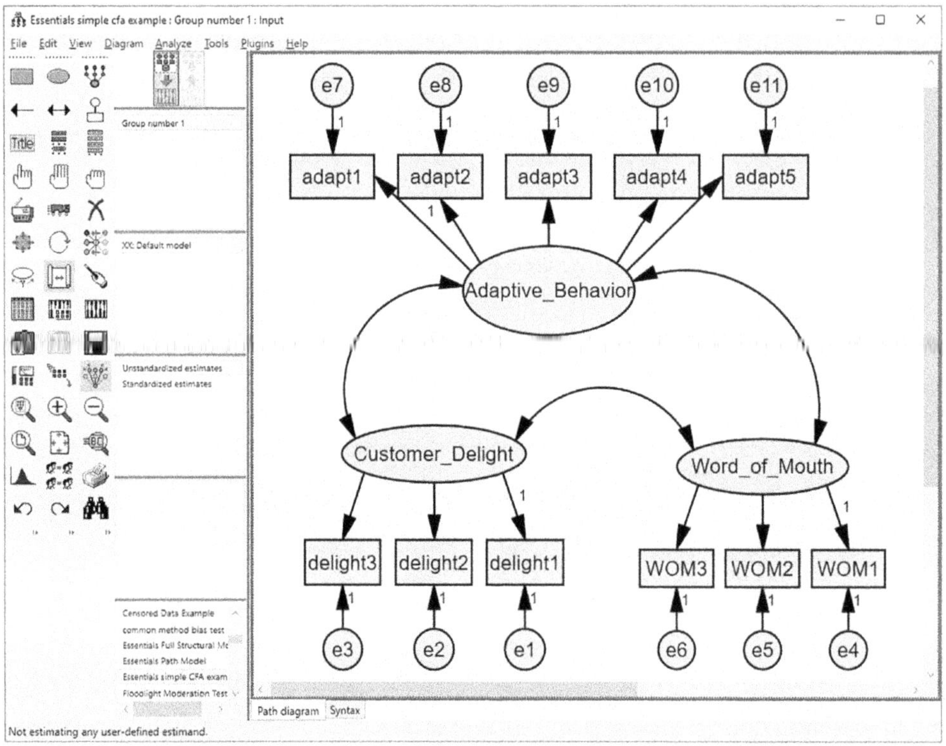

Figure 4.7 Three Construct CFA Model in AMOS

Before you run the CFA analysis, you need to select the "Analysis Properties" icon . This will start a pop-up window that will ask how much detail you want in the output of the analysis. Go to the "Output" tab at the top of the pop-up window, which will give all the possible options. I prefer to select "Minimization History, Standardized Estimates, and Square Multiple Correlations". You can also select "Modification Indices" and even change the threshold for how big a modification index needs to be in order to be visible. Other analysis options provide more information in the output, but I find that these options are all you really need for a simple CFA.

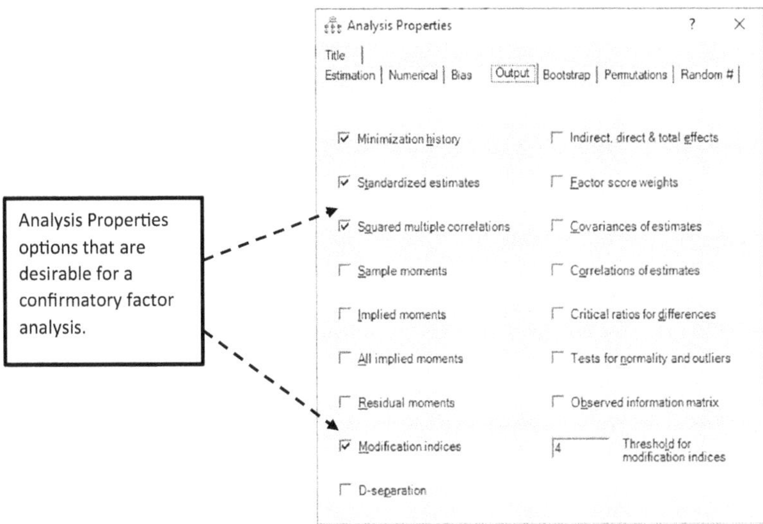

Figure 4.8 Analysis Properties Output Screen

After selecting these options, cancel out of this window and then hit the "Run Analysis" button . Once the analysis is complete, you will see either an "OK" or "XX" in the "models" window. An "OK" means the model ran to completion; a "XX" means there is an error and the analysis did not finish. If an analysis is completed, you will also see the chi-square and degrees of freedom listed in the "Computational Summary" window.

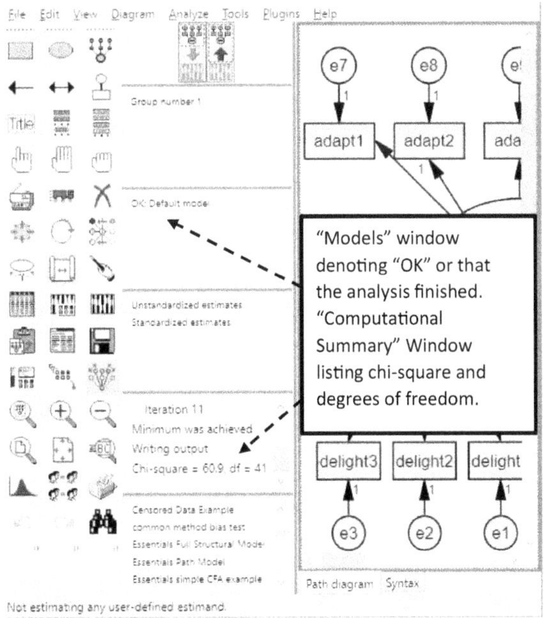

Figure 4.9 Models and Computational Summary Window

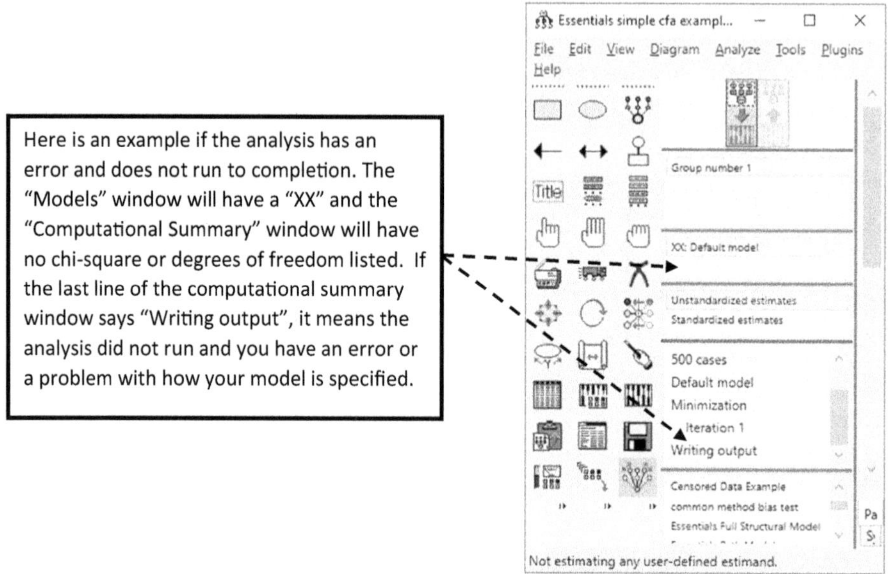

Figure 4.10 Example of Analysis Failing to Run to Completion

Let's now take a look at the output. To get to the output results, you need to hit the "View Text" button. This icon looks similar to the data file icon; make sure you choose the right one. Once selected, the output will come up in a separate window. You can see on the left-hand side links to different output results. The first link is "Analysis Summary", and this just gives the time and date of analysis (not that useful). The next link is "Notes for Group". This link will state your sample size and if the model is recursive or non-recursive. In a CFA, you should never have a non-recursive model. More information on what a non-recursive model is appears on page 310.

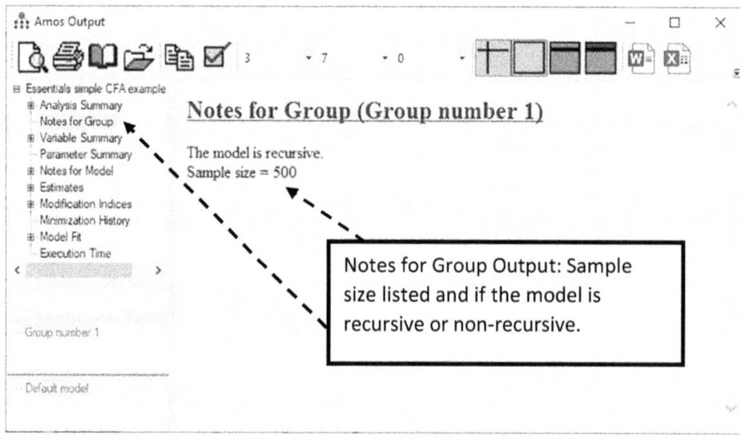

Figure 4.11 Notes for Group Output

The next tab is "Variable Summary". An example of the output is provided in Figure 4.12. This is a breakdown of your model that lists each variable and if it is an independent or dependent variable. You will see that all unobserved latent variables and all error terms in the CFA analysis are listed as independents and all indicators are listed as dependent variables.

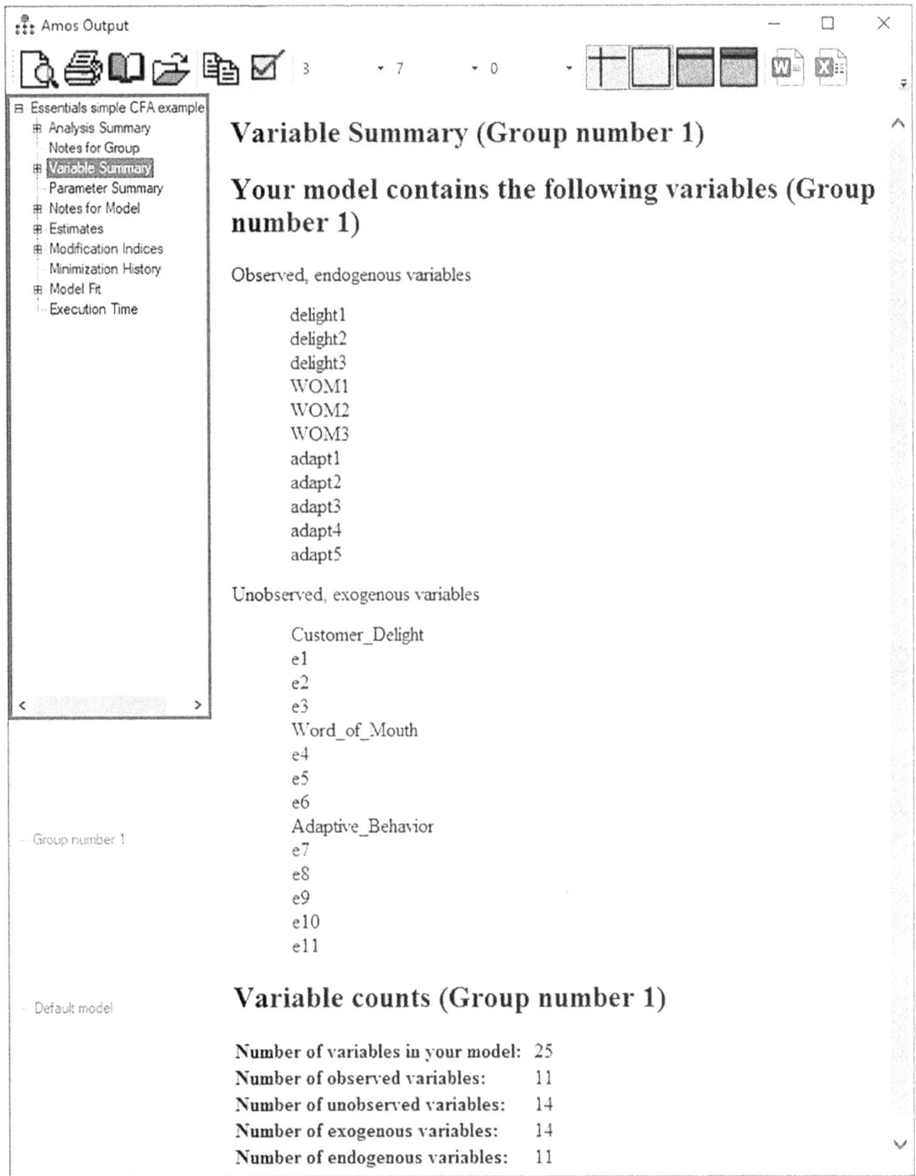

Figure 4.12 Variable Summary Output

The next link is "Parameter Summary". This is a detailed breakdown of all the parameters in your model.

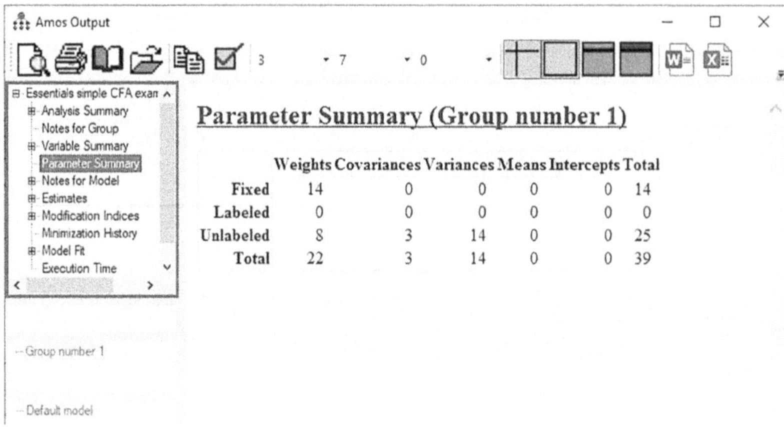

Figure 4.13 Parameter Summary Output

Next is the "Notes for Model" link; this will list your degrees of freedom in your model along with the chi-square test. The Notes for Model output will also be where AMOS presents error messages if your model does not run to completion.

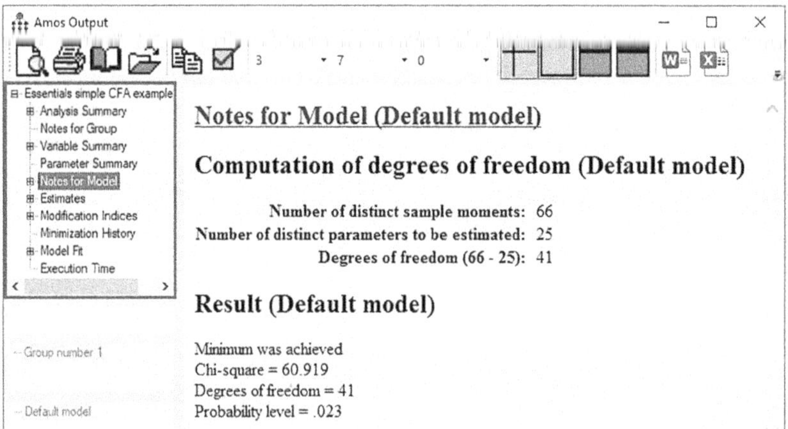

Figure 4.14 Notes for Model Output

The next tab is the "Estimates" tab. This tab is where a lot of the information you need will be located. In the Estimates tab, you will find the unstandardized and standardized regression weights (for a CFA, these are referred to as factor loadings). The first regression weights presented are the unstandardized regression weights. Next, you will see the column "S.E.", which stands for Standard Error. The next column is the critical ratio (C.R.); this is the t-value to determine significance. The next column is the p-value. If the p-value is under .001, it will just be listed as stars. Right under the unstandardized regression weights is the standardized regression weights. You will notice that it does not include C.R. or p-values. These values are the same as the unstandardized values above. Normally, in a CFA, you present standardized regression weights (factor loadings) along with the t-values for each. You need to pay close attention that you choose the corresponding t-value from the unstandardized regression output when presenting the standardized factor loadings and t-values. After the standardized weights, the "Estimates" tab will provide information on your covariances and correlations. These values can help determine if you have a possible multicollinearity issue. At the bottom of the page will be the squared multiple correlations (R^2). If you remember from earlier, this is nothing more than a standardized regression weight that is squared. For a full example of the "Estimates" output, see Figure 4.15.

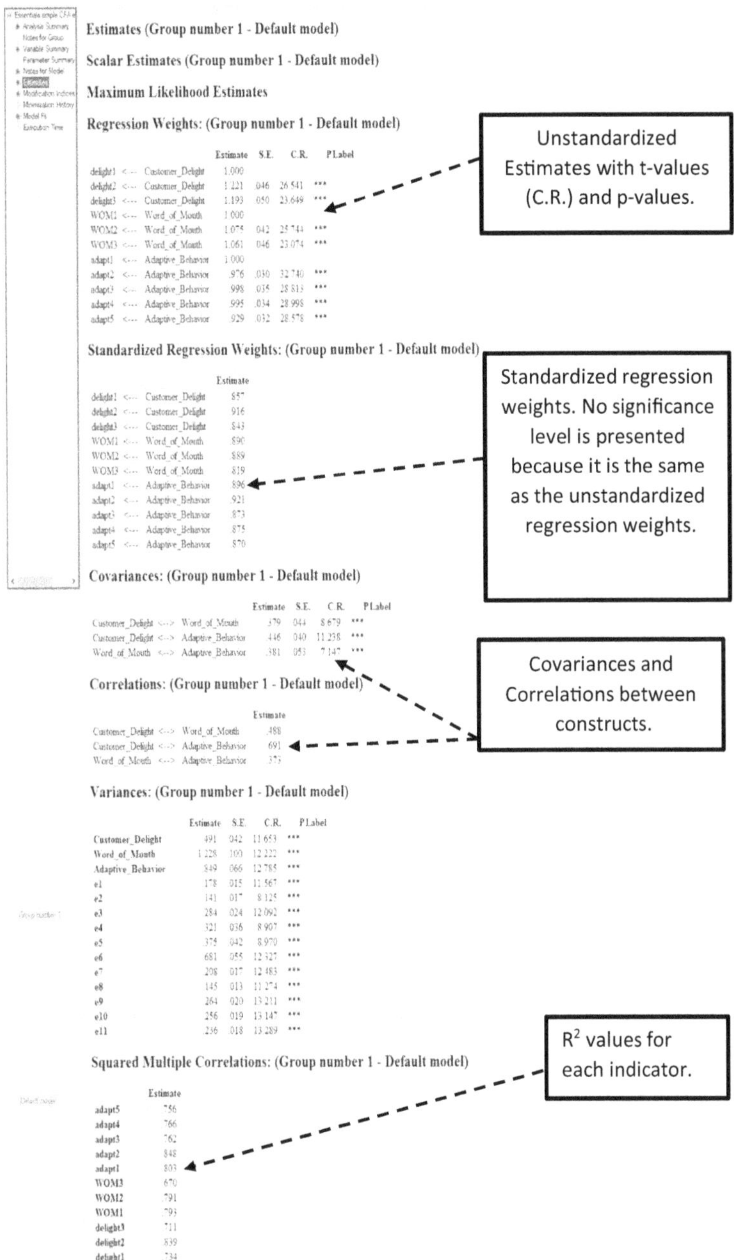

Figure 4.15 Estimates Output in AMOS

The next tab I want to discuss is the "Model Fit" tab. This tab provides you with a list of various model fit indices. On the first line, you will see NPAR, which stands for number of parameters. The next column, CMIN, is your chi-square value, while DF is the degrees of freedom in the model and P is the p-value for a chi-square test. The last column, CMIN/DF, is the relative chi-square test or, specifically, chi-square divided by the number of degrees of freedom. In this tab, your model will be listed as the "Default" model. AMOS gives you an overabundance of fit tests, but I will highlight here the ones I think are most relevant.

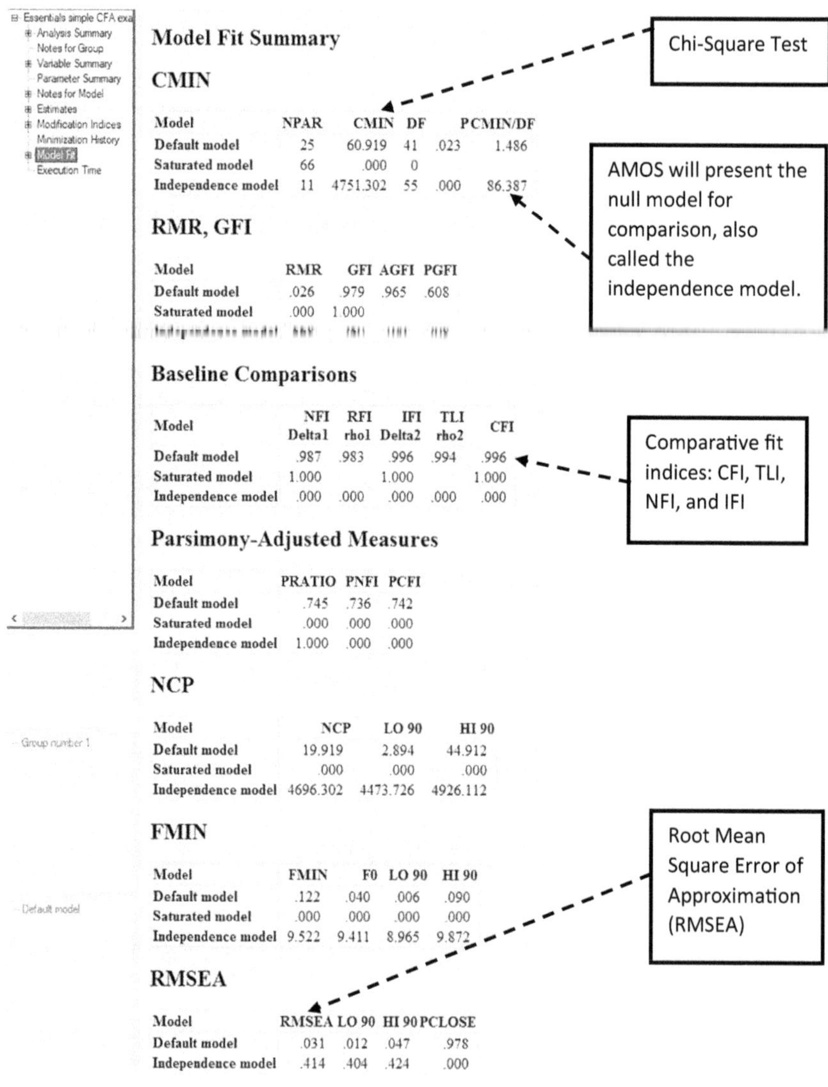

Model Fit Summary

CMIN

Model	NPAR	CMIN	DF	P	CMIN/DF
Default model	25	60.919	41	.023	1.486
Saturated model	66	.000	0		
Independence model	11	4751.302	55	.000	86.387

RMR, GFI

Model	RMR	GFI	AGFI	PGFI
Default model	.026	.979	.965	.608
Saturated model	.000	1.000		
Independence model	[illegible]	[illegible]	[illegible]	[illegible]

Baseline Comparisons

Model	NFI Delta1	RFI rho1	IFI Delta2	TLI rho2	CFI
Default model	.987	.983	.996	.994	.996
Saturated model	1.000		1.000		1.000
Independence model	.000	.000	.000	.000	.000

Parsimony-Adjusted Measures

Model	PRATIO	PNFI	PCFI
Default model	.745	.736	.742
Saturated model	.000	.000	.000
Independence model	1.000	.000	.000

NCP

Model	NCP	LO 90	HI 90
Default model	19.919	2.894	44.912
Saturated model	.000	.000	.000
Independence model	4696.302	4473.726	4926.112

FMIN

Model	FMIN	F0	LO 90	HI 90
Default model	.122	.040	.006	.090
Saturated model	.000	.000	.000	.000
Independence model	9.522	9.411	8.965	9.872

RMSEA

Model	RMSEA	LO 90	HI 90	PCLOSE
Default model	.031	.012	.047	.978
Independence model	.414	.404	.424	.000

Figure 4.16 Model Fit Output

Below the Estimates tab in the output is the "Modification Indices" tab (you will see this tab only if you requested this in the Analysis Properties Window). The values listed are modifications for possible covariances and also modifications if a regression weight (path) was added. With the covariances data, the M.I. value is how much the chi-square value would decrease if you added the covariance. The second column "Par Change" is how much a parameter would change if this covariance was added. See Figure 4.17.

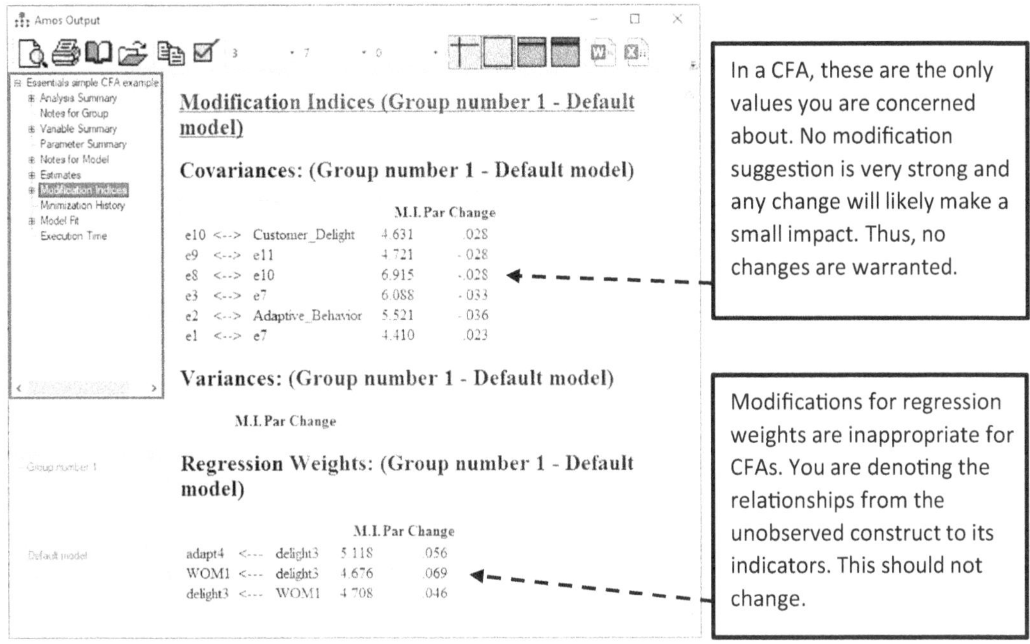

Figure 4.17 Modification Indices Output

The last links to be discussed in the output are "Execution Time" and "Minimization History". The execution time tab tells you how long the analysis took, which is not that useful. The minimization history tab tells you how many iterations were needed for the analysis to come to completion. Neither of these links is especially pertinent when it comes to reporting results.

Overall, if we look at the results from the CFA, we can be encouraged that each unobservable construct is being reflected in its indicators. From the "Estimates" tab, we can see that all of our indicators significantly loaded on the specified unobservable construct. All loadings were also at an acceptable level (> .70), which denotes that each indicator is explaining an acceptable amount of the variance. From the "Model Fit" output, we can see that the relative chi-square fit test is just above 1.0, which means an acceptable fit is achieved. As well, the comparative fit indices of CFI, TLI, and IFI are all above .90, further supporting the fit of the model to the data. Lastly, our RMSEA value is .03, providing additional support that the model "fits" the data. From this CFA, there is evidence that our indicators are measuring their intended concept.

Standardized Residuals

Along with modification indices, AMOS also provides a test of model misspecification through standardized residuals. The standardized residuals are the difference between the observed covariance matrix and the estimated covariance matrix for each pair of observed variables. You will specifically need to request for this information to be presented in the analysis of a SEM model. In the Analysis Properties Window, you will see a tab called "Output" and at the bottom of the window is a checkbox option for "Residual Moments". You will need to select this box to see the Standardized Residuals in the analysis. After running the analysis, you will need to go into the output under the Estimates link and then select the Matrices option. AMOS will provide you with the unstandardized and standardized residuals, but only the standardized residuals need to be examined. Because the data is standardized, the unit of measurement is transformed to allow for easier comparison. If a residual value exceeds 2.58, then the residual of the observed and estimated covariance matrix is determined to be large (Joreskog and Sorbom 1988) and a sign of possible model misspecification. In the example output (see Figure 4.18), you can see that the biggest residual is 1.199, the difference of delight3 and adapt4. These indicators are across constructs, so no adjustment would be made in this instance. If the high residual value was within construct, then you would consider adding a covariance between the constructs' error terms.

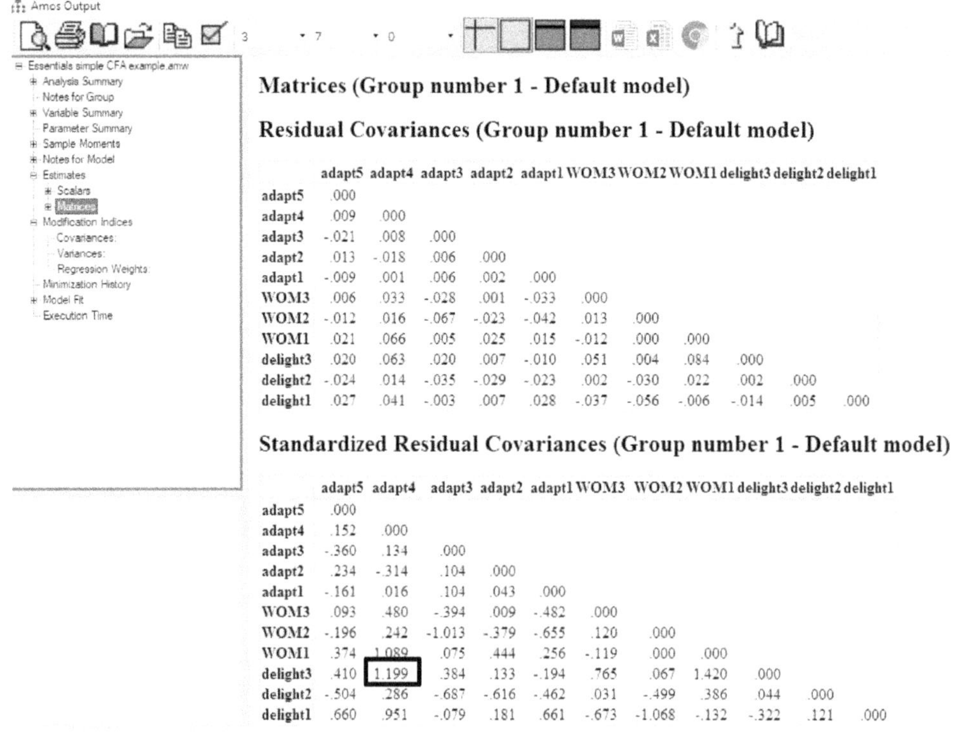

Matrices (Group number 1 - Default model)

Residual Covariances (Group number 1 - Default model)

	adapt5	adapt4	adapt3	adapt2	adapt1	WOM3	WOM2	WOM1	delight3	delight2	delight1
adapt5	.000										
adapt4	.009	.000									
adapt3	-.021	.008	.000								
adapt2	.013	-.018	.006	.000							
adapt1	-.009	.001	.006	.002	.000						
WOM3	.006	.033	-.028	.001	-.033	.000					
WOM2	-.012	.016	-.067	-.023	-.042	.013	.000				
WOM1	.021	.066	.005	.025	.015	-.012	.000	.000			
delight3	.020	.063	.020	.007	-.010	.051	.004	.084	.000		
delight2	-.024	.014	-.035	-.029	-.023	.002	-.030	.022	.002	.000	
delight1	.027	.041	-.003	.007	.028	-.037	-.056	-.006	-.014	.005	.000

Standardized Residual Covariances (Group number 1 - Default model)

	adapt5	adapt4	adapt3	adapt2	adapt1	WOM3	WOM2	WOM1	delight3	delight2	delight1
adapt5	.000										
adapt4	.152	.000									
adapt3	-.360	.134	.000								
adapt2	.234	-.314	.104	.000							
adapt1	-.161	.016	.104	.043	.000						
WOM3	.093	.480	-.394	.009	-.482	.000					
WOM2	-.196	.242	-1.013	-.379	-.655	.120	.000				
WOM1	.374	1.089	.075	.444	.256	-.119	.000	.000			
delight3	.410	1.199	.384	.133	-.194	.765	.067	1.420	.000		
delight2	-.504	.286	-.687	-.616	-.462	.031	-.499	.386	.044	.000	
delight1	.660	.951	-.079	.181	.661	-.673	-1.068	-.132	-.322	.121	.000

Figure 4.18 Standardized Residuals Output

Assessing Convergent and Discriminant Validity of Your Measures

After initially establishing that each indicator is loading on its respective construct and the model has an acceptable fit to the data, we now need to assess the convergent and discriminant validity of your measures. Just to recap, the basic difference between convergent and discriminant validity is that convergent validity tests whether indicators will converge to measure a single concept, whereas discriminant validity tests to see if a construct is unrelated or distinguishes from other constructs. A CFA is a good first step in determining validity, but the results of a CFA alone will not be able to confirm convergent and discriminant validity. The framework outlined by Fornell and Larcker (1981) is an excellent method for assessing this type of validity and is one of the most widely used approaches with many researchers today.

To assess convergent validity, Fornell and Larcker state that you need to calculate the Average Variance Extracted (AVE) for each construct. An AVE is calculated by getting the R^2 value for each indicator in a construct, adding them together, and dividing by the total number of indicators. The AVE number needs to be higher than .50 to denote that your indicators have convergent validity on your construct.

With discriminant validity, you need to calculate the shared variance between constructs. To get this shared variance, a correlation analysis needs to be done between constructs (not indicators, but constructs). To perform a correlation analysis between constructs, you first need to form a composite variable for each construct. This is done by taking the scores of the indicators for each construct, summing them, and then dividing by the total number. This single composite score for each construct will be used in the correlation analysis. Once you get the correlation between constructs, you will then square those values. The resulting value should be less than the average variance extracted (AVE) for each construct. If so, you have support for discriminant validity. For simplicity, I have also seen where the square root of the AVE is compared to the original correlation of each construct. By doing it this way, you do not have to square every correlation, which could be a large number with a big model. Let's look at an example and calculate the AVEs for our constructs used in the CFA analysis.

Adaptive Behavior R^2	*Customer Delight R^2*	*Positive Word of Mouth R^2*
adapt1 = .80	delight1 = .73	WOM1 = .79
adapt2 = .84	delight2 = .83	WOM2 = .79
adapt3 = .76	delight3 = .71	WOM3 = .67
adapt4 = .76		
adapt5 = .75		
AVE = .78	**AVE = .75**	**AVE = .75**

With all the AVEs for each construct having a value greater than .50, there is support that there is convergent validity for the indicators of each unobservable variable. After assessing convergent validity, let's now investigate the discriminant validity of the constructs. The first thing we need to do is create a composite score for each construct. We will do this in the SPSS data file.

In SPSS, you need to go to the "Transform" menu at the top and then select "Compute Variable". Let's start by computing the composite variable for Adaptive Behavior. The first thing you need to do is create a new name for the composite variable. I have called the new variable "comp_adapt", which denotes composite variable of the Adaptive Behavior construct. Next, you need to go to the "Numeric Expression" box, where you will input the formula desired. We want to initially sum all the adapt (1–5) indicators. You can select an indicator and then use the arrow key to insert that variable name in the numeric expression window. This just keeps you from having to type in all the names manually. Once you have denoted that all adapt indicators should be summed (make sure to put a parenthesis around the summation), then you need to divide by the total number of indicators. Once you hit the "OK" button at the bottom, SPSS will form the composite variable in the last column of your data file. You will need to repeat these steps for all the other constructs so we can perform a correlation analysis with all the composite variables that are formed.

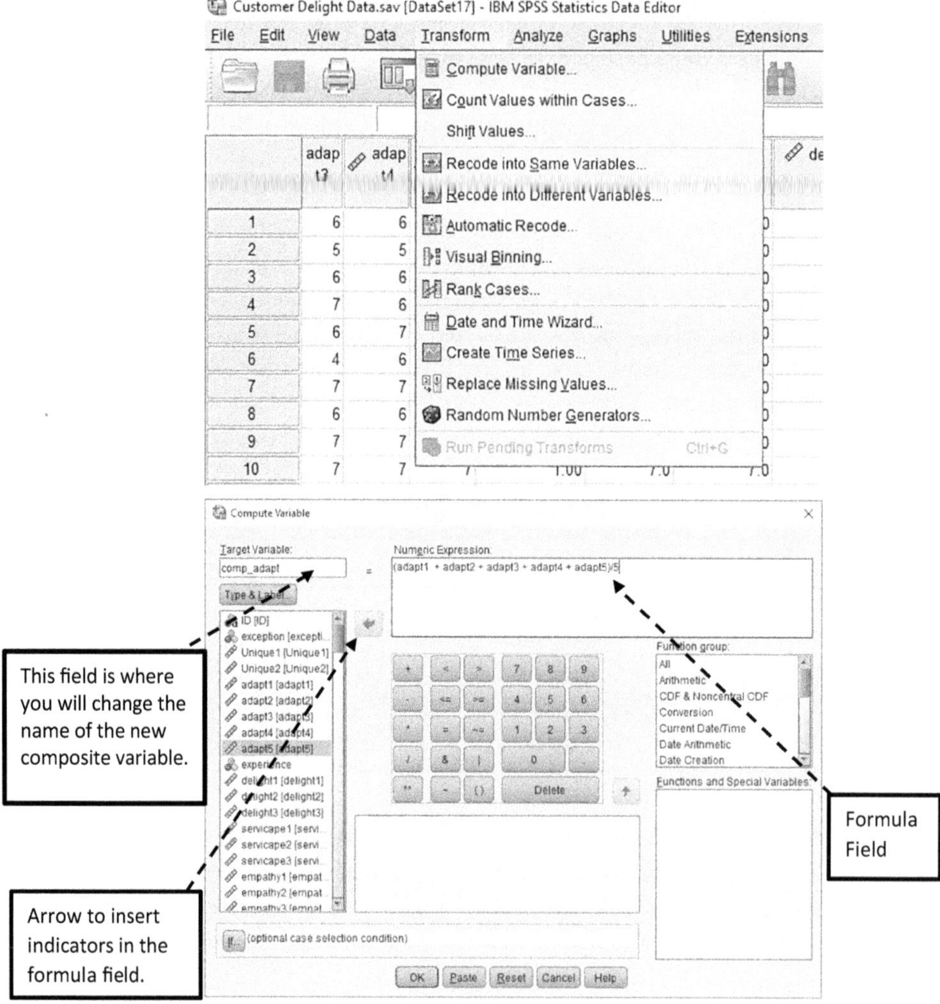

Figure 4.19 Compute Composite Variable

Here is an example of a correlation analysis with our three composite constructs.

Correlation between Constructs	*Adaptive Behavior*	*Customer Delight*	*Positive WOM*
Adaptive Behavior	1		
Customer Delight	.65	1	
Positive WOM	.34	.44	1

To determine the shared variance between each construct, you will square the correlations and compare them to the AVE values for each construct. Let's examine the discriminant validity of Adaptive Behavior. The shared variance between Adaptive Behavior and Customer Delight is $(.65)^2 = .42$, which is far lower than the AVE for Adaptive Behavior (.78) or Customer Delight (.75). Thus, there is evidence that these constructs discriminate from one another. Similarly, the shared variance between Adaptive Behavior and Positive Word of Mouth $(.34)^2 = .11$ is lower than the AVE values for either construct. You will need to examine every correlation and perform this comparison of shared variance to AVE to determine if you have any discriminant validity problems in your model. With our current example, all AVE values exceed the shared variance between constructs, thus supporting the discriminant validity of our constructs in the model.

Heterotrait-Monotrait Ratio of Correlations (HTMT)

While Fornell and Larcker's (1981) recommendation of examining shared variance to assess discriminant validity has been extremely popular in the past, recent research has started to question how sensitive this test is in capturing discriminant validity issues between constructs (Henseler et al. 2015). Subsequently, the heterotrait-monotrait ratio of correlations (HTMT) technique was offered as a better approach to determine discriminant validity between constructs. The HTMT method examines the ratio of between-trait correlations to within-trait correlations of two constructs. Put another way, it examines the correlations of indicators across constructs to the correlations of indicators within a construct. The mathematical formula for HTMT is:

$$\text{HTMT}_{ij} = \frac{1}{K_i K_j} \sum_{g=1}^{K_i} \sum_{h=1}^{K_j} r_{ig,jh} \div \left(\frac{2}{K_i\left(K_i - 1\right)} \sum_{g=1}^{K_i - 1} \sum_{h=g+1}^{K_i} r_{ig,ih} \cdot \frac{2}{K_j\left(K_j - 1\right)} \sum_{g=1}^{K_j - 1} \sum_{h=g+1}^{K_j} r_{jg,jh} \right)^{\frac{1}{2}}$$

If you were like me the first time I saw that formula, you are thinking, "What in the world does all this mean?" While the formula might look a little scary, when you break it down into its parts, it is pretty simple. So, let's take this formula and put it into layman's terms using an example. Let's say we wanted to determine if there was any discriminant validity problems between our constructs of Adaptive Behavior and Positive Word of Mouth. The first thing we need to assess is the value for the average heterotrait correlations. This value is the average of all the correlations across indicators of Adaptive Behavior and Positive Word of Mouth. Next, we need to determine the average monotrait correlation value. You will have an average monotrait correlation value for each of your constructs. This is the average of the correlations of indicators within a construct. So, let's look at our formula again in a simplified form.

HTMT Formula:

$$\frac{\textit{Average of the indicator correlations across Adaptive Behavior and Positive WOM}}{\sqrt{\textit{Average Correlation within Adaptive Behavior indicators} * \textit{Average Correlation within Positive WOM indicators}}}$$

Let's look at the correlation matrix of the two construct's indicators to help clarify the issue.

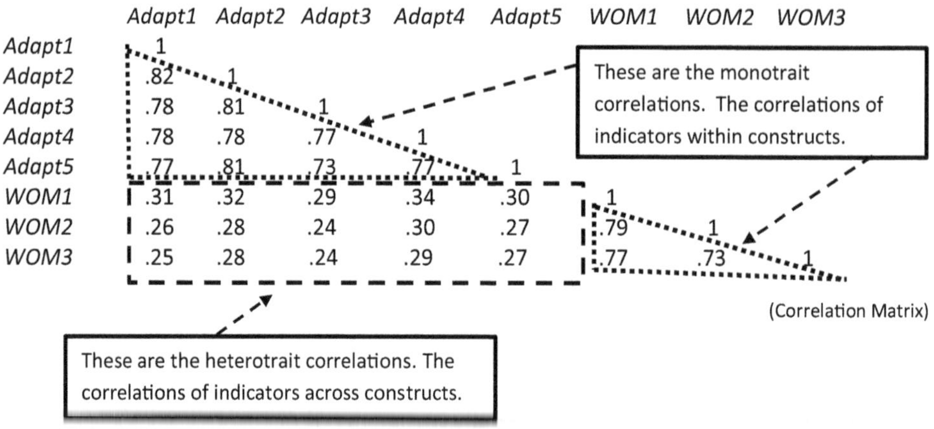

	Adapt1	*Adapt2*	*Adapt3*	*Adapt4*	*Adapt5*	*WOM1*	*WOM2*	*WOM3*
Adapt1	1							
Adapt2	.82	1						
Adapt3	.78	.81	1					
Adapt4	.78	.78	.77	1				
Adapt5	.77	.81	.73	.77	1			
WOM1	.31	.32	.29	.34	.30	1		
WOM2	.26	.28	.24	.30	.27	.79	1	
WOM3	.25	.28	.24	.29	.27	.77	.73	1

Figure 4.20 HTMT Correlations

Heterotrait Correlations:

.31 + .32 + .29 + .34 + .30 + .26 + .28 + .24 + .30 + .27 + .25 + .28 + .24 + .29 + .27 = 4.24/15

Average Heterotrait correlation = .282

Monotrait Correlations:

Adaptive Behavior = .82 + .78 + .78 + .77 + .81 + .78 + .81 + .77 + .73 + .77 = 7.82/10

Average monotrait correlation for Adaptive Behavior = .782

Positive Word of Mouth = .79 + .77 + .73 = 2.29/3

Average monotrait correlation for Positive Word of Mouth = .763

$$\text{HTMT} = \frac{.282}{\sqrt{.782 * .763}} = \frac{.282}{.7724} = .365$$

The HTMT value across the Adaptive Behavior and Positive Word of Mouth constructs is .365. Kline (2011) states that if a HTMT value is greater than .85, then you have discriminant validity problems. Values under .85 indicate that discriminant validity is established and the two constructs are distinctively different from one another. In our example, we can conclude that discriminant validity has been established across the constructs of Adaptive Behavior and

Positive Word of Mouth. If you had other constructs in your model, you would need to get an HTMT value for each pair of constructs to show discriminant validity across your model.

I would love to tell you that AMOS has an easy function to handle HTMT, but right now it does not. Hand calculating HTMT is a little tedious, and there are other options. You can get your correlation matrix and import it into an Excel spreadsheet and then highlight the cells you need to average. This is a little quicker than doing it by hand. There is also a plugin, created for AMOS by James Gaskin, that will calculate all the HTMT values in a model. That plugin can be found at http://statwiki.kolobkreations.com/index.php?title=Main_Page. There is a growing trend to use the HTMT method to assess discriminant validity because it is purported to be the best balance between high detection and low false positive rates in determining the discriminant validity of a construct (Voorhees et al. 2016).

If I Have a Weak Factor Loading, Should I Drop It?

If you have a factor loading that is near or below the .70 threshold, it does not mean you need to drop the indicator from the analysis. Complex or newly developed constructs will often have numerous indicators in an attempt to capture a comprehensive aspect of a construct. If you have numerous indicators that are strongly loading on the unobserved construct and an AVE value that is still exceeding .50, then I would suggest keeping the indicator. The weaker indicator could very well be helping to capture a unique component of the construct. That said, if the construct is nowhere near the threshold (< .60), this item is contributing very little in understanding the unobservable construct. With a factor loading lower than .60, you are barely explaining a third of the variance in the indicator. If this is the case, you should strongly consider dropping this indicator. This poor-performing indicator can create more unexplained variance in your model and ultimately hurt your ability to achieve convergent and discriminant validity.

A word of caution should be given about deleting indicators in the measurement analysis. If you collect data on some phenomenon and in the analysis decide to start dropping indicators from your constructs, then you really need to have a second data collection to verify that your revised scales (without the dropped items) are valid. Having a single sample and dropping indicators sets you up for criticism that you are capitalizing on chance. If you cannot verify that changes you made in the scales are stable and not based on the unique aspects of that specific data collection, then criticism could ensue in regards to the validity of your results. That is why pretesting a survey or scales is so important, especially with an indicator that is being adapted into a new context or even if a relatively new construct is being measured. The pretest should be where indicators are dropped, and your final data collection should verify the structure and measurement of each construct established at the end of the pretest.

How to Calculate Composite Reliability

I have discussed earlier that reliability of indicators can be explored by calculating Cronbach's alpha, but this test has had its detractors. Yang and Green (2011) has noted that Cronbach's alpha is known to overestimate and underestimate values and is "not to be construed as a coefficient of internal consistency but rather an estimate of reliability based on the internal consistency of items" (p. 389). In the face of this criticism, a test called "composite reliability" has been offered as a better alternative to Cronbach's alpha, especially when using SEM (Hair et al.

2009). This reliability test is calculated based on the factor loadings of indicators obtained from a confirmatory factor analysis. The only downside to this test is that AMOS does not calculate composite reliability and so you have to calculate it by hand (or, if you are savvy enough, design a script to calculate it). To calculate composite reliability, you need the standardized factor loadings of each construct. Here is how to calculate a composite reliability for each construct:

$$\frac{(\text{sum of standardized loadings})^2}{(\text{sum of standardized loadings})^2 + (\text{sum of indicator measurement error})}$$

For example, let's take the construct of Adaptive Behavior.

Standardized Factor loadings from the CFA

Adapt1 = .896
Adapt2 = .920
Adapt3 = .872
Adapt4 = .875
Adapt5 = .869

An indicator's measurement error is calculated by taking 1 minus the R^2 value for an indicator of a construct (this is the variance you are not explaining).

$$\frac{(.896 + .920 + .872 + .875 + .869)^2}{(.896 + .920 + .872 + .875 + .869)^2 + (1 - (.896)^2 + 1 - (.920)^2 + 1 - (.872)^2 + 1 - (.875)^2 + 1 - (.869)^2)}$$

$$=$$

$$\frac{19.64}{19.64 + 1.069} = .948$$

The composite reliability for the Adaptive Behavior construct is .94. You may notice that the composite reliability technique and Cronbach's alpha will produce slightly different values. Though Cronbach's alpha may the easiest and most widely used analysis for reliability, I find composite reliability to be a better representation of the reliability of indicators when the measurement model is included as well.

What If I Have a Standardized Factor Loading Greater Than 1?

A standardized factor loading greater than 1 is stating that you are explaining more than 100% of the variance in an indicator. In this instance, you will also see a negative number in your error term, which is often called a "Heywood case". The causes of a Heywood case are often the result of an outlier, multicollinearity between indicators, or a mis-specified model. You will see Heywood cases more often when a construct has only two indicators. Possible solutions are to remove a covariance between indicator error terms, deleting the problematic indicator, dropping outliers, adding another indicator to the unobserved variable, or dropping the maximum likelihood estimation in favor of GLS (generalized least squares—this can be done the Analysis Properties window). If you are only concerned with the standardized factor loadings (and not the unstandardized), I have seen Heywood cases addressed by constraining the unobserved variable's variance to "1" and then labelling all the paths from the unobservable construct to all the indicators the same term (Like an "A"). By labeling all of the paths to the indicators the same name, it will constrain all the paths to be equal. So, the unstandardized estimates will all be the same using this technique, but the standardized estimates will reflect the difference in the indicators. This is not an ideal method to address a Heywood case, but it is an option if all else fails.

Note: you can have unstandardized loadings greater than 1 and it is perfectly acceptable.

How Do I Report My CFA Results?

One of the challenges in performing research is analyzing the data, but an equally challenging task is how to report my findings when I am writing it up for a journal or publication. I will give you two templates to follow for writing up CFA results in a table format. There are many acceptable formats to report CFA results, but these templates allow the reader to view all the necessary information and at the same time present it in a succinct manner. Before figuring out the format, you need to assess what information needs to be included. A table should include the actual wording of your indicators as they were presented in the survey; factor loadings, t-values, reliabilities, and model fit statistics are advisable when you want a reader to consider your findings. I include the actual indicator wording in the analysis because it gives a clue to strong or weak indicators. It allows the reader to determine the face validity of your indicators and also can provide insight for the reader on how exactly the construct was captured. Lastly, you need to denote what indicators were constrained for identification purposes or, specifically, which indicator was used to set the metric for each construct. See examples of CFA results presented in Table 4.1.

Example 4.1:

Table 4.1 Confirmatory Factor and Reliability Analysis

Constructs	*Standardized Factor Loading*	*t-value*
Perceived Adaptive Behavior (C.R. = .94)		
The service experience was:		
-Customized to address my particular need	.89	**
-Adapted based on my situation	.92	32.74
-Tailored to address my concerns	.87	28.81
-Modified to my exact circumstance	.87	28.99
-Focused on my individual situation	.86	28.57
Customer Delight (C.R. = .89)		
Based on the service employee's actions did you feel:		
-Delighted	.85	**
-Elated	.91	26.54
-Gleeful	.84	23.64
Positive Word of Mouth (C.R. = .89)		
Based on your experience:		
-I would likely say positive things about [this service provider]	.89	**
-I would speak favorably of [this service provider] to others	.88	25.74
-I would recommend [this service provider] to others	.81	23.07

Model Fit Statistics (χ^2 = 60.91, df = 41; CFI = 0.99, TLI = 0.99, RMSEA = 0.03).

** = Items constrained for identification purposes.
C.R. = Composite Reliability

Example 4.2:

Table 4.1 Confirmatory Factor and Reliability Analysis

Constructs	*Standardized Factor Loading*	*t-value*
Perceived Adaptive Behavior *(Citation where indicators come from)*	(C.R. = .94)	
The service experience was:		
-Customized to address my particular need	.89	**
-Adapted based on my situation	.92	32.74
-Tailored to address my concerns	.87	28.81
-Modified to my exact circumstance	.87	28.99
-Focused on my individual situation	.86	28.57
Customer Delight *(Citation where indicators come from)*	(C.R. = .89)	
Based on the service employee's actions did you feel:		
-Delighted	.85	**
-Elated	.91	26.54
-Gleeful	.84	23.64
Positive Word of Mouth *(Citation where indicators come from)*	(C.R. = .89)	
Based on your experience:		
-I would likely say positive things about [this service provider]	.89	**
-I would speak favorably of [this service provider] to others	.88	25.74
-I would recommend [this service provider] to others	.81	23.07

Model Fit Statistics (χ^2 = 60.91, df = 41; CFI = 0.99, TLI = 0.99, RMSEA = 0.03).

** = Items constrained for identification purposes.
C.R. = Composite Reliability

Measurement Model Invariance Across Groups

Up to this point, we have discussed performing a CFA with a single group. With SEM requiring a large sample size, it is pretty common to collect data from two different methods such as online and face-to-face surveys. You will also come across instances where you are surveying two different groups but still trying to use the same measures for each group. A measurement model invariance test is often required in those occurrences. This test is done to determine if the factor loadings of indicators in a CFA do not differ across groups. You will most often see this test performed (and required by reviewers) when you have to survey two groups and your survey items are slightly altered because of the group dynamics. An example would be if you were asking first-time customers and repeat customers the same questions but needed to make sure that the meaning of the indicators have not changed now that one group has more experience with the service. A measurement model invariance test determines if your indicators are actually measuring the same thing across groups. If lack of measurement invariance is found, this indicates that the meaning of the unobservable construct is shifting across groups or possibly over time. Ultimately, you are seeing if your factor structure of your CFA is equivalent across groups.

There are five potential invariance tests to assess if you have differences in your indicators across groups. The first test that needs to be performed is called *configural invariance*. This initial test will examine if the overall structure of your measurement model is equivalent across groups. In essence, you are assessing the extent to which the same number of factors best represent the data for both groups. To accomplish this, you need to set up a two group analysis, which will examine if model fit is established across the groups. If strong model fit is present across both groups, then you can say with confidence that the data is invariant across the groups from a configural or structural perspective.

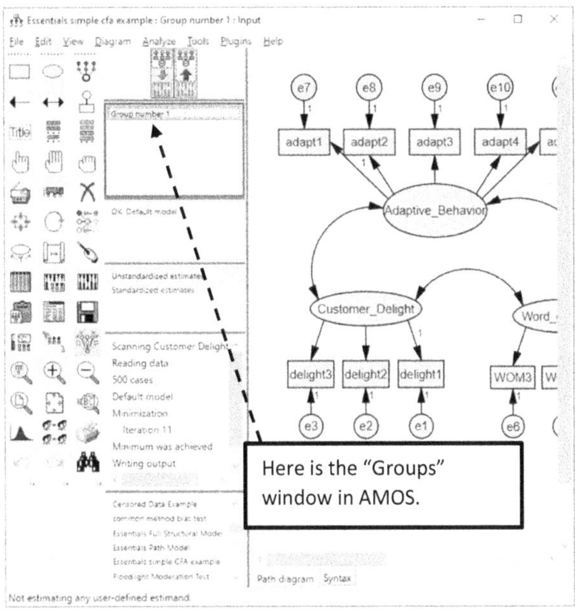

Figure 4.21 Groups Window on Graphics Page

Let's look at how to set up a multi-group analysis and test for configural invariance. Referring back to our original example, we now want to see if first-time customers are different from repeat customers. The first step is to go to the "Groups" area in AMOS. If no groups are specified, AMOS will default to one group and call it "Group number 1". You will need to double click into "Group number 1" to bring up the "Manage Groups" window.

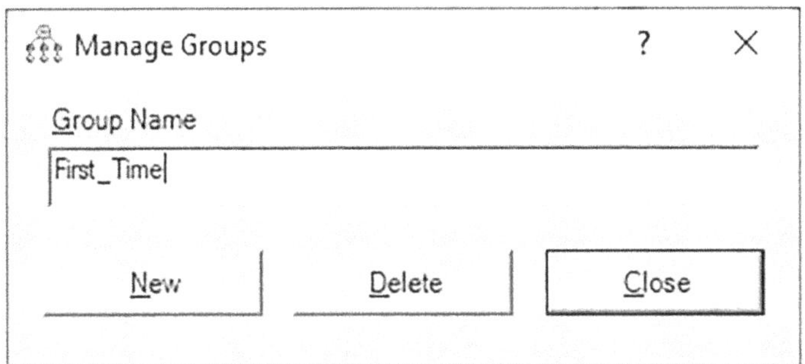

Figure 4.22 Manage Groups Pop-Up Window

(You can also access the "Manage Groups" window by going to the "Analyze" menu at the top of AMOS and then select Manage Groups). In the Manage Groups window, change the name of the group to whatever you desire. I am calling the first group "First_Time" to represent the first-time customers. To create a second group, you need to hit the "New" button on the bottom of the Manage Groups window. This will form a new group (AMOS will call it Group 2 by default) and you should change the name to represent the second group. I'll call the second group "Repeat". After forming the groups, you need to tell AMOS where the data is for each group. Select the data file icon and then select the first group "First_Time". Next, you can click the file name button and read the data file in for the first group. If the data for the second group is in a separate file, then you will click the second group "Repeat" and perform the same process of reading the data file into the group. If the groups are in the same data file, you will read in the same data file for each group, then you will need to hit the "Grouping Variable" button. This will ask what variable name the group distinction is in your data. Next, you need to click the "Group Value" button, and this is where you can note which value corresponds to which group. For instance, I have a column in the "Customer Delight Data" called "experience" which lists if the customer was a first-time or repeat customer. Customers who are new customers are listed as a "2" and customers who are repeat customers are a "1".

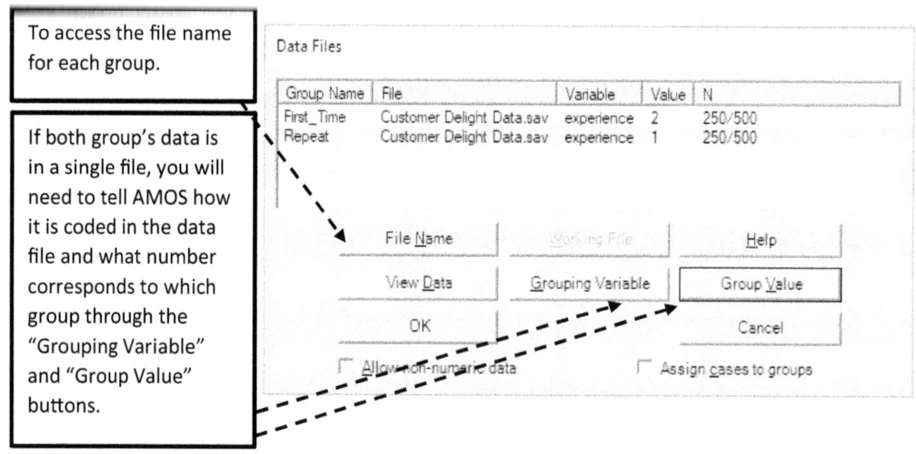

Figure 4.23 Data Files for Multiple Groups

After reading in the data for each group, you will need to uniquely label every parameter in your CFA for each group. You can imagine what a pain this would be to do this individually, but AMOS has a function that will do it for you. Hit the button (Multiple Group Analysis). Once you select this button, the following pop-up window will appear (See Figure 4.24). You can go ahead and hit "OK". It is just stating that it is going to label every parameter and suggest potential model comparisons across the groups.

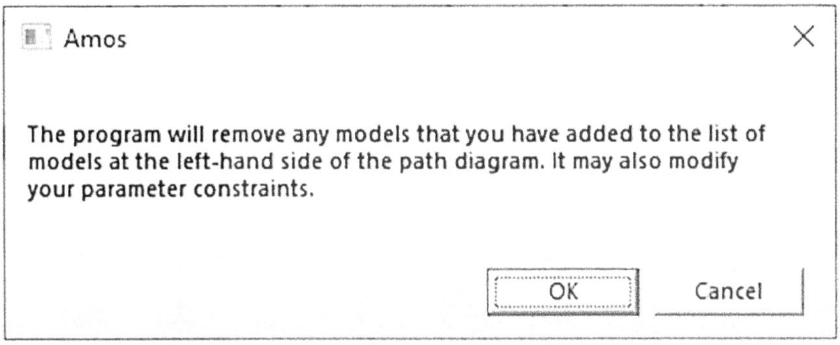

Amos

The program will remove any models that you have added to the list of models at the left-hand side of the path diagram. It may also modify your parameter constraints.

OK Cancel

Figure 4.24 Multiple Group Warning Message

The next window that will appear is the multiple group "Models" window. Since you just requested both groups' parameters to be labeled, AMOS will provide an unconstrained model where no parameters are constrained across the groups. It will also provide you with up to 8 constrained models. The first one is a measurement weights comparison where AMOS will constrain the measurement weights (factor loadings) for each group to be equal. Subsequent models can constrain structural weights, covariances, and errors. In a measurement model invariance test of a CFA, AMOS will propose three constrained models. I usually just hit "OK" here and let AMOS give me the models whether I will specifically use them or not. You do have the option of unchecking the boxes for a specific model if you do not want to see a specific aspect of the model constrained.

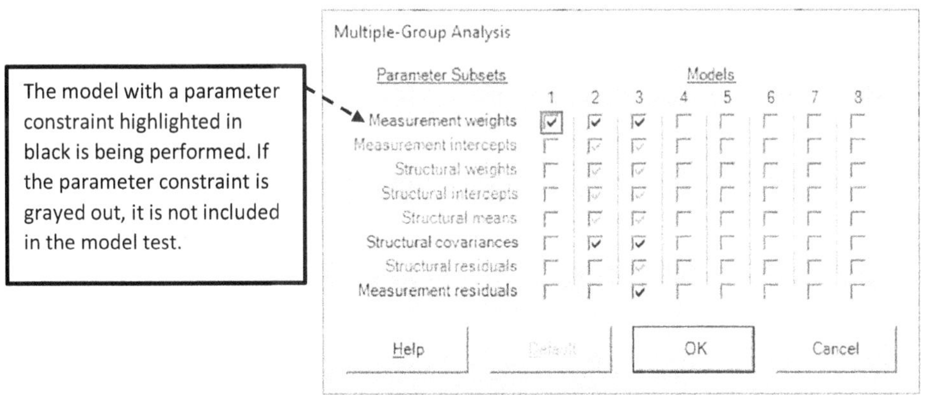

Figure 4.25 Models for Multigroup Comparison

After hitting "OK" you can go back to the main window and see on the left-hand side your groups (First_Time and Repeat). Right below that will be the unconstrained model along with all the constrained models. See Figure 4.26 for an example of what your model should look like for running the analysis. Note, if you ask AMOS to label all your parameters, it will use the letter "a" for factor loadings, "v" for error terms, and "ccc" for covariances.

In the "Groups" window you can see both groups. You can select each one to see the specifics of the group.

Unconstrained and Constrained Models

You can see where AMOS has uniquely labeled the factor loading from Customer Delight to delight2 as "a1_1" for the First_Time Group and "a1_2" for Repeat group. Your first denoted group will have all parameters listed as an _1 and your second group is listed as an _2.

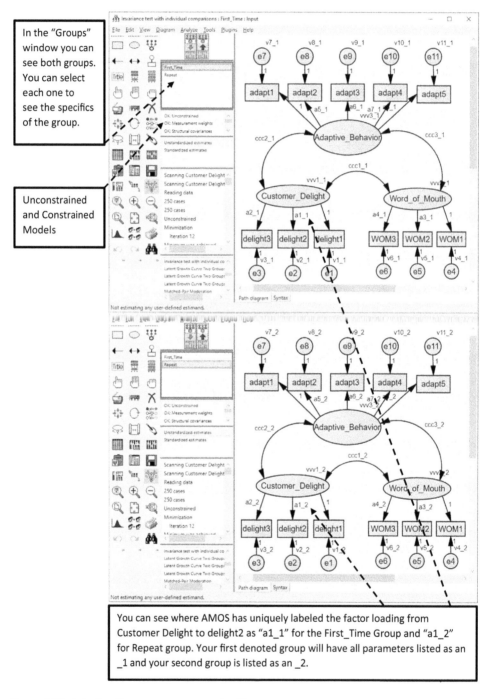

Figure 4.26 Labeling Parameters across the Groups

After labeling your groups and setting up your models, click the run analysis button  and then let's look at the output.

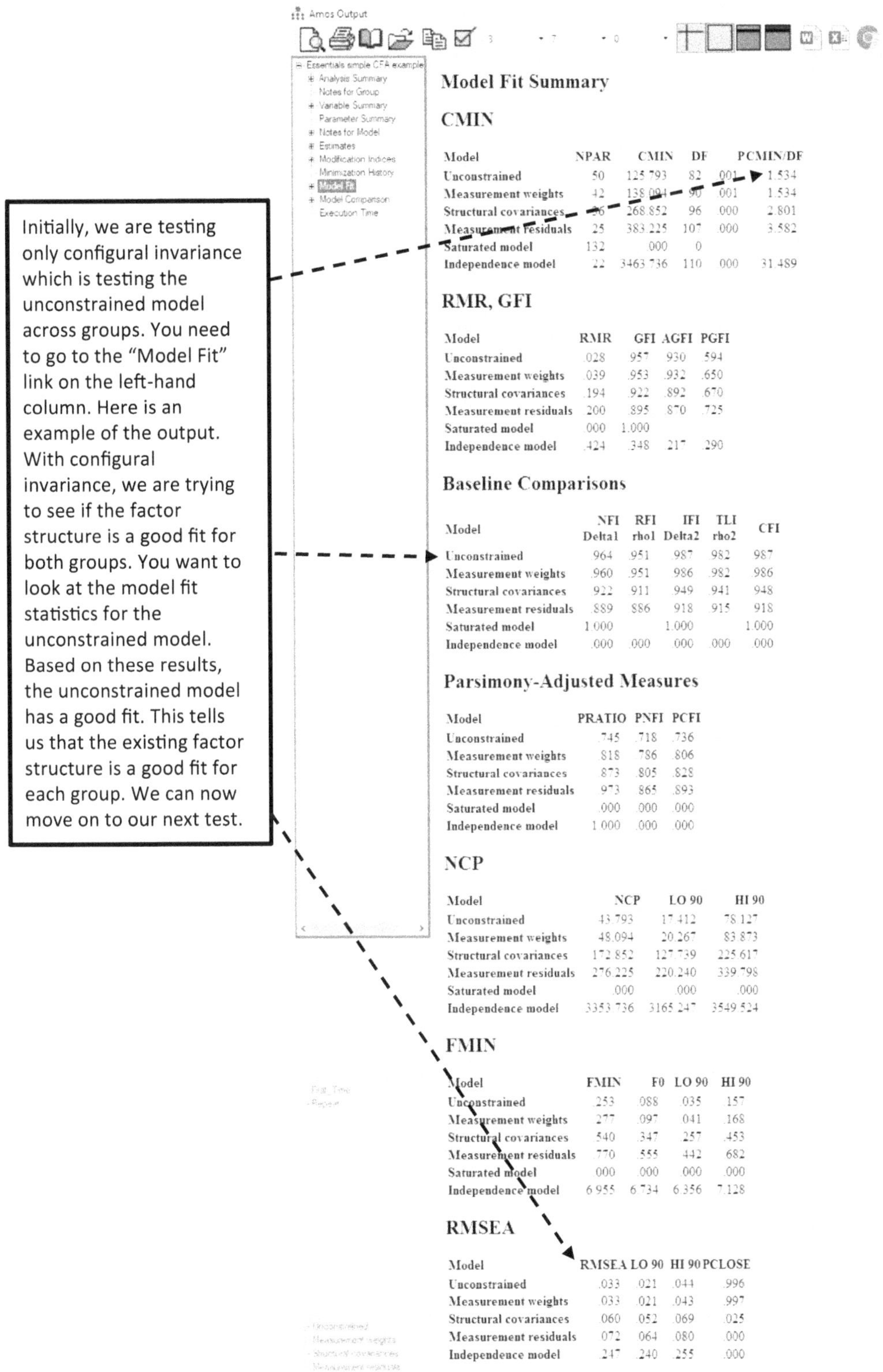

Model Fit Summary

CMIN

Model	NPAR	CMIN	DF	P	CMIN/DF
Unconstrained	50	125.793	82	.001	1.534
Measurement weights	42	138.094	90	.001	1.534
Structural covariances	36	268.852	96	.000	2.801
Measurement residuals	25	383.225	107	.000	3.582
Saturated model	132	.000	0		
Independence model	22	3463.736	110	.000	31.489

RMR, GFI

Model	RMR	GFI	AGFI	PGFI
Unconstrained	.028	.957	.930	.594
Measurement weights	.039	.953	.932	.650
Structural covariances	.194	.922	.892	.670
Measurement residuals	.200	.895	.870	.725
Saturated model	.000	1.000		
Independence model	.424	.348	.217	.290

Baseline Comparisons

Model	NFI Delta1	RFI rho1	IFI Delta2	TLI rho2	CFI
Unconstrained	.964	.951	.987	.982	.987
Measurement weights	.960	.951	.986	.982	.986
Structural covariances	.922	.911	.949	.941	.948
Measurement residuals	.889	.886	.918	.915	.918
Saturated model	1.000		1.000		1.000
Independence model	.000	.000	.000	.000	.000

Parsimony-Adjusted Measures

Model	PRATIO	PNFI	PCFI
Unconstrained	.745	.718	.736
Measurement weights	.818	.786	.806
Structural covariances	.873	.805	.828
Measurement residuals	.973	.865	.893
Saturated model	.000	.000	.000
Independence model	1.000	.000	.000

NCP

Model	NCP	LO 90	HI 90
Unconstrained	43.793	17.412	78.127
Measurement weights	48.094	20.267	83.873
Structural covariances	172.852	127.739	225.617
Measurement residuals	276.225	220.240	339.798
Saturated model	.000	.000	.000
Independence model	3353.736	3165.247	3549.524

FMIN

Model	FMIN	F0	LO 90	HI 90
Unconstrained	.253	.088	.035	.157
Measurement weights	.277	.097	.041	.168
Structural covariances	.540	.347	.257	.453
Measurement residuals	.770	.555	.442	.682
Saturated model	.000	.000	.000	.000
Independence model	6.955	6.734	6.356	7.128

RMSEA

Model	RMSEA	LO 90	HI 90	PCLOSE
Unconstrained	.033	.021	.044	.996
Measurement weights	.033	.021	.043	.997
Structural covariances	.060	.052	.069	.025
Measurement residuals	.072	.064	.080	.000
Independence model	.247	.240	.255	.000

Figure 4.27 Model Fit with Multiple Group Analysis

The next model you want to assess is the *metric invariance*. (This is usually what most reviewers are concerned with in assessing invariance between groups.) Metric invariance establishes the equivalence of the basic "meaning" of the construct via the factor loadings across the groups. In essence, are your indicators measuring the same thing across the groups? With this multi-group analysis, you will constrain the factor loadings for each group to be equal. You will then look at the change in chi-square (from the unconstrained model) to the constrained model of factor loadings across the groups to see if there is a significant difference. If it is significant, then the meaning of your unobservable constructs is different across groups (You want non-significance here.) On the upside, once you have tested the configural invariance, it is a pretty easy process to find the metric invariance. Going back to the main graphics page in AMOS, we have already set up the two group analysis. We have also requested a constrained model where the factor loadings are constrained across the groups. In the model window, you will see it listed as "Measurement weights".

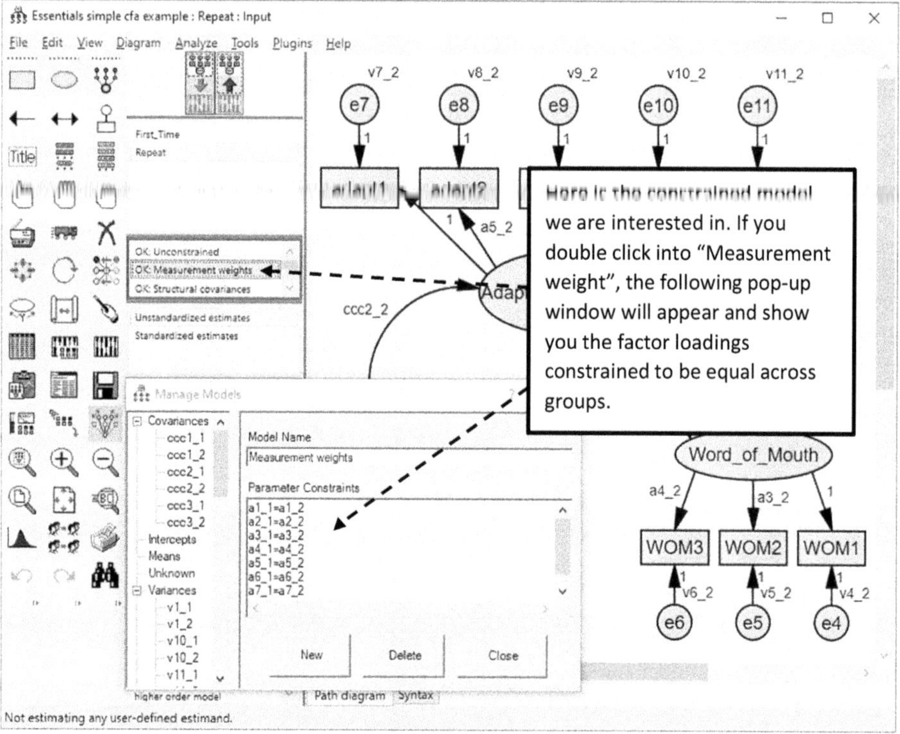

Figure 4.28 Measurement Invariance Constraints

Let's run the analysis again and return to the output. To assess metric invariance, you need to go to the "Model Comparison" link on the left-hand side of the output. The model comparison output compares the unconstrained model to all the constrained models you requested. For the metric invariance test, we are concerned only about the difference between the unconstrained and constrained measurement weights model. You can see below that once we constrained the 8 factor loadings across the groups and compared it to the unconstrained model, there was a non-significant difference in the chi-square value. Just to clarify, we had 11 total factor loadings but 3 are constrained to 1 in order to set the metric. Thus, only 8 factor loadings are freely estimated.

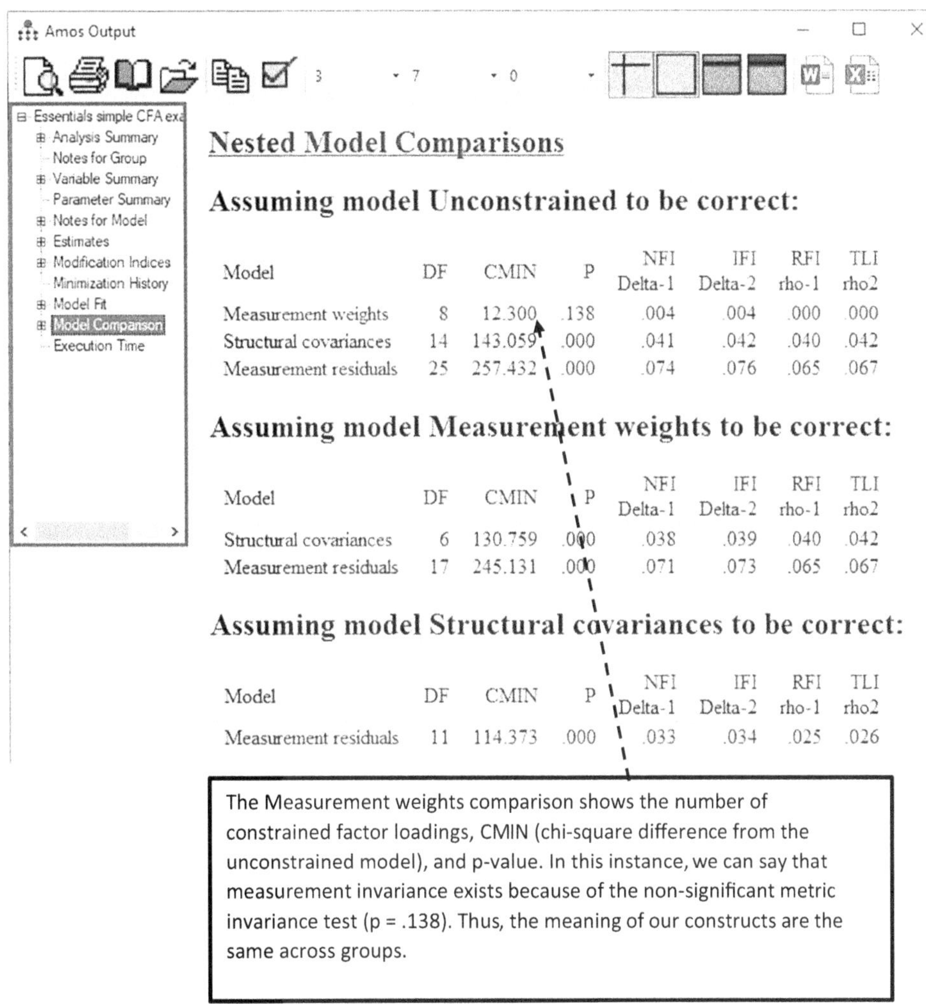
Amos Output
Essentials simple CFA exa
Analysis Summary
Notes for Group
Variable Summary
Parameter Summary
Notes for Model
Estimates
Modification Indices
Minimization History
Model Fit
Model Comparison
Execution Time

Nested Model Comparisons

Assuming model Unconstrained to be correct:

Model	DF	CMIN	P	NFI Delta-1	IFI Delta-2	RFI rho-1	TLI rho2
Measurement weights	8	12.300	.138	.004	.004	.000	.000
Structural covariances	14	143.059	.000	.041	.042	.040	.042
Measurement residuals	25	257.432	.000	.074	.076	.065	.067

Assuming model Measurement weights to be correct:

Model	DF	CMIN	P	NFI Delta-1	IFI Delta-2	RFI rho-1	TLI rho2
Structural covariances	6	130.759	.000	.038	.039	.040	.042
Measurement residuals	17	245.131	.000	.071	.073	.065	.067

Assuming model Structural covariances to be correct:

Model	DF	CMIN	P	NFI Delta-1	IFI Delta-2	RFI rho-1	TLI rho2
Measurement residuals	11	114.373	.000	.033	.034	.025	.026

The Measurement weights comparison shows the number of constrained factor loadings, CMIN (chi-square difference from the unconstrained model), and p-value. In this instance, we can say that measurement invariance exists because of the non-significant metric invariance test (p = .138). Thus, the meaning of our constructs are the same across groups.

Figure 4.29 Model Comparison of Constraint Models

For many research studies, this is as far as you need to go. In some instances, further invariance testing is beneficial. There are three more potential tests for invariance that build off the metric invariance test. With each test, more and more constraints are added to the constraint model. These tests are run the same way as the metric invariance test, except they are listed as different models in AMOS.

1. *Scalar invariance*—this is where you constrain factor loadings and measurement intercepts (means) and compare this to the unconstrained model. In AMOS, that constrained model is called "Measurement intercepts".
2. *Factor variance invariance*—this test constrains factor loadings, covariances, and variances of the constructs across groups. This constrained model is called "Structural covariance".
3. *Error variance invariance*—this is the most restrictive model; it constrains factor loadings, covariance, variances in the construct, and also error terms of indicators. In AMOS, this is referred to as the "Measurement Residuals" model comparison. It is highly unlikely to get a non-significant finding with this test especially if you have a lot of indicators in your model.

Again, with any of these tests, you are trying to determine if a significant chi-square difference exists between the unconstrained and constrained models. The goal is to have a non-significant finding, noting that the measurement properties do not differ across the groups.

Full vs. Partial Metric Invariance

The test described in the previous section is considered a "full" invariance test. When a model gets more complex, it is increasingly difficult to achieve full invariance. Partial invariance is where multiple estimates/factor loadings per construct need to be equivalent (but not all). Based on Hair et al. (2009), if two parameters per construct are found to be invariant, then partial invariance is found and the research can move forward. If full invariance is not supported, the researcher can systematically "free" the constraints on each factor that have the greatest impact on chi-square to achieve a non-significant invariance test.

How Do I Know Which Parameter to Free in a Partial Invariance Test?

If you have a significant chi-square invariance test, you need to see what indicators/factor loadings are differing across the groups. You can look at the individual factor loadings for each group and see where you have large differences across the groups. It may just be one construct causing the significant invariance test. Sometimes the differences in loadings are minimal and give you little direction in finding the indicator that is not invariant across the groups. The best way I have found is to perform an individual chi-square difference test on the indicators of each construct. It is a little tedious but is the best way to see exactly where your measurement problem is compared to just eyeballing differences in factor loadings.

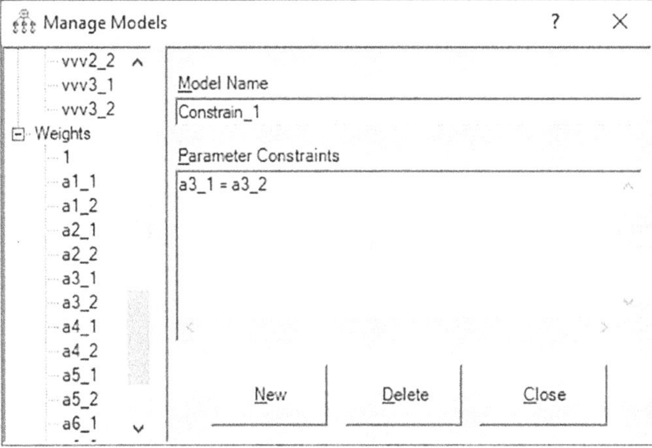

Figure 4.30 Constrain One Path Across the Groups

Let's say in our example, we think there is an invariance problem with the Positive Word of Mouth construct. The first thing I want to do is create a new constrained model in AMOS that will allow me to constrain only one factor loading at a time. First, let's go to the models window in AMOS and double click on the "Unconstrained" model. This will bring up the "Manage Models" pop-up window. I want to select the "New" button at the bottom to form a new model. A new window will pop up where you need to label the model. I like to call the new model simply "Constrain 1". The first indicator in Word of Mouth (WOM1) is constrained to 1 to set the metric, so this item will not help us. The second indicator (WOM2) is labeled a3_1 (or a3_2 for second group). I want to constrain just this indicator to be equal across the groups and to see if there is a significant chi-square difference just for this one factor loading. In the pop-up window, I denote that a3_1 = a3_2. (If you double click on the variables on the left-hand side, it will pull the variable over to the parameter constraint field without having to type it in.) After constraining this one factor loading, I hit the "Close" button and then run the analysis again. Let's now look at the output in the "Model Comparison" window.

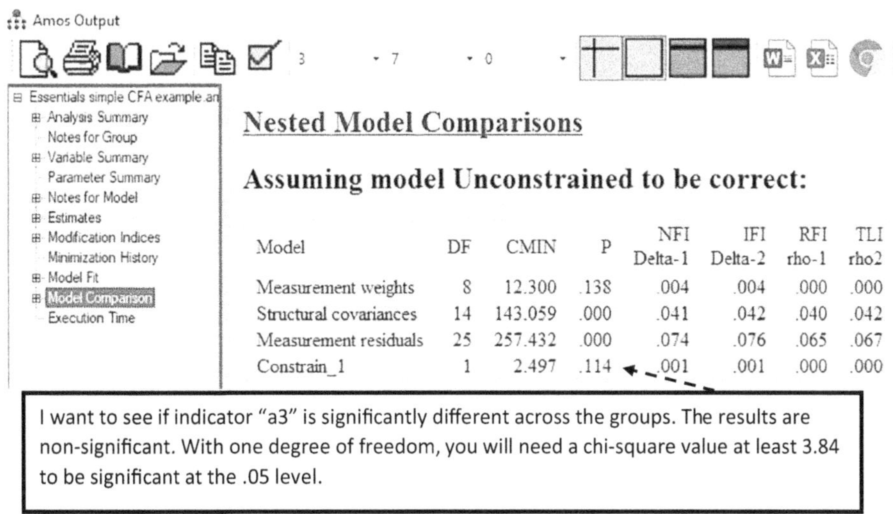

Nested Model Comparisons

Assuming model Unconstrained to be correct:

Model	DF	CMIN	P	NFI Delta-1	IFI Delta-2	RFI rho-1	TLI rho2
Measurement weights	8	12.300	.138	.004	.004	.000	.000
Structural covariances	14	143.059	.000	.041	.042	.040	.042
Measurement residuals	25	257.432	.000	.074	.076	.065	.067
Constrain_1	1	2.497	.114	.001	.001	.000	.000

Figure 4.31 Model Comparison of Constrained Parameter

Let's go back to the AMOS graphics screen and double click the "Constrain 1" model in the models window. This will bring up the pop-up window again. Let's now look at WOM3 which is labeled as 'a4'. Erase all the 'a3' constraints from the constraint window and replace it with 'a4' constraints. Let's run the analysis again and go back to the "Model Comparison" window.

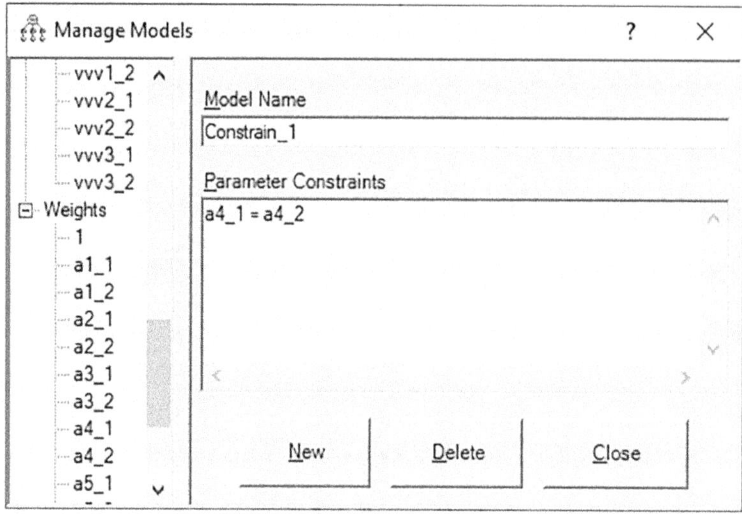

Figure 4.32 Constrain WOM3 across Groups

We can see that constraining just "a4" across the groups did find a significant difference (p-value of 0.013). You can now run a partial metric invariance test where you are constraining the factor loadings to be equal across the groups except for WOM3 (a4), which is now not constrained across the groups. If you are still not achieving a non-significant invariance test, you will need to see if other individual factor loadings are significantly different across the groups. You may have to perform this individual constraint test for multiple constructs if you are having a problem zeroing in on where the invariance problem lies. As I said, this can be time consuming and laborious, but it is necessary to achieve partial metric invariance.

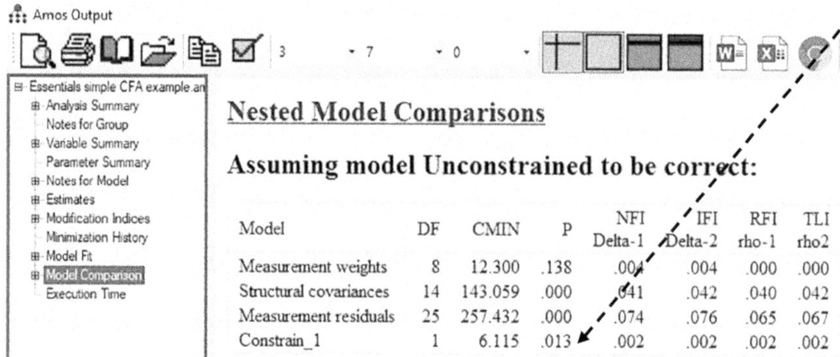

Nested Model Comparisons

Assuming model Unconstrained to be correct:

Model	DF	CMIN	P	NFI Delta-1	IFI Delta-2	RFI rho-1	TLI rho2
Measurement weights	8	12.300	.138	.004	.004	.000	.000
Structural covariances	14	143.059	.000	.041	.042	.040	.042
Measurement residuals	25	257.432	.000	.074	.076	.065	.067
Constrain_1	1	6.115	.013	.002	.002	.002	.002

Figure 4.33 Model Comparison Results for WOM3

Another way to assess exactly where you have an invariance issue in your model is to create a separate model comparison test for each factor loading. By doing this, you can see where the potential invariance issues are across the whole model instead of performing multiple tests one at a time. In our example, we have 8 factor loadings that are constrained to be equal across the groups (the factor loadings that are set to "1" are excluded). To perform the invariance test this way, you would need to bring up the Manage Models window, then name the model comparison "a1 test", and then constrain the a1_1 parameter to be equal to a1_2 parameter. You would repeat this process and create 8 new models that would test each factor loading that is labeled separately.

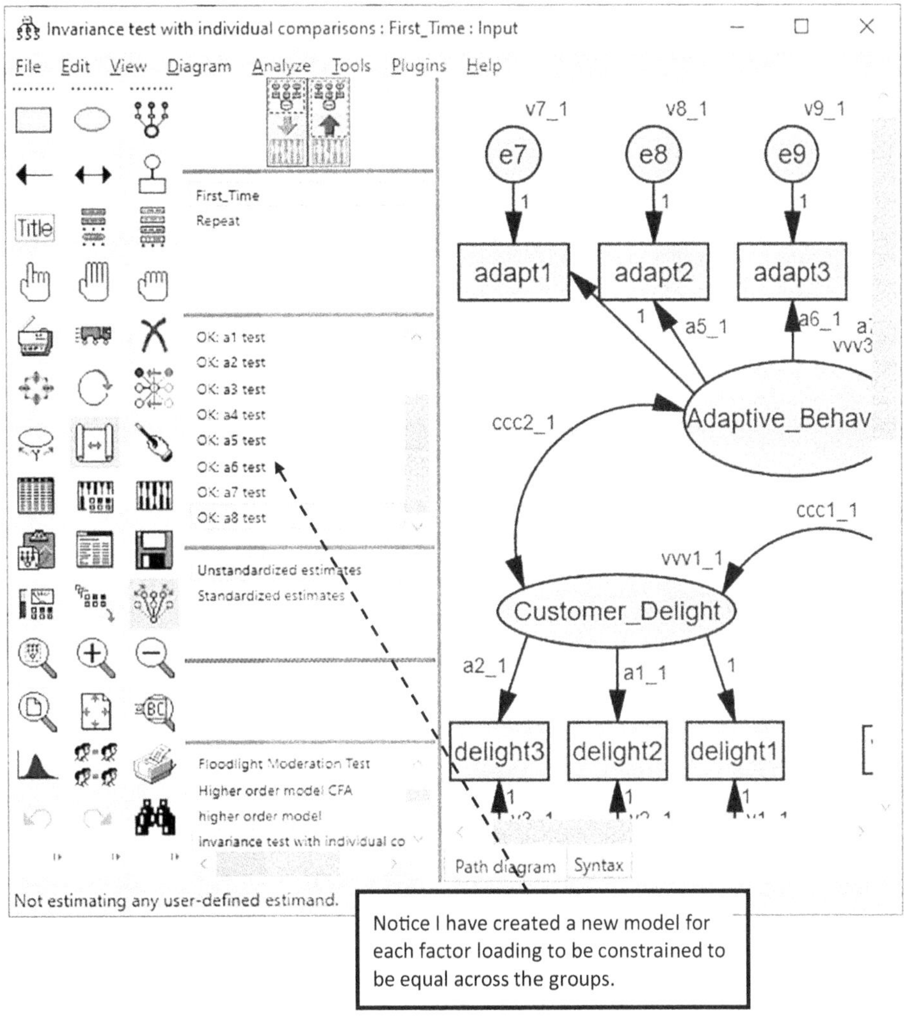

Figure 4.34 Multiple Parameter Constraints Across Groups

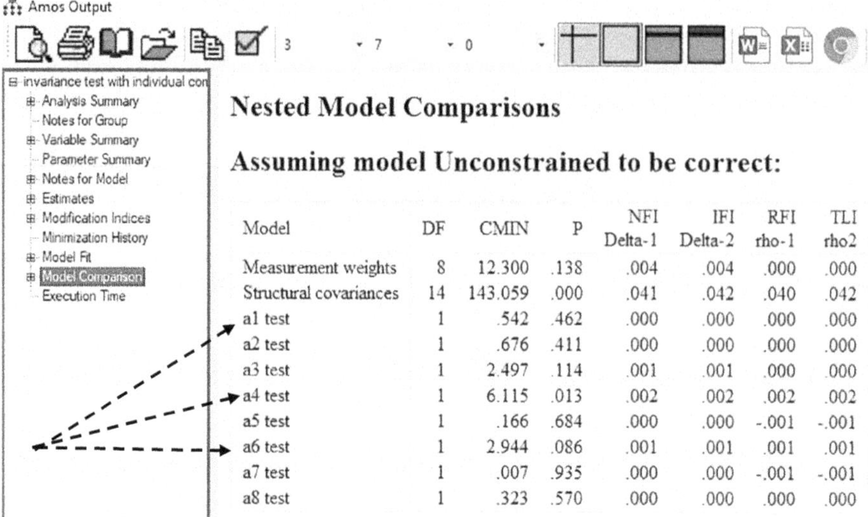

Model	DF	CMIN	P	NFI Delta-1	IFI Delta-2	RFI rho-1	TLI rho2
Measurement weights	8	12.300	.138	.004	.004	.000	.000
Structural covariances	14	143.059	.000	.041	.042	.040	.042
a1 test	1	.542	.462	.000	.000	.000	.000
a2 test	1	.676	.411	.000	.000	.000	.000
a3 test	1	2.497	.114	.001	.001	.000	.000
a4 test	1	6.115	.013	.002	.002	.002	.002
a5 test	1	.166	.684	.000	.000	-.001	-.001
a6 test	1	2.944	.086	.001	.001	.001	.001
a7 test	1	.007	.935	.000	.000	-.001	-.001
a8 test	1	.323	.570	.000	.000	.000	.000

Figure 4.35 Multiple Parameter Constraint Output

After running the analysis again, if we go to the results and click on the Model Comparison link, you will see the individual invariance tests for each factor loading. The test of all 8 factor loadings are presented at once so you can see exactly where your invariance problems lie in your model. In this instance, it appears that only a4 (WOM3) has a significant invariance test. All other factor loadings are invariant across the groups. Again, this is just another option in invariance testing. You can create one new constrained model and test each factor loading one by one, or you can create a constrained model for every factor loading at the beginning and see all the invariance tests at once.

In the event that you cannot achieve even partial metric invariance, you have a serious measurement problem that will not let you proceed. You will ultimately need to go back to the data collection phase and determine how you can assess the same construct across different groups.

Common Method Bias

Over the last 10 years, more and more attention has been paid to the idea of common method bias (CMB) in the measurement analysis phase. Common method bias is the inflation (or in rare cases deflation) of the true correlation among observable variables in a study. Research has shown that because respondents are replying to survey questions about independent and dependent variables at the same time, this can artificially inflate the covariation (which lead to biased parameter estimates). Here are some ways to control for common method bias:

1. *Harman's Single Factor Test*—this simplistic test performs an EFA with all the indicators in your model to determine if one single factor will emerge. If a single factor does appear, then common method bias is said to be present in the data. You will also see a Harman's

single factor test performed with a CFA where all indicators are purposely loaded on one factor to determine model fit. If you have an acceptable model fit with the one construct model, then you have a method bias. There is an ongoing debate as to whether Harman's single factor test is an appropriate test to determine common method bias. On one side, researchers have questioned this approach and have concluded that it is insufficient to determine if common method bias is present (Malhotra et al. 2007; Chang et al. 2010). Other researchers (Fuller et al. 2016) have argued that if common method bias is strong enough to actually bias results, then Harman's single factor test is sensitive enough to determine if a problem exists. While Harman's single factor test is easy to implement, it is a relatively insensitive test to determine common method bias compared to other post-hoc tests. In my opinion, if you know a test is inferior to others, then there is very little justification for using this method.

2. *Marker-Variable Technique*—to use this test, the researcher has to plan ahead in the survey design phase of your research. This technique requires you to introduce a variable in a survey that is theoretically unrelated to any other construct in your study. This "mole" variable is also called the marker variable. CMB is assessed by examining the correlation between the marker variable and the unrelated variables of your study. Theoretically, the correlation between your marker variable and the variables of the study should be low. If the correlations are not low, there is a good chance you are going to have a significant method bias. To determine if this bias is present, you need to partial out the effect of the marker variable from all the correlations across constructs. In essence, you are going to strip out any inflated correlation because of a method bias from your other constructs.

Here is how to obtain the adjusted correlation between constructs with the marker variable's influence removed:

R^A = Adjusted Correlation
R^M = Correlation of Marker Variable
R^U = Unadjusted Correlation

$$R^A = \frac{R^U - R^M}{1 - R^M}$$

In the past, a researcher would use the lowest correlation of the marker variable and another construct in the model to be the correlation that needs to be partialed out of all other correlations. Lindell and Whitney (2001) state you should use the second smallest correlation of your marker variable and a variable in your study so that you do not capitalize on chance. They make the argument that it provides a more conservative estimate.

Let's look at an example to add more context to this discussion. Using our CFA example from before, I have initially formed composite variables for each construct in the model, and I have also included a marker variable. The marker variable was a construct called Price Consciousness, which is how price sensitive a customer is. This unrelated construct should have a low correlation to the other constructs of the model. Next, I am going to perform a correlation analysis with those variables of the model along with the marker variable of price consciousness. Here is an example of the correlation analysis before any adjustments are made.

Correlation	*Adaptive Behavior*	*Customer Delight*	*WOM*	*Price Con*
Adaptive Behavior	1			
Customer Delight	.65	1		
Positive Word of Mouth	.34	.44	1	
Price Consciousness (Marker)	.04	.05	.07	1

Let's initially examine the correlation of Adaptive Behavior and Customer Delight. The unadjusted correlation is .65. The second lowest correlation of Price Consciousness (marker) to any other construct in the model is .05. Next, let's get the adjusted correlation for Adaptive Behavior and Customer Delight.

$$\frac{.65-.05}{1-.05}=\frac{.60}{.95}=.63$$

The adjusted correlation is .63. Since we are parceling out a level of correlation, your adjusted correlation should be smaller. You will need to find the adjusted correlation for each value in the correlation analysis for the constructs of your model.

Here is the adjusted correlation for each construct with the marker variable's influence removed from the other constructs.

Correlation	*Adaptive Behavior*	*Customer Delight*	*WOM*	*Price Con*
Adaptive Behavior	1			
Customer Delight	.63	1		
Positive Word of Mouth	.30	.41	1	
Price Consciousness (Marker)	.04	.05	.07	1

Once you get the adjusted correlation for every construct of your study, you will then use this adjusted correlation matrix as your input for your AMOS model. To see how to use a correlation matrix as the input of your model, see Chapter 5.

The downside of using this technique is you are asking an "out of the blue" question in your survey, which could confuse the respondent. The biggest concern is this technique almost necessitates that you use composite variables in your analysis. One of the primary strengths of SEM is to model measurement error. With this technique of using an adjusted correlation matrix as your input, you are just examining the relationships between composite variables, which could present a slightly different picture of your results compared to a model that had all the indicators for each construct included in the analysis.

3. *Include a Latent Common Method Factor*—the most popular way to handle common method bias is to include a common method factor in your CFA. A common method factor is a latent variable that has a direct relationship with each construct's indicators. The common method factor will represent and account for variance across constructs (due to the potential methods bias). You will first model your CFA, then you will include a latent

variable in the model with no indicators. Label this variable "Common_Method" or whatever you want in order to remember that this is the common method construct. From this common method construct, you will start drawing relationships from the construct to all the indicators in the model. You will include a direct relationship from the unobserved common method latent construct to every indicator in the model. You might want to go about this in a systematic manner so that you do not miss a relationship to an indicator. With a CFA that has a large number of constructs, this can be a substantial number of relationships, so my best advice is to start adding relationships one construct at a time until all the indicators have a relationship to the unobservable common method factor.

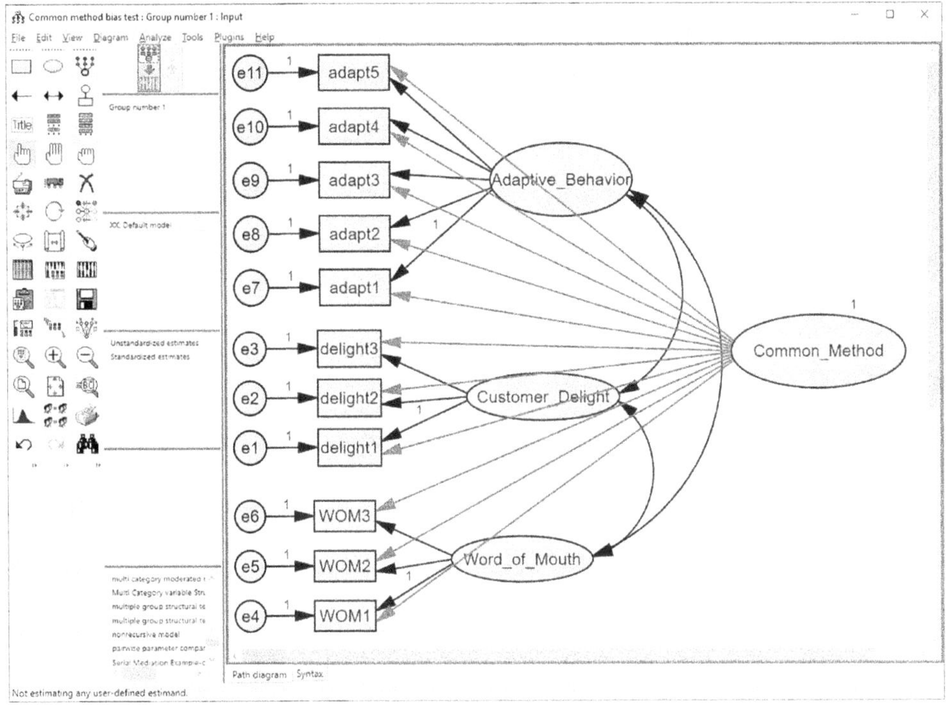

Figure 4.36 Example of Common Method Factor With a Relationship to Every Indicator

After drawing a path from the common method construct to all the indicators, you will need to constrain all the relationships from the common method factor to be equal. We are doing this to see what is the common influence across all the indicators. If common method bias is present, it should affect all the variables of the survey equally. Right click on one of the relationships (arrows) from the common method construct; the Object Properties window should appear. Under the Parameters tab at the top, put a letter in the "regression weight" line. In this example, I labeled the regression weight simply "a", but you could call it anything you want. After labeling the parameter, you can cancel out of this screen.

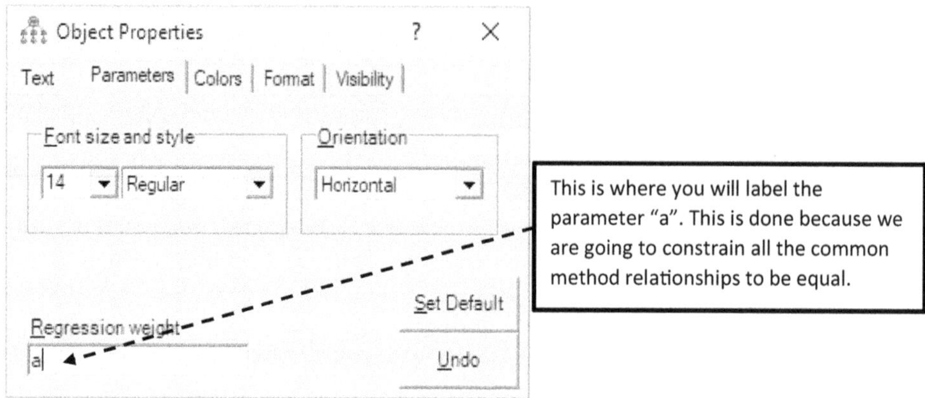

Figure 4.37 Constraining All Relationships to "a" in Common Method Bias Test

You can go into each relationship and constrain all the parameters to the letter "a", but this might be extremely time consuming if you have a large number of indicators. AMOS has a function that lets you copy a constraint to other relationships. So, we will copy this constraint of letter "a" and paste it in all other relationships from the common method construct. To do this, the first thing you need to do is select all the other relationships from the common method variable (do not select the one that is already constrained with an "a"). The easiest way to do this is to use the [select icon] (select) button and select each relationship. You can also hold down the left-click button on your mouse and drag over the relationships, and it will also highlight them.

Next, you need to select the "Drag Properties" button [Drag Properties icon]. A pop-up window will appear. Select "Parameter Constraints" in the Drag Properties window. Now, go back to the relationship that has the regression weight labeled "a" and drag the "a" to all the other highlighted relationships. Make sure the "Drag Properties" pop-up window is active on the screen, or it will not perform the drag function. The Drag Properties icon is a handy function, especially if you have a larger number of indicators.

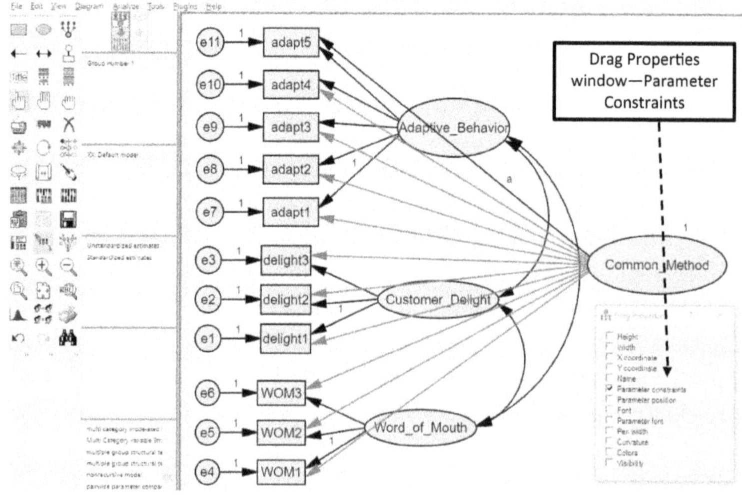

Figure 4.38 Using the Drag Function to Constrain All the Relationships to "a"

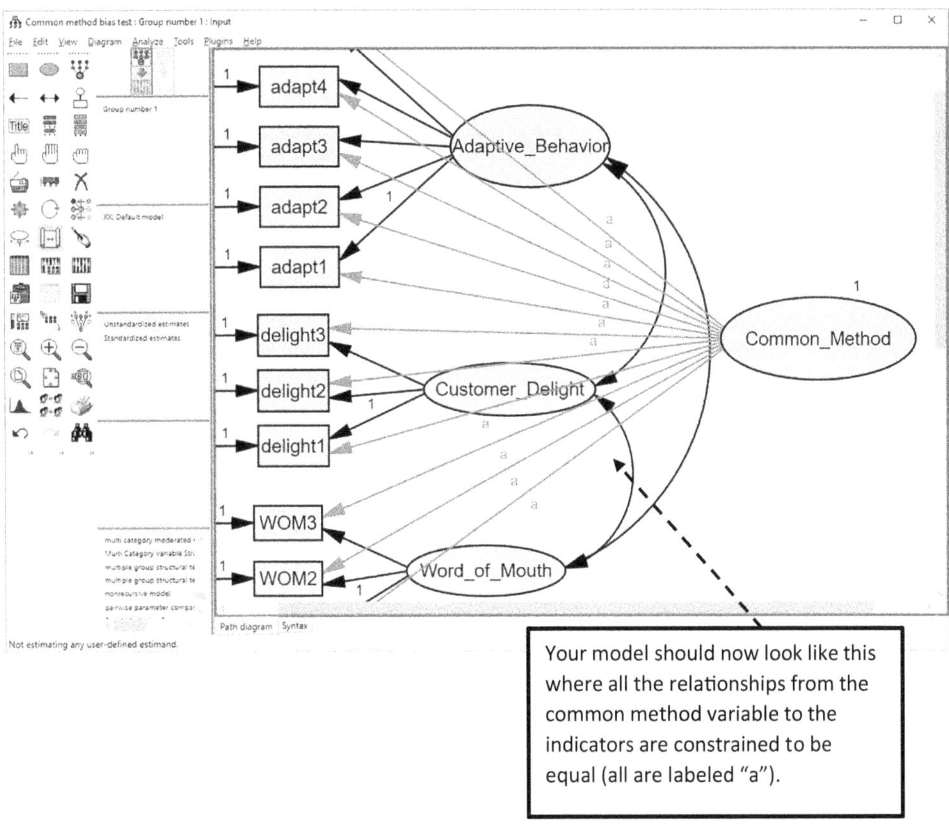

Figure 4.39 Example of All Relationships Constrained in Common Method Test

Before moving forward, it is a good idea to hit the "Deselect All Objects" icon so that you are not having any unintended action with the highlighted relationships from the common method factor. After constraining all the relationships to be equal, you next need to right click in the unobservable common method variable. The Object Properties window will appear. You should set the variance of the unobserved construct to "1". This is done because we are concerned only about the impact of the potential bias to the indicators of our model.

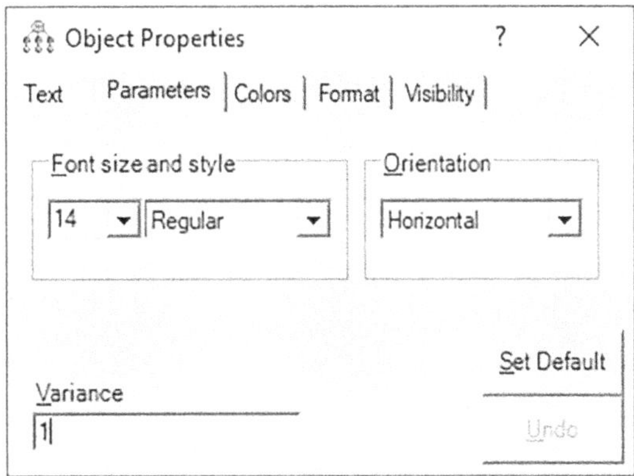

Figure 4.40 Setting the Variance to "1" in Unobservable Common Method Variable

Next, you will run the analysis for the model [icon]. AMOS will initially warn you that your unobserved variables in the CFA do not have a covariance to the common_method construct. You do not need to covary your constructs in the model with the common_method construct. Just hit the "Proceed with the Analysis" button to continue without adding additional covariances. After the analysis finishes, go into the output and go to the model fit link. With the common method test, we will perform a chi-square difference test to determine if bias is present. Specifically, you are concerned with the chi-square values of the CFA model. The CFA comparison will examine what the chi-square value was for your CFA when the common method construct was not included, and then a comparison will be made to the chi-square value of the CFA when the common method construct was included. In the analysis, you should see only 1 degree of freedom difference between the two models. Remember, we constrained all the relationships in the common method construct model to be equal. Hence, we need to see if the difference in chi-square is significant which would indicate a common method bias.

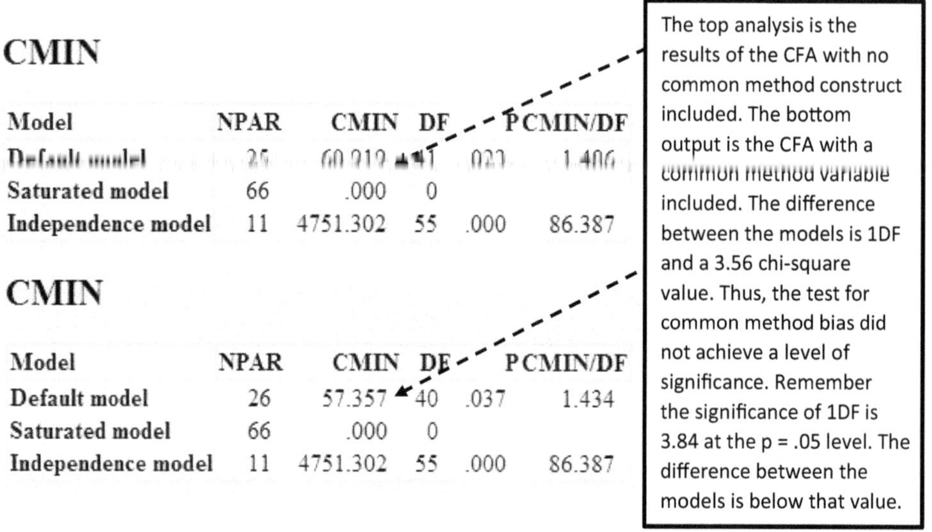

The top analysis is the results of the CFA with no common method construct included. The bottom output is the CFA with a common method variable included. The difference between the models is 1DF and a 3.56 chi-square value. Thus, the test for common method bias did not achieve a level of significance. Remember the significance of 1DF is 3.84 at the p = .05 level. The difference between the models is below that value.

CMIN

Model	NPAR	CMIN	DF	P	CMIN/DF
Default model	25	60.919	41	.023	1.486
Saturated model	66	.000	0		
Independence model	11	4751.302	55	.000	86.387

CMIN

Model	NPAR	CMIN	DF	P	CMIN/DF
Default model	26	57.357	40	.037	1.434
Saturated model	66	.000	0		
Independence model	11	4751.302	55	.000	86.387

Figure 4.41 Difference of Chi-Square for Common Method Test

What If My Test for Common Method Bias Is Significant?

You will need to include the common method variable and its relationships to all the indicators when you start testing the structural relationships between constructs. By including the common method variable in the testing of the structural relationships, you are controlling for the potential bias of the common method. If you want to see exactly where the potential bias is originating from, you can go to the standardized regression weights of the CFA output that has the common method construct included. In the standardized regression weights, examine the relationships from the common method construct to the indicators and observe which indicator is loading at a high level. This is a good indication of where the common method bias is coming from that is causing a significant chi-square difference test between the original CFA and the CFA with a common method variable included.

What if My Common Method Bias Test Is Non-Significant?

You can state in your research that common method bias is not a substantial concern in your research (do not state that it is not present—it could be present but at very low levels). In your research, you could even present the chi-square difference test showing that common method bias was not prevalent. With a non-significant common method bias test, there is no need to include the common method latent factor in the structural analysis. Your common method test has shown that this potential bias is not a concern moving forward.

What Is a Second Order Confirmatory Factor Analysis Model?

A second order CFA is a "higher order" construct that is measured by latent constructs. For instance, let's say we want to model a construct called "Unique Experience". This construct is the degree to which customers think their experience was unique or different compared to a normal experience. This second order construct of "Unique Experience" is made up of two constructs called "Surprise" and "Empathy". The surprise construct is to what degree the customer was surprised by the experience delivered and empathy is how empathic was the employee to the needs of the customer. See Figure 4.42.

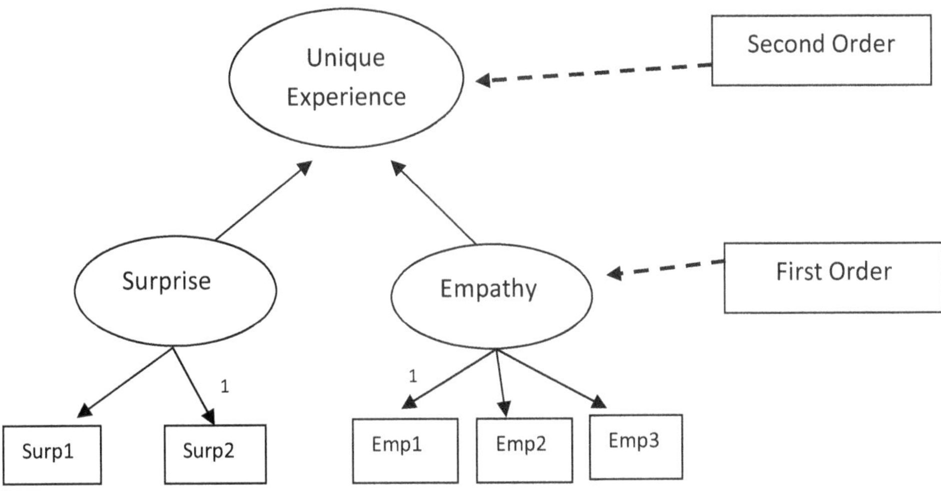

Figure 4.42 Example of Second Order Model With Two First Order Dimensions

In this example, the higher order construct of "Unique Experience" is made up or formed by two first order unobservable constructs. Empathy is measured with three indicators, and Surprise is measured with two indicators. With complex constructs, it is not unusual to have a second order construct made up of multiple first order constructs. Second order constructs are sometimes also referred to as higher order constructs. Assessing the validity of a second order construct will take place in the first order level. For this example, the constructs of Surprise and Empathy would be included in a CFA to determine the validity of the indicators to their constructs. Investigating the relationships from the first order constructs to the second order construct would not take place in a CFA. This would be assessed in the structural model where the between-construct relationships are examined.

You cannot create a composite variable of your second order construct. Trying to combine multiple constructs to form a composite variable is inappropriate. You can form composite variables of the first order constructs and then form relationships to the second order construct. With second order constructs, the first order constructs are conceptualizing the second order concept. Since multiple different constructs are coming together to define another concept, the idea of reflective and formative indicators needs to be discussed.

Reflective vs. Formative Indicators

Based on classical test theory (Lord and Novick 1968), when an unobservable variable causes changes in its indicators, the specification of these indicators is reflective (Fornell and Bookstein 1982) or effect indicators (Bollen and Lennox 1991). By far, this is the most common type of measurement model in which the direction of influence flows from the unobserved construct to its indicators (MacKenzie et al. 2005). With this type of measurement model, the unobserved construct is itself responsible for explaining the variation in its indicators. Thus, all indicators should be relatively correlated because each indicator is a reflection or manifestation of the effects of the unobserved, or latent, construct. The assessment of reliability, unidimensionality, discriminant validity, and convergent validity are all meaningful tests with reflective indicators. Additionally, reflective indicators are assumed to be interchangeable because they all represent aspects of the same conceptual domain (i.e., the unobservable construct; MacKenzie et al. 2005). Lastly, in specifying a model with reflective indicators, the error terms in the model are associated with each individual indicator rather than with the latent construct.

Alternatively, measurement models specified such that the direction of influence flows *from* the indicators *to* the unobservable construct are said to be comprised of formative or causal indicators (Bollen and Lennox 1991). With this type of measurement model, the underlying assumptions differ dramatically from the assumptions of a measurement model specified with reflective indicators. In fact, a measurement model with formative indicators involves the construction of an index rather than a scale. The indicators in a formative model are meant to contain the full meaning of the unobservable construct. In essence, the measures or indicators define and encompass the meaning of the latent construct.

Since formative indicators do not derive their meaning *from* the unobservable construct but instead define the unobservable construct, formative measures are not required to be positively correlated with each other. Thus, it would be perfectly acceptable for formative indicators of an unobservable construct to be uncorrelated or even negatively correlated with another. Nunnally and Bernstein (1994) note that two formative indicators can be negatively correlated and still serve as meaningful indicators of an unobservable construct. Thus, it is not necessarily the case that a set of formative indicators has a similar theme or content (Jarvis et al. 2003). Unlike reflective indicators, each formative indicator describes a part of the unobserved construct. Thus, formative indicators are not interchangeable, and dropping a formative indicator from a measurement model specification can result in a change in the definition of an unobservable construct. In fact, Bollen and Lennox (1991) state that "omitting an indicator is omitting a part of the construct" (p. 308). This emphasizes why the process of defining a construct with a measurement model composed of formative indicators is such an important process; by doing so, the researcher is actually describing and specifying what dimensions are forming the latent construct.

Because the underlying assumptions of a measurement model specified by formative indicators require no correlation among indicators, traditional procedures to assess internal consistency/reliability and construct validity are not appropriate. Bagozzi (1994) notes "reliability in the internal consistency sense and construct validity in terms of convergent and discriminant validity are not meaningful when indexes are formed as a linear sum of measurements" (p. 333). Similarly, Bollen and Lennox (1991) state that since "causal indicators are not invalidated by low internal consistency . . . to assess validity we need to examine other variables that are effects of the latent construct" (p. 312).

Though traditional validity concerns are not relevant for formative indicators, Diamantopoulos and Winklhofer (2001) detail four areas of concern with formative indicators that must be addressed. The first one is content specification. This concern is based around the idea that you have fully specified all the dimensions that will "form" this construct. The next area is indicator specification. This concern details that you have included enough indicators or items in your model to fully capture the particular aspect of the construct. Next is indicator collinearity: multicollinearity between indicators is problematic with formative indicators. Excessive collinearity among indicators makes it difficult to separate the distinct influence of indicators on the unobserved construct. The last concern is external validity. A formative indicator model should have the ability to extend into multiple contexts.

The last distinction between formative and reflective indicators relates to the specification of error terms. In a reflective measurement model, error terms are associated with each indicator. A formative measurement model, however, must by definition represent error on the construct level. Thus, error must be assessed for the set of indicators (i.e., the index) rather than on the individual indicator level. This construct level error evaluation is meant to capture the missing facets or causes of the construct (Diamantopoulos 2006). Figure 4.43 contains some examples of formative models.

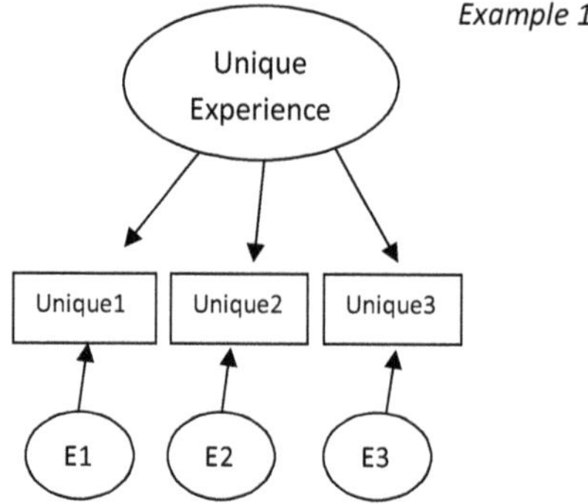

Example 1 is the most common method of measurement where a construct is "reflective" of its indicators. Error is modeled on the indicator level.

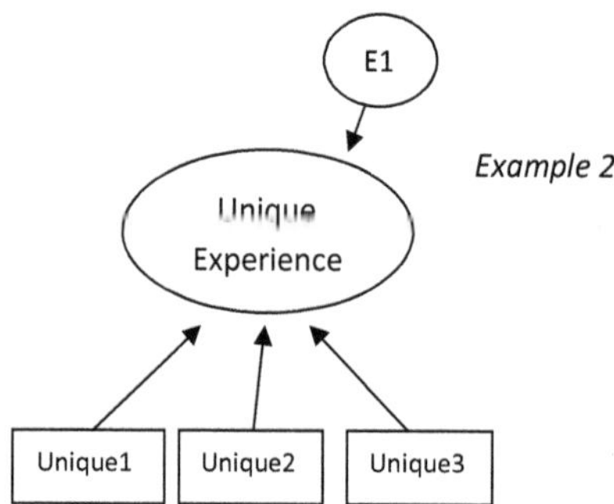

Example 2 is a formative first order construct. You will rarely see a construct like this. A formative construct is often developed by numerous different concepts coming together to "form" a new unobservable construct. Notice that error is modeled on the construct level now.

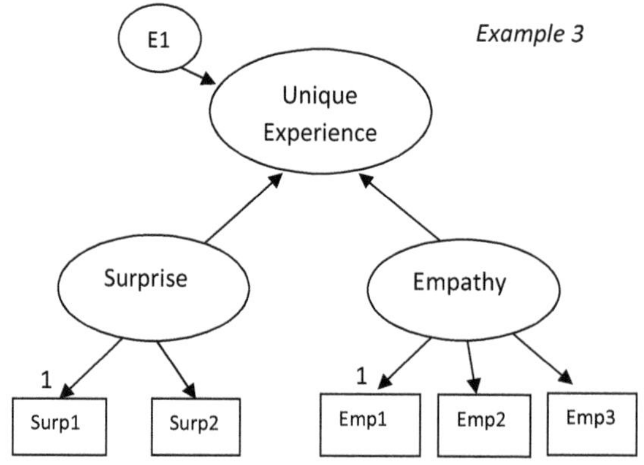

Example 3 is the most common type of formative construct. The first order constructs are reflective but the relationships from the first order constructs to the second order construct is formative.

Figure 4.43a Examples of Acceptable and Unacceptable Second Order Models

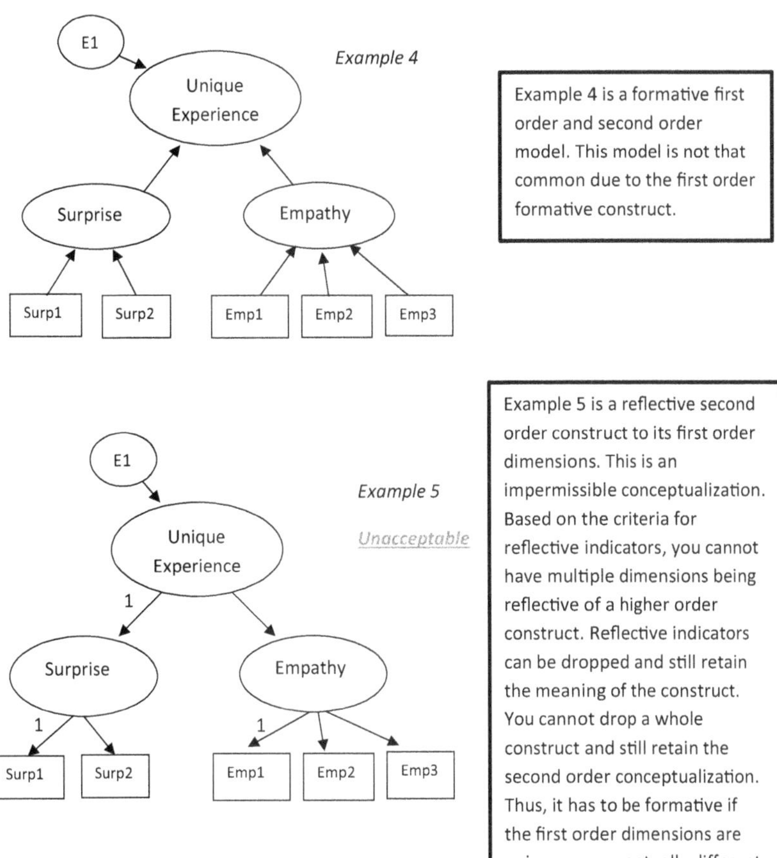

E1
Unique Experience
Example 4
Example 4 is a formative first order and second order model. This model is not that common due to the first order formative construct.
Surprise
Empathy
Surp1
Surp2
Emp1
Emp2
Emp3
E1
Example 5
Unacceptable
Unique Experience
1
Surprise
Empathy
1
1
Surp1
Surp2
Emp1
Emp2
Emp3
Example 5 is a reflective second order construct to its first order dimensions. This is an impermissible conceptualization. Based on the criteria for reflective indicators, you cannot have multiple dimensions being reflective of a higher order construct. Reflective indicators can be dropped and still retain the meaning of the construct. You cannot drop a whole construct and still retain the second order conceptualization. Thus, it has to be formative if the first order dimensions are unique or conceptually different.

Figure 4.43b Examples of Acceptable and Unacceptable Second Order Models (Continued)

Potential Identification Problems With Formative Indicators

A formative construct will have identification problems in SEM if additional steps are not taken. The first way to rectify the identification problem is to include two reflective indicators from the formative unobservable construct. These two reflective indicators should try to capture the overall theme of the formative construct. You need to know if your conceptualization has a formative construct before data collection takes place, because you will need to ask these dedicated questions solely for identification of the formative construct. This is by far the most preferred way to solve the identification issues of formative constructs. You will also see this technique called a MIMIC model, which stands for multiple indicator multiple cause model. With this type of model, you have both formative and reflective relationships included in the measurement of a concept. The second way to solve the identification problem is to have a relationship from the formative construct to two unobservable constructs in the model that are reflective. In essence, you are achieving identification through the paths to other reflective constructs. See Figure 4.44.

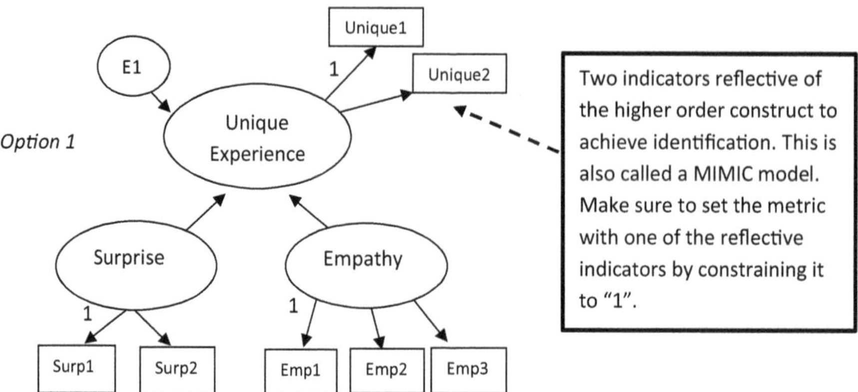

Figure 4.44a Ways to Achieve Identification With a Second Order Formative Construct

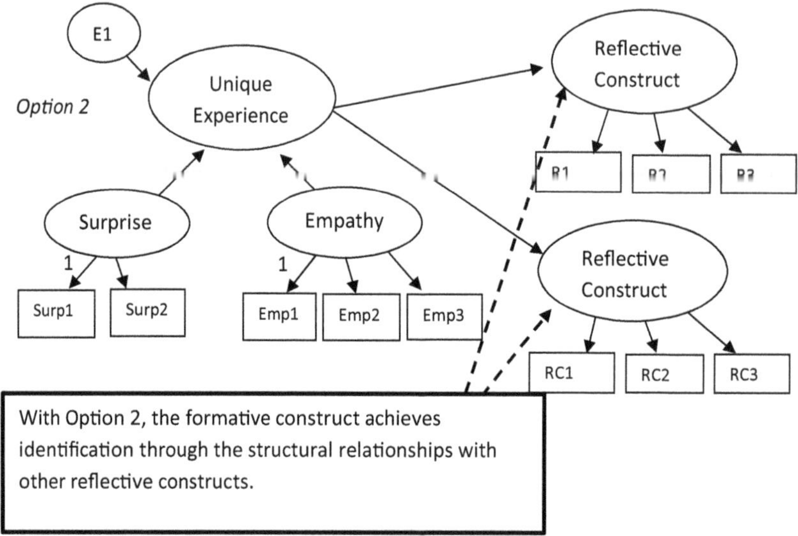

Figure 4.44b Ways to Achieve Identification With a Second Order Formative Construct

In My Opinion: Identification With Formative Indicators

In my opinion, the MIMIC model approach is far superior to the option of achieving identification through the structural relationships with other reflective constructs. I have found that the second option of using structural paths for identification will often wreck your model fit and can have adverse effects on your structural relationships. In my previous work, I have tested both methods for identification in a model, and the second option (structural path for identification) has consistently produced worse results.

If you know you have a formative construct, ask the two identification questions in your survey and use the MIMIC model approach. It is not dependent on other constructs and allows for a cleaner analysis.

Dependent Relationships With Formative Constructs

As stated earlier, a formative construct is defined by its indicators. A change in a formative unobserved construct cannot take place without a change also taking place in the indicators. Hence, I think it is a good idea to discuss the appropriate way to model relationships in a SEM model with formative constructs. If a formative construct is directly influenced by its indicators, then any antecedent/predictor constructs must have a relationship to these indicators instead of the higher order construct. A common mistake is for a predictor construct to have a direct relationship to a higher order formative construct. The higher order construct cannot change without a change in the first order constructs. Thus, if a formative construct is a dependent variable, the predictor construct needs to form a relationship to the first order constructs to have an influence on the overall formative construct. For further discussion on why endogenous formative constructs need to have relationships modeled on the first order level, see Lee and Cadogan (2013).

While relationships for dependent formative constructs need to be modeled on the first order level, this same requirement is not necessary when the formative construct is a predictor or independent variable. When a formative construct is treated as an independent variable, the relationship can be modeled from the higher or second order level. A higher order formative construct is an index of the first order influences and the overall effect needs to be used as the predictor. Thus, relationships can be modeled from the higher order level when the formative construct is a predictor of another construct.

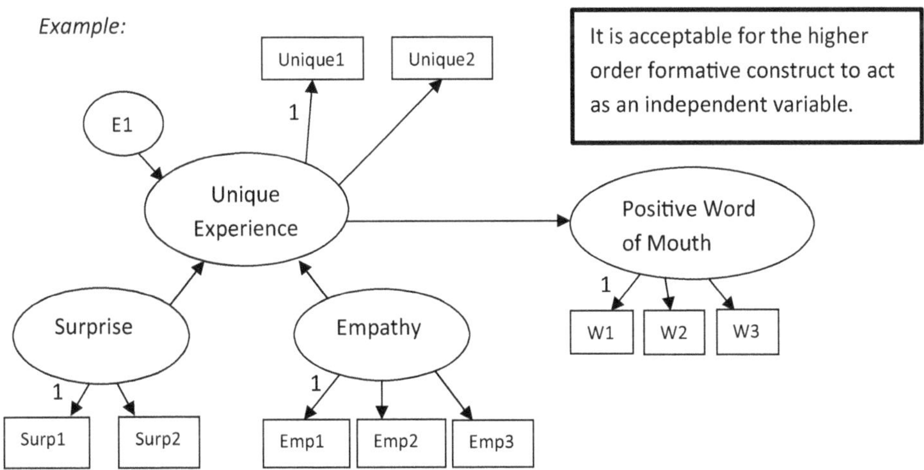

Figure 4.45a Second Order Constructs as Independent and Dependent Variables

Example:

It is unacceptable to have a direct relationship to the higher order construct when it is formative. The influence of an independent variable should be on the first order level.

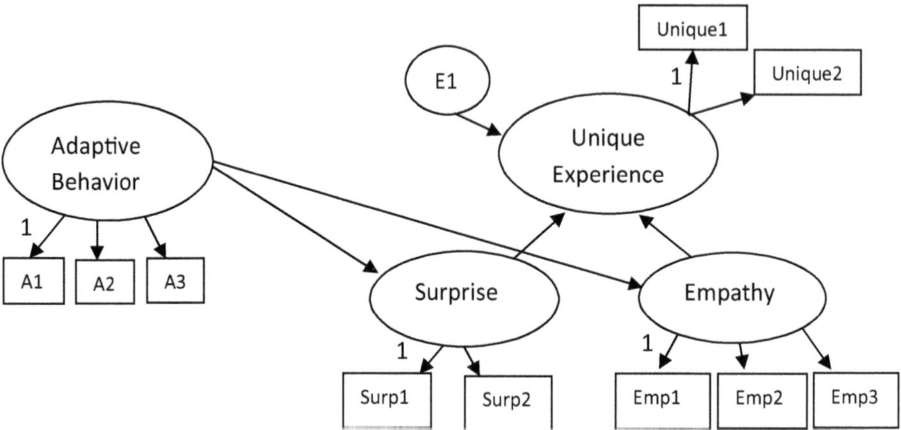

Figure 4.45b Second Order Constructs as Independent and Dependent Variables

Higher Order Formative Construct Example

Let's look at an example of a higher order (second order) construct that has formative indicators in AMOS. Using our example from earlier in the chapter, the higher order construct of Unique Experience is formed by two first order constructs of Surprise and Empathy. We have also included two reflective indicators off the higher order construct for identification purposes called Unique1 and Unique2. The higher order construct is proposed to have a positive relationship to Positive Word of Mouth by customers. Before examining the relationships of the first order to second order constructs, we need to address some validity issues of the reflective constructs. In this model, the construct of Surprise, Empathy and Positive Word of Mouth are all measured as constructs that have reflective indicators. We would need to initially assess the convergent and discriminant validity of those constructs before moving on to the higher order conceptualization. As discussed earlier in the chapter, a researcher would need to run a CFA and assess reliability along with convergent and discriminant validity.

In running the CFA, we are not including any formative relationships; we are only assessing the constructs with reflective indicators first. See Figure 4.46.

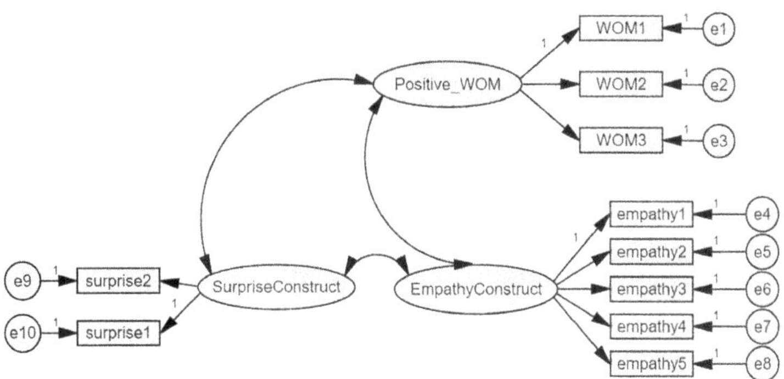

Figure 4.46 Example of CFA With First Order Constructs

The results of the CFA (Figure 4.47) show us that each construct's indicators load to a significant degree with all the factor loadings in excess of .70. Further analysis finds that all reliabilities exceed the recommended cutoff and the AVE for each construct is above .50, indicating convergent validity and no shared variance exceeds the AVE for each construct. Lastly, the model fit for the CFA is acceptable as well.

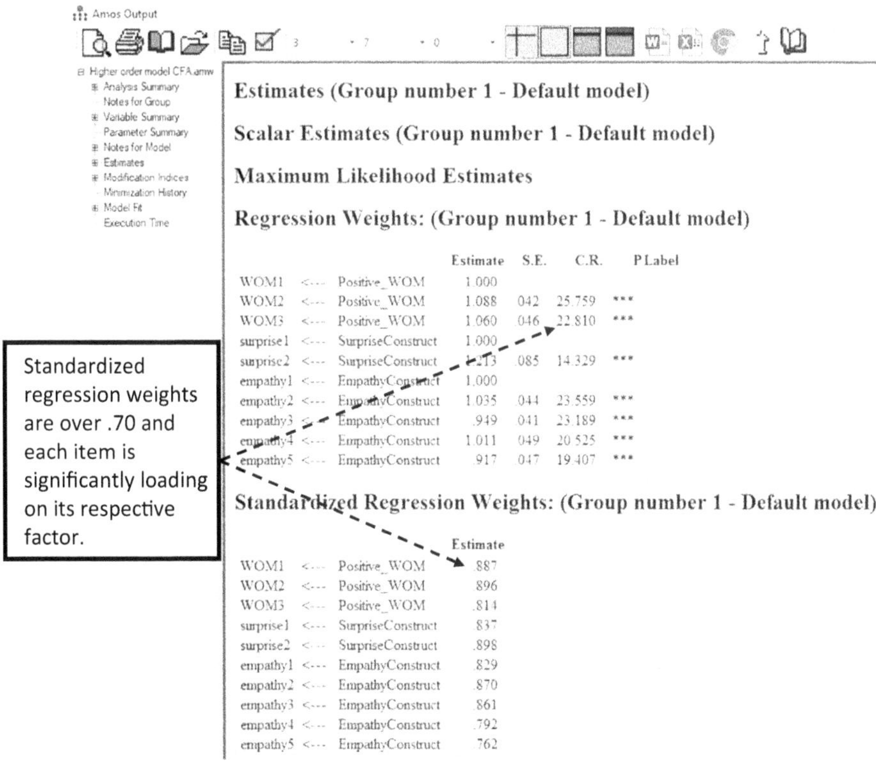

Estimates (Group number 1 - Default model)

Scalar Estimates (Group number 1 - Default model)

Maximum Likelihood Estimates

Regression Weights: (Group number 1 - Default model)

			Estimate	S.E.	C.R.	P	Label
WOM1	<---	Positive_WOM	1.000				
WOM2	<---	Positive_WOM	1.088	.042	25.759	***	
WOM3	<---	Positive_WOM	1.060	.046	22.810	***	
surprise1	<---	SurpriseConstruct	1.000				
surprise2	<---	SurpriseConstruct	1.213	.085	14.329	***	
empathy1	<---	EmpathyConstruct	1.000				
empathy2	<---	EmpathyConstruct	1.035	.044	23.559	***	
empathy3	<---	EmpathyConstruct	.949	.041	23.189	***	
empathy4	<---	EmpathyConstruct	1.011	.049	20.525	***	
empathy5	<---	EmpathyConstruct	.917	.047	19.407	***	

Standardized Regression Weights: (Group number 1 - Default model)

			Estimate
WOM1	<---	Positive_WOM	.887
WOM2	<---	Positive_WOM	.896
WOM3	<---	Positive_WOM	.814
surprise1	<---	SurpriseConstruct	.837
surprise2	<---	SurpriseConstruct	.898
empathy1	<---	EmpathyConstruct	.829
empathy2	<---	EmpathyConstruct	.870
empathy3	<---	EmpathyConstruct	.861
empathy4	<---	EmpathyConstruct	.792
empathy5	<---	EmpathyConstruct	.762

Figure 4.47 Estimates Output for CFA Model

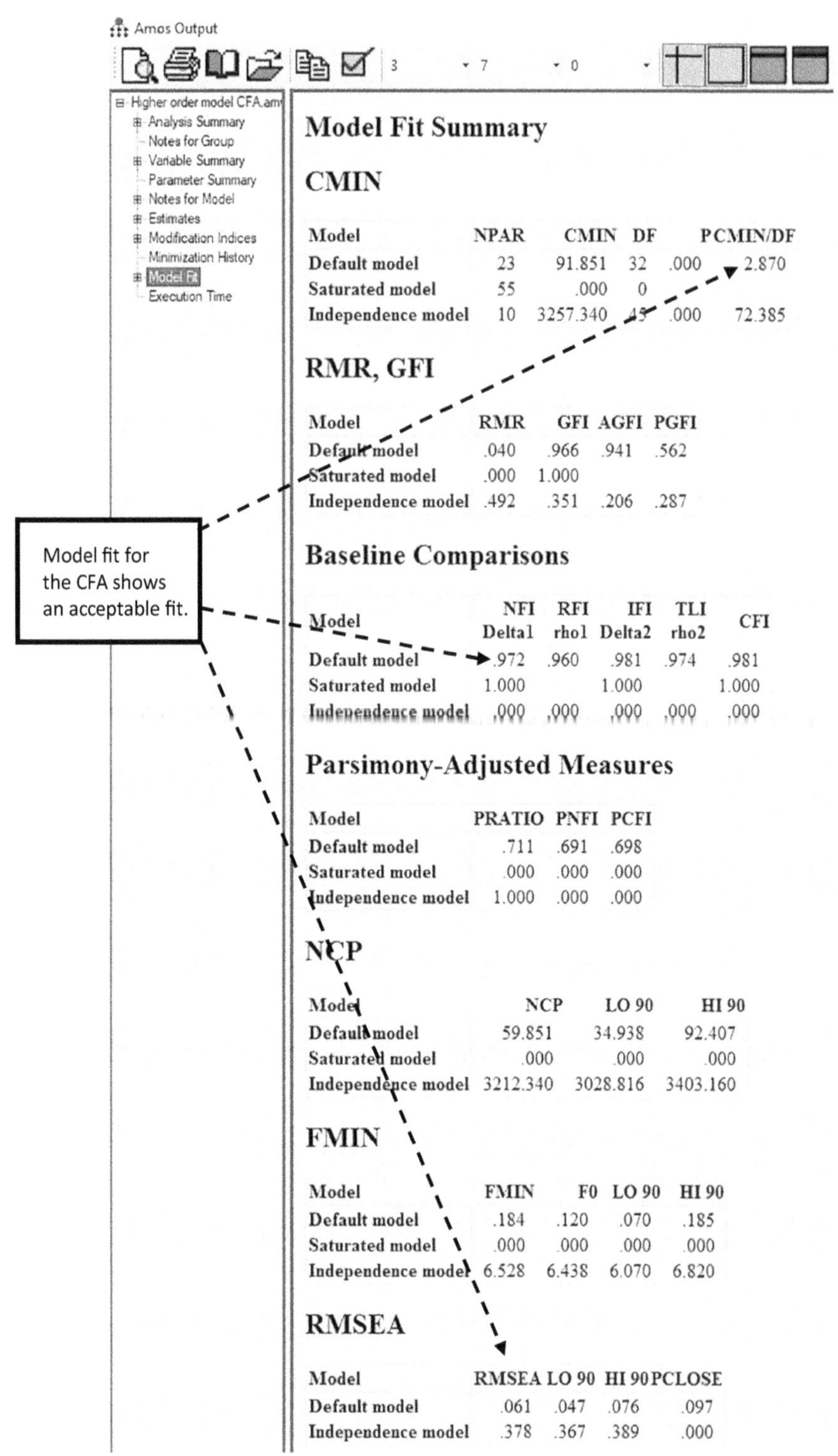

Model Fit Summary

CMIN

Model	NPAR	CMIN	DF	P	CMIN/DF
Default model	23	91.851	32	.000	2.870
Saturated model	55	.000	0		
Independence model	10	3257.340	45	.000	72.385

RMR, GFI

Model	RMR	GFI	AGFI	PGFI
Default model	.040	.966	.941	.562
Saturated model	.000	1.000		
Independence model	.492	.351	.206	.287

Baseline Comparisons

Model	NFI Delta1	RFI rho1	IFI Delta2	TLI rho2	CFI
Default model	.972	.960	.981	.974	.981
Saturated model	1.000		1.000		1.000
Independence model	.000	.000	.000	.000	.000

Parsimony-Adjusted Measures

Model	PRATIO	PNFI	PCFI
Default model	.711	.691	.698
Saturated model	.000	.000	.000
Independence model	1.000	.000	.000

NCP

Model	NCP	LO 90	HI 90
Default model	59.851	34.938	92.407
Saturated model	.000	.000	.000
Independence model	3212.340	3028.816	3403.160

FMIN

Model	FMIN	F0	LO 90	HI 90
Default model	.184	.120	.070	.185
Saturated model	.000	.000	.000	.000
Independence model	6.528	6.438	6.070	6.820

RMSEA

Model	RMSEA	LO 90	HI 90	PCLOSE
Default model	.061	.047	.076	.097
Independence model	.378	.367	.389	.000

Figure 4.48 Model Fit Statistics From CFA Analysis

After establishing the validity of the reflective constructs, we can now examine the higher order relationships along with the structural relationship to Positive Word of Mouth.

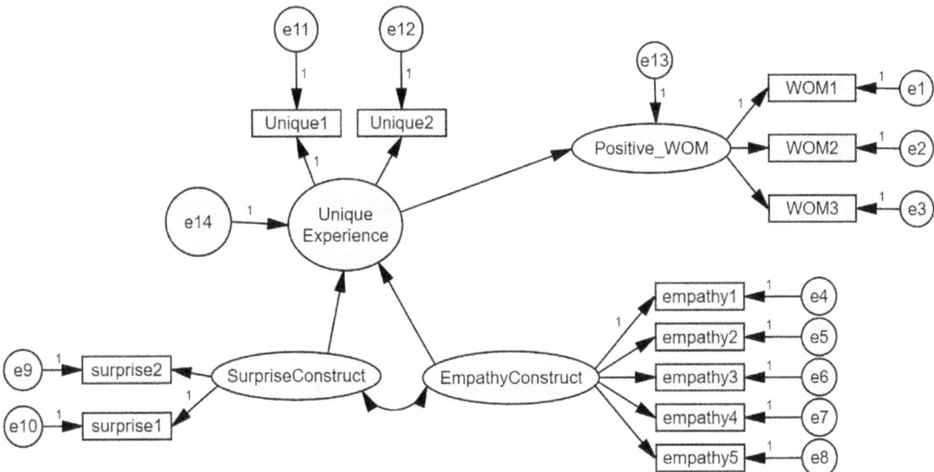

Figure 4.49 Second Order Construct Modeled in AMOS

Notice that the two first order constructs have a formative relationship to the higher order construct of Unique Experience. The higher order construct also has two reflective indicators (Unique 1 and Unique2) for identification purposes. Since the first order constructs have a direct influence to the higher order construct of Unique Experience, a dedicated error term must be included on the higher order construct. In this instance, that error term is labeled "e14". AMOS will treat the two first order constructs like independent variables, so you will need to include a covariance between the first order constructs. If there are other independent variables in the model, you will need to include a covariance from the first order constructs to those independent variables as well. One last thing to pay special attention to is setting the metric with the identification indicators. In one of the two identification indicators, you will have to constrain the relationship to "1" to set the metric. In this example, I constrained the relationship to Unique1 to a value of "1". Lastly, you will see the structural relationship included from the higher order construct of Unique Experience to the construct of Positive Word of Mouth. Let's now look at the results.

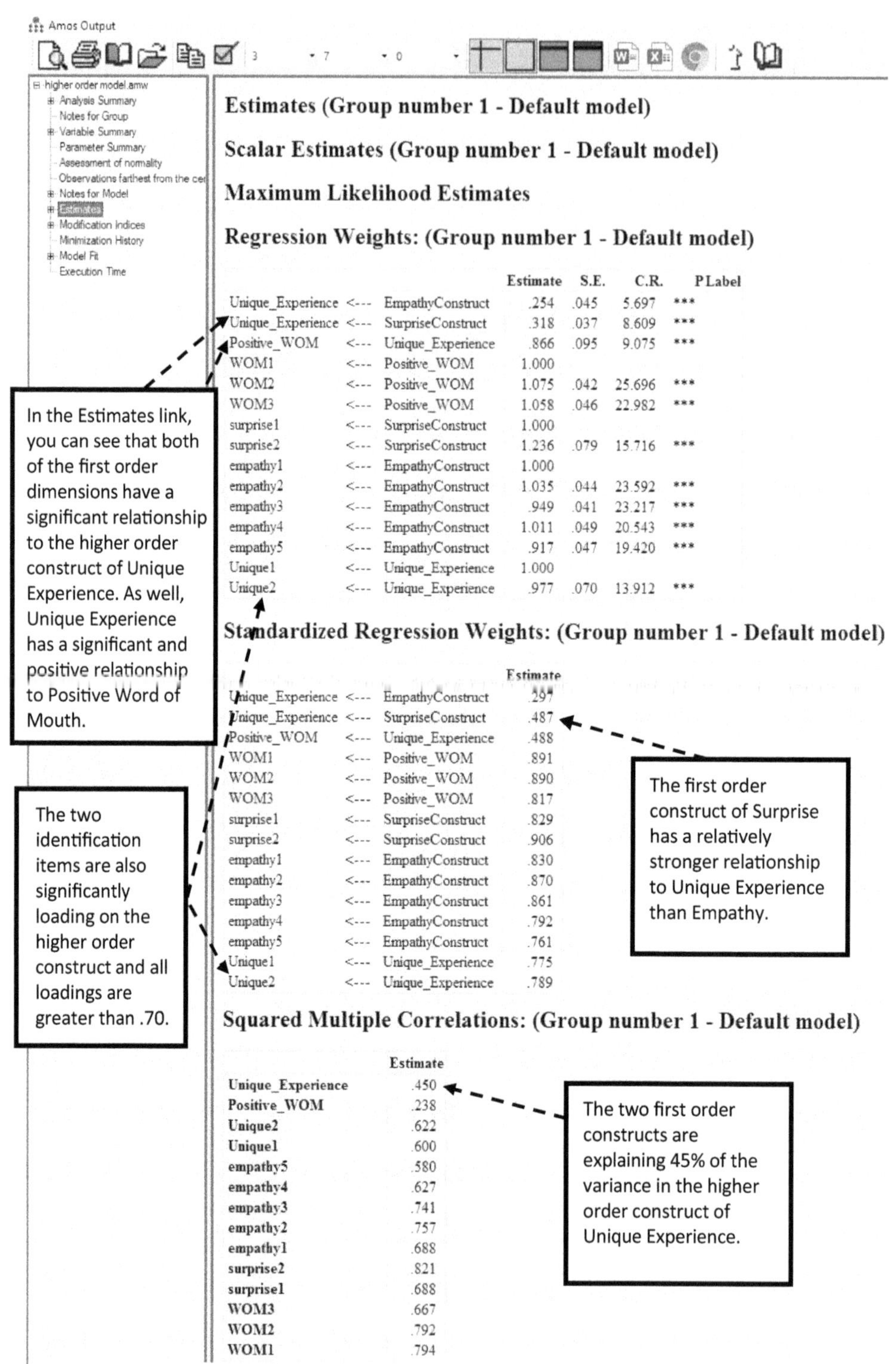

Amos Output
higher order model.amw
Analysis Summary
Notes for Group
Variable Summary
Parameter Summary
Assessment of normality
Observations farthest from the ce
Notes for Model
Estimates
Modification Indices
Minimization History
Model Fit
Execution Time
Estimates (Group number 1 - Default model)
Scalar Estimates (Group number 1 - Default model)
Maximum Likelihood Estimates
Regression Weights: (Group number 1 - Default model)
Estimate S.E. C.R. P Label
Unique_Experience <--- EmpathyConstruct .254 .045 5.697 ***
Unique_Experience <--- SurpriseConstruct .318 .037 8.609 ***
Positive_WOM <--- Unique_Experience .866 .095 9.075 ***
WOM1 <--- Positive_WOM 1.000
WOM2 <--- Positive_WOM 1.075 .042 25.696 ***
WOM3 <--- Positive_WOM 1.058 .046 22.982 ***
surprise1 <--- SurpriseConstruct 1.000
surprise2 <--- SurpriseConstruct 1.236 .079 15.716 ***
empathy1 <--- EmpathyConstruct 1.000
empathy2 <--- EmpathyConstruct 1.035 .044 23.592 ***
empathy3 <--- EmpathyConstruct .949 .041 23.217 ***
empathy4 <--- EmpathyConstruct 1.011 .049 20.543 ***
empathy5 <--- EmpathyConstruct .917 .047 19.420 ***
Unique1 <--- Unique_Experience 1.000
Unique2 <--- Unique_Experience .977 .070 13.912 ***
Standardized Regression Weights: (Group number 1 - Default model)
Estimate
Unique_Experience <--- EmpathyConstruct .297
Unique_Experience <--- SurpriseConstruct .487
Positive_WOM <--- Unique_Experience .488
WOM1 <--- Positive_WOM .891
WOM2 <--- Positive_WOM .890
WOM3 <--- Positive_WOM .817
surprise1 <--- SurpriseConstruct .829
surprise2 <--- SurpriseConstruct .906
empathy1 <--- EmpathyConstruct .830
empathy2 <--- EmpathyConstruct .870
empathy3 <--- EmpathyConstruct .861
empathy4 <--- EmpathyConstruct .792
empathy5 <--- EmpathyConstruct .761
Unique1 <--- Unique_Experience .775
Unique2 <--- Unique_Experience .789
Squared Multiple Correlations: (Group number 1 - Default model)
Estimate
Unique_Experience .450
Positive_WOM .238
Unique2 .622
Unique1 .600
empathy5 .580
empathy4 .627
empathy3 .741
empathy2 .757
empathy1 .688
surprise2 .821
surprise1 .688
WOM3 .667
WOM2 .792
WOM1 .794
In the Estimates link, you can see that both of the first order dimensions have a significant relationship to the higher order construct of Unique Experience. As well, Unique Experience has a significant and positive relationship to Positive Word of Mouth.
The two identification items are also significantly loading on the higher order construct and all loadings are greater than .70.
The first order construct of Surprise has a relatively stronger relationship to Unique Experience than Empathy.
The two first order constructs are explaining 45% of the variance in the higher order construct of Unique Experience.

Figure 4.50 Estimates Output of Second Order Model

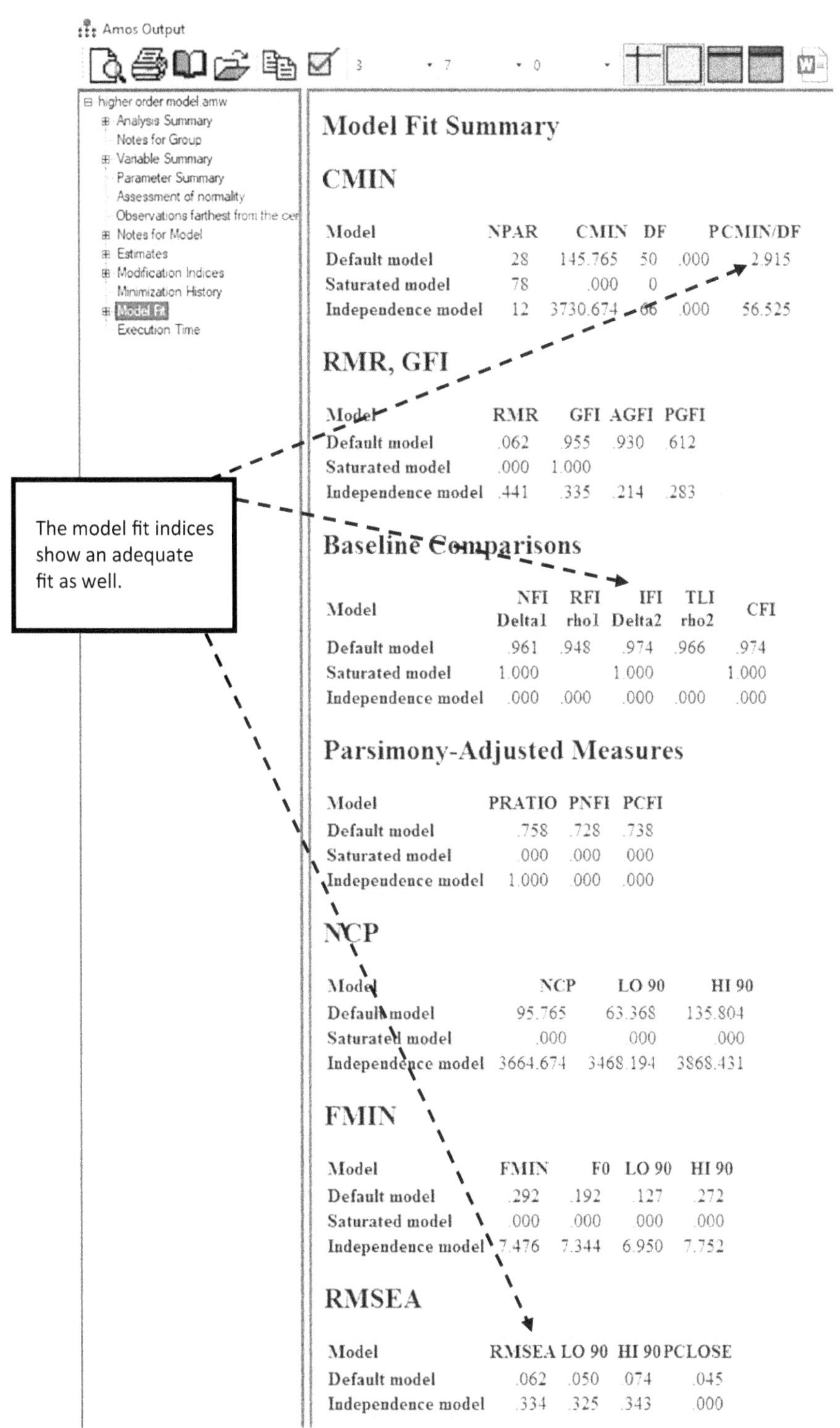

Model Fit Summary

CMIN

Model	NPAR	CMIN	DF	P	CMIN/DF
Default model	28	145.765	50	.000	2.915
Saturated model	78	.000	0		
Independence model	12	3730.674	66	.000	56.525

RMR, GFI

Model	RMR	GFI	AGFI	PGFI
Default model	.062	.955	.930	.612
Saturated model	.000	1.000		
Independence model	.441	.335	.214	.283

Baseline Comparisons

Model	NFI Delta1	RFI rho1	IFI Delta2	TLI rho2	CFI
Default model	.961	.948	.974	.966	.974
Saturated model	1.000		1.000		1.000
Independence model	.000	.000	.000	.000	.000

Parsimony-Adjusted Measures

Model	PRATIO	PNFI	PCFI
Default model	.758	.728	.738
Saturated model	.000	.000	.000
Independence model	1.000	.000	.000

NCP

Model	NCP	LO 90	HI 90
Default model	95.765	63.368	135.804
Saturated model	.000	.000	.000
Independence model	3664.674	3468.194	3868.431

FMIN

Model	FMIN	F0	LO 90	HI 90
Default model	.292	.192	.127	.272
Saturated model	.000	.000	.000	.000
Independence model	7.476	7.344	6.950	7.752

RMSEA

Model	RMSEA	LO 90	HI 90	PCLOSE
Default model	.062	.050	.074	.045
Independence model	.334	.325	.343	.000

Figure 4.51 Model Fit Statistics of Second Order Model

How Do I Present the Result of My Higher Order Formative Model?

The results of the CFA for the first order dimensions should be presented in a dedicated CFA table. For the first order constructs' relationship to the higher order construct, I prefer to put this information in a structural relationship table. I also like to include the actual wording of the identification items to give the reader more information. See the following example.

Example 4.3:

	Standardized Estimates	*t-values*
Relationship to Higher Order Construct of Unique Experience		
Surprise → Unique Experience	.49	8.60
Empathy → Unique Experience	.30	5.69
Structural Relationships		
Unique Experience → Positive Word of Mouth	.49	9.07

Model fit: χ^2 = 145.76, df = 50, p < .001, CFI = .97, IFI = .97, RMSEA = .06

Note: Two identification items were included on the higher order construct of Unique Experience. Both items significantly loaded on the higher order construct with factor loadings greater than .70. The wording for those items were:

—If I had to sum up my experience, I felt my experience was distinctive (Unique1)

—If I had to sum up my experience, I felt my experience was special (Unique2)

Error Messages in AMOS

If you encounter an error message in AMOS while testing your measurement model, here are some of the most common causes I have found along with potential remedies.

1. The model is unidentified—after running the analysis, this error message will appear in the "Notes for Model" link of the output.

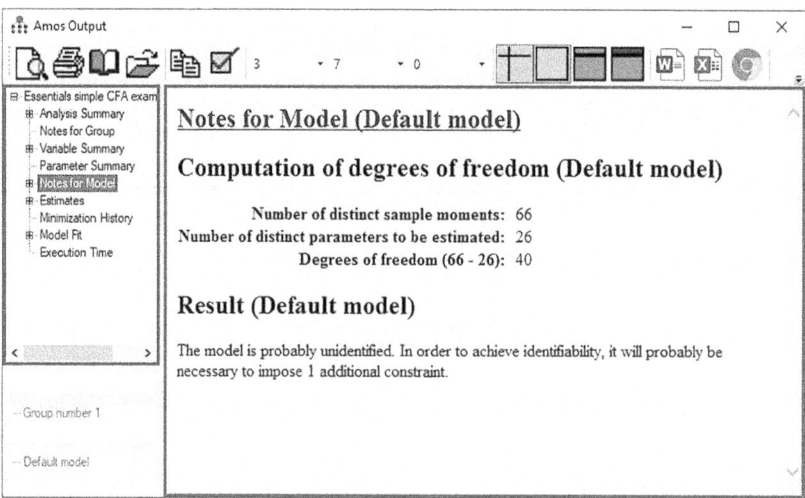

Figure 4.52 Error Message for Unidentified Model

This unidentified model means you are trying to estimate more parameters than observations. This can often be caused by including too many relationships or covariances in your model. Among the more likely reasons for this message is that you failed to set the metric with one of your items in a construct, or you have deleted an item from a construct and that specific item was set to "1" to set the metric for the construct. Once you have deleted the item and not set another indicator to 1, AMOS will give you an unidentified model error message. Another reason for an unidentified model error could be that you deleted an indicator but failed to delete the corresponding error term. The error term is essentially a stand-alone construct still in the model. This will also prompt an unidentified model error message.

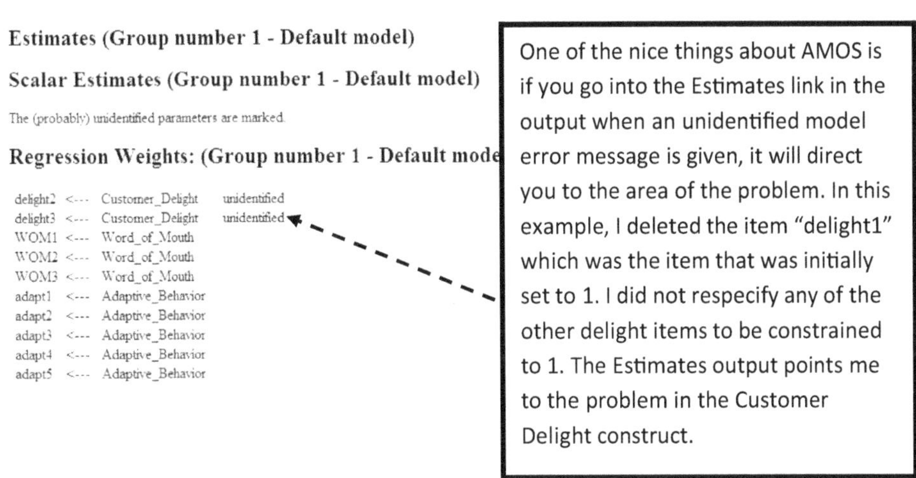

Figure 4.53 Estimates Output Showing Unidentified Indicators

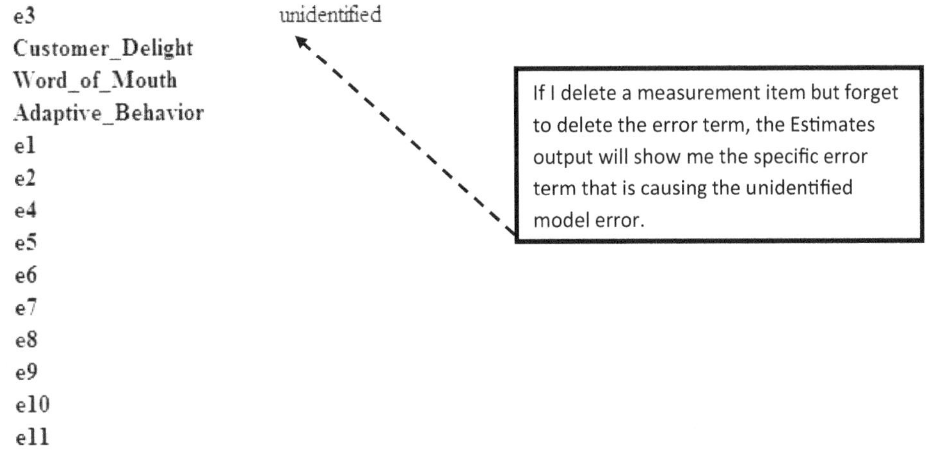

Figure 4.54 Unidentified Message in Error Terms

2. Not an observed variable message—one of the messages you might receive from AMOS is that your observed variable cannot be found in the data. In our CFA example, we had a measurement indicator that was named "delight2". If I misspelled this name during the input to "delightt2", there is no data that matches that exact name. Hence, AMOS will give you an error message that you have a variable in a square/rectangle and it has no data associated with that variable name. You can also get the "not an observable variable" message if the variable name is correct, but there is no data under that name in the data file. If the column under that name is blank, you will get this message.

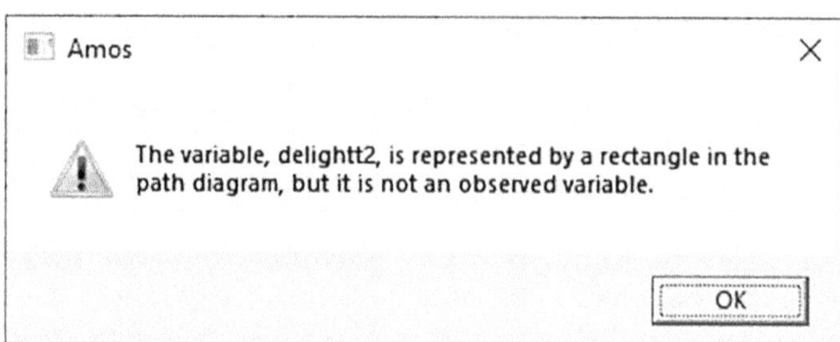

Figure 4.55 Not an Observed Variable Error Message

3. Missing covariance message—all independent variables need to have a covariance added. If you forget to add the covariance between constructs, AMOS will give you a warning message that two independent constructs are not correlated. AMOS will let you proceed with the analysis without adding a covariance between the constructs, but the majority of the time you will need to include the missing covariance.

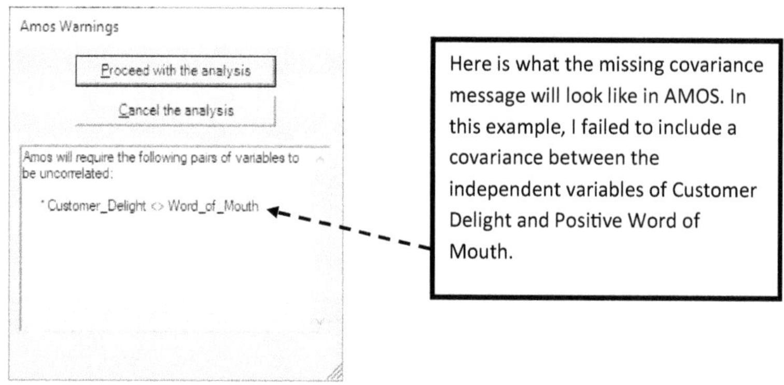

Figure 4.56 Missing Covariance Message in AMOS

Definitions of Constructs Used in Examples for This Chapter:

Adaptive Behavior: customer's perception that an employee adapted/modified their normal job performance to meet their needs. This adaptation can be through verbal interaction, service performance, or meeting special requests. Construct was measured with a 7-point Likert scale of Strongly Disagree to Strongly Agree.

Customer Delight: customer's profoundly positive emotional state resulting from expectations being exceeded to a surprising degree. Construct was measured with a 7-point Likert scale of Strongly Disagree to Strongly Agree.

Positive Word of Mouth: customer's intention to spread positive information to others about a previous experience. Construct was measured with a 7-point Likert scale of Strongly Disagree to Strongly Agree.

Unique Experience: customer's perception that an experience was distinctive or different compared to a normal experience with the retailer. Construct is a higher order construct that is measured by the first order dimensions of surprise and empathy.

Surprise: the degree that a customer is astonished by the experience delivered in the service/retail setting. Construct was measured with a 7-point Likert scale of Strongly Disagree to Strongly Agree.

Empathy: The level of compassion directed at the customer from the employee in meeting the needs of the customer. Construct was measured with a 7-point Likert scale of Strongly Disagree to Strongly Agree.

Highlights of the Chapter:

1. Confirmatory factor analysis (CFA) is a statistical technique that analyzes how well your indicators measure your unobserved constructs.
2. Exploratory factor analysis (EFA) differs from CFA in that all indicators across all constructs are allowed to freely load together. A CFA specifically denotes the relationships from indicator to construct.
3. Factor loadings, similar to regression weights, estimate the direct effects of unobservable constructs on their indicators. Factor loadings are presented in unstandardized or standardized formats. The standardized format is on a 0-to-1 scale.
4. An acceptable standardized factor loading for an indicator is greater than .70. The explained variance of an indicator is calculated by taking the square of the standardized factor loading. If the standardized factor loading is .70, then the explained variance in that indicator (R^2) is $.70^2 = .50$, or 50% of the variance.
5. Each unobserved construct must "set the metric" with one of its indicators. This is done by constraining one of the indicators to 1.0. The indicator that is set to one is also known as the reference item and is setting the measurement range for the other indicators.
6. Model fit statistics will determine if the estimated covariance matrix is a close representation of the observed covariance matrix. Prominent model fits statistics are:

   a. Chi-square test—you want a non-significance test result. A significant test result means the observed and estimated covariance matrix are significantly different.
   b. CFI, IFI, NFI, RFI, and TLI—these are all comparative statistics. Values over .90 mean you have an acceptable model fit.
   c. RMSEA—this a badness of fit measure. Values less than .08 are acceptable, but a preferred result is less than .05.

7. Modification indices are suggestions to alter a model to increase the fit of the model to the data. Modification indices will not be produced if there is missing data.

8. In a CFA, the only modification indices that are a concern are the potential error covariances that can be added within a construct. Error terms should not be covaried across constructs.
9. In the AMOS output, factor loadings and squared multiple correlations (R^2) are located under the "Estimates" link in the output. Model fit statistics have a link simply titled "Model Fit".
10. Standardized residuals is another analysis that will indicate model misspecification along with potential error covariances to improve fit.
11. To assess convergent and discriminant validity, the Fornell and Larcker (1981) method is a good template. Convergent validity is determined by calculating the average variance extracted for each construct. The average variance extracted should exceed .50 to support convergent validity claims. Discriminant validity is assessed by determining the shared variance between constructs. The shared variance between constructs should not exceed the average variance extracted determined for each construct.
12. The heterotrait-monotrait ratio of correlations (HTMT) is another method to determine discriminant validity. This method examines the correlations within construct indicators as well as the correlations of indicators across constructs.
13. Composite reliability is an assessment of internal consistency that is based on the standardized factor loadings of the CFA. This reliability test does have advantages over other reliability tests such as Cronbach's alpha.
14. Standardized factor loadings greater than 1 or error terms that are negative (also known as a Heywood case) are impermissible solutions.
15. Measurement invariance is often done to assess if differences in the measurement of a construct appear across two different groups. Often, your goal is to show that the measurement of your constructs is valid across two different groups. Invariance testing frequently takes place through configural invariance testing, metric invariance testing, and scalar invariance testing.
16. Partial metric invariance is where invariance across the groups is established but not all indicators are constrained within a construct.
17. Common method bias is where an inflation of estimates takes place because the independent variables and dependent variables were measured at the same time.
18. Common method bias can be addressed through Harman's single factor test, the marker variable technique, and including a latent unmeasured common method factor.
19. A second order or higher order construct is where multiple constructs form the higher order concept. Formative indicators are required for a higher order construct.
20. Formative constructs often have identification issues that require additional identification indicators to be included that represent the overall concept of the formative construct. A MIMIC model approach is most often used to address the identification issues with formative models.

References

Bagozzi, Richard P. (1994), *Structural Equation Models in Marketing Research: Basic Principles*. Cambridge, MA: Blackwell.

Bentler, P.M. and D.G. Bonett. (1980), "Significance Tests and Goodness of Fit in the Analysis of Covariance Structures", *Psychological Bulletin*, 88 (3), 588–606.

Bollen, Kenneth and Richard Lennox. (1991), "Conventional Wisdom on Measurement: A Structural Equation Perspective", *Psychological Bulletin*, 110 (2), 305–314.

Byrne, Barbara M. (1989), *A Primer of LISREL: Basic Applications and Programming for Confirmatory Factor Analytic Models*. New York, NY: Springer-Verlag.

Chang, Sea-Jin, Arjen van Witteloostuijn, and Lourraine Eden. (2010), "From the Editors: Common Method Variance in International Business Research", *Journal of International Business Studies*, 41 (2), 178–184.

Diamantopoulos, Adamantios. (2006), "The Error Term in Formative Measurement Models: Interpretation and Modeling Implications", *Journal of Modeling in Management*, 1 (1), 7–17.

Diamantopoulos, Adamantios and Heidi M. Winklhofer. (2001), "Index Construction With Formative Indicators: An Alternative to Scale Development", *Journal of Marketing Research*, 38 (May), 269–277.

Fornell, Claes and Fred L. Bookstein. (1982), "Two Structural Equation Models: LISREL and PLS Applied to Consumer Exit-Voice Theory", *Journal of Marketing Research*, 19 (November), 440–452.

Fornell, Claes and David F. Larcker. (1981), "Evaluating Structural Equation Models and Unobservable Variables and Measurement Error", *Journal of Marketing Research*, 18 (February), 39–50.

Fuller, Christie M., Marcia J. Simmering, Guclu Atinc, Yasemin Atinc, and Barry J. Babin. (2016), "Common Methods Variance Detection in Business Research", *Journal of Business Research*, 69 (8), 3192–3198.

Gerbing, David W. and James C. Anderson. (1984), "On the Meaning of Within-Factor Correlated Measurement Errors", *Journal of Consumer Research*, 11 (1), 572–580.

Hair, Joseph F., William C. Black, Barry J. Babin, and Rolph E. Anderson. (2009), *Multivariate Data Analysis* (7th ed.). Upper Saddle River, NJ: Prentice Hall.

Henseler, Jorg, Christian M. Ringle, and Mario Sarstedt. (2015), "A New Criterion for Assessing Discriminant Validity in Variance-Based Structural Equation Modeling", *Journal of the Academy of Marketing Science*, 43 (1), 115–135.

Hu, L. and P.M. Bentler. (1999), "Cutoff Criteria for Fit Indexes in Covariance Structure Analysis: Conventional Criteria Versus New Alternatives", *Structural Equation Modeling*, 6 (1), 1–55.

Jarvis, Cheryl Burke, Scott B. MacKenzie, and Philip M. Podsakoff. (2003), "A Critical Review of Construct Indicators and Measurement Model Misspecification in Marketing and Consumer Research", *Journal of Consumer Research*, 30 (2), 199–218.

Joreskog, Karl G. (1999), "How Large Can a Standardized Coefficient Be?" Retrieved October 2018 from: www.ssicentral.com/lisrel/techdocs/HowLargeCanaStandardizedCoefficientbe.pdf.

Joreskog, Karl G. and Dag Sorbom. (1988), *LISREAL 7: A Guide to the Program and Applications*. Chicago, IL: SPSS, Inc.

Kline, Rex B. (2011), *Principles and Practice of Structural Equation Modeling* (3rd ed.). New York, NY: Guilford Press.

Lee, Nick and John W. Cadogan. (2013), "Problems With Formative and Higher Order Reflective Variables", *Journal of Business Research*, 66 (2), 242–247.

Lindell, Michael K. and David J. Whitney. (2001), "Accounting for Common Method Variance in Cross-Sectional Research Designs", *Journal of Applied Psychology*, 86 (1), 114–121.

Lord, Frederic M. and Melvin R. Novick. (1968), *Statistical Theories of Mental Test Scores*. Reading, MA: Addison-Wesley.

MacCallum, Robert C., M.W. Browne, and H.M. Sugawara. (1996), "Power Analysis and Determination of Sample Size for Covariance Structure Modeling", *Psychological Methods*, 1 (2), 130–149.

MacKenzie, Scott B., Philip M. Podsakoff, and Cheryl Burke Jarvis. (2005), "The Problem of Measurement Model Misspecification in Behavioral and Organizational Research and Some Recommended Solutions", *Journal of Applied Psychology*, 90 (4), 710–730.

Malhotra, Naresh K., Ashutosh Patil, and Sung S. Kim. (2007), "Bias Breakdown", *Marketing Research*, 19 (1), 24–29.

Marsh, Herbert W., Kit-Tai Hau, and Zhonglin Wen. (2004), "In Search of Golden Rules: Comment on Hypothesis-Testing Approaches to Setting Cutoff Values for Fit Indexes and Dangers in Overgeneralizing Hu and Bentler's (1999) Findings", *Structural Equation Modeling*, 11 (3), 320–341.

Nunnally, Jum C. and Ira H. Bernstein. (1994), *Psychometric Theory* (3rd ed.). New York, NY: McGraw-Hill.

Schumacker, Randall E. and Richard G. Lomax. (2004), *A Beginner's Guide to Structural Equation Modeling* (2nd ed.). Mahwah, NJ: Erlbaum.

Sharma, Subhash, Soumen Mukherjee, Ajith Kumar, and William R. Dillon. (2005), "A Simulation Study to Investigate the Use of Cutoff Values for Assessing Model Fit in Covariance Structure Models", *Journal of Business Research*, 58 (7), 935–943.

Voorhees, Clay, Michael K. Brady, Roger Calantone, and Edward Ramirez. (2016), "Discriminant Validity Testing in Marketing: An Analysis, Causes for Concern, and Proposed Remedies", *Journal of the Academy of Marketing Science*, 44 (1), 119–134.

Yang, Yanyun and Samuel B. Green. (2011), "Coefficient Alpha: A Reliability Coefficient for the 21st Century", *Journal of Psychoeducational Assessment*, 29 (4), 377–392.

Chapter 5

Path and Full Structural Models

Path Analysis

So far, we have talked only about the measurement model; now let's talk about the structural model. The structural model's focus is on examining the relationships *between* constructs. Hence, we will look at how independent constructs influence dependent constructs or, in more complex models, how dependent variables influence other dependent variables. The first type of structural model we will examine is called a path analysis. In a path analysis, you are assessing only relationships between constructs (no measurement model items included). It is inappropriate to examine a path analysis until you have performed a measurement model analysis to determine if your measures are valid. Once the measurement model has been established, you can form composite variables for each construct. A path analysis examines the structural relationships between composite variables. Refer to Chapter 4 on how to form composite variables in SPSS.

Adding to our existing example, let's say we have a simple model where we want to test if "Adaptive Behavior" and another construct called "Servicescape" directly influence perceptions of Customer Delight. Just to clarify, Servicescape refers to customers' perceptions about the built environment in which the service takes place, which could include atmosphere, furniture, and other things related to the environment such as displays, colors, etc. From the Customer Delight construct, let's explore if it has a relationship to Positive Word of Mouth (WOM) and another construct called "Tolerance to Future Failures". The Tolerance to Future Failures construct is how likely a customer is to be tolerant to a service failure in the future.

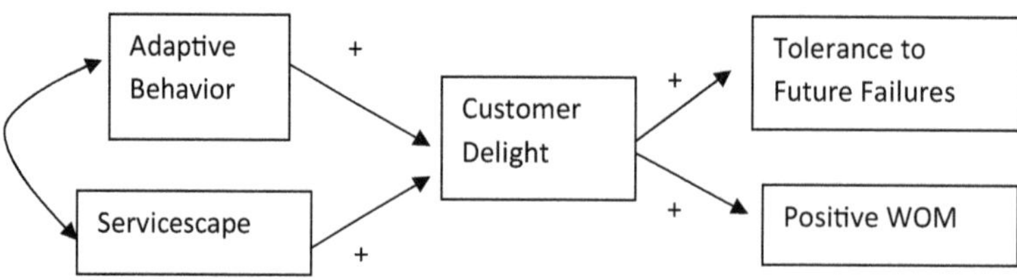

Figure 5.1 Structural Model With Composite Variables

After forming composite variables of each construct and saving the file in SPSS, you will need to read in the revised data file to AMOS. By forming a composite of a construct's multiple indicators, you have now graphically changed the construct from being a "circle" to a "square". In essence, you have made the construct an observable. So in a path model, we will be using only squares to graphically represent the constructs. The next thing you need to do is drag in the composite constructs from the variable view to the work area.

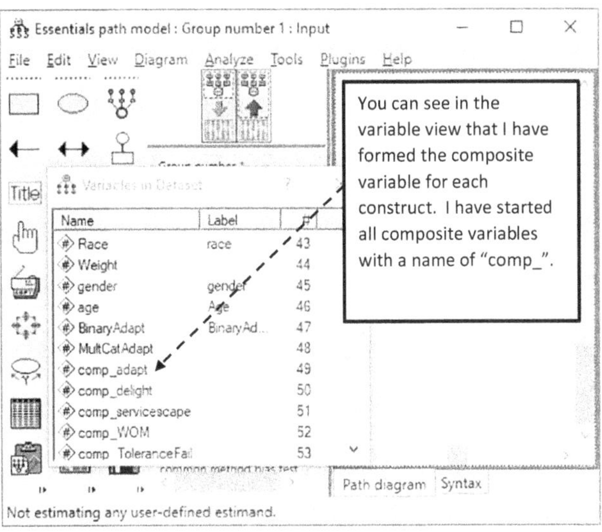

Figure 5.2 Composite Variables Used in Path Analysis

Next, you will have to add directional arrows to denote a relationship. You also need to let all the independent variables covary. In this model, comp_adapt and comp_servicescape are allowed to covary. Lastly, you need to add an error term to all dependent variables. Make sure to label each error term as well. See Figure 5.3 of a path model in graphical form in AMOS.

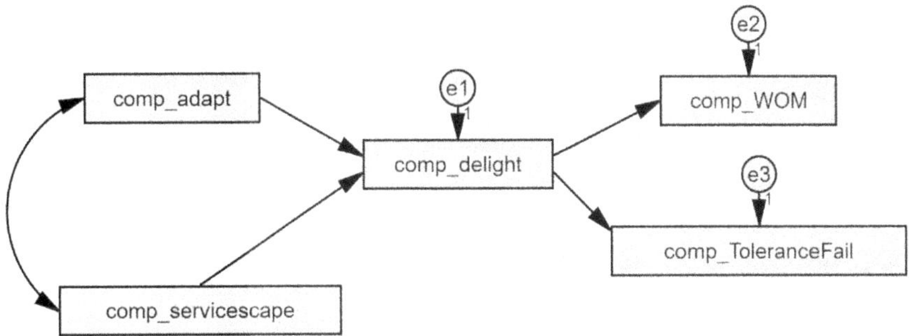

Figure 5.3 Path Model Drawn in AMOS

After forming the model, you will need to run the analysis [run icon]. Make sure the "Models" window says "OK" and the computational summary window lists the chi-square value and degrees of freedom. If this is present, then you can go to the output and see your results.

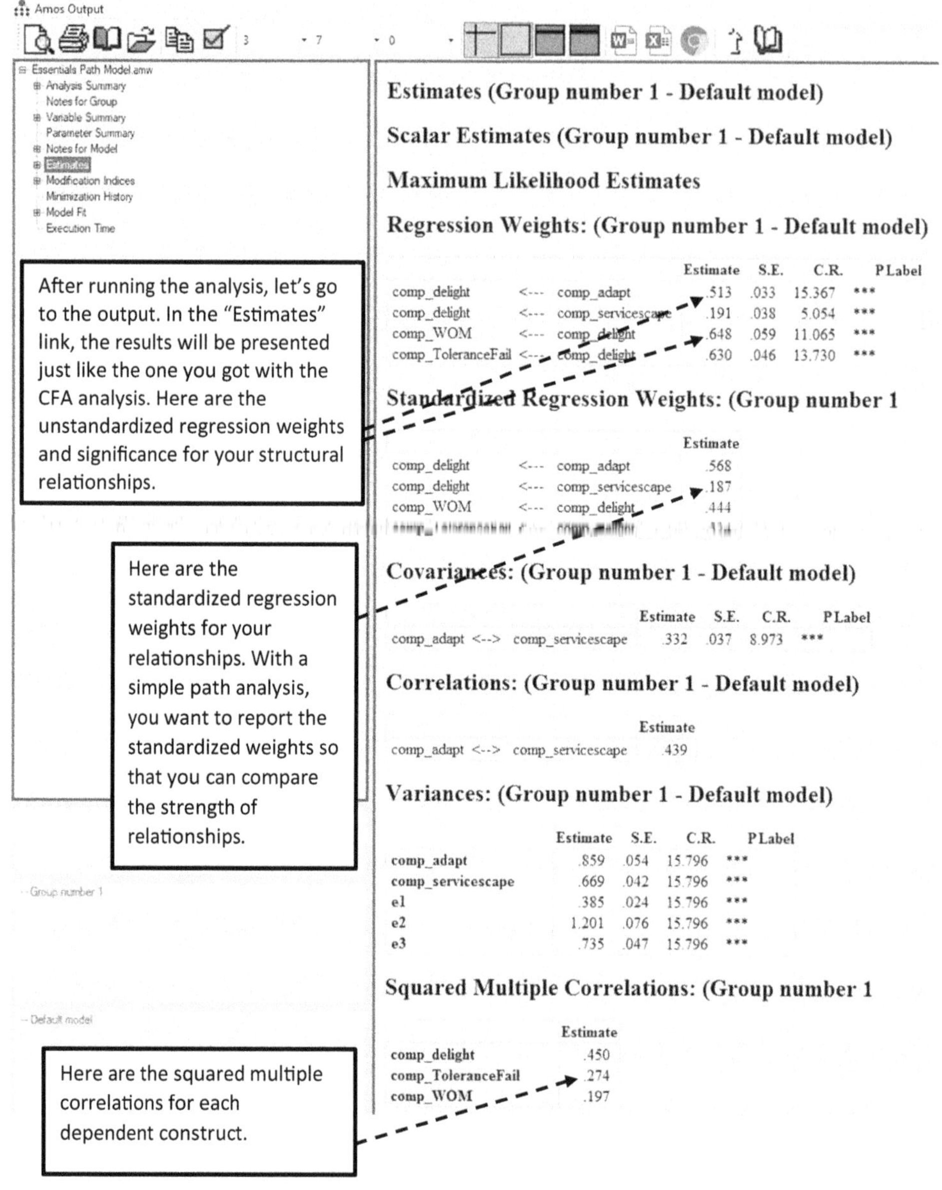

Figure 5.4 Estimates Output for Path Model

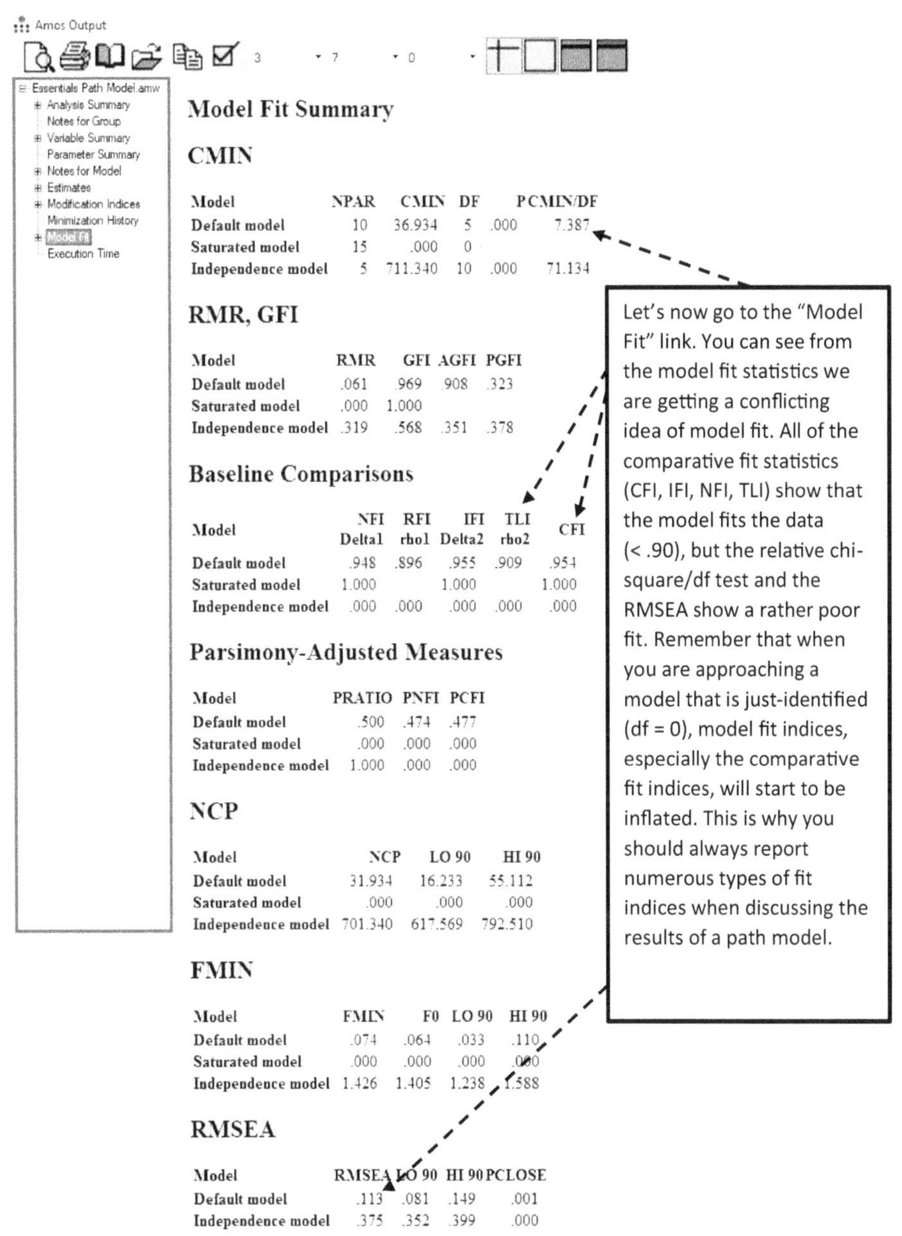

Model Fit Summary

CMIN

Model	NPAR	CMIN	DF	P	CMIN/DF
Default model	10	36.934	5	.000	7.387
Saturated model	15	.000	0		
Independence model	5	711.340	10	.000	71.134

RMR, GFI

Model	RMR	GFI	AGFI	PGFI
Default model	.061	.969	.908	.323
Saturated model	.000	1.000		
Independence model	.319	.568	.351	.378

Baseline Comparisons

Model	NFI Delta1	RFI rho1	IFI Delta2	TLI rho2	CFI
Default model	.948	.896	.955	.909	.954
Saturated model	1.000		1.000		1.000
Independence model	.000	.000	.000	.000	.000

Parsimony-Adjusted Measures

Model	PRATIO	PNFI	PCFI
Default model	.500	.474	.477
Saturated model	.000	.000	.000
Independence model	1.000	.000	.000

NCP

Model	NCP	LO 90	HI 90
Default model	31.934	16.233	55.112
Saturated model	.000	.000	.000
Independence model	701.340	617.569	792.510

FMIN

Model	FMIN	F0	LO 90	HI 90
Default model	.074	.064	.033	.110
Saturated model	.000	.000	.000	.000
Independence model	1.426	1.405	1.238	1.588

RMSEA

Model	RMSEA	LO 90	HI 90	PCLOSE
Default model	.113	.081	.149	.001
Independence model	.375	.352	.399	.000

Amos Output
Essentials Path Model.amw
Analysis Summary
Notes for Group
Variable Summary
Parameter Summary
Notes for Model
Estimates
Modification Indices
Minimization History
Model Fit
Execution Time
Let's now go to the "Model Fit" link. You can see from the model fit statistics we are getting a conflicting idea of model fit. All of the comparative fit statistics (CFI, IFI, NFI, TLI) show that the model fits the data (< .90), but the relative chi-square/df test and the RMSEA show a rather poor fit. Remember that when you are approaching a model that is just-identified (df = 0), model fit indices, especially the comparative fit indices, will start to be inflated. This is why you should always report numerous types of fit indices when discussing the results of a path model.

Figure 5.5 Model Fit Indices for Path Model

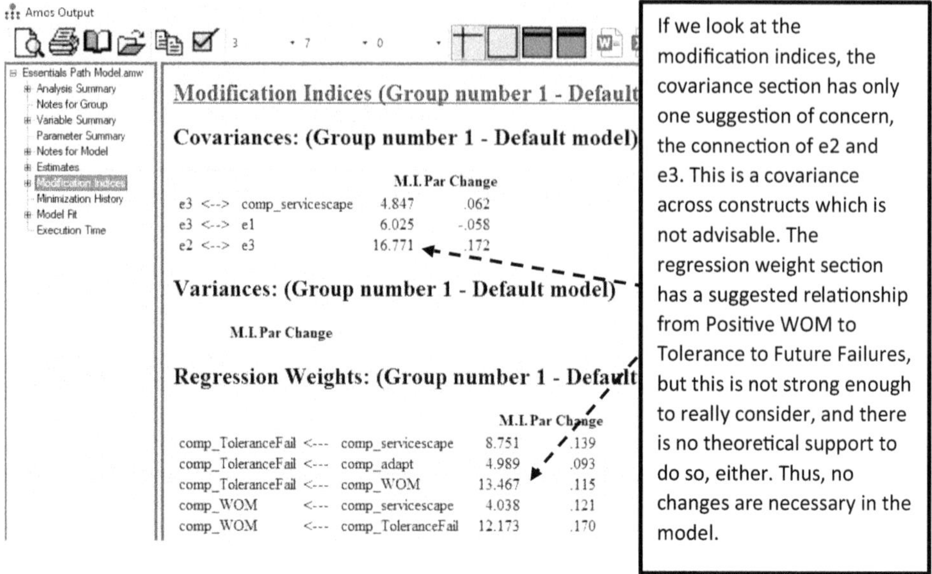

Figure 5.6 Modification Indices for Path Model

Looking at the overall results of our path model test, it appears that both constructs of Adaptive Behavior and Servicescape have a relationship to Customer Delight. The standardized regression weights tell us that Adaptive Behavior had a relatively stronger influence on Customer Delight (.568) compared to Servicescape (.187). The influence of Customer Delight on Positive Word of Mouth and Tolerance to Future Failures was also significant. Again, examining the standardized regression weights lets us see that Customer Delight had a stronger relative influence on Tolerance to Future Failures (.524) than on Positive WOM (.444), though both were significant.

One thing to take notice in a SEM model is whether the regression weights are positive or negative. In our example, all of the relationships are positive, which means the dependent construct is being positively influenced. Based on our results when Customer Delight increases, you will also see increases in an evaluation of Positive WOM and Tolerance to Future Failures. If the regression weights were negative, that means the dependent variable is being weakened. So, if the relationship from Customer Delight to Positive WOM was negative, this would indicate that when Customer Delight evaluations increase, Positive WOM evaluations would decrease. In essence, a positive influence means that both your constructs in the relationship are moving/changing in the same direction, whereas a negative influence means your constructs in the relationship are moving in opposite directions.

The squared multiple correlation (R^2) for Customer Delight was .450, with the other dependent variables of Tolerance to Failure (.274) and Positive Word of Mouth (.197) showing an acceptable level of variance being explained. Unlike a CFA, there is no set or suggested criteria necessary to be explained with the squared multiple correlation values of the overall construct. These R^2 values are based on the structural relationships and exhibit how much of the variance in the dependent variable is explained by the antecedent relationships of other variables. The R^2 values of a dependent variable is influenced by how many antecedent relationships are present. In our example, Positive Word of Mouth has an influence only from Customer Delight, and the R^2 value of Positive Word of Mouth is how much of the variance is being explained by Customer Delight. With new and hard-to-capture concepts, having a R^2 of 30% might be really good while having a R^2 of 30% might be quite inadequate with a well-established construct that has numerous antecedent relationships included in the model.

The overall results for our path model in regard to model fit is a little troubling. One of the biggest drawbacks to using a path model is that you are not accounting for measurement error, which could explain some of the variance in your model. When a composite variable is formed, all the unexplained error in the measurement items are lumped together, which makes it hard to explain the variance in a model (thus having a weaker model fit). With few degrees of freedom, some model fit indices will be inflated, while others such RMSEA and relative chi-square/df test are more true to assessing how the model fits the data. Though using a path model is easy and efficient, it has issues in assessing model fit. Using a path model is very similar to other statistical techniques (e.g., PROCESS) that use composite variables, but many of those other techniques do not even assess model fit. In my opinion, if you are going to use SEM for your research, it is always better to use a full structural model that models not only measurement items but also structural relationships. More to come in this chapter about how to set up a full structural model in AMOS.

Can I Use a Correlation Matrix as My Data Input?

Yes, AMOS allows you to use a correlation matrix as data input, but you need to include the standard deviation, mean, and sample size for each construct. Typically, you will see path models used when the data input is a correlation matrix instead of the raw data. For many correlation analyses, the researcher is using composite variables to determine the correlation between constructs. This makes it easy to transition to a path model in SEM. You can use a correlation matrix as the data input in a full structural model, but you would have to perform a correlation analysis with every indicator in the model. This could get a little burdensome and prone to input errors.

To use a correlation matrix as the input, you need to have the data set up in a very specific format in SPSS. Using our path model example, Figure 5.7 shows the specific format in SPSS if we wanted to use a correlation matrix as the input for the path model. If it is not in this format, AMOS will not be able to read the data. Note that in the first column you need to label it "rowtype_" and the second column "varname_". The next columns will be your construct names. In the first row will be your sample size, and the next rows will be your correlations between constructs. The next to last row is standard deviation, and the last row is the mean of the construct.

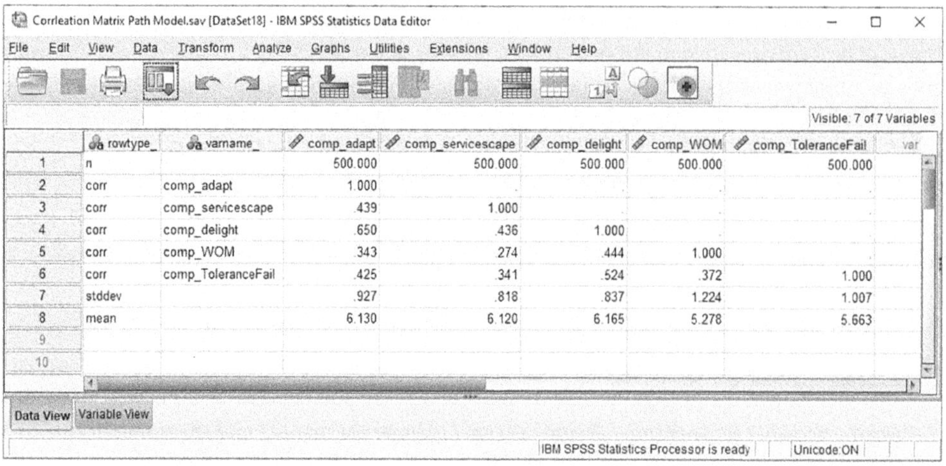

Correlation Matrix Path Model.sav [DataSet18] - IBM SPSS Statistics Data Editor

	rowtype_	varname_	comp_adapt	comp_servicescape	comp_delight	comp_WOM	comp_ToleranceFail
1	n		500.000	500.000	500.000	500.000	500.000
2	corr	comp_adapt	1.000				
3	corr	comp_servicescape	.439	1.000			
4	corr	comp_delight	.650	.436	1.000		
5	corr	comp_WOM	.343	.274	.444	1.000	
6	corr	comp_ToleranceFail	.425	.341	.524	.372	1.000
7	stddev		.927	.818	.837	1.224	1.007
8	mean		6.130	6.120	6.165	5.278	5.663

Figure 5.7 Correlation Matrix Used as Input for Path Model

If you so desire, you can also use the covariance matrix as input. See Figure 5.8 for an example of the specific format needed in SPSS to use the covariance matrix as input.

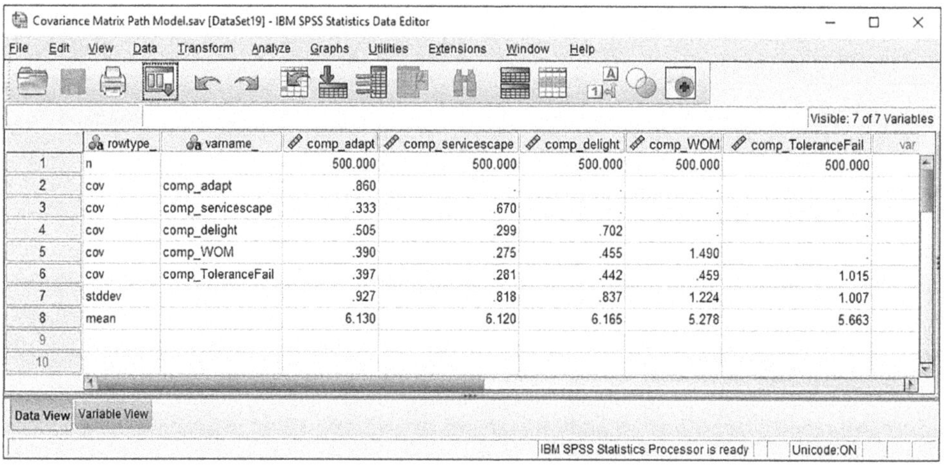

Covariance Matrix Path Model.sav [DataSet19] - IBM SPSS Statistics Data Editor

	rowtype_	varname_	comp_adapt	comp_servicescape	comp_delight	comp_WOM	comp_ToleranceFail
1	n		500.000	500.000	500.000	500.000	500.000
2	cov	comp_adapt	.860				
3	cov	comp_servicescape	.333	.670			
4	cov	comp_delight	.505	.299	.702		
5	cov	comp_WOM	.390	.275	.455	1.490	
6	cov	comp_ToleranceFail	.397	.281	.442	.459	1.015
7	stddev		.927	.818	.837	1.224	1.007
8	mean		6.130	6.120	6.165	5.278	5.663

Figure 5.8 Covariance Matrix Used as Input for Path Model

I have included an example that shows the analysis of the path model run with the correlation matrix and another one run with the raw data. The results are near identical. Often, research papers will provide the correlation matrix along with means and standard deviations. If you want to see if a researcher ran the data correctly, you can use that data given as your input and see if the analysis produces similar results to the one provided in the research article.

Correlation Matrix Data Input

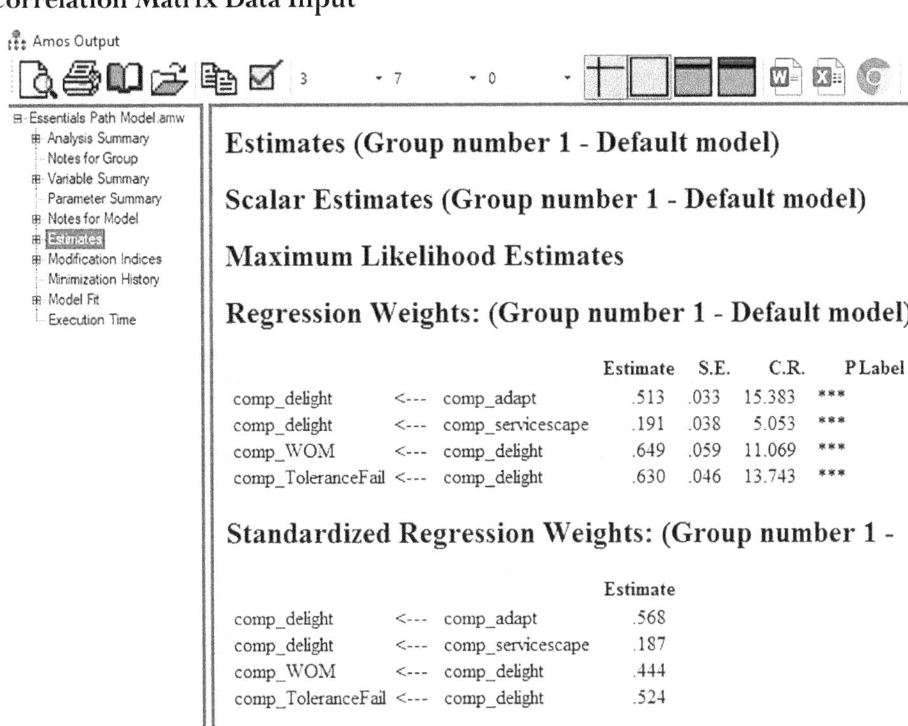

Estimates (Group number 1 - Default model)

Scalar Estimates (Group number 1 - Default model)

Maximum Likelihood Estimates

Regression Weights: (Group number 1 - Default model)

			Estimate	S.E.	C.R.	P	Label
comp_delight	<---	comp_adapt	.513	.033	15.383	***	
comp_delight	<---	comp_servicescape	.191	.038	5.053	***	
comp_WOM	<---	comp_delight	.649	.059	11.069	***	
comp_ToleranceFail	<---	comp_delight	.630	.046	13.743	***	

Standardized Regression Weights: (Group number 1 -

			Estimate
comp_delight	<---	comp_adapt	.568
comp_delight	<---	comp_servicescape	.187
comp_WOM	<---	comp_delight	.444
comp_ToleranceFail	<---	comp_delight	.524

Raw Data (Covariance) Input

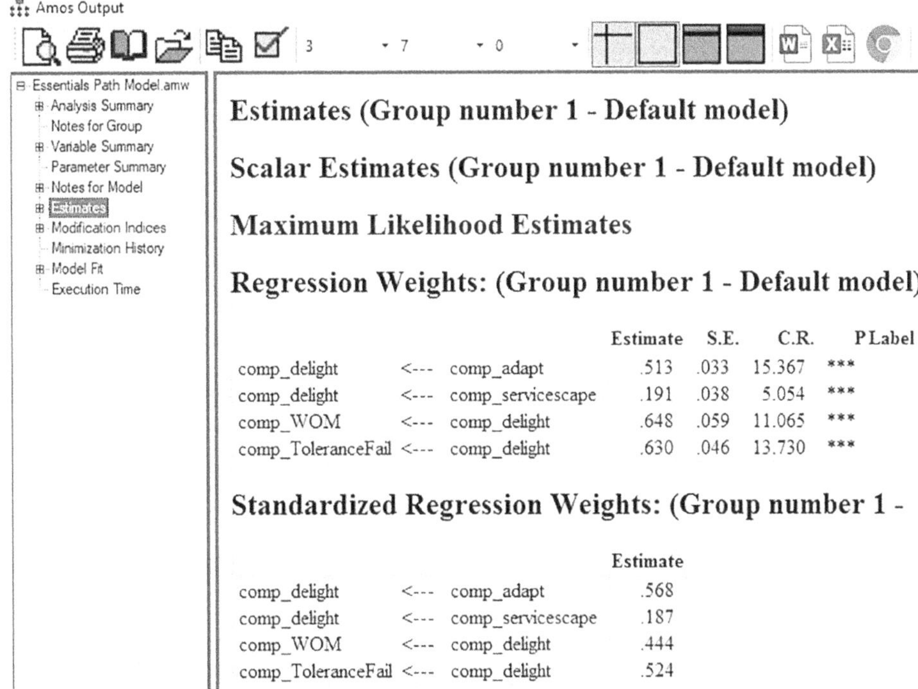

Estimates (Group number 1 - Default model)

Scalar Estimates (Group number 1 - Default model)

Maximum Likelihood Estimates

Regression Weights: (Group number 1 - Default model)

			Estimate	S.E.	C.R.	P	Label
comp_delight	<---	comp_adapt	.513	.033	15.367	***	
comp_delight	<---	comp_servicescape	.191	.038	5.054	***	
comp_WOM	<---	comp_delight	.648	.059	11.065	***	
comp_ToleranceFail	<---	comp_delight	.630	.046	13.730	***	

Standardized Regression Weights: (Group number 1 -

			Estimate
comp_delight	<---	comp_adapt	.568
comp_delight	<---	comp_servicescape	.187
comp_WOM	<---	comp_delight	.444
comp_ToleranceFail	<---	comp_delight	.524

Figure 5.9 Comparison of Covariance and Correlation Matrix Input in AMOS

Notice that in the example, only the composite variables were used and, thus, a path model would be appropriate to use. If you had a full structural model where you wanted to include every indicator in the model test, then you would create a correlation/covariance matrix that included all indicators to be tested in the model. This would be a very large correlation/covariance matrix depending on the number of indicators to be included. Regardless of whether it is a composite variable or individual indicators, AMOS will allow you to run the analysis from a correlation or covariance matrix.

If you are looking for an easy way to find the correlation matrix and covariance matrix along with means and standard deviations for each construct, SPSS has numerous options to find this information. One of the best options is to use the correlation analysis function and ask for additional information. To view a correlation matrix in SPSS, you will go to "Analyze" in the top menu, select "Correlate", and then select "Bivariate". You will include the variables you want a correlation matrix for and then hit the "Options" button. You can then select the checkbox of "Means and standard deviations". The next checkbox of "Cross-product deviations and covariances" will give you the covariance matrix.

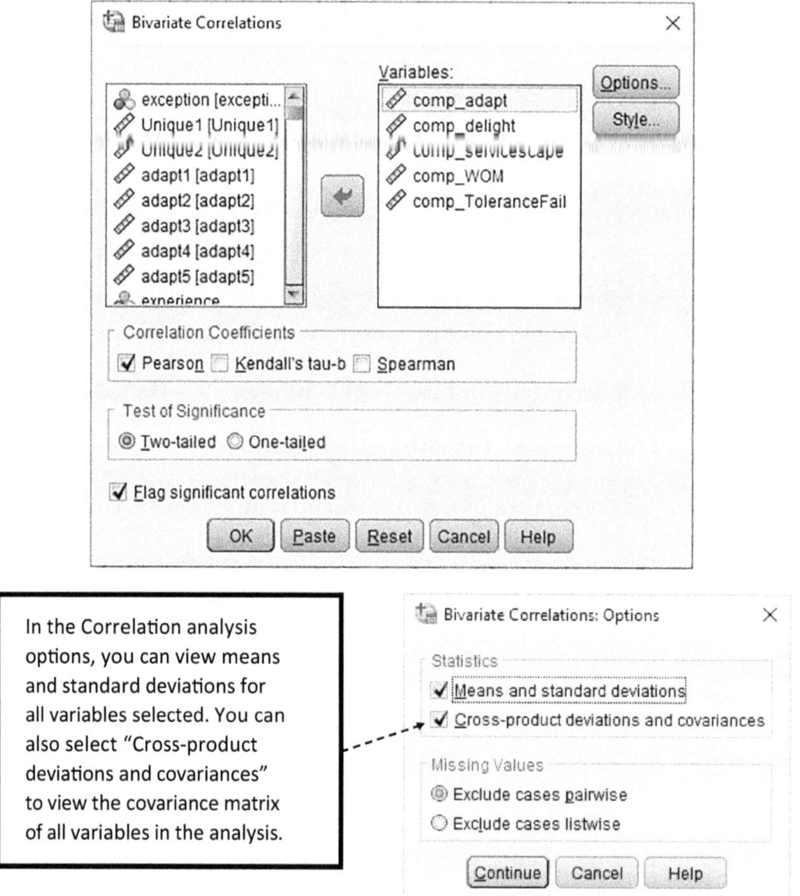

Figure 5.10 Perform Correlation Analysis in SPSS

Descriptive Statistics

	Mean	Std. Deviation	N
comp_adapt	6.1296	.92752	500
comp_delight	6.1653	.83796	500
comp_servicescape	6.1207	.81860	500
comp_WOM	5.2780	1.22408	500
comp_ToleranceFail	5.6630	1.00758	500

Correlations

		comp_adapt	comp_delight	comp_servicescape	comp_WOM	comp_ToleranceFail
comp_adapt	Pearson Correlation	1	.650**	.439**	.343**	.425**
	Sig. (2-tailed)		.000	.000	.000	.000
	Sum of Squares and Cross-products	429.282	251.920	166.181	194.519	198.338
	Covariance	.860	.505	.333	.390	.397
	N	500	500	500	500	500
comp_delight	Pearson Correlation	.650**	1	.436**	.444**	.524**
	Sig. (2-tailed)	.000		.000	.000	.000
	Sum of Squares and Cross-products	251.920	350.388	149.136	227.185	220.609
	Covariance	.505	.702	.299	.455	.442
	N	500	500	500	500	500
comp_servicescape	Pearson Correlation	.439**	.436**	1	.274**	.341**
	Sig. (2-tailed)	.000	.000		.000	.000
	Sum of Squares and Cross-products	166.181	149.136	334.386	137.005	140.332
	Covariance	.333	.299	.670	.275	.281
	N	500	500	500	500	500
comp_WOM	Pearson Correlation	.343**	.444**	.274**	1	.372**
	Sig. (2-tailed)	.000	.000	.000		.000
	Sum of Squares and Cross-products	194.519	227.185	137.005	747.691	229.176
	Covariance	.390	.455	.275	1.498	.459
	N	500	500	500	500	500
comp_ToleranceFail	Pearson Correlation	.425**	.524**	.341**	.372**	1
	Sig. (2-tailed)	.000	.000	.000	.000	
	Sum of Squares and Cross-products	198.338	220.609	140.332	229.176	506.590
	Covariance	.397	.442	.281	.459	1.015
	N	500	500	500	500	500

**. Correlation is significant at the 0.01 level (2-tailed).

Figure 5.11 Example of Output Using a Correlation Analysis

Full Structural Model Analysis

A full structural model assesses the relationships between constructs but also includes the measurement indicators for each variable. A full structural model will allow you to account for the measurement error in a construct's indicators while also assessing the relationships between constructs. You will initially draw all the constructs and indicators like you did in the CFA, then you will start including the direct paths between constructs. This is a more robust model and will account for each indicator individually. Unlike a composite variable path model, each indicator of a construct is included along with its effect on other constructs.

Let's go back to the path model example and look at it as a full structural model. With the full structural model, the unobserved constructs and indicators are modeled along with the relationships between constructs. See Figure 5.12.

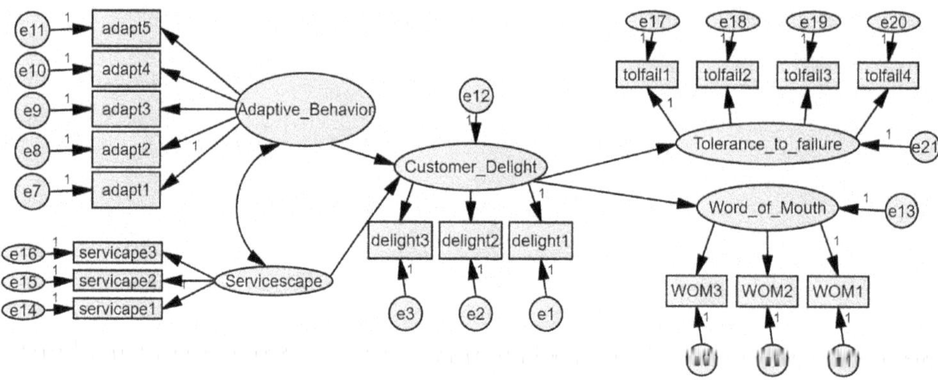

Figure 5.12 Full Structural Model Drawn in AMOS

Just like in the path model, you need to include error terms for each dependent construct and to make sure all error terms are labeled. In the CFA, all constructs were considered independent constructs, but that is not the case in a full structural model. A construct is considered an independent if it has a structural relationship that influences another construct and is not being influenced by any other construct in the model. In this example, Adaptive Behavior and Servicescape are the only independent variables. Since these two constructs are considered independent, a covariance needs to be added between them.

After adding the structural relationships and labeling all error terms, you are ready to run the analysis. A full structural analysis will give you not only the structural relationships between constructs but also the measurement properties or factor loadings for each construct. With a full structural model, the degrees of freedom will be substantially higher, which should alleviate any model fit inflation that happens when a model is close to just-identified. Let's take a closer look at the output of this full structural model test; see Figure 5.13.

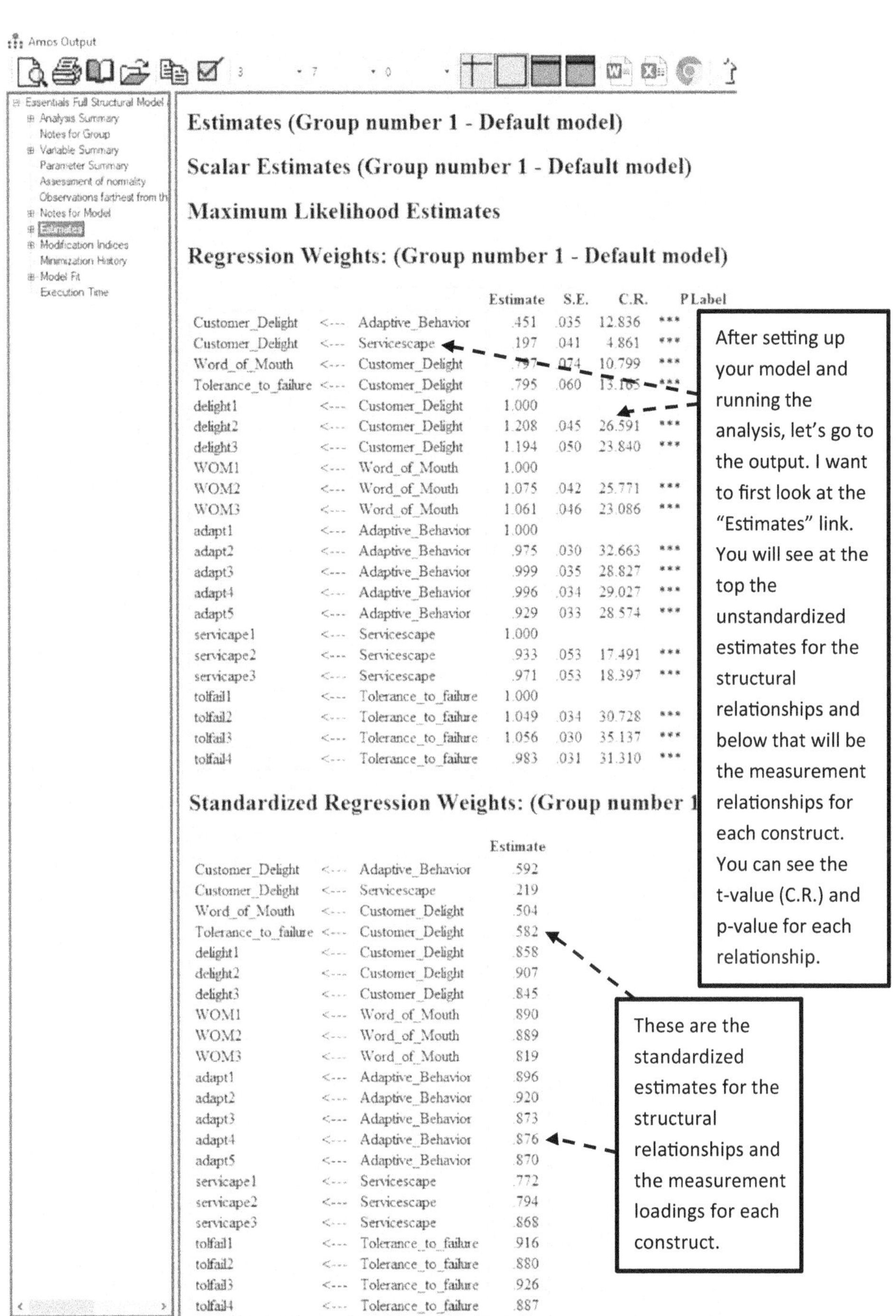

Amos Output

Essentials Full Structural Model
Analysis Summary
Notes for Group
Variable Summary
Parameter Summary
Assessment of normality
Observations farthest from th
Notes for Model
Estimates
Modification Indices
Minimization History
Model Fit
Execution Time

Estimates (Group number 1 - Default model)

Scalar Estimates (Group number 1 - Default model)

Maximum Likelihood Estimates

Regression Weights: (Group number 1 - Default model)

			Estimate	S.E.	C.R.	P	Label
Customer_Delight	<---	Adaptive_Behavior	.451	.035	12.836	***	
Customer_Delight	<---	Servicescape	.197	.041	4.861	***	
Word_of_Mouth	<---	Customer_Delight	.797	.074	10.799	***	
Tolerance_to_failure	<---	Customer_Delight	.795	.060	13.165	***	
delight1	<---	Customer_Delight	1.000				
delight2	<---	Customer_Delight	1.208	.045	26.591	***	
delight3	<---	Customer_Delight	1.194	.050	23.840	***	
WOM1	<---	Word_of_Mouth	1.000				
WOM2	<---	Word_of_Mouth	1.075	.042	25.771	***	
WOM3	<---	Word_of_Mouth	1.061	.046	23.086	***	
adapt1	<---	Adaptive_Behavior	1.000				
adapt2	<---	Adaptive_Behavior	.975	.030	32.663	***	
adapt3	<---	Adaptive_Behavior	.999	.035	28.827	***	
adapt4	<---	Adaptive_Behavior	.996	.034	29.027	***	
adapt5	<---	Adaptive_Behavior	.929	.033	28.574	***	
servicape1	<---	Servicescape	1.000				
servicape2	<---	Servicescape	.933	.053	17.491	***	
servicape3	<---	Servicescape	.971	.053	18.397	***	
tolfail1	<---	Tolerance_to_failure	1.000				
tolfail2	<---	Tolerance_to_failure	1.049	.034	30.728	***	
tolfail3	<---	Tolerance_to_failure	1.056	.030	35.137	***	
tolfail4	<---	Tolerance_to_failure	.983	.031	31.310	***	

Standardized Regression Weights: (Group number 1

			Estimate
Customer_Delight	<---	Adaptive_Behavior	.592
Customer_Delight	<---	Servicescape	.219
Word_of_Mouth	<---	Customer_Delight	.504
Tolerance_to_failure	<---	Customer_Delight	.582
delight1	<---	Customer_Delight	.858
delight2	<---	Customer_Delight	.907
delight3	<---	Customer_Delight	.845
WOM1	<---	Word_of_Mouth	.890
WOM2	<---	Word_of_Mouth	.889
WOM3	<---	Word_of_Mouth	.819
adapt1	<---	Adaptive_Behavior	.896
adapt2	<---	Adaptive_Behavior	.920
adapt3	<---	Adaptive_Behavior	.873
adapt4	<---	Adaptive_Behavior	.876
adapt5	<---	Adaptive_Behavior	.870
servicape1	<---	Servicescape	.772
servicape2	<---	Servicescape	.794
servicape3	<---	Servicescape	.868
tolfail1	<---	Tolerance_to_failure	.916
tolfail2	<---	Tolerance_to_failure	.880
tolfail3	<---	Tolerance_to_failure	.926
tolfail4	<---	Tolerance_to_failure	.887

Figure 5.13 Estimates Output for Full Structural Model

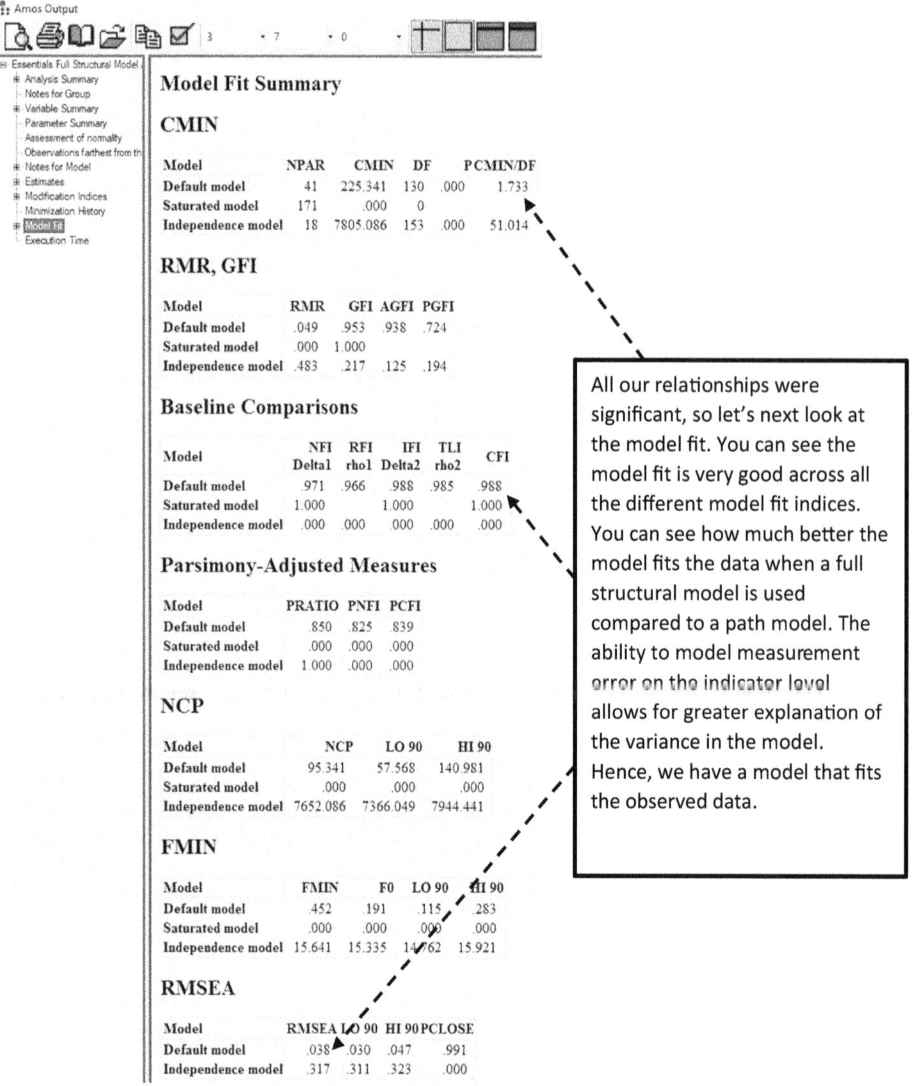

Model Fit Summary

CMIN

Model	NPAR	CMIN	DF	P	CMIN/DF
Default model	41	225.341	130	.000	1.733
Saturated model	171	.000	0		
Independence model	18	7805.086	153	.000	51.014

RMR, GFI

Model	RMR	GFI	AGFI	PGFI
Default model	.049	.953	.938	.724
Saturated model	.000	1.000		
Independence model	.483	.217	.125	.194

Baseline Comparisons

Model	NFI Delta1	RFI rho1	IFI Delta2	TLI rho2	CFI
Default model	.971	.966	.988	.985	.988
Saturated model	1.000		1.000		1.000
Independence model	.000	.000	.000	.000	.000

Parsimony-Adjusted Measures

Model	PRATIO	PNFI	PCFI
Default model	.850	.825	.839
Saturated model	.000	.000	.000
Independence model	1.000	.000	.000

NCP

Model	NCP	LO 90	HI 90
Default model	95.341	57.568	140.981
Saturated model	.000	.000	.000
Independence model	7652.086	7366.049	7944.441

FMIN

Model	FMIN	F0	LO 90	HI 90
Default model	.452	.191	.115	.283
Saturated model	.000	.000	.000	.000
Independence model	15.641	15.335	14.762	15.921

RMSEA

Model	RMSEA	LO 90	HI 90	PCLOSE
Default model	.038	.030	.047	.991
Independence model	.317	.311	.323	.000

Figure 5.14 Model Fit Statistics for Full Structural Model

Next, let's look at the modification indices. With the full structural model, we should have already assessed the measurement model when we performed a CFA; thus, our focus is not on adjusting/covarying error terms with constructs. At this point, the modifications that concern us are the regression weights between constructs. As you can see, there are no modifications that are substantial or worthy of consideration (See Figure 5.15). The modification indices will suggest unacceptable alterations such as indicators having structural relationships with other indicators. Even if the modification index is high, these are nonsensical suggestions and should not be considered.

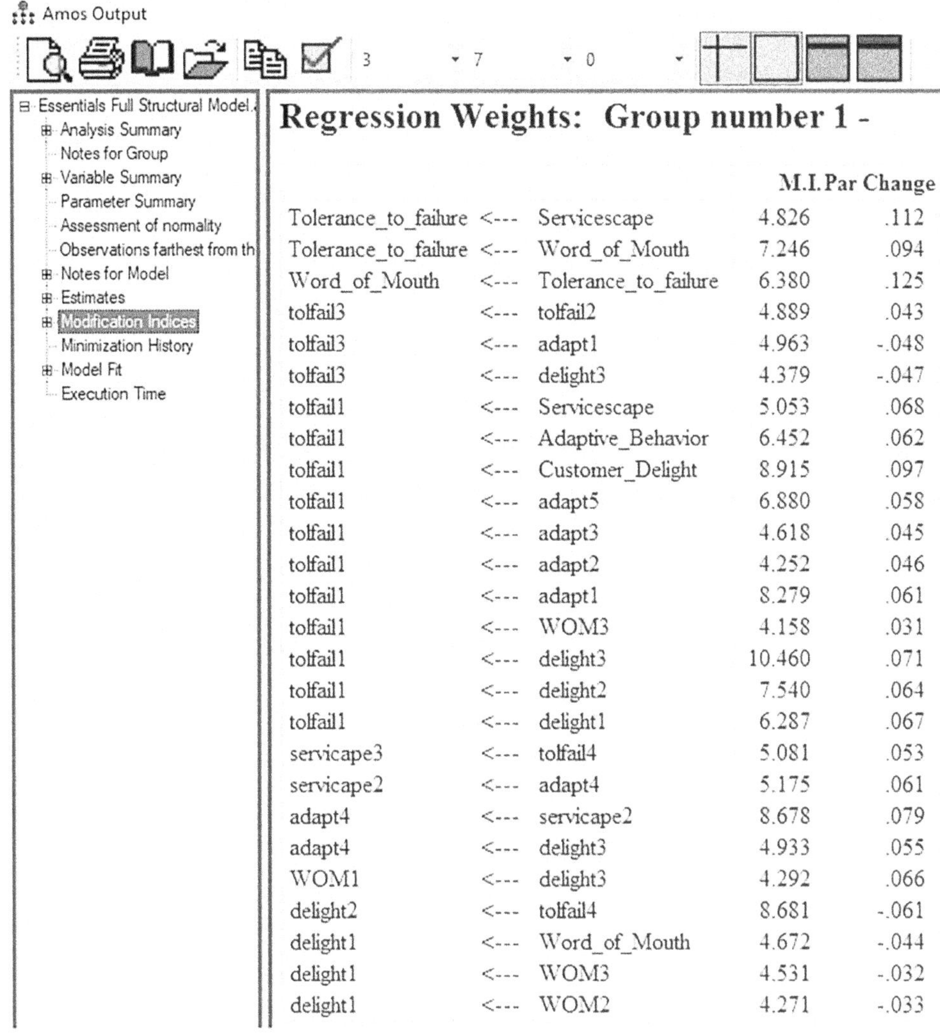

Regression Weights: Group number 1 -

			M.I.	Par Change
Tolerance_to_failure	<---	Servicescape	4.826	.112
Tolerance_to_failure	<---	Word_of_Mouth	7.246	.094
Word_of_Mouth	<---	Tolerance_to_failure	6.380	.125
tolfail3	<---	tolfail2	4.889	.043
tolfail3	<---	adapt1	4.963	-.048
tolfail3	<---	delight3	4.379	-.047
tolfail1	<---	Servicescape	5.053	.068
tolfail1	<---	Adaptive_Behavior	6.452	.062
tolfail1	<---	Customer_Delight	8.915	.097
tolfail1	<---	adapt5	6.880	.058
tolfail1	<---	adapt3	4.618	.045
tolfail1	<---	adapt2	4.252	.046
tolfail1	<---	adapt1	8.279	.061
tolfail1	<---	WOM3	4.158	.031
tolfail1	<---	delight3	10.460	.071
tolfail1	<---	delight2	7.540	.064
tolfail1	<---	delight1	6.287	.067
servicape3	<---	tolfail4	5.081	.053
servicape2	<---	adapt4	5.175	.061
adapt4	<---	servicape2	8.678	.079
adapt4	<---	delight3	4.933	.055
WOM1	<---	delight3	4.292	.066
delight2	<---	tolfail4	8.681	-.061
delight1	<---	Word_of_Mouth	4.672	-.044
delight1	<---	WOM3	4.531	-.032
delight1	<---	WOM2	4.271	-.033

Figure 5.15 Modification Indices for Full Structural Model

The overall results of the full structural model show that the relationships from Adaptive Behavior and Servicescape to Customer Delight were significant. Additionally, the relationships from Customer Delight to Positive Word of Mouth and Tolerance to Future Failures were also significant. If you compare the results from the path model to the full structural model, you will see that all the structural relationships are stronger in the full structural model, and this is a function of explaining more of the variance in the model with the indicators included. This is also reflected with the stronger model fit indices for the full structural model over the path model. Overall, a full structural model will provide a stronger test in assessing relationships between constructs than using a path model.

One function not yet discussed is the "View Output Path Diagram" function. After you run your analysis, you can go back to the graphics window and view the standardized or unstandardized results for every path on the actual diagram. The view output path diagram function is what will display these values on the model. This function is located at the top of the graphics window right above the "Groups" window. The graphic interface looks like this: . It is represented with an arrow pointed up. You have to run the analysis first, but then you can click this button and it will give you the regression coefficients for each parameter. It will not give you significance of a parameter; just the regression value. If you want the values to go away, just hit the input path diagram button, which is the part of this interface with the arrow pointed down.

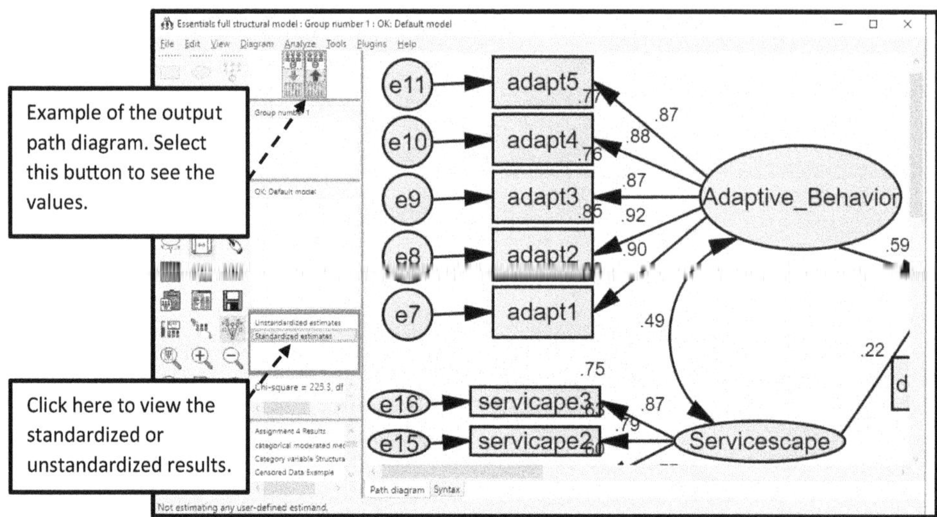

Figure 5.16 View Input/Output Results on the Graphic Interface Page

How Do I Report My Full Structural Model Results?

With the structural model, it is a good idea to present standardized regression weights, t-values, model fit statistics, and R^2 values. I like to present R^2 values of the dependent constructs so the reader can see how much of the variance is being explained with my independent variables. I also like to state if my hypotheses were supported or not. I feel like there is no need to present the measurement indicators again because you should have presented this with a confirmatory factor analysis prior to performing the structural analysis. Ultimately, you want to say a lot in a little amount of space. Presenting your results in a table should be done in a manner where the reader can see all the necessary information to determine the final results of your SEM test. This is not the only way to present structural results, but it is a good template.

Example 5.1:

Table 5.1 Structural Model Test Results

Hypothesized Relationships	*Standardized Estimates*	*t-values*	*Hypothesis Supported*
H1: Adaptive Behavior → Customer Delight	.592	12.83	Supported
H2: Servicescape → Customer Delight	.219	4.86	Supported
H3: Customer Delight → Positive Word of Mouth	.504	10.79	Supported
H4: Customer Delight → Tolerance for future Failures	.582	13.16	Supported
Squared Multiple Correlation (R^2):			
Customer Delight	.525		
Positive Word of Mouth	.254		
Tolerance for Future Failures	.339		
Model Fit Statistics:			
χ^2 = 225.34, df = 130, $p < .001$, CFI = .98, IFI = .98, RMSEA = .03			

Using Specification Search to Aid in Model Trimming and Fit

After you have conceptualized your model, you can use the specification search function to aid in trimming/fitting of your model. Trimming a model means removing some paths that might not be contributing much to the overall model. The specification search function will propose numerous different proposed models to see which one has the best model fit. This will let you know if dropping a relationship will actually improve your model. Where modification indices are looking to add relationships, the specification search tool explores the opposite by examining how your model improves by removing relationships. After the model is initially specified, the first step is to select the specification search icon that looks like: . The specification search window will then come up on the screen (see Figure 5.17).

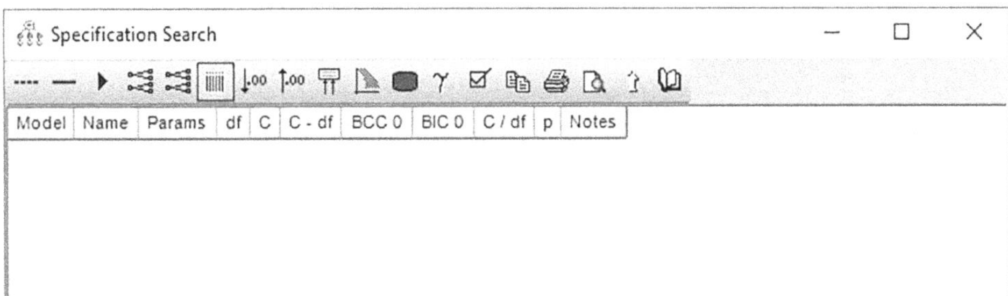

Figure 5.17 Specification Search Window

All functions in this window are accomplished through the banner icons at the top:

The icon allows you to select a relationship or covariance and make it optional.

The icon denotes that relationships are required (not optional).

The icon  performs the specification search.

The icon 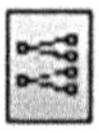 shows all optional arrows.

The icon 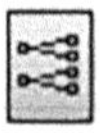 hides all optional arrows.

The icon  shows summary of results.

The icon  decreases decimal places in the results.

The icon  increases the decimal places in the results.

The icon  shows a short list of the top 10 best potential models. This is handy if you have a lot of potential models.

The icon  shows diagrams of results.

The icon  shows the path diagram.

The icon  shows parameter estimates on the path diagram.

The icon  takes you to the options menu.

The icon  allows you to copy rows of results to the clipboard.

Note the values:

Params = number of parameters in the model
Df = degrees of freedom
C = chi-square value
C-df = chi-square minus degrees of freedom
C/df = chi-square value divided by degrees of freedom
P = p value from chi-square test

After the specification search window comes up, select the  icon and start selecting which relationships you want to be optional. In our previously used structural model, I decided to make all the structural relationships optional. A relationship that is selected to be optional will be highlighted (pink by default). You will also notice that most of the icons on the left-hand side ribbon are grayed out. When the specification search window is active, most functions will take place in the specification window.

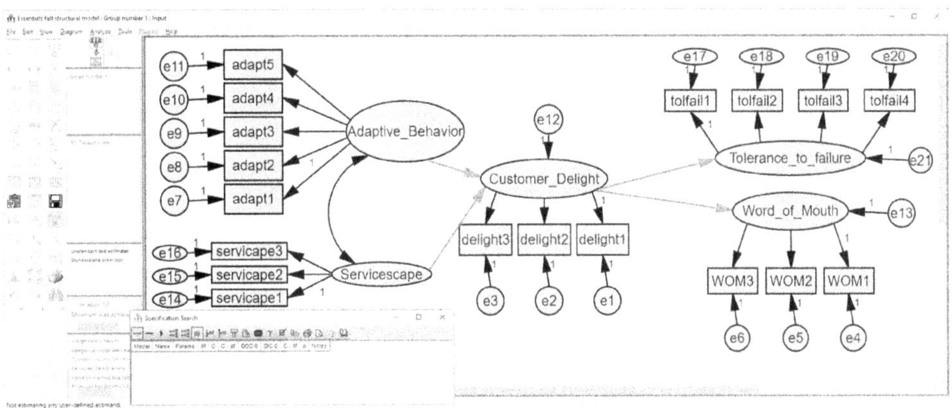

Figure 5.18 Setting Optional Paths in the Specification Search Window

After specifying the optional relationships in the model, we are almost ready to run the analysis. Before we do that, I like to see different options for the results in the output, so I will select the "Options" icon, and this will bring up a pop-up window. In that pop-up window make sure you are in the "Current Results" tab at the top. Scroll down on the display option and select "Derived fit indices". This will provide you with the RMSEA and CFI fit indices of all the potential models proposed.

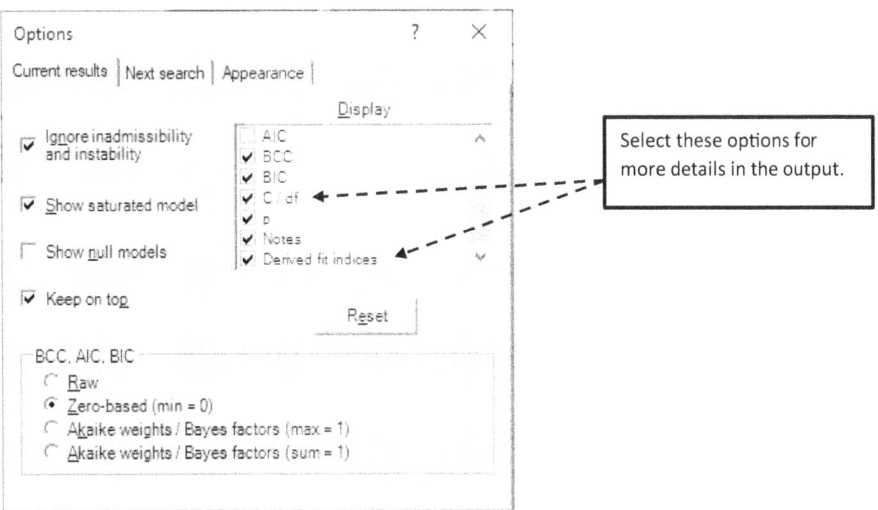

Figure 5.19 Options Window in Specification Search Functions

After selecting these options for more details, hit the cancel button (or X button in the right corner) and then run the analysis by selecting the ▶ icon. In the specification search window, all the possible combinations of your model will appear with the relationships denoted as optional. An example of the output is in Figure 5.20.

Specification Search

Model	Name	Params	df	C	C - df	BCC 0	BIC 0	C / df	p	Notes	RMSEA	CFI 1	CFI 2
1	Default model	37	134	801.593	667.593	567.935	551.393	5.982	0.000		0.100	0.913	0.832
2	Default model	38	133	532.282	399.282	300.703	288.297	4.002	0.000		0.078	0.948	0.899
3	Default model	38	133	642.793	509.793	411.215	398.808	4.833	0.000		0.088	0.933	0.872
4	Default model	38	133	671.760	538.760	440.181	427.775	5.051	0.000		0.090	0.930	0.864
5	Default model	38	133	693.146	560.146	461.568	449.161	5.212	0.000		0.092	0.927	0.859
6	Default model	39	132	366.062	234.062	136.562	128.291	2.773	0.000		0.060	0.969	0.941
7	Default model	39	132	420.562	288.562	191.063	182.792	3.186	0.000		0.066	0.962	0.927
8	Default model	39	132	507.174	375.174	277.674	269.404	3.842	0.000		0.075	0.951	0.906
9	Default model	39	132	511.530	379.530	282.031	273.760	3.875	0.000		0.076	0.950	0.904
10	Default model	39	132	529.161	397.161	299.661	291.391	4.009	0.000		0.078	0.948	0.900
11	Default model	39	132	560.242	428.242	330.743	322.472	4.244	0.000		0.081	0.944	0.892
12	Default model	40	131	249.461	118.461	22.041	17.906	1.904	0.000		0.043	0.985	0.970
13	Default model	40	131	343.215	212.215	115.794	111.659	2.620	0.000		0.057	0.972	0.947
14	Default model	40	131	390.463	259.463	163.043	158.907	2.981	0.000		0.063	0.966	0.935
15	Default model	40	131	398.604	267.604	171.184	167.049	3.043	0.000		0.064	0.965	0.933
16	Default model	41	130	225.341	95.341	***0.000***	***0.000***	***1.733***	***0.000***		***0.038***	0.988	0.976
[illegible]	[illegible]	[illegible]	0	[illegible]	[illegible]	[illegible]	[illegible]					1.000	1.000

Figure 5.20 Potential Models Given in Specification Search Function

In this output, 16 different possible models are suggested. You will see that in the output, the best-fitting model will be in bold. For the CFI fit index, the bold value will be the saturated model, which gives you a value of "1". With the CFI results, you are looking for the second-best results. If you want to see the specifics on which relationships were included/excluded with each model, you need to double click into the model number. Based on the results, model 16 had the best results, which was the original model where all relationships were included. The second-best model was model 12, which had the relationship from Servicescape to Customer Delight removed, but all other relationships were included. If you are struggling to get a good model fit, this is a good tool to help "trim" your model.

What Are Alternative Models, and Why Should I Be Concerned With Them?

In the past, a heavy emphasis was placed on the idea of alternative models, or the ability to show the superiority of your research model compared to other potential rival models. While still a valid procedure, the popularity of requiring alternative models in research has waned. The main reason is that researchers would put up these "straw-man" models that were obviously worse than the original model. This did not really show the superiority of the original model; it just showed that some alternatives were really poor

(Edwards 2008). There is a very good discussion about how to form and test alternative models in SEM from the work of MacCallum et al. (1993). The authors detail the process of using the "replacing rule", under which the predictors and dependent variables may be swapped to see if the relationship is better in reverse than initially predicted. Additionally, the authors suggest using trimmed models or models where the relationships are directed to different dependent variables than initially proposed. Lastly, if there are rival explanations to a construct or concept, assessing the competing models will add credence to the findings.

If you are going to propose a viable rival model, the way to assess the superiority of a model is often through the model fit statistics. Looking at the model fit tests, you can see if your original model is a better fit than the "alternative" model. To do this, you can examine the fit indices, or you can look at the chi-square values for each model and perform a difference test based on the degrees of freedom. As stated earlier, you could also use the specification search tool to examine "trimmed" models to see if they have a better fit. The idea of examining potential alternative models is a good idea and adds some validity that your proposed model is capturing the observed covariance matrix. One should use caution that proposing a rival/alternative model is not just an exercise in trying to find the worst-fitting model because this provides little justification for the superiority of the original model.

How Do I Add a Control Variable to My Structural Model?

At times, you might want to control for other potential influences in your model. Common control variables are demographics of a sample (gender, age, income) but can also be attitudinal or psychographic measures. With a control variable, you are accounting for the potential influence of these variables in order to get unbiased estimates. To put it another way, you are examining relationships in the model while controlling for the influence of a specific variable. Do not underestimate the importance of control variables. A control variable can help with model fit and can assist in significance of relationships between constructs. The right control variable is the difference between an ill-fitting model that has very little significance between constructs and an acceptable model with strong relationships. It is a good idea in the survey development phase to ask questions to be used as control variables. You may find that a control variable is the key to understanding the nature of a relationship when a complex model is required.

To include a control variable, you will drag that item from your variable list to the model window. You will then place a direct relationship from the control variable to each dependent variable in the model. You will also need to add a covariance relationship from the control variable to all the independent (exogenous) constructs in the model. In our full structural model example, let's say that I needed to account for the "Age" of the respondent. The age of the customer might influence expectations of how the service should go and the likelihood of being delighted. I am going to include the "Age" observable variable in the model and add relationships to all the dependent variables to control for the potential influence of this variable on the ultimate influence of the dependent variables. You can add as many control variables as you like as long as you think the variable might have an influence on a potential relationship in the model. See the example in AMOS of what it looks like with a control variable added to the model in Figure 5.21. After including the control variable, you can run the analysis. See Figure 5.22 for an example of the output.

e11
adapt5
e10
adapt4
e9
adapt3
e8
adapt2
e7
adapt1
Adaptive_Behavior
e12
Customer_Delight
e17
e18
e19
e20
tolfail1
tolfail2
tolfail3
tolfail4
Tolerance_to_failure
e21
Word_of_Mouth
e13
e16
servicape3
e15
servicape2
e14
servicape1
Servicescape
delight3
delight2
delight1
e3
e2
e1
Age
WOM3
WOM2
WOM1
e6
e5
e4

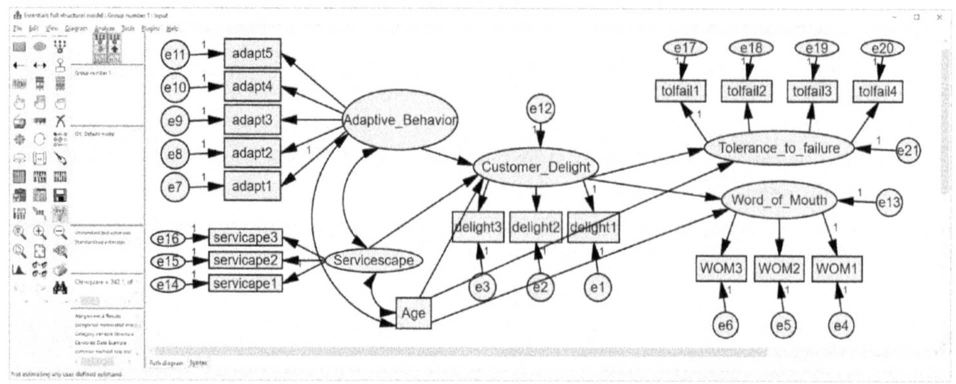

Figure 5.21 Full Structural Model Including Control Variable of Age

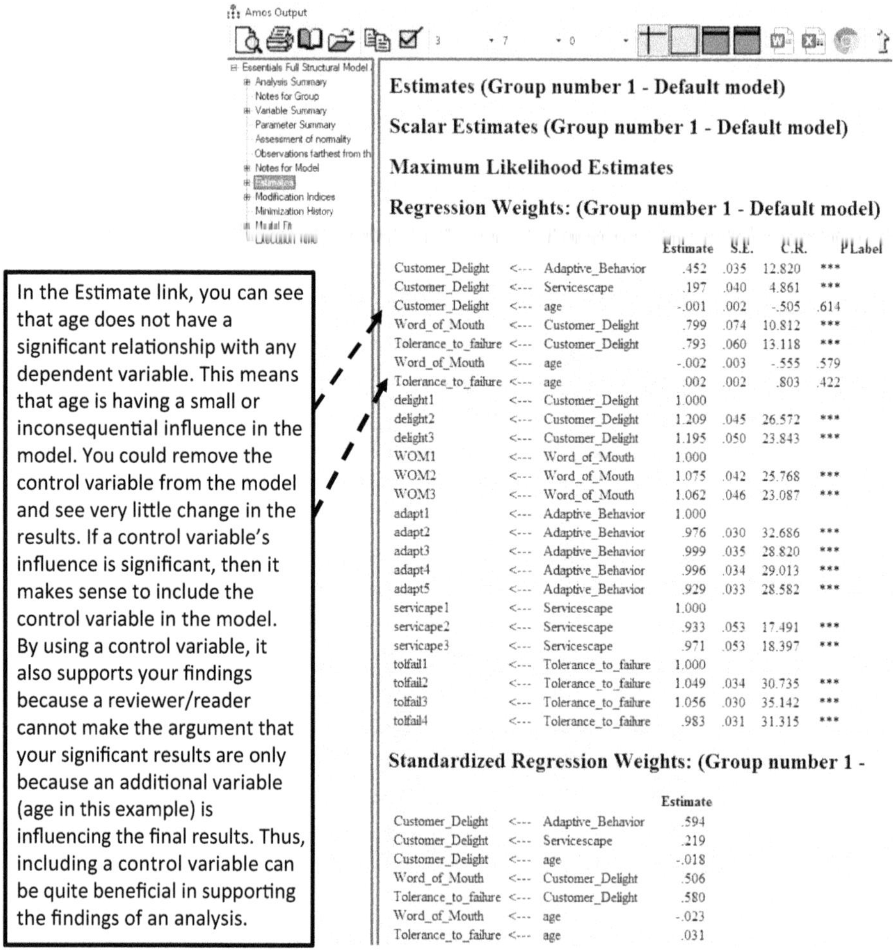

Amos Output
Essentials Full Structural Model
Analysis Summary
Notes for Group
Variable Summary
Parameter Summary
Assessment of normality
Observations farthest from th
Notes for Model
Estimates
Modification Indices
Minimization History
Model Fit
In the Estimate link, you can see that age does not have a significant relationship with any dependent variable. This means that age is having a small or inconsequential influence in the model. You could remove the control variable from the model and see very little change in the results. If a control variable's influence is significant, then it makes sense to include the control variable in the model. By using a control variable, it also supports your findings because a reviewer/reader cannot make the argument that your significant results are only because an additional variable (age in this example) is influencing the final results. Thus, including a control variable can be quite beneficial in supporting the findings of an analysis.

Estimates (Group number 1 - Default model)

Scalar Estimates (Group number 1 - Default model)

Maximum Likelihood Estimates

Regression Weights: (Group number 1 - Default model)

			Estimate	S.E.	C.R.	P	Label
Customer_Delight	<---	Adaptive_Behavior	.452	.035	12.820	***	
Customer_Delight	<---	Servicescape	.197	.040	4.861	***	
Customer_Delight	<---	age	-.001	.002	-.505	.614	
Word_of_Mouth	<---	Customer_Delight	.799	.074	10.812	***	
Tolerance_to_failure	<---	Customer_Delight	.793	.060	13.118	***	
Word_of_Mouth	<---	age	-.002	.003	-.555	.579	
Tolerance_to_failure	<---	age	.002	.002	.803	.422	
delight1	<---	Customer_Delight	1.000				
delight2	<---	Customer_Delight	1.209	.045	26.572	***	
delight3	<---	Customer_Delight	1.195	.050	23.843	***	
WOM1	<---	Word_of_Mouth	1.000				
WOM2	<---	Word_of_Mouth	1.075	.042	25.768	***	
WOM3	<---	Word_of_Mouth	1.062	.046	23.087	***	
adapt1	<---	Adaptive_Behavior	1.000				
adapt2	<---	Adaptive_Behavior	.976	.030	32.686	***	
adapt3	<---	Adaptive_Behavior	.999	.035	28.820	***	
adapt4	<---	Adaptive_Behavior	.996	.034	29.013	***	
adapt5	<---	Adaptive_Behavior	.929	.033	28.582	***	
servicape1	<---	Servicescape	1.000				
servicape2	<---	Servicescape	.933	.053	17.491	***	
servicape3	<---	Servicescape	.971	.053	18.397	***	
tolfail1	<---	Tolerance_to_failure	1.000				
tolfail2	<---	Tolerance_to_failure	1.049	.034	30.735	***	
tolfail3	<---	Tolerance_to_failure	1.056	.030	35.142	***	
tolfail4	<---	Tolerance_to_failure	.983	.031	31.315	***	

Standardized Regression Weights: (Group number 1 -

			Estimate
Customer_Delight	<---	Adaptive_Behavior	.594
Customer_Delight	<---	Servicescape	.219
Customer_Delight	<---	age	-.018
Word_of_Mouth	<---	Customer_Delight	.506
Tolerance_to_failure	<---	Customer_Delight	.580
Word_of_Mouth	<---	age	-.023
Tolerance_to_failure	<---	age	.031

Figure 5.22 Estimates Output With Control Variable of Age Included

Two Group Analysis

A two group analysis can see if differences exist in the relationships proposed in a model across groups. Performing a two group analysis is very similar to the discussion about measurement invariance in Chapter 4. Let's continue with the example used in the full structural analysis of Adaptive Behavior and Servicescape leading to Customer Delight, which influences Positive Word of Mouth and Tolerance to Future Failures. The example going forward is for a full structural analysis, but the exact same process can be used for a path model. After initially drawing out your model in AMOS, you need to specify the two groups. For this example, the two groups will be (1) new customers and (2) repeat customers. We will see if first-time customers differ in their evaluation and attitudes compared to repeat customers who have been through the experience before. In the "Models" window, the default value will be one group labeled "Group 1". We need to create two groups for the analysis. The first step is to rename the "Group 1" label to something meaningful. To do this, you need to initially double click in this Group 1 label. A pop-up "Manage Groups" window will appear where you can change the name of the group. Let's call the first group "First_Time" to represent the first-time customers. You will then need to hit the "New" button at the bottom of the manage groups pop-up window to form another group. Let's call the second group "Repeat" to represent the repeat customers.

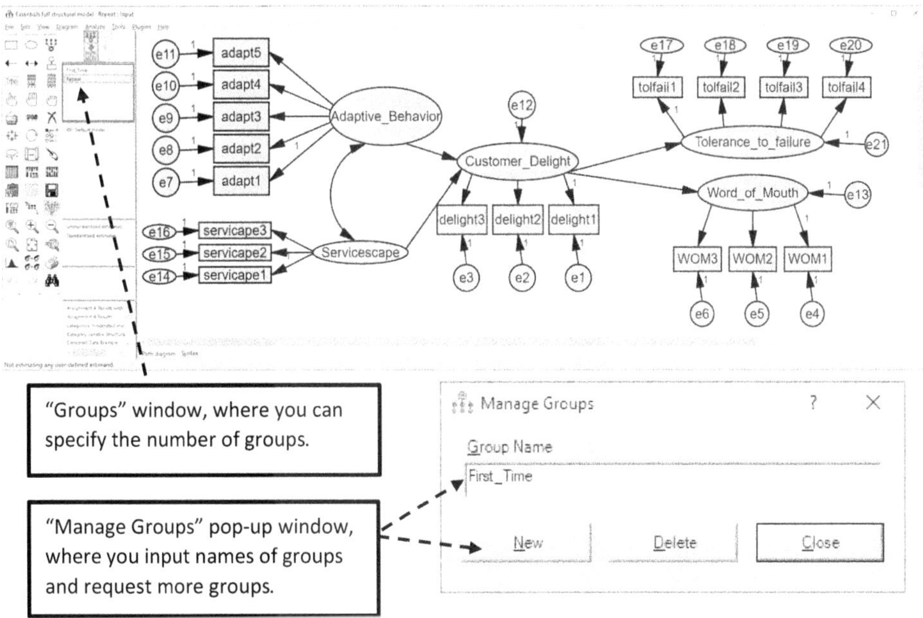

Figure 5.23 Setting Up Two Groups in a Structural Model

After forming the groups, you need to specify where the data is for each group. Each group can have a separate data file or can be in the same data file, but you will need to specify the values of each group for AMOS. Hit the "Data Files Button" and then select the "File Name" button and find your data file. For this example, the file name is called Customer Delight Data. In this file, I have a column called "experience" that is populated with a 1 or a 2 value. The "1s" denote repeat customers and the "2s" denote first-time customers. If you are using the same data file for both groups, you will need to use the "Group Variable" function to tell AMOS what column the group differences are in. You will also have to tell AMOS what value corresponds with which group using the "Group Value" button.

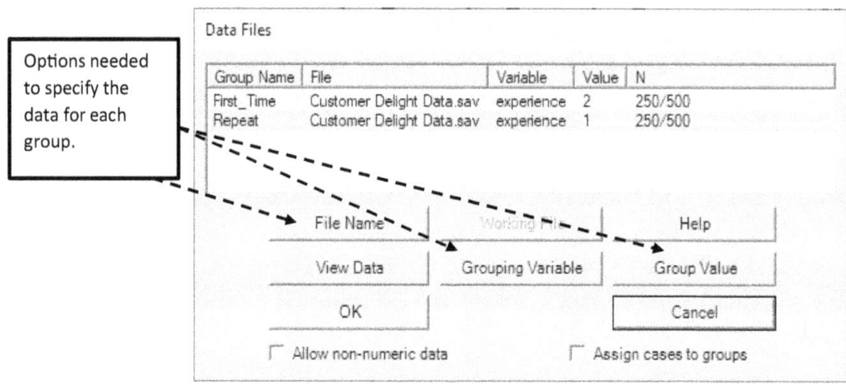

Figure 5.24 Reading in the Data File for Each Group in the Analysis

In this example, we have an even split of the total 500 sample. With a two group analysis, you need to make sure each group has a sufficient sample size to accurately capture the relationships within each group. This can be a downside with two group analyses because each group has to have a sufficient sample for power reasons, which means the overall sample size can be quite large.

After reading in the data file for each group, you need to hit the "OK" button. To run a two group analysis, you will have to label every parameter and error term for each group. AMOS has a function for this so that you do not have to label everything individually. You will need to use the "Multi-Group" analysis button, which looks like a double headed icon . After selecting this icon, you will initially get a pop-up warning window. This warning window is just stating that it is going to set up potential models to test in AMOS and, if existing models are already set up, AMOS will delete those previous models. In essence, it is going to start with the default models of a two group comparison.

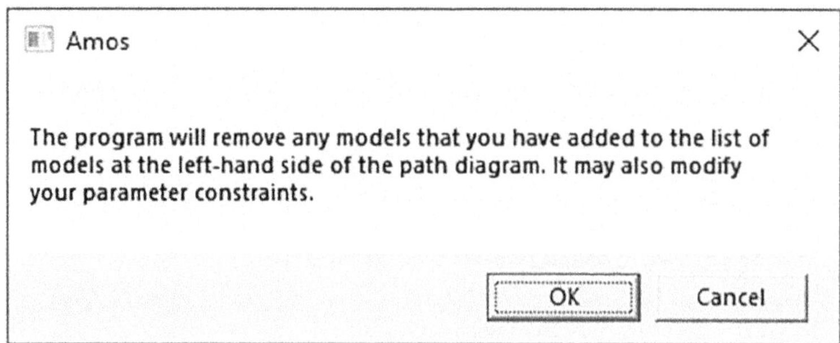

Figure 5.25 Warning Message Using Multiple Group Analysis

Select the "OK" button on this warning window. Next, a pop-up "Multiple-Group Analysis" window will appear and will let you know what potential models are being suggested to test. The type of model AMOS will suggest will depend on the complexity of your model. In this example, AMOS suggested five potential models. The checkmarks in this pop-up window denote if you want these different parameters constrained to be equal across the groups. I usually just hit "OK" and let AMOS create the models even if I am not going to use that specific model. It takes more time to deselect the parameters you do not need. If I have extra models I do not need, I just ignore that output.

After hitting "OK", you will see in the models window an unconstrained model across the two groups, and then you will see five different models that are constraining the two groups.

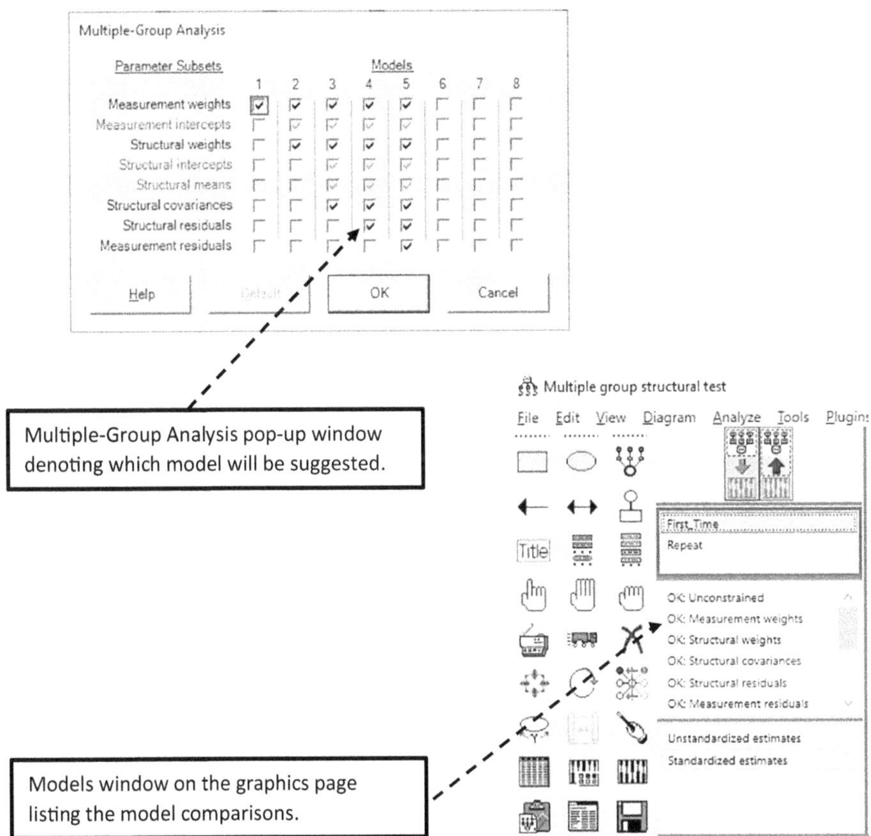

Figure 5.26 Comparison Models in Multiple Group Analysis

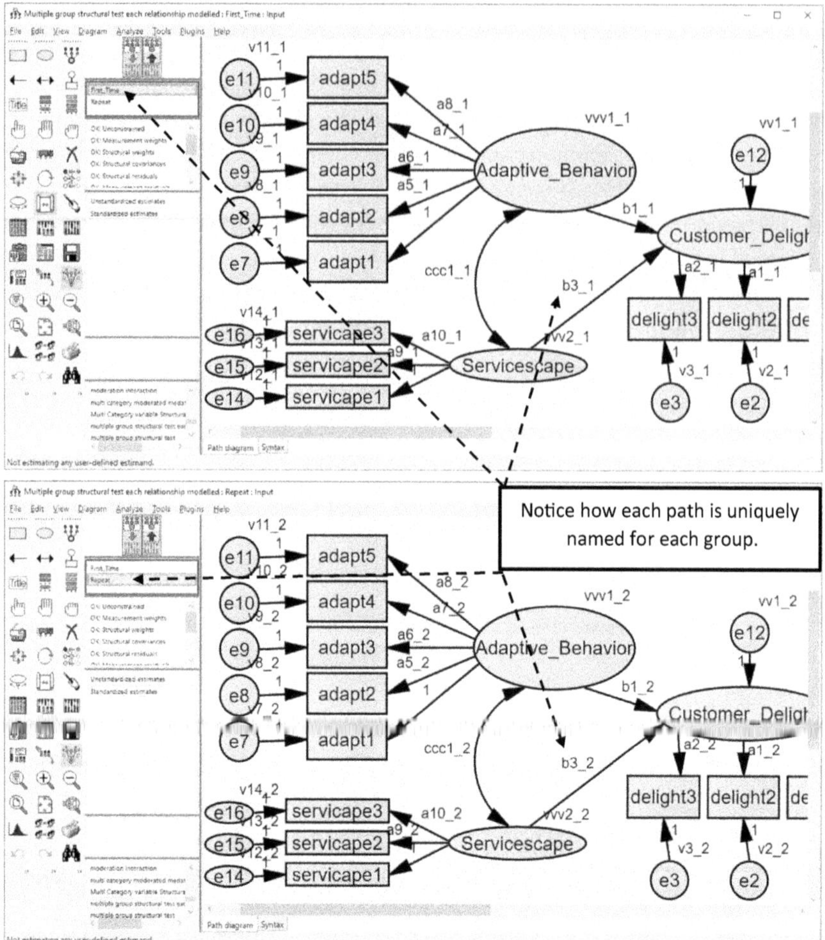

Figure 5.27 Unique Parameter Labeling for Each Group

In a two group analysis, if you use the multigroup analysis icon to label your parameters across the groups, AMOS will use an "a" and a number for factor loadings and a "b" and a number for structural relationships between constructs. It is very important that every parameter has a unique name across the groups. For instance, the structural relationship from Servicescape to Customer Delight is labeled "b3_1" for the first-time customer group and "b3_2" for the repeat customer group. This similar notation lets you know that "b3" is the specific relationship from Servicescape to Customer Delight but the underscore numbers after "b3" lets you know which group for clarification purposes.

In Chapter 4, we talked about how to test for invariance, and specifically metric invariance was a test of factor loadings being constrained across the groups. The measurement weights model in AMOS specifically constrains all factor loadings (or parameters listed as an "a") to be equal across the groups. The structural weights model constrains the factor loadings but also constrains the relationships between constructs to be equal. If you double click into the structural weights model on the graphics screen, you will see the measurement and structural relationships constrained. See Figure 5.28.

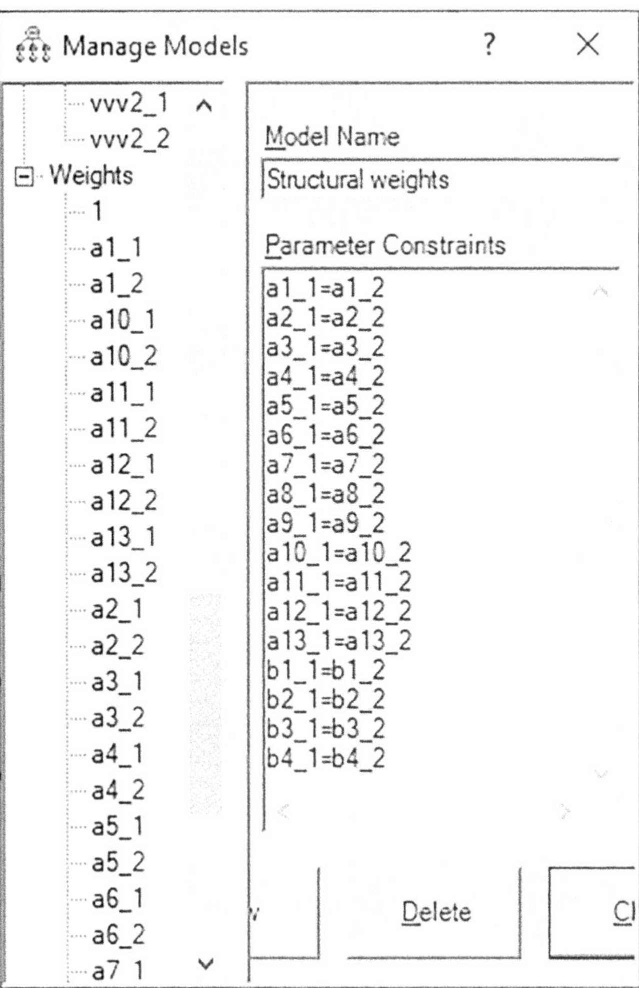

Figure 5.28 Parameters Constrained to be Equal Across the Groups

If we run the two group analysis with the structural weights model, this will tell us if first-time and repeat customers are different *as a whole*. This analysis is examining *all* of the relationships in the model across the groups. If we find differences in this model, it tells us only that the groups are significantly different as a whole; it gives us no indication exactly where in the model they are different. You might have one relationship that is extremely different across the groups and all other relationships were non-significant. When you examine the relationships as a whole, you cannot tell where in the model any differences are coming from. Hence, we need to form a new model that is not a default model listed by AMOS. In the models window, if you double click on the last model "Measurement Residuals", the managed models pop-up window will appear. At the bottom of the window is a button called "New". Select this button, and a new model will be created that is currently blank. You need to first title this model. We are going to call this model "Constrain 1". Next, we constrain one structural relationship at a time to see if the specific relationship is different across the groups. Remember that structural relationships are labeled as "b" and a number in AMOS. Let's look at the first structural relationship of Adaptive Behavior to Customer Delight.

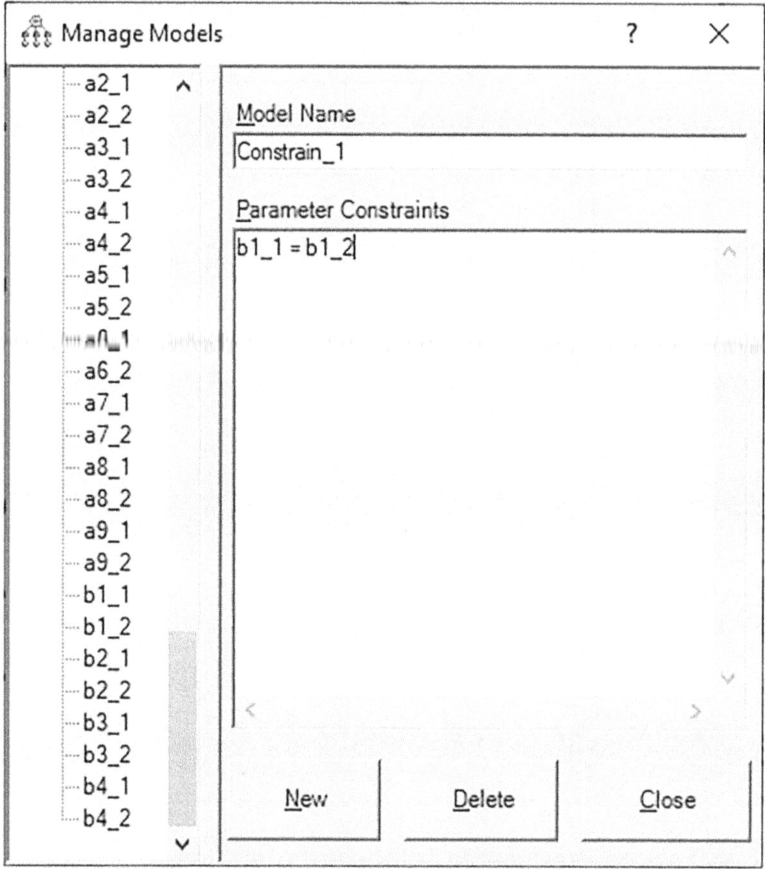

Figure 5.29 Adaptive Behavior to Customer Delight Constrained to be Equal Across the Groups

This relationship is labeled as b1 (b1_1 for first-time customers and b1_2 for repeat customers). We need to constrain this specific relationship to be equal across the groups to see if differences are present. In the "constrain 1" model, you are going to constrain b1_1 to be equal to b1_2. Note if you double click on the value listed in the left-hand menu, it will automatically include this in the parameter constraint window. After constraining this relationship to be equal across the groups, hit the close button, and then we are ready to run the analysis. Once the analysis has finished, you first go to the Model Comparison link in the output. This will tell you if there is a difference in chi-square values across your models. The output in this section will show comparisons of the different models listed. In the first section, you will see a subheading that says, "Assuming model Unconstrained to be correct". This compares all the constrained models listed by AMOS to the unconstrained model where no relationships were constrained to be equal. In this first section, we are concerned with the "Constrain 1" model, where we are testing the relationship from Adaptive Behavior to Customer Delight.

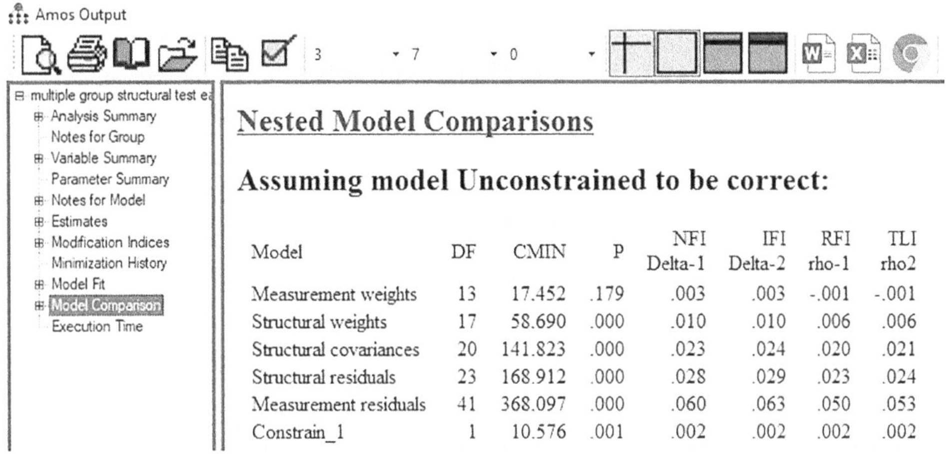

Nested Model Comparisons

Assuming model Unconstrained to be correct:

Model	DF	CMIN	P	NFI Delta-1	IFI Delta-2	RFI rho-1	TLI rho2
Measurement weights	13	17.452	.179	.003	.003	-.001	-.001
Structural weights	17	58.690	.000	.010	.010	.006	.006
Structural covariances	20	141.823	.000	.023	.024	.020	.021
Structural residuals	23	168.912	.000	.028	.029	.023	.024
Measurement residuals	41	368.097	.000	.060	.063	.050	.053
Constrain_1	1	10.576	.001	.002	.002	.002	.002

Figure 5.30 Model Comparison Results

The results of the "Constrain 1" model show that the chi-square difference for the one parameter that we constrained is 10.57, which is a p-value at the .001 level (Remember that with one degree of freedom, significance at the .05 level requires a chi-square value of at least 3.84). These results for the Constrain 1 model mean that the relationship of Adaptive Behavior to Customer Delight is significantly different across the groups. Now that we know a significant difference is present, we need to see which group has a stronger or weaker effect on the relationship. To do this, we need to go to the Estimates link in the output. In the Estimates output, we are going to examine the strength of the relationships across the two groups. There is a "Groups" window on the left hand side of the Estimates output. You need to first select the group you are interested in, and this will present the relationships for that specific group. See Figures 5.31 and 5.32.

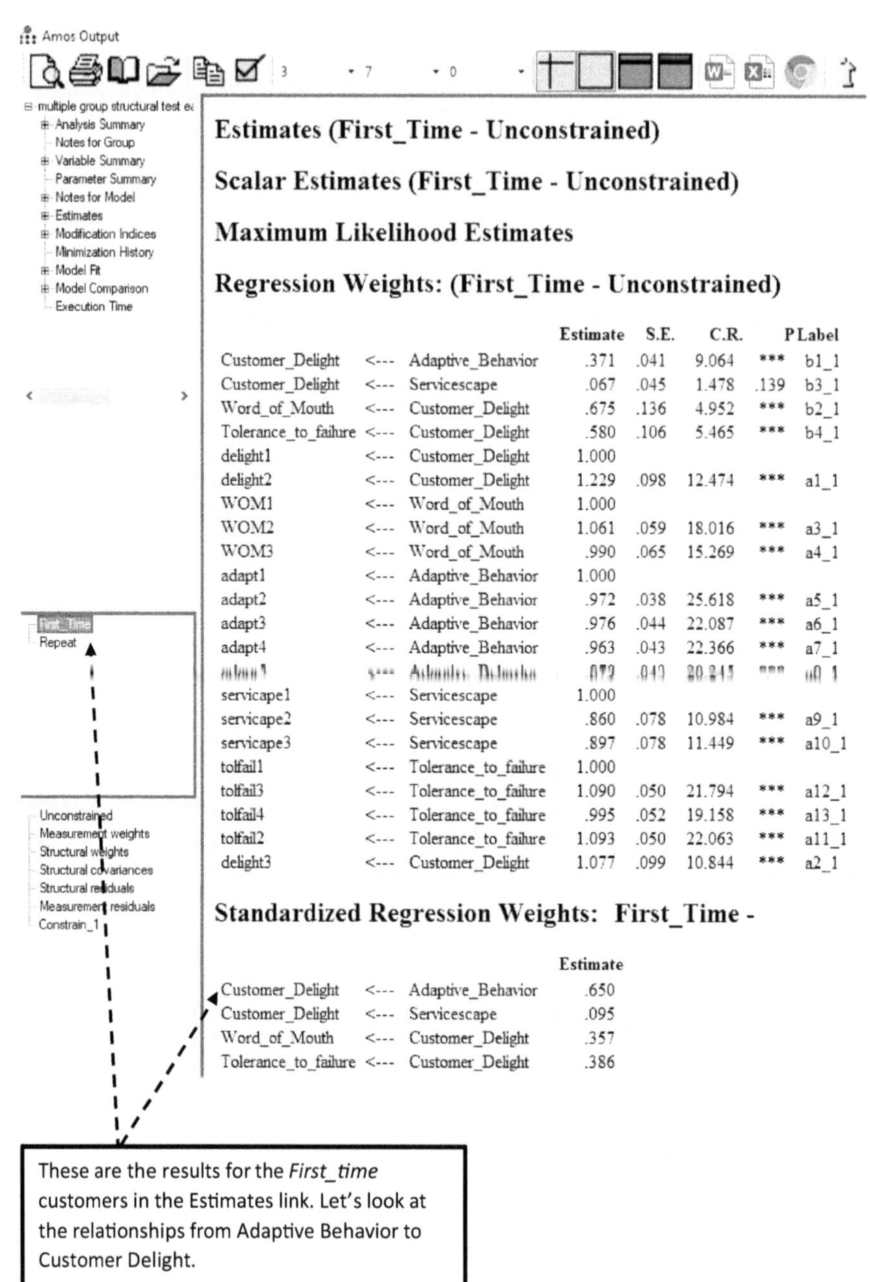

Figure 5.31 Estimates Output for First-Time Group

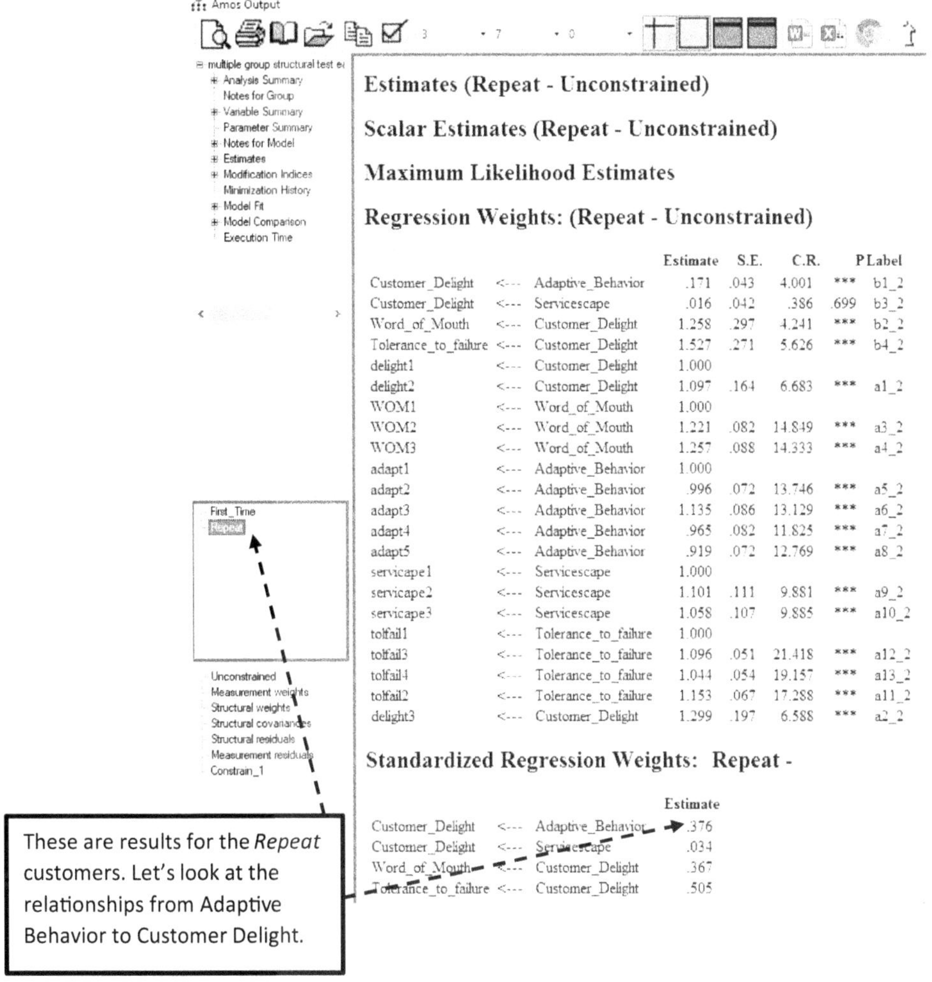

Estimates (Repeat - Unconstrained)

Scalar Estimates (Repeat - Unconstrained)

Maximum Likelihood Estimates

Regression Weights: (Repeat - Unconstrained)

			Estimate	S.E.	C.R.	P	Label
Customer_Delight	<---	Adaptive_Behavior	.171	.043	4.001	***	b1_2
Customer_Delight	<---	Servicescape	.016	.042	.386	.699	b3_2
Word_of_Mouth	<---	Customer_Delight	1.258	.297	4.241	***	b2_2
Tolerance_to_failure	<---	Customer_Delight	1.527	.271	5.626	***	b4_2
delight1	<---	Customer_Delight	1.000				
delight2	<---	Customer_Delight	1.097	.164	6.683	***	a1_2
WOM1	<---	Word_of_Mouth	1.000				
WOM2	<---	Word_of_Mouth	1.221	.082	14.849	***	a3_2
WOM3	<---	Word_of_Mouth	1.257	.088	14.333	***	a4_2
adapt1	<---	Adaptive_Behavior	1.000				
adapt2	<---	Adaptive_Behavior	.996	.072	13.746	***	a5_2
adapt3	<---	Adaptive_Behavior	1.135	.086	13.129	***	a6_2
adapt4	<---	Adaptive_Behavior	.965	.082	11.825	***	a7_2
adapt5	<---	Adaptive_Behavior	.919	.072	12.769	***	a8_2
servicape1	<---	Servicescape	1.000				
servicape2	<---	Servicescape	1.101	.111	9.881	***	a9_2
servicape3	<---	Servicescape	1.058	.107	9.885	***	a10_2
tolfail1	<---	Tolerance_to_failure	1.000				
tolfail3	<---	Tolerance_to_failure	1.096	.051	21.418	***	a12_2
tolfail4	<---	Tolerance_to_failure	1.044	.054	19.157	***	a13_2
tolfail2	<---	Tolerance_to_failure	1.153	.067	17.288	***	a11_2
delight3	<---	Customer_Delight	1.299	.197	6.588	***	a2_2

Standardized Regression Weights: Repeat -

			Estimate
Customer_Delight	<---	Adaptive_Behavior	.376
Customer_Delight	<---	Servicescape	.034
Word_of_Mouth	<---	Customer_Delight	.367
Tolerance_to_failure	<---	Customer_Delight	.505

Figure 5.32 Estimates Output for Repeat Group

If you look at the Adaptive Behavior to Customer Delight relationship across both groups, you will see that the first-time customers have a much stronger relationship than the repeat customers. Thus, we can conclude that adapting a service for a first-time customer has a significantly stronger influence on Customer Delight than with repeat customers. You can see the standardized regression weight for first-time customers (.650) is substantially stronger than with repeat customers (.376).

If you would like to test the next relationship of Servicescape to Customer Delight (labeled as b3), then go back into the "Constrain 1" model on the graphics page and replace the b1 constraint for a b3 constraint. After you do this, close the window and run the analysis again. The first step is to go to the output section and examine the model comparison output again. This will let you know if you even have a significant difference across the groups for this specific relationship.

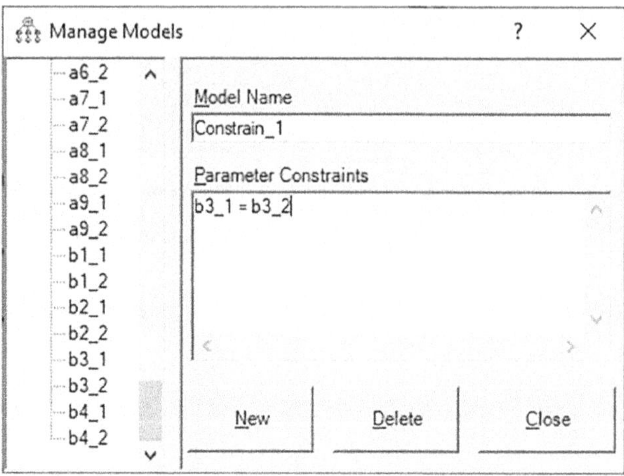

Figure 5.33 Servicescape to Delight Constrained

Amos Output

multiple group structural test e
Analysis Summary
Notes for Group
Variable Summary
Parameter Summary
Notes for Model
Estimates
Modification Indices
Minimization History
Model Fit
Model Comparison
Execution Time

Nested Model Comparisons

Assuming model Unconstrained to be correct:

Model	DF	CMIN	P	NFI Delta-1	IFI Delta-2	RFI rho-1	TLI rho2
Measurement weights	13	17.452	.179	.003	.003	-.001	-.001
Structural weights	17	58.690	.000	.010	.010	.006	.006
Structural covariances	20	141.823	.000	.023	.024	.020	.021
Structural residuals	23	168.912	.000	.028	.029	.023	.024
Measurement residuals	41	368.097	.000	.060	.063	.050	.053
Constrain_1	1	.663	.415	.000	.000	.000	.000

Figure 5.34 Model Comparison Results for Constrained Relationships

The results of this test (Constrain 1) show that there is no significant difference between the groups for the Servicescape to Customer Delight relationship ($\Delta\chi^2/1df = 0.663$). Thus, the groups are very similar in its relationship from Servicescape to Customer Delight. To fully understand the differences across the groups, you will need to individually constrain all the other relationships in the model. With a big model, this can be tedious to individually test each relationship, but it is necessary to see exactly where differences lie across the groups.

Another option instead of testing one relationship at a time is to create a separate model test for each structural relationship in the model. By doing this, you can see the differences across groups for every structural relationship at once instead of running the same test over and over. For instance, in our example, we have four structural relationships. We could create four additional model tests, and instead of calling the structural test "Constrain 1", we can call the test "b1 test", "b2 test", "b3 test", and "b4 test". With the b1 test, we would constrain b1_1 = b1_2. We would repeat this with each of the structural tests.

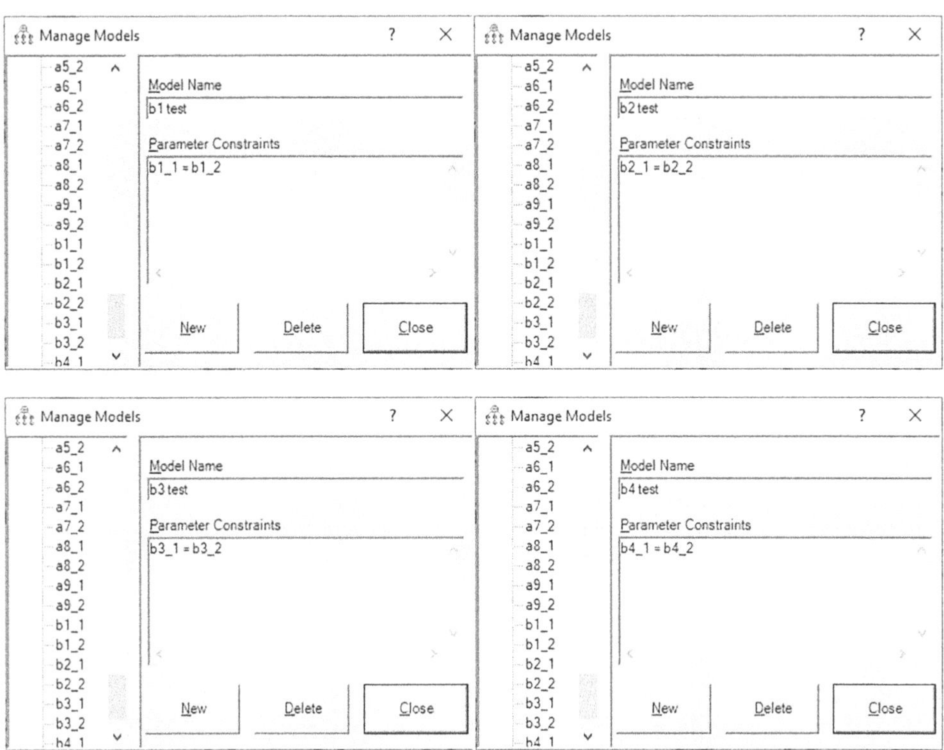

Figure 5.35 Constraining Every Structural Path Across the Groups

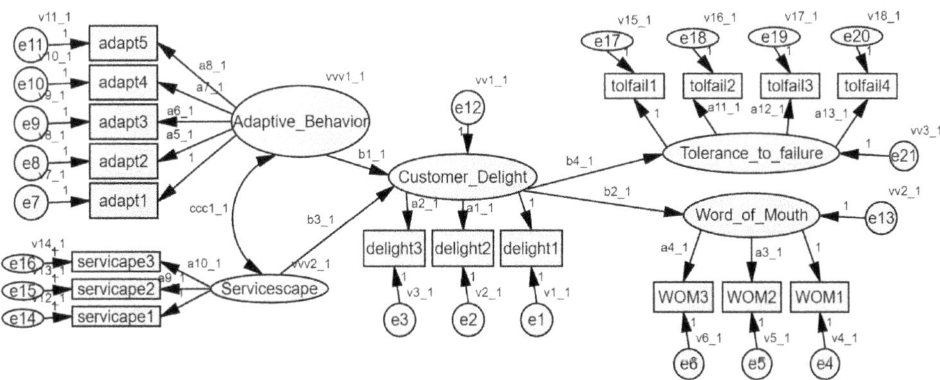

Figure 5.36 Example of a Full Structural Model Labeled

After creating a separate model test for each structural relationship, you are now ready to run your analysis and go back to the model comparison output. In the output, you can see the individual structural relationships that are tested (b1–b4).

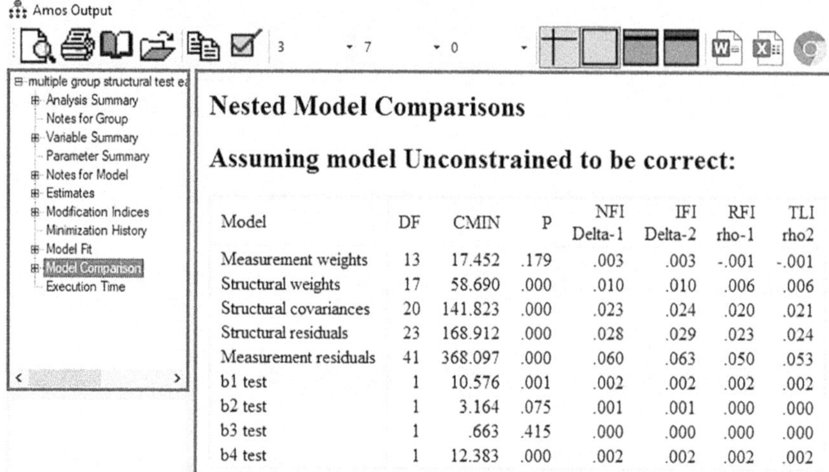

Nested Model Comparisons

Assuming model Unconstrained to be correct:

Model	DF	CMIN	P	NFI Delta-1	IFI Delta-2	RFI rho-1	TLI rho2
Measurement weights	13	17.452	.179	.003	.003	-.001	-.001
Structural weights	17	58.690	.000	.010	.010	.006	.006
Structural covariances	20	141.823	.000	.023	.024	.020	.021
Structural residuals	23	168.912	.000	.028	.029	.023	.024
Measurement residuals	41	368.097	.000	.060	.063	.050	.053
b1 test	1	10.576	.001	.002	.002	.002	.002
b2 test	1	3.164	.075	.001	.001	.000	.000
b3 test	1	.663	.415	.000	.000	.000	.000
b4 test	1	12.383	.000	.002	.002	.002	.002

Figure 5.37 Model Comparison Results With Individual Structural Paths Constrained

Now we can see all the structural relationships tested at once. We see that b1 and b4 are significantly different across the groups, but b2 and b3 are non-significant. As stated before, you would need to go back into the Estimates output to see which relationship is stronger or weaker across the groups.

Model Fit Summary

CMIN

Model	NPAR	CMIN	DF	P	CMIN/DF
Unconstrained	82	418.338	260	.000	1.609
Measurement weights	69	435.790	273	.000	1.596
Structural weights	65	477.028	277	.000	1.722
Structural covariances	62	560.161	280	.000	2.001
Structural residuals	59	587.249	283	.000	2.075
Measurement residuals	41	786.435	301	.000	2.613
b1 test	81	428.914	261	.000	1.643
b2 test	81	421.502	261	.000	1.615
b3 test	81	419.001	261	.000	1.605
b4 test	81	430.721	261	.000	1.650
Saturated model	342	.000	0		
Independence model	36	6131.469	306	.000	20.037

Figure 5.38 Model Fit Results for Multiple Group Analysis

One last thing we need to address is model fit statistics with our two group analysis. If we go into the Model Fit output, we do not get fit statistics for each group. With a two group analysis, AMOS will give you a model fit across the two groups. It examines how the model fits the data in the presence of both groups. In the output, we are only concerned with the "Unconstrained" model fit statistics. This is assessing model fit across both groups. All other model fit statistics are not that helpful in a two group analysis.

What if I Have More Than Two Groups in My Analysis?

Let's say you have three groups in your analysis and want to see if the groups are significantly different from one another. AMOS will let you set up a third group in the models window and will run the analysis across all three groups. The problem is that AMOS examines these potential differences *as a whole* across the groups. It will let you know if your relationships are significantly different across all three groups, but it will not break out where the differences are coming from. For instance, imagine you run the three group analysis and it says *all* of your relationships are significantly different across the groups. Those results may be that group 1 and 2 are highly different and group 3 is not really different from either group. The analysis will simply tell you if there is a difference across all the groups. The difference across group 1 and 2 may be so strong that the analysis states there is a difference across all groups. Consequently, setting up a third group in AMOS is not that beneficial and provides little information about where differences lie. To perform an analysis with three groups, you will have to perform multiple two group analyses. So with three groups, you would need to perform a two group analysis between groups 1 and 2, groups 1 and 3, and groups 2 and 3. This is the only way to see differences between the groups and also determine if specific relationships are different across the groups. It is not an ideal solution because it is labor intensive, but it will give you the answers you need until AMOS comes up with an update that will allow you to examine differences across more than two groups.

When I Try to Run My Structural Analysis, I Get an Error Message About My Matrix Not Being Positive Definite

You will get this message when you have a negative eigenvalue in your matrix. A non-positive matrix is often the result of multicollinearity. For instance, let's say you are examining the eating habits of children and you have two variables of "child height" and "child weight". The linear correlation between these two constructs might be nearly perfect and the covariance matrix would not be positive definite. You can also get a non-positive matrix with a small sample size simply due to sampling fluctuation. Lastly, you could also get a non-positive matrix if you have large amounts of missing data. With a simple mean replacement (which I don't recommend), this might be the cause of the non-positive matrix. To see if this is the problem, try another method of data replacement. More than likely, a non-positive matrix is multicollinearity between two constructs. If the problem is multicollinearity, you will need to remove covariances of error terms or, in the worst-case scenario, remove a structural relationship between the two highly correlated variables. Ultimately, you might even need to drop one of the problematic variables from the model if the issue persists.

Can I Correlate the Error Terms of Two Unobservable Constructs in a Full Structural Model?

The majority of the time, correlating error terms of unobservable constructs is not permissible, but there are some exceptions. If two constructs are systematically correlated with one another but not causally correlated, then you can correlate the error terms. This would be where two constructs are highly correlated with one another but not dependent on one another. Again, very rarely will you allow the error terms of unobservable constructs to covary.

How Do I Present the Results of My Two Group Analysis?

Here is a way you can present your results in a table format that will be easy for the reader to understand. In a two group analysis, you need to present the relationship strength (standardized coefficient) and t-values for each relationship. You also need to show the significance of the comparison across groups. This can be done by presenting the chi-square differences across both groups when that specific relationship is constrained.

Example 5.2:

Table 5.1 Multiple Group Difference Test

Hypothesized Relationships	*First-Time Customers*	*Repeat Customers*	*Group Differences*
	Standardized Estimates (t-values)	Standardized Estimates (t-values)	$\Delta\ \chi^2/1$ df
H1: Adaptive Behavior → Customer Delight	.650 (9.06)	.376 (4.00)	10.57*
H2: Servicescape → Customer Delight	.095 (1.47)	.034 (0.38)	0.66 n.s.
H3: Customer Delight → Positive Word of Mouth	.357 (4.95)	.367 (4.24)	3.16 n.s.
H4: Customer Delight → Tolerance for Future Failures	.386 (5.46)	.505 (5.62)	12.38*

Model Fit Across the Groups: χ^2 = 418.33, df = 260, p < .001, CFI = .97, IFI = .97, RMSEA = .03

Note: *= p < .001; n.s. = not significant

How Do I Search for Multivariate Outliers?

If your model fit is poor and the modification indices are providing no help, you might want to examine the multivariate outliers in your data set. A multivariate outlier is a collection of unusual or "out-of-the-norm" scores across multiple variables. Let's go back to the full structural model example. If you go into the Analysis Properties function and go to the "Output" tab, you will see an option on the right-hand side called "Test for normality and outliers". See Figure 5.39.

After making this selection, cancel out of the window and run the analysis. In the output, you need to select the option titled "Observations farthest from the centroid". The

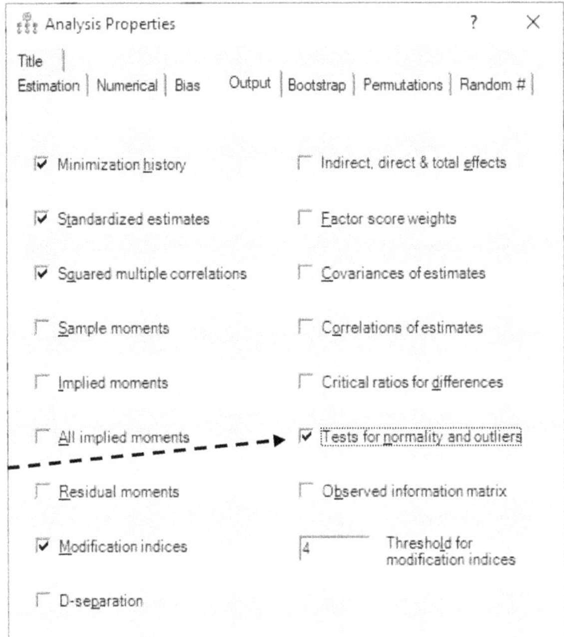

Figure 5.39 Request a Test for Normality and Outliers in the Analysis Properties Window

results will give a Mahalanobis d-square result. This statistic represents the squared distance from the centroid of a data set. The bigger the distance, the farther the item is from the mean distribution. AMOS also presents two additional statistics, p1 and p2. The p1 column shows the probability of any observation exceeding the squared Mahalanobis distance of that observation. The p2 column shows the probability that the largest squared distance of any observation would exceed the Mahalanobis distance computed. Arbuckle (2017) provides a heuristic for determining which observations may be outliers stating that small numbers in the p1 column are to be expected. Small numbers in the p2 column, on the other hand, indicate observations that are improbably far from the centroid under the hypothesis of normality. If you have p1 and p2 values that are less than .001, these are cases denoted as outliers. Figure 5.40 shows an example of the output when I ran the outlier analysis for the full structural model.

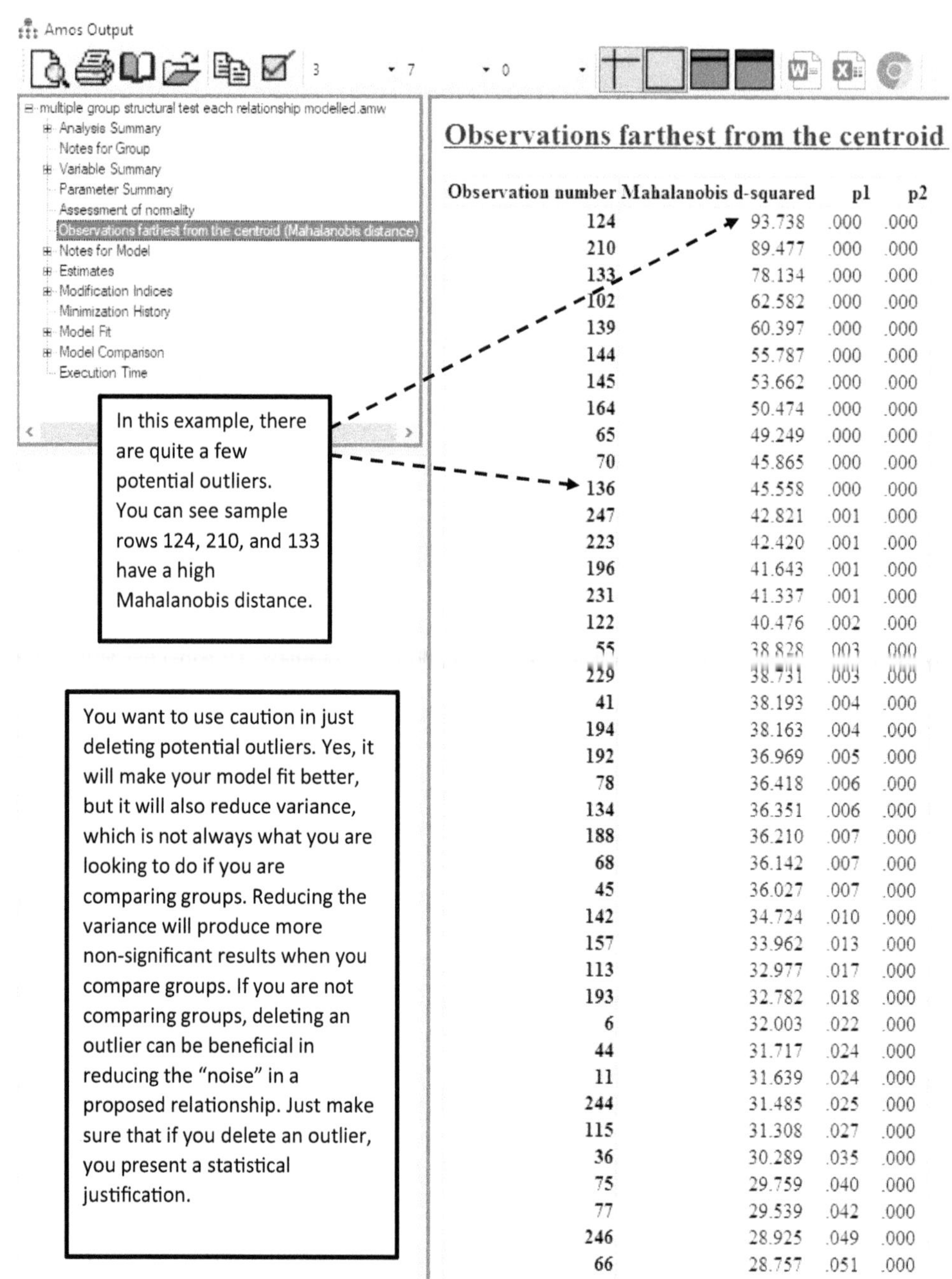

Observations farthest from the centroid

Observation number	Mahalanobis d-squared	p1	p2
124	93.738	.000	.000
210	89.477	.000	.000
133	78.134	.000	.000
102	62.582	.000	.000
139	60.397	.000	.000
144	55.787	.000	.000
145	53.662	.000	.000
164	50.474	.000	.000
65	49.249	.000	.000
70	45.865	.000	.000
136	45.558	.000	.000
247	42.821	.001	.000
223	42.420	.001	.000
196	41.643	.001	.000
231	41.337	.001	.000
122	40.476	.002	.000
55	38.828	.003	.000
229	38.731	.003	.000
41	38.193	.004	.000
194	38.163	.004	.000
192	36.969	.005	.000
78	36.418	.006	.000
134	36.351	.006	.000
188	36.210	.007	.000
68	36.142	.007	.000
45	36.027	.007	.000
142	34.724	.010	.000
157	33.962	.013	.000
113	32.977	.017	.000
193	32.782	.018	.000
6	32.003	.022	.000
44	31.717	.024	.000
11	31.639	.024	.000
244	31.485	.025	.000
115	31.308	.027	.000
36	30.289	.035	.000
75	29.759	.040	.000
77	29.539	.042	.000
246	28.925	.049	.000
66	28.757	.051	.000

Figure 5.40 Test of Outliers Using Mahalanobis Distance

How Do I Determine if My Data Is *Not* Normally Distributed (Non-Normal)?

In the Analysis Properties function, the output tab has a function called "Test for normality and outliers". After selecting this function, run the analysis. In the output, there is a link called "Assessment of normality". This output will give the minimum and maximum values for each variable along with the skewness and kurtosis of the data.

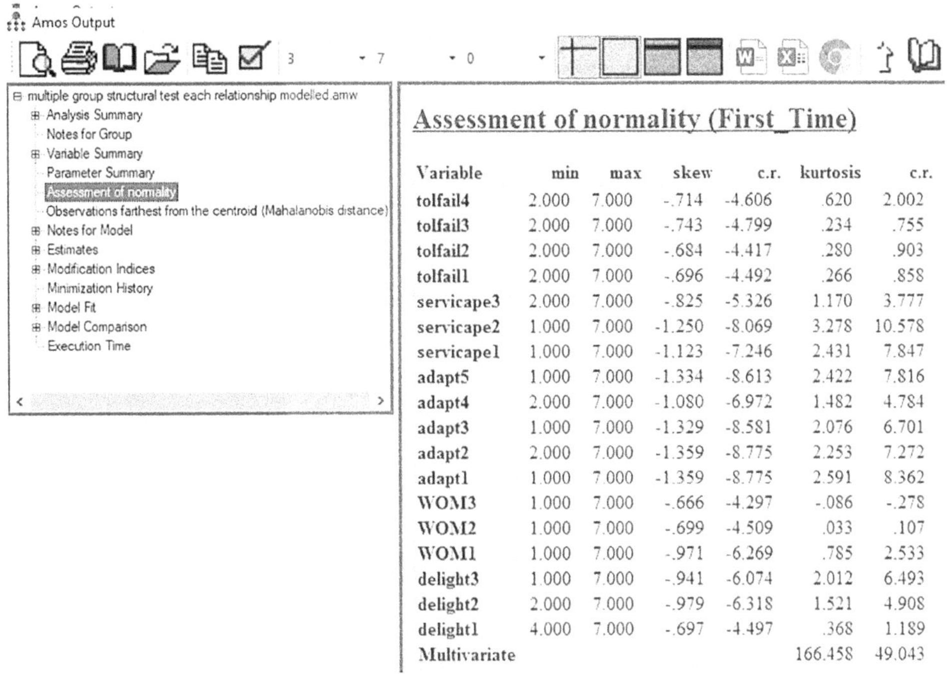

Assessment of normality (First_Time)

Variable	min	max	skew	c.r.	kurtosis	c.r.
tolfail4	2.000	7.000	-.714	-4.606	.620	2.002
tolfail3	2.000	7.000	-.743	-4.799	.234	.755
tolfail2	2.000	7.000	-.684	-4.417	.280	.903
tolfail1	2.000	7.000	-.696	-4.492	.266	.858
servicape3	2.000	7.000	-.825	-5.326	1.170	3.777
servicape2	1.000	7.000	-1.250	-8.069	3.278	10.578
servicape1	1.000	7.000	-1.123	-7.246	2.431	7.847
adapt5	1.000	7.000	-1.334	-8.613	2.422	7.816
adapt4	2.000	7.000	-1.080	-6.972	1.482	4.784
adapt3	1.000	7.000	-1.329	-8.581	2.076	6.701
adapt2	2.000	7.000	-1.359	-8.775	2.253	7.272
adapt1	1.000	7.000	-1.359	-8.775	2.591	8.362
WOM3	1.000	7.000	-.666	-4.297	-.086	-.278
WOM2	1.000	7.000	-.699	-4.509	.033	.107
WOM1	1.000	7.000	-.971	-6.269	.785	2.533
delight3	1.000	7.000	-.941	-6.074	2.012	6.493
delight2	2.000	7.000	-.979	-6.318	1.521	4.908
delight1	4.000	7.000	-.697	-4.497	.368	1.189
Multivariate					166.458	49.043

Figure 5.41 Assessment of Normality Result

Skew—is the tilt in the distribution. The more common type is right skew, where the smaller tail points to the right. Less common is left skew, where the smaller tail points left. Negative skew is left-leaning, positive skew right-leaning.

Kurtosis—is the peakedness of a distribution. Negative kurtosis indicates too many cases in the tails of the distribution. Positive kurtosis indicates too few cases in the tails.

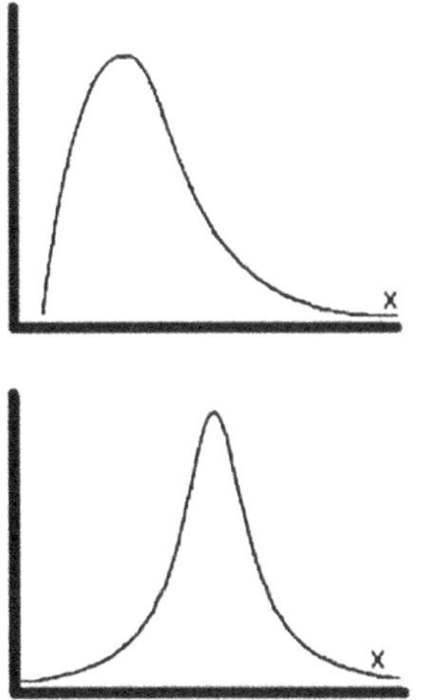

Figure 5.42 Examples of Skew and Kurtosis

Your data is still considered to be normal if your skew values range between −2 and +2. For kurtosis, the range is −10 to +10 to still be considered normally distributed. Based on our results, we can see that both the skew and kurtosis are in an acceptable range to be considered "normal".

If your data is non-normal, you can use another estimation method (GLM instead of maximum likelihood), which does not assume multivariate normality. A more common technique to address non-normality is to run your model with the bootstrap technique. Bootstrapping is a resampling procedure of the original data to determine if your estimated relationships fall within a confidence interval. For a detailed explanation on how to use bootstrapping to assess a model that has non-normal data, see page 287 in Chapter 10.

What if I Get an Error Message in the Analysis That Says "Iteration Limit Reached"?

The default iteration limit in the analysis function of AMOS is 50. If you get an error message that says the iteration limit has been reached and the analysis did not run to completion, it usually means that you are having an issue with the error term of an indicator or construct. You can increase the iteration limit to see if the analysis will run to completion. To do so, you need to go into the Analysis Properties function and then go to the "Numerical" tab at the top of the pop-up window. In the iteration limit option, you can change this to 1,000 and then run the analysis again. Even if the iteration limit was not reached, more than likely you still have a problem in the model. Often when you have a model that reaches an iteration limit of 50, increasing the iteration to 5,000 will still not fix the problem. If you receive an error message about the iteration limit, it is a good idea to go into the output and look at the "Notes for model" link. This will usually give you a good idea where the problem is in your model. If you have a negative error variance, this can cause the iteration limit message to appear. Your best bet is to find the specific indicator or construct that is having issues and remove error covariances or remove the indicator all together.

In My Opinion: Covariance-Based SEM vs. Variance-Based SEM

Variance-based or partial least squares SEM (PLS-SEM) has become more popular because of its flexibility and potential problem-solving capabilities to address the challenges that are present with covariance-based SEM. For instance, PLS-SEM can be used with small samples, uses weighted scores for greater explained variance, can handle non-normal data, and is best used for "exploratory" research. While at face value this seems like a great alternative to covariance-based SEM, if you look deeper, PLS-SEM is a problematic alternative. First, PLS-SEM does not calculate any model fit statistics. One of the primary advantages to SEM is the ability to assess a whole structural model. This is done via the fit statistics that compare the estimated covariance matrix to the observed covariance matrix. In PLS-SEM, model fit is ignored, which means model misspecification may be present, and it is simply not being assessed. This seems especially reckless with large and complex models.

Second, PLS-SEM is presented as an especially valuable technique for exploratory research compared to covariance-based SEM, which is confirmatory in nature (Peng and Lai 2012). Before a study takes place, the researcher should *a priori* have an idea of how the constructs should influence one another and what indicators are needed to capture the constructs. The theory used by the researcher should be the basis of the hypotheses between constructs. In essence, a study should either support or fail to support the hypotheses that were outlined *a priori*. This should be consistent whether you are using PLS-SEM or covariance-based SEM. PLS-SEM has been used as an "exploratory" attempt to understand a model but has been often categorized as data driven modeling (Ronkko et al. 2016) where relationships are simply added or subtracted based on the data and not theory. This data driven approach has the possibility of capitalizing on chance and would be advisable only if a second sample could confirm the findings of the first model.

Third, PLS-SEM allows the researcher to vary the weights of indicators in a construct. This is done to increase the reliability of the construct, but recent research has found that it has no relative impact on a construct's reliability and often inflates correlations between constructs (Ronkko et al. 2016). Fourth, PLS-SEM is lauded as a program that will work with small samples compared to covariance-based SEM that requires a larger sample. The appropriate sample size for a SEM model should be based on the complexity of the model and not the software. Sample size should be based on the necessary power to find an effect. For those looking for more information on this topic, McQuitty (2004) does a good job of outlining the necessary sample size needed based on complexity of the model. A simple model with few degrees of freedom could be grossly underpowered with a small sample. A small sample can bias results with a covariance-based SEM approach, but previous research has found the PLS-SEM was just as problematic in regards to a small sample size bias (Chumney 2013; Reinartz et al. 2009).

Fifth, PLS-SEM uses Ordinary Least Squares (OLS) regression, which has the same assumptions about normality of data as covariance-based SEM. Previous research has even noted that PLS has no more benefits of handling non-normal data than other covariance-based programs (Dijkstra 2015). Lastly and most concerning, PLS-SEM is widely known to produce inconsistent and biased estimations (Ronkko et al. 2016). The research by Reinartz et al. (2009) found that estimations were biased from 6% to 19% based on the strength of the path estimate. Overall, the evidence against using PLS-SEM is strong and convincing. In my opinion, I would encourage you to stick to a covariance-based SEM approach.

Definitions of Constructs Used in Examples for This Chapter:

Adaptive Behavior: customer's perception that an employee adapted/modified their normal job performance to meet their needs. This adaptation can be through verbal interaction, service performance, or meeting special requests. Construct was measured with a 7-point Likert scale of Strongly Disagree to Strongly Agree.

Customer Delight: customer's profoundly positive emotional state resulting from expectations being exceeded to a surprising degree. Construct was measured with a 7-point Likert scale of Strongly Disagree to Strongly Agree.

Positive Word of Mouth: customer's intention to spread positive information to others about a previous experience. Construct was measured with a 7-point Likert scale of Strongly Disagree to Strongly Agree.

Servicescape: customer's perceptions about the built environment that the service takes place, which could include atmosphere, furniture, and other things related to the environment such as displays, colors, and cleanliness. Construct was measured with a 7-point Likert scale of Strongly Disagree to Strongly Agree.

Tolerance to Future Failures: likelihood that a customer is understanding of a service failure with future interactions. Construct was measured with a 7-point Likert scale of Strongly Disagree to Strongly Agree.

First-Time Customer (Group)—customers who are experiencing the service for the first time.

Repeat Customer (Group)—customers who have previous experience with the service.

Highlights of the Chapter:

1. Path analysis examines the relationships between constructs via composite variables. These composite variables do not include the measurement properties of the construct.
2. AMOS will let you use a correlation or a covariance matrix as the data input in designing a model. The correlation/covariance matrix has to be in a specific format outlined in the chapter, or AMOS will not be able to read the data.
3. A full structural model examines the relationships between constructs but also includes the measurement indicators for each variable.
4. The specification search function can be used to see how your model fit is adjusted for better or for worse when you "trim" relationships from the model. This function will look at all possible combinations with relationships included or deleted in the model.
5. Alternative models allow you to show the superiority of your model compared to other rival models. The replacing rule method is a good way to conceptualize an alternative model for testing.
6. Control variables let you account for potential influences in your model relationships. Including a control variable is done by adding an observable variable that has a direct relationship to all the dependent variables in the model.
7. A two group analysis examines if structural relationships are significantly different across the groups. The significance testing is done through a chi-square difference test.
8. An error message of non-positive definite matrix means you have a negative eigenvalue in your matrix. This is often caused by multicollinearity issues.
9. Multivariate outliers can be assessed by calculating the Mahalanobis distance, or distance from the centroid of the data set.
10. Non-normality of the data can be determined by the skew and kurtosis of the data. Skew is the tilt of the distribution, and kurtosis is the peakedness of the distribution.
11. The iteration limit in AMOS is 50. If you get an error message that says the iteration limit has been reached and the analysis did not run to completion, you most likely have

a problem with an error term of an indicator. You can raise the iteration limit to a higher number, but this will often not fix the underlying problem.

References

Arbuckle, James L. (2017), *IBM SPSS AMOS 25 User's Guide*, IBM Corporation.

Chumney, F.L. (2013), *Structural Equation Models With Small Samples: A Comparative Study of Four Approaches*. Doctoral dissertation, University of Nebraska-Lincoln.

Dijkstra, Theo K. (2015), "PLS and CB SEM, a Weary and a Fresh Look at Presumed Antagonists" (keynote address), Presented at the 2nd International Symposium on PLS Path Modeling. Sevilla, Spain. Retrieved from: www.researchgate.net/publication/277816598_PLS_CB_SEM_a_weary_and_a_fresh_look_at_presumed_antagonists_keynote_address.

Edwards, Jeffrey R. (2008), "Seven Alternative Model Specifications in Structural Equation Modeling: Facts, Fictions, and Truth", in Charles E. Lance and Robert J. Vandenberg (eds.) *Statistical and Methodological Myths and Urban Legends*. New York, NY: Taylor & Francis Group.

MacCallum, Robert C., Duane T. Wegener, Bert N. Uchino, and Leandre R. Fabrigar. (1993), "The Problem of Equivalent Models in Applications of Covariance Structure Analysis", *Psychological Bulletin*, 114 (1), 185–199.

McQuitty, Shaun. (2004), "Statistical Power and Structural Equation Models in Business Research", *Journal of Business Research*, 57 (2), 175–183.

Peng, David Xiaosong and Fujun Lai. (2012), "Using Partial Least Squares in Operation Management Research: A Practical Guideline and Summary of Past Research", *Journal of Operations Management*, 30 (6), 467–480.

Reinartz, Werner, Michael Haenlein, and Jorg Henseler. (2009), "An Empirical Comparison of the Efficacy of Covariance-Based and Variance-Based SEM", *International Journal of Research in Marketing*, 26 (4), 332–344.

Ronkko, Mikko., Cameron N. McIntosh, John Antonakis, and Jeffrey R. Edwards. (2016), "Partial Least Squares Path Modeling: Time for Some Serious Second Thoughts", *Journal of Operations Management*, 47–48 (November), 9–27.

Chapter 6

Mediation

Introduction to Mediation

Up to this point, we have focused on how one construct can directly influence another construct in a SEM model. Let's now examine how the influence between two constructs may take an indirect path through a third variable called a mediator. In these situations, the third variable will intervene on the influence of the two constructs (Hair et al. 2009). In testing if "mediation" or the presence of a mediator is in a model, you need to understand some of the terminology that is used, such as direct effect, indirect effect, and total effects. A direct effect is simply a direct relationship between an independent variable and a dependent variable. An indirect effect is the relationship that flows from an independent variable to a mediator and then to a dependent variable. The term total effect is the combined influence of the direct effect between two constructs and the indirect effect flowing through the mediator.

Mediation can take numerous forms in a model. You can have what is called full mediation (also called indirect only mediation) where the direct effect between two constructs is non-significant, but an indirect effect through a mediator does have a significant relationship. Partial mediation is another form that mediation can take. This is where the direct effect between two constructs is significant, and so is the indirect effect through a mediator. Lastly, you can have complementary and competitive mediation. Complementary mediation is where the direct effect and the indirect effect have a similar influence in regard to directionality. For instance, the direct effect may a have positive influence, and the indirect effect has a positive influence as well. A competitive mediation is where you have different directionality between the direct effect and indirect effect. The direct effect might have a negative influence, but the indirect effect might have a positive influence. With this type of mediation, the presence of the mediator can change the directionality of the influence.

Let's look at a simple mediation model to give some context to our discussion. We have an independent variable (we will label it "X") that has a proposed direct influence on a dependent variable (we will call it "Y"). We will also propose that the influence of X to Y might flow through a mediator variable (we will call it "M"). We have three variables in this simple model. We are going to examine the direct effect of X to Y and also the indirect effect of X to M to Y. The indirect effect is calculated by taking the product of the X to M relationship and the M to Y relationship. We will simply multiply the regression coefficients for each of those relationships to get the indirect effect.

From a statistical standpoint, you will often see the paths in a mediation model referred to as the "A path", the "B path", and the "C path". The commonly referred-to A path is the relationship from the independent variable to the mediator (X to M). The B path is used to refer to the relationship from the mediator to the dependent variable (M to Y). The C path is used when referring to the direct path from the independent variable to the dependent variable (X to Y). This is common vernacular when discussing mediation, and you need to take note of these parameter labels. To help clarify our discussion, the different types of mediation are represented in graphical form. See Example 6.1.

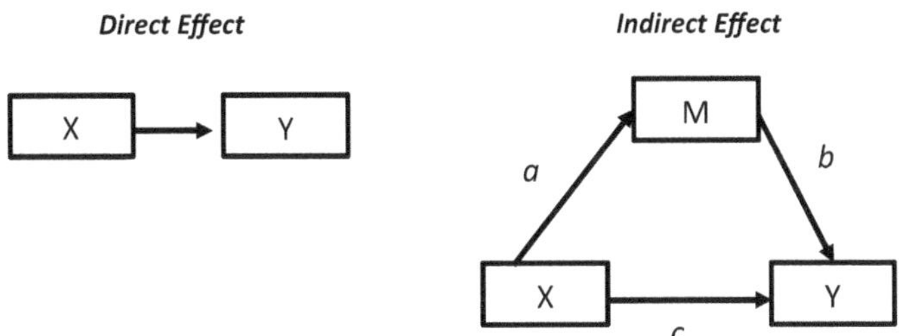

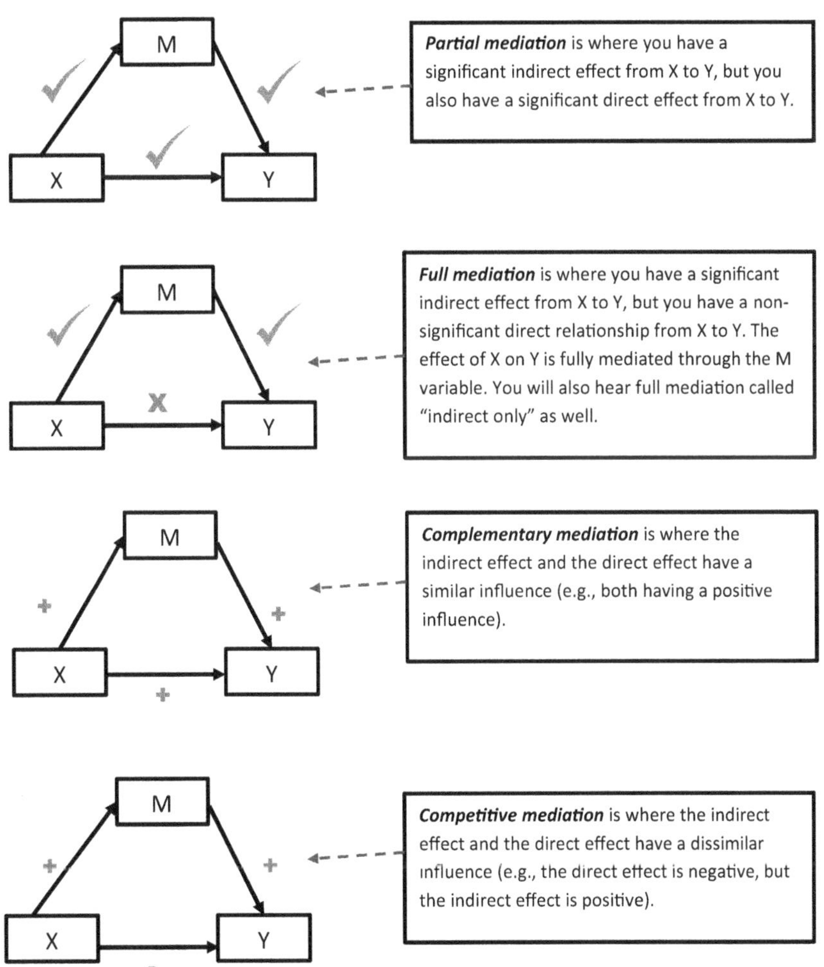

The indirect effect can take different forms:
M
X
Y
Partial mediation is where you have a significant indirect effect from X to Y, but you also have a significant direct effect from X to Y.
M
X
Y
Full mediation is where you have a significant indirect effect from X to Y, but you have a non-significant direct relationship from X to Y. The effect of X on Y is fully mediated through the M variable. You will also hear full mediation called "indirect only" as well.
M
+
+
X
Y
+
Complementary mediation is where the indirect effect and the direct effect have a similar influence (e.g., both having a positive influence).
M
+
+
X
Y
-
Competitive mediation is where the indirect effect and the direct effect have a dissimilar influence (e.g., the direct effect is negative, but the indirect effect is positive).

How to Test for Mediation

The research by Baron and Kenny (1986) was one of the fundamental frameworks for how to test mediation. Over the years, research has refined their initial work on testing mediation. I think it is a worthy pursuit to discuss where mediation testing started and where it has progressed today. Baron and Kenny (1986) stated there were four steps to testing mediation:

Step 1—make sure that X has a significant influence on Y (C path; absent of M at this point).
Step 2—test that X has a significant influence on M (A path; no Y included); this needs to be significant for mediation to be present.
Step 3—test that X has an influence on M and that M has an influence on Y (A and B paths); both paths need to be significant.
Step 4—test the direct and indirect relationships simultaneously and determine if and what type of indirect effect is present (A, B, and C paths are all being evaluated).

The Baron and Kenny method was based on finding the unstandardized coefficients for each relationship and then determining significance using a Sobel test. As research has progressed, this method of testing mediation has changed, and Sobel testing has been rejected as a valid means of testing mediation. For a good discussion on why Sobel testing should no longer be used in assessing mediation, see Zhao et al. (2010). Even the initial steps outlined by Baron and Kenny have changed as well. The first step that the C path needs to be significant is not a requirement anymore. Indirect effects can be present even if a non-significant C path is initially found. The justification is based on the idea that there are suppressor effects that prevent the C path from being significant, but the indirect effect is still present. The idea that the A path and the B path have to individually be significant has been rejected as well. Hayes (2018) notes that an indirect effect is the product of the A and B paths, and statistical significance of either the A path or the B path is not a requirement for mediation.

The revised method is now concerned with assessing the indirect effect by examining the product of the A path and the B path while controlling for the direct effect of the C path. Since the Sobel test is flawed for this type of test, the more accepted approach in mediation testing is to use a bootstrap technique to determine significance. A bootstrap technique treats your data sample like a pseudo-population and then takes a random sample with replacement to determine if your indirect effect falls within a confidence interval. You can request the number of bootstrap samples to increase the accuracy of predictions (the higher, the better). I find that a bootstrap sample of 5,000 is sufficiently large, and any greater number of samples will produce very little difference. Note that with a bootstrap sample, the computer program will generate a completely different sample every time you run the analysis. With 5,000 samples, the differences will be small, but the exact numbers in the results will not be the same if you run the analysis twice. To control for this, you can ask AMOS to always use the same "seed" number, which will produce the exact same results if you run the bootstrap analysis again. Having a set "seed number" is a good idea because it keeps you from getting slightly different results every time you run the analysis for the exact same model. I will discuss how to set the seed number in AMOS later in the chapter on page 194. Lastly, you need to be aware that when you sample with replacement, the same case can appear in more than one generated data set. Overall, the bootstrap technique has become the accepted method because of its ease and accuracy of results.

Let's look at an example in AMOS of a mediation test. Using the full structural model example from earlier, we want to examine if the construct of Adaptive Behavior has an indirect effect through Customer Delight to the construct of Positive Word of Mouth. Notice that I am including a direct path from Adaptive Behavior to Positive Word of Mouth. This will allow us to see what type of mediation is present in the analysis.

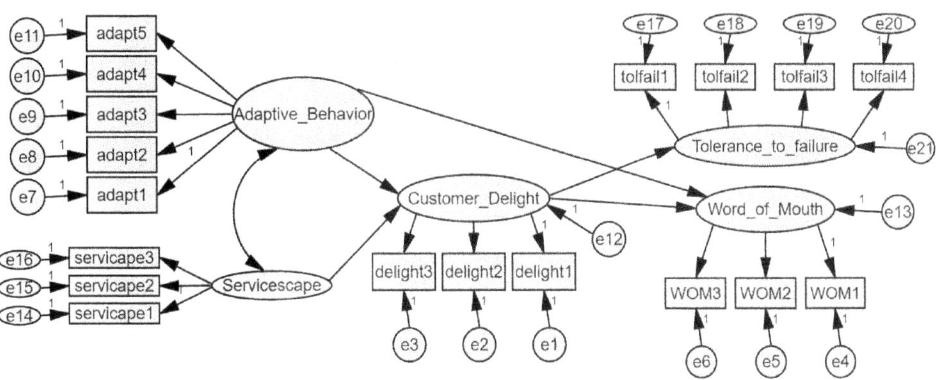

Figure 6.1 Mediation Test of Adaptive Behavior Through Customer Delight to Positive Word of Mouth

To determine if the indirect effect of Adaptive Behavior to Positive Word of Mouth is significant, we need to request from AMOS the indirect, direct, and total effects in the output. This will give all possible indirect effects in the model. To do this, select the Analysis Properties button [icon], and when the Analysis Properties pop-up window appears, go to the Output tab at the top. On that tab, you will see at the top right an option for "Indirect, direct, and total effects". Select this option.

Next, we need to request a bootstrap analysis in AMOS. To do this, go to the bootstrap tab at the top of the Analysis Properties window. On that tab will be a checkbox called "Perform bootstrap"; click that box. AMOS will initially give you a default number of

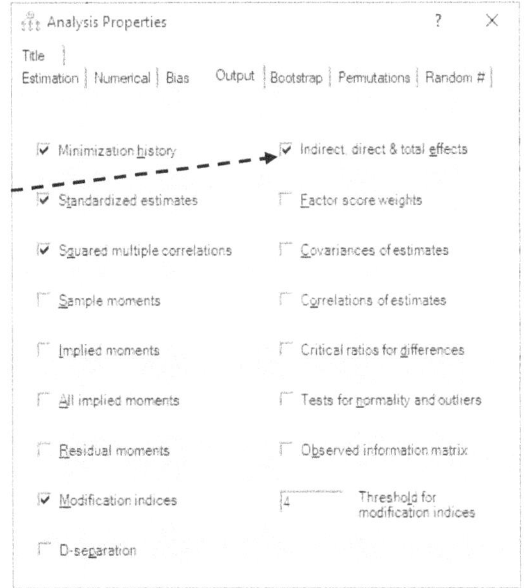

Figure 6.2 Request Indirect Effect in Analysis Properties Window

200 samples. This is way too small. Change the number of samples to 5,000. You will also need to select the "Bias-corrected confidence intervals" checkbox. AMOS will default a 90% confidence interval, but significance in most research is at the .05 level, so you need to change this to a 95% confidence level. I typically leave all the other options on this page blank. See Figure 6.3. After selecting the option of indirect effects in the output and asking AMOS to perform a bootstrap, you can cancel out of the Analysis Properties window and then run the analysis.

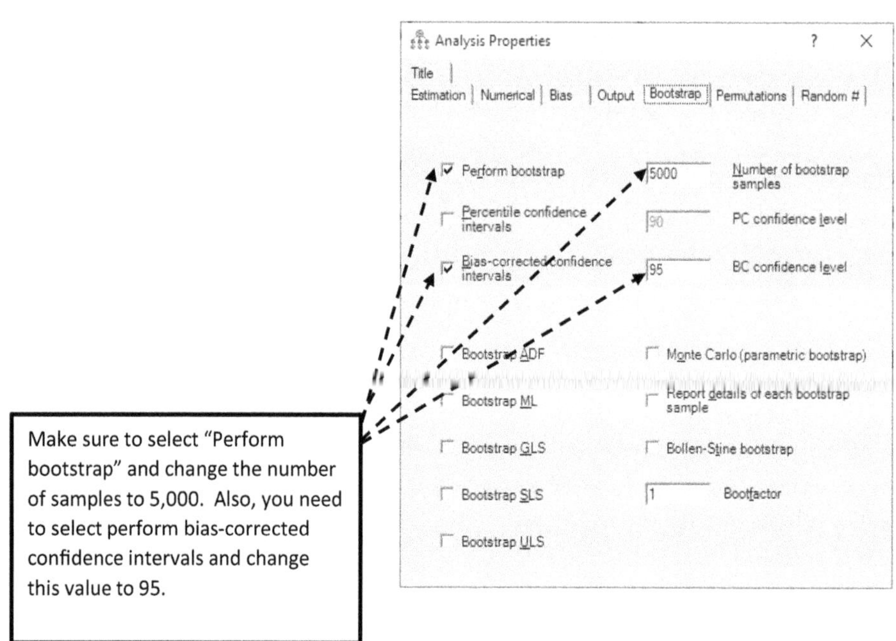

Figure 6.3 Request a Bootstrap and Confidence Intervals

Let's look at the output to determine if mediation is present. In the Estimates link, you want to select the "Matrices" link. This will let you see the total effects, direct effects, and indirect effects for each relationship in your model. We want to select the indirect effects. AMOS will give you the option to examine the unstandardized or standardized indirect effect. With most mediation analyses, you will see the unstandardized indirect effect reported. If you were looking to compare indirect effects within a model, you could easily do so with the standardized indirect effects, but normally, the unstandardized indirect effects are reported. In the “Indirect Effects” tab, you will see all the possible indirect effects in your model. We are concerned only with the relationship of Adaptive Behavior to Positive Word of Mouth through Customer Delight. In our model, we have only one possible mediator from Adaptive Behavior to Positive Word of Mouth, so the indirect effect listed must be through the mediator of Customer Delight. (If you have more than one mediator, I will discuss this on page 182.) If we look at the intersection of Adaptive Behavior and Positive Word of Mouth, the unstandardized indirect effect is .333. Again, to calculate an indirect effect, it is a very simple process. The indirect effect is the product of the A path and the B path. The unstandardized regression coefficient for the relationship from Adaptive Behavior to Customer Delight (A path) was .450. The unstandardized regression coefficient for the relationship from Customer Delight to Positive Word of Mouth (B path) was .740. Multiplying these two values together gives us the indirect effect (.450*.740 =.333).

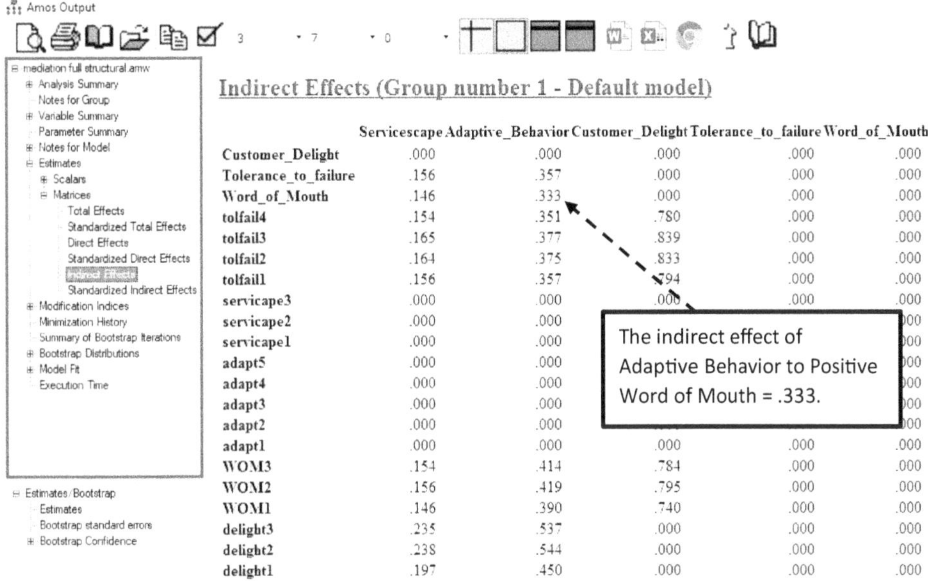

Indirect Effects (Group number 1 - Default model)

	Servicescape	Adaptive_Behavior	Customer_Delight	Tolerance_to_failure	Word_of_Mouth
Customer_Delight	.000	.000	.000	.000	.000
Tolerance_to_failure	.156	.357	.000	.000	.000
Word_of_Mouth	.146	.333	.000	.000	.000
tolfail4	.154	.351	.780	.000	.000
tolfail3	.165	.377	.839	.000	.000
tolfail2	.164	.375	.833	.000	.000
tolfail1	.156	.357	.794	.000	.000
servicape3	.000	.000	.000	.000	.000
servicape2	.000	.000	[illegible]	[illegible]	[illegible]
servicape1	.000	.000	[illegible]	[illegible]	[illegible]
adapt5	.000	.000	[illegible]	[illegible]	[illegible]
adapt4	.000	.000	[illegible]	[illegible]	[illegible]
adapt3	.000	.000	[illegible]	[illegible]	[illegible]
adapt2	.000	.000	[illegible]	[illegible]	[illegible]
adapt1	.000	.000	.000	.000	.000
WOM3	.154	.414	.784	.000	.000
WOM2	.156	.419	.795	.000	.000
WOM1	.146	.390	.740	.000	.000
delight3	.235	.537	.000	.000	.000
delight2	.238	.544	.000	.000	.000
delight1	.197	.450	.000	.000	.000

Figure 6.4 Indirect Effects Results in Matrices Link

We now know the indirect effect, but we still need to know if the indirect effect is significant and if it falls within the 95% confidence interval generated by our bootstrap. The indirect effects tab will give us the indirect effect but nothing else. We need to go to the bootstrap analysis section to find the other information. On the left-hand side, in a box below the output links is a section called "Estimates/Bootstrap". Under that link will be another option called "Bias-corrected percentile method". This is where we will find all the information we are looking for in regards to confidence intervals and significance levels. With the confidence intervals, you are going to get an upper bound and lower bound estimate of the indirect effect based on your bootstrap of 5,000 samples. If the range for the upper and lower bound estimates do not cross over zero, then the indirect effect is considered significant. AMOS will also give you a p-value if you need to show the specific level of significance in the bootstrap test.

Note, you have to be in the "Indirect effects" link at the top of the window to even access the bootstrap analysis in the bottom window. If you are not on the indirect effects tab at the top, the bootstrap analysis will be grayed out and inaccessible.

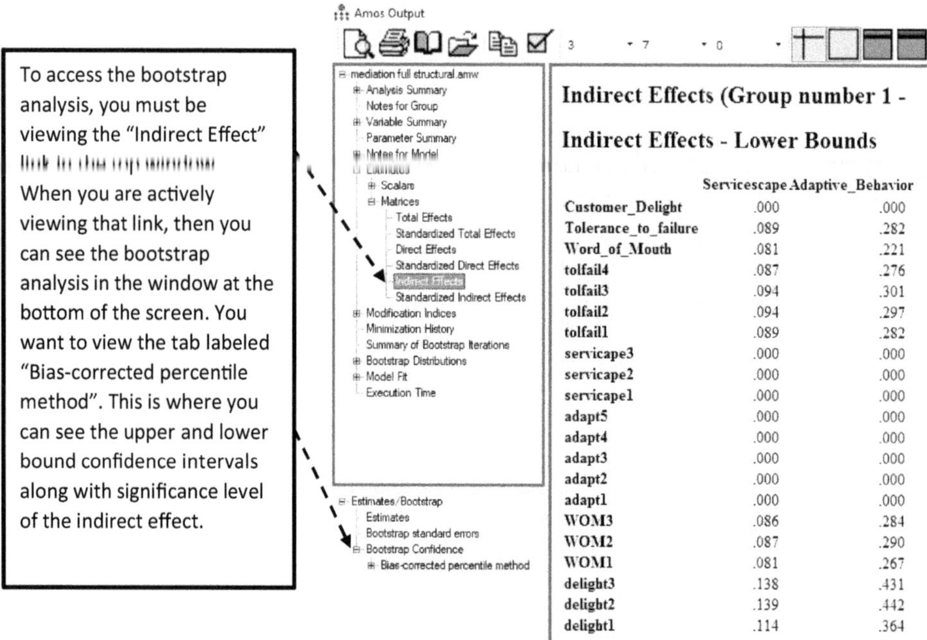

	Servicescape	Adaptive_Behavior
Customer_Delight	.000	.000
Tolerance_to_failure	.089	.282
Word_of_Mouth	.081	.221
tolfail4	.087	.276
tolfail3	.094	.301
tolfail2	.094	.297
tolfail1	.089	.282
servicape3	.000	.000
servicape2	.000	.000
servicape1	.000	.000
adapt5	.000	.000
adapt4	.000	.000
adapt3	.000	.000
adapt2	.000	.000
adapt1	.000	.000
WOM3	.086	.284
WOM2	.087	.290
WOM1	.081	.267
delight3	.138	.431
delight2	.139	.442
delight1	.114	.364

Figure 6.5 Accessing Confidence Intervals in Results

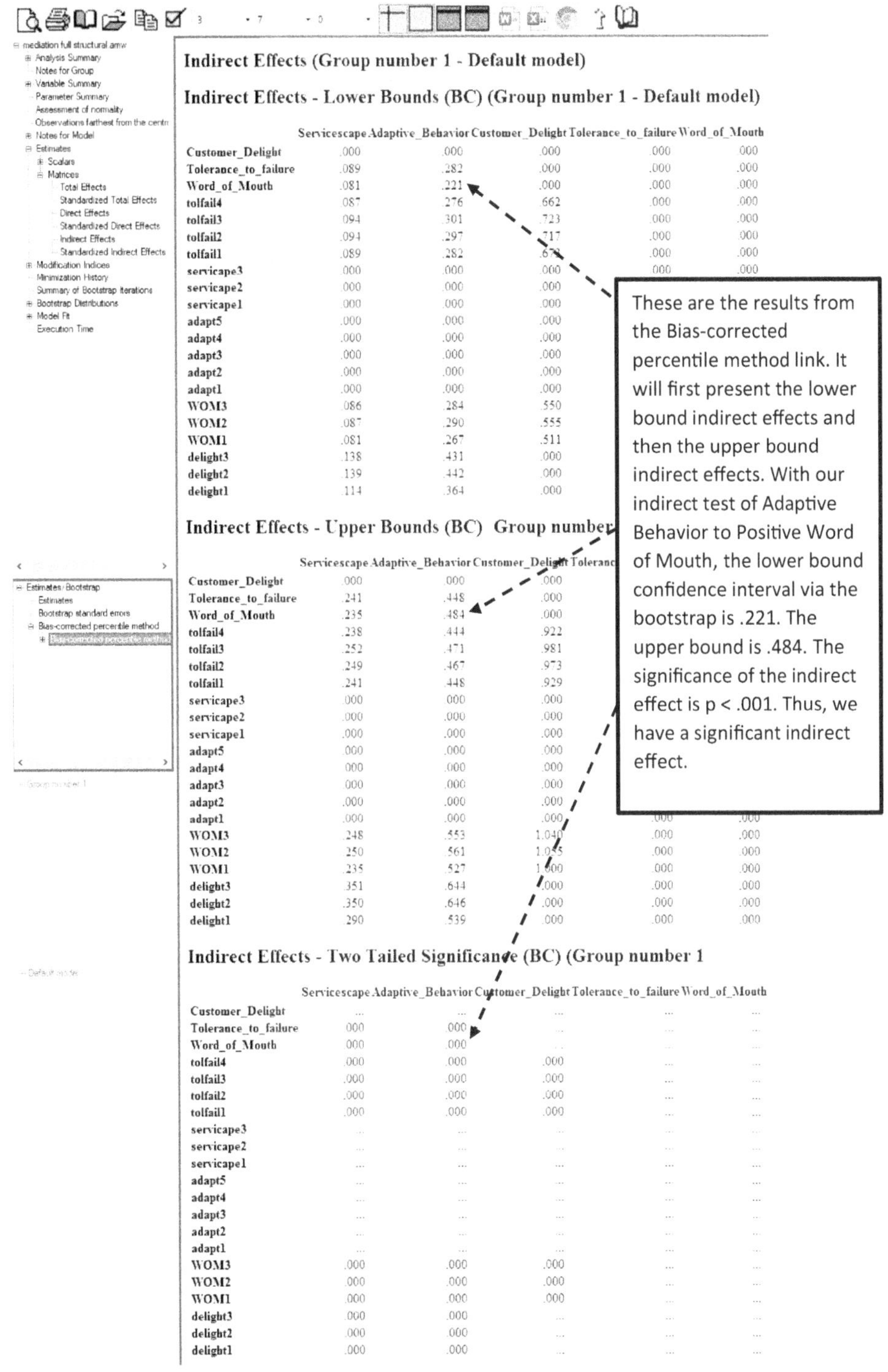

Indirect Effects (Group number 1 - Default model)

Indirect Effects - Lower Bounds (BC) (Group number 1 - Default model)

	Servicescape	Adaptive_Behavior	Customer_Delight	Tolerance_to_failure	Word_of_Mouth
Customer_Delight	.000	.000	.000	.000	.000
Tolerance_to_failure	.089	.282	.000	.000	.000
Word_of_Mouth	.081	.221	.000	.000	.000
tolfail4	.087	.276	.662	.000	.000
tolfail3	.094	.301	.723	.000	.000
tolfail2	.094	.297	.717	.000	.000
tolfail1	.089	.282	.67[illegible]	.000	.000
servicape3	.000	.000	.000	.000	.000
servicape2	.000	.000	.000		
servicape1	.000	.000	.000		
adapt5	.000	.000	.000		
adapt4	.000	.000	.000		
adapt3	.000	.000	.000		
adapt2	.000	.000	.000		
adapt1	.000	.000	.000		
WOM3	.086	.284	.550		
WOM2	.087	.290	.555		
WOM1	.081	.267	.511		
delight3	.138	.431	.000		
delight2	.139	.442	.000		
delight1	.114	.364	.000		

Indirect Effects - Upper Bounds (BC) Group number

	Servicescape	Adaptive_Behavior	Customer_Delight	Toleranc	
Customer_Delight	.000	.000	.000		
Tolerance_to_failure	.241	.448	.000		
Word_of_Mouth	.235	.484	.000		
tolfail4	.238	.444	.922		
tolfail3	.252	.471	.981		
tolfail2	.249	.467	.973		
tolfail1	.241	.448	.929		
servicape3	.000	.000	.000		
servicape2	.000	.000	.000		
servicape1	.000	.000	.000		
adapt5	.000	.000	.000		
adapt4	.000	.000	.000		
adapt3	.000	.000	.000		
adapt2	.000	.000	.000		
adapt1	.000	.000	.000	.000	.000
WOM3	.248	.553	1.040	.000	.000
WOM2	.250	.561	1.0[illegible]5	.000	.000
WOM1	.235	.527	1.[illegible]00	.000	.000
delight3	.351	.644	.000	.000	.000
delight2	.350	.646	.000	.000	.000
delight1	.290	.539	.000	.000	.000

Indirect Effects - Two Tailed Significance (BC) (Group number 1

	Servicescape	Adaptive_Behavior	Customer_Delight	Tolerance_to_failure	Word_of_Mouth
Customer_Delight	...	...	...	...	...
Tolerance_to_failure	.000	.000	...	...	...
Word_of_Mouth	.000	.000	...	...	...
tolfail4	.000	.000	.000	...	...
tolfail3	.000	.000	.000	...	...
tolfail2	.000	.000	.000	...	...
tolfail1	.000	.000	.000	...	...
servicape3	...	...	...	...	...
servicape2	...	...	...	...	...
servicape1	...	...	...	...	...
adapt5	...	...	...	...	...
adapt4	...	...	...	...	...
adapt3	...	...	...	...	...
adapt2	...	...	...	...	...
adapt1	...	...	...	...	...
WOM3	.000	.000	.000	...	...
WOM2	.000	.000	.000	...	...
WOM1	.000	.000	.000	...	...
delight3	.000	.000	...	...	...
delight2	.000	.000	...	...	...
delight1	.000	.000	...	...	...

Figure 6.6 Upper and Lower Confidence Intervals Along With Significance

Based on these results, we can conclude that Adaptive Behavior has a significant indirect effect on Positive Word of Mouth through the construct of Customer Delight. We know that the indirect effect is significant, but now we need to assess what type of mediation is present. Is it full mediation or partial mediation through the Customer Delight construct? To accomplish this, we need to examine the C path, or the direct path, from Adaptive Behavior to Positive Word of Mouth in the "Estimates" link in the output. We can see that Adaptive Behavior has a non-significant relationship to Positive Word of Mouth (p = .455). This means that the influence of Adaptive Behavior on Positive Word of Mouth is fully mediated through the construct of Customer Delight.

Amos Output

			Estimate	S.E.	C.R.	P	Label
Customer_Delight	<---	Adaptive_Behavior	.450	.035	12.779	***	
Customer_Delight	<---	Servicescape	.197	.041	4.847	***	
Word_of_Mouth	<---	Customer_Delight	.740	.106	7.005	***	
Tolerance_to_failure	<---	Customer_Delight	.794	.060	13.150	***	
Word_of_Mouth	<---	Adaptive_Behavior	.057	.077	.747	.455	
delight1	<---	Customer_Delight	1.000				
delight2	<---	Customer_Delight	1.209	.045	26.627	***	
delight3	<---	Customer_Delight	1.194	.050	23.846	***	
WOM1	<---	Word_of_Mouth	1.000				
WOM2	<---	Word_of_Mouth	1.074	.042	25.774	***	
WOM3	<---	Word_of_Mouth	1.061	.046	23.087	***	
adapt1	<---	Adaptive_Behavior	1.000				
adapt2	<---	Adaptive_Behavior	.975	.030	32.661	***	
adapt3	<---	Adaptive_Behavior	.999	.035	28.818	***	
adapt4	<---	Adaptive_Behavior	.996	.034	29.028	***	
adapt5	<---	Adaptive_Behavior	.929	.033	28.572	***	

Figure 6.7 Examining the Direct Effect in Mediation Test

Since we have only one mediator, we can easily assess if a significant indirect effect is from Adaptive Behavior to the other dependent variable of Tolerance to Future Failures. We need to change the C path, or the direct effect, from Adaptive Behavior to Tolerance to Future Failures, and then we can run the exact same indirect, direct, and total effects analysis as we did before.

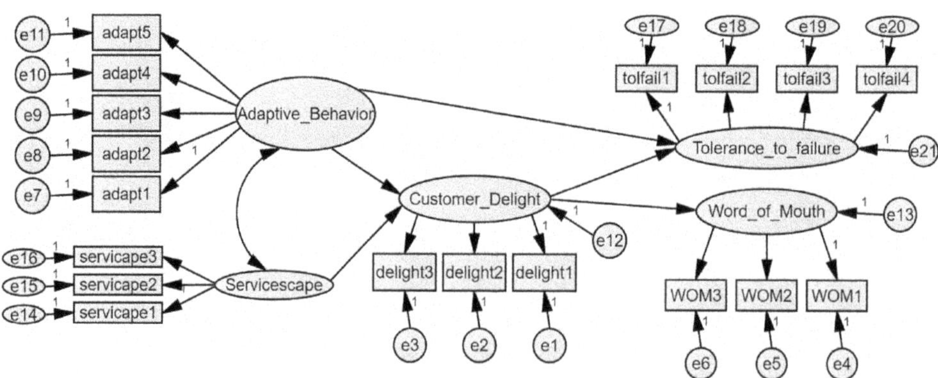

Figure 6.8 Mediation Test From Adaptive Behavior Through Customer Delight to Tolerance to Future Failures

The indirect effect of Adaptive Behavior to Tolerance to Future Failures is .313. Next, let's look at the same output for the confidence intervals generated by our bootstrap. The lower bound confidence interval is .231 and the upper bound is .426. Since this confidence interval did not cross zero, we know that the indirect effect is significant. Examining the two-tail significance test in the output, the indirect effect is significant at the p < .001 level.

The last thing we need to do is assess the C path or direct effect from Adaptive Behavior to Tolerance to Future Failures to determine the type of mediation that is present. In the output of the Estimates link (Figure 6.11), you will see that the direct relationship from Adaptive Behavior to Tolerance to Future Failures has a non-significant relationship (p. = .119). Thus, we have a significant indirect effect and non-significant direct effect, meaning that Customer Delight fully mediates the relationship of Adaptive Behavior to Tolerance to Future Failures. If you have only one potential mediator in your model, AMOS will give you all possible indirect effects, which is a nice function and can save you time especially if you have a large number of independent and dependent variables.

Indirect Effects

	Servicescape	Adaptive_Behavior
Customer_Delight	.000	.000
Tolerance_to_failure	.137	.313
Word_of_Mouth	.156	.356

Figure 6.9 Indirect Effects Results for Adaptive Behavior to Tolerance to Future Failures

Lower Bound Estimate

Indirect Effects - Lower Bounds

	Servicescape	Adaptive_Behavior
Customer_Delight	.000	.000
Tolerance_to_failure	.072	.231
Word_of_Mouth	.088	.267

Upper Bound Estimate

Indirect Effects - Upper Bounds

	Servicescape	Adaptive_Behavior
Customer_Delight	.000	.000
Tolerance_to_failure	.225	.426
Word_of_Mouth	.240	.457

Figure 6.10 Upper and Lower Bound Estimates of Confidence Interval

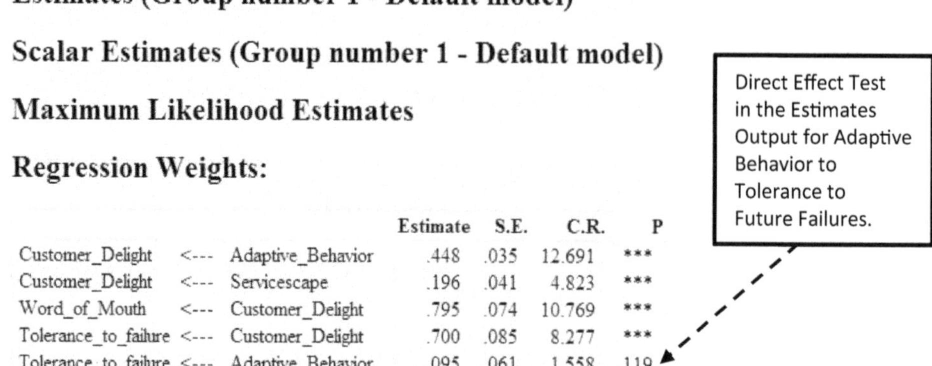

Estimates (Group number 1 - Default model)

Scalar Estimates (Group number 1 - Default model)

Maximum Likelihood Estimates

Regression Weights:

			Estimate	S.E.	C.R.	P
Customer_Delight	<---	Adaptive_Behavior	.448	.035	12.691	***
Customer_Delight	<---	Servicescape	.196	.041	4.823	***
Word_of_Mouth	<---	Customer_Delight	.795	.074	10.769	***
Tolerance_to_failure	<---	Customer_Delight	.700	.085	8.277	***
Tolerance_to_failure	<---	Adaptive_Behavior	.095	.061	1.558	.119

Direct Effect Test in the Estimates Output for Adaptive Behavior to Tolerance to Future Failures.

Figure 6.11 Direct Effect From Adaptive Behavior to Tolerance to Future Failures

How Do I Report the Results of My Mediation Test?

Your mediation test should always compliment the findings from the structural analysis. The structural results will let the reader know the specifics of the A path and B path. When presenting the mediation part of the analysis, it is a good idea to present the indirect effect, the lower and upper bound confidence intervals, the significance of the indirect effect, and the direct effect. By including all of this information, the reader can fully evaluate the mediation properties of your results.

Example 6.2:

Table 6.1 Test for Mediation Using a Bootstrap Analysis With a 95% Confidence Interval

Relationships	*Direct Effect*	*Indirect Effect*	*Confidence Interval*		*p-value*	*Conclusion*
			Low	*High*		
Adaptive Behavior → Customer Delight → Positive Word of Mouth	.057 (0.74)	.333	.221	.484	< .001	Full Mediation
Adaptive Behavior → Customer Delight → Tolerance for Future Failures	.095 (1.55)	.313	.231	.426	< .001	Full Mediation

Note: Unstandardized coefficients reported. Values in parentheses are t-values. Bootstrap sample = 5,000 with replacement.

Can I Use a Correlation Matrix or Summary Data to Test Mediation in AMOS?

Up to this point, we have tested mediation using the raw data. AMOS will allow you to test mediation with a correlation/covariance matrix as your input, but it will require some additional steps. For simplicity, let's use our existing example, except we are going to test for mediation with a path model that has composite variables. If we are looking to test that Adaptive Behavior has a significant indirect effect to Positive Word of Mouth, we need to make sure the summary data is in a format that AMOS can read. For a review of how to use a correlation or covariance matrix as input data, see Chapter 5, page 133.

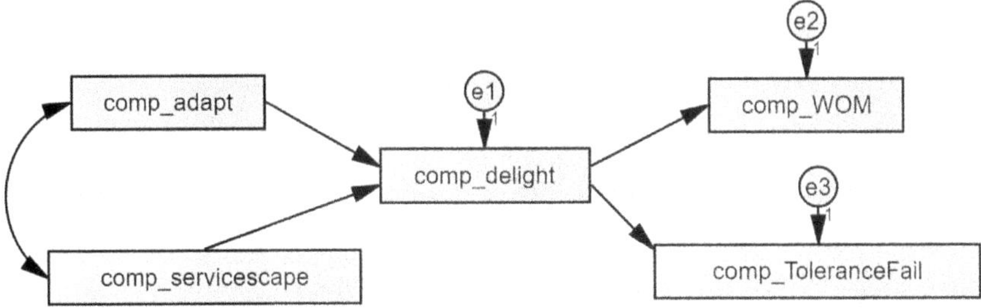

Figure 6.12 Mediation Test With a Simple Path Model

Once you have formatted and saved your summary data, you need to make sure AMOS has the new data file as the input. In the Analysis Properties window, select the "Indirect, direct, and total effects" option again. With the Bootstrap tab, select "Perform Bootstrap" and change the number of bootstraps to 5,000. Select the "Bias-corrected confidence intervals" and change the confidence interval to 95. Since you do not have raw data, you also need to select "Monte Carlo (parametric) bootstrap" option. With a Monte Carlo bootstrap, the bootstrap sample's means, variances, and covariances will match the summary data input. In essence, it runs a simulation that will match the summary data provided. If you do not select the Monte Carlo option, AMOS will give you an error message and say it cannot run the bootstrap without the raw data. After making these selections, you are ready to run the analysis. The format for the output with the Monte Carlo simulation will look exactly like the output for the mediation test that used the raw data. Thus, you will need to go to the same place in the output to find your results.

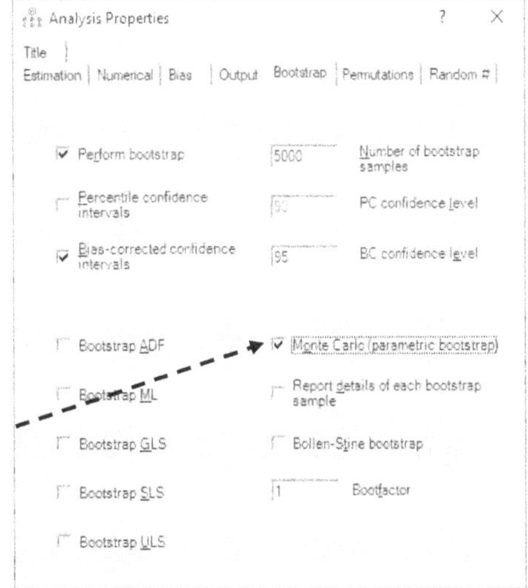

Figure 6.13 Monte Carlo Simulation Needed for Bootstrap With Summary Data Input

What if I Have Multiple Mediators in My Model?

As stated earlier, when you request indirect effects in AMOS, this will give you all the possible indirect effects in your model. If you have a single mediator, this function is quite handy, but if you have multiple possible mediators in a model, this function can be problematic. The reason for this problem is AMOS will assess the indirect effect from an independent to a dependent variable through all possible mediators. The program will try to examine the total indirect effect though all possible mediators. This type of analysis is not that helpful because mediation really needs to be assessed with each individual mediator instead of the collective group. To find the indirect effect between two variables when there are numerous possible mediators, we have to use a different method from how we assessed mediation in the previous example.

To examine the individual relationships in a multiple mediator model, AMOS has a function called "estimands" that will allow you greater flexibility in the analysis of complex models. The estimands function is syntax based. There are no icons or drop-down menus we can use to accomplish our task of examining a specific indirect effect when multiple mediators are present. Thus, we are going to use the syntax-based estimands function to examine a specific indirect effect within a larger model.

Let's go back to our earlier mediation example of Adaptive Behavior having an indirect effect to the constructs of Positive Word of Mouth and Tolerance to Future Failures through the mediator of Customer Delight. Now let's add a second mediator called "Satisfaction". This is a measure of how simply satisfied a customer was in the experience. Hence, we want to see if Adaptive Behavior by an employee has a stronger indirect effect to the dependent variables through Customer Delight than simple Satisfaction with the experience. This is called a parallel mediation test because there are parallel paths from the independent to the dependent variable.

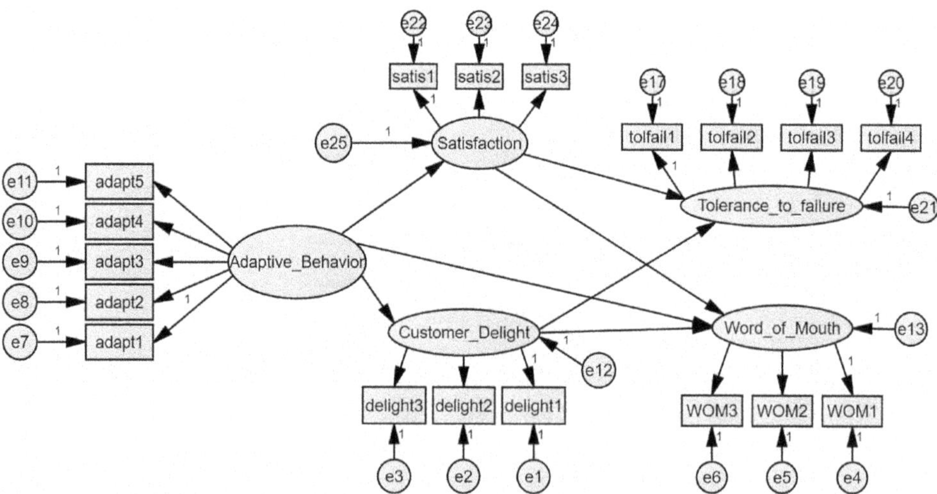

Figure 6.14 Multiple Mediator Model in AMOS

When you have multiple mediators, AMOS will require you to denote what specific relationships you are concerned with in testing for the indirect effect. To do this, you need to label all the indirect parameters for the specific relationships you are concerned with in the model. You will need to label the A path and the B path, and, if you so desire, the C path, but this path is not necessary since it is a direct effect in the model. Saying that, I like to label the C path, too. Ultimately, we are labeling these parameters so AMOS knows which relationships you want to isolate and examine. Let's say we want to initially explore the indirect effect of Adaptive Behavior to Positive Word of Mouth through the construct of Customer Delight, but now the construct of Satisfaction is included in the model. First, you are going to label the A path in the mediation test by double clicking on the arrow from Adaptive Behavior to Customer Delight and bringing up the Object Properties for that specific arrow. (You can right click on the arrow and select Object Properties, too.) You need to label this specific parameter. You can call it anything you want, but I am going to label it "A_Path" just to make it easier to interpret when we get the final output.

The A_Path label will be in the regression weight field of the Object Properties window. Note that you cannot have spaces in the name you give the parameter. I am going to select the arrow from Customer Delight to Positive Word of Mouth and label that relationship "B_Path". Now you are ready to use the estimands function. At the very bottom left-hand side of the screen will be a default field of AMOS stating "not estimating any user-defined estimand". If you click on this message, AMOS will prompt you to either select an estimand or define a new estimand.

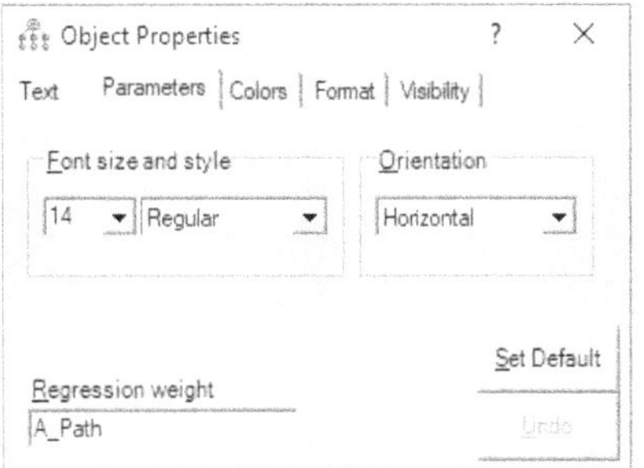

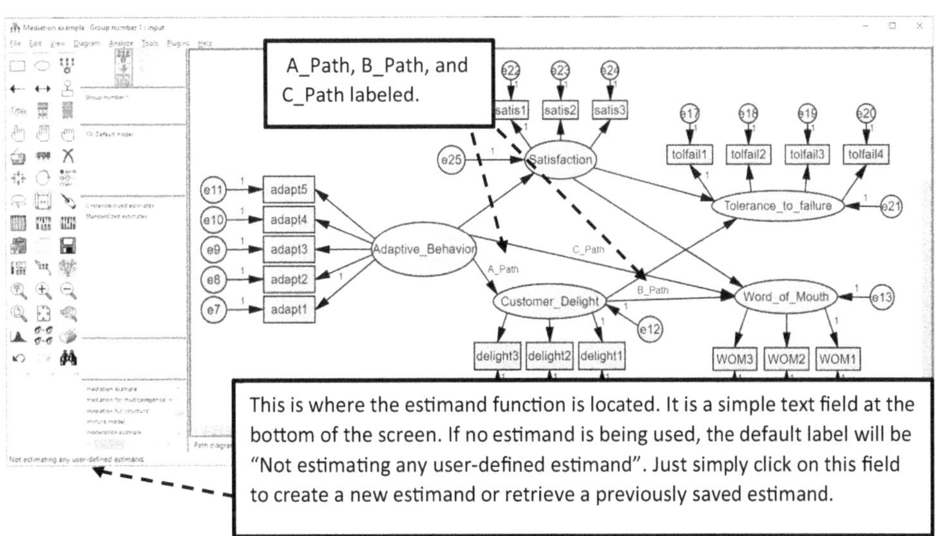

Figure 6.15 Labeling Parameters for Mediation Testing

Let's choose to define a new estimand option. The estimand pop-up window will appear. In the syntax window, we need to specify how AMOS should analyze the indirect effect. Remember that earlier, I said the indirect effect is the A path multiplied by the B path. Let's call our new indirect analysis simply "indirecttest", and then you will put an equal sign and specify the labels for the paths of the indirect effect you want to test. We are going to multiply the path labeled "A_Path" by the path labeled "B_Path". See Figure 6.16. After you have specified the function in the window, you need to make sure you do not have any syntax errors. You will need to select the check syntax icon in the window. If you have any errors, they will be listed in the description section at the bottom. If no errors are present, the description section will say "Syntax is OK'.

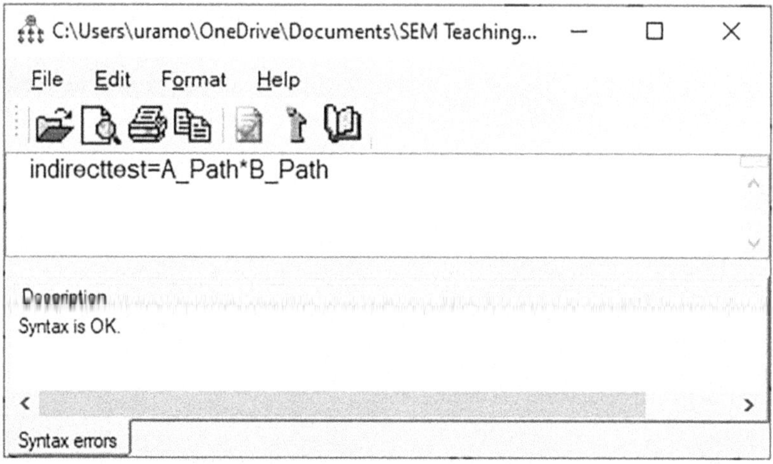

Figure 6.16 Using Estimand Function to Calculate Indirect Effect

Please note that an estimand function will work only with a bootstrap analysis. If you do not have a bootstrap analysis selected in the analysis options, an error warning window will appear. It is a good idea to save this estimand function so that you do not have to type in the syntax relationships again for future mediation tests. If you are trying to retrieve a previously saved estimand, you will choose the "select estimand" function instead of defining a new estimand. After saving the estimand, you can close out the pop-up window and run the analysis . Let's go to the output and see the results (Figure 6.17). In the Estimates link, you need to choose the "Scalars" option. Within this link, you will see an option titled "User-defined estimands"; select this option. The results presented will be the indirect effect for the specific relationship you denoted in the estimand function. The indirect effect of Adaptive Behavior to Positive Word of Mouth through Customer Delight is .384. Again, this is just isolating a specific indirect effect in a model where multiple mediators are present. Note that the indirect effect is different with the multiple mediator model (.384) compared to the single mediator model we tested earlier (.333) even though we are testing the same relationship. The indirect effect with the multiple mediator model is now accounting for differences with the second mediator (satisfaction) included in the model.

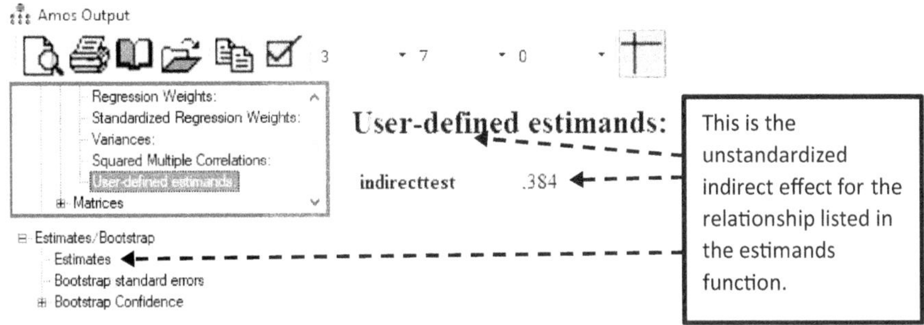

Figure 6.17 User Defined Estimand Test of Indirect Effects

With the "User-defined estimands" option selected, you can now go to the bootstrap analysis and selected the "Bias-corrected percentile method" option. This will give you the indirect effect, confidence interval, and significance for the indirect effect. Note that if you do not have the "User-defined estimands" option selected, all the bootstrap analysis will be grayed out.

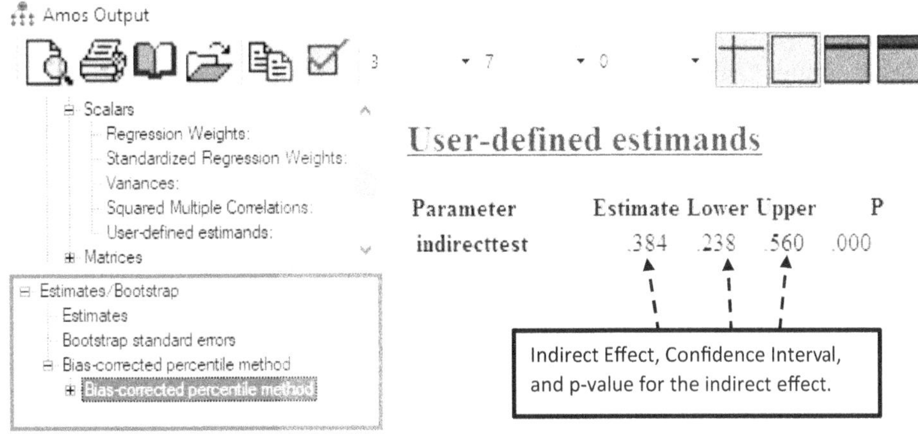

Figure 6.18 Bias-Corrected Percentile Method Results for Indirect Effect Test

A positive and significant indirect effect was found. We now need to assess the C path, or the direct relationship from Adaptive Behavior to Positive Word of Mouth, to determine what type of mediation is present. The results from the Estimates output (Figure 6.19) notes that Adaptive Behavior does not have a significant relationship to Positive Word of Mouth ($p = 0.482$), so we have full mediation. Take note in the Estimates output that our labels for each relationship are displayed in the output as well.

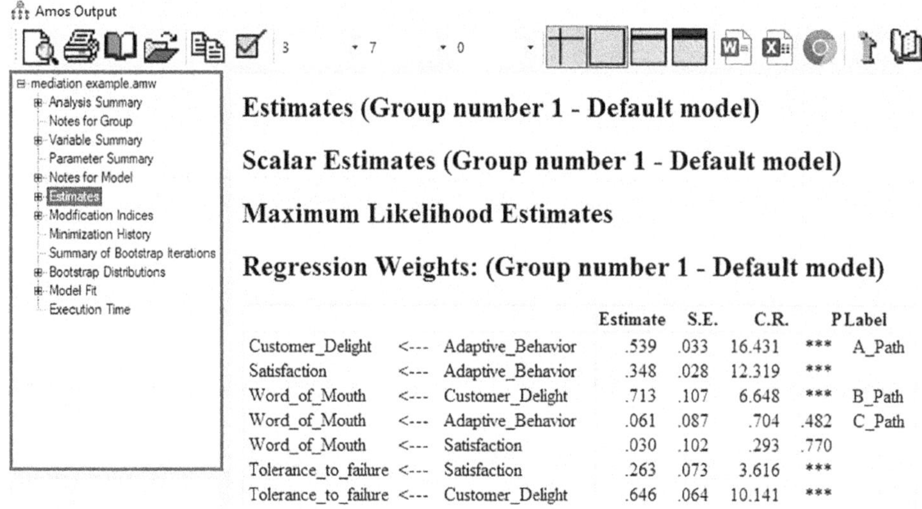
Amos Output

mediation example.amw
Analysis Summary
Notes for Group
Variable Summary
Parameter Summary
Notes for Model
Estimates
Modification Indices
Minimization History
Summary of Bootstrap Iterations
Bootstrap Distributions
Model Fit
Execution Time

Estimates (Group number 1 - Default model)

Scalar Estimates (Group number 1 - Default model)

Maximum Likelihood Estimates

Regression Weights: (Group number 1 - Default model)

			Estimate	S.E.	C.R.	P	Label
Customer_Delight	<---	Adaptive_Behavior	.539	.033	16.431	***	A_Path
Satisfaction	<---	Adaptive_Behavior	.348	.028	12.319	***	
Word_of_Mouth	<---	Customer_Delight	.713	.107	6.648	***	B_Path
Word_of_Mouth	<---	Adaptive_Behavior	.061	.087	.704	.482	C_Path
Word_of_Mouth	<---	Satisfaction	.030	.102	.293	.770	
Tolerance_to_failure	<---	Satisfaction	.263	.073	3.616	***	
Tolerance_to_failure	<---	Customer_Delight	.646	.064	10.141	***	

Figure 6.19 Examining the Direct Effect in Mediation Test

We have found the indirect effect from Adaptive Behavior to Positive Word of Mouth through Customer Delight, but now let's examine the indirect relationship from Adaptive Behavior through the Satisfaction construct to Positive Word of Mouth. The first thing you need to do is label the indirect paths when Satisfaction is the mediator. You can handle this two ways: (1) you can delete the existing parameter names and label the relationship from Adaptive Behavior to Satisfaction as the "A_Path" and the relationship from Satisfaction to Positive Word of Mouth as "B_Path"; or (2) you can label the parameters a completely new name that is unique to only those paths. For instance, you could label the relationship from Adaptive Behavior to Satisfaction as "X_Path" and the relationship from Satisfaction to Positive Word of Mouth as "Y_Path".

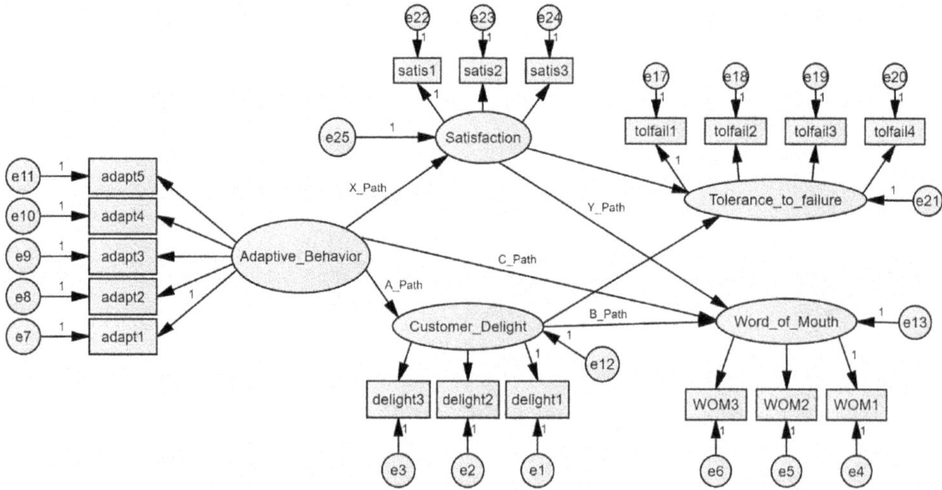

Figure 6.20 Labeling the Paths of Both Mediators

Choose which method works best for you. The advantage to labeling all the relationships unique names is it allows you to see multiple indirect effects simultaneously using the estimands function. Let's look at an example where we can isolate and analyze multiple indirect effects through the estimand function.

First, we need to go back into your estimands function and select "edit" estimand. This will bring up the existing estimand function. The first indirect test through Customer Delight was called "Indirecttest". We need to come up with another name for the indirect test going through Satisfaction. Let's call that indirect test "Sat_indirecttest". For this test, we will write the formula for the indirect effect like we did with the previous test. With this test, we multiply the "X_Path" by the "Y_Path" to get the indirect effect. Make sure you run the syntax check again. If the description says "Syntax is OK", save the new function and then cancel out of the window. If you have a problem with the syntax, this is primarily because the labels in the estimand function are not matching the labels in the model (or the labels are completely missing from the model). After saving the estimand, you are now ready to run the analysis again.

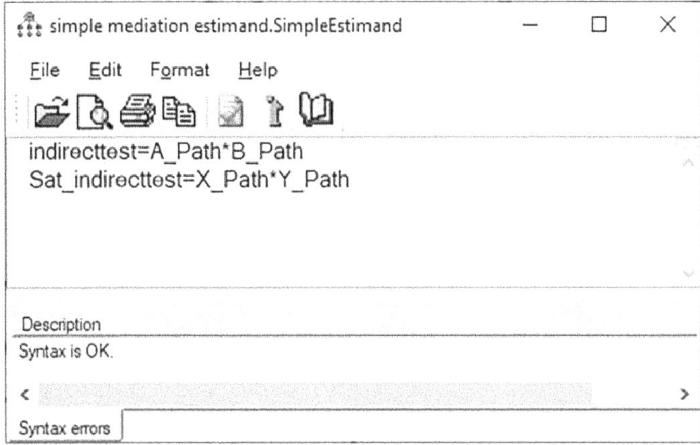

Figure 6.21 Estimand Function to Calculate Each Indirect Effect

In the output, go back to the User-defined estimands option and then select the Bias-corrected percentile method. You can see now that both the "indirecttest" and "Sat_indirecttest" are listed (Figure 6.22). This gives us the indirect effect for each test along with a confidence interval and p-value. The indirect effect through the Satisfaction construct is non-significant with a p-value of .804. Notice how the confidence interval in the nonsignificant indirect effect crosses zero. Again, these results are the unstandardized coefficients. If you need to see the standard error for each indirect test, there is an option listed above the Bias-corrected percentile method option that is simply called bootstrap standard errors. Selecting this option will allow you to see the standard errors for each indirect test you specified.

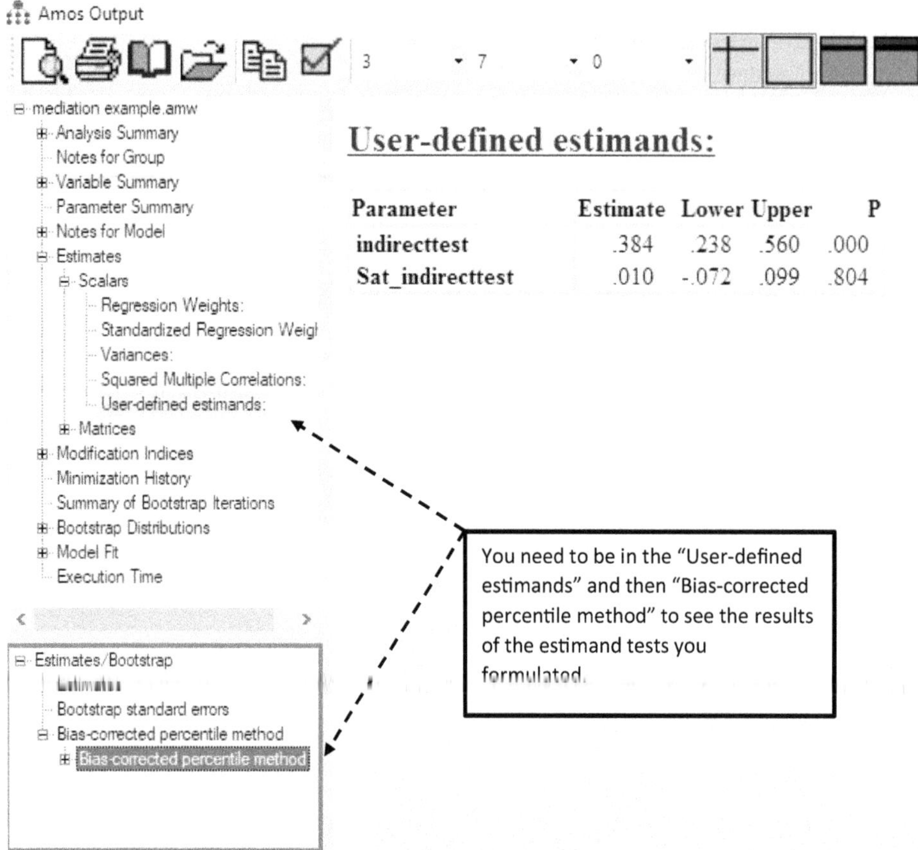

Parameter	Estimate	Lower	Upper	P
indirecttest	.384	.238	.560	.000
Sat_indirecttest	.010	-.072	.099	.804

Figure 6.22 Indirect Effects and Confidence Intervals for Both User-Defined Functions

Based on these results, we can conclude that the influence of Adaptive Behavior to Positive Word of Mouth flows only through customers' perceptions of delight. If you have more relationships to test, you can label those parameters and make adjustments in the estimands function. By using the estimands function, you have the ability to isolate an indirect effect even when multiple mediators are present.

How Do I Test Serial Mediation?

Serial mediation, also called chain mediation, is where the influence of the independent variable flows through multiple mediators before impacting the dependent variable. Serial mediation often takes place where the first mediator will have a direct relationship with a second mediator before ultimately having a relationship to the final dependent variable. With this type of mediation, you have to account for the indirect effect across multiple constructs.

To test this type of mediation, we are going to use the estimands function again. Let's use our mediation example again, but this time let's include another variable called "Loyalty", which is the degree to which a customer is faithful to a retailer/service provider. With the revised model, Adaptive Behavior will have a relationship to Customer Delight, which impacts Positive Word of Mouth, and now Positive Word of Mouth influences Loyalty.

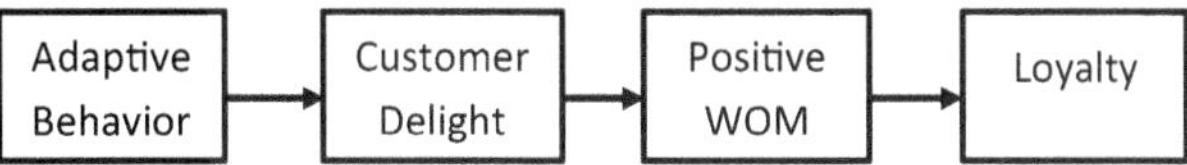

In this revised model, the influence or effect of Adaptive Behavior is proposed to flow through Customer Delight and Positive Word of Mouth to Loyalty. Put another way, the indirect effect of Adaptive Behavior to Loyalty flows through both constructs of Customer Delight and Positive Word of Mouth. Our first step is to draw out our revised model in AMOS. Next, we need to label the arrows (parameters) between each construct. To be consistent, let's label the path from the independent variable to the first mediator (Adaptive Behavior to Customer Delight) as the "A_Path". The path to the ultimate dependent variable from the mediator (Positive Word of Mouth to Loyalty) we will label the "B_Path". The path between the two mediators (Customer Delight to Positive Word of Mouth) we will call the "D_path". I don't want to call that relationship "C_path"; let's save that label for the direct effect from Adaptive Behavior to Loyalty. I also want to avoid labeling a parameter starting with the letter "E". That letter is saved for error terms. Again, the labels are arbitrary; just make sure you give it a label that is unique and one that helps you recognize a specific path in the output. See Figure 6.23.

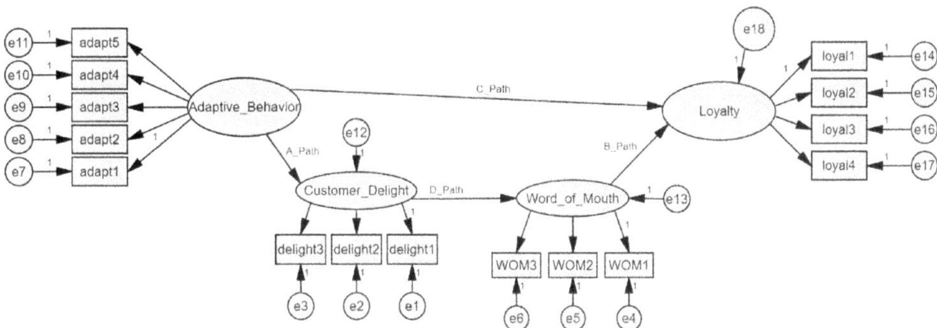

Figure 6.23 Serial Mediation Model in AMOS

Now that we have uniquely labeled the parameters, we need to use the estimand function by defining a new function. To calculate the indirect effect in serial mediation, you need to multiply the intermediating relationships together. Specifically, you will multiply the regression coefficient for each intervening relationship. In our example, we are going to multiply the "A_Path" times the "D_Path" times the "B_Path". This will give us the serial indirect effect. In the estimands function, let's call our indirect test "SerialMediation". In the syntax, we will specify the formula for the indirect relationship. After doing this, we make sure to check for syntax errors, and then we can save and exit the pop-up window. The analysis is now ready to be run. Going to the output, we return to the Estimates link and then the Scalars option. Select the User-Defined estimands. We can then go to the Bias-corrected percentile method to see the full indirect effect details.

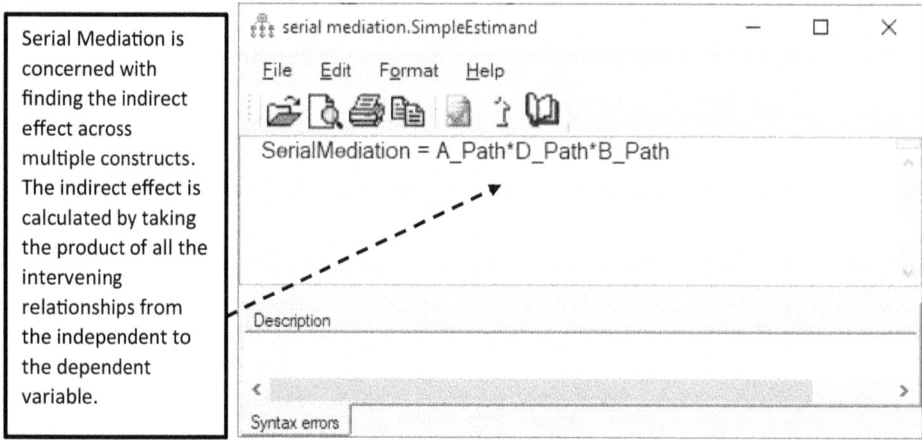

Figure 6.24 Estimand Function Calculating Serial Mediation

The results of the indirect effect through both intervening variables to Loyalty was .055, and it is significant at the p = .002 level. We initially can determine that the serial mediation is significant, but we need to examine the direct effects to determine the type of mediation that is present (see Figure 6.26). The direct effect (C_Path) is significant with a p value = .001. These results show that both the indirect effect and the direct effect are significant. This means partial mediation is present with this serial mediation test.

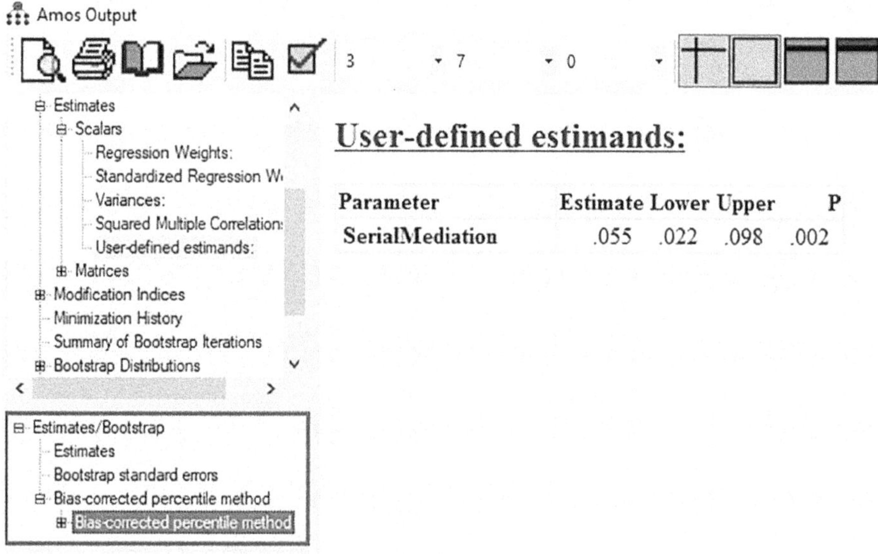

Figure 6.25 Serial Mediation Results Along with Confidence Interval

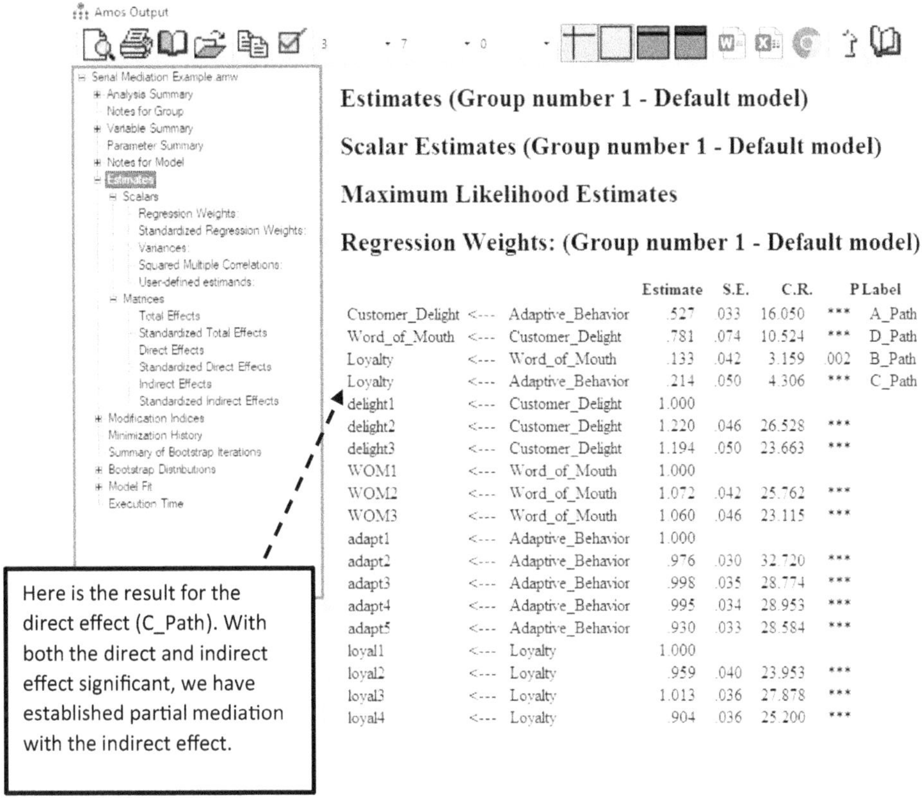

Estimates (Group number 1 - Default model)

Scalar Estimates (Group number 1 - Default model)

Maximum Likelihood Estimates

Regression Weights: (Group number 1 - Default model)

			Estimate	S.E.	C.R.	P	Label
Customer_Delight	<---	Adaptive_Behavior	.527	.033	16.050	***	A_Path
Word_of_Mouth	<---	Customer_Delight	.781	.074	10.524	***	D_Path
Loyalty	<---	Word_of_Mouth	.133	.042	3.159	.002	B_Path
Loyalty	<---	Adaptive_Behavior	.214	.050	4.306	***	C_Path
delight1	<---	Customer_Delight	1.000				
delight2	<---	Customer_Delight	1.220	.046	26.528	***	
delight3	<---	Customer_Delight	1.194	.050	23.663	***	
WOM1	<---	Word_of_Mouth	1.000				
WOM2	<---	Word_of_Mouth	1.072	.042	25.762	***	
WOM3	<---	Word_of_Mouth	1.060	.046	23.115	***	
adapt1	<---	Adaptive_Behavior	1.000				
adapt2	<---	Adaptive_Behavior	.976	.030	32.720	***	
adapt3	<---	Adaptive_Behavior	.998	.035	28.774	***	
adapt4	<---	Adaptive_Behavior	.995	.034	28.953	***	
adapt5	<---	Adaptive_Behavior	.930	.033	28.584	***	
loyal1	<---	Loyalty	1.000				
loyal2	<---	Loyalty	.959	.040	23.953	***	
loyal3	<---	Loyalty	1.013	.036	27.878	***	
loyal4	<---	Loyalty	.904	.036	25.200	***	

Figure 6.26 Examining the Direct Effect in Serial Mediation Test

This test had only two mediators, but you could have more than two mediators in a serial mediation test. If you have three mediators, the process would be exactly the same. You would label all the parameters and then get the product of all the relationships from the independent to dependent variable through the mediators. Using the estimands function will make this a relatively easy process.

Since the indirect effect from Adaptive Behavior to Loyalty could go only through the two specified intervening constructs, we should be able to get the same results from the "indirect effects" output that AMOS initially gives us. In the output, let's go to the Estimates tab, "Matrices" option, and then down to the Indirect Effects. You will see that AMOS gives us all possible indirect effects. The indirect effect of Adaptive Behavior to Loyalty is .055, the same as the estimands function we ran earlier.

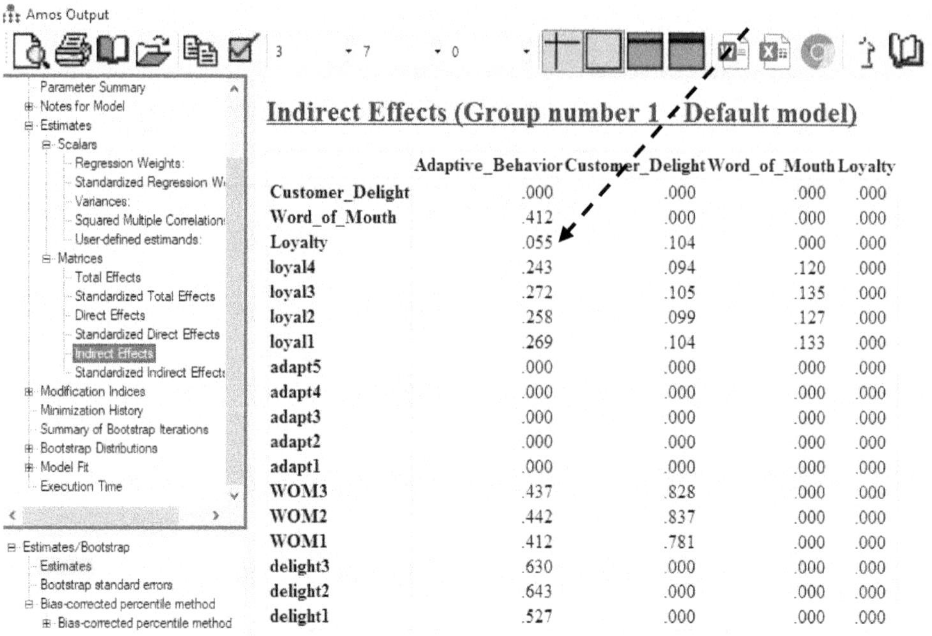

Indirect Effects (Group number 1 - Default model)

	Adaptive_Behavior	Customer_Delight	Word_of_Mouth	Loyalty
Customer_Delight	.000	.000	.000	.000
Word_of_Mouth	.412	.000	.000	.000
Loyalty	.055	.104	.000	.000
loyal4	.243	.094	.120	.000
loyal3	.272	.105	.135	.000
loyal2	.258	.099	.127	.000
loyal1	.269	.104	.133	.000
adapt5	.000	.000	.000	.000
adapt4	.000	.000	.000	.000
adapt3	.000	.000	.000	.000
adapt2	.000	.000	.000	.000
adapt1	.000	.000	.000	.000
WOM3	.437	.828	.000	.000
WOM2	.442	.837	.000	.000
WOM1	.412	.781	.000	.000
delight3	.630	.000	.000	.000
delight2	.643	.000	.000	.000
delight1	.527	.000	.000	.000

Figure 6.27 Results From the Dedicated Indirect Effect Test in AMOS

If we go to the Bias-corrected percentile method from these indirect effects where the bootstrap analysis is presented, you get the same confidence interval and p-value as the one listed in the estimands output. See Figure 6.28 to view the full output of this bootstrap analysis.

Remember, these results are similar only because the indirect effect is going through the only two intervening variables in the model. In this example, the indirect effect from Adaptive Behavior to Loyalty has no other possible indirect effect but through the two mediators. If other mediators were included, or if you had two competing serial mediations, you would definitely need to use the estimands function.

These are the same upper and lower bound confidence intervals along with the same p-value as the estimand test of mediation.

Indirect Effects (Group number 1 - Default model)

Indirect Effects - Lower Bounds (BC) (Group number

	Adaptive_Behavior	Customer_Delight	Word_of_Mouth	Loyalty
Customer_Delight	.000	.000	.000	.000
Word_of_Mouth	.314	.000	.000	.000
Loyalty	.022	.040	.000	.000
loyal4	.160	.037	.045	.000
loyal3	.175	.041	.050	.000
loyal2	.167	.038	.047	.000
loyal1	.172	.040	.049	.000
adapt5	.000	.000	.000	.000
adapt4	.000	.000	.000	.000
adapt3	.000	.000	.000	.000
adapt2	.000	.000	.000	.000
adapt1	.000	.000	.000	.000
WOM3	.339	.668	.000	.000
WOM2	.345	.684	.000	.000
WOM1	.314	.619	.000	.000
delight3	.537	.000	.000	.000
delight2	.556	.000	.000	.000
delight1	.453	.000	.000	.000

Indirect Effects - Upper Bounds (BC) (Group number

	Adaptive_Behavior	Customer_Delight	Word_of_Mouth	Loyalty
Customer_Delight	.000	.000	.000	.000
Word_of_Mouth	.520	.000	.000	.000
Loyalty	.098	.182	.000	.000
loyal4	.334	.166	.200	.000
loyal3	.374	.186	.227	.000
loyal2	.353	.176	.215	.000
loyal1	.368	.182	.220	.000
adapt5	.000	.000	.000	.000
adapt4	.000	.000	.000	.000
adapt3	.000	.000	.000	.000
adapt2	.000	.000	.000	.000
adapt1	.000	.000	.000	.000
WOM3	.550	1.005	.000	.000
WOM2	.553	1.011	.000	.000
WOM1	.520	.952	.000	.000
delight3	.734	.000	.000	.000
delight2	.739	.000	.000	.000
delight1	.607	.000	.000	.000

Indirect Effects - Two Tailed Significance (BC)

	Adaptive_Behavior	Customer_Delight	Word_of_Mouth	Loyalty
Customer_Delight	...	...	...	...
Word_of_Mouth	.000	...	...	...
Loyalty	.002	.003	...	...

Figure 6.28 Confidence Intervals From Dedicated Indirect Effect Test in AMOS

Setting the Seed in Bootstrapping

Bootstrapping is a technique where numerous samples with replacement are drawn in order to determine the confidence interval of an indirect effect. Every time you run a bootstrap, you have a different potential set of samples and your results could slightly change. When you request a sample of at least 5,000, these differences will be small, but you might find that your numbers change every time you run the same analysis. AMOS has addressed this issue by coming up with a "seed" that captures the exact method the samples were drawn. By setting the seed number, you can tell AMOS to draw the exact same sample as before so that you have consistent results and your numbers will not slightly change with every run of the analysis.

To set the seed number, you need to go into the Analysis Properties option and go to the tab labeled "Random #" which is usually the last tab. This option will display the "Seed for random numbers". The default is the number 1. You can change this numerical value to any number you want (there is no significance in the number); just make sure to retain the number you used for the bootstrap. If you have a coauthor that wants to run your model, they will get slightly different results unless you give them the seed number used in the original analysis.

There is also another option in this window called "Use original random number generator". If you select this option, AMOS will randomly choose a seed number for every analysis. This means you will get a different set of samples for every analysis. Note that it will not give the exact seed number used with this option.

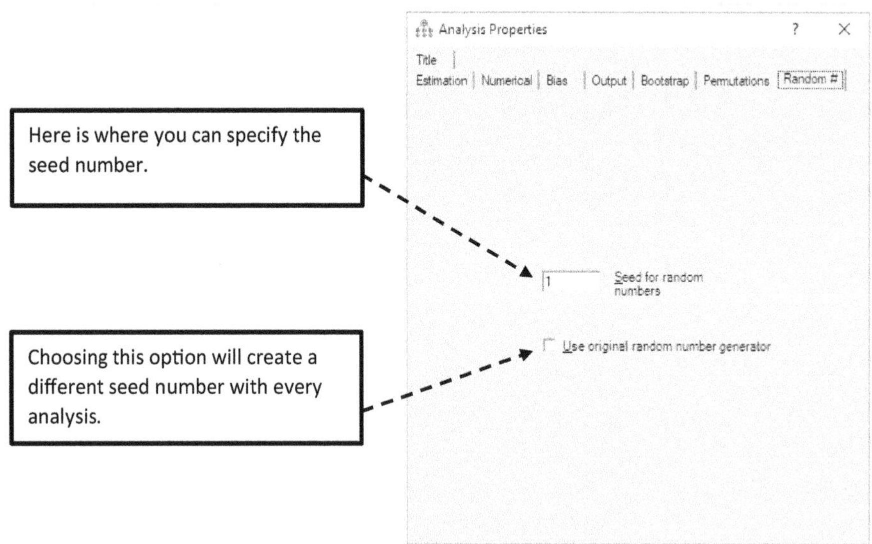

Figure 6.29 Using the Analysis Properties Window to Change the Seed Number in Bootstrapping

To provide greater clarity to the bootstrap analysis, I will often change the seed number and run the analysis again to see the consistency of the results. Please note that I am not saying you should change the seed number and keep running the analysis until you find the results you want. I am just saying that running the bootstrap more than once can provide insight into the consistency of the results you are reporting. You might find that the first sample was slightly higher in estimates than when you run it again. Your ultimate goal is to provide an accurate picture of your results to the reader.

Definitions of Constructs Used in Examples for This Chapter:

Adaptive Behavior: customer's perception that an employee adapted/modified their normal job performance to meet their needs. This adaptation can be through verbal interaction, service performance, or meeting special requests. Construct was measured with a 7-point Likert scale of Strongly Disagree to Strongly Agree.

Customer Delight: customer's profoundly positive emotional state resulting from expectations being exceeded to a surprising degree. Construct was measured with a 7-point Likert scale of Strongly Disagree to Strongly Agree.

Positive Word of Mouth: customer's intention to spread positive information to others about a previous experience. Construct was measured with a 7-point Likert scale of Strongly Disagree to Strongly Agree.

Satisfaction: evaluation of one's expectations compared to performance. Construct was measured with a 7-point Likert scale of Strongly Disagree to Strongly Agree.

Servicescape: customer's perceptions about the built environment that the service takes place, which could include atmosphere, furniture, and other things related to the environment such as displays, colors, and cleanliness. Construct was measured with a 7-point Likert scale of Strongly Disagree to Strongly Agree.

Tolerance to Future Failures: likelihood that a customer is understanding of a service failure with future interactions. Construct was measured with a 7-point Likert scale of Strongly Disagree to Strongly Agree.

Loyalty: the degree to which a customer is faithful to a retailer/service provider. Construct was measured with a 7-point Likert scale of Strongly Disagree to Strongly Agree.

Highlights of the Chapter:

1. Mediation is a test to determine if the influence of an independent variable to a dependent variable takes place through an intervening variable called a mediator.
2. Mediation can be full or partial. Full mediation is where the indirect effect is significant but the direct effect is non-significant. Partial mediation is where the indirect and direct effects are significant.
3. Complementary mediation is where the indirect and directs effect have a similar influence. Competitive mediation is where the indirect effect and the direct effect have a dissimilar influence.
4. We have moved away from the Baron and Kenny (1986) method in mediation testing to using bootstrapping. A bootstrap technique treats your data sample like a pseudo-population and then takes a random sample with replacement to determine if your indirect effect falls within a confidence interval.
5. It is advisable to use at least 5,000 samples in a bootstrap analysis.
6. The indirect effect is calculated by getting the regression coefficient from the independent variable to the mediator (A path) and multiplying it by the regression coefficient from the mediator to the dependent variable (B path).

7. You can use a correlation/covariance matrix as your input for a mediation test, but you will need to use a Monte Carlo parametric bootstrap.
8. Parallel mediation is where you have multiple possible mediators from an independent variable to a dependent variable in a model. To isolate the effect of a specific mediator, you will need to use the estimands function in AMOS.
9. Serial mediation is a multiple mediator model that takes place when the first mediator will have a direct relationship with a second mediator before ultimately having a relationship to the final dependent variable.
10. The "seed" number in bootstrapping allows AMOS to draw the exact same sample as a prior run so that you will not have slightly different results with each bootstrap analysis.

References

Baron, R.M. and Kenny, D.A. (1986), "The Moderator-Mediator Variable Distinction in Social Psychological Research: Conceptual, Strategic, and Statistical Considerations", *Journal of Personality and Social Psychology*, 51 (6), 1173–1182.

Hair, Joseph F., William C. Black, Barry J. Babin, and Rolph E. Anderson. (2009), *Multivariate Data Analysis* (7th ed.). Upper Saddle River, NJ: Prentice Hall.

Hayes, Andrew. (2018), *Introduction to Mediation, Moderation, and Conditional Process Analysis* (2nd ed.). New York, NY: Guilford Press.

Zhao, Xinshu, John G. Lynch, and Qimei Chen. (2010), "Reconsidering Baron and Kenny: Myths and Truths about Mediation Analysis", *Journal of Consumer Research*, 37 (August), 197–206.

Chapter 7

Moderation

Introduction to Moderation

Moderation is where the direct influence of an independent variable on a dependent variable is altered or changed because of a third variable. This third variable, called the "moderator", can influence the strength (and sometimes sign) of the relationship from the independent variable to the dependent variable. A moderator is said to "interact" with the independent variable to determine the influence on the dependent variable. Thus, you will hear the term "interaction" when testing for moderation where the combined effect of the independent variable and the moderator is examined.

There are numerous ways to test for moderation using SEM. The first method I will discuss is the "interaction term" method. An interaction term is where you form a product term of the independent variable and the moderator. This interaction term will then let you know if the presence of the moderator is significantly influencing the relationship from the independent variable to the dependent variable. If your moderator is a continuous variable, the interaction term method is the preferred option in moderation testing. Before moving on to an example, we need to address the potential graphing discrepancy with moderation. For many researchers trying to represent moderation graphically in a publication, they will simply draw a line from the moderator that intersects the influence from the independent to the dependent variable. You cannot graphically draw a moderator like this in AMOS. It will not simply let you draw a moderator arrow that is intercepting a direct effect between two variables. I just wanted to clarify this point that AMOS will not reproduce moderation the same way it is often graphically represented.

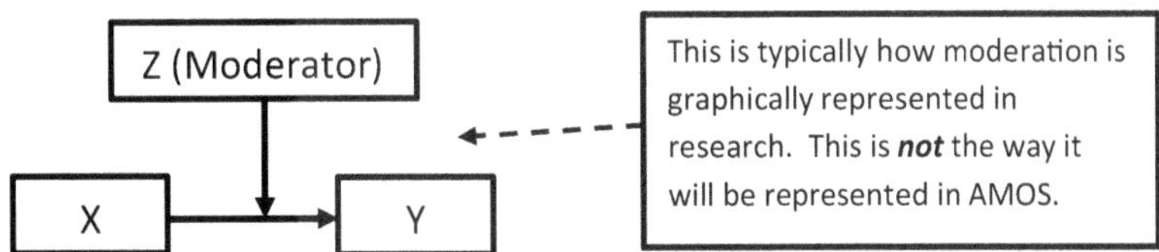

Let's look at a moderation example that uses an interaction term. For simplicity, I am going to use a path model with composite variables to initially show how a moderation test is performed. Later in the chapter, I will show you how to perform a moderation test with a full structural model.

Using our example from the path model test, adapting a service will lead to Customer Delight, which will impact customers' likelihood to spread Positive Word of Mouth. If we say that the relationship from Adaptive Behavior to Customer Delight is moderated by how friendly the employee was during the service, we need to see how the interaction of Adaptive Behavior and Friendliness influence Customer Delight.

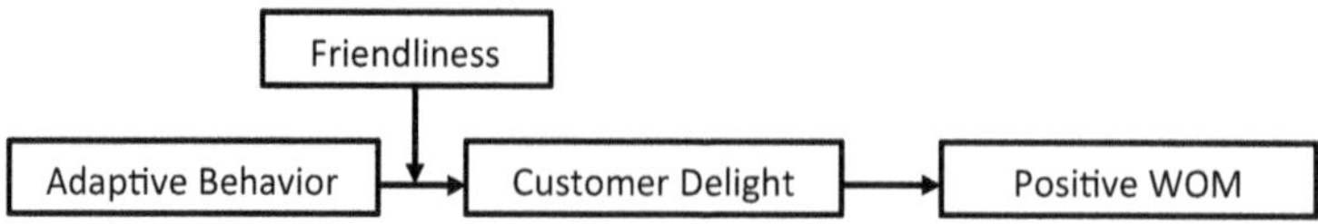

To assess this interaction, we need to form a product term of Adaptive Behavior and Friendliness. A problem that can occur with a product term is the issue of high collinearity with the original constructs which can cause problems in the analysis (Frazier et al. 2004). One way to circumnavigate this problem is to mean center the variables in your data. There has been an ongoing debate on whether mean centering is necessary. Previous research has stated the results are essentially the same whether you mean center or leave the data in its raw form (Echambadi and Hess 2007; Hayes 2018). While the differences between these methods are minimal, the advantage of mean centering the data is not only are you accounting for potential collinearity issues, but it also makes the interpretation of results easier. Thus, the recommendation to mean center your data before analyzing the data is encouraged (Dawson 2014).

In testing for moderation, we need to mean center the independent variable and the moderator before we form the product term. To mean center the data, we first need to get the mean for the independent variable and moderator. In SPSS, go to the "Analyze" option on the top menu, then go to "Descriptive Statistics" and then "Descriptives". This will bring up a descriptives pop-up window. Since this is a path model, we are concerned only with the composite variables of the independent variable and moderator. In the Descriptives window, you need to select your independent variable (comp_adapt) and moderator (comp_Friendly) and hit "OK". This will give us the mean value for each composite variable. Adaptive Behavior was 6.12 and Friendliness was 5.78 (on a 1–7 Likert Scale).

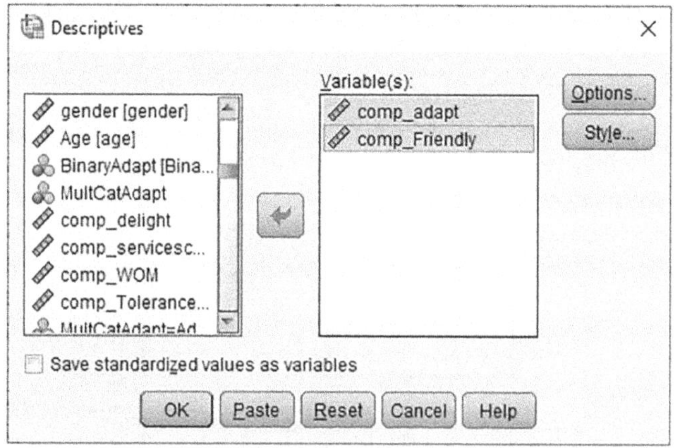

Descriptive Statistics

	N	Minimum	Maximum	Mean	Std. Deviation
comp_adapt	500	1.60	7.00	6.1296	.92752
comp_Friendly	500	1.00	7.00	5.7867	1.37746
Valid N (listwise)	500				

Figure 7.1 Finding the Mean and Standard Deviation for a Variable in SPSS

Once we have the mean values, we need to form a new variable that is mean centered. In SPSS, go to the "Transform" menu option and "Compute Variable". This function will allow us to create a new variable that is going to mean center the original variable. For Adaptive Behavior, let's call the new variable "centerAdapt" and in the numeric expression we will subtract the mean from the original variable of "comp_Adapt" (composite variable of Adaptive Behavior). Let's do the same thing with the moderator. We will call that variable "centerFriend". The new variables will be listed in the last columns of the SPSS data file.

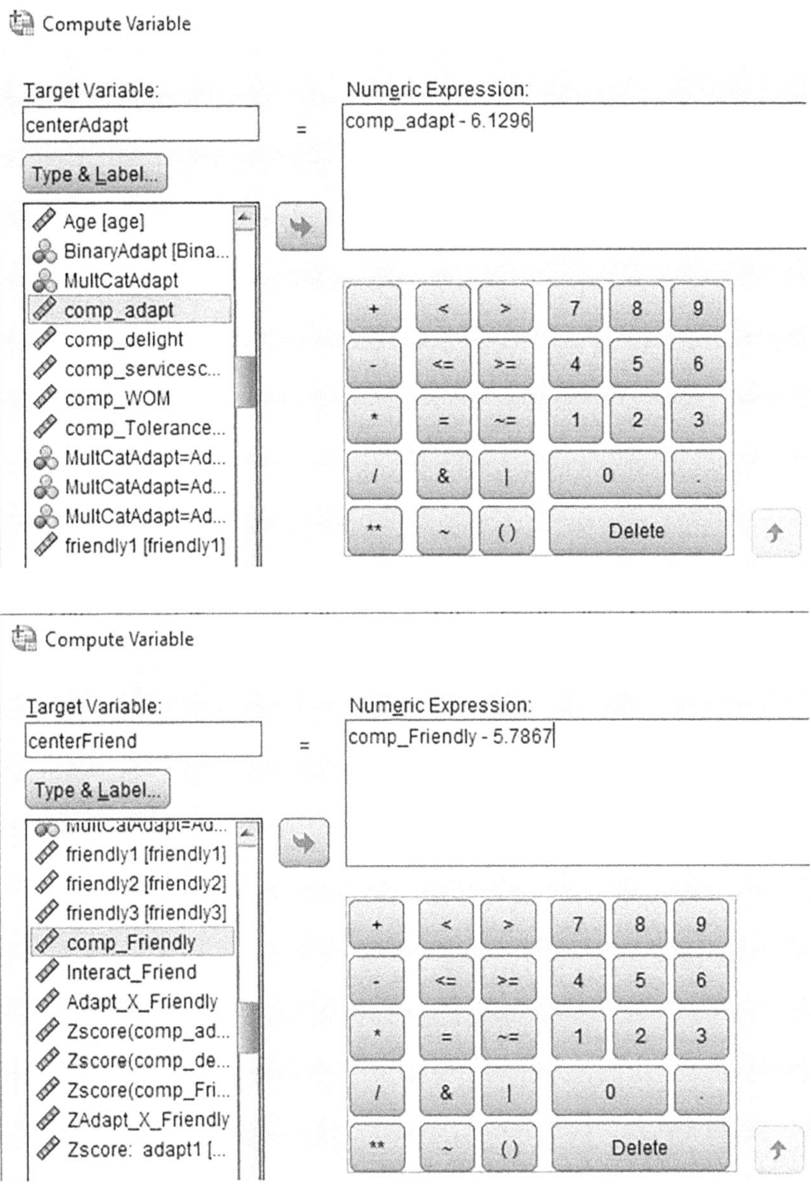

Figure 7.2 Mean Centering a Variable in SPSS

If you are concerned that the new variable is mean centered correctly, you can do a simple test in SPSS to verify your results. In SPSS, go to the "Analyze" menu option, "Descriptive Statistics", and then "Descriptives". The pop-up window will appear, and this time you will select the recently formed mean centered variables of centerAdapt and then centerFriend. Hit the OK button and run the analysis. You can see that the mean for those variables is listed as a zero. The standard deviation is the exact same for the mean centered and original variables. You will also notice that the minimum and maximum values have changed from the original variables. The subtraction of the mean from all the variables has altered these values now. Again, if you are curious if a variable was actually mean centered, here is a quick way to tell.

Table 7.1 SPSS Results Verifying the Variables Are Mean Centered

Descriptive Statistics

	N	Minimum	Maximum	Mean	Std. Deviation
centerAdapt	500	-4.53	.87	.0000	.92752
centerFriend	500	-4.79	1.21	.0000	1.37746
Valid N (listwise)	500				

Once we have created the new centered variables, we need to create a product term (interaction) variable. Let's go back to the "Compute Variable" function in SPSS. Now we are going to multiply the two centered variables of "centerAdapt" and "centerFriend". This will create an interaction term that we are going to need to assess moderation. Let's call the interaction variable "CenterAdapt_X_Friend". Once we have formed the mean centered variables and the interaction variable, we are ready to save the data and then go to AMOS to draw our moderation model in the graphics window.

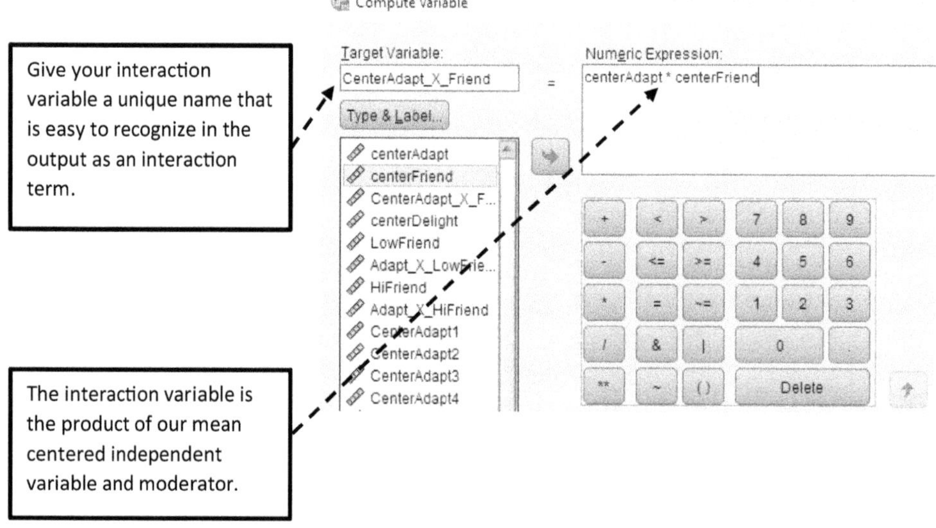

Figure 7.3 Forming an Interaction Term of Adaptive Behavior and Friendliness in SPSS

In AMOS, to test for moderation you need to include a path from the moderator and interaction variable to the dependent variable, which in this example is Customer Delight. We will have three paths leading to Customer Delight: the path from the independent variable, the moderator, and the mean centered interaction of those two constructs. Note that you need only to bring in the centered interaction variable to AMOS; all other constructs can be the original composite variables. Once these constructs and paths have been added to the model, we are ready to run the analysis.

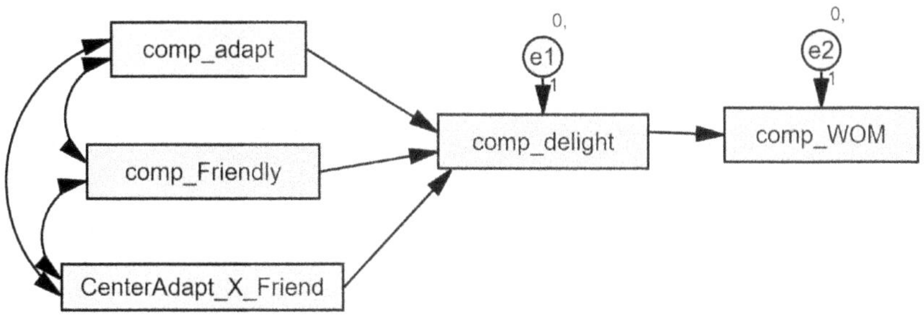

Figure 7.4 Simple Moderation Model in AMOS

Let's go to the "Estimates" link in the output. Notice that our interaction term is positive and significant (See Figure 7.5). This means that the relationship from Adaptive Behavior is being positively strengthened to Customer Delight by Friendliness. If the interaction was significant but negative, this would indicate that in the presence of the moderator, the relationship from Adaptive Behavior to Customer Delight is weakened. Our moderator has a significant direct relationship to Customer Delight; but even if it was non-significant, that is okay because we are really concerned only with the interaction to determine if moderation is present. If our interaction term was non-significant, then we could say that there is evidence that the construct of Friendliness is not moderating the relationship from Adaptive Behavior to Customer Delight.

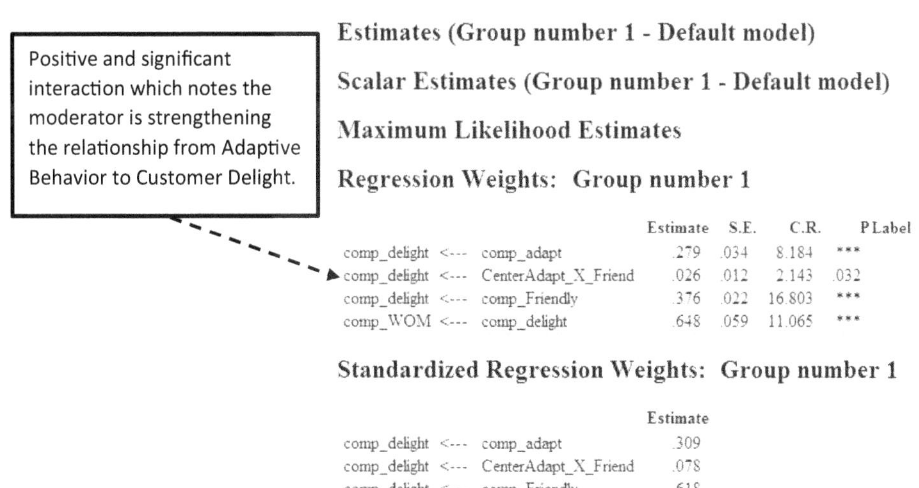

Estimates (Group number 1 - Default model)

Scalar Estimates (Group number 1 - Default model)

Maximum Likelihood Estimates

Regression Weights: Group number 1

			Estimate	S.E.	C.R.	P	Label
comp_delight	<---	comp_adapt	.279	.034	8.184	***	
comp_delight	<---	CenterAdapt_X_Friend	.026	.012	2.143	.032	
comp_delight	<---	comp_Friendly	.376	.022	16.803	***	
comp_WOM	<---	comp_delight	.648	.059	11.065	***	

Standardized Regression Weights: Group number 1

			Estimate
comp_delight	<---	comp_adapt	.309
comp_delight	<---	CenterAdapt_X_Friend	.078
comp_delight	<---	comp_Friendly	.618
comp_WOM	<---	comp_delight	.444

Figure 7.5 Estimates Output of Moderation Test

Just to recap, in testing for moderation with a continuous variable, you need to form a mean centered interaction term that is a product of the moderator and independent variable. In AMOS, you will form a direct relationship from the independent variable, moderator, and mean centered interaction to the specified dependent variable. From there, you will examine the interaction term in the analysis to determine if the "interaction" between the moderator and independent variable is influencing the strength of the relationship of the independent variable to the dependent variable.

Probing the Interaction

In our moderation example, we can see that the interaction is significant and positive, but we do not know much else about the interaction or ultimately how the moderator influences the relationship from the independent variable to the dependent variable. Next, we can "probe the interaction", which means we are going to explore how the relationship from the independent variable to the dependent variable changes in different levels of the moderator. This is especially important when the independent variable has a weak relationship to the dependent variable, but the interaction of the moderator and the independent variable is significant. In those instances, we want to see where the relationship from the independent variable to the dependent variable changes when the moderator is at different levels. To accomplish this testing of different levels of a moderator, we are initially going to explore how to examine a moderator at low levels by creating a new "low level moderator" that is one standard deviation below the mean of the original moderator. Conversely, we are going to create a "high level moderator" test in which we examine the moderator at one standard deviation above the mean. This type of probing the interaction where you are choosing a specific point below and above the mean is called a spotlight analysis. It is also called a "pick-a-point approach" to moderation testing. Ultimately, probing the interaction gives you a better picture of how moderation is working in your model.

The first step is find the standard deviation for the moderator construct. In our previous moderator example, we needed to find the mean of the moderator. In that same output, the standard deviation is provided as well (the Descriptives output). Based on that information, we know the standard deviation for the moderator of Friendliness is 1.37746. Let's probe the interaction when the moderator is low. We need to form a new variable in the data set that represents the moderator at low levels.

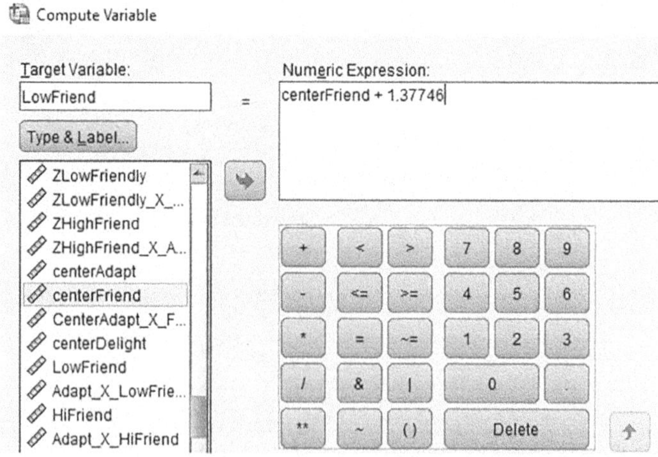

Descriptive Statistics

	N	Minimum	Maximum	Mean	Std. Deviation
comp_adapt	500	1.60	7.00	6.1296	.92752
comp_Friendly	500	1.00	7.00	5.7867	1.37746
Valid N (listwise)	500				

Figure 7.6 Computing a Low Moderator Value to Probe the Interaction

Let's call the new variable "LowFriend". In the "Transform" menu in SPSS, we go to the "Compute Variable" function. We label our new construct and then take the mean centered composite variable of the moderator of "centerFriend" and ***add*** the standard deviation to it. I know it seems odd to get the low moderator value by adding the standard deviation, but this is the necessary process to represent the low levels of the moderator. Once you have formed the "LowFriend" moderator, you need to create an interaction term with the low level moderator (LowFriend) and the mean centered independent variable of Adaptive Behavior (centerAdapt).

Just to clarify, the interaction term will multiply "LowFriend" (mean centered moderator plus one standard deviation) by the mean centered independent variable "centerAdapt". Let's call the interaction term for the low moderator "Adapt_X_LowFriend". Once you have formed this low moderator and interaction variable, we are ready to go back to AMOS and form a model for moderation testing. In AMOS, we will test this moderation the same way as we did before, except we are now using the low moderator and the interaction with the low moderator. To be efficient in creating the moderation model test, we can drag in the mean centered interaction of the Adaptive Behavior variable and low level moderator. We will also need to drag in the mean centered low level moderator variable. Lastly, we can leave the independent variable in the model as the original composite variable that was used in the first moderation test. Once you have the model drawn, we can run the analysis and then go to the Estimates link in the output.

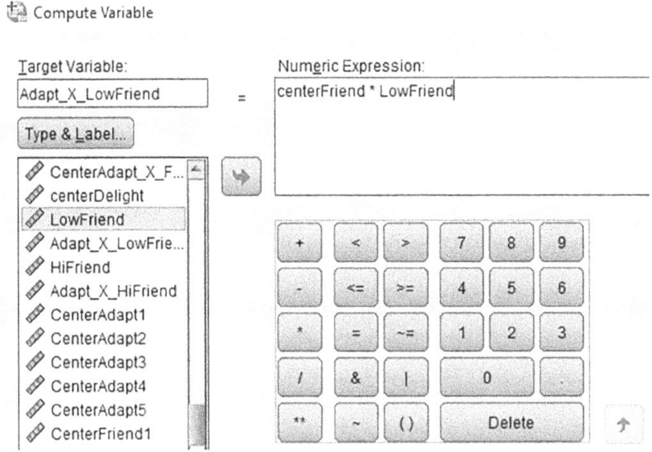

Figure 7.7 Forming an Interaction Term With Low Moderator Value

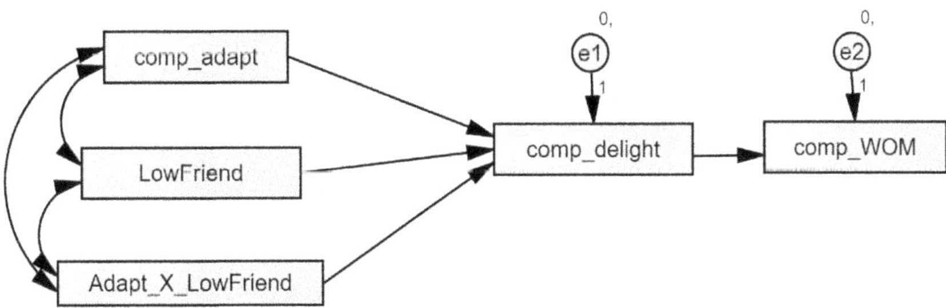

Figure 7.8 Moderation Test With Interaction Term Including the Low Level of the Moderator

In the output, the only relationship we are concerned with is that of Adaptive Behavior to Customer Delight. We want to see how this relationship changes when low friendliness is included. Notice that the interaction results and moderator relationship to Customer Delight did not change from the original analysis. The results show that when the employee had a low degree of Friendliness, the relationship from Adaptive Behavior to Customer Delight is still significant but weaker. The original test had an unstandardized regression weight from Adaptive Behavior to Customer Delight of .279, and now under low levels of the moderator, the relationship has weakened to .244.

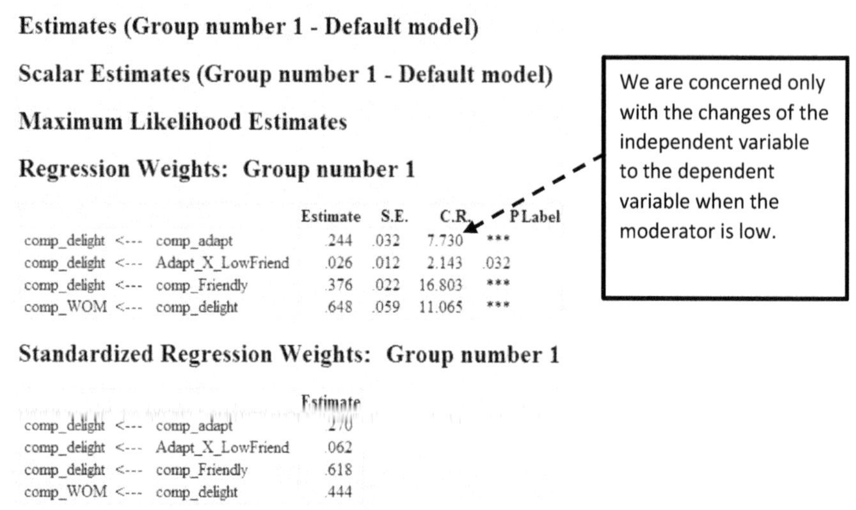
Estimates (Group number 1 - Default model)

Scalar Estimates (Group number 1 - Default model)

Maximum Likelihood Estimates

Regression Weights: Group number 1

			Estimate	S.E.	C.R.	P	Label
comp_delight	<---	comp_adapt	.244	.032	7.730	***	
comp_delight	<---	Adapt_X_LowFriend	.026	.012	2.143	.032	
comp_delight	<---	comp_Friendly	.376	.022	16.803	***	
comp_WOM	<---	comp_delight	.648	.059	11.065	***	

Standardized Regression Weights: Group number 1

			Estimate
comp_delight	<---	comp_adapt	.270
comp_delight	<---	Adapt_X_LowFriend	.062
comp_delight	<---	comp_Friendly	.618
comp_WOM	<---	comp_delight	.444

Figure 7.9 Estimates Output With Low Moderator Interaction Term

We have examined the relationship when the moderator is low; let's now examine when the moderator is strong or at high levels. In SPSS, let's form a new variable called "HiFriend" which denotes high friendliness by the employee. We will take the mean centered variable of Friendliness, and this time we will ***subtract*** the standard deviation to get the high level moderator. After that, we will form an interaction term with "HiFriend" and the mean centered Adaptive Behavior construct "centerAdapt". Let's call the interaction term "Adapt_X_HiFriend". Once these variables have been created and you have saved the SPSS file, you can drag in the high moderator variables in AMOS and then you are ready to run the analysis again.

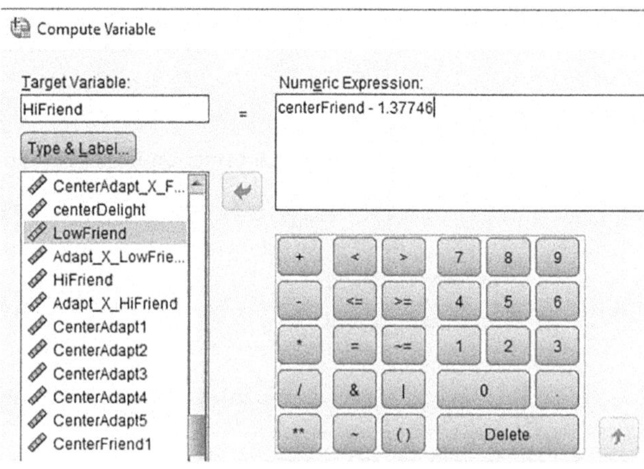

Figure 7.10 Computing the High Level of the Moderator in SPSS

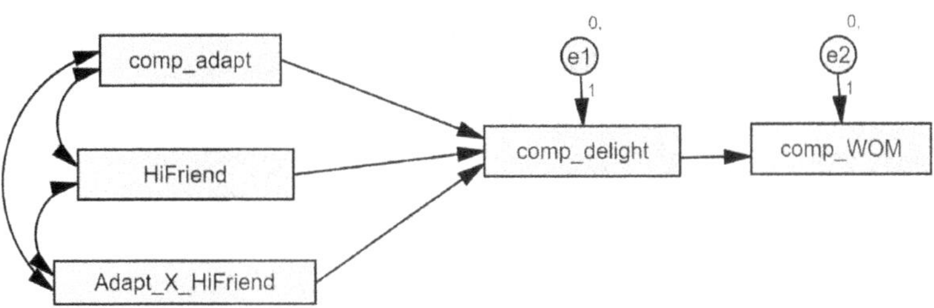

Figure 7.11 AMOS Model With Interaction Term Including the High Level of the Moderator

When we go to the Estimates link in the output, the relationship from Adaptive Behavior to Customer Delight is positive and significant again at high levels of the moderator. Hence, the construct of Friendliness is moderating the relationship of Adaptive Behavior to Customer Delight when Friendliness levels are weak and strong. When the moderator was high, the relationship from Adaptive Behavior to Customer Delight strengthened even more than the initial test. The regression weight with high levels of the moderator was .315 compared to the first mean centered test of .279. By probing the interaction, you get a better picture of the relationship from the independent variable to the dependent variable in the presence of the moderator.

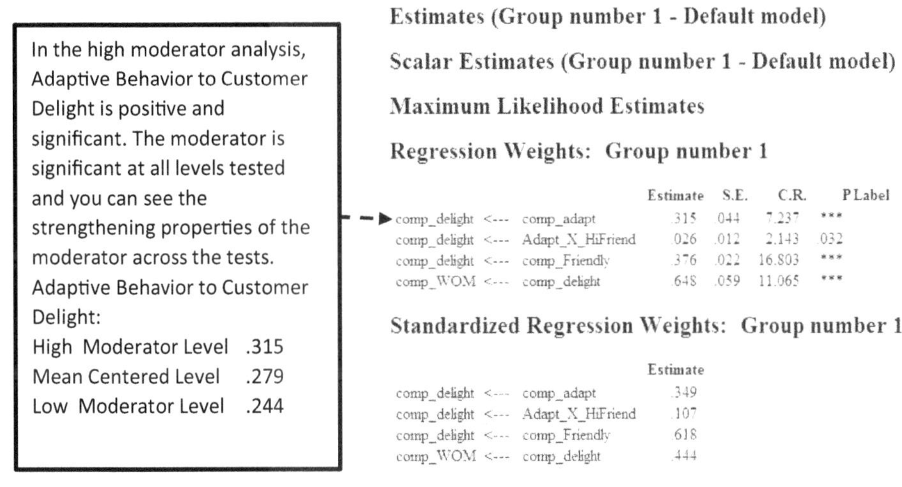
In the high moderator analysis, Adaptive Behavior to Customer Delight is positive and significant. The moderator is significant at all levels tested and you can see the strengthening properties of the moderator across the tests.

Adaptive Behavior to Customer Delight:

High Moderator Level	.315
Mean Centered Level	.279
Low Moderator Level	.244

Estimates (Group number 1 - Default model)

Scalar Estimates (Group number 1 - Default model)

Maximum Likelihood Estimates

Regression Weights: Group number 1

			Estimate	S.E.	C.R.	P	Label
comp_delight	<---	comp_adapt	.315	.044	7.237	***	
comp_delight	<---	Adapt_X_HiFriend	.026	.012	2.143	.032	
comp_delight	<---	comp_Friendly	.376	.022	16.803	***	
comp_WOM	<---	comp_delight	.648	.059	11.065	***	

Standardized Regression Weights: Group number 1

			Estimate
comp_delight	<---	comp_adapt	.349
comp_delight	<---	Adapt_X_HiFriend	.107
comp_delight	<---	comp_Friendly	.618
comp_WOM	<---	comp_delight	.444

Figure 7.12 Estimates Output for Moderator at High Levels

With moderation testing, you want to interpret and present the unstandardized results of your analysis. The interaction term in a moderation test will not be properly standardized and is not interpretable (Frazier et al. 2004). Thus, you need to focus on the unstandardized results in testing for moderation.

Up to this point, we have discussed probing an interaction where you are choosing a specific point above and below the mean of the moderator to determine how the moderator influences the relationship from the independent variable to the dependent variable. You can also use a floodlight analysis (Spiller et al. 2013) to probe an interaction where it does not look at a specific point above and below the mean; rather, it examines all possible points of the moderator to determine exactly where the interaction becomes significant. A floodlight analysis uses an approach that was initially introduced by Johnson and Neyman (1936). To examine the influence of all possible moderator values, a bootstrap is performed where you can see the regression weight of the interaction at different levels of the moderator. A confidence interval is also performed to let the reader know the level of significance at each level. The specific point where an interaction becomes significant is often referred to as the Johnson-Neyman point. You will also hear the term "regions of significance" to refer to a range of values that represent significance of the interaction of the moderator. Ultimately, the floodlight analysis is quite handy in telling you exactly what level of the moderator must be present to significantly influence the relationship from the independent variable to the dependent variable.

With having to calculate all possible values of the moderator, you can see where this would be impractical without some computational muscle. Many programs like SPSS, SAS, R, and others implement macros that can accomplish this analysis for you. I have even seen some researchers perform a quasi-floodlight analysis where they will pick numerous points below and above the mean of the moderator to assess the level of significance at different points. This is probably closer to a "pick-a-point" or spotlight analysis than a true floodlight analysis.

Probing an interaction via a floodlight analysis has grown in popularity because it allows a reader the ability to assess exactly where a relationship significantly changes in the presence of a moderator. Instead of examining a specific point, the reader now has the ability to see the entire range of the data. Saying that, you will often see a floodlight analysis presented in a graphical form to give the reader an easier interpretation of the data.

There is good news and bad news in regards to performing a floodlight analysis in AMOS. The bad news is that AMOS does not have a function that will calculate a floodlight analysis or even give you Johnson-Neyman points. The good news is that there are some researchers, such as James Gaskin, who are kind enough to develop and share a plugin for AMOS that will perform this analysis. A simple search on the internet will direct you to those plugins. To view an example of a floodlight analysis in graphical form, see Figure 7.13.

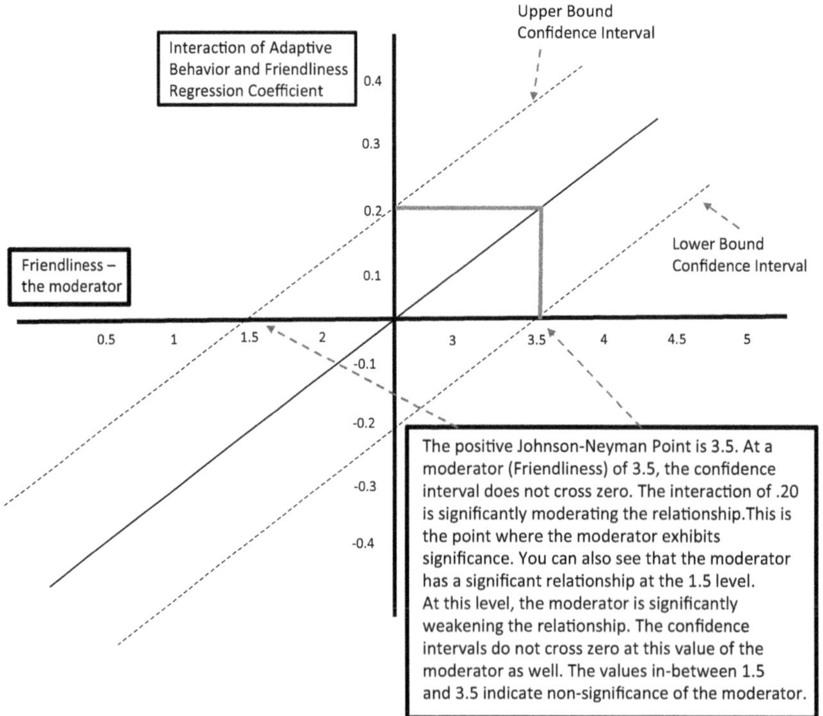
Upper Bound
Confidence Interval
Interaction of Adaptive
Behavior and Friendliness
Regression Coefficient
0.4
0.3
0.2
0.1
-0.1
-0.2
-0.3
-0.4
Lower Bound
Confidence Interval
Friendliness –
the moderator
0.5
1
1.5
2
3
3.5
4
4.5
5
The positive Johnson-Neyman Point is 3.5. At a moderator (Friendliness) of 3.5, the confidence interval does not cross zero. The interaction of .20 is significantly moderating the relationship.This is the point where the moderator exhibits significance. You can also see that the moderator has a significant relationship at the 1.5 level.
At this level, the moderator is significantly weakening the relationship. The confidence intervals do not cross zero at this value of the moderator as well. The values in-between 1.5 and 3.5 indicate non-significance of the moderator.

Figure 7.13 Example of Floodlight Analysis

Testing Moderation in a Full Structural Model

The previous examples describe how to test for moderation in a path model, or specifically, with composite variables. What if you want to test moderation in a full structural model? There are three different ways that moderation can be assessed in a full structural model. These three ways are (1) the mixed model method, (2) the full indicator interaction method, and (3) the matched-pairs method. Each method has advantages and disadvantages in assessing moderation. First, let's talk about the mixed model method.

Mixed Model Method

The mixed model method includes latent unobservable variables with the independent and dependent variables in a model but include a composite moderator variable along with a composite interaction term. This is not a true test of a full structural model because you have both latent unobservable constructs and composite variables included in the same model. Using our previous example of Adaptive Behavior to Customer Delight that is moderated by Friendliness, let's examine how this method is performed in AMOS. The variables of Adaptive Behavior, Customer Delight, and Positive Word of Mouth are latent unobservable constructs with all the indicators included. The moderator of Friendliness is a composite variable formed from the average of the moderator indicators. To get the interaction term, you need to form a composite variable of the independent variable of Adaptive Behavior. After getting composite variables for both Friendliness and Adaptive Behavior, you will need to mean center both of those composite variables. Once you have centered both composite variables, you will get the product of those variables to represent the interaction term. In this example, the interaction variable is "CenterAdapt_X_Friendly". In forming the model, the independent variable of Adaptive Behavior is included as a latent variable with the indicators included. The moderator of Friendliness is included as a composite variable and the interaction term is a composite variable of the interaction of the mean centered moderator and independent variable. Let's look at the results.

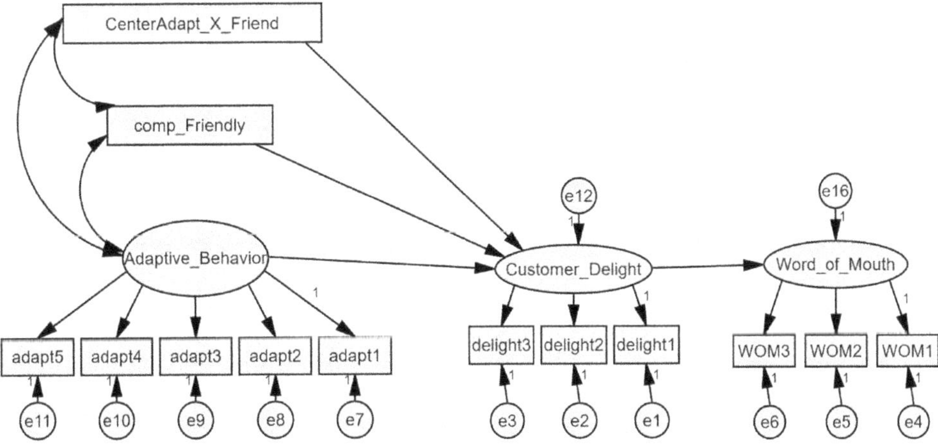

Figure 7.14 Example of Mixed Model Method in AMOS

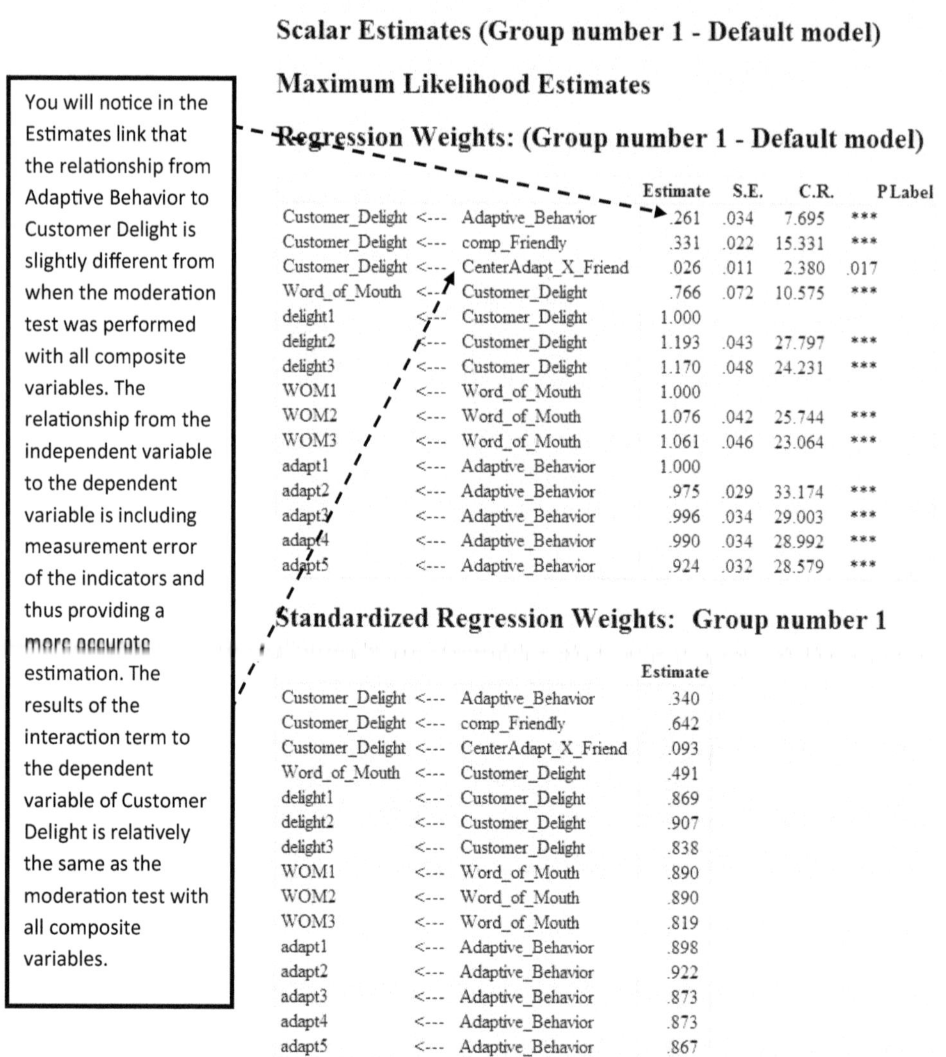

You will notice in the Estimates link that the relationship from Adaptive Behavior to Customer Delight is slightly different from when the moderation test was performed with all composite variables. The relationship from the independent variable to the dependent variable is including measurement error of the indicators and thus providing a more accurate estimation. The results of the interaction term to the dependent variable of Customer Delight is relatively the same as the moderation test with all composite variables.

Estimates (Group number 1 - Default model)

Scalar Estimates (Group number 1 - Default model)

Maximum Likelihood Estimates

Regression Weights: (Group number 1 - Default model)

			Estimate	S.E.	C.R.	P	Label
Customer_Delight	<---	Adaptive_Behavior	.261	.034	7.695	***	
Customer_Delight	<---	comp_Friendly	.331	.022	15.331	***	
Customer_Delight	<---	CenterAdapt_X_Friend	.026	.011	2.380	.017	
Word_of_Mouth	<---	Customer_Delight	.766	.072	10.575	***	
delight1	<---	Customer_Delight	1.000				
delight2	<---	Customer_Delight	1.193	.043	27.797	***	
delight3	<---	Customer_Delight	1.170	.048	24.231	***	
WOM1	<---	Word_of_Mouth	1.000				
WOM2	<---	Word_of_Mouth	1.076	.042	25.744	***	
WOM3	<---	Word_of_Mouth	1.061	.046	23.064	***	
adapt1	<---	Adaptive_Behavior	1.000				
adapt2	<---	Adaptive_Behavior	.975	.029	33.174	***	
adapt3	<---	Adaptive_Behavior	.996	.034	29.003	***	
adapt4	<---	Adaptive_Behavior	.990	.034	28.992	***	
adapt5	<---	Adaptive_Behavior	.924	.032	28.579	***	

Standardized Regression Weights: Group number 1

			Estimate
Customer_Delight	<---	Adaptive_Behavior	.340
Customer_Delight	<---	comp_Friendly	.642
Customer_Delight	<---	CenterAdapt_X_Friend	.093
Word_of_Mouth	<---	Customer_Delight	.491
delight1	<---	Customer_Delight	.869
delight2	<---	Customer_Delight	.907
delight3	<---	Customer_Delight	.838
WOM1	<---	Word_of_Mouth	.890
WOM2	<---	Word_of_Mouth	.890
WOM3	<---	Word_of_Mouth	.819
adapt1	<---	Adaptive_Behavior	.898
adapt2	<---	Adaptive_Behavior	.922
adapt3	<---	Adaptive_Behavior	.873
adapt4	<---	Adaptive_Behavior	.873
adapt5	<---	Adaptive_Behavior	.867

Figure 7.15 Estimates Output for Mixed Model Moderation Test

While this is not a true test of a full structural model because of the mix of latent and composite variables, this approach can still provide an accurate examination of how a moderator can influence the relationships between latent constructs. To probe the interaction using this method, you would need to form a new composite moderator that represented the low and high values of the construct (mean centered composite moderator plus or minus 1 standard deviation). You would then need to create a new composite interaction term that was the product of the composite independent variable and the new high/low composite moderator variable. The process of probing the interaction is similar to the earlier discussion of probing an interaction in a path model that has all composite variables.

Full Indicator Interaction Method

The full indicator interaction method tests all variables, including the interaction term, as a latent unobservable construct. The process of creating a latent interaction term between the independent variable and the moderator is more complex and laborious than previous methods. Let's use our moderation example again, but this time all the independent and dependent variables will be represented as an unobservable latent construct, and now the moderator will be represented as a latent construct as well. The question remains, how do you form the interaction term when the independent variable and moderator are unobservable and represented by the individual indicators? Testing of moderation becomes more complicated with a full structural model because you need to form an interaction term for each indicator across the two constructs.

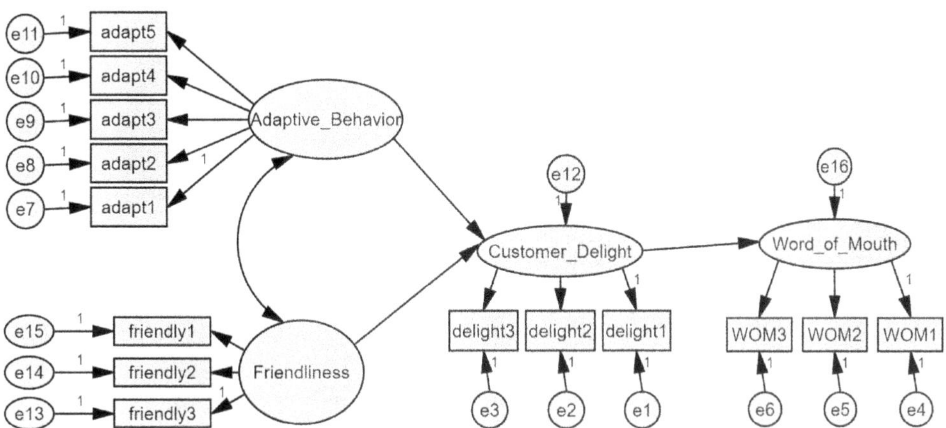

Figure 7.16 Full Structural Model to Be Tested in AMOS

Yes, you read that right. An interaction term for each pair of indicators across the independent and moderator variable. If you have a large number of indicators for either construct, you will have a substantial number of interaction terms to create. To clarify this point, the first indicator in the Friendliness construct "friendly1" will need to form a separate interaction for each one of the five adapt indicators. You will then repeat this process for "friendly2" and "friendly3" until you have 15 interaction terms across the two constructs.

The first step in creating your interaction terms is to mean center all the indicators for your moderator and your independent variable. After you have mean centered all those indicators, you can then start forming the interaction terms across all the indicators in SPSS (Using the Transform function/Compute Variable). For the adapt1 and friendly1 interaction,

I have decided to call the new variable "CAdapt1XFriend1". You need to form a unique name for every pairing of the indicators. Once those interaction terms are created, we need to go back to AMOS and create an unobservable interaction construct. Let's call the unobservable interaction "Interaction_A_X_F" and then include the 15 interaction indicators to this unobservable construct. Lastly, we need to make sure a direct relationship is going from Adaptive Behavior, Friendliness, and the new interaction term (Interaction_A_X_F) to the variable of Customer Delight. The only mean centered indicators that need to be brought into the AMOS model are the interaction terms. The other constructs can be the original indicators. After drawing the model with the unobserved independent and dependent variables, moderator, and interaction term, we are ready to run the analysis. To see a graphical representation of this analysis, see Figure 7.17.

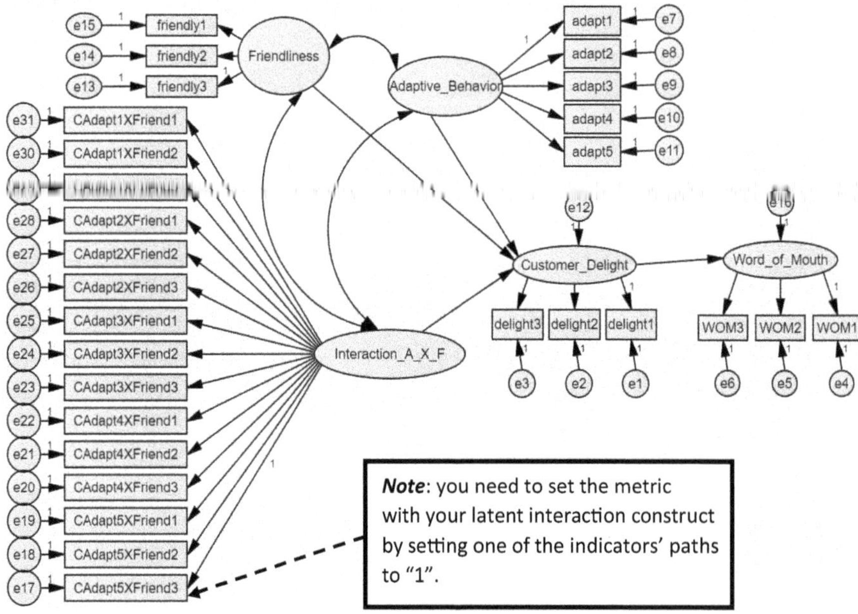

Figure 7.17 Full Indicator Interaction Term Test in AMOS

In the output of this moderation test, we have similar results to the test that was performed using the path model (composite variables) and the mixed method approach. The full indicator interaction method did produce slightly different results from those of the other tests but as a whole is still consistent with the findings of previous tests. See Figure 7.18 for the full structural model results.

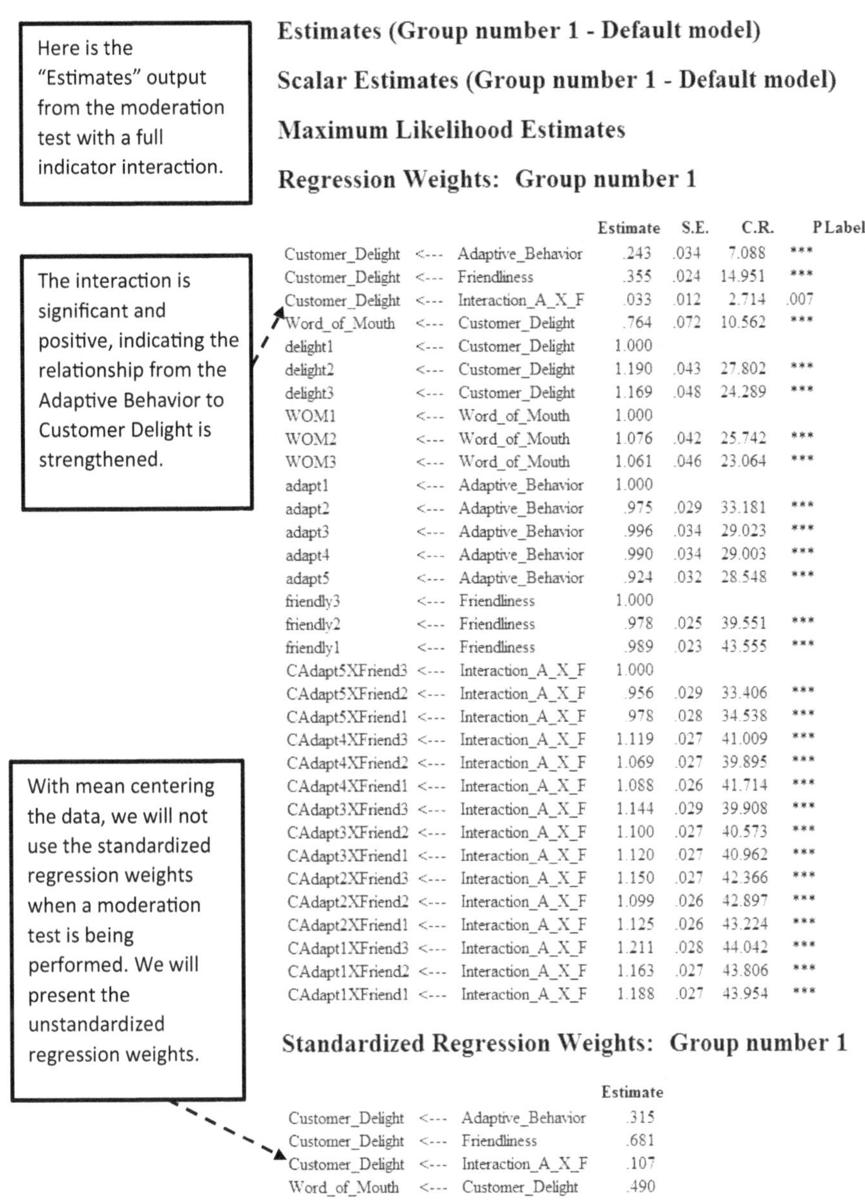

Here is the "Estimates" output from the moderation test with a full indicator interaction.
The interaction is significant and positive, indicating the relationship from the Adaptive Behavior to Customer Delight is strengthened.
With mean centering the data, we will not use the standardized regression weights when a moderation test is being performed. We will present the unstandardized regression weights.

Estimates (Group number 1 - Default model)

Scalar Estimates (Group number 1 - Default model)

Maximum Likelihood Estimates

Regression Weights: Group number 1

			Estimate	S.E.	C.R.	P	Label
Customer_Delight	<---	Adaptive_Behavior	.243	.034	7.088	***	
Customer_Delight	<---	Friendliness	.355	.024	14.951	***	
Customer_Delight	<---	Interaction_A_X_F	.033	.012	2.714	.007	
Word_of_Mouth	<---	Customer_Delight	.764	.072	10.562	***	
delight1	<---	Customer_Delight	1.000				
delight2	<---	Customer_Delight	1.190	.043	27.802	***	
delight3	<---	Customer_Delight	1.169	.048	24.289	***	
WOM1	<---	Word_of_Mouth	1.000				
WOM2	<---	Word_of_Mouth	1.076	.042	25.742	***	
WOM3	<---	Word_of_Mouth	1.061	.046	23.064	***	
adapt1	<---	Adaptive_Behavior	1.000				
adapt2	<---	Adaptive_Behavior	.975	.029	33.181	***	
adapt3	<---	Adaptive_Behavior	.996	.034	29.023	***	
adapt4	<---	Adaptive_Behavior	.990	.034	29.003	***	
adapt5	<---	Adaptive_Behavior	.924	.032	28.548	***	
friendly3	<---	Friendliness	1.000				
friendly2	<---	Friendliness	.978	.025	39.551	***	
friendly1	<---	Friendliness	.989	.023	43.555	***	
CAdapt5XFriend3	<---	Interaction_A_X_F	1.000				
CAdapt5XFriend2	<---	Interaction_A_X_F	.956	.029	33.406	***	
CAdapt5XFriend1	<---	Interaction_A_X_F	.978	.028	34.538	***	
CAdapt4XFriend3	<---	Interaction_A_X_F	1.119	.027	41.009	***	
CAdapt4XFriend2	<---	Interaction_A_X_F	1.069	.027	39.895	***	
CAdapt4XFriend1	<---	Interaction_A_X_F	1.088	.026	41.714	***	
CAdapt3XFriend3	<---	Interaction_A_X_F	1.144	.029	39.908	***	
CAdapt3XFriend2	<---	Interaction_A_X_F	1.100	.027	40.573	***	
CAdapt3XFriend1	<---	Interaction_A_X_F	1.120	.027	40.962	***	
CAdapt2XFriend3	<---	Interaction_A_X_F	1.150	.027	42.366	***	
CAdapt2XFriend2	<---	Interaction_A_X_F	1.099	.026	42.897	***	
CAdapt2XFriend1	<---	Interaction_A_X_F	1.125	.026	43.224	***	
CAdapt1XFriend3	<---	Interaction_A_X_F	1.211	.028	44.042	***	
CAdapt1XFriend2	<---	Interaction_A_X_F	1.163	.027	43.806	***	
CAdapt1XFriend1	<---	Interaction_A_X_F	1.188	.027	43.954	***	

Standardized Regression Weights: Group number 1

			Estimate
Customer_Delight	<---	Adaptive_Behavior	.315
Customer_Delight	<---	Friendliness	.681
Customer_Delight	<---	Interaction_A_X_F	.107
Word_of_Mouth	<---	Customer_Delight	.490

Figure 7.18 Estimates Output for Full Indicator Interaction Term

To be blunt, testing for moderation in a full indicator interaction model can be a tedious process. In this example, the moderator had only three indicators, which is usually the minimum number needed to even assess the reliability of a construct's measures. If the moderator had five indicators like the independent variable, that number of interaction terms balloons from 15 to 25. Subsequently, there is no shortage of critics for the full indicator interaction method. Researchers such as Ping (1998) note that models that have constructs with a large number of indicators will be creating a very large number of interaction indicators that can create covariance matrix issues where the model will result in nonconvergence. As well, the increased number of interaction indicators can negatively impact model fit estimation. Lastly, Ping notes that reusing the same indicator to form multiple interaction terms can also be problematic. Marsh et al. (2004) further state that using the same indicator to form numerous interaction indicators can create artificially correlated residuals. While this method allows us to use a full structural model with latent variables, it has its drawbacks as well.

As for probing the interaction, this full indicator interaction method is similar to the process outlined earlier for the path model and the mixed method approach. With the path model example, we subtracted or added the standard deviation from the composite moderator variable to get the high and low levels of the variable. In a full indicator interaction model, you need to find the standard deviation for each indicator of your moderator variable. With each indicator, you will subtract its specific standard deviation to get a high level indicator and you will add that standard deviation to get the low level indicator. After forming the new indicators for the moderator variable, you are ready to create an interaction term. Each low/high level indicator needs to be multiplied by every mean centered indicator of the independent variable. Just as before, you will have 15 interaction terms with the low level moderator and a separate 15 interaction terms with the high level moderator. For instance, if you are running the high/strong level moderator analysis, you first want to make sure your unobserved

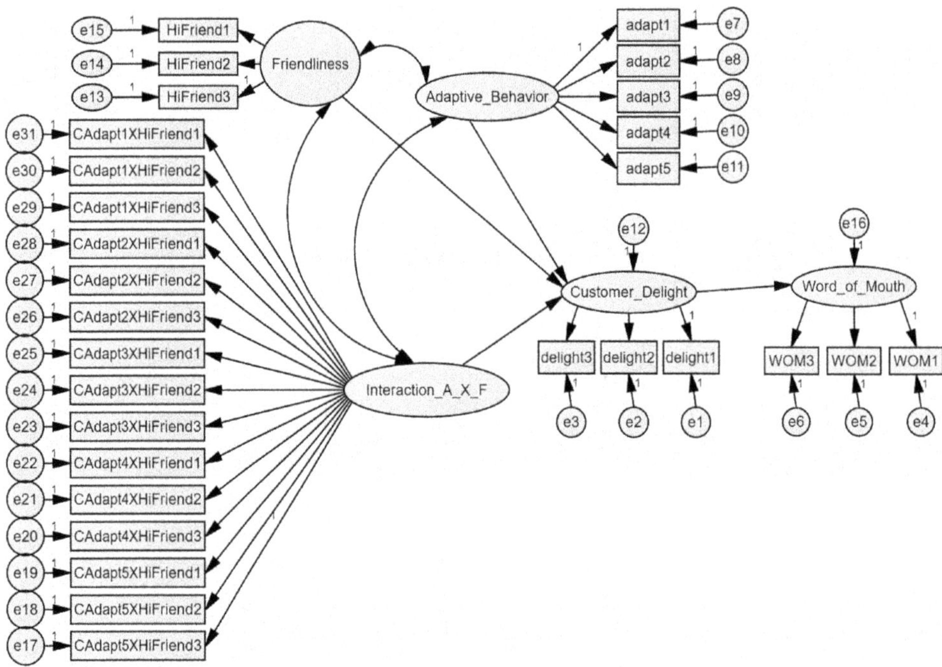

Figure 7.19 Full Indicator Interaction Term With High Levels of the Moderator

moderator (Friendliness) has the high level indicators attached to the construct. With the unobserved interaction variable (Interaction_A_X_F), you need to include the 15 newly formed interaction terms for the high level of the moderator. See Figure 7.19 for a graphical representation. To perform the low level moderation test, you simply change out the indicators to the low levels for the moderator and the unobserved interaction variable.

When we probed the interaction with a path model, the only results that changed from the initial analysis was the independent to dependent relationship (Adaptive Behavior to Customer Delight). With a moderation test in a full indicator interaction model, you will often see the "probing" relationships that include the moderator be slightly different from the initial test. This is often a rounding issue that takes place when each indicator has to be uniquely changed and then multiplied by the indicators of the independent variable. Subsequently, you are looking at the collective effect of these indicators when assessing structural relationships. When we are probing an interaction, those relationships are not our primary focus. Our main concern is the change from the independent to dependent variable with different levels of the moderator. In Figures 7.20 and 7.21, you will see the results for the high and low level interaction tests for the full indicator interaction model.

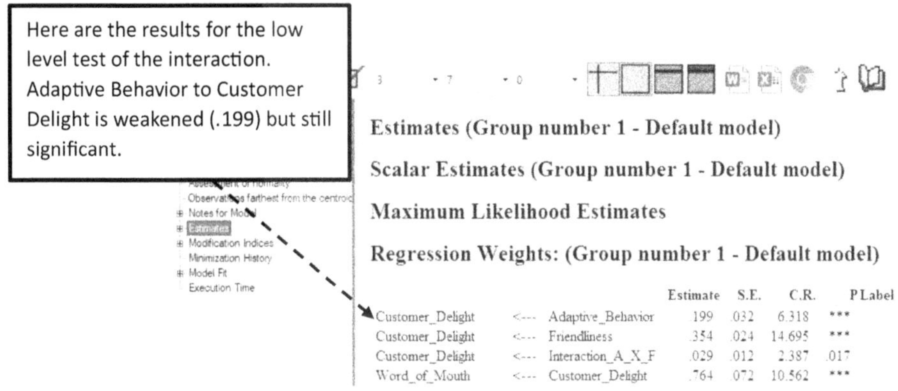

Figure 7.20 Estimates Output for Low Level Full Indicator Interaction Term

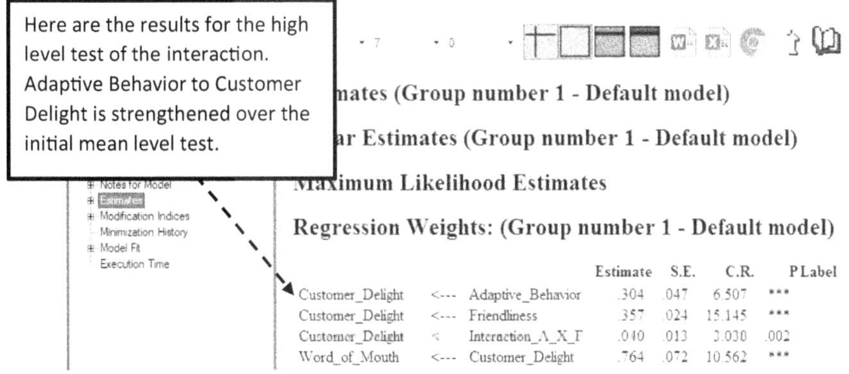

Figure 7.21 Estimates Output for High Level Full Indicator Interaction Term

Matched-Pairs Method

The matched-pairs method is a moderation test that uses latent constructs in a full structural model but circumnavigates some of the issues that were present with the full indicator interaction method. The matched-pairs method uses a condensed interaction term instead of modeling every possible indicator interaction. Marsh et al. (2004) note that a matched-pair method follows two criteria: (1) the indicators of a moderator and independent variable are accounted for in the interaction term, and (2) no indicator will be reused to form an interaction term. Let's consider an example of what this looks like. To make things easy, let's imagine that the moderator of Friendliness has three indicators and the independent variable of Adaptive Behavior has three indicators. The matched-pairs method would form an interaction term by creating a latent variable that included interaction indicators. The indicators would be created with one indicator of the moderator by one indicator of the independent variable until all the indicators had been used once and no indicator was reused to form the interaction indicators. In the example provided, the latent interaction term is formed by multiplying the first Friendliness indicator by the first Adaptive Behavior indicator. The process is repeated for Friendliness 2 and Adaptive Behavior 2 along with Friendliness 3 and Adaptive Behavior 3. See the graphical presentation provided in Figure 7.22.

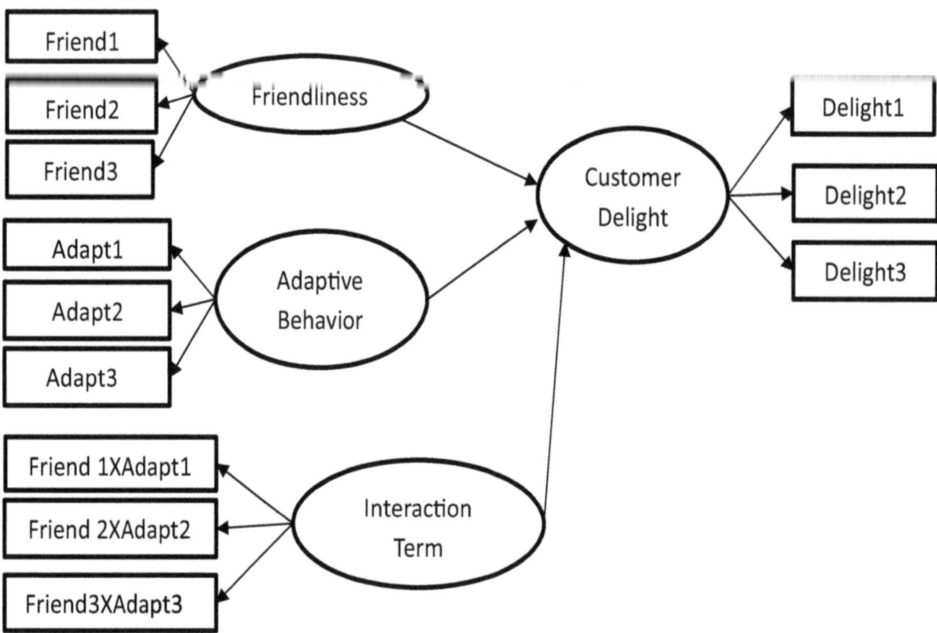

Figure 7.22 Example of a Matched Pairs Moderation Test

I know many of you at this point have the question, which of the different possible interaction combinations should I use as my matched-pair? As well, what if I don't have the same number of indicators for my moderator and independent variable? How do I form the matched-pair? Marsh et al. (2008) note that all possible interactions should initially be assessed and then the best (highest loading) interaction indicators are used where no indicator is used more than once. In the example, where you have three indicators in the moderator and the independent variable, you would choose three interaction indicators that would use all indicators once and not reuse any indicator. You would initially create an interaction term with all possible interaction indicators, choose the three with the highest factor loadings, and follow the rules of using all indicators and not reusing one. If you have differing number of indicators from the moderator and the independent variable, you will choose the construct with the lowest number of indicators, and that will be your number of interaction indicators to include in the newly formed interaction term. Again, you would assess all possible interaction indicators and choose the interactions that used all of the indicators of the smaller construct along with possible combinations of the larger construct. In essence, the smaller construct will use all indicators at least once with a combination of indicators of the larger construct. The overt problem with this method when the number of indicators differ across constructs is that you are not using all of the indicators to form your interaction variable. Some of the indicators of the larger construct will be left out.

Let's look at a matched-pair example with our existing example of Friendliness moderating the relationship from Adaptive Behavior to Customer Delight. To form the interaction term, we need to first assess which matched-pair needs to be included, since we have five indicators in the Adaptive Behavior construct and three indicators in the Friendliness construct. In the previous example of the full indicator interaction, we included all possible interactions in the interaction term construct. Looking at those results (Figure 7.18), the best matched-pair based on factor loadings is Adapt1&Friend1, Adapt2&Friend2, and Adapt4&Friend3. Notice that the smaller construct of Friendliness includes all the indicators at least once, but we are using only a subset of three indicators from Adaptive Behavior. In AMOS, we are going to model all constructs as latent unobservables with the indicators included along with the new interaction latent construct that has the three matched-pairs included as the indicators; see Figure 7.23. Let's look at the results in AMOS.

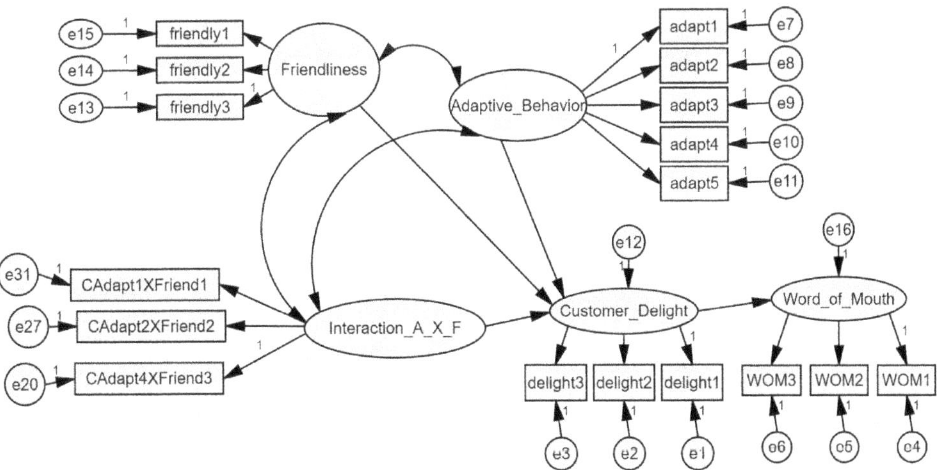

Figure 7.23 Matched-Pairs Moderation Test Drawn in AMOS

Regression Weights: (Group number 1 - Default model)

			Estimate	S.E.	C.R.	P	Label
Customer_Delight	<---	Adaptive_Behavior	.243	.035	7.045	***	
Customer_Delight	<---	Friendliness	.355	.024	14.927	***	
Customer_Delight	<---	Interaction_A_X_F	.030	.011	2.636	.008	
Word_of_Mouth	<---	Customer_Delight	.764	.072	10.559	***	
delight1	<---	Customer_Delight	1.000				
delight2	<---	Customer_Delight	1.190	.043	27.802	***	
delight3	<---	Customer_Delight	1.169	.048	24.288	***	
WOM1	<---	Word_of_Mouth	1.000				
WOM2	<---	Word_of_Mouth	1.076	.042	25.742	***	
WOM3	<---	Word_of_Mouth	1.061	.046	23.065	***	
adapt1	<---	Adaptive_Behavior	1.000				
adapt2	<---	Adaptive_Behavior	.975	.029	33.212	***	
adapt3	<---	Adaptive_Behavior	.996	.034	29.012	***	
adapt4	<---	Adaptive_Behavior	.990	.034	28.999	***	
adapt5	<---	Adaptive_Behavior	.924	.032	28.566	***	
friendly3	<---	Friendliness	1.000				
friendly2	<---	Friendliness	.978	.025	39.572	***	
friendly1	<---	Friendliness	.989	.023	43.541	***	
CAdapt4XFriend3	<---	Interaction_A_X_F	1.000				
CAdapt2XFriend2	<---	Interaction_A_X_F	.973	.017	57.352	***	
CAdapt1XFriend1	<---	Interaction_A_X_F	1.053	.018	59.943	***	

The matched-pair results show that the interaction term relationship to Customer Delight is very near to the results of the full indicator interaction method without having to add nearly as many interaction indicators to the model.

Figure 7.24 Estimates Output for Matched-Pairs Moderation Test

To probe the interaction with the matched-pair approach, you will need to get the high and low values of the moderator and multiply those values by the three indicators of the independent variable that is selected to be "matched" with the moderator.

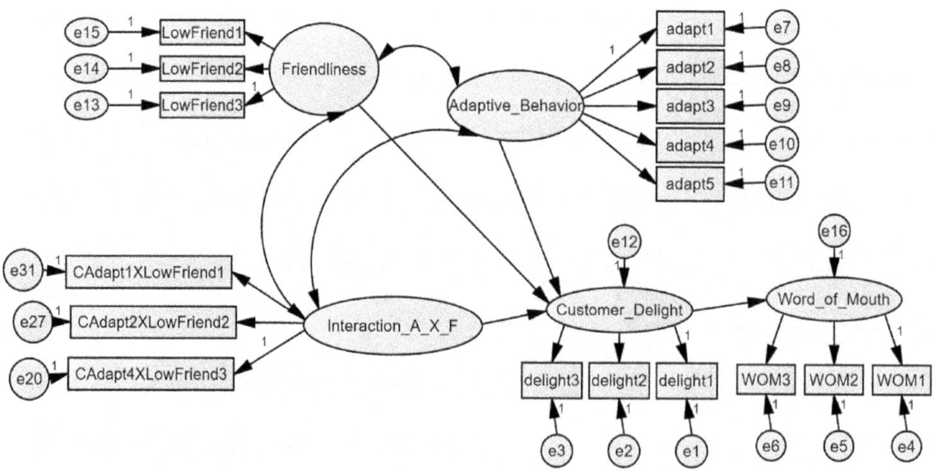

Figure 7.25 Matched-Pairs Moderation Test With Low Level Moderator

Figure 7.26 displays the results of the moderator Friendliness at low levels using the matched-pair method.

Estimates (Group number 1 - Default model)

Scalar Estimates (Group number 1 - Default model)

Maximum Likelihood Estimates

Regression Weights: (Group number 1 - Default model)

			Estimate	S.E.	C.R.	P	Label
Customer_Delight	<---	Adaptive_Behavior	.200	.031	6.350	***	
Customer_Delight	<---	Friendliness	.355	.024	14.656	***	
Customer_Delight	<---	Interaction_A_X_F	.027	.011	2.369	.018	
Word_of_Mouth	<---	Customer_Delight	.764	.072	10.560	***	

Figure 7.26 Estimates Output for Matched-Pairs Moderation Test With Low Level Moderator

Figure 7.27 displays the results of the moderator Friendliness at high levels using the matched-pair method.

Estimates (Group number 1 - Default model)

Scalar Estimates (Group number 1 - Default model)

Maximum Likelihood Estimates

Regression Weights: (Group number 1 - Default model)

			Estimate	S.E.	C.R.	P	Label
Customer_Delight	<---	Adaptive_Behavior	.302	.048	6.237	***	
Customer_Delight	<---	Friendliness	.356	.024	15.052	***	
Customer_Delight	<---	Interaction_A_X_F	.035	.013	2.782	.005	
Word_of_Mouth	<---	Customer_Delight	.764	.072	10.556	***	

Figure 7.27 Estimates Output for Matched Pairs Moderation Test With High Level Moderator

Table 7.2 Comparison of the Moderation Results Across Methods

	Path Model	*Mixed Method*	*Full Indicator*	*Matched-Pair*
Adaptive Behavior → Customer Delight	.279 (8.18)	.261 (7.69)	.243 (7.08)	.243 (7.04)
Friendliness → Customer Delight	.376 (16.80)	.331 (15.33)	.355 (14.95)	.355 (14.92)
Interaction Term → Customer Delight	.026 (2.14)	.026 (2.38)	.033 (2.71)	.030 (2.63)
Customer Delight → Positive Word of Mouth	.648 (11.06)	.766 (10.57)	.764 (10.56)	.764 (10.55)
Model Fit:	χ^2 = 5.30	χ^2 = 90.42	χ^2 = 5769.81	χ^2 = 172.64
	df = 3	df = 60	df = 370	df = 112
	CFI = .99	CFI = .99	CFI = .81	CFI = .99
	TLI = .99	TLI = .99	TLI = .80	TLI = .99
	RMSEA = .04	RMSEA = .03	RMSEA = .17	RMSEA = .03

Note: Unstandardized results presented with t-values in parentheses.

In Table 7.2, you can see a comparison of the different moderation testing techniques. While there is consistency in the results, each one of these methods of moderation testing has a drawback. The path model is the simplest way to test moderation, but you are not assessing any of the measurement error in the model with this method, and the path model is near saturation, which can skew model fit results. The mixed method approach accounts for the measurement error in the independent and dependent variables but fails to run a latent interaction test and, subsequently, does not account for measurement error in the moderator. The full indicator interaction method is the most laborious approach and has serious concerns in regards to assessing the fit of a model. In this example, the model fit is unacceptable with the inclusion of so many interaction indicators in the model. The last approach of matched-pair runs the moderation test in a full structural model with latent constructs, but the interaction term accounts for only some of the influence of the independent variable because it had a larger number of indicators than the moderator. As stated earlier, each method has its drawbacks, but based on this analysis, the advised approach to moderation testing would be the mixed method or matched-pair technique.

How Do I Present My Moderation Results?

When you are presenting results for a moderation test in a table format, it is a good idea to include the following results with the presentation of the structural regression weights of the constructs. There is no need to have a dedicated table for moderation when it can complement the structural results. Specifically, for the moderation test, I like to include the relationship from the moderator and the interaction term to the dependent variable. Showing the results of probing the interaction is also advisable. Lastly, including a graph is sometimes nice to let the reader see the interaction between variables.

Example 7.1:

Table 7.3 Structural and Moderation Test Results (Matched-Pair method)

Hypothesized Relationships	*Unstandardized Estimates*	*t-values*	*Hypothesis Supported*
H1: Adaptive Behavior → Customer Delight	.243	7.04	Supported
H2: Customer Delight → Positive Word of Mouth	.764	10.55	Supported
Moderation Test			
Friendliness → Customer Delight	.355	14.92	
H3: Adaptive Behavior ***X*** Friendliness → Customer Delight	.030	2.63	Supported
Probing the Interaction of Friendliness			
Low level: Adaptive Behavior → Customer Delight	.199	6.30	
Mean level: Adaptive Behavior → Customer Delight	.243	7.04	
High level: Adaptive Behavior → Customer Delight	.305	6.36	

Mean Center vs. Z Score in Moderation Testing

Instead of creating a new variable where you are subtracting the variable's mean, SPSS gives you another option to center the data by "standardizing" the indicators (or converting it to a Z score). With mean centering, you are changing the mean value, but the standard deviation and scale remain the same. This is not the case with Z scores. If you convert your data to a Z score, SPSS will rescale the data so that one unit in the data is equivalent to one standard deviation. Both methods will center the mean to zero, but using Z scores will also completely rescale the data.

To create a Z score with your data, you need to go to the "Analyze" menu option in SPSS, then select "Descriptive Statistics" and then choose "Descriptives". A pop-up window will appear where you will include the variables of the moderator and the independent variable in the "Variables" option. You will also see at the bottom of the pop-up window a checkbox that states "Save Standardized Values as Variables". Check this box and hit OK.

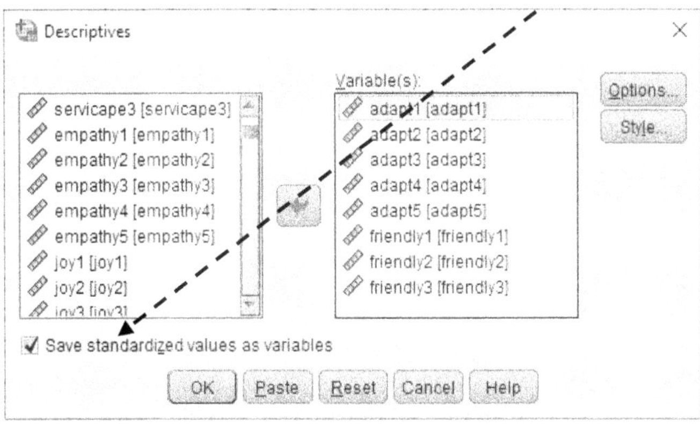

Figure 7.28 Creating Z Scores of Variables in SPSS

SPSS will create a new variable for each one of the variables selected in the Descriptives window. At the end of the data, SPSS will add a "Z" in the front of the newly formed variable along with the original variable name. See Figure 7.29.

Customer Delight Data.sav [DataSet17] - IBM SPSS Statistics Data Editor

File Edit View Data Transform Analyze Graphs Utilities Extensions Window Help

Visible: 178 of 178 Variables

		Zadapt1	Zadapt2	Zadapt3	Zadapt4	Zadapt5
7	3	.86092	.84933	.86291	.88342	.81230
8	2	-.11077	-.17396	-.08534	-.07060	-.20308
9	2	.86092	.84933	.86291	.88342	.81230
10	3	.86092	.84933	.86291	.88342	.81230
11	3	.86092	.84933	.86291	.88342	.81230

Data View Variable View

IBM SPSS Statistics Processor is ready | Unicode:ON

Figure 7.29 Example of Variables Transformed Into Z Scores in SPSS

These standardized variables are now mean centered and rescaled. You will then use these Z score indicators to create interaction terms just like we did with the mean centered example. I have included an example of what the graphic depiction would look like in AMOS. Notice that the interaction terms are all reformed with the Z scores and all the labels have a Z at the front to denote a Z score interaction.

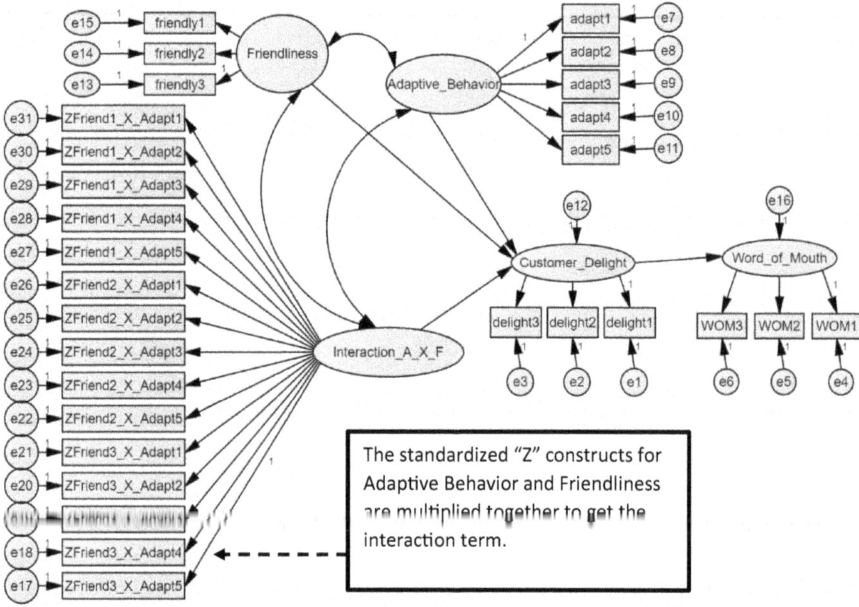

Figure 7.30 Example of Z Scores Used in Moderation Testing

Let's now look at the results of our full structural moderation test with the standardized Z score interactions and compare the results to the mean centered moderation test.

Estimates output from the manual mean centered analysis.

Regression Weights: Group number 1

			Estimate	S.E.	C.R.	P	Label
Customer_Delight	<---	Adaptive_Behavior	.243	.034	7.088	***	
Customer_Delight	<---	Friendliness	.355	.024	14.951	***	
Customer_Delight	<---	Interaction_A_X_F	.033	.012	2.714	.007	
Word_of_Mouth	<---	Customer_Delight	.764	.072	10.562	***	

Estimates output from the Z Score variables.

Regression Weights: Group number 1

			Estimate	S.E.	C.R.	P	Label
Customer_Delight	<---	Adaptive_Behavior	.243	.034	7.088	***	
Customer_Delight	<---	Friendliness	.355	.024	14.951	***	
Customer_Delight	<---	Interaction_A_X_F	.048	.018	2.714	.007	
Word_of_Mouth	<---	Customer_Delight	.764	.072	10.562	***	

Figure 7.31 Comparison of Mean Centered and Z Score Results

Comparison of the results shows a small difference in the unstandardized regression weights of the interaction variable. The t-value for the interaction is exactly the same across the different tests. The standardized regression weights are also exactly the same across the two tests. Any differences that are present across the two moderation tests is a result of rescaling the data with the Z scores and rounding considerations with the mean centered option. The results are essentially equivalent.

Probing the interaction with a Z score moderation test is accomplished in a slightly different manner. Transforming the data to a Z score rescales the data where 1 unit (or a value of 1) is 1 standard deviation. To create the high moderation variable, you would need to take the Z score for each indicator of the moderator and subtract a value of 1. For the low moderation, you would add a value of 1 to all the Z scores for the indicators of the moderator. After that, you would form your interaction terms with the Z score Hi/Low moderator indicators multiplied by the independent variables' Z score indicators.

Whether you use mean centering or Z scores, both methods should help to account for any potential multicollinearity between the moderator and the independent variable. While the Z score option may save you some time, you need to be aware that Z scores will rescale your data and subsequently impact standard deviation values. With a mean centered value, your standard deviation does not change from the original data, and the scale is still the same. One unit with a mean centered value is still one unit.

Moderation Testing With a Categorical Moderator

You can use a categorical variable as a moderator in AMOS. The way to test a categorical moderator is the exact same process used to perform a two group analysis that was discussed in Chapter 5. For instance, let's say we have a categorical moderator that captures the customer's previous experience with the retailer. One of the categories will be "first-time customers" and the second category will be "repeat customers". This categorical variable is proposed to moderate the relationship from Adaptive Behavior to Customer Delight. In essence, we are hypothesizing that adapting a service will have a stronger relationship to customer delight with first-time customers compared to repeat customers. To test this moderator, we will set up a two group analysis in AMOS where we will form two groups and then label all the parameters differently across the groups. For a detailed explanation on two group analysis, see page 149 in Chapter 5. Once we have labeled all the parameters for each group, we are ready to specify the relationships that need to be tested across the groups. AMOS will initially give you different potential models that will constrain different aspects of the model to be equal across the groups and compare this to the unconstrained model. We need to create a new model comparison (we can call it "Constrain 1") because we are concerned only if the relationship from Adaptive Behavior to Customer Delight is significantly different across the categories of the moderator. We are going to constrain that one path in the model and compare the results to the unconstrained model and initially see if a chi-square difference is significant across the groups. In the labeled model in Figure 7.32, the path we will focus in on is b1_1 (Adaptive Behavior to Customer Delight).

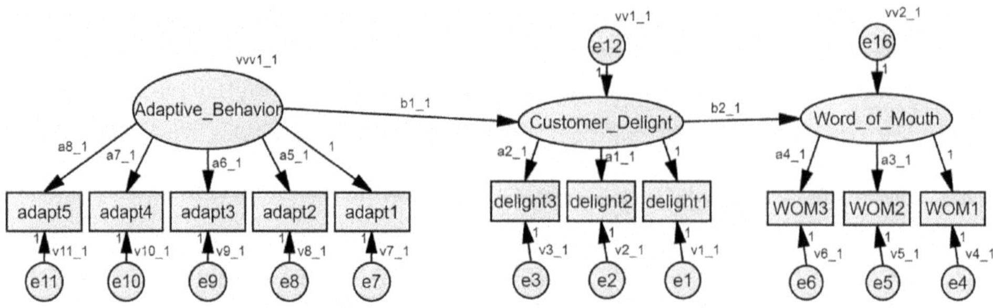

Figure 7.32 Categorical Moderator Tested in a Two Group Model

The "Constrain 1" model test is going to constrain the b1_1 (first-time customer) relationship to the b1_2 (repeat customer) relationship. No other model comparisons are of interest at this point. After forming the new comparison model, we are ready to run the analysis.

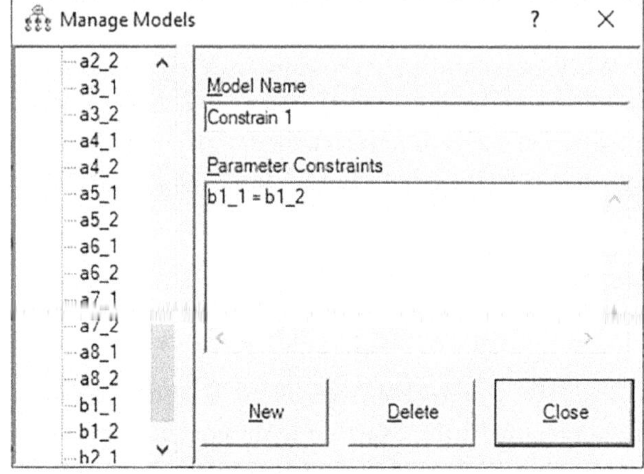

Figure 7.33 Constraining Adaptive Behavior to Customer Delight to Be Equal Across the Groups

After running the analysis, the first area in the output we want to examine is the "Model Comparison" link. This will give us the chi-square difference across the groups for the relationship we are testing. The results of the test show us that the "Constrain 1" model comparison had a chi-square difference of 15.007, which is significant at the $p < .001$ level.

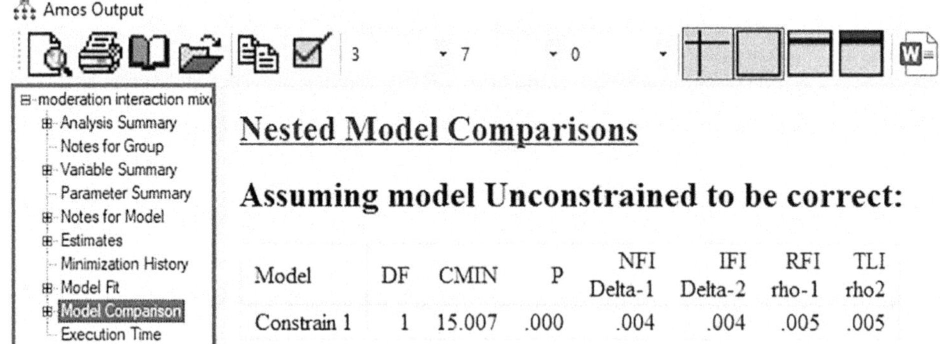

Nested Model Comparisons

Assuming model Unconstrained to be correct:

Model	DF	CMIN	P	NFI Delta-1	IFI Delta-2	RFI rho-1	TLI rho2
Constrain 1	1	15.007	.000	.004	.004	.005	.005

Figure 7.34 Chi-Square Difference Test Across the Groups

We now know the relationship is different across the groups, but I do not know if a specific category is strengthening/weakening a relationship compared to another category. To find out this information, we need to go to the "Estimates" link in the output and examine the regression coefficients across the groups.

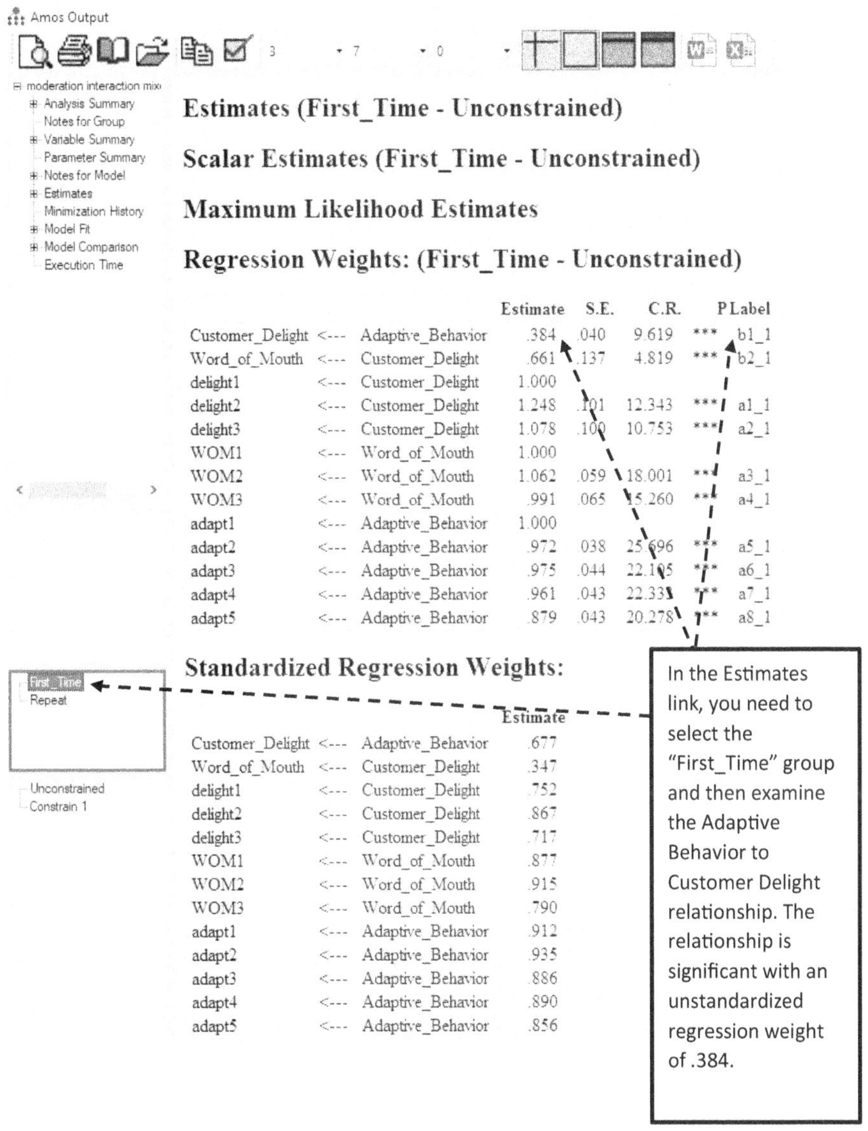

			Estimate	S.E.	C.R.	P	Label
Customer_Delight	<---	Adaptive_Behavior	.384	.040	9.619	***	b1_1
Word_of_Mouth	<---	Customer_Delight	.661	.137	4.819	***	b2_1
delight1	<---	Customer_Delight	1.000				
delight2	<---	Customer_Delight	1.248	.101	12.343	***	a1_1
delight3	<---	Customer_Delight	1.078	.100	10.753	***	a2_1
WOM1	<---	Word_of_Mouth	1.000				
WOM2	<---	Word_of_Mouth	1.062	.059	18.001	***	a3_1
WOM3	<---	Word_of_Mouth	.991	.065	15.260	***	a4_1
adapt1	<---	Adaptive_Behavior	1.000				
adapt2	<---	Adaptive_Behavior	.972	.038	25.696	***	a5_1
adapt3	<---	Adaptive_Behavior	.975	.044	22.105	***	a6_1
adapt4	<---	Adaptive_Behavior	.961	.043	22.331	***	a7_1
adapt5	<---	Adaptive_Behavior	.879	.043	20.278	***	a8_1

			Estimate
Customer_Delight	<---	Adaptive_Behavior	.677
Word_of_Mouth	<---	Customer_Delight	.347
delight1	<---	Customer_Delight	.752
delight2	<---	Customer_Delight	.867
delight3	<---	Customer_Delight	.717
WOM1	<---	Word_of_Mouth	.877
WOM2	<---	Word_of_Mouth	.915
WOM3	<---	Word_of_Mouth	.790
adapt1	<---	Adaptive_Behavior	.912
adapt2	<---	Adaptive_Behavior	.935
adapt3	<---	Adaptive_Behavior	.886
adapt4	<---	Adaptive_Behavior	.890
adapt5	<---	Adaptive_Behavior	.856

Figure 7.35 Examining the Direct Effects in the Estimates Output for the First-Time Group

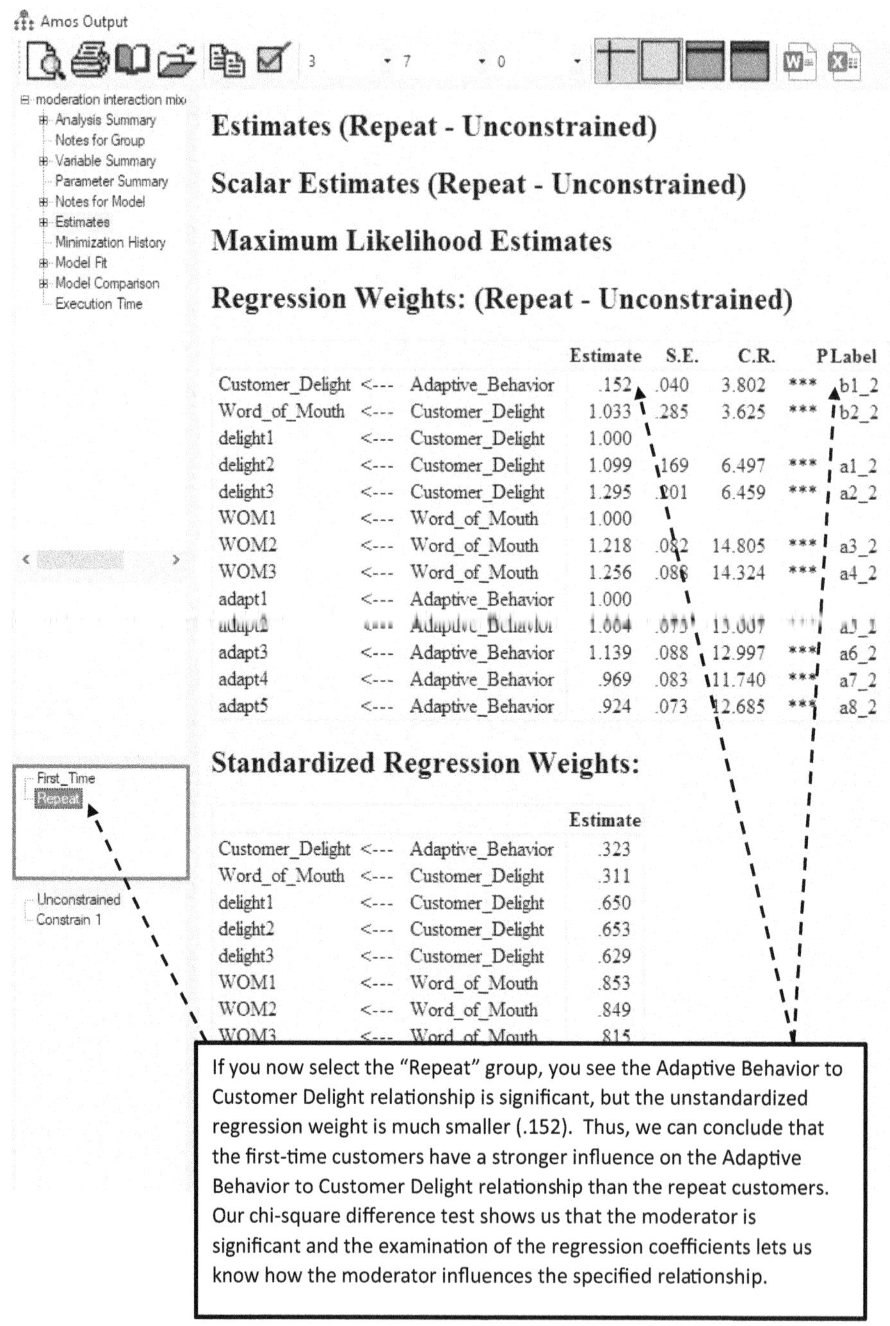
Amos Output
moderation interaction mix
Analysis Summary
Notes for Group
Variable Summary
Parameter Summary
Notes for Model
Estimates
Minimization History
Model Fit
Model Comparison
Execution Time
First_Time
Repeat
Unconstrained
Constrain 1
Estimates (Repeat - Unconstrained)
Scalar Estimates (Repeat - Unconstrained)
Maximum Likelihood Estimates
Regression Weights: (Repeat - Unconstrained)
Standardized Regression Weights:
If you now select the "Repeat" group, you see the Adaptive Behavior to Customer Delight relationship is significant, but the unstandardized regression weight is much smaller (.152). Thus, we can conclude that the first-time customers have a stronger influence on the Adaptive Behavior to Customer Delight relationship than the repeat customers. Our chi-square difference test shows us that the moderator is significant and the examination of the regression coefficients lets us know how the moderator influences the specified relationship.

			Estimate	S.E.	C.R.	P	Label
Customer_Delight	<---	Adaptive_Behavior	.152	.040	3.802	***	b1_2
Word_of_Mouth	<---	Customer_Delight	1.033	.285	3.625	***	b2_2
delight1	<---	Customer_Delight	1.000				
delight2	<---	Customer_Delight	1.099	.169	6.497	***	a1_2
delight3	<---	Customer_Delight	1.295	.201	6.459	***	a2_2
WOM1	<---	Word_of_Mouth	1.000				
WOM2	<---	Word_of_Mouth	1.218	.082	14.805	***	a3_2
WOM3	<---	Word_of_Mouth	1.256	.088	14.324	***	a4_2
adapt1	<---	Adaptive_Behavior	1.000				
adapt2	<---	Adaptive_Behavior	1.064	.075	13.007	***	a5_2
adapt3	<---	Adaptive_Behavior	1.139	.088	12.997	***	a6_2
adapt4	<---	Adaptive_Behavior	.969	.083	11.740	***	a7_2
adapt5	<---	Adaptive_Behavior	.924	.073	12.685	***	a8_2

			Estimate
Customer_Delight	<---	Adaptive_Behavior	.323
Word_of_Mouth	<---	Customer_Delight	.311
delight1	<---	Customer_Delight	.650
delight2	<---	Customer_Delight	.653
delight3	<---	Customer_Delight	.629
WOM1	<---	Word_of_Mouth	.853
WOM2	<---	Word_of_Mouth	.849
WOM3	<---	Word_of_Mouth	.815

Figure 7.36 Examining the Direct Effects in the Estimates Output for the Repeat Group

With categorical moderation testing, we are not creating interaction terms like with moderation testing with a continuous variable. We treat the different categories of the moderator like they are two separate groups. These groups are then compared to determine if the relationship of interest is different across the groups and which group is stronger/weaker compared to the other.

In this example, I used first-time/repeat customers, but the moderation test could have been a demographic variable such as Male/Female. Examples of other variables for moderation testing could have been customers that just wanted dessert/customers that wanted a full meal. It could even be the actions of the employee such as the employee broke a rule to make a customer happy/employee did not break a rule to make a customer happy. The categorical moderator just needs to be a distinct category. Presenting the results of a categorical moderation test will be similar to the presentation of a two group analysis. You will present the regression weights and t-values across the groups. You will also need to present the chi-square difference test. Since we are not mean centering the data, you can also present the standardized regression weights if you want.

In My Opinion: Treating a Continuous Variable as a Categorical Variable in Moderation Testing

In the past, I would see numerous research studies where a researcher would take a continuous variable and artificially break the variable into two categories. For instance, you would see a variable like Ease of Use on a 7-point Likert scale that would be broken into two categories of (a) Hard to use and (b) Easy to use. The division of the continuous variable was usually split at the mean of the data. This two category Ease of Use construct would then be used for a moderation test as the categorical moderator. There are numerous problems with taking a continuous variable and splitting it into a categorical variable. First, the data might be extremely skewed where the mean of the data is a 6 on a 1-to-7 scale. You would probably see values listed as a 5 combined into the low ease of use category based on where the mean lies. If you had a full range of scores, a 5 might actually be considered a high ease of use response. Put another way, you are actually taking relatively high ease of use scores and calling them low because of the skewness of the data. Second, I often feel the cut point that distinguishes categories is determined by which alternative produces the best results for the researcher. I have heard of researchers using three different cut point options and the one they ultimately choose is the one that lines up with their hypotheses. It feels very opportunistic when you are arbitrarily dividing a continuous variable into categories. That said, I feel the best option for testing moderation with a continuous variable is to use an interaction term. By using an interaction term, you also avoid the criticism that you are just capitalizing on chance because of how this data set was divided.

Calculating Categorical Moderation via Pairwise Parameter Comparison

With a categorical moderator, you can also assess moderation by a function called the pairwise parameter comparison in AMOS. With this method, you still have to form the groups and label the parameters, but you do not have to individually constrain the relationship of interest.

The pairwise parameter comparison will show you all the possible constraints of parameters. I will warn you that this is only a good option if you have a very small number of parameters; otherwise, you will be drowning in all the possible combinations of parameter comparisons. To make things simplistic, let's use the path model example (composite variables) and test if first-time customers/repeat customers are moderating the relationship from Adaptive Behavior to Customer Delight. After forming the model, creating the groups, and labeling all the parameters, go into the Analysis Properties window . In the Output tab, you will see a checkbox on the right-hand side that says "Critical ratios for differences"; let's check that box. After doing that, cancel out of the window and run your analysis.

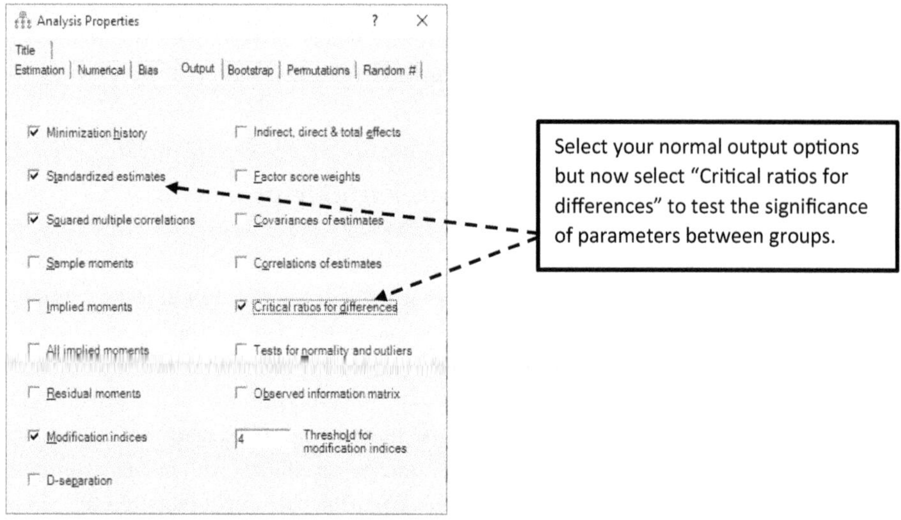

Figure 7.37 Critical Ratios for Differences Function Located in the Analysis Properties Window

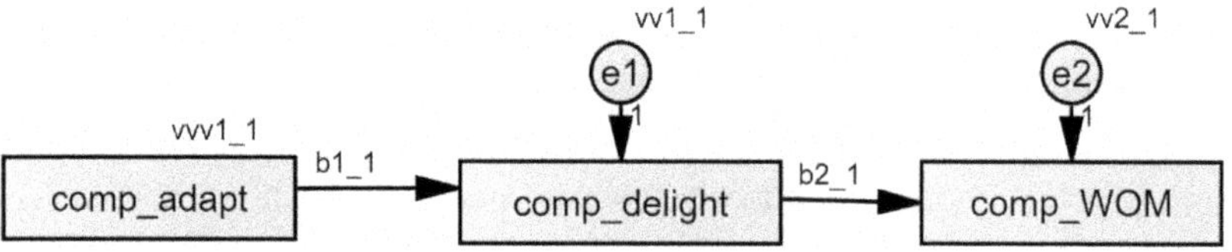

Figure 7.38 Labeled Model to Test With Critical Ratios for Differences

Once the analysis finishes running, go into the output. You need to click the link titled "Pairwise Parameter Comparison". This output will give the critical ratio (t-value) for every possible parameter comparison across the groups. It constrains all possible parameters across the groups and present the results of those comparisons. The parameter comparison that we are concerned with is the one from Adaptive Behavior to Customer Delight, labeled b1_1 (for first-time customers) and b1_2 (repeat customers). To find the b1 parameter comparison, you will need to find the b1_1 on the column value and b1_2 on the row level.

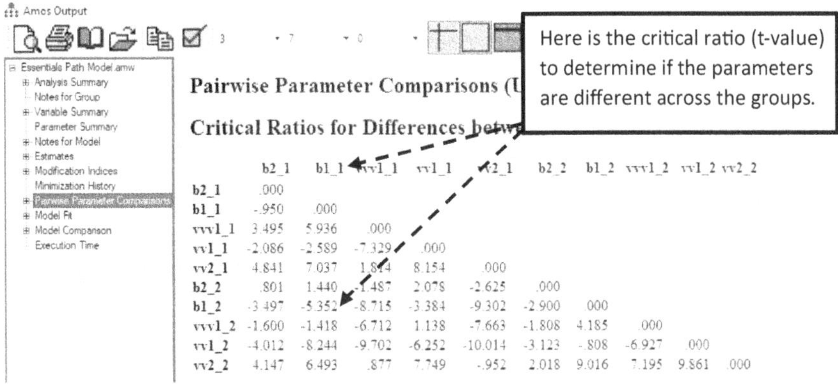

Pairwise Parameter Comparisons (U

Critical Ratios for Differences betw

	b2_1	b1_1	vvv1_1	vv1_1	vv2_1	b2_2	b1_2	vvv1_2	vv1_2	vv2_2
b2_1	.000									
b1_1	-.950	.000								
vvv1_1	3.495	5.936	.000							
vv1_1	-2.086	-2.589	-7.329	.000						
vv2_1	4.841	7.037	1.844	8.154	.000					
b2_2	.801	1.440	-1.487	2.078	-2.625	.000				
b1_2	-3.497	-5.352	-8.715	-3.384	-9.302	-2.900	.000			
vvv1_2	-1.600	-1.418	-6.712	1.138	-7.663	-1.808	4.185	.000		
vv1_2	-4.012	-8.244	-9.702	-6.252	-10.014	-3.123	-.808	-6.927	.000	
vv2_2	4.147	6.493	.877	7.749	-.952	2.018	9.016	7.195	9.861	.000

Figure 7.39 Critical Ratios for Differences Output

If you look at where they intersect, the critical ratio value says 5.352, which is significant. The value is negative, but we are concerned only with the absolute value presented. After determining that the relationship is significantly different, you can go to the Estimates output and see the differences of regression weights across the groups.

I do not recommend this option in testing categorical moderation because the pairwise parameter output is so hard to use. If you have a full structural model, you will be scrolling 40 columns to the right and 45 rows down to see the parameter of interest. It can be extremely difficult to find your specific parameter of interest in a large model (especially one that is a full structural model).

Moderated Mediation With a Continuous Moderator

In more complex models, you may have a mediation model that also has a moderator on one of the indirect paths. Not only are you trying to determine if mediation is present, but you are also trying to see if a moderator is changing the strength of the indirect effect. The easiest way to tackle this issue is to use the estimands function in AMOS outlined in the mediation section starting on page 182. Let's look at our moderation example again, only now we are going to examine if the moderator is influencing the indirect effect. Our simple mediation test will be if Adaptive Behavior leads to Customer Delight, which leads to Positive Word of Mouth. Our moderator will be the construct of Friendliness, which positively influences the relationship from Adaptive Behavior to Customer Delight. See the graphical representation that follows.

In AMOS, we drag in our constructs and include the paths for mediation. We also include the moderator and the interaction term into the model. Note the interaction term needs to be created by the mean centered variables as outlined in the moderation examples presented earlier. After we have drawn the model, we label all the parameter estimates. This will be necessary when we start using the estimands function in AMOS. See Figure 7.40.

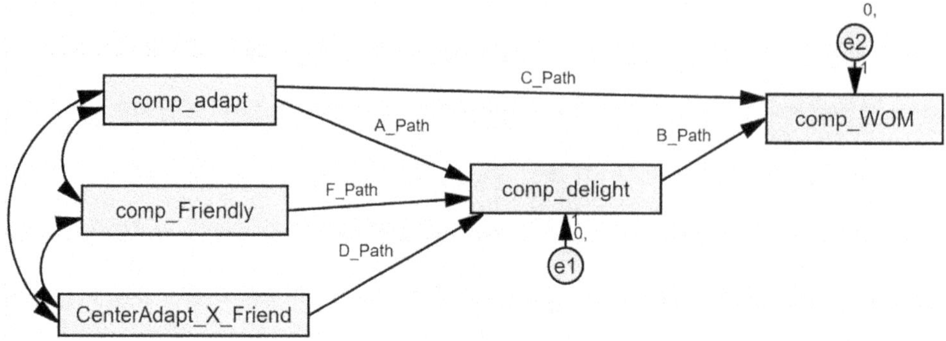

Figure 7.40 Moderated Mediation Model With Parameters Labeled

In the estimands function, we are going to examine the indirect effects at different levels of the moderator. In AMOS, we are going to select the "Define new estimands" function which will bring up a pop-up window. The indirect effect is the product of the A_Path and the B_Path. Initially, we are going to tell AMOS to calculate the labeled parameter "A_Path" by the "B_Path". This is going to determine the indirect effect in the presence of the moderator. Make sure the moderator and interaction term are included in the model; we are not trying to piecemeal the analysis. Next, we need to "probe" the indirect effect to determine how the moderator influences the indirect effect when it is at different levels. In the estimands function, let's label these tests "OneStandBelow" and "OneStandAbove". This will denote that the moderator is one standard deviation below the mean and one standard deviation above the mean. The standard deviation for Friendliness is 1.37746.

To probe the moderator at different levels, we initially take the path from the interaction term to the mediator (D_Path) and multiply it by the standard deviation of the moderator. We then take this value and multiply it by the path from the independent variable to the mediator (A_Path). Next, the product of those values will be multiplied by the path from the mediator to the dependent variable (B_Path). To help clarify this, let's look at an example of what the formula would look like in the estimand function: (A_Path+(D_Path*1.37746))*B_Path. This would represent the one standard deviation above test. The One Standard Below formula would be exactly the same, except the interaction parameter (D_Path) would be multiplied by the negative of the standard deviation. See the example of the formulas in the estimand formula window in Figure 7.41.

Normally, in a moderation test, you would need to form your new "Hi and Low" mean centered variables and interactions in SPSS but the estimands function will allow us to save some time by calculating them all at once. Once you have saved the new estimand function, make sure to run the syntax check. Remember that an estimands function will not run unless a bootstrap analysis is being performed. You need to go into the Analysis Properties, select

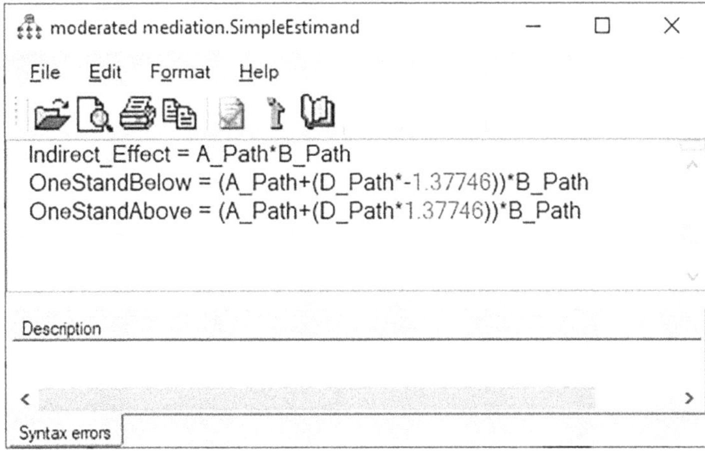

Figure 7.41 Estimand Function Testing Indirect Effects at Different Levels of the Moderator

Regression Weights: (Group number 1 - Default model)

			Estimate	S.E.	C.R.	P	Label
comp_delight	<---	comp_adapt	.279	.034	8.184	***	A_Path
comp_delight	<---	CenterAdapt_X_Friend	.026	.012	2.143	.032	D_Path
comp_delight	<---	comp_Friendly	.376	.022	16.803	***	F_Path
comp_WOM	<---	comp_delight	.558	.077	7.264	***	B_Path
comp_WOM	<---	comp_adapt	.126	.069	1.810	.070	C_Path

Figure 7.42 Estimates Output Examining Interaction and Direct Effects in Model

perform bootstrap and change the samples to 5,000, and then change the confidence interval to 95%. You are now ready to run the analysis. Let's initially go to the Estimates link in the output.

From these results, we can see that the A_Path is significant along with the B_Path. We also see a significant interaction. Notice the C_Path or direct effect of Adaptive Behavior to Customer Delight is non-significant. This is good initial information, but we still do not know about the indirect effect or how the moderator influences the indirect effect. Under the Estimates link, let's go to the "Scalars" option and then select the "User-defined estimand" link. This will initially give us the indirect effect for all our outlined tests in the estimands function. If you select the "Bias-corrected percentile method" at the bottom, you will have the bootstrap results that you need. As you can see in the output of Figure 7.43, the indirect effect in the presence of the moderator is .156, and per the bootstrap, that is within the confidence interval at a $p < .001$ level. You will also see the indirect effects when we probed the interaction at one standard deviation below and above the mean. The results show than when the moderator is low, the indirect effect is .136, which is still significant. Conversely, when the moderator is high, the indirect effect is .176 and significant as well.

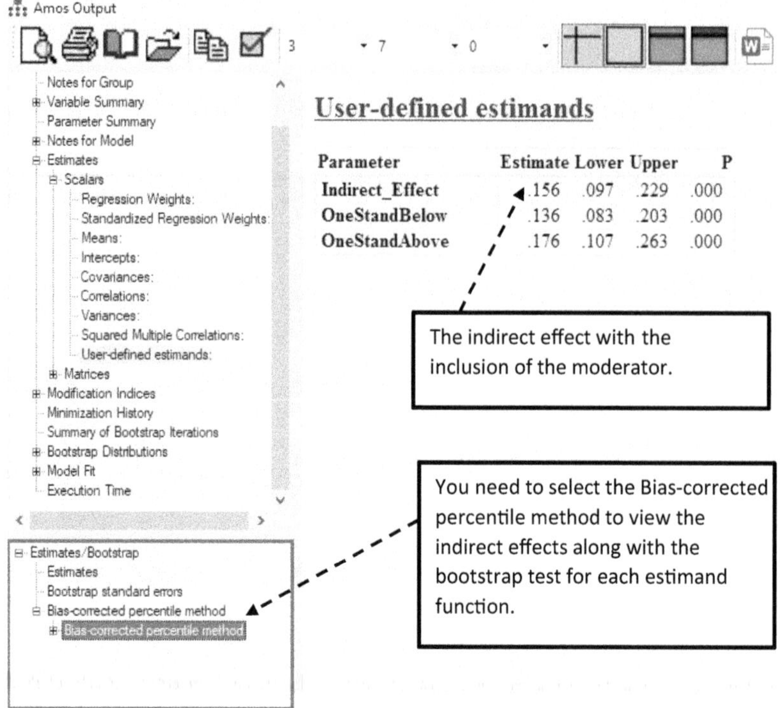

Figure 7.43 User Defined Estimand Showing Indirect Effects at Different Levels of the Moderator

The last test we need to assess is if the construct of Friendliness is significantly moderating the indirect effect. We saw earlier that the interaction was significant but that just tests the "A_Path". We need to assess if the indirect effect is being moderated. This is assessed by the index of moderated mediation value. This value is calculated by getting the product of the interaction term (D_Path) to the mediator by the relationship of the mediator to the dependent variable (B_Path). This analysis examines if the slope is significantly different than zero, which indicates that moderated mediation is taking place. Since there is only one mediator, AMOS will give us this information in the Indirect Effects output along with a bootstrap analysis to determine if the index of moderated mediation is significant. In the Estimates link, you need to go to the "Matrices" option. In the unstandardized indirect effects, you will see the indirect effect of the interaction term (through customer delight) to positive word of mouth. That value is .015.

Indirect Effects (Group number 1 - Default model)

	CenterAdapt_X_Friend	comp_Friendly	comp_adapt	comp_delight
comp_delight	.000	.000	.000	.000
comp_WOM	.015	.210	.156	.000

Figure 7.44 Indirect Effect to Determine Index of Moderated Mediation

We now need to go to the Bias-corrected percentile method option to see if it is significant. The results give us the lower and upper bound of the bootstrap test. We can also see that the index of moderated mediation is significant with a p = .039. Thus, we can conclude that the indirect effect is moderated by Friendliness. Note that we do not need the index of moderated mediation for our high or low estimates of the moderator. Our primary concern in testing the index of moderation mediation is the original mean value in the indirect test.

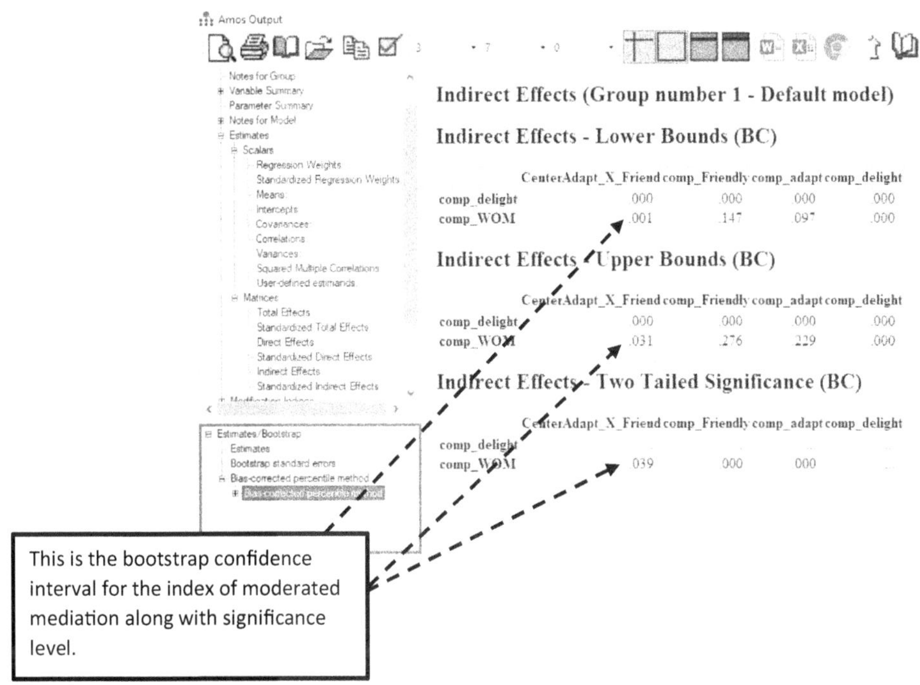

Figure 7.45 Confidence Interval for Index of Moderated Mediation

With the index of moderated mediation, we used the AMOS indirect effect results because the interaction was only going through the single mediator of Customer Delight to Positive Word of Mouth. There was only one possible indirect path from the interaction term to Positive Word of Mouth. If you have multiple mediators that you are testing simultaneously, you would be better off using the estimands function. In that situation, you will denote what specific relationships you wanted to isolate in the bigger model. In our example, the estimands formula for the index of moderated mediation would be the D_Path (interaction term to customer delight) multiplied by the B_Path (Customer Delight to Positive Word of Mouth).

How Do I Report the Results of My Moderated Mediation Test?

There is a lot of information to present in a moderated mediation test. Here is one example of how to present your results. You need to include the structural results, the tests of the indirect effect, the probing of the indirect effect, and the index of moderated mediation.

Example 7.2:

Table 7.4 Test for Moderated Mediation Using 95% Confidence Interval

Direct Relationships			*Unstandardized Coefficient*	*t-values*
Adaptive Behavior → Customer Delight			.279	8.18
Customer Delight → Positive Word of Mouth			.558	7.26
Friendliness → Customer Delight			.376	16.80
Adaptive Behavior **X** Friendliness → Customer Delight			.026	2.14
Moderated Indirect Relationship	*Direct Effect*	*Indirect Effect*	*Confidence Interval Low/High*	*p-value*
Adaptive Behavior → Customer Delight → Positive Word of Mouth*	.126 (1.81)	.156	.097 /.229	< .001
Probing Moderated Indirect Relationships				
Low Levels of Friendliness:		.136	.083 /.203	<.001
High Levels of Friendliness:		.176	.107 /.263	<.001
Index of Moderated Mediation		.015	.001 /.031	.039

Note: * = The indirect effect is moderated by the construct of Friendliness.
Unstandardized coefficients reported. Value in parentheses is t-value. Bootstrap Sample = 5,000 with replacement.

Moderated Mediation With a Categorical Moderator

In the preceding example, we explored moderated mediation with a moderator that was continuous. Let's now examine how moderated mediation is performed when the moderator is a categorical variable. With a categorical moderator, we will not be forming an interaction term but will be assessing the moderator with a two group analysis. Let's go back to our simple example, Adaptive Behavior will influence feelings of Customer Delight which will influence Positive Word of Mouth intentions. The categorical moderator will be if the customer was a first-time customer or a repeat customer. In the data, the column "experience" has the repeat customers listed as a 1 and the first-time customers listed as a 2. We are going to draw our simple mediation model but also create separate groups for our moderator. For more information on setting up groups in two group analysis, see page 149.

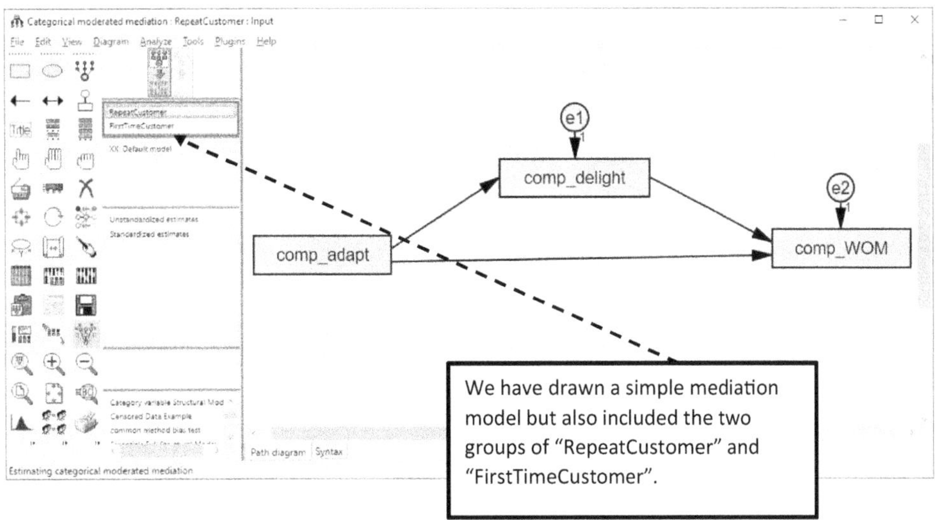

Figure 7.46 Simple Mediation Model With Moderator Denoted as Two Groups

Now that we have drawn our model and created the groups, we need to label the parameters for *each* group. The labels need to be unique for each group. The reason we are labeling the parameters is because we are going to use the estimand function to help determine if moderated mediation is present. Let's select the "FirstTimeCustomer" group and then select (double click) the parameter from Adaptive Behavior to Customer Delight. This will bring up the Object Properties box where we will label this path the "A_Path". You can call it anything you like; the name is arbitrary. By default, a checkbox on the Object Properties page is selected, called "All groups". If this box is selected, it will use the same label name for this parameter across all the groups. We want to label all parameters uniquely across the groups, so uncheck this box. You will have to uncheck the box with each parameter you are trying to label in the first group.

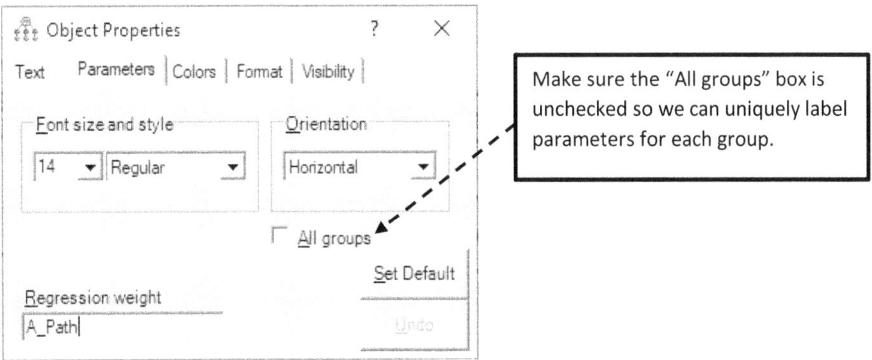

Figure 7.47 Uniquely Labeling Parameters Across the Groups

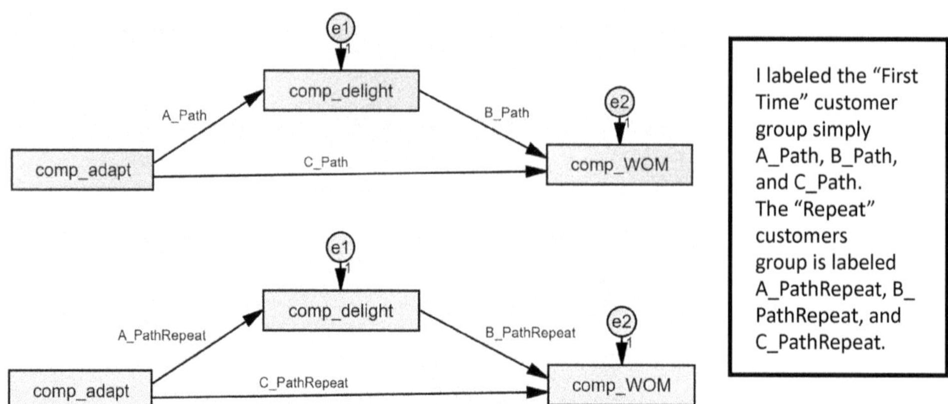

Figure 7.48 First Time and Repeat Group's Parameter Labels

After setting up our groups and labeling all the parameters uniquely for each group, we are ready to set up the estimand formula. Remember from our previous mediation discussions that the indirect effect is the product of the A_Path and the B_Path. To test if our categorical moderator is influencing the indirect effect, we are going to determine the difference between the indirect effects in the presence of the moderator. Put more succinctly, we are going to take the difference of the indirect effects across the groups. After that, we will then run a bootstrap analysis to see if the differences are significant.

In the estimands function, we want to define a new estimand. I will call the test "ModMediation". In the estimands function, I am going to find the indirect effect for the first-time customer group (A_Path*B_Path) and then I am going to specify the repeat customer group (A_PathRepeat*B_PathRepeat). I am going to subtract the indirect effect of the repeat customer group from the first-time customer group. This function will give us the difference of the indirect effects.

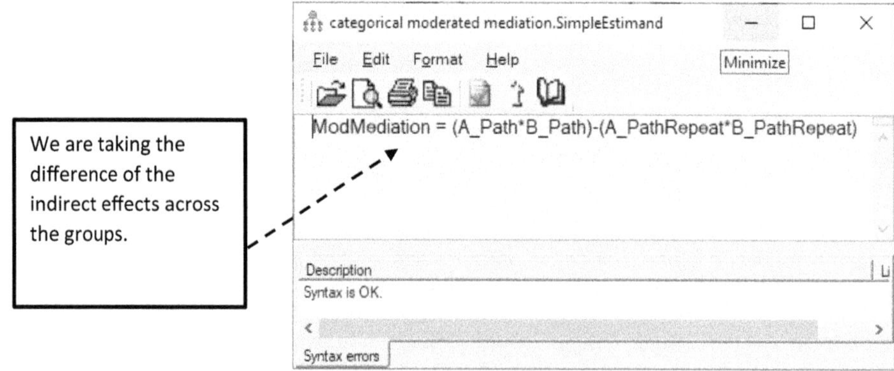

Figure 7.49 Estimand Function Examining the Differences Across the Group's Indirect Effects

Once we have set up the estimands function, we can check the syntax and then hit the save button and exit the screen. Before we run the analysis, you need to make sure you have gone to the Analysis Properties window and selected the "indirect, direct, and total effects" button in the output. You also need to perform a bootstrap analysis with 5,000 samples and a confidence interval of 95%. After making these selections, you are ready to run the analysis.

In the output, let's go to the "Estimates" link and then go to the "Scalars" option where we will select the "User-defined estimands". This will initially just show us the difference of the indirect effects (.121), but we still don't know if the difference is significant. Let's now select the "Bias-corrected percentile method" link on the left-hand side that is at the bottom of the page. This will give us the bootstrap analysis for the difference of indirect effects. The results show that the lower bound confidence interval crosses zero, which means there is a nonsignificant result in the difference between the indirect effects. Thus, we can conclude that the status of the customer (first-time or repeat) does not significantly moderate the mediation of Adaptive Behavior through Customer Delight to Positive Word of Mouth.

User-defined estimands:

Parameter	Estimate	Lower	Upper	P
ModMediation	.121	-.040	.273	.135

Figure 7.50 Difference of Indirect Effects in User Defined Estimand

If the results had been significant, we would then look at the indirect effects for each group to see which one was stronger. We would find that by going to the "Estimates" link, then the "Matrices" option where we would select indirect effects. We would have to select the group we wanted to see from the groups window on the left-hand side. In this example, the indirect effect for repeat customers was .089 and for first-time customers .209. If we had found a significant moderated mediation test, then we could conclude that the indirect effect is significantly strengthened by first-time customers compared to repeat customers.

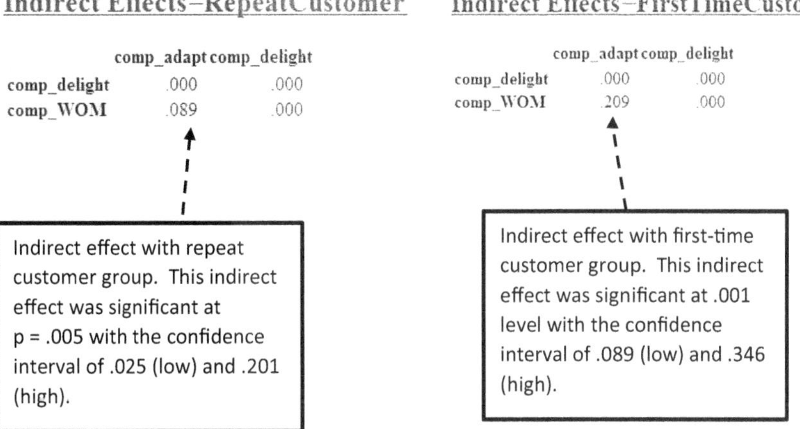

Indirect Effects-RepeatCustomer
comp_adapt comp_delight
comp_delight .000 .000
comp_WOM .089 .000
Indirect Effects-FirstTimeCustomer
comp_adapt comp_delight
comp_delight .000 .000
comp_WOM .209 .000
Indirect effect with repeat customer group. This indirect effect was significant at p = .005 with the confidence interval of .025 (low) and .201 (high).
Indirect effect with first-time customer group. This indirect effect was significant at .001 level with the confidence interval of .089 (low) and .346 (high).

Figure 7.51 Examining the Indirect Effects of Each Group

Note that both of the indirect effects are significant for each group but the difference between the indirect effects is not significant, noting that moderated mediation is not present. One thing to remember is the difference of indirect effects will be dependent on how you order the groups in the estimand function. Our moderated mediation difference could have easily been −.121 if we would have subtracted the first-time customer group from the repeat customers. Just be mindful that the sign of the effect is dependent on the groups and which one is listed first in the estimands window.

Definitions of Constructs Used in Examples for This Chapter:

Adaptive Behavior: customer's perception that an employee adapted/modified their normal job performance to meet their needs. This adaptation can be through verbal interaction, service performance, or meeting special requests. Construct was measured with a 7-point Likert scale of Strongly Disagree to Strongly Agree.

Customer Delight: customer's profoundly positive emotional state resulting from expectations being exceeded to a surprising degree. Construct was measured with a 7-point Likert scale of Strongly Disagree to Strongly Agree.

Positive Word of Mouth: customer's intention to spread positive information to others about a previous experience. Construct was measured with a 7-point Likert scale of Strongly Disagree to Strongly Agree.

Friendliness: perception that an employee was kind or caring during a customer interaction. Construct was measured with a 7-point Likert scale of Strongly Disagree to Strongly Agree.

Experience: Categorical/Dichotomous construct: customers who had no prior experience with the service provider were classified as "first-time customers" and coded as a "2" in the data. Customers who had a prior experience with the service provider were classified as "repeat customers" and were coded as a "1".

Highlights of the Chapter:

1. Moderation is where the direct influence of an independent variable on a dependent variable is altered or changed because of a third variable. This third variable is called the "moderator".
2. With a continuous moderator, an interaction term is created by getting the product of the independent variable and the moderator.
3. When forming an interaction term, it is a good idea to mean center your independent variable and moderator before forming the product term.
4. Probing an interaction can take place through a spotlight analysis. This type of analysis usually examines the moderator at high and low levels by examining 1 standard deviation below and above the mean with the moderator.
5. You can also use a floodlight analysis to probe an interaction which looks at all possible values of the moderator to determine when an interaction with an independent variable becomes significant. The point of significance is often called a Johnson-Neyman point.

6. Testing a full structural model with a moderator can be accomplished in one of three ways: (1) the mixed model method, (2) the full indicator interaction method, or (3) the matched-pairs method.
7. Instead of mean centering your data, you can also use Z scores. Z scores will rescale your data and standard deviation scores.
8. A categorical moderator in SEM is tested in a two group analysis. The different categories of the moderator are treated as different groups.
9. It is unadvisable to take a continuous variable and split the data to create a categorical moderator variable. If a moderator is in a continuous format, then interaction testing is recommended.
10. Moderated mediation is where you are trying to determine if a moderator is influencing the indirect relationship from the independent variable to the ultimate dependent variable.
11. You need to assess the index of moderated mediation to determine if a moderator is significantly impacting an indirect effect.
12. Moderated mediation with a categorical moderator is tested by examining the difference of the indirect effects across the categories and using a bootstrap to determine if the difference is at a significant level.

References

Dawson, Jeremy F. (2014), "Moderation in Management Research", *Journal of Business and Psychology*, 29 (1), 1–19.

Echambadi, Raj and James D. Hess. (2007), "Mean-Centering Does Not Alleviate Collinearity Problems in Moderated Multiple Regression Models", *Marketing Science*, 26 (3), 438–445.

Frazier, Patricia A., Andrew P. Tix, and Kenneth E. Barron. (2004), "Testing Moderator and Mediator Effects in Counseling Psychology", *Journal of Counseling Psychology*, 51 (1), 115–134.

Hayes, Andrew. (2018), *Introduction to Mediation, Moderation, and Conditional Process Analysis* (2nd ed.). New York, NY: Guilford Press.

Johnson, Palmer O. and Jerzy Neyman. (1936), "Tests of Certain Linear Hypotheses and Their Application to Some Educational Problems", *Statistical Research Memoirs*, 1, 57–93.

Marsh, Herbert W., Zhonglin Wen, and Kit-Tai Hau. (2004), "Structural Equation Models of Latent Interactions: Evaluation of Alternative Estimation Strategies and Indicator Construction", *Psychological Methods*, 9 (3), 275–300.

Marsh, Herbert W., Zhonglin Wen, and Kit-Tai, Hau. (2008), "Structural Equation Models of Latent Interaction and Quadratic Effects", in Gregory Hancock and Ralph D. Mueller (eds.) *Structural Equation Modeling: A Second Course*. Greenwich, CT: Information Age.

Ping, R.A. Jr. (1998), "EQS and LISREL Examples Using Survey Data", in R.E. Schumacker and G.A. Marcoulides (eds.) *Interaction and Nonlinear Effects in Structural Equation Modeling*. Mahwah, NJ: Erlbaum.

Spiller, Stephen A., Gavan J. Fitzsimons, John G. Lynch Jr., and Gary H. McClelland. (2013), "Spotlights, Floodlights, and the Magic Number Zero: Simple Effects Tests in Moderated Regression", *Journal of Marketing Research*, 50 (2), 277–288.

Chapter 8

Using Categorical Independent Variables in SEM

Binary Categorical Variables in SEM

AMOS has the assumption that the dependent variables are continuous, but you can use categorical variables as independent constructs in an AMOS model. The only way this can be done is by dummy coding the categorical variable into a "0" and "1". Once dummy coding takes place in SPSS, we can use this dichotomous variable in the analysis as an independent variable. Let's go back to our path analysis example. In that example, we said that the construct of Adaptive Behavior will influence customers' feelings of delight which influence Positive Word of Mouth.

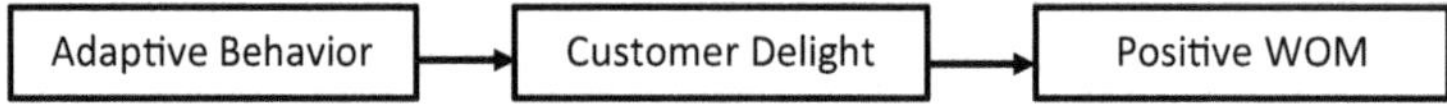

Initially, in our path model example, Adaptive Behavior was measured on a 7-point Likert scale. Now, let's say we performed an experiment and the employee either adapted the service experience for the customer (treatment) or they did not adapt the experience (control). After the experience, customers were asked questions about feelings of delight and intentions to spread word of mouth. In the data, all respondents who had an adapted service were coded as a "1", and all respondents who did not receive an adapted service were coded as a "0". The column label for this dummy coding is called "BinaryAdapt". After the category variable has been dummy coded, we can set up the model in AMOS and run the analysis.

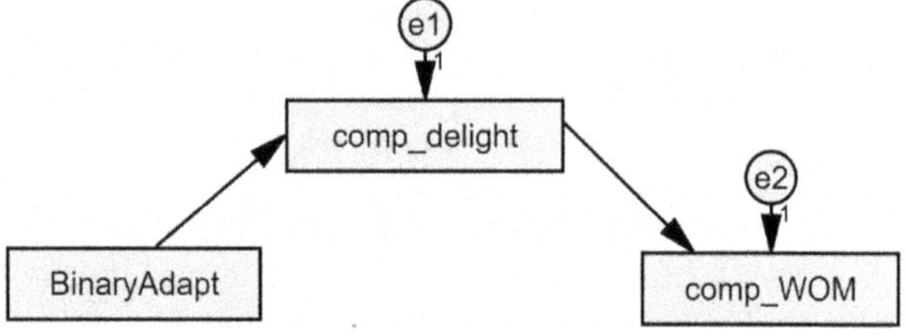

Figure 8.1 Binary Independent Variable Model

The output in the Estimates link (See Figure 8.2) shows us that the binary variable of Adaptive Behavior to Customer Delight is significant. The unstandardized estimate is .820. You don't want to look at the standardized estimates with a dummy coded variable. Since the estimate is positive, this means that values coded as a 1 (employees adapted the service) had a stronger effect on Customer Delight than the group coded as a 0 (employees did not adapt the service). If the unstandardized coefficient was a negative, this would mean the group coded as a "0" had a stronger relationship to Customer Delight. To add greater context to these findings, the regression coefficient of the binary variable is nothing more than the mean difference of the Customer Delight construct across the groups. If you examine the mean of Customer Delight for the group that adapted the service and the group that did not adapt the service, the difference of those values is the regression coefficient of the binary variable in AMOS.

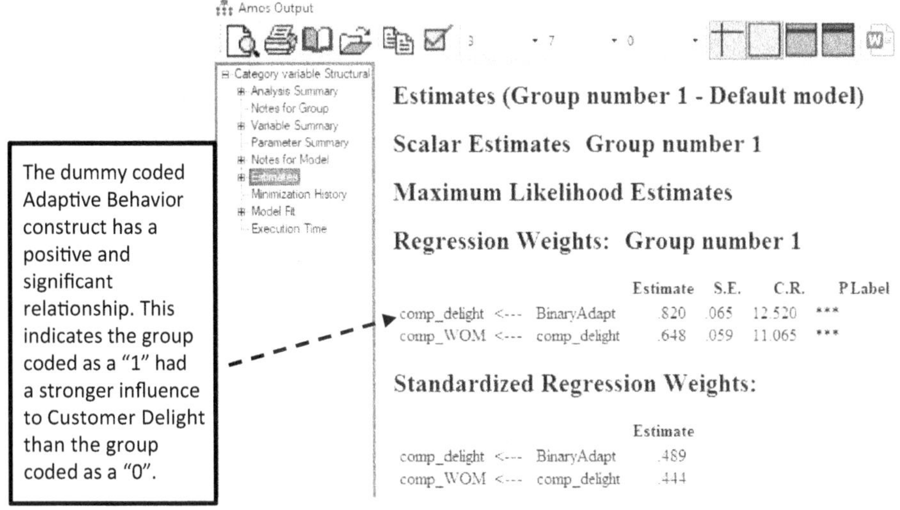

Figure 8.2 Estimates Output for Binary Independent Variable Model

The regression coefficient for the categorical variable to the dependent variable is the difference of means in the dependent variable across the groups. Not Adapted group (coded as 0) Customer Delight mean = 5.734. The Adapted group (coded as 1) Customer Delight mean = 6.5539. The difference: 6.5539 – 5.734 = .820.

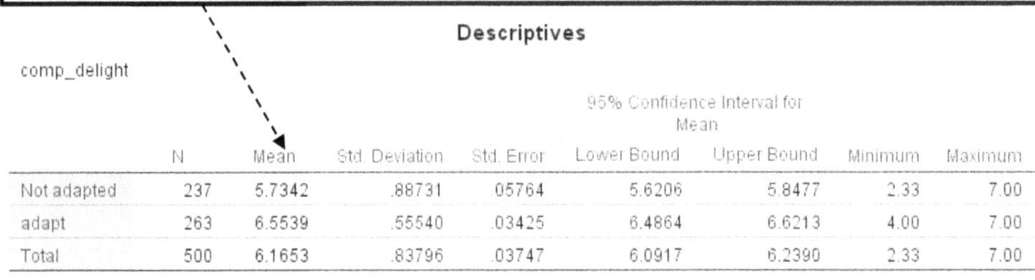

Descriptives

comp_delight

	N	Mean	Std. Deviation	Std. Error	95% Confidence Interval for Mean Lower Bound	95% Confidence Interval for Mean Upper Bound	Minimum	Maximum
Not adapted	237	5.7342	.88731	.05764	5.6206	5.8477	2.33	7.00
adapt	263	6.5539	.55540	.03425	6.4864	6.6213	4.00	7.00
Total	500	6.1653	.83796	.03747	6.0917	6.2390	2.33	7.00

Figure 8.3 Binary Independent Variable Regression Weight Based on Difference of Means

Mediation with Binary Categorical Independent Variables

Mediation with a categorical independent variable is run very similarly to a mediation analysis with a continuous variable. The independent variable will need to be coded as a "1" or a "0" for the groups. In this example, customers who received no adaptation in the service were coded as a "0" and those customers that did receive an adapted service was coded as a "1". Next, you will create the model in AMOS with the categorical independent variable, and you will also add the direct effect parameter to determine what type of mediation is present. Since our interest is in the indirect effect, we will run a bootstrap with 5,000 samples and also include a 95% confidence interval. Having selected these options, we are ready to run the analysis.

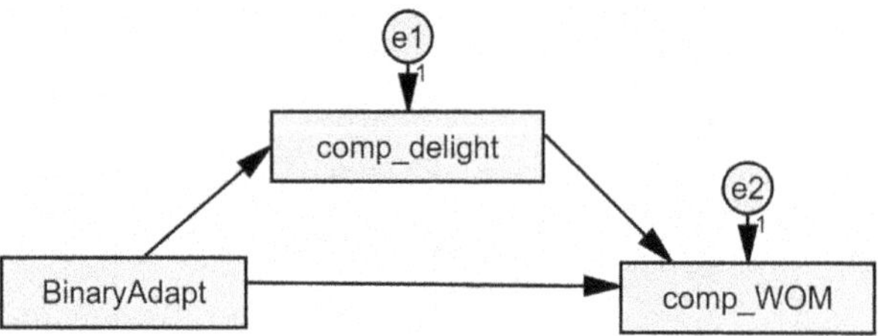

Figure 8.4 Mediation Model With Binary Independent Variable

In the results, we are examining if the indirect effect is significantly different across the categories. We will calculate the indirect effect as we have in the previous examples of multiplying the path from the independent variable to the mediator by the relationship from the mediator to the dependent variable. The relationship from the binary variable to the mediator (A path) is the difference of means of the mediator across the groups. This difference will then be multiplied by the path from the mediator to the dependent variable (B path). Since the independent variable is dummy coded as a 1 or 0, the indirect effect would be considered the "relative indirect effect". The same would apply with the direct effect from the binary variable to the dependent variable (C path). This would be considered a "relative direct effect". Since your independent variable is dichotomous and the mediator is continuous, you need to be clear that this is the relative effect on the dependent variable.

Let's look at the Estimates output to initially examine the direct effects.

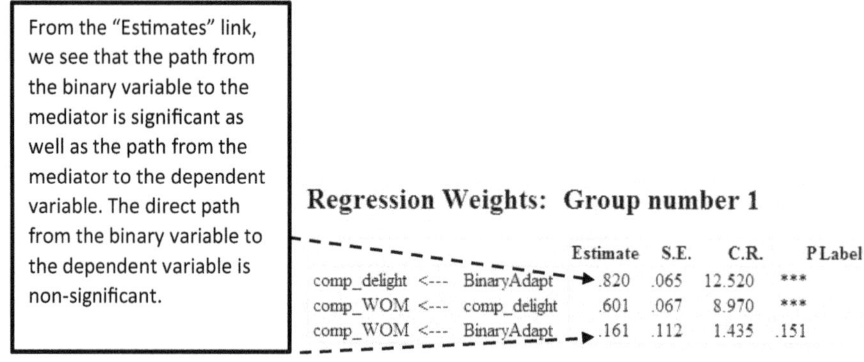

Regression Weights: Group number 1

			Estimate	S.E.	C.R.	P	Label
comp_delight	<---	BinaryAdapt	.820	.065	12.520	***	
comp_WOM	<---	comp_delight	.601	.067	8.970	***	
comp_WOM	<---	BinaryAdapt	.161	.112	1.435	.151	

Figure 8.5 Relative Direct Effects From the Estimates Output

Next, let's examine the indirect effect. In the Estimates link in the output, select the "Matrices" option and then select the indirect effects option (note that you have to ask for indirect effects in the Analysis Properties window). The results show that the indirect effect has a value of .493. The indirect effect is positive, which initially tells us the independent variable coded as a "1" has a relatively stronger indirect influence on the dependent variable. We need to determine if this relative indirect effect is significant.

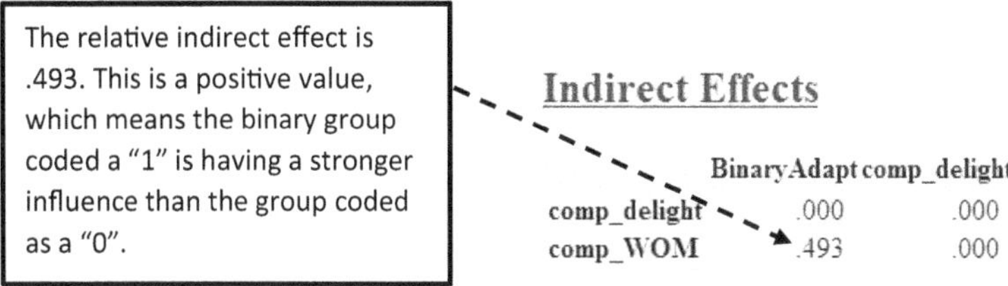

Figure 8.6 Relative Indirect Effects of the Binary Adaptive Behavior Construct to Positive Word of Mouth

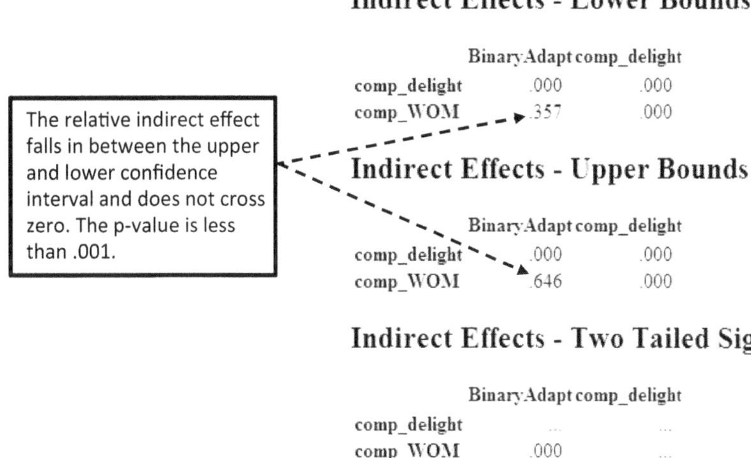

Figure 8.7 Confidence Interval of the Relative Indirect Effect

Once you are in the indirect effects option, you need to select the Bias-corrected percentile method option that is at the bottom of the output screen. This will give us the significance and confidence intervals of the indirect test. The bootstrap analysis shows that the upper and lower bound confidence intervals do not cross zero; thus the indirect effect is statistically significant. Ultimately, we can conclude that the relative indirect effect of adapting a service has a significantly stronger influence on the construct of positive word of mouth than the group that did not adapt the service.

Many categorical independent variables take the form of an experiment where you have a manipulation and a control group. In testing the relative indirect effect, you are trying to assess not only if the manipulation group has a direct effect to a mediator, but whether the influence of the manipulation group impacts the ultimate dependent variable. In our results, the relative direct effect was insignificant, but the addition of a mediator shows that an indirect effect is present to the dependent variable. In essence, the influence of the manipulation group was fully mediated to the dependent variable. Just because an independent variable is categorical does not mean you cannot assess if an indirect effect is present in your model. AMOS may require that the dependent variables are continuous, but you can evaluate independent variables in numerous formats if it is coded appropriately.

Multicategorical Independent Variables in SEM

In our previous example, our independent variable had only two categories (Treatment and Control group). The dummy coding for this two group category was straightforward and easy, with one group getting labeled a "1" and the other a "0". When you have more than two groups in your independent variable, the dummy coding for this categorical variable becomes more complex. With three categories, you need to create three separate dummy coded variables in your data set. Let's go back to our categorical example.

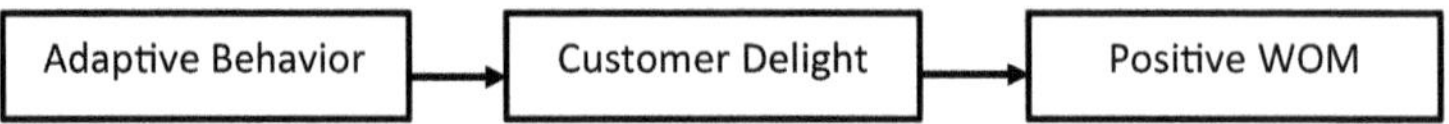

We initially had the Adaptive Behavior construct as a binary construct where customers either received an adaptive service or not. Now let's change the Adaptive Behavior construct to have three categories. The first category is the employee did not adapt the service. The second category is the employee adapted the service at the beginning of the experience, and the last category is the employee adapted the service at the end of the experience. These three categories will let us know when adapting an experience influences Customer Delight the most. We now have three separate categories that need to be analyzed. If we look in SPSS, I have a column titled "MultCatAdapt", which has the three categories listed as a 1, 2, or 3.

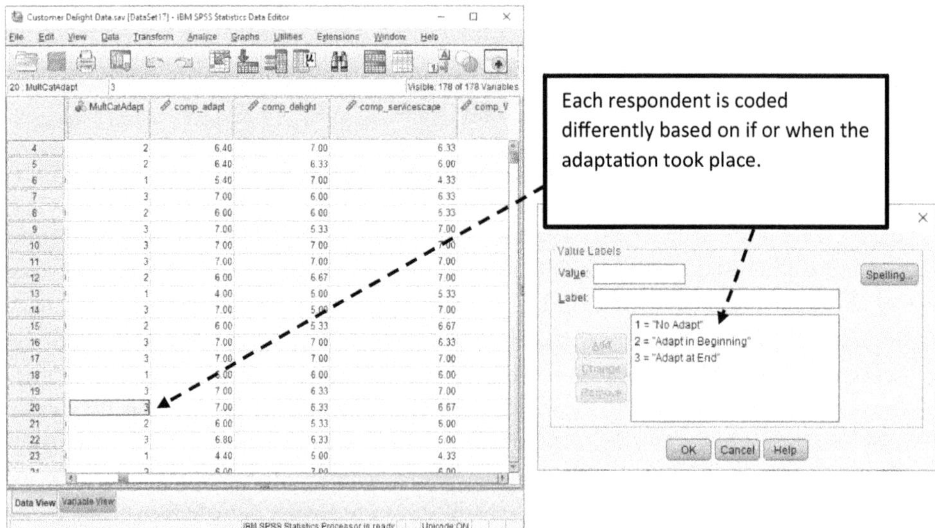

Figure 8.8 Coding Multicategorical Variables in SPSS

You now need to convert this multicategorical data into multiple binary variables. There is a handy function in SPSS that will perform this transformation for you. In SPSS, go to the "Transform" menu option at the top and then select "Create Dummy Variables". A pop-up window will appear. In this window, select the "MultCatAdapt" variable to dummy code and bring it over into the dummy code window. Make sure the "create main-effect dummies" is selected. Next, you need to choose a "root name". This dummy code function in SPSS will start creating numerous different variables based on the categories in your specified variable (MultCatAdapt). SPSS will just start labeling them the root name and then a number. I am going to call the root name for all the dummy variables "TimeAdapt". You can hit the OK button after these options are selected. In the SPSS file, the very last columns now will have the new variables created. The way SPSS dummy codes multiple categories is that a variable is created where the first category is listed as a 1 and all other categories are listed as a 0. The same process takes place for the other created variables where a specified category is listed as 1 and all other categories are listed as a 0. SPSS will dummy code the variables as either a presence (1) or absence (0). Since we had three categories in our MultCatAdapt column, SPSS will create three new dummy coded variables. While TimeAdapt1, TimeAdapt2, and TimeAdapt3 are okay as labels, I find it is always better to go back and change the labels to accurately reflect each category. TimeAdapt1 was when no adaptation took place. I am going to change that label to be "NoAdapt". TimeAdapt 2 was the adaptation in the beginning and TimeAdapt3 was at the end. I am going to change those labels to "AdaptBegin" and "AdaptEnd", respectively. Changing these labels to a more accurate category name will be beneficial when you run the AMOS analysis with these dummy coded variables. This should complete the process of dummy coding your variable that had multiple categories.

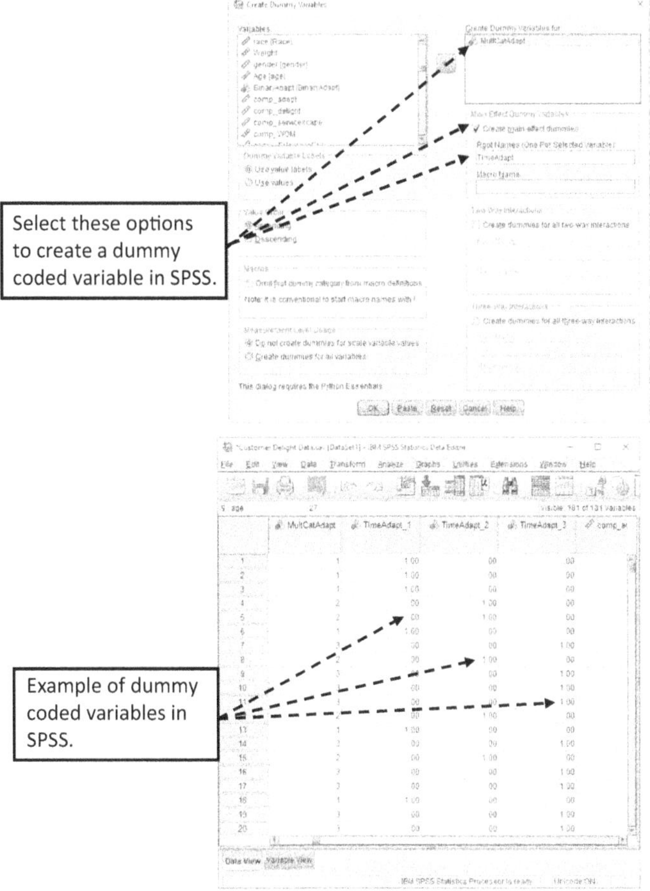

Figure 8.9 Using the Dummy Code Function in SPSS

With a multicategorical analysis, one of our initial categories has to be used as a "reference" category, or, to put it another way, a comparison category to all the other categories. In this example, I am going to use the no adaptation category as a reference group. I can choose whatever group I want as the reference group, but it makes sense to use a category that is similar to a control group as the reference. To test our categorical independent variable, we are going to include two variables at the front of the model instead of just one. The two newly formed categorical variables of "AdaptBegin" and "AdaptEnd" will now act as the independent variable at the front of the model. Note that the no adaptation group is coded as zero in both groups of "AdaptBegin" and "AdaptEnd". Again, that group will be used a reference in the analysis.

We want to understand the collective effect of the categories, so we are not going to test each category individually. We are going to include both the "AdaptBegin" and "AdaptEnd" in the model. The "AdaptBegin" variable is where we will be testing those customers who had an adapted service at the beginning of the experience compared to those that had no experience adapted. Similarly, the "AdaptEnd" category is going to compare the customers who had an adaptation that took place at the end of the experience compared to those that did not have an adapted experience. After drawing the model, let's run the analysis and go to the output and examine the "Estimates" link in the results.

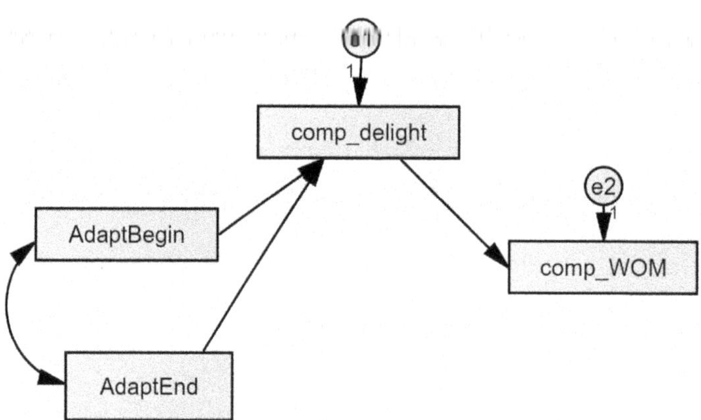

Figure 8.10 Multicategorical Independent Variable in AMOS

Regression Weights: Group number 1

			Estimate	S.E.	C.R.	P	Label
comp_delight	<---	AdaptBegin	.837	.077	10.934	***	
comp_delight	<---	AdaptEnd	1.112	.074	14.946	***	
comp_WOM	<---	comp_delight	.648	.059	11.065	***	

Figure 8.11 Estimates Output With Regression Weights of Multicategorical Variable

First, we are concerned only with the unstandardized results with the dummy coded variables. A standardized dummy variable is nonsensical. Remember that the regression weight listed from the dummy variable to Customer Delight is just the differences of means of the groups. In our results, customers in the "AdaptBegin" group were significantly different from those in the no adapt group, with the AdaptBegin group having a relatively stronger relationship to Customer Delight than the no adapt group.

Since the regression coefficient is positive, we know that the group labeled a 1 (Adapted at the Beginning group) is the relatively stronger group. In the AdaptEnd group, we see a positive and significant relationship to Customer Delight as well. The AdaptEnd group has a relatively bigger influence to Customer Delight than the AdaptBegin group. The difference in Customer Delight for the AdaptEnd group was greater than the difference in the AdaptBegin group. Thus, we can conclude that the AdaptEnd group has a relatively stronger effect to Customer Delight than the AdaptBegin group compared to those that did not have an adapted experience.

I know the next question many of you will have: how do I just compare the groups of those that adapted the service at the beginning to those that adapted the service at the end? If you are concerned only with the comparison of those groups and are not concerned with the "no adaptation" group, you can recode the adapt in the beginning and adapt at the end groups into a dichotomous variable of 1 or 0 and then run the analysis again with this new variable. This new test will specifically test the differences between these groups.

Mediation With Multicategorical Independent Variables

To test for mediation with a multicategorical independent variable, we will initially have to dummy code all the categories of the independent variable into separate variables. This is accomplished in the same way as discussed in the previous section about multicategorical variables. We are dummy coding the multiple categories because one of the categories will be used as a reference to compare the other categories.

Let's continue the multicategorical example used earlier of Adaptive Behavior leads to Customer Delight which leads to Positive Word of Mouth. In the previous example, we simply examined the structural relationships between the variables. Now, let's determine if our categorical independent variable (Adaptive Behavior) has an indirect effect on Positive Word of Mouth through Customer Delight. Thus, we are going to add another relationship directly from the independent variable to the dependent variable to assess the direct effects in a mediation test. I am going to dummy code the variables the same as the previous example. The dummy coded variable "AdaptBegin", where the adaptation of the service took place at the beginning of the service, will be listed as a "1", and all other categories will be listed as a "0". The "AdaptEnd" variable will have the adaptation of the service at the end category listed as a "1" and all other categories listed as a "0". The reference group will be the "no adaptation" category. It will be coded as a zero in both of the newly formed dummy variables.

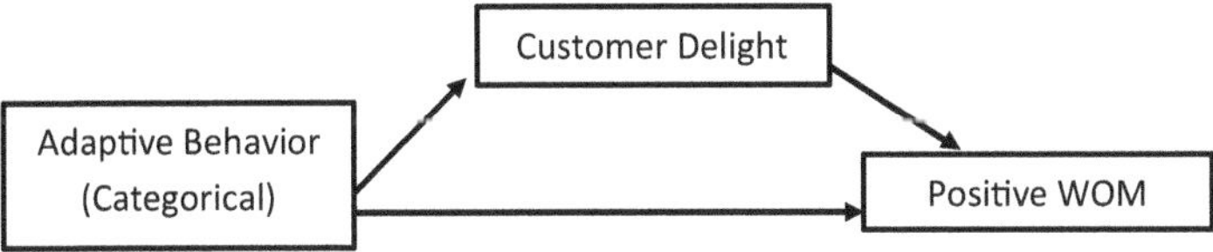

Since we have two new dummy coded variables now acting as the independent variable, we will have to assess the indirect effect coming from each variable. We have only one mediator in this example, so we can initially just use the indirect effects tests that are provided by AMOS. We could also use the estimand function to find the indirect effect. I will show the results using both methods. Let's look at the indirect effects test in AMOS first.

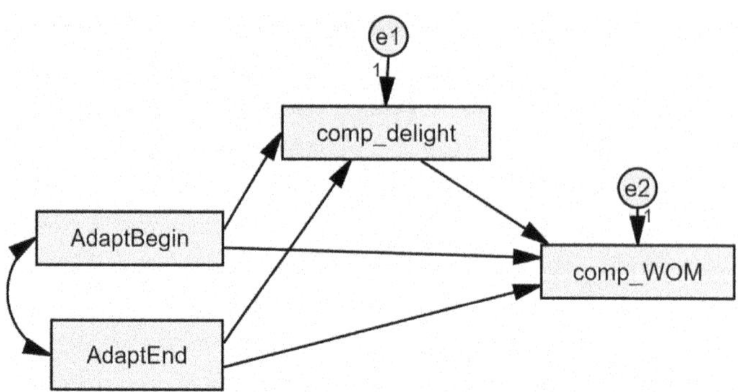

Figure 8.12 Multicategorical Mediation Model With Direct and Indirect Effects Included

You need to initially draw your model with both the categorical dummy variables having a path to the mediator and also to the dependent variable. After drawing the model, you need to request the "direct, indirect, and total effects" options in the Analysis Properties. You also need to request a bootstrap with 5,000 samples and a confidence interval at 95%. After making these selections, you are ready to run the analysis.

In the output, let's go the "Estimates" link and then the "Matrices" option, and then select the unstandardized indirect effects. The results of the analysis indicate that both indirect effects are positive, which indicates that the reference group is relatively weaker for each category. We can also see that the indirect effect for the AdaptEnd group has a relatively stronger indirect effect than the AdaptBegin group compared to the reference group. The AdaptEnd group has an indirect effect of .622, and the AdaptBegin group has an indirect effect of .469.

Indirect Effects Group number 1

	AdaptEnd	AdaptBegin	comp_delight
comp_delight	.000	.000	.000
comp_WOM	.622	.469	.000

Figure 8.13 Relative Indirect Effects for Each Categorical Independent Variable

We now need to determine if the indirect effects for each categorial variable are significant. In the output, we are currently selecting the unstandardized indirect effects in the "Estimates" link. You need to select the "Bias-corrected percentile method" option that is located at the bottom left-hand side of the screen. The results provide the bootstrap analysis results. The results of our bootstrap show that each indirect effect is significant and that no confidence interval crosses over zero. Thus, we can conclude that adapting a service at the beginning of an experience has a significant indirect effect to Positive Word of Mouth through Customer Delight. Similarly, adapting a service at the end of an experience also has a significant indirect effect to Positive Word of Mouth. Compared to the group that did not receive an adaptation in the service, the group that had an adaptation at the end of the service had a relatively stronger indirect influence to Positive Word of Mouth than the group that adapted the service at the beginning of the experience.

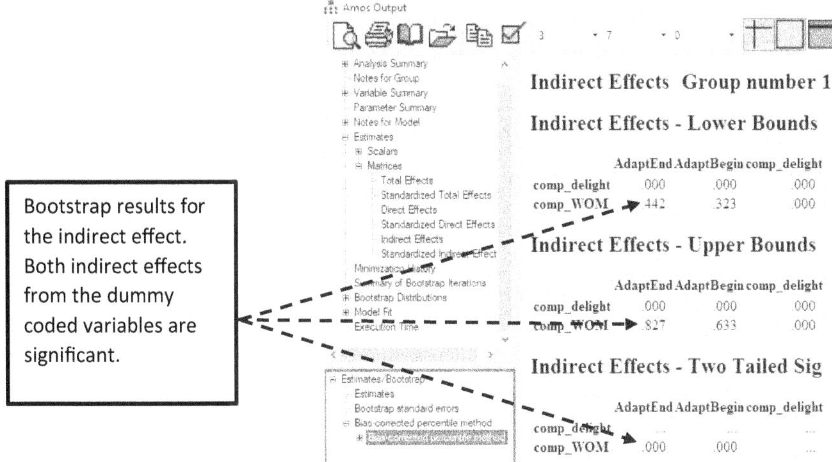

Indirect Effects - Lower Bounds

	AdaptEnd	AdaptBegin	comp_delight
comp_delight	.000	.000	.000
comp_WOM	.442	.323	.000

Indirect Effects - Upper Bounds

	AdaptEnd	AdaptBegin	comp_delight
comp_delight	.000	.000	.000
comp_WOM	.827	.633	.000

Indirect Effects - Two Tailed Sig

	AdaptEnd	AdaptBegin	comp_delight
comp_delight	...	...	...
comp_WOM	.000	.000	...

Figure 8.14 Confidence Intervals for Both Categories of the Independent Variable

To add greater clarity to the mediation test, let's look at the direct effects for each categorical dummy variable in the "Estimates" link. See Figure 8.15. The AdaptBegin variable does not have a direct relationship to positive word of mouth ($p = .164$), which means the indirect effect is taking place fully through the Customer Delight construct. Conversely, the AdaptEnd dummy variable has a significant direct effect. This indicates that the influence of the adapt at the end of the service group is partially mediated through Customer Delight but has a direct influence as well.

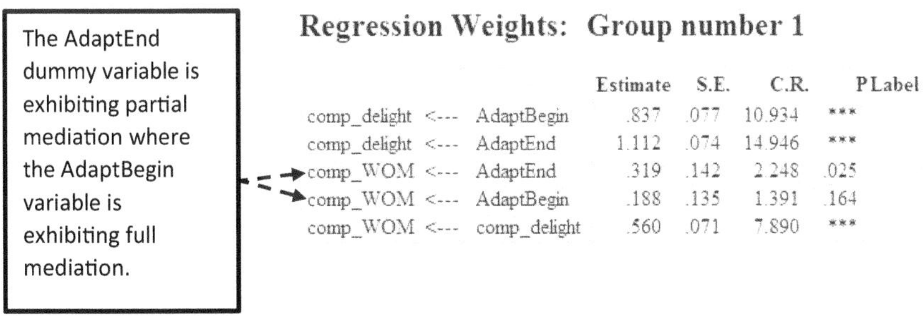

The AdaptEnd dummy variable is exhibiting partial mediation where the AdaptBegin variable is exhibiting full mediation.

Regression Weights: Group number 1

			Estimate	S.E.	C.R.	P	Label
comp_delight	<---	AdaptBegin	.837	.077	10.934	***	
comp_delight	<---	AdaptEnd	1.112	.074	14.946	***	
comp_WOM	<---	AdaptEnd	.319	.142	2.248	.025	
comp_WOM	<---	AdaptBegin	.188	.135	1.391	.164	
comp_WOM	<---	comp_delight	.560	.071	7.890	***	

Figure 8.15 Direct Effects From the Categorical Dummy Variables

We used the indirect effects test in AMOS to find our results, and this is an easy way to find mediation if you have only one possible indirect path. Since there was only one mediator between the independent variable and the dependent variable, the indirect path could take place in only one method. If we had more than one option for the indirect effect, we would not want to use the indirect effect test through AMOS. We would be better off using the estimands function. To use this function, we would initially have to label all the parameters across the model. See Figure 8.16.

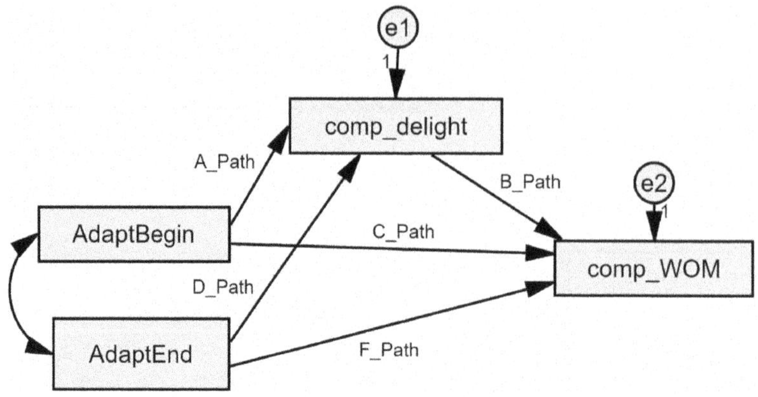

Figure 8.16 **Fully Labeled Model to Assess Mediation of Multicategorical Variable**

In the estimands function, I am going to "Define new Estimand" to calculate the indirect effect for each dummy coded variable. I'll call the indirect test for the adapt at the beginning group simply "Indirect_Effect_AdaptBegin" and call the indirect test for the adapt at the end group "Indirect_Effect_AdaptEnd". An estimands function requires a bootstrap analysis to be performed. Make sure to select a bootstrap sample of 5,000 and a confidence interval of 95%. At this point, you are ready to run your analysis.

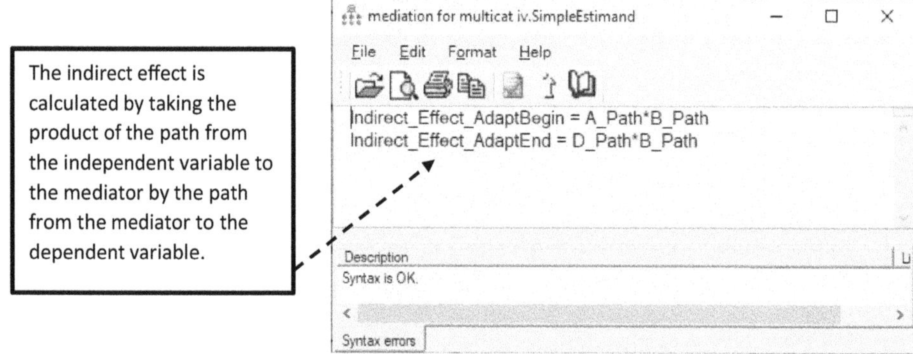

Figure 8.17 **Estimands Function Needed to Assess Indirect Effects of a Dummy Coded Variable**

In the Estimates link of the output, you need to select the "Scalars" option and then the "User-Defined estimands" output. This will initially just give you the indirect effects, but if you also select the "Bias-corrected percentile method" at the bottom of the output, this will give you the indirect effects along with the bootstrap analysis. See Figure 8.18. The results of the estimands function mirror the same results that we received from the indirect effects test in AMOS. If you have a simple mediation analysis where there is only one mediator, then using the indirect effects test in AMOS is a little quicker. If you have more than one potential mediator or just want more specificity in the analysis, then using the estimands function is the preferred option.

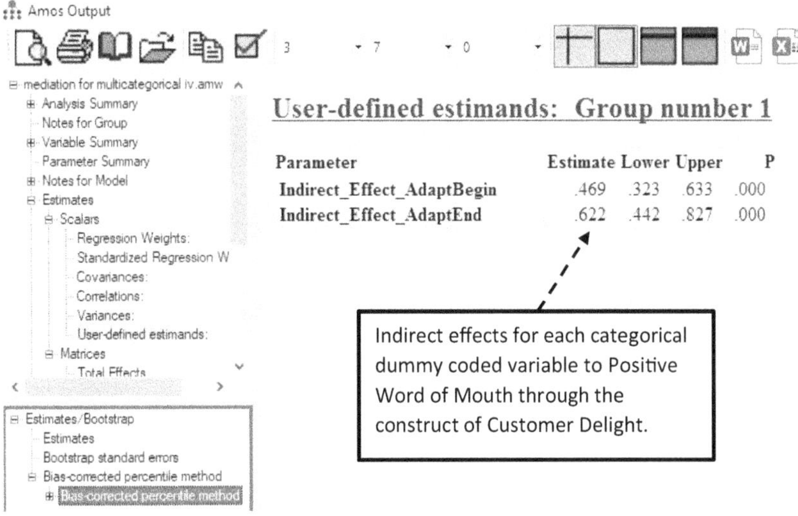

Figure 8.18 User Defined Estimands That Includes Confidence Intervals for Each Indirect Effect

Moderated Mediation With a Multicategorical Independent Variable

So far, we have examined multicategorical independent variables in a simple structural model test and then a mediation test. Let's extend our example now to assess moderated mediation with multicategorical independent variables. We are going to use the same example as before, except this time we will add a moderator. The moderator in this test is a construct called "Need for Speed in a Transaction", and in order to simplify things, let's just call the construct "Speedy". This construct represents a customer's need for a speedy service experience. In other words, how fast or slow does the customer want the experience to take place. The speed of the service experience can influence the customer's desire to adapt a service. Adaptation can often slow down the service because you are leaving a normal manner of operations to adapt the service to the customer. This moderator is proposed to work in a negative manner with the relationship of Adaptive Behavior and Customer Delight. When a customer is high in Need for Speed, then the relationship from Adaptive Behavior to Customer Delight will be weakened. Conversely, if a customer has a low Need for Speed, the Adaptive Behavior to Customer Delight should be strengthened. See the graphic representation that follows.

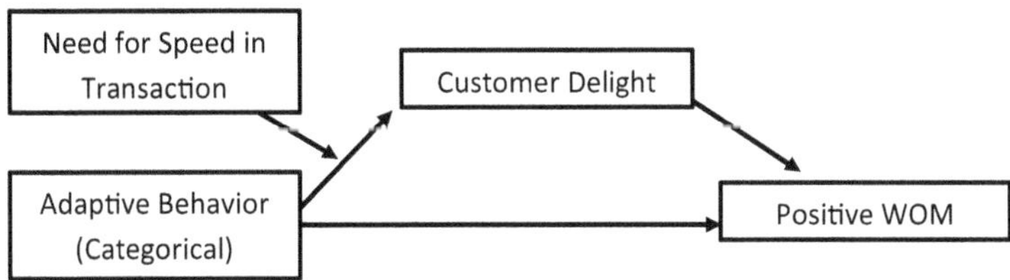

To set up this test, we are going to dummy code the categorical variable again. We are going to use the same names for the constructs as before. Since we are testing moderation with a continuous variable, we need to form an interaction term. The first thing you need to do is mean center the moderator. Since the independent variables are dummy coded to ones and zeroes, there is no need to mean center those variables. After you have centered the data with the moderator, you need to create an interaction term for both of the dummy coded independent variables (AdaptBegin and AdaptEnd). I will call these variables "AdaptBegin_X_CenterSpeedy" and "AdaptEnd_X_CenterSpeedy". Once we have the interaction terms created in SPSS, then you are ready to draw the model in AMOS. See Figure 8.19.

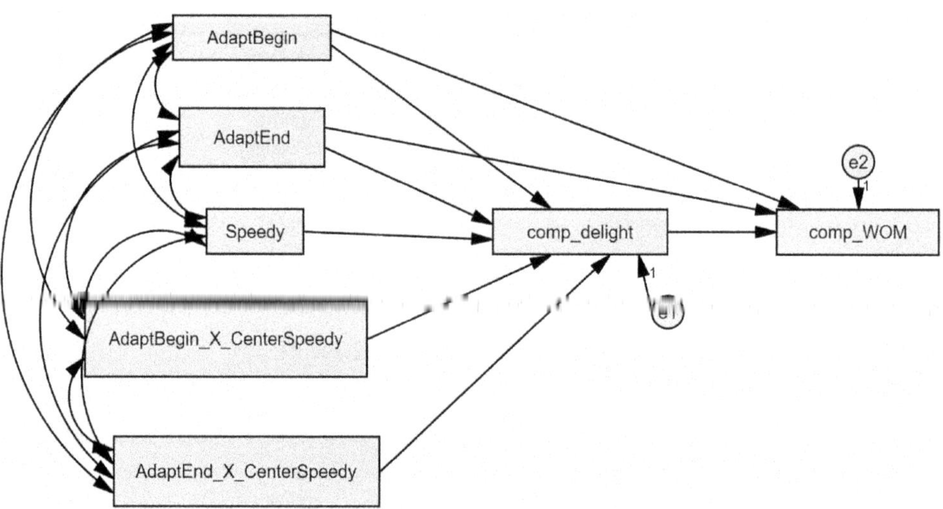

Figure 8.19 Moderated Mediation Test With Dummy Coded Independent Variables and Interaction Terms

Both of the independent dummy coded variables will have a relationship to Customer Delight and Positive Word of Mouth in order to test the mediation properties. Next, you will include the moderator and the two newly created interaction terms, and they will have a direct influence on Customer Delight. At this point, we have two dummy coded variables acting as the independent variable, a continuous moderator, and two interaction terms with the dummy coded variables.

To test for mediation, we will also use a bootstrap analysis and examine the significance of the indirect effects in the presence of the moderator. Lastly, we are going to use the estimands function in AMOS to help probe the interaction of the indirect effect of the categorical variables to the construct of Positive Word of Mouth. After drawing the model, we need to label all the parameters in the model. Since we have two categorical independent variables, I am going to label the path from "AdaptBegin" to Customer Delight as "A_PathBegin". I will call the relationships from "AdaptEnd" to Customer Delight "A_PathEnd". I will use the same pattern with the direct effects, labeling them "C_PathBegin" and "C_PathEnd". See Figure 8.20 to see all the labels for the remaining paths in the model. You can see that each label has a unique name.

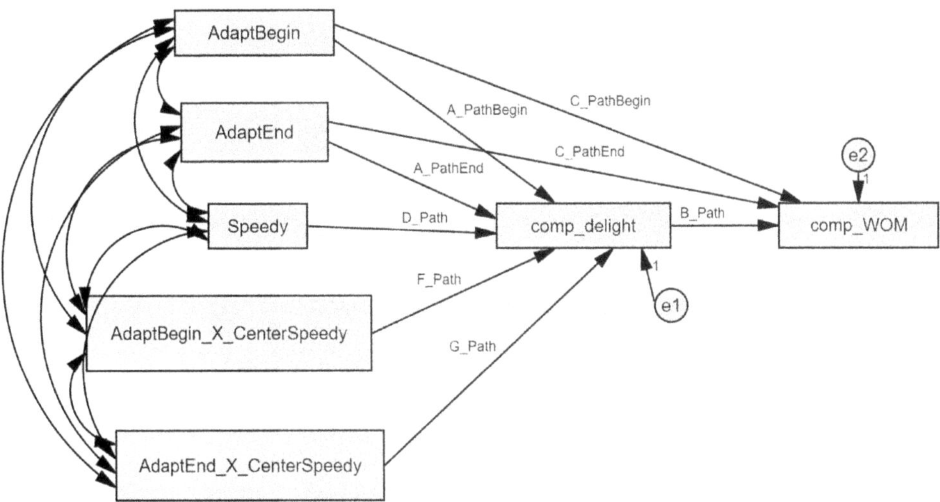

Figure 8.20 **Fully Labeled Moderated Mediation Test of Multicategorical Independent Variable**

We now need to use the estimands function in AMOS to determine the indirect effect and how it changes with the moderator. We are initially going to examine the indirect path for each categorical variable. We are then going to probe the interaction of the indirect effect. The standard deviation for our moderator (Need for Speed) was 1.08418. Now we are going to probe when the moderator is low for the first categorical variable of AdaptBegin. To do this, we take the interaction estimate (F_Path in this example) and multiply that by the standard deviation to get the effect at one standard deviation above the mean. We are also going to multiply the negative of the standard deviation to get the effect that is one standard deviation below the mean. This revised interaction term will be added to the "A_Path" and then multiplied to the "B_Path". I know that might sound complicated, but it is really pretty simple when you see it in the estimand window (Figure 8.21). To test the indirect effect at high levels of the moderator (Need for Speed), the name "SpeedHiatBegin" will be used as the name for the test when adaptation at the beginning group is compared to the no adaptation group. The other categorical variable of adapting the service at the end of the experience has a test name of "SpeedHiatEnd". The low level of the moderator in the indirect effect is similarly named of "SpeedLowatEnd" and "SpeedLowatBegin". Notice that with the moderator going one standard deviation below the mean, we need to have the sign as a negative.

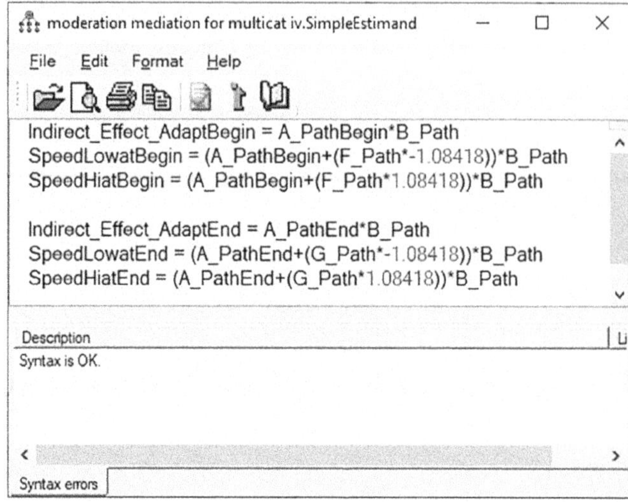

Figure 8.21 Estimands Function for Indirect Effects in the Presence of the Moderator

After noting the estimands for both categorical variables, you need to check the syntax before moving forward. With an estimands function, you need to make sure you ask for a bootstrap analysis with 5,000 samples with a 95% confidence interval. Once making those selections, you are ready to run the analysis.

In the Estimates link of the output, you can see the regression estimates for each path in the model. From this analysis, we can see that both the categorical variables have a positive and significant relationship to Customer Delight. Remember the regression coefficient for the dummy coded category variables is simply a difference of mean from the Customer Delight variable across the groups. The results also show us that the interaction term for both the "AdaptBegin" and "AdaptEnd" to Customer Delight is negative and significant. This lets us know that the Adaptive Behavior to Customer Delight relationship is weakened in the presence of the moderator (Need for Speed). Lastly, you can see that the direct effect from the "Adapt-Begin" construct is non-significant but that the direct effect from "AdaptEnd" is significant.

Regression Weights: (Group number 1 - Default model)

			Estimate	S.E.	C.R.	P	Label
comp_delight	<---	AdaptEnd	1.050	.077	13.725	***	A_PathEnd
comp_delight	<---	Speedy	.194	.051	3.777	***	D_Path
comp_delight	<---	AdaptBegin_X_CenterSpeedy	-.151	.074	-2.029	.042	F_Path
comp_delight	<---	AdaptEnd_X_CenterSpeedy	-.199	.069	-2.881	.004	G_Path
comp_delight	<---	AdaptBegin	.773	.077	10.002	***	A_PathBegin
comp_WOM	<---	comp_delight	.560	.071	7.890	***	B_Path
comp_WOM	<---	AdaptEnd	.319	.142	2.248	.025	C_PathEnd
comp_WOM	<---	AdaptBegin	.188	.135	1.391	.164	C_PathBegin

Figure 8.22 Estimates Output for the Relative Direct Effects and Interaction Terms

After assessing the direct effects, let's now look at the estimand function for the indirect effects along with how the indirect effect changes when we probe the interaction. In the "Estimates" link in the output, we need to go to "Scalars" and then choose "User-defined estimands". This will initially list the indirect effects. If we go to the Bias-corrected percentile method option at the bottom of the output, you can see the indirect effects along with the bootstrap confidence intervals for all the tests listed in the Estimands. See Figure 8.23.

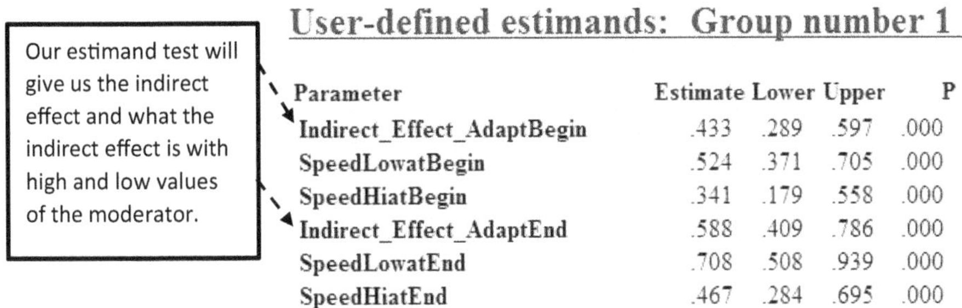

Our estimand test will give us the indirect effect and what the indirect effect is with high and low values of the moderator.

User-defined estimands: Group number 1

Parameter	Estimate	Lower	Upper	P
Indirect_Effect_AdaptBegin	.433	.289	.597	.000
SpeedLowatBegin	.524	.371	.705	.000
SpeedHiatBegin	.341	.179	.558	.000
Indirect_Effect_AdaptEnd	.588	.409	.786	.000
SpeedLowatEnd	.708	.508	.939	.000
SpeedHiatEnd	.467	.284	.695	.000

Figure 8.23 User Defined Estimand That Provides Confidence Intervals for Indirect Effects at Different Levels of the Moderator

With the first categorical variable of "AdaptBegin", we see the indirect effect of .433, which is significant at the $p < .001$ level. If you look at the high and low values of the moderator, each has a significant indirect effect, but the pattern produces an interesting story. When the moderator is low or customers have a low need for speed in the interaction, the indirect effect is .524, but when customers have a high need for speed, the indirect effect is .341. These results show that when customers have a high need for speed in the interaction, the relationship from Adaptive Behavior to Customer Delight is weaker than when customers have a low need for speed in the interaction. All our indirect estimates are significant and positive, which indicates that customers who have an adaptation at the beginning of the experience have a relatively stronger indirect effect on Positive Word of Mouth compared to the group that had no adaptation in the service. As for the second categorical variable of "AdaptEnd", the indirect effect was positive and significant with a value of .588. The low and high tests of the moderator found a similar pattern as the first categorical variable. When the need for speed was low, adapting the service at the end produced an indirect effect of .708. When the need for speed was high, adapting a service at the end had a value of .467. Again, when customers had a high need for speed, adapting the service had a weaker influence on spreading positive word of mouth about the experience compared to those that had a low need for speed in the service.

From our user-defined estimand, we have examined the indirect effect in the presence of the moderator. At this point, we need to assess if the moderator significantly moderates the indirect effect. This will be accomplished by examining the index of moderated mediation for each categorical variable in the model. The index of moderated mediation is the path from the interaction variable to the mediator multiplied by the path from the mediator to the dependent variable. If we go to the "Estimates" link in the output, then go to the "Matrices" option, and then select indirect effects (make sure the indirect effects option is selected in the Analysis Properties window), we see the indirect effect for AdaptBegin_X_CenterSpeedy and Positive Word of Mouth is −.111. The indirect effect for AdaptEnd_X_CenterSpeedy and Positive Word of Mouth is −.0842. If you go to the Bias-corrected percentile method on the left-hand side, you can see the bootstrap confidence intervals for both of those indirect effects. In this case, they are both significant. The negative value lets us know the slope is moving in the opposite direction or specifically that the indirect effect is weakening. The significance of the index of moderated mediation lets us know that, yes, moderated mediation is taking place in the model.

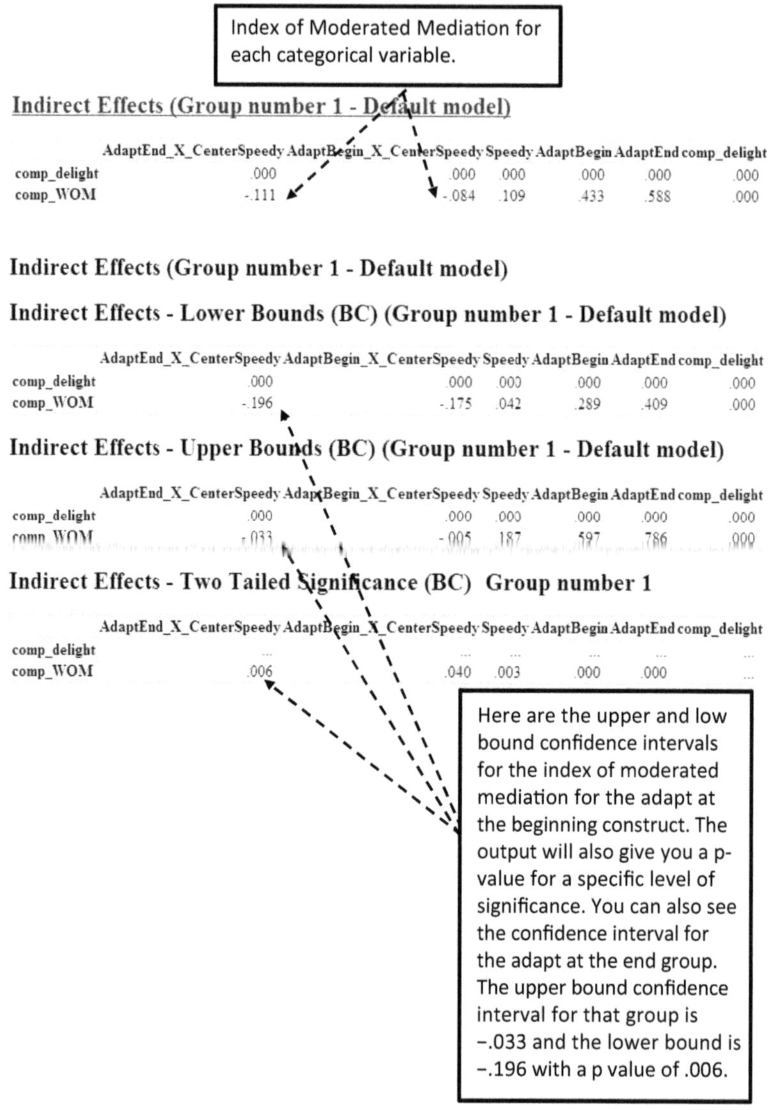

Indirect Effects (Group number 1 - Default model)

	AdaptEnd_X_CenterSpeedy	AdaptBegin_X_CenterSpeedy	Speedy	AdaptBegin	AdaptEnd	comp_delight
comp_delight	.000	.000	.000	.000	.000	.000
comp_WOM	-.111	-.084	.109	.433	.588	.000

Indirect Effects (Group number 1 - Default model)

Indirect Effects - Lower Bounds (BC) (Group number 1 - Default model)

	AdaptEnd_X_CenterSpeedy	AdaptBegin_X_CenterSpeedy	Speedy	AdaptBegin	AdaptEnd	comp_delight
comp_delight	.000	.000	.000	.000	.000	.000
comp_WOM	-.196	-.175	.042	.289	.409	.000

Indirect Effects - Upper Bounds (BC) (Group number 1 - Default model)

	AdaptEnd_X_CenterSpeedy	AdaptBegin_X_CenterSpeedy	Speedy	AdaptBegin	AdaptEnd	comp_delight
comp_delight	.000	.000	.000	.000	.000	.000
comp_WOM	-.033	-.005	.187	.597	.786	.000

Indirect Effects - Two Tailed Significance (BC) Group number 1

	AdaptEnd_X_CenterSpeedy	AdaptBegin_X_CenterSpeedy	Speedy	AdaptBegin	AdaptEnd	comp_delight
comp_delight	...	...	...	...	...	...
comp_WOM	.006	.040	.003	.000	.000	...

Figure 8.24 Index of Moderated Mediation and Confidence Intervals for Dummy Coded Indirect Effects Test

How Do I Report the Results of My Multicategorical Moderated Mediation Test?

With multiple categories, you need to make sure the reader can easily find the statistical tests for each group. The categories and reference group also need to be overtly clear to the reader. I have provided two possible examples on how to present your results.

Example 8.1:

Table 8.1 Test for Categorial Moderated Mediation Using 95% Confidence Interval

Relationships Compared to the Reference Group of No Adaptation	*Unstandardized Coefficient*	*t-values*
Adaptive Behavior at the Beginning of the Experience → Customer Delight	.77	10.00
Adaptive Behavior at the End of the Experience → Customer Delight	1.05	13.72
Customer Delight → Positive Word of Mouth	.56	7.89
Test of Moderator		
Speed → Customer Delight	.19	3.77
Adapt at the Beginning of the Experience **X** Speed → Customer Delight	−.15	−2.03
Adapt at the End of the Experience **X** Speed → Customer Delight	−.19	−2.88

Moderated Indirect Relationship	*Direct Effect*	*Indirect Effect*	*Confidence Low*	*Interval High*	*p-value*
Adapt at Beginning → Customer Delight → Positive Word of Mouth*	.18 (1.39)	.43	.29	.60	<.001
Adapt at End → Customer Delight → Positive Word of Mouth*	.31 (2.24)	.58	.41	.80	<.001
Probing Moderated Indirect Relationships					
Adapt at the Beginning					
Low Levels of Speed:		.52	.37	.70	<.001
High Levels of Speed:		.34	.17	.55	<.001
Adapt at the End					
Low Levels of Speed:		.70	.51	.94	<.001
High Levels of Speed:		.46	.28	.70	<.001
Index of Moderated Mediation for Adapt at Beginning		−.08	−.17	−.005	.04
Index of Moderated Mediation for Adapt at End		−.11	−.20	−.03	.006

Note: Speed = Need for Speed in Transaction. Bootstrap Sample = 5,000 with replacement. Reference Group in this test was customers who did not get their experience adapted at all.

* = The indirect effect is moderated by the construct of Need for Speed in the transaction.

Example 8.2:

Table 8.2: Test for Categorial Moderated Mediation Using 95% Confidence Interval

Adapt at the Beginning compared to the reference group of No Adaption		*Unstandardized Coefficient*		*t-values*	
Adaptive Behavior at the Beginning of the Experience → Customer Delight		.77		10.00	
Adapt at the Beginning of the Experience **X** Speed → Customer Delight		−.15		−2.03	
Moderated Indirect Relationship	*Direct Effect*	*Indirect Effect*	*Confidence Interval* *Low*	*High*	*p-value*
Adapt at Beginning → Customer Delight → Positive Word of Mouth*	.18 (1.39)	.43	.29	.60	<.001
Probing Moderated Indirect Relationships					
Low Levels of Speed:		.52	.37	.70	<.001
High Levels of Speed:		.34	.17	.55	<.001
Index of Moderated Mediation for Adapt at Beginning		−.08	−.17	−.005	.04
Adapt at the End compared to the reference group of No Adaption		*Unstandardized Coefficient*		*t-values*	
Adaptive Behavior at the End of the Experience → Customer Delight		1.05		13.72	
Adapt at the End of the Experience **X** Speed → Customer Delight		-.19		-2.88	
Moderated Indirect Relationship	*Direct Effect*	*Indirect Effect*	*Confidence Interval* *Low*	*High*	*p-value*
*Adapt at End → Customer Delight → Positive Word of Mouth**	.31 (2.24)	.58	.41	.80	<.001
Probing Moderated Indirect Relationships					
Low Levels of Speed:		.70	.51	.94	<.001
High Levels of Speed:		.46	.28	.70	<.001
Index of Moderated Mediation for Adapt at End		−.11	−.20	−.03	.006

Note: Customer delight had a significant direct relationship to Positive Word of Mouth (β =.56 t-value = 7.89).

—Speed = Need for Speed in Transaction. * = The indirect effect is moderated by the construct of Need for Speed in the transaction.
—Need for speed had a significant direct relationship to customer delight (β = .[illegible]; t-value = 3.77).
—Reference Group in this test was customers who did not get their experience adapted at all.

Definitions of Constructs Used in Examples for This Chapter:

Adaptive Behavior: customer's perception that an employee adapted/modified their normal job performance to meet their needs. This adaptation can be through verbal interaction, service performance, or meeting special requests.

Binary Adaptive Behavior: 1 = customers who had an experience adapted; 0 = customers who did not have an experience adapted

Multicategorical Adaptive Behavior: 1 = customers who did not have an adapted experience; 2 = customers experienced an adaptation at the beginning of the experience; 3 = customers experienced an adaptation at the end of the experience.

Customer Delight: customer's profoundly positive emotional state resulting from expectations being exceeded to a surprising degree. Construct was measured with a 7-point Likert scale of Strongly Disagree to Strongly Agree.

Positive Word of Mouth: customer's intention to spread positive information to others about a previous experience. Construct was measured with a 7-point Likert scale of Strongly Disagree to Strongly Agree.

Need for Speed in a Transaction: customer's need for a quick transaction time.

Highlights of the Chapter:

1. Binary categorical variables can be used as independent variables in SEM, but they will need to be dummy coded into "1s" and "0s".
2. The regression coefficient of a binary categorical independent variable is simply the mean difference of the dependent variable across the categories.
3. The positive or negative sign of a regression coefficients for a binary categorical independent variable will determine which group has a stronger influence. Positive regression coefficients denote a stronger influence with a category that is dummy coded as a "1". Negative regression coefficients denote a stronger influence with a category that is dummy coded as a "0". The directionality of the sign with an indirect effect also denotes which category has a relatively stronger effect.
4. Multicategorical independent variables (more than two categories) have to dummy code a new variable for each category. One of the categories has to be a "reference category" for comparison purposes.
5. With a multicategorical independent variable, you will have multiple dummy coded variables that replace the single independent variable as it relates to conceptualization in AMOS.
6. In a moderated mediation model with a multicategorical independent variable, you will have multiple dummy coded variables acting as the independent variable. You will also have multiple interaction terms for each dummy coded construct that represents the categories of the independent variable. You will also need to assess the index of moderated mediation for each interaction term created to determine if moderated mediation is present.

Chapter 9

Latent Growth Curve Models

Introduction to Latent Growth Curve Models

Latent growth curve models allow us to see the "growth" or change over numerous time points for a respondent. This type of analysis works well for longitudinal data collection, especially with test-retest situations. If a respondent was measured at only two time points, we could use a two group analysis to determine differences of the two time points. When you have more than two time points, latent growth curve modeling can be quite handy. This type of modeling allows us to see the change over all the time points. Latent growth curve modeling works best for linear relationships, but it can determine the quadratic nature of the data if that is a concern. With a latent growth curve model, you are going to determine the intercept and slope of a value. If you are looking to forecast values into the future, it is advisable to have equal intervals between your time periods. Otherwise, the growth curve will have a "generalized" prediction in trying to account for the diversity of time frames. Saying that, if you are more concerned with the actual growth over the time period than future prediction, then you can use unequal time intervals. The real benefit of latent growth curves is to determine if there is a significant difference between groups in the "growth curve—slope/intercept". Obviously, understanding if change or "growth" over a period of time is important, but without a reference group you are not sure if this change really matters. That is why latent growth curves are well suited for experimental design research that is longitudinal or is a test-retest format.

Let's look at an example about a snack shop at a golf course. The snack shop wants to know if using environmentally sustainable packaging for their snacks would increase purchase behaviors of golfers. To test this out, they ran an experiment with golfers who make a reservation to play golf every Saturday and who typically purchase snacks after their round is over. A random group of those golfers after completing a round of golf were presented snack options to purchase that were packaged in environmentally sustainable materials. The cost was initially the same; just the packaging changed. Another group was selected as a control group, and they were presented snack options with the original packaging that did not mention being environmentally sustainable. The golf shop was going to see if spending patterns changed for the group that had an environmentally sustainable package. The snack shop tracked the purchases over four Saturdays. Dollar amount spent on snacks was captured and gender was also recorded, with 1 denoting males and 0 denoting females. Lastly, the snack shop coded which experimental group the golfers were in by a column called "sustain". Customers who got environmentally sustainable packaging for their snacks were coded as a "0", and those that received the original package with no mention of sustainability were coded as a "1".

Once our data is coded in SPSS, we are ready to draw a growth curve model in AMOS. To perform a latent growth curve, you need to go to the "plugins" tab at the top and then select "Growth Curve Model". You will then see a pop-up window asking how many time points you have. Select four and hit OK.

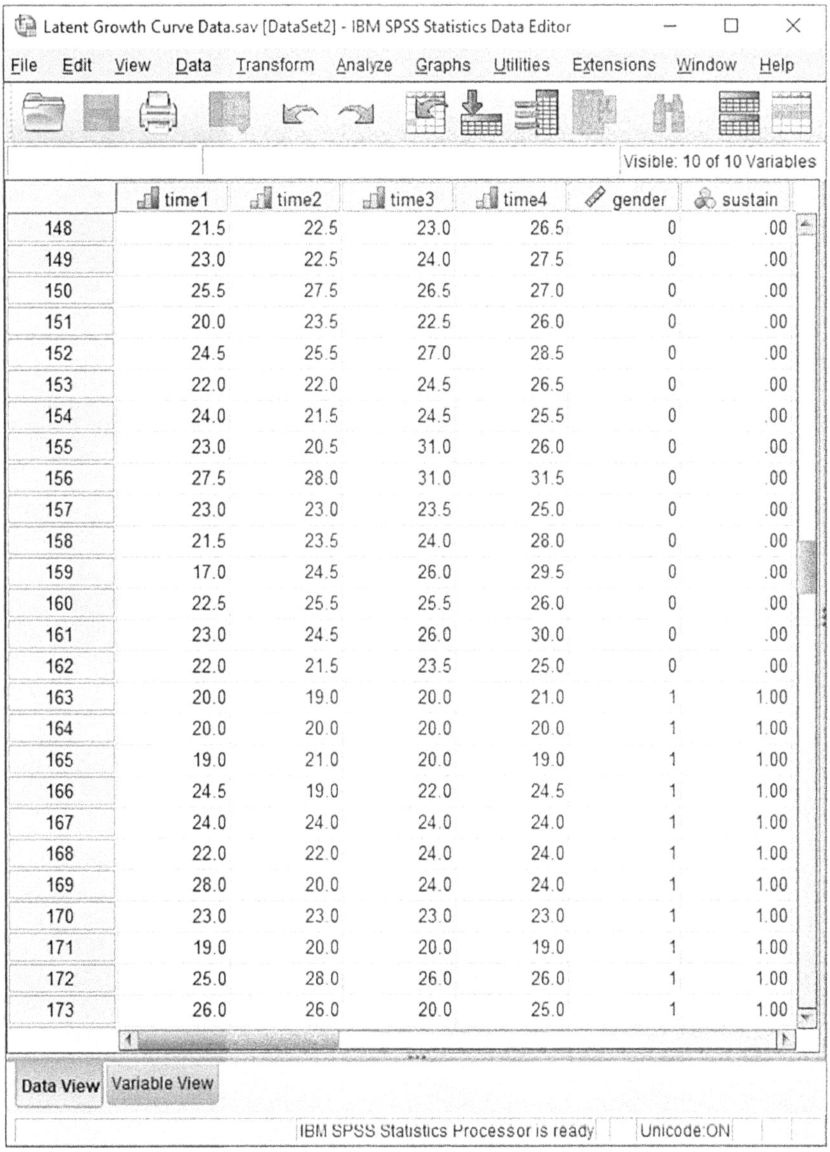

Latent Growth Curve Data.sav [DataSet2] - IBM SPSS Statistics Data Editor

File Edit View Data Transform Analyze Graphs Utilities Extensions Window Help

Visible: 10 of 10 Variables

	time1	time2	time3	time4	gender	sustain
148	21.5	22.5	23.0	26.5	0	.00
149	23.0	22.5	24.0	27.5	0	.00
150	25.5	27.5	26.5	27.0	0	.00
151	20.0	23.5	22.5	26.0	0	.00
152	24.5	25.5	27.0	28.5	0	.00
153	22.0	22.0	24.5	26.5	0	.00
154	24.0	21.5	24.5	25.5	0	.00
155	23.0	20.5	31.0	26.0	0	.00
156	27.5	28.0	31.0	31.5	0	.00
157	23.0	23.0	23.5	25.0	0	.00
158	21.5	23.5	24.0	28.0	0	.00
159	17.0	24.5	26.0	29.5	0	.00
160	22.5	25.5	25.5	26.0	0	.00
161	23.0	24.5	26.0	30.0	0	.00
162	22.0	21.5	23.5	25.0	0	.00
163	20.0	19.0	20.0	21.0	1	1.00
164	20.0	20.0	20.0	20.0	1	1.00
165	19.0	21.0	20.0	19.0	1	1.00
166	24.5	19.0	22.0	24.5	1	1.00
167	24.0	24.0	24.0	24.0	1	1.00
168	22.0	22.0	24.0	24.0	1	1.00
169	28.0	20.0	24.0	24.0	1	1.00
170	23.0	23.0	23.0	23.0	1	1.00
171	19.0	20.0	20.0	19.0	1	1.00
172	25.0	28.0	26.0	26.0	1	1.00
173	26.0	26.0	20.0	25.0	1	1.00

Data View Variable View

IBM SPSS Statistics Processor is ready Unicode:ON

Figure 9.1 Data Collected at Four Different Time Points

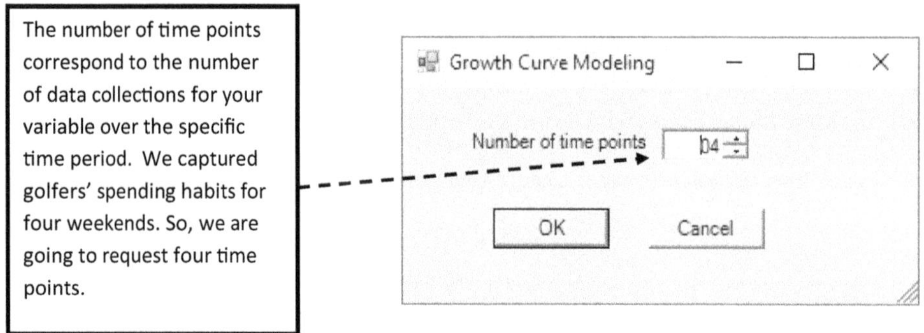

The number of time points correspond to the number of data collections for your variable over the specific time period. We captured golfers' spending habits for four weekends. So, we are going to request four time points.
Growth Curve Modeling
Number of time points
04
OK
Cancel

Figure 9.2 AMOS Latent Growth Curve Popup Window

After doing this, AMOS will populate a generic growth curve model with four time points. The growth model will have two unobservable variables listed as "ICEPT", which stands for intercept, and the second variable is called "SLOPE", which represents how steep or flat the "growth" or change is taking place. From the intercept construct, you will see parameters drawn to four different observables. You will notice that the parameters from the intercept construct to each observable is constrained to a value of "1". This is done so that regardless of the data point, the intercept (or starting point) should be the same for each time period. The slope has default values spaced out over four time periods (0, .33, .67, 1). I prefer to change these to meaningful time periods. The line to the first time period is listed as a "0". We are going to keep this value as a "0" because we

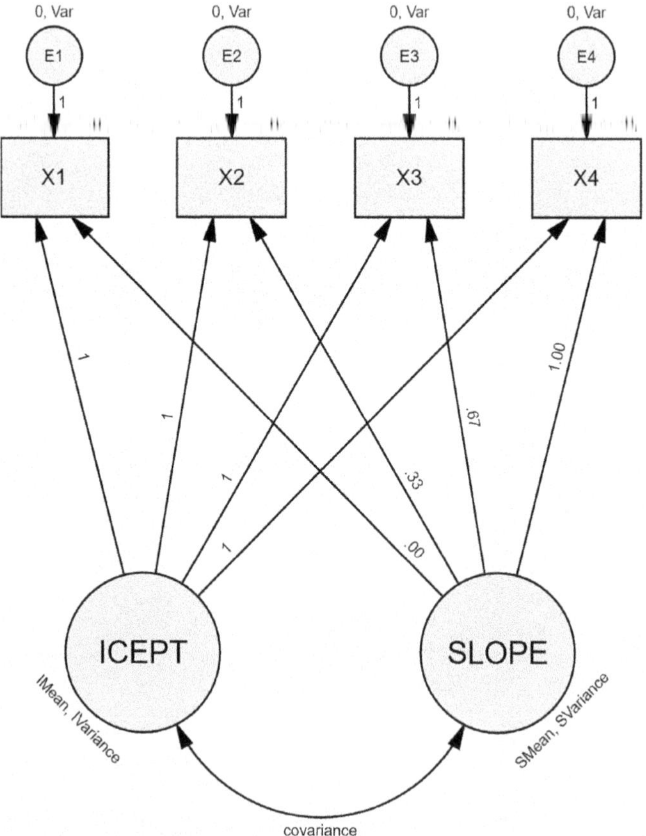

Figure 9.3 Latent Growth Curve With Intercept and Slope Modeled

want the first time period to reflect the intercept. Subsequently, the parameters for the next time periods will be labeled 1, 2, and 3. AMOS will also label the intercept mean and variance along with the slope mean and variance (imean, ivariance, smean, svariance). You need to remove these labels. If you had only one group, the labels would be fine; but since we have two groups, we need to remove those labels. Our two groups are (1) the customers who got an environmentally sustainable package; and (2) customers who did not get an environmentally sustainable package. The covariance between the slope and intercept constructs is also labeled, and we will remove that label as well. You can just double click into the labels which will bring up the Object Properties window. You will then just erase the labels for the mean and variance. As for the covariance label, do the same thing and remove that label.

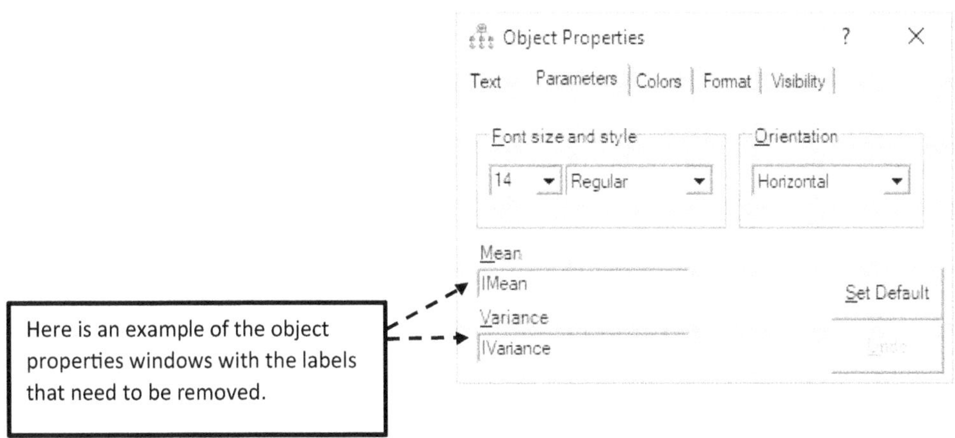

Figure 9.4 Object Properties Window With Mean and Variance Labeled

You will see four observables, X1–X4; these are the time points where we captured sales figures at the four different points of time. The sales figures are simply labeled Time 1–4 in the data file. In AMOS, you now need to view the variables of your data set and drag in the time points to the observables in the model. One last thing to note is that the error variances for the time periods are all equal. You will see that AMOS puts a label in the error variance of "var". This is to denote that the error variances for all time periods should be equal. I will remove this label as well so that the variance for each time period can be individually captured.

Next, you need to set up the two groups in AMOS. For a detailed discussion on how to set up groups in AMOS, see page 149. I am going to call one group "SustainPackage" for the group of individuals that were presented snacks in environmentally sustainable packages. The second group, labeled "NoSustain", was the group that was presented snacks in the original package that did not have any reference to environmental sustainability.

In the data, the individuals who had sustainable packaging were listed as a "0" in the sustain column and the individuals who had no environmental labeling on their snacks were listed as a

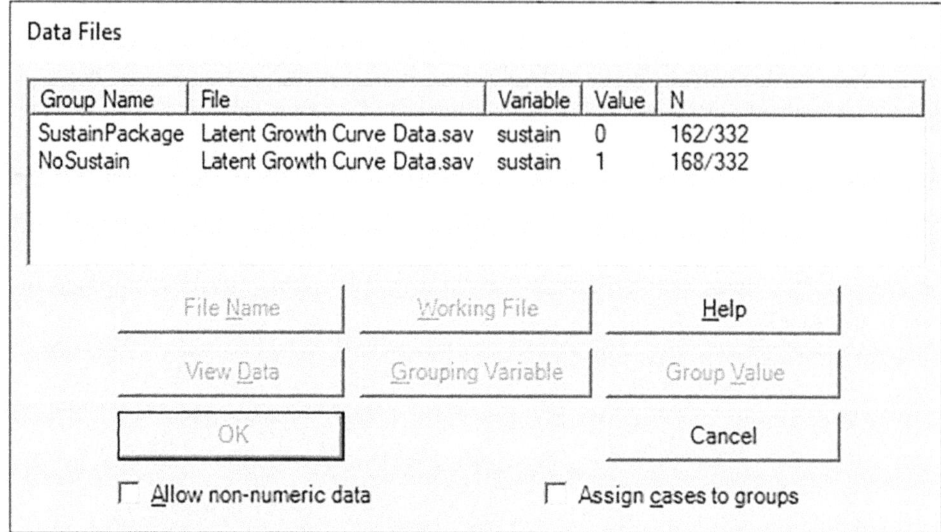

Figure 9.5 Denoting Data File Location for Each Group

"1". After setting up the groups, you need to read in the data for each group. The next step is to let AMOS uniquely label the means, variances, and covariances for each group. To do this, select the "multi-group analysis" button . This will give you a prompt that it is going to label all the parameters and suggest potential models with constrained parameters to test. Hit OK and let AMOS label all the parameters.

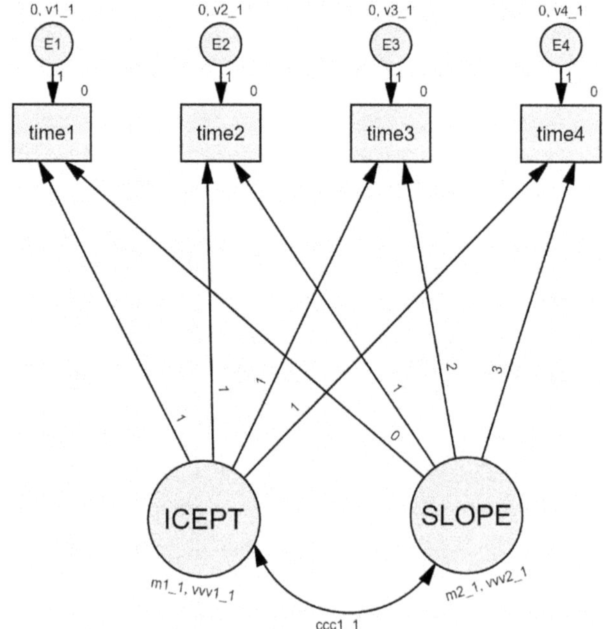

Figure 9.6 Labeled Latent Growth Model

This is what your model should look like after the parameter labeling of both groups. AMOS has labeled the mean for the intercept as m1_1 for the "SustainPackage" group. If you selected the other group (NoSustain), that mean value would be labeled as m1_2. You will see that the mean, variance, and covariance parameters all have a unique label name. Once you let AMOS label the parameters, it will suggest model comparisons across the groups. One of the potential models that AMOS suggests is called "Structural Means". This model comparison will constrain the means for the intercept and slope to be equal across the groups. This is the model comparison test that we are primarily concerned with going forward. We want to know if the intercept and slope is significantly different across the groups. See Figure 9.7 to see what the structural means test looks like.

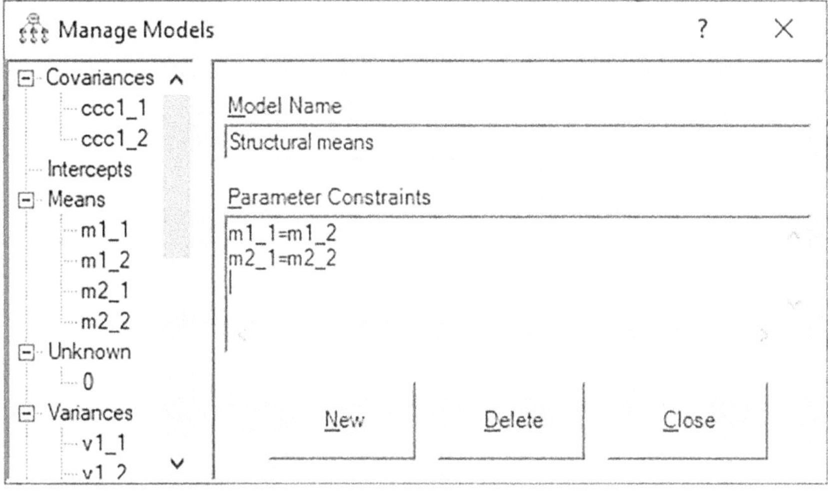

Figure 9.7 Structural Means Comparison Test

After setting up the groups and labeling the parameters, we now need to ask for AMOS to estimate the means and intercepts in the output. When we go to the Analysis Properties window under the Estimation tab, there is a checkbox called "Estimate means and intercepts" that we need to select. After doing this, we can cancel out of the window and run the analysis. Let's initially go to the model fit statistics in the output. In the model fit output (Figure 9.8), we are only concerned with the unconstrained model. Based on these results, the model fit is acceptable, so we can move on to the next analysis, which is the model comparison test. In the model comparison test option, we are going to examine the structural means test, which constrained the means for the intercept and slope to be equal across the groups.

If we see a significant chi-square test, then we can say with confidence that the groups are significantly different. The results of the structural means comparison (Figure 9.9) shows a significant difference between the groups. With 2 degrees of freedom constrained, the chi-square difference was 222.85, which is significant at the $p < .001$ level. Now that we know that the groups are different, we need to see the intercept and slope for each group to determine where the differences lie. In the "Estimates" link in the output, we are going to examine the means for the intercept and slope for each group.

Model Fit Summary

CMIN

Model	NPAR	CMIN	DF	P	CMIN/DF
Unconstrained	18	58.884	10	.000	5.888
Measurement weights	18	58.884	10	.000	5.888
Structural means	16	281.742	12	.000	23.479
Structural covariances	13	352.504	15	.000	23.500
Measurement residuals	9	379.035	19	.000	19.949
Saturated model	28	.000	0		
Independence model	16	843.541	12	.000	70.295

Baseline Comparisons

Model	NFI Delta1	RFI rho1	IFI Delta2	TLI rho2	CFI
Unconstrained	.930	.916	.941	.929	.941
Measurement weights	.930	.916	.941	.929	.941
Structural means	.666	.666	.676	.676	.676
Structural covariances	.582	.666	.593	.675	.594
Measurement residuals	.551	.716	.563	.727	.567
Saturated model	1.000		1.000		1.000
Independence model	.000	.000	.000	.000	.000

Figure 9.8 Model Fit Statistics Across the Model Comparisons

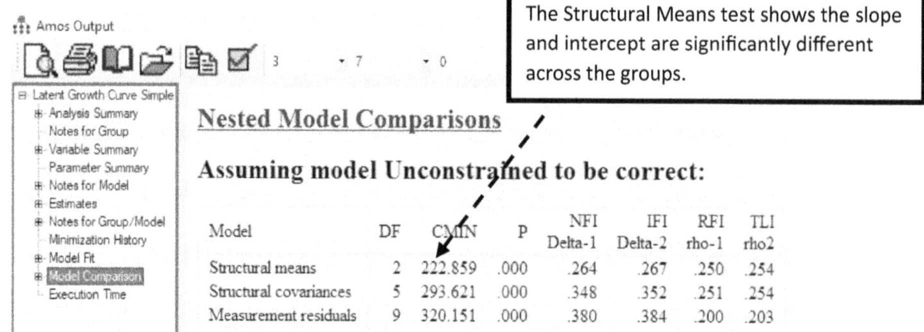

Nested Model Comparisons

Assuming model Unconstrained to be correct:

Model	DF	CMIN	P	NFI Delta-1	IFI Delta-2	RFI rho-1	TLI rho2
Structural means	2	222.859	.000	.264	.267	.250	.254
Structural covariances	5	293.621	.000	.348	.352	.251	.254
Measurement residuals	9	320.151	.000	.380	.384	.200	.203

Figure 9.9 Chi-Square Difference Test from the Model Comparison Results

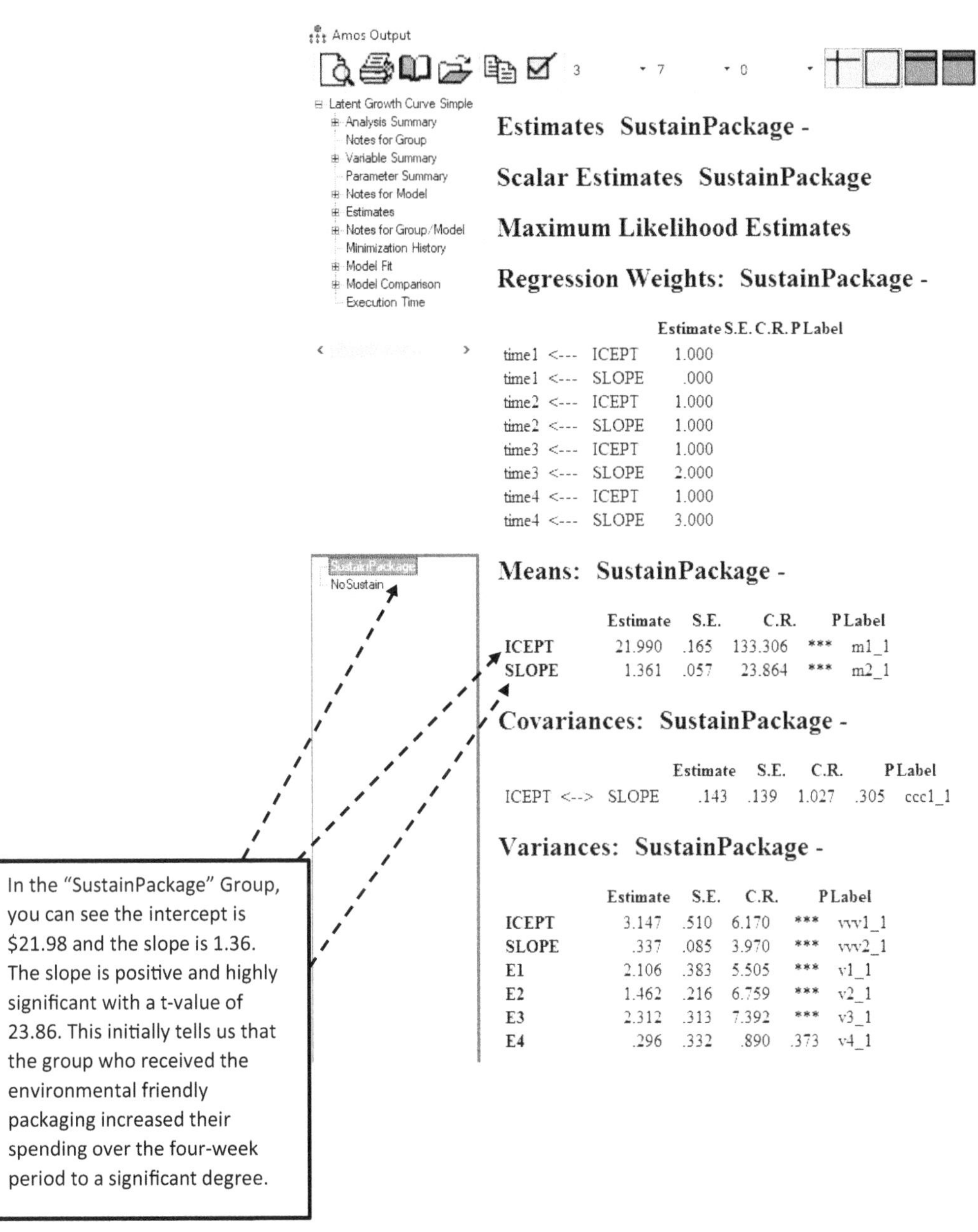

Amos Output
Latent Growth Curve Simple
Analysis Summary
Notes for Group
Variable Summary
Parameter Summary
Notes for Model
Estimates
Notes for Group/Model
Minimization History
Model Fit
Model Comparison
Execution Time
SustainPackage
NoSustain
Estimates SustainPackage -
Scalar Estimates SustainPackage
Maximum Likelihood Estimates
Regression Weights: SustainPackage -
Estimate S.E. C.R. P Label
time1 <--- ICEPT 1.000
time1 <--- SLOPE .000
time2 <--- ICEPT 1.000
time2 <--- SLOPE 1.000
time3 <--- ICEPT 1.000
time3 <--- SLOPE 2.000
time4 <--- ICEPT 1.000
time4 <--- SLOPE 3.000
Means: SustainPackage -
Estimate S.E. C.R. P Label
ICEPT 21.990 .165 133.306 *** m1_1
SLOPE 1.361 .057 23.864 *** m2_1
Covariances: SustainPackage -
Estimate S.E. C.R. P Label
ICEPT <--> SLOPE .143 .139 1.027 .305 ccc1_1
Variances: SustainPackage -
Estimate S.E. C.R. P Label
ICEPT 3.147 .510 6.170 *** vvv1_1
SLOPE .337 .085 3.970 *** vvv2_1
E1 2.106 .383 5.505 *** v1_1
E2 1.462 .216 6.759 *** v2_1
E3 2.312 .313 7.392 *** v3_1
E4 .296 .332 .890 .373 v4_1
In the "SustainPackage" Group, you can see the intercept is $21.98 and the slope is 1.36. The slope is positive and highly significant with a t-value of 23.86. This initially tells us that the group who received the environmental friendly packaging increased their spending over the four-week period to a significant degree.

Figure 9.10 Estimates Output for the Sustainable Packaging Group

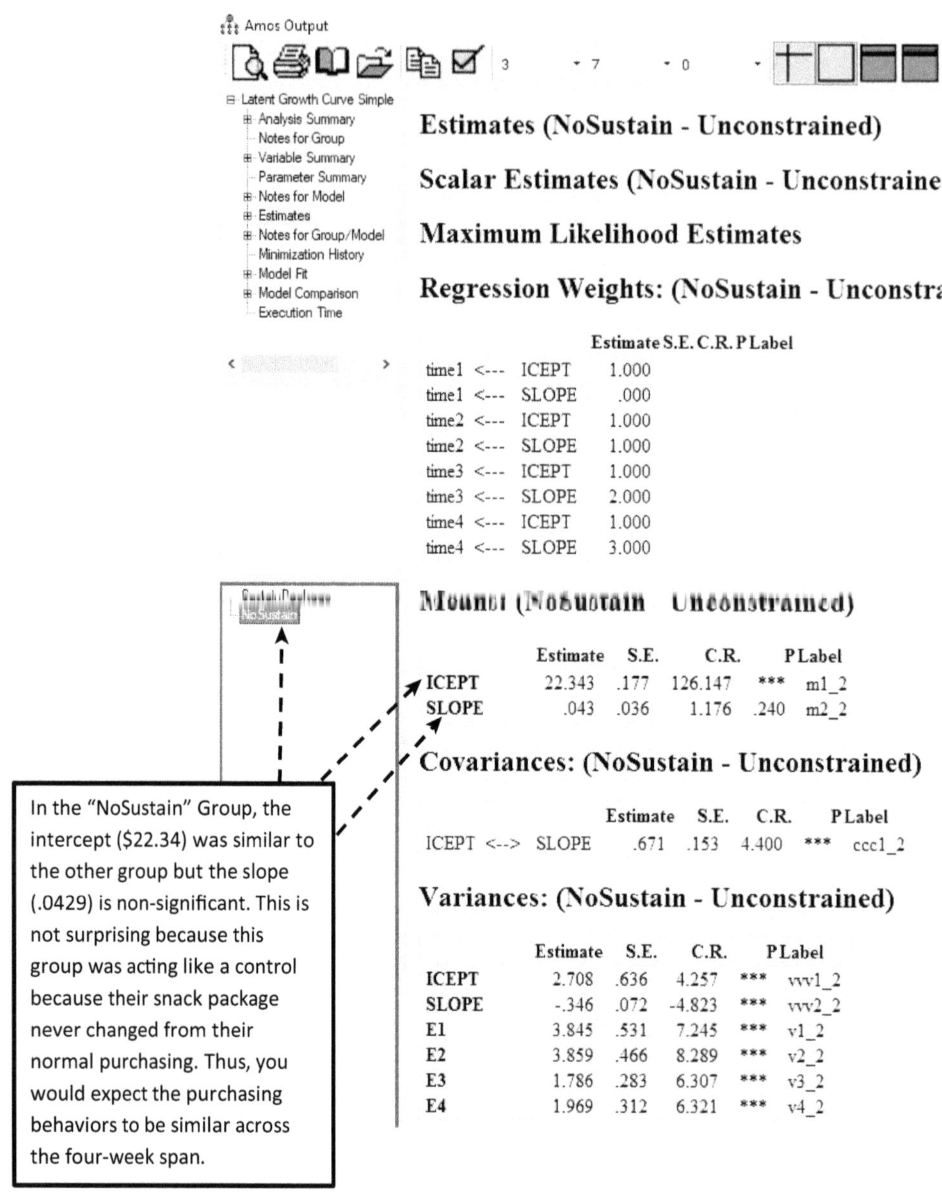

Figure 9.11 Estimates Output for the No Sustainable Packaging Group

The results of our experiment show that the group that had their snacks in environmentally sustainable packaging purchased snacks at a significantly higher rate than those customers whose snacks did not list the packaging as being sustainable. Over the four-week time period, there was a significant change in spending behavior.

The reason I prefer to do a comparison with latent growth curves is that it gives you greater context to your research question. We could have run a latent growth curve with just the environmentally sustainable packaging group and the slope would be significant, so we see a change in behavior; but I do not know if that change is significant compared to a control group. You could make the argument that the first time period could act like a control group and then see if there is a significant change over time. I don't prefer this option because it assumes that the intercept would be the exact same for each group. Especially with experimental manipulations, the first time point or intercept might be dramatically different. Ultimately, we are looking to see if the growth/change over time is significant in comparison to a group in an initial status and one that has experienced a manipulation. For instance, you see many latent growth curve examples that use student testing. Let's say we instituted a new curriculum for half of a high school's seniors in a school and the other half received the existing curriculum. If we just run a latent growth curve on the seniors who got the new curriculum, we could see if growth in test scores took place, but we don't know if the new curriculum is better than the old one without a comparison. If we compare the groups and see no significant difference in slopes across either curriculum, this will let us know that growth/change may be taking place, but it is not significantly better than the curriculum they started with before the test. Saying all this, latent growth curves are beneficial, but comparison of latent growth curves is where you can get real insight.

Including Predictors Into a Latent Growth Curve Model

In the previous example, we had two groups and we simply tracked spending behaviors across the groups. With many latent growth curve models, you will want to include a predictor of the intercept and slope; specifically, the variable or construct that would influence the intercept and growth over the time period. Using our environmentally sustainable packaging example, let's say we think that females are going to be more responsive to this type of packaging than males and we want to see if gender has an impact on the intercept and slope. Initially, we are going to draw and label the latent growth model the same as before, but this time we are going to include a gender construct (males coded as a 1, females coded as a 0) and have a path drawn directly from the predictor variable to the unobserved intercept and slope. The path from the predictor directly to the unobservables (slope and intercept) will now change these variables from an independent to a dependent variable. This means you will need to include error terms on the unobservable intercept and slope variable.

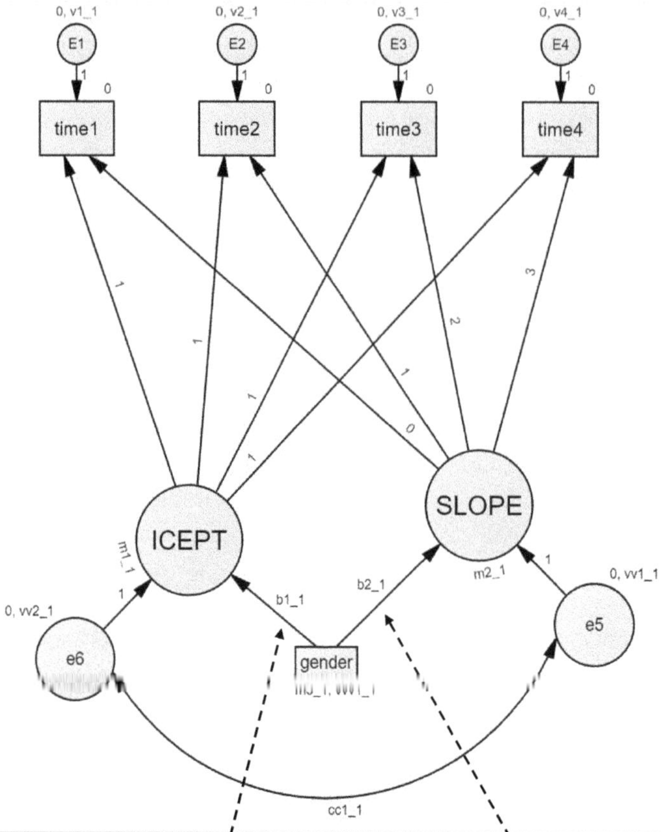

We have added the construct of gender with a direct path to the intercept and slope. Notice that we have labeled those paths. The "SustainPackage" group is labeled b1_1 and b2_1. The "NoSustain" group is labeled b1_2 and b2_2. Make sure you are including error terms on the intercept and slope with the inclusion of a predictor/independent variable. You will also need to covary the error terms for the intercept and slope.

Figure 9.12 Latent Growth Curve With Predictor Variable of Gender Modeled

If you are not recreating the model and are just trying to add a predictor to an existing latent growth curve model, you need to delete the existing parameter names for the variance of the intercept and slope. AMOS will give you a warning/error message if you try to have the variances labeled for the unobservable variable while including an error term. You also want to make sure that you correlate the error terms for the intercept and the slope of unobservable variables. If you want to compare the influence of gender across the groups, you will need to uniquely label the parameters from gender to the intercept and slope for each group. You can choose to select the multi-group analysis button again and it will relabel all your parameters again, or you can just label them individually. If you choose to have AMOS relabel all your parameters again, it will give you numerous potential models for comparison. In this example we are really concerned with only two tests: Test 1, which asks if the slope and intercept are different between the groups; and Test 2, which asks whether the influence of gender is significantly different across the groups. All other model comparison tests will not help us much. Once we have formed the model and asked for AMOS to "Estimate means and intercepts" in the output, we are ready to run the analysis.

When you have AMOS label your parameters, two model comparisons will be of primary concern: the structural intercepts, and the structural weights comparison. The "Structural intercepts" comparison will constrain the means for the intercept and slope to be the same, and it will also constrain the parameters from the independent variable (gender) to the slope and intercept. This comparison test will let you know if the intercept and slope are significantly different across the groups with the inclusion of the predictor variable (gender). The second comparison, called the "Structural weights", will only constrain the parameters from the independent variable to the intercept and slope. This specific test will allow to you to examine if the predictor variable is having a significant influence in the growth model across the groups. Again, AMOS will give you more models for comparison, but these are the ones you need to focus on going forward. Let's run the analysis and examine the model comparison link in the output.

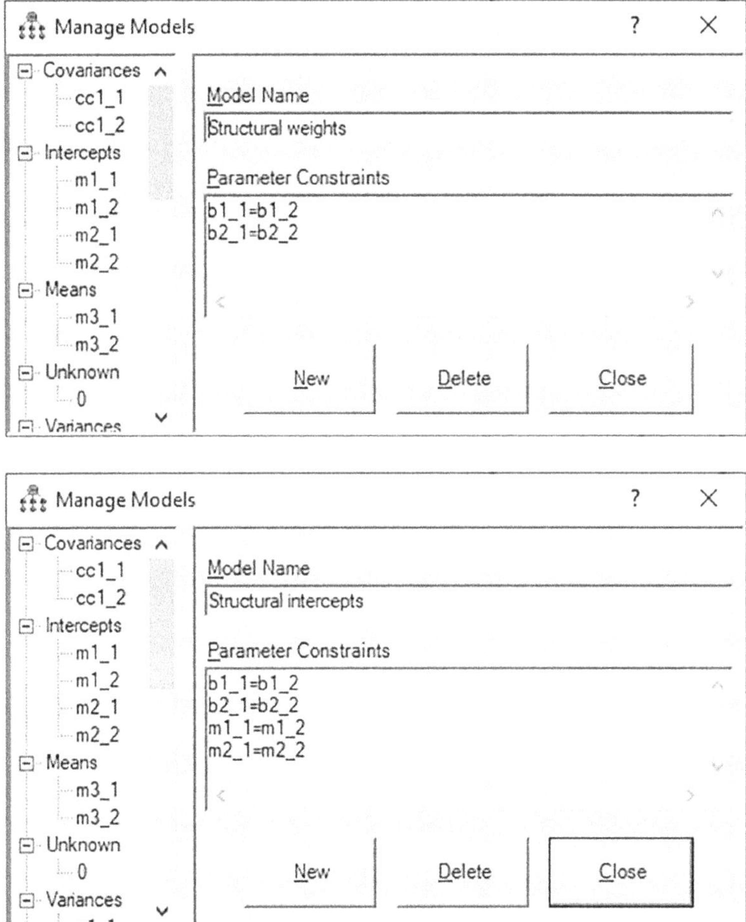

Figure 9.13 Manage Models Window Showing Structural Weight and Intercepts Comparison

The results show us that the structural intercept comparison was significant, which means the slope and intercept are significantly different across the two groups when accounting for the influence of gender. The specific test for gender called the structural weights was also significant, providing evidence that gender had a significant influence across the groups.

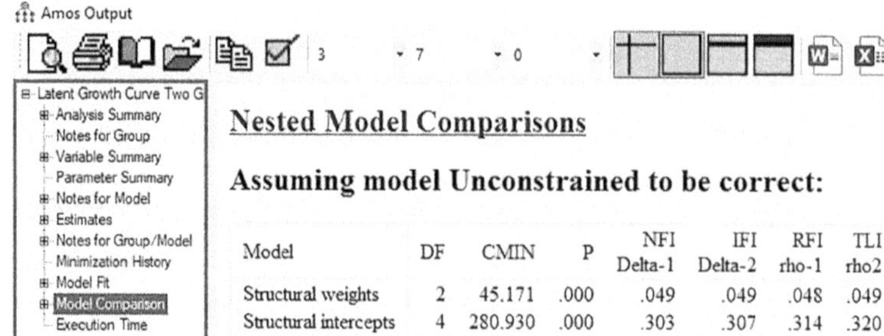

Nested Model Comparisons

Assuming model Unconstrained to be correct:

Model	DF	CMIN	P	NFI Delta-1	IFI Delta-2	RFI rho-1	TLI rho2
Structural weights	2	45.171	.000	.049	.049	.048	.049
Structural intercepts	4	280.930	.000	.303	.307	.314	.320

Figure 9.14 Chi-Square Difference Test for Structural Weights and Intercepts Model Comparison

After finding a significant difference between the groups, let's go to the "Estimates" link in the output, where we will examine the results of each group. See Figures 9.15 and 9.16.

In the environmentally sustainable group, you can see that gender has a significant and negative direct influence of the intercept and slope. Remember, males were coded as a 1 and females as a 0. This means females had a stronger influence on the starting intercept and slope than males. In the intercepts section in the output, you will see the intercept is significant and slope for the "SustainPackage" group is positive and significant denoting that spending patterns increased in the positive for this group. Notice that the slope is a little stronger now that we are including the predictor of gender than the first analysis that had no predictors.

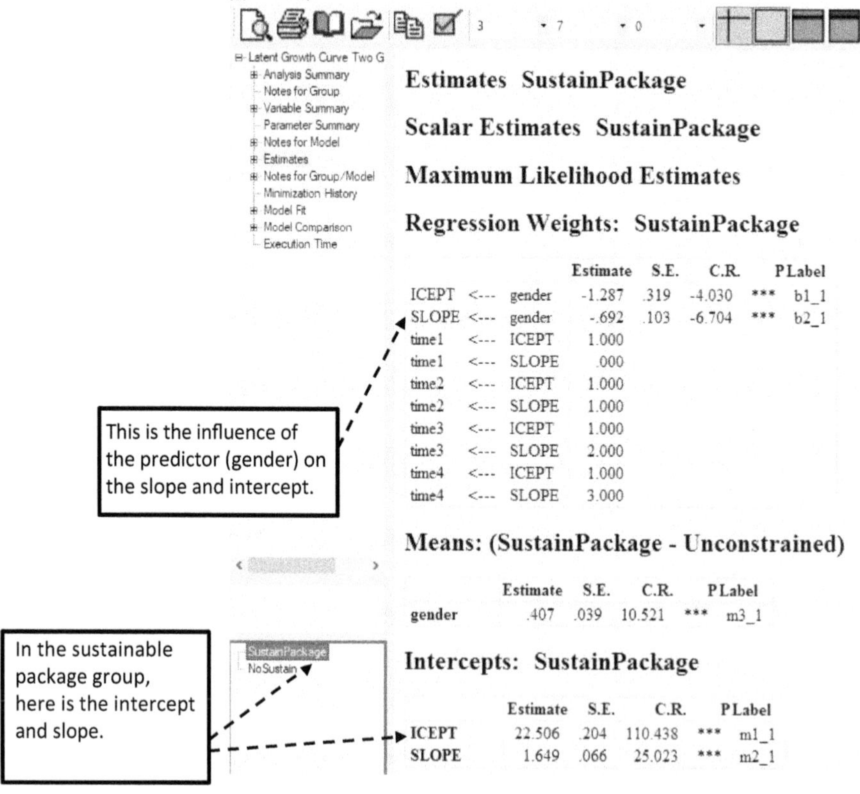

Estimates SustainPackage

Scalar Estimates SustainPackage

Maximum Likelihood Estimates

Regression Weights: SustainPackage

			Estimate	S.E.	C.R.	P	Label
ICEPT	<---	gender	-1.287	.319	-4.030	***	b1_1
SLOPE	<---	gender	-.692	.103	-6.704	***	b2_1
time1	<---	ICEPT	1.000				
time1	<---	SLOPE	.000				
time2	<---	ICEPT	1.000				
time2	<---	SLOPE	1.000				
time3	<---	ICEPT	1.000				
time3	<---	SLOPE	2.000				
time4	<---	ICEPT	1.000				
time4	<---	SLOPE	3.000				

Means: (SustainPackage - Unconstrained)

	Estimate	S.E.	C.R.	P	Label
gender	.407	.039	10.521	***	m3_1

Intercepts: SustainPackage

	Estimate	S.E.	C.R.	P	Label
ICEPT	22.506	.204	110.438	***	m1_1
SLOPE	1.649	.066	25.023	***	m2_1

Figure 9.15 Estimates Output of the Sustainable Package Group Including Regression Weights of Predictors Along With Intercept and Slope Values

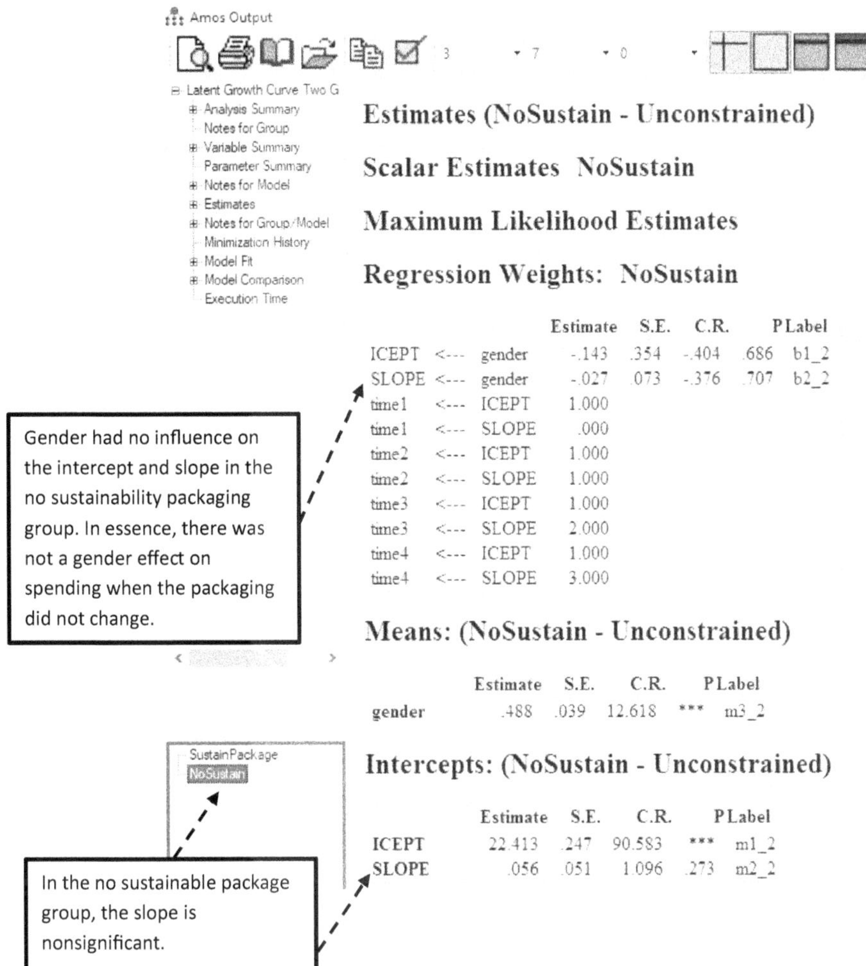

Figure 9.16 Estimates Output of the No Sustainable Package Group Including Regression Weights of Predictors Along With Intercept and Slope Values

In the group that did not have environmentally sustainable packaging listed on their snacks, gender did not have a significant difference on slope or intercept. Additionally, the "NoSustain" group did not have a significant slope denoting that the change over the four time periods was not significant.

Our ultimate results show that the environmentally sustainable packaging had a significant positive "growth" or change over the four-week time period in customers purchasing behavior compared to customers who did not have any sustainability packaging information presented on their snacks. Additionally, female customers responded more strongly to the environmentally sustainable packaging than males.

How Do I Present My Latent Growth Curve Results?

There are many alternative templates you can use to present your latent growth curve results, but I find it is a good idea to present the mean values of the construct captured over the time periods for both groups. I also like to present the slope and intercept. Lastly, including the regression coefficients of a predictor variable should also be presented. Here is one template you can use:

Example 9.1:

Table 9.1 Latent Growth Curve Results

Construct Measured	*Mean Values*			
	Time 1	*Time 2*	*Time 3*	*Time 4*
Spending Behavior (No Environmental Package)	22.72	21.95	22.30	22.63
Spending Behavior (Environmental Package)	22.18	23.16	24.64	26.09
Relationships	*Estimate*	*t-value*		
No Environmental Package Group				
Intercept	22.41	90.58		
Slope	0.05	1.09		
Gender to Intercept	−0.143	−0.40		
Gender to Slope	−0.027	−0.37		
Environmental Package Group				
Intercept	22.50	110.43		
Slope	1.64	25.02		
Gender to Intercept	−1.286	−4.02		
Gender to Slope	−0.692	−6.70		
Chi-Square Difference test of gender across the groups				
$\Delta\chi^2$/2df = 45.17; p < .001				

Model Fit Across the Groups: χ^2 = 66.59, df = 14, p<.001, CFI=.94, IFI=.94, RMSEA=.10
Note: Gender was coded as a 1 for males and a 0 for females.

Latent Growth Curves With Nonlinear Patterns

Up to this point, we have examined latent growth curves that were linear in nature. Latent growth curves can assess nonlinear patterns as well. If you think your data might have linear and quadratic components, latent growth curves can assess the growth between time points and also assess the potential curvilinear nature of the data. In our latent growth curve example, AMOS will initially default a model with two unobserved variables of intercept and slope. If you think a quadratic component is present, you need to add a third unobservable variable. Let's call this third unobservable "Quadratic". We are going to include a parameter to each time period (observables) in the model. To reflect the quadratic nature of this test, we will place a "−1" for time period 1. For time periods 2 and 3, we will label the parameter a "1"; and for the last time period, we will label that parameter a "−1". With the Quadratic unobservable, we are going to examine the mean values. A negative mean value in the Quadratic variable means that either the data is curving upward or the change in values are increasing steeply over time. A positive mean indicates that the data is curving downward or the values are decreasing steeply over time. We are also going to add a covariance between all the unobservables in the model.

Let's run the analysis and go to the "Estimates" link in the output.

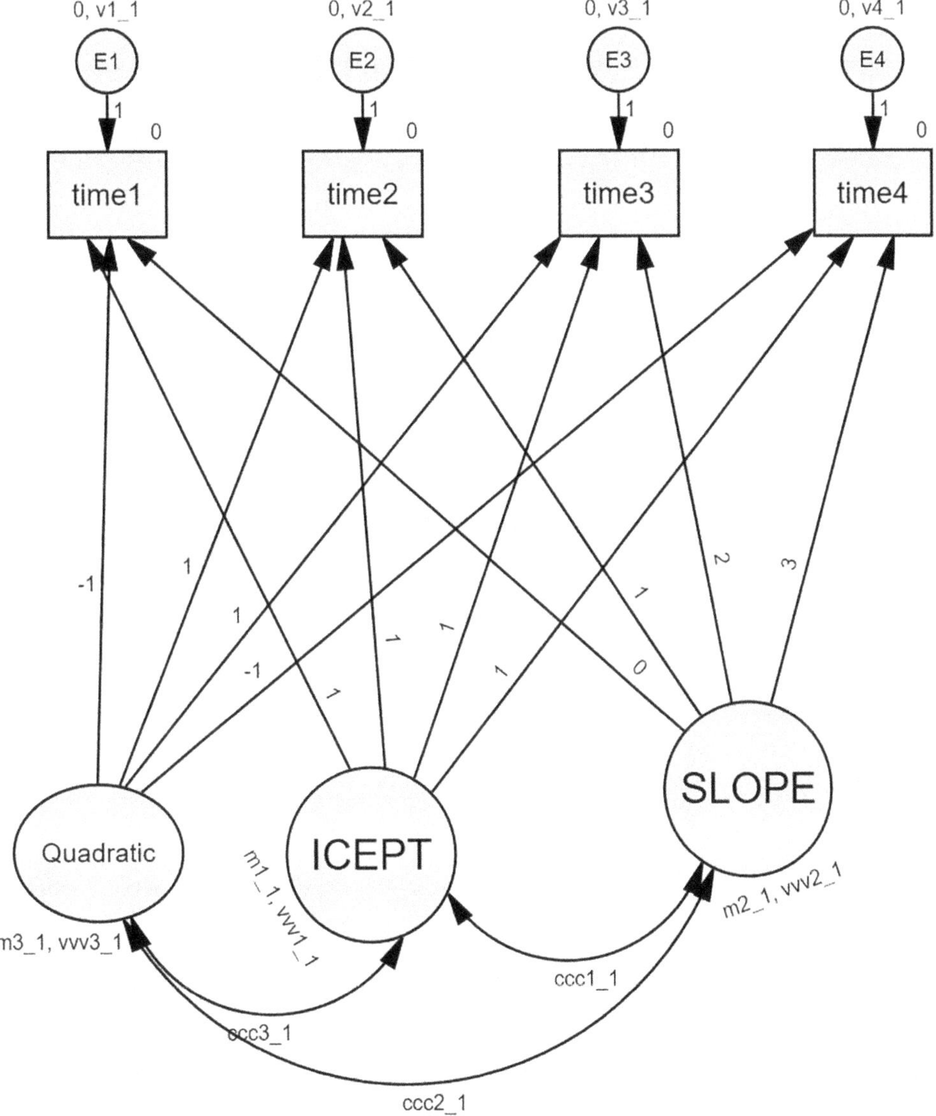

Figure 9.17 AMOS Latent Growth Curve Model Testing for a Curvilinear Pattern

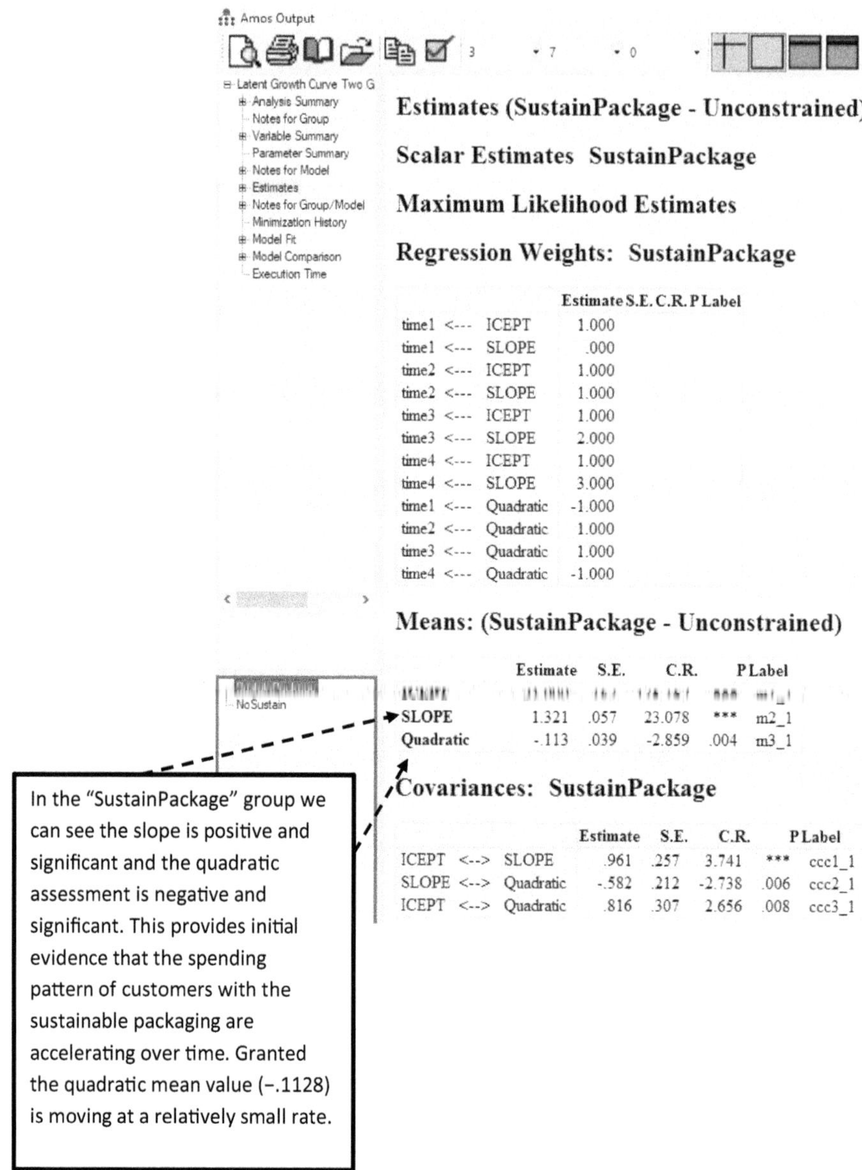

Figure 9.18 Estimates Output Testing the Quadratic Effects for the Sustainable Package Group

I solely used the sustainability packaging group in this example, but if you want to perform a two group analysis to see if the intercept, slope, and quadratic pattern are different across the groups, you just need to label the mean and variance for each group and then constrain those values across the groups. In the example provided, I labeled the quadratic variable's mean m3_2 and the variance vvv3_2. So, in the comparison test, you would constrain slope, intercept, and quadratic pattern to be equal across the groups. You can then run a two group analysis which would tell you if there were differences across the groups and also determine if the quadratic nature of the data was significant across the groups.

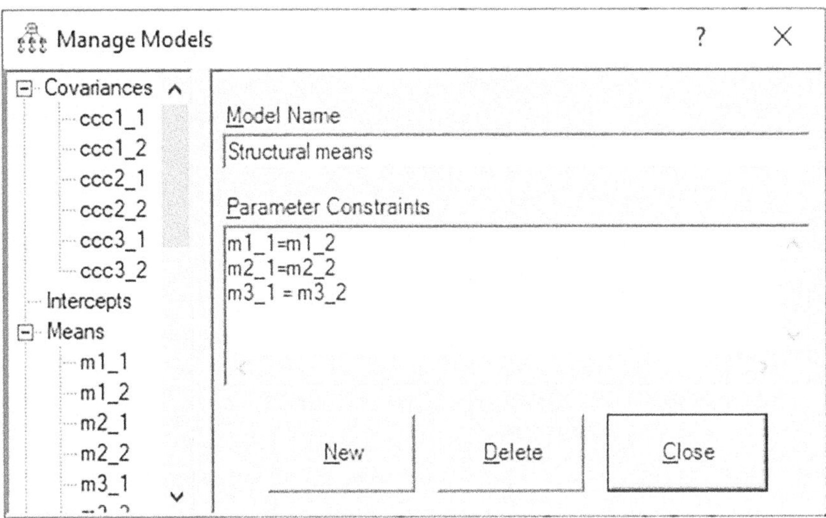

Figure 9.19 Constraining Parameters Across the Groups for the Slope, Intercept, and Quadratic Variable.

Latent Growth Curves Across Two Domains

There are situations where you want to test two domains together in a latent growth curve model. If we believe that the growth or change of one variable is also correlated with the change or growth of another variable, we may want to test a latent growth curve model with two domains. In essence, you will learn more by understanding the collective impact rather than testing them individually. To do this, you need to have two sets of intercepts and slopes in the model. For instance, let's say we also want to see how much a customer tips when the packaging is environmentally sustainable on their snacks. We would initially draw a growth model for the spending patterns of snacks from our original example, and then we would have to draw another intercept and slope along with observables. In the second domain, we have tracked tipping amounts across the four-week time period. With two domains included in one model, we need to make sure that all parameters and variables are uniquely named. For the tipping domain, I am simply adding "Tip" to the front of all the names. I have also covaried all the intercepts and slopes across the domains. If we think that both domains are connected, the intercepts and slopes need to include a covariance. After setting up your model with both domains, you can then view the output and examine the estimated means of the intercept and slope as noted in the previous examples. In the output, we would examine if the intercept and slope changed over the four time periods while considering the second domain. To see an example of how to set up a latent growth curve with two domains, see Figure 9.20.

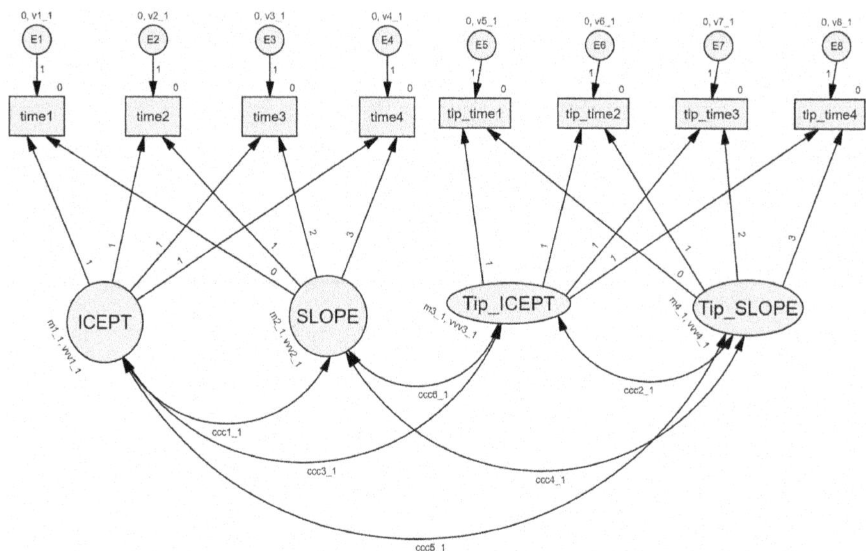

Figure 9.20 Example of a Latent Growth Curve Model With Two Domains

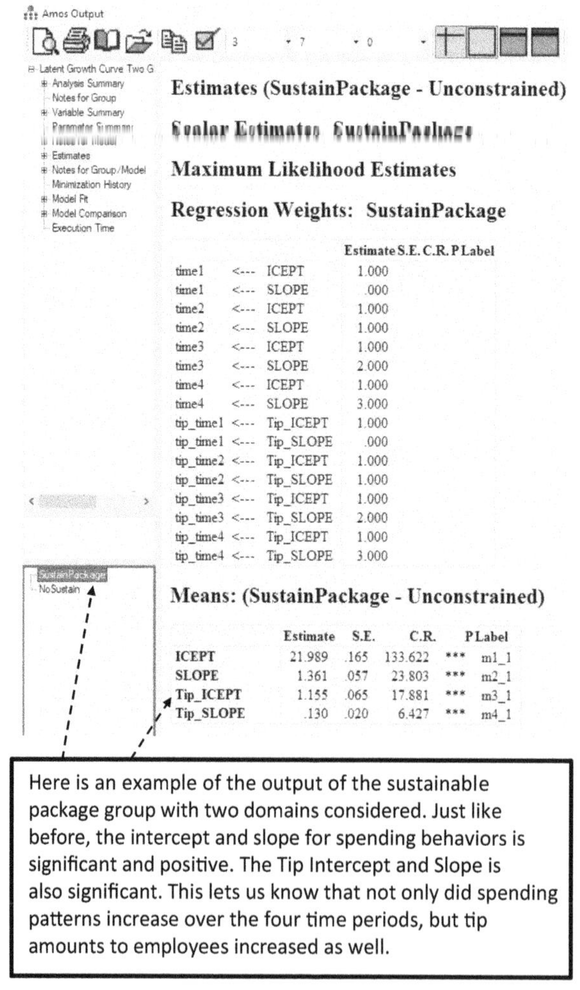

Estimates (SustainPackage - Unconstrained)

Scalar Estimates (SustainPackage)

Maximum Likelihood Estimates

Regression Weights: SustainPackage

			Estimate	S.E.	C.R.	P	Label
time1	<---	ICEPT	1.000				
time1	<---	SLOPE	.000				
time2	<---	ICEPT	1.000				
time2	<---	SLOPE	1.000				
time3	<---	ICEPT	1.000				
time3	<---	SLOPE	2.000				
time4	<---	ICEPT	1.000				
time4	<---	SLOPE	3.000				
tip_time1	<---	Tip_ICEPT	1.000				
tip_time1	<---	Tip_SLOPE	.000				
tip_time2	<---	Tip_ICEPT	1.000				
tip_time2	<---	Tip_SLOPE	1.000				
tip_time3	<---	Tip_ICEPT	1.000				
tip_time3	<---	Tip_SLOPE	2.000				
tip_time4	<---	Tip_ICEPT	1.000				
tip_time4	<---	Tip_SLOPE	3.000				

Means: (SustainPackage - Unconstrained)

	Estimate	S.E.	C.R.	P	Label
ICEPT	21.989	.165	133.622	***	m1_1
SLOPE	1.361	.057	23.803	***	m2_1
Tip_ICEPT	1.155	.065	17.881	***	m3_1
Tip_SLOPE	.130	.020	6.427	***	m4_1

Here is an example of the output of the sustainable package group with two domains considered. Just like before, the intercept and slope for spending behaviors is significant and positive. The Tip Intercept and Slope is also significant. This lets us know that not only did spending patterns increase over the four time periods, but tip amounts to employees increased as well.

Figure 9.21 Estimates Output for Sustainable Packaging Group Examining the Domains of Spending and Tipping

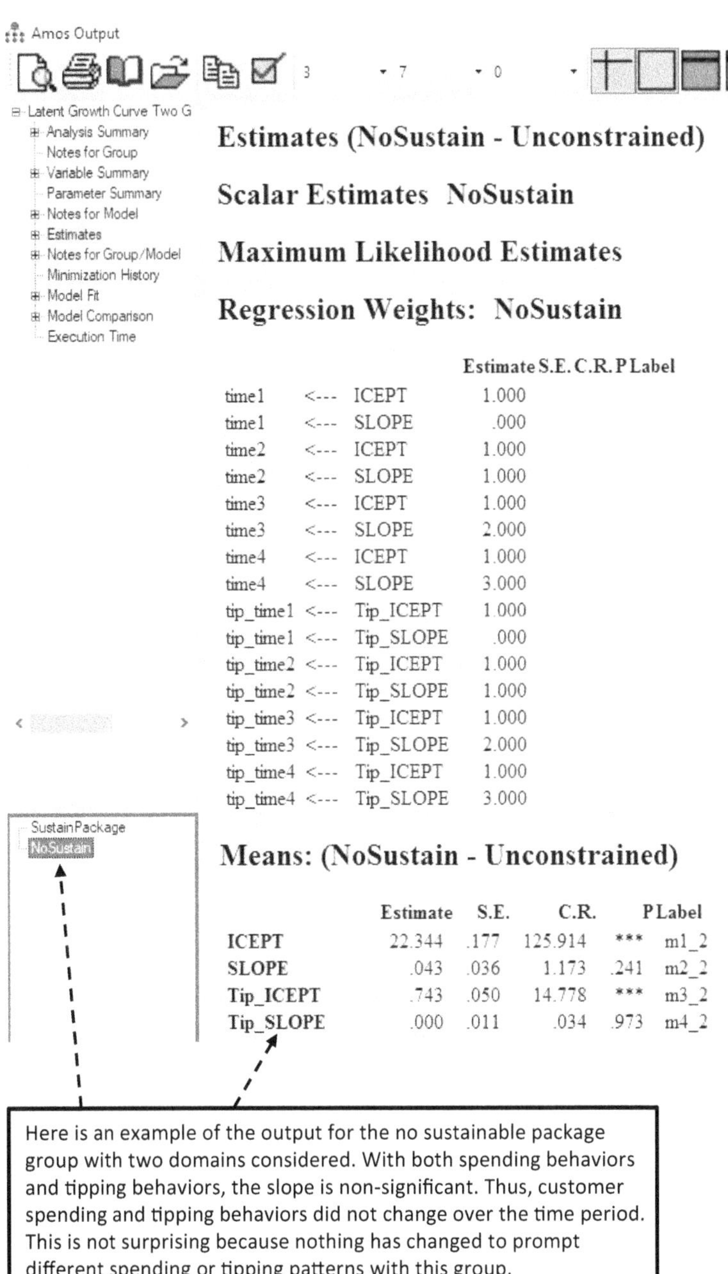

Amos Output
Latent Growth Curve Two G
Analysis Summary
Notes for Group
Variable Summary
Parameter Summary
Notes for Model
Estimates
Notes for Group/Model
Minimization History
Model Fit
Model Comparison
Execution Time
SustainPackage
NoSustain

Estimates (NoSustain - Unconstrained)

Scalar Estimates NoSustain

Maximum Likelihood Estimates

Regression Weights: NoSustain

			Estimate	S.E.	C.R.	P	Label
time1	<---	ICEPT	1.000				
time1	<---	SLOPE	.000				
time2	<---	ICEPT	1.000				
time2	<---	SLOPE	1.000				
time3	<---	ICEPT	1.000				
time3	<---	SLOPE	2.000				
time4	<---	ICEPT	1.000				
time4	<---	SLOPE	3.000				
tip_time1	<---	Tip_ICEPT	1.000				
tip_time1	<---	Tip_SLOPE	.000				
tip_time2	<---	Tip_ICEPT	1.000				
tip_time2	<---	Tip_SLOPE	1.000				
tip_time3	<---	Tip_ICEPT	1.000				
tip_time3	<---	Tip_SLOPE	2.000				
tip_time4	<---	Tip_ICEPT	1.000				
tip_time4	<---	Tip_SLOPE	3.000				

Means: (NoSustain - Unconstrained)

	Estimate	S.E.	C.R.	P	Label
ICEPT	22.344	.177	125.914	***	m1_2
SLOPE	.043	.036	1.173	.241	m2_2
Tip_ICEPT	.743	.050	14.778	***	m3_2
Tip_SLOPE	.000	.011	.034	.973	m4_2

Here is an example of the output for the no sustainable package group with two domains considered. With both spending behaviors and tipping behaviors, the slope is non-significant. Thus, customer spending and tipping behaviors did not change over the time period. This is not surprising because nothing has changed to prompt different spending or tipping patterns with this group.

Figure 9.22 Estimates Output for the No Sustainable Packaging Group Examining the Domains of Spending and Tipping

If we wanted to see if the "growth" was significantly different across the groups, we could initially set up a model comparison test where we are going to constrain the intercept and slope for both domains to be equal across the groups and compare it to an unconstrained model. We have labeled the means for all the unobservables as m1–m4 with the "_1" group being the sustainable package group and the "_2" group being the no sustainable packaging group.

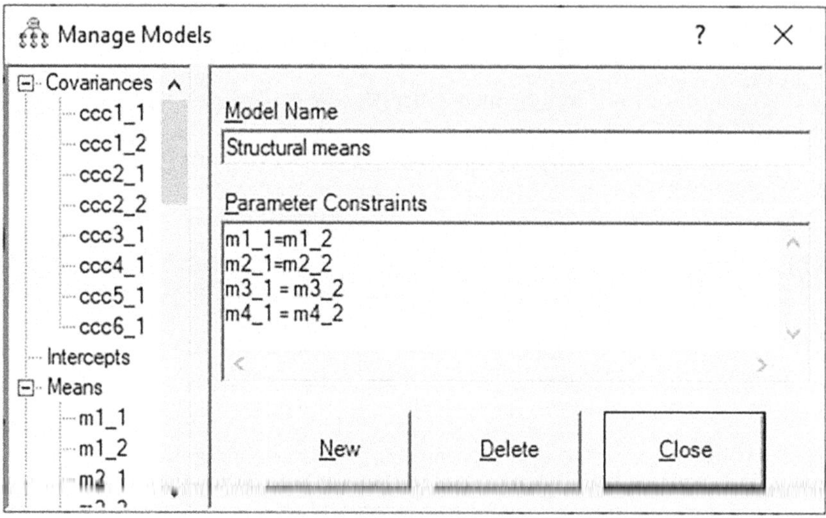

Figure 9.23 Constraining Parameters Across Groups for Both Domains

After constraining the means to be equal across the groups, let's run the analysis and go to the output. The model comparison option in the output will let us know the chi-square difference across the groups. Since we have constrained four different means, we should have a 4 degree of freedom difference from the unconstrained model.

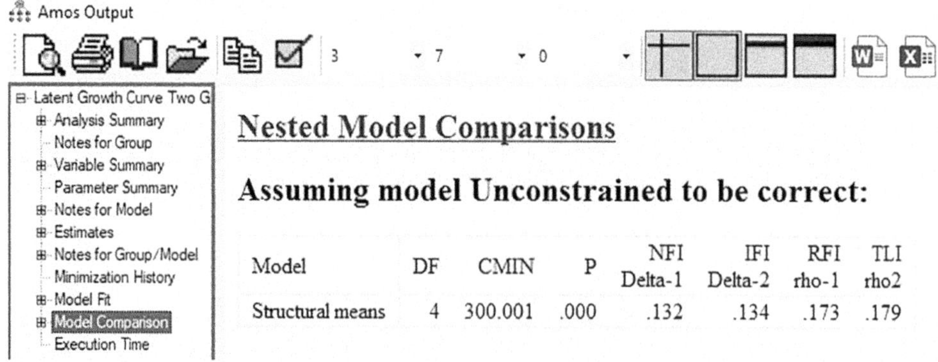

Nested Model Comparisons

Assuming model Unconstrained to be correct:

Model	DF	CMIN	P	NFI Delta-1	IFI Delta-2	RFI rho-1	TLI rho2
Structural means	4	300.001	.000	.132	.134	.173	.179

Figure 9.24 Chi-Square Difference Test With Parameters for Both Domains Constrained

The results of the model comparison test show that constraining those means to be equal across the groups produced a chi-square difference of 300.001, which is significant at a $p < .001$ level. Hence, we can conclude that the groups are significantly different, and based on the latent growth analysis, spending and tipping patterns significantly increased when sustainable packaging was introduced at the golf snack shop.

Definitions of Constructs Used in Examples for This Chapter:

Sustainable Package: participants were presented snack options that were in environmentally sustainable packages.

Non-Sustainable Package: participants were presented snack options in the original packaging that made no mention of sustainability in the packaging.

Tipping: How much a customer tipped an employee during a service/retail experience.

Highlights of the Chapter:

1. Latent growth curve models examine the change or "growth" over numerous time periods. To assess if the growth is significant, the intercept and slope of the growth/change is examined.
2. Latent growth curves are ideal in examining the growth across groups or the growth over a control group. Significant differences across the groups is determined through a chi-square difference test.
3. You can also include predictor variables in a latent growth curve to examine how this independent variable influences the intercept and slope of the growth curve.
4. With AMOS, you can assess if your growth pattern is curvilinear. The curvilinear unobservable construct added to the model will access mean values where a negative value means the data is curving upward and positive value means the data is curving downward.
5. AMOS will allow you to examine the growth of two domains simultaneously rather than having to examine them individually.

Chapter 10

Advanced Topics in SEM

Using Weighted Scores in AMOS

If your data sample is skewed to the point that a certain group is underrepresented, you might want to use a weighted score where underrepresented groups will have a stronger weight in the analysis. An example of this might be where 80% of your sample is female and you need to let the males in the sample have a stronger weight because they are underrepresented. Other examples of this can be where your sample is heavily skewed to one race and you want to include weights to the other races in order to represent a certain population. Weighting a score can be done for lots of reasons, but ultimately it is done so that your sample represents a specified group or population.

Let's use our structural model example again that Adaptive Behavior influences Customer Delight which influences Positive Word of Mouth. In our data collection, 80% of the respondents were Caucasian and 20% were African American. If we know that the customers of the retailer who were surveyed has a demographic makeup of 70% Caucasian and 30% African American, then our sample is underrepresenting the African American group, and we might want to give their responses more weight in the analysis.

If we look at the specifics of our data file (Figure 10.1), there is a column labeled "Race" where a "1" denotes a customer is Caucasian and a "2" represents a customer that is African American. Next, you need to determine the weight that needs to be applied across the data. To calculate the weight, you can use the following formula:

% of the population/% of the sample in the data

If we know that 30% of our customers are African American and 20% of our sample is African American, then the weighting for this group is:

30 / 20 = 1.50

For the Caucasian group who are overrepresented (with 80% of the sample), the weight of their scores is:

70 / 80 = 0.875

Weightings that are greater than 1 mean that those respondents are given more weight or importance in the analysis. Weightings less than 1 mean that the respondents' scores are given less emphasis in the analysis. After finding the weighting for each race, you need to form a new column in your SPSS data, and you can call it "weight". For all the respondents, who are classified as a "1" in Race, you will include a weight of 0.875. For all respondents with a 2 in the Race field, you will include a weight of 1.50. See Figure 10.1.

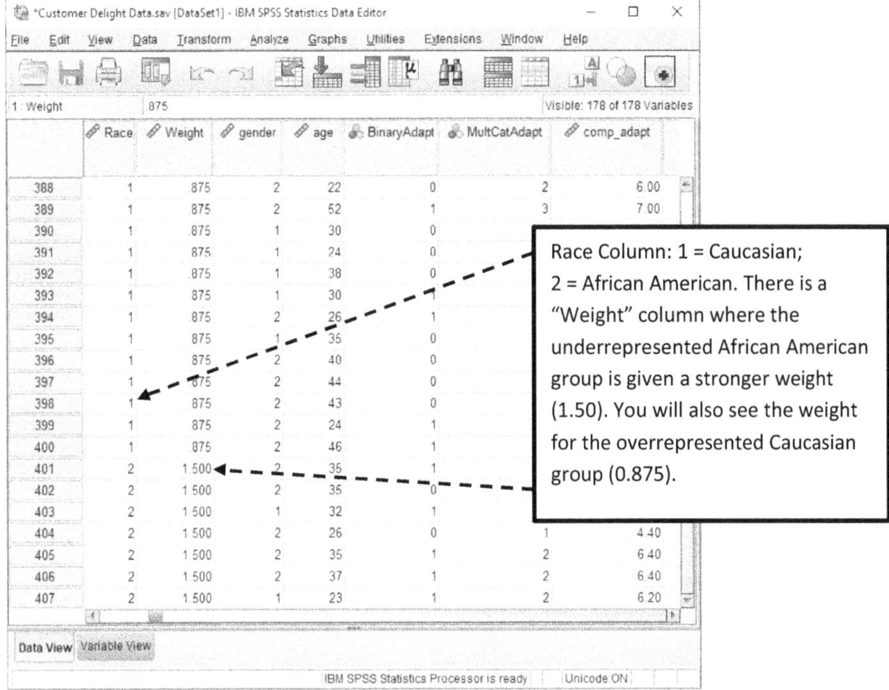

Figure 10.1 Scores Weighted in SPSS

After establishing the weights for each group, you need to apply the weights to the data. SPSS has a helpful function that will apply a weight to a whole row (or respondent). In the "Data" menu option at the top of SPSS, there is a function at the bottom called "Weight Cases". After selecting that option, you will see a pop-up menu. This menu will ask what column you want to use as the weight for the data. I labeled the column simply "Weight". After selecting the "Weight" variable, hit the OK button. The weight will now be applied to all of the data. See Table 10.1 to view an example with the weight function on and off in SPSS.

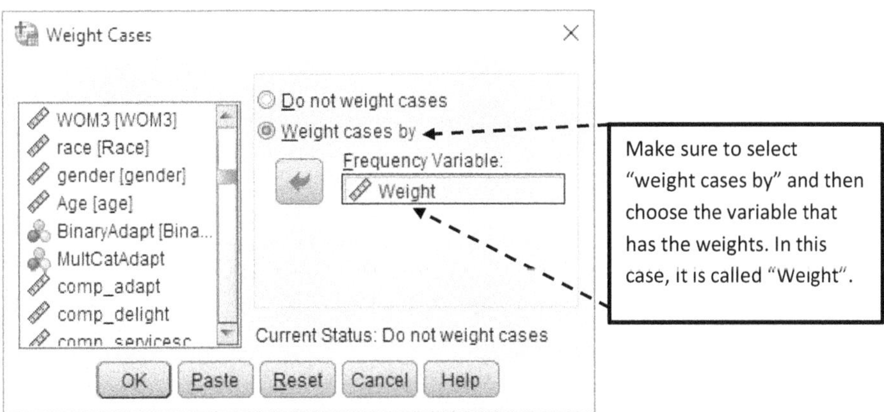

Figure 10.2 Weight Cases Pop-Up Window in SPSS

Table 10.1 Descriptive Statistics With Scores Weighted and Unweighted

Descriptive Statistics

	N	Minimum	Maximum	Mean	Std. Deviation
adapt1	500	1	7	6.11	1.029
adapt2	500	2	7	6.17	.977
adapt3	500	1	7	6.09	1.055
adapt4	500	2	7	6.07	1.048
Valid N (listwise)	500				

Simple analysis of the Adaptive Behavior indicators. Examine the means and standard deviations with the weights not included.

Descriptive Statistics

	N	Minimum	Maximum	Mean	Std. Deviation
adapt1	500	1	7	6.10	1.017
adapt2	500	2	7	6.15	.977
adapt3	500	1	7	6.07	1.053
adapt4	500	2	7	6.07	1.040
Valid N (listwise)	500				

With the weights included you can see the means and standard deviations are different.

Please note that SPSS will continue to run subsequent analyses with the weighted scores until you tell SPSS to stop weighting the scores. To turn off the weightings, just go back into the "Weight Cases" pop up menu, select "Do not weight cases", and hit OK.

After applying the weight in SPSS and saving the data file, you would think that it would be a simple process of pulling in these revised scores to AMOS, but you would be wrong. If you have a weighted score saved in the SPSS data and try to use it in AMOS, you will get an error message. This error message states that AMOS will not recognize the weights and AMOS will give each case a weighing of 1 (which means no weighting at all). To use a weighted score, we have to use a work-around.

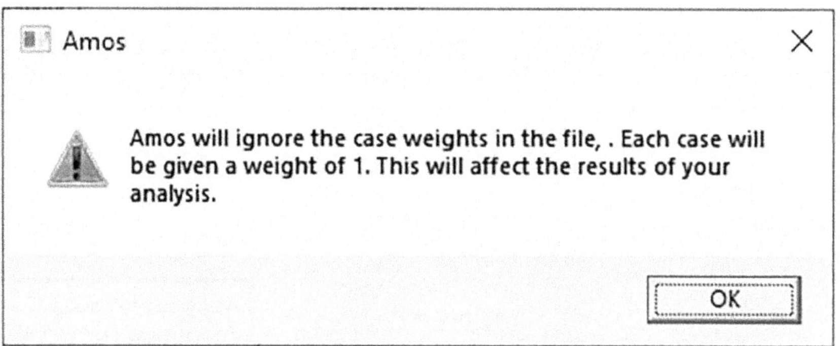

Figure 10.3 AMOS Error Message When Trying to Use a Weighted Score Data File

Let's go back to the SPSS file where our data is located. To work around this problem, we are going to get the covariance matrix of the weighted scores. We will also get the weighted means and standard deviations for each indicator or construct. Once we get this information, we will create a new SPSS file that will set up the adjusted data as a covariance matrix that we can use as input in AMOS. If you are examining a path model, this is a pretty easy process. If you are testing a full structural model, then it gets more laborious because you need to form a covariance matrix that includes every indicator in the model.

For instance, let's use our three construct model that we have used previously (Adaptive Behavior → Customer Delight → Positive WOM) and set this up as a weighted score. After applying the weight in SPSS, we could use the correlation function in SPSS to get the means, standard deviations, and covariance matrix, but the results will be in a very unfriendly format. Another option presents the results in a little more manageable form: the reliability analysis option in SPSS.

In this function, we would include all the indicators for each of the three variables. We are not concerned with the reliability across all three constructs; we are just going to choose some options in this analysis to give us the means, standard deviation, and covariance matrix. To do this, we go to the "Analyze" function at the top menu in SPSS, then "Scale", and then we select "Reliability Analysis".

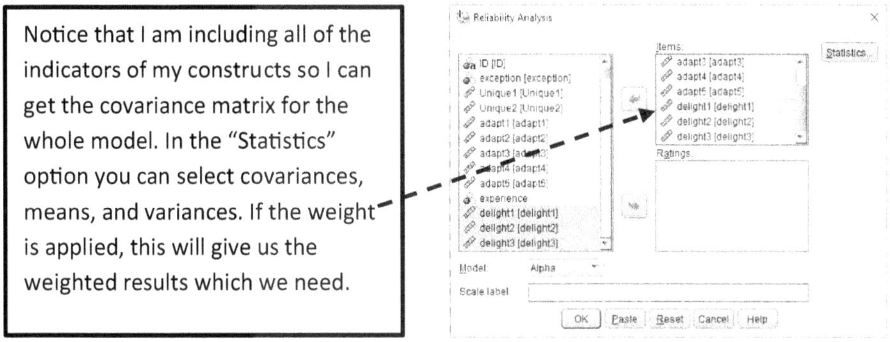

Notice that I am including all of the indicators of my constructs so I can get the covariance matrix for the whole model. In the "Statistics" option you can select covariances, means, and variances. If the weight is applied, this will give us the weighted results which we need.

Figure 10.4 Using the Reliability Analysis Function to get a Covariance Matrix

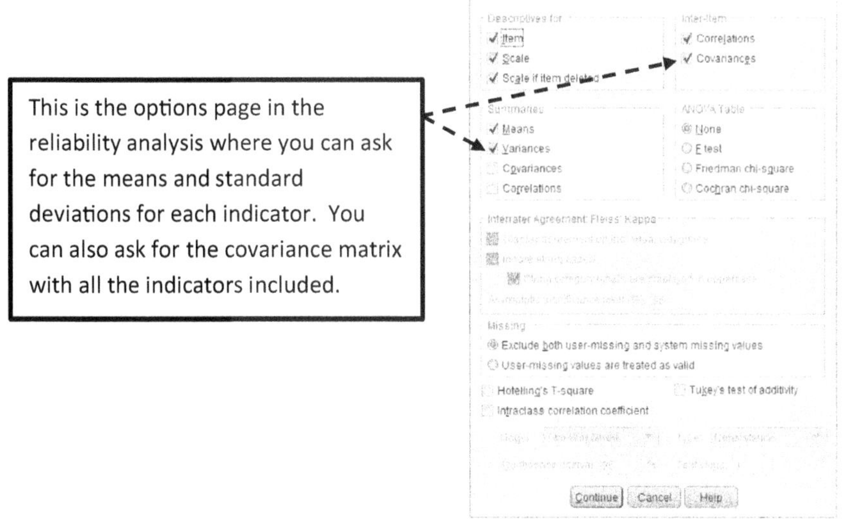

Figure 10.5 Statistic Option in Reliability Analysis

To see the full output of this analysis, see Figure 10.6. Once we have this information, we can set up a separate file that will be used as the input for AMOS. To see how to use a covariance matrix as input in AMOS, refer to page 133. Obviously, this would have been easier if we could have just brought in the weighted scores directly from SPSS, but this alternative will give us the same results. It is a little more labor intensive to set up the weighted covariance input file, but you can still perform your analysis with weighted scores through this alternative way.

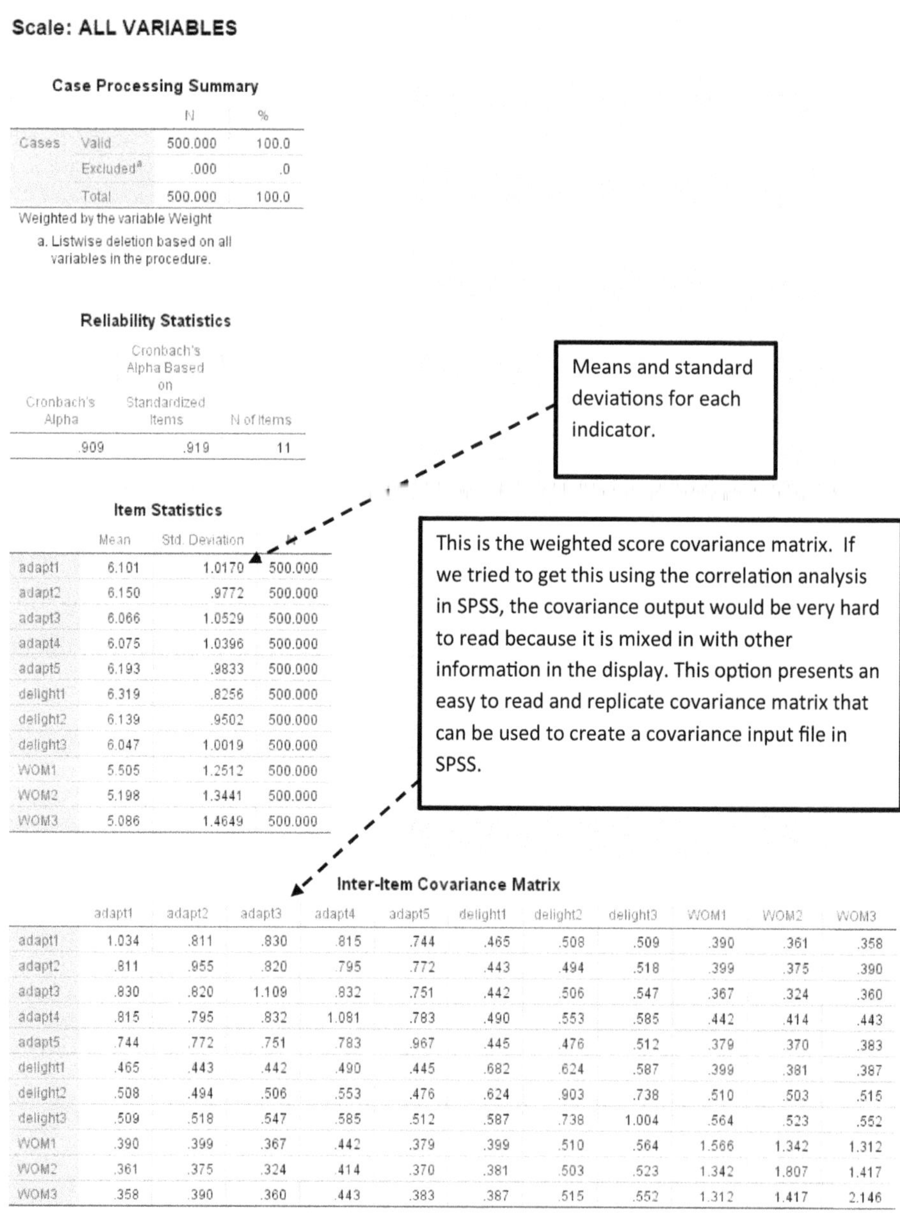

Scale: ALL VARIABLES

Case Processing Summary

		N	%
Cases	Valid	500.000	100.0
	Excluded[a]	.000	.0
	Total	500.000	100.0

Weighted by the variable Weight

a. Listwise deletion based on all variables in the procedure.

Reliability Statistics

Cronbach's Alpha	Cronbach's Alpha Based on Standardized Items	N of Items
.909	.919	11

Item Statistics

	Mean	Std. Deviation	N
adapt1	6.101	1.0170	500.000
adapt2	6.150	.9772	500.000
adapt3	6.066	1.0529	500.000
adapt4	6.075	1.0396	500.000
adapt5	6.193	.9833	500.000
delight1	6.319	.8256	500.000
delight2	6.139	.9502	500.000
delight3	6.047	1.0019	500.000
WOM1	5.505	1.2512	500.000
WOM2	5.198	1.3441	500.000
WOM3	5.086	1.4649	500.000

Inter-Item Covariance Matrix

	adapt1	adapt2	adapt3	adapt4	adapt5	delight1	delight2	delight3	WOM1	WOM2	WOM3
adapt1	1.034	.811	.830	.815	.744	.465	.508	.509	.390	.361	.358
adapt2	.811	.955	.820	.795	.772	.443	.494	.518	.399	.375	.390
adapt3	.830	.820	1.109	.832	.751	.442	.506	.547	.367	.324	.360
adapt4	.815	.795	.832	1.081	.783	.490	.553	.585	.442	.414	.443
adapt5	.744	.772	.751	.783	.967	.445	.476	.512	.379	.370	.383
delight1	.465	.443	.442	.490	.445	.682	.624	.587	.399	.381	.387
delight2	.508	.494	.506	.553	.476	.624	.903	.738	.510	.503	.515
delight3	.509	.518	.547	.585	.512	.587	.738	1.004	.564	.523	.552
WOM1	.390	.399	.367	.442	.379	.399	.510	.564	1.566	1.342	1.312
WOM2	.361	.375	.324	.414	.370	.381	.503	.523	1.342	1.807	1.417
WOM3	.358	.390	.360	.443	.383	.387	.515	.552	1.312	1.417	2.146

Means and standard deviations for each indicator.
This is the weighted score covariance matrix. If we tried to get this using the correlation analysis in SPSS, the covariance output would be very hard to read because it is mixed in with other information in the display. This option presents an easy to read and replicate covariance matrix that can be used to create a covariance input file in SPSS.

Figure 10.6 Reliability Analysis Output Using Weighted Scores

How to Use Bootstrapping to Account for Non-Normal Data

One of the fundamental assumptions with SEM is that your data is normally distributed. Having non-normal data can lead to chi-square values being inflated and thus can lead researchers to start making changes or alterations in a model that are not really needed. To address the issue of having non-normal data, you can look for multivariate outliers, and this might address your issues in a small sample. The best and most frequently used technique to address non-normality is to use a bootstrap in the analysis. In the mediation discussion in Chapter 6, I go into detail about what is a bootstrap and how it is performed for mediation testing. We are going to use a very similar process here in using bootstrapping to assess a model with non-normal data.

After you have formed your model in AMOS and determined that your data is non-normal (see page 165), you need to run your analysis with a bootstrap sample. To accomplish this, you will go into the Analysis Properties window and then select the Bootstrap tab at the top. You will need to select the option that says "Perform bootstrap". You will need to change the number of samples from 200 to 5,000. Having a sample of 5,000 is sufficiently large to achieve stability in the results. You will then select the "Bias-corrected confidence intervals" option and change the confidence interval from 90 to 95. Next, you will need to select the option "Bootstrap ML" in order to run the bootstrap via maximum likelihood. After those options are checked, you are ready to run the analysis again.

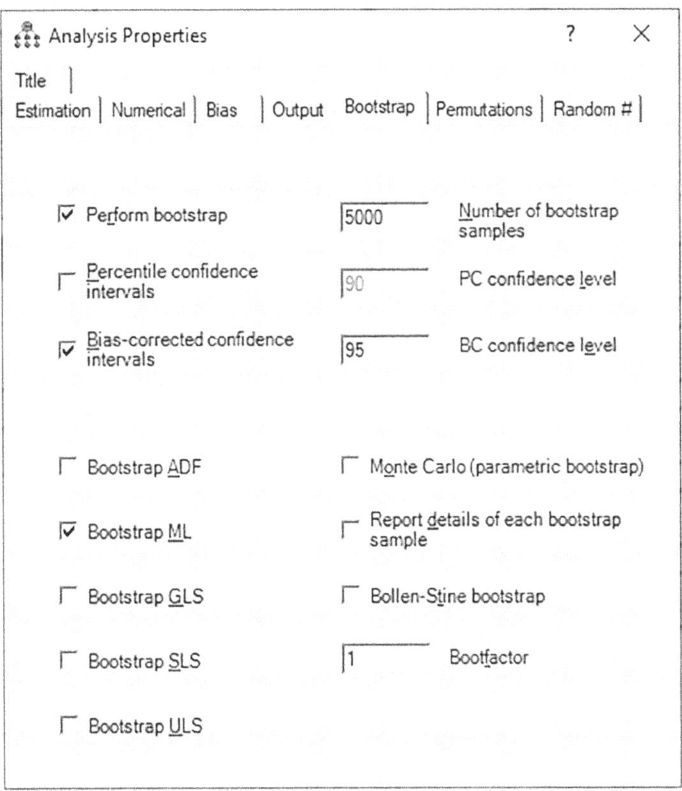

Figure 10.7 Performing ML Bootstrap in Analysis Properties Window

Let's use our full structural model example from Chapter 5 and assume our data is not normally distributed. This example states that Adaptive Behavior and Servicescape is going to positively influence Customer Delight feelings, which are going to positively influence the dependent variables of Tolerance to Future Failures and Intentions to Spread Positive Word of Mouth.

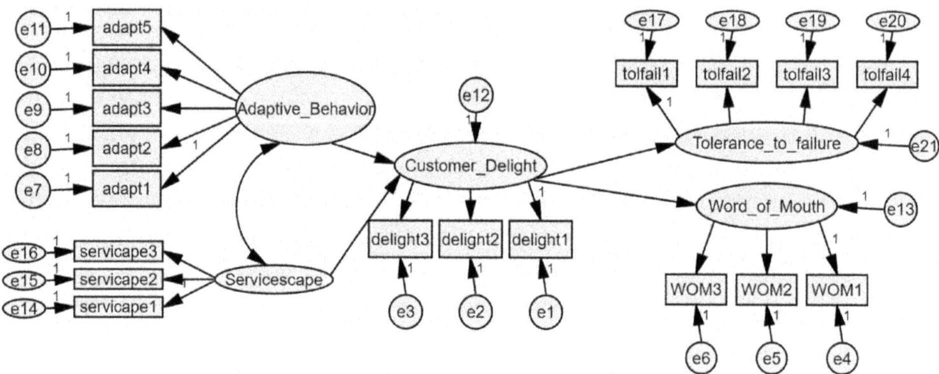

Figure 10.8 Full Structural Model in AMOS to Test Non-Normal Data

After drawing the model and selecting the bootstrapping options just detailed, you are ready to run your analysis. In the output, go to the "Estimates" link and you will see the unstandardized and standardized estimates of your model. This is information we will need, but we also need to find the bootstrap estimates for each hypothesized relationship.

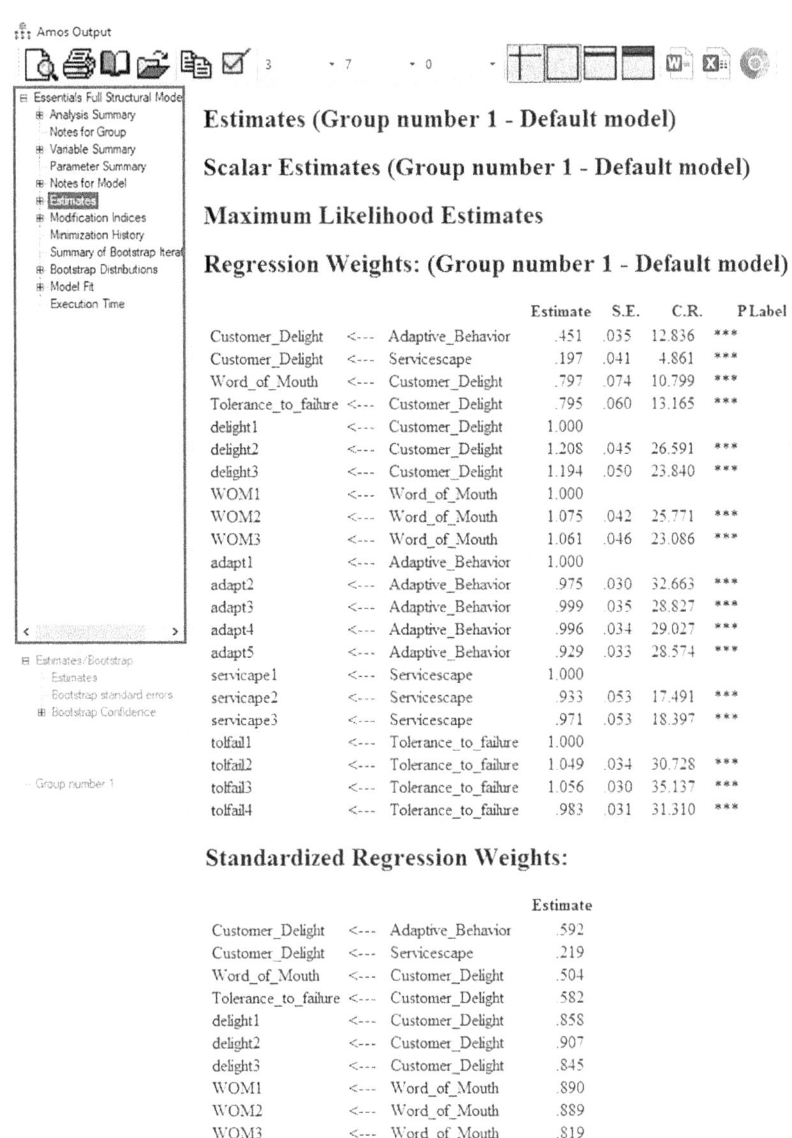

Estimates (Group number 1 - Default model)

Scalar Estimates (Group number 1 - Default model)

Maximum Likelihood Estimates

Regression Weights: (Group number 1 - Default model)

			Estimate	S.E.	C.R.	P	Label
Customer_Delight	<---	Adaptive_Behavior	.451	.035	12.836	***	
Customer_Delight	<---	Servicescape	.197	.041	4.861	***	
Word_of_Mouth	<---	Customer_Delight	.797	.074	10.799	***	
Tolerance_to_failure	<---	Customer_Delight	.795	.060	13.165	***	
delight1	<---	Customer_Delight	1.000				
delight2	<---	Customer_Delight	1.208	.045	26.591	***	
delight3	<---	Customer_Delight	1.194	.050	23.840	***	
WOM1	<---	Word_of_Mouth	1.000				
WOM2	<---	Word_of_Mouth	1.075	.042	25.771	***	
WOM3	<---	Word_of_Mouth	1.061	.046	23.086	***	
adapt1	<---	Adaptive_Behavior	1.000				
adapt2	<---	Adaptive_Behavior	.975	.030	32.663	***	
adapt3	<---	Adaptive_Behavior	.999	.035	28.827	***	
adapt4	<---	Adaptive_Behavior	.996	.034	29.027	***	
adapt5	<---	Adaptive_Behavior	.929	.033	28.574	***	
servicape1	<---	Servicescape	1.000				
servicape2	<---	Servicescape	.933	.053	17.491	***	
servicape3	<---	Servicescape	.971	.053	18.397	***	
tolfail1	<---	Tolerance_to_failure	1.000				
tolfail2	<---	Tolerance_to_failure	1.049	.034	30.728	***	
tolfail3	<---	Tolerance_to_failure	1.056	.030	35.137	***	
tolfail4	<---	Tolerance_to_failure	.983	.031	31.310	***	

Standardized Regression Weights:

			Estimate
Customer_Delight	<---	Adaptive_Behavior	.592
Customer_Delight	<---	Servicescape	.219
Word_of_Mouth	<---	Customer_Delight	.504
Tolerance_to_failure	<---	Customer_Delight	.582
delight1	<---	Customer_Delight	.858
delight2	<---	Customer_Delight	.907
delight3	<---	Customer_Delight	.845
WOM1	<---	Word_of_Mouth	.890
WOM2	<---	Word_of_Mouth	.889
WOM3	<---	Word_of_Mouth	.819
adapt1	<---	Adaptive_Behavior	.896
adapt2	<---	Adaptive_Behavior	.920
adapt3	<---	Adaptive_Behavior	.873
adapt4	<---	Adaptive_Behavior	.876
adapt5	<---	Adaptive_Behavior	.870
servicape1	<---	Servicescape	.772
servicape2	<---	Servicescape	.794
servicape3	<---	Servicescape	.868
tolfail1	<---	Tolerance_to_failure	.916
tolfail2	<---	Tolerance_to_failure	.880
tolfail3	<---	Tolerance_to_failure	.926
tolfail4	<---	Tolerance_to_failure	.887

Figure 10.9 Estimates Output of Regression Weights in Full Structural Model

After viewing the "Estimates" link, you need to go to the "Scalars" link and then select "Regression Weights". This will initially just show you the unstandardized estimates that you just saw in the "Estimates" link. After you have selected the "Regression Weights" link, there should be additional links that become available at the bottom left part of the page. These links are "Bootstrap errors" and "Bias-corrected percentile method". Select the "Bias-corrected percentile method". This link will present the unstandardized regression estimates, but it will also present a bootstrap confidence interval for each estimate. The bootstrap estimate will let you know if your unstandardized estimates fall within the 95% confidence interval when 5,000 bootstrap samples were used to "normalize" the data.

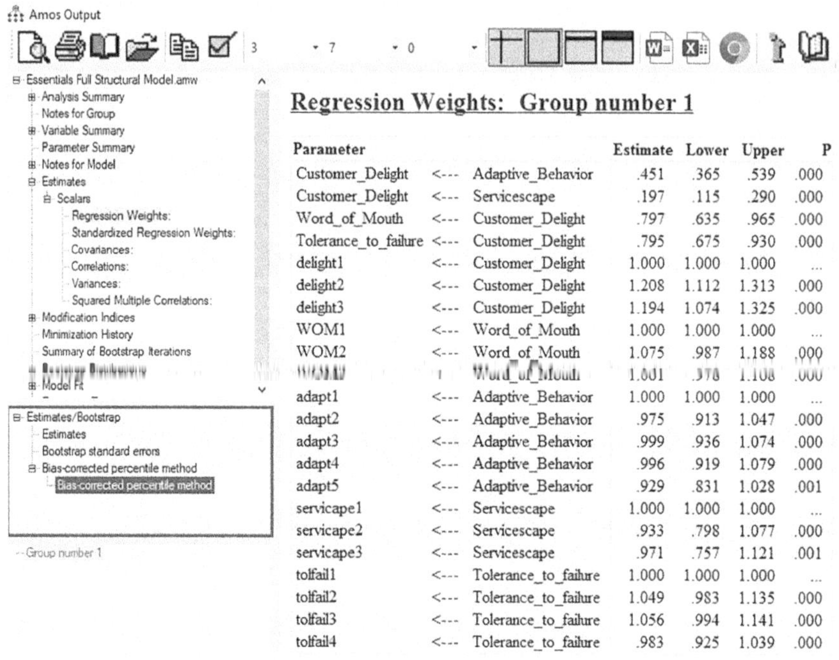

Regression Weights: Group number 1

Parameter			Estimate	Lower	Upper	P
Customer_Delight	<---	Adaptive_Behavior	.451	.365	.539	.000
Customer_Delight	<---	Servicescape	.197	.115	.290	.000
Word_of_Mouth	<---	Customer_Delight	.797	.635	.965	.000
Tolerance_to_failure	<---	Customer_Delight	.795	.675	.930	.000
delight1	<---	Customer_Delight	1.000	1.000	1.000	...
delight2	<---	Customer_Delight	1.208	1.112	1.313	.000
delight3	<---	Customer_Delight	1.194	1.074	1.325	.000
WOM1	<---	Word_of_Mouth	1.000	1.000	1.000	...
WOM2	<---	Word_of_Mouth	1.075	.987	1.188	.000
[illegible]	[illegible]	Word_of_Mouth	1.001	.978	1.108	.000
adapt1	<---	Adaptive_Behavior	1.000	1.000	1.000	...
adapt2	<---	Adaptive_Behavior	.975	.913	1.047	.000
adapt3	<---	Adaptive_Behavior	.999	.936	1.074	.000
adapt4	<---	Adaptive_Behavior	.996	.919	1.079	.000
adapt5	<---	Adaptive_Behavior	.929	.831	1.028	.001
servicape1	<---	Servicescape	1.000	1.000	1.000	...
servicape2	<---	Servicescape	.933	.798	1.077	.000
servicape3	<---	Servicescape	.971	.757	1.121	.001
tolfail1	<---	Tolerance_to_failure	1.000	1.000	1.000	...
tolfail2	<---	Tolerance_to_failure	1.049	.983	1.135	.000
tolfail3	<---	Tolerance_to_failure	1.056	.994	1.141	.000
tolfail4	<---	Tolerance_to_failure	.983	.925	1.039	.000

Figure 10.10 Unstandardized Regression Weights With Confidence Intervals Based on Bootstrap

In this example, all estimates fall within a confidence interval that does not include zero. You can also see a p-value for each bootstrap confidence interval. Thus, we can conclude that our estimates are valid based on the bootstrapping technique to normalize the data.

One of the primary concerns with non-normal data is the inflation of model fit estimates. To assess model fit with the bootstrap samples, we are going to use to the Bollen-Stine method. This method will allow us to see if the proposed model fits the data when the bootstrap samples are used as the input. AMOS can be a little quirky when asking for a Bollen-Stine bootstrap. If we simply ask for the Bollen-Stine option in Analysis Properties when "Bias-corrected confidence interval" is selected, AMOS will not produce the estimate. If you select the Bollen-Stine bootstrap, you have to uncheck the "Bias-corrected confidence interval" option. Thus, I run the bootstrap initially with the Bias-corrected confidence intervals and get the information I need, and then I run a separate analysis for the Bollen-Stine bootstrap with the Bias-corrected confidence intervals option not checked.

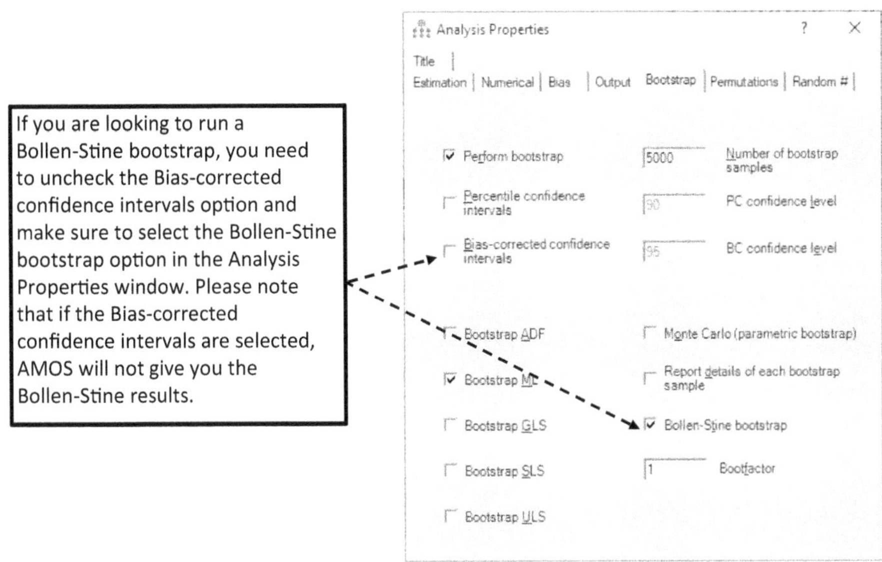

Figure 10.11 Selecting Bollen-Stine Bootstrap in Analysis Properties Window

After selecting the Bollen-Stine option and running the analysis again, let's initially examine the model fit estimates in the output. We can see that the model fit for our model has a chi-square value of 225.34 with 130 degrees of freedom.

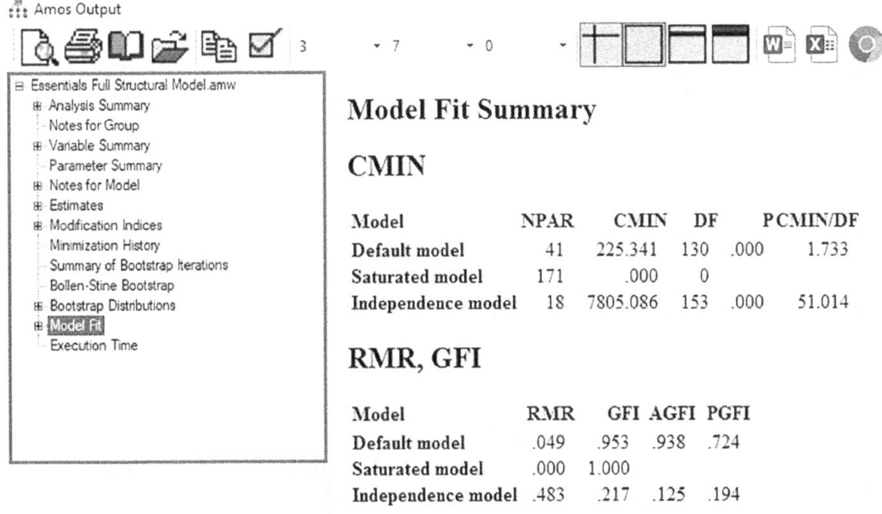

Model Fit Summary

CMIN

Model	NPAR	CMIN	DF	P	CMIN/DF
Default model	41	225.341	130	.000	1.733
Saturated model	171	.000	0		
Independence model	18	7805.086	153	.000	51.014

RMR, GFI

Model	RMR	GFI	AGFI	PGFI
Default model	.049	.953	.938	.724
Saturated model	.000	1.000		
Independence model	.483	.217	.125	.194

Figure 10.12 Model Fit Statistics in AMOS

If we select the Bootstrap distributions link on the left-hand side, we can see the distribution of chi-square values across the 5,000 bootstrap samples that were run with the proposed model. You can see the mean value was 188.04 and that our initial chi-square value of 225.34 is clearly within the distribution that ranges from 91.35 to 366.43.

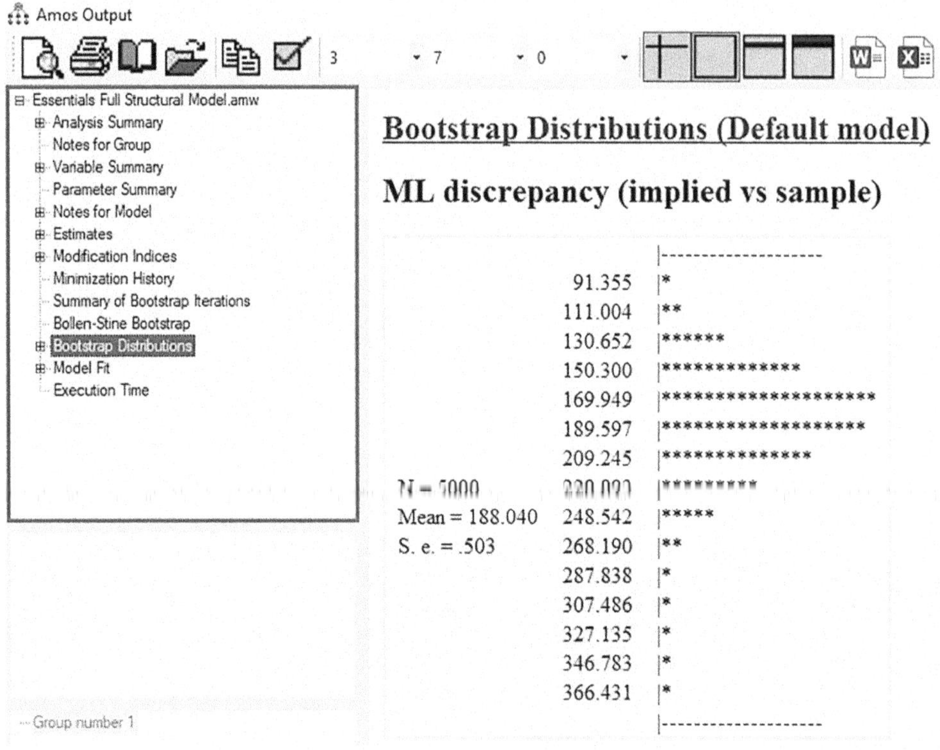

Figure 10.13 Bootstrap Distribution of Chi-Square Values

Next, we need to examine the Bollen-Stine bootstrap which is accessed via a separate link above the Bootstrap distributions option. Clicking on this link will bring up the Bollen-Stine test results. The Bollen-Stine test will initially tell you how many bootstrap samples fit the model better than the initial estimate, and it will also tell you how many samples fit equally well or actually fit worse. Your goal is to have a Bollen-Stine bootstrap that is non-significant because this means the model still has an adequate "fit" with the bootstrap samples. If you have a significant Bollen-Stine estimate, then it states your model fit is problematic based on the bootstrap estimates that are trying to "normalize" the data. In this example, 4,300 samples fit better, 700 samples fit worse, and the Bollen-Stine estimate was a p-value of .14. Thus, we can conclude that the model still has an adequate fit with the bootstrap samples.

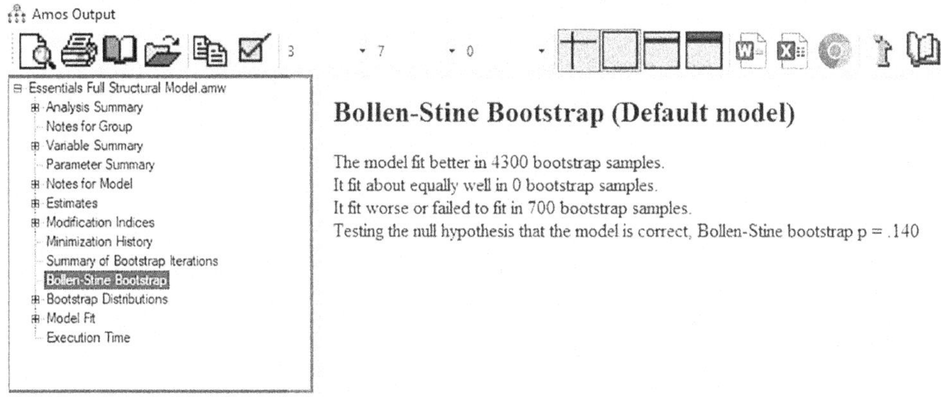
Amos Output
Essentials Full Structural Model.amw
Analysis Summary
Notes for Group
Variable Summary
Parameter Summary
Notes for Model
Estimates
Modification Indices
Minimization History
Summary of Bootstrap Iterations
Bollen-Stine Bootstrap
Bootstrap Distributions
Model Fit
Execution Time
Bollen-Stine Bootstrap (Default model)
The model fit better in 4300 bootstrap samples.
It fit about equally well in 0 bootstrap samples.
It fit worse or failed to fit in 700 bootstrap samples.
Testing the null hypothesis that the model is correct, Bollen-Stine bootstrap p = .140

Figure 10.14 Bollen-Stine Bootstrap Results in AMOS

If the Bollen-Stine bootstrap is rejected (found a significant result $p < .05$), this should give the researcher pause in moving forward because the result means the model is not fitting the data. Saying that, the Bollen-Stine is very sensitive to sample size, and it is advisable to use numerous goodness (and badness) of fit indices to determine model fit. Bollen-Stine accesses only chi-square values, but it is always advisable to use numerous different model fit options in presenting results.

Mixture Modeling

Mixture modeling is a type of modeling where data is divided into subgroups and classified. Using a Bayesian analysis, all data that is unclassified will then be assigned to a group based on the existing criteria of the data that has already been assigned. For instance, let's say we are trying to classify the type of academic student for a master's program admission. We want to know what criteria we can use to predict if an applicant will be a good student. To do this, we have to create some "training data". We have 100 students that have already gone through the program, and at graduation they were classified as either "Excellent", "Average", or "Below Average". Next, we need to see what categories or criteria we can observe before a potential student starts the program that can help us understand the likelihood a student will be classified as Excellent, Average, or Below Average. The master's program director thinks there are three criteria that can help project how successful an applicant would be in the master's program. These three criteria are GPA from their undergraduate degree, what they scored on the GMAT test, and what letter grade they received on the principles of finance course in their undergraduate degree. Again, we are examining criteria that could help classify a student before given admittance. The goal is to avoid admitting "Below Average" students. In our training data, we will need to input the GPA, GMAT, and finance scores for each student that has been classified.

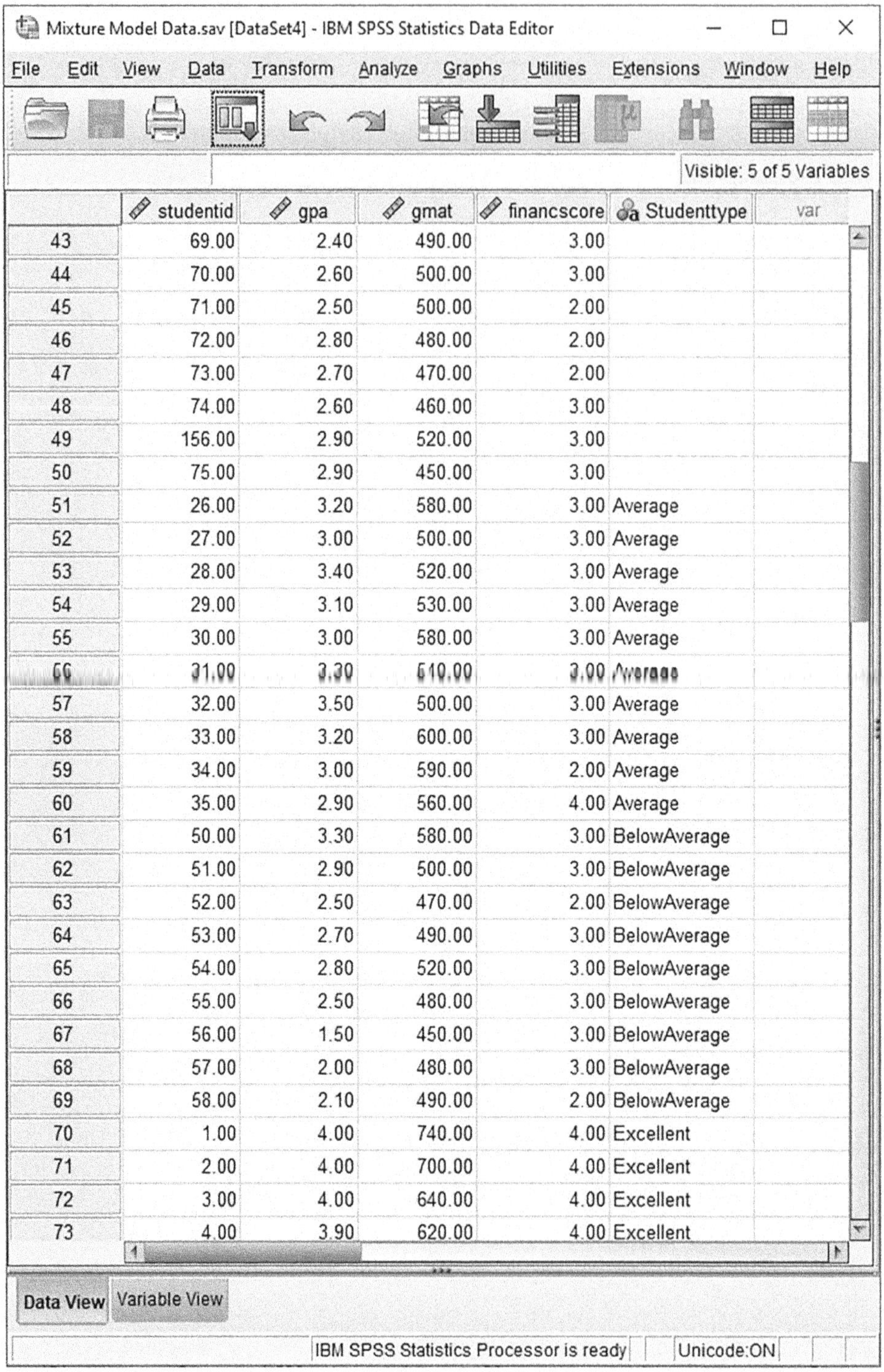

Mixture Model Data.sav [DataSet4] - IBM SPSS Statistics Data Editor

File Edit View Data Transform Analyze Graphs Utilities Extensions Window Help

Visible: 5 of 5 Variables

	studentid	gpa	gmat	financscore	Studenttype	var
43	69.00	2.40	490.00	3.00		
44	70.00	2.60	500.00	3.00		
45	71.00	2.50	500.00	2.00		
46	72.00	2.80	480.00	2.00		
47	73.00	2.70	470.00	2.00		
48	74.00	2.60	460.00	3.00		
49	156.00	2.90	520.00	3.00		
50	75.00	2.90	450.00	3.00		
51	26.00	3.20	580.00	3.00	Average	
52	27.00	3.00	500.00	3.00	Average	
53	28.00	3.40	520.00	3.00	Average	
54	29.00	3.10	530.00	3.00	Average	
55	30.00	3.00	580.00	3.00	Average	
56	31.00	3.30	510.00	3.00	Average	
57	32.00	3.50	500.00	3.00	Average	
58	33.00	3.20	600.00	3.00	Average	
59	34.00	3.00	590.00	2.00	Average	
60	35.00	2.90	560.00	4.00	Average	
61	50.00	3.30	580.00	3.00	BelowAverage	
62	51.00	2.90	500.00	3.00	BelowAverage	
63	52.00	2.50	470.00	2.00	BelowAverage	
64	53.00	2.70	490.00	3.00	BelowAverage	
65	54.00	2.80	520.00	3.00	BelowAverage	
66	55.00	2.50	480.00	3.00	BelowAverage	
67	56.00	1.50	450.00	3.00	BelowAverage	
68	57.00	2.00	480.00	3.00	BelowAverage	
69	58.00	2.10	490.00	2.00	BelowAverage	
70	1.00	4.00	740.00	4.00	Excellent	
71	2.00	4.00	700.00	4.00	Excellent	
72	3.00	4.00	640.00	4.00	Excellent	
73	4.00	3.90	620.00	4.00	Excellent	

Data View Variable View

IBM SPSS Statistics Processor is ready Unicode:ON

Figure 10.15 Mixture Model Data With Classifications in SPSS

Let's say we get 50 new applicants for the program. We will need the GPA, GMAT, and finance score for each of these applicants as well. The first thing we need to do is to create a unique id for each applicant and enter the decision criteria (GPA, GMAT, finance score) in a separate row for each applicant. Next, we will create a column at the end of the data labeled "Studenttype". After entering the 50 new applicants, we will bring in the 100 students used as "training" information. This group will look exactly the same as the applicants in format, except they will have a classification as Excellent, Average, or Below Average in the "Studenttype" field. The 50 new applicants will have no classification at this point. Ultimately, we want AMOS to run a Bayesian analysis and code the 50 new students as either an Excellent, Average, or Below Average Student.

After getting your training data and new data in SPSS, you are ready to go to AMOS. In AMOS, you are going to create three groups. You will have a group for each category or classification of student (Excellent, Average, and Below Average). You will then need to read in the data for each group. The different classifications will often be in one file, so you will need to select the grouping variable and find the column name the classifications are in (Studenttype is this example). After that, you can select the "Group Value" and choose the classification for each group. See Figure 10.16. On this data file window, make sure to click "Allow non-numeric data" and "Assign cases to groups"; otherwise, AMOS cannot read the classification of each data row. As well, you want AMOS to assign unlabeled data to a group with mixture modeling. If you do not select these, you will get an error message.

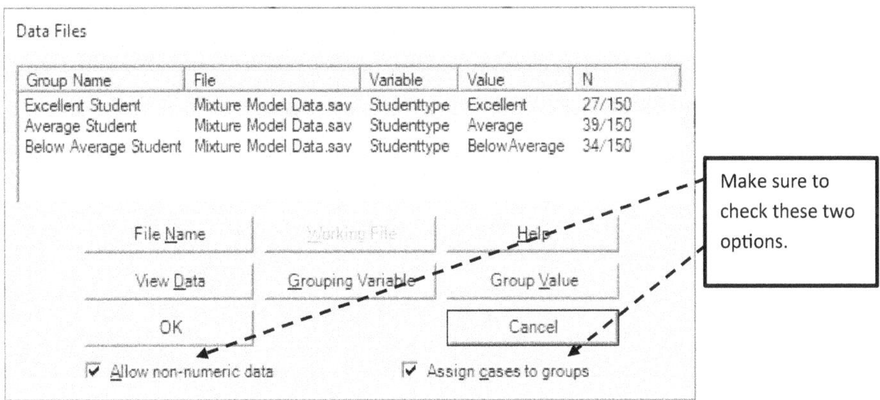

Figure 10.16 Reading in Data Files for Each Classification in Mixture Model

Next, you need to drag in all the predictor variables into the AMOS graphics window and draw a covariance between all the variables. With mixture modeling you need to constrain (1) the variances of constructs; and (2) the covariances between constructs to be equal across *all* the groups. In a construct you just dragged into AMOS, right click and go to Object Properties. In the parameters tab at the top, go to the variance field and label it "v1". Make sure the "All groups" button is checked as well in the Object Properties window. This will label the variance the exact same across the groups as "v1". You will then go and uniquely label each variance for every variable, repeating the same process as the variable labeled "v1". Next, you will go to the covariances (right click and go to Object Properties) and uniquely name each covariance, again making sure the "All groups" option is checked. This will constrain all your groups (classifications) to be equal in regard to variance and covariance.

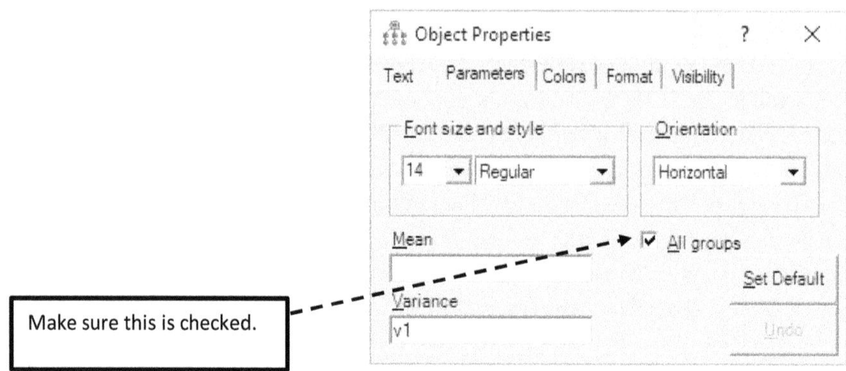

Figure 10.17 Labeling Variances in Object Properties Window

Here is what your model should look like after all the constraints have been applied.

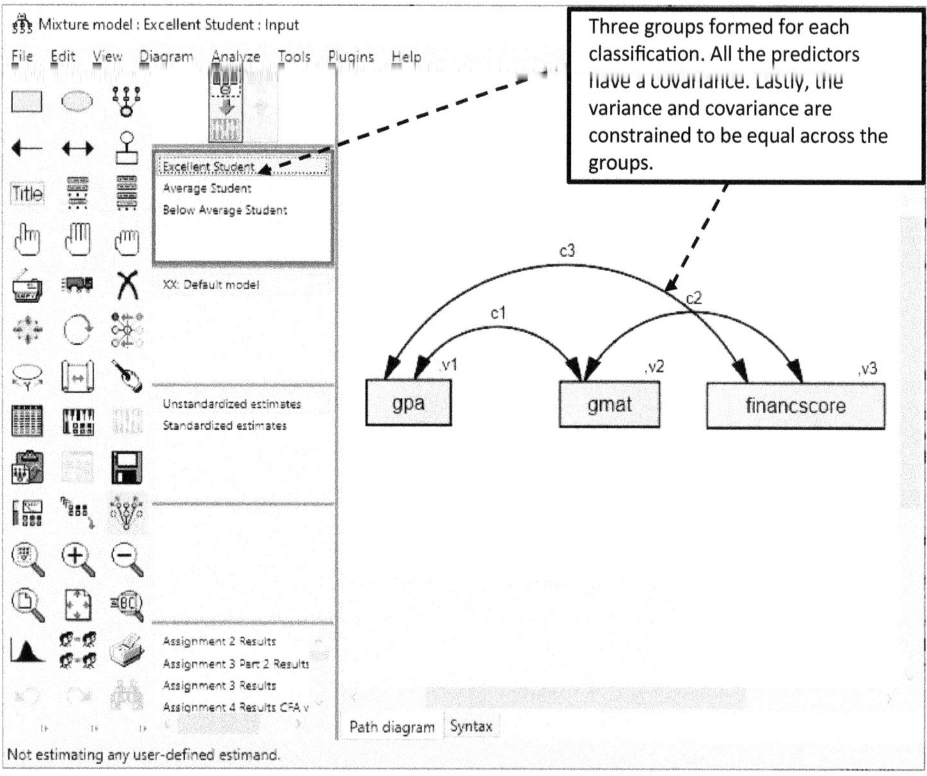

Figure 10.18 Labeled Mixture Model in AMOS

Now select the Bayesian Analysis button [icon], and you will see a pop-up window appear. Using the training data, the analysis will start sampling your training data multiple times over to determine the probability of your unclassified data fitting into a classification group. Initially, the Bayesian window will have a red frowny face at the top, which means the Bayesian estimation is not ready. When that red face turns to a yellow smiling face, your estimation is ready to be interpreted.

The Bayesian window will provide a lot descriptives about your classifications. There is a tab at the top of the window that will allow you to see the information for each group. You can see the "Average" student has a mean GMAT score of 552, a GPA of 3.21, and an average finance score of 2.99 on a 1-to-4 scale. As well, the analysis will give you the maximum and minimum score to classify as an "Average" student. In the Below Average group, the initial results show that students that have a GPA less than a 2.50 and a score under 500 on the GMAT have a high probability of being classified as a below average student.

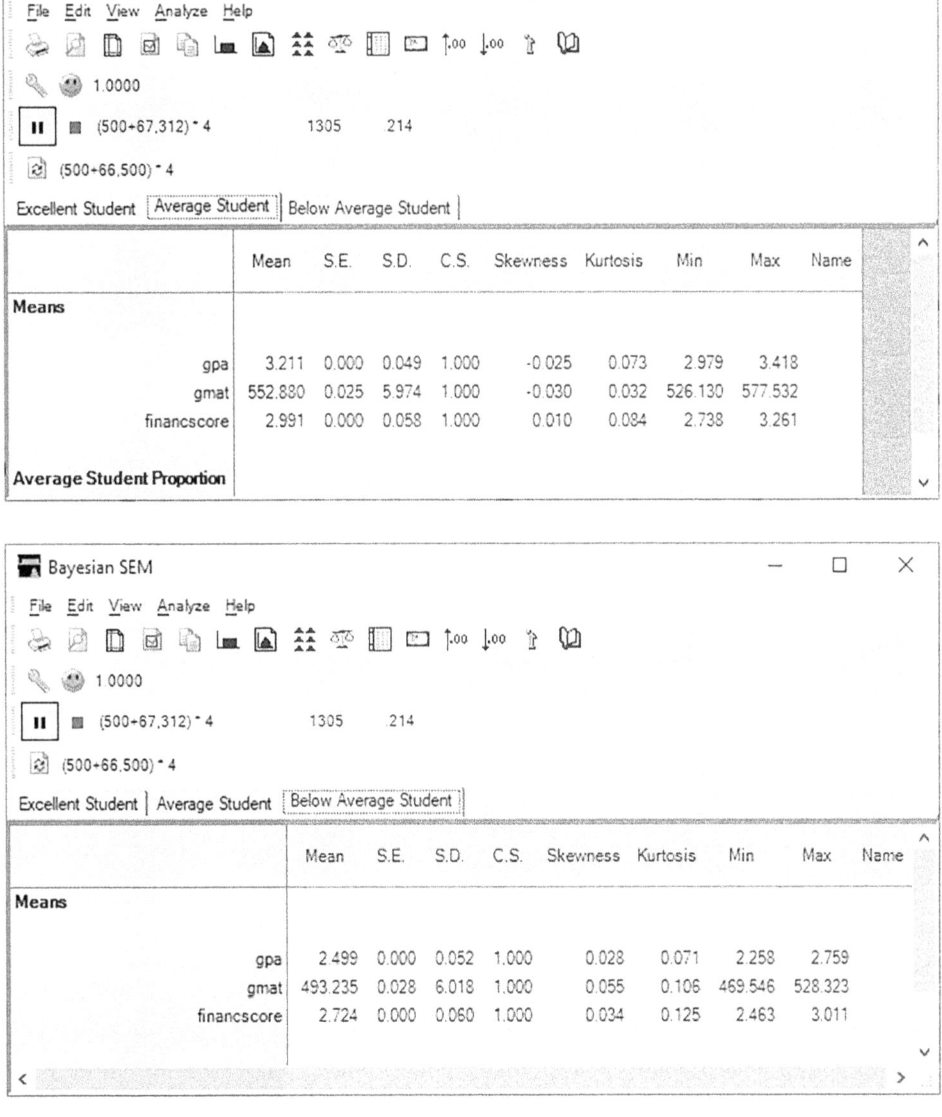

	Mean	S.E.	S.D.	C.S.	Skewness	Kurtosis	Min	Max	Name
Means									
gpa	3.211	0.000	0.049	1.000	-0.025	0.073	2.979	3.418	
gmat	552.880	0.025	5.974	1.000	-0.030	0.032	526.130	577.532	
financscore	2.991	0.000	0.058	1.000	0.010	0.084	2.738	3.261	
Average Student Proportion									

	Mean	S.E.	S.D.	C.S.	Skewness	Kurtosis	Min	Max	Name
Means									
gpa	2.499	0.000	0.052	1.000	0.028	0.071	2.258	2.759	
gmat	493.235	0.028	6.018	1.000	0.055	0.106	469.546	528.323	
financscore	2.724	0.000	0.060	1.000	0.034	0.125	2.463	3.011	

Figure 10.19 Bayesian Estimation for Average and Below Average Students

Posterior Predictive Distributions

	gpa	gmat	financscore	P(Excellent)	P(Average)	P(BelowAverage)
1	4	610	4	**0.99**	0.01	0.00
2	3.7	600	3	0.12	**0.88**	0.00
3	3.8	580	3	0.11	**0.89**	0.00
4	4	600	4	**0.99**	0.01	0.00
5	3.9	620	3	0.31	**0.69**	0.00
6	3.8	580	4	**0.96**	0.04	0.00
7	3.6	590	4	**0.94**	0.06	0.00
8	3.7	580	4	**0.95**	0.05	0.00
9	3.8	600	3	0.16	**0.84**	0.00
10	4	620	4	**0.99**	0.01	0.00
11	3.5	630	4	**0.97**	0.03	0.00
12	3.7	600	4	**0.97**	0.03	0.00
13	3.8	620	3	0.24	**0.76**	0.00
14	3.6	590	4	**0.94**	0.06	0.00
15	3.5	590	4	**0.92**	0.08	0.00
16	[illegible]	610	[illegible]	0.07	[illegible]	0.01
17	3.7	600	4	**0.97**	0.03	0.00
18	4	590	4	**0.99**	0.01	0.00

Figure 10.20 Posterior Predictions for Each Classification

To see how the Bayesian analysis classified the new applicants, you need to look at the posterior predictions [button]. When you click on this button, you will initially see the rows blinking with changing numbers, but after a few seconds the numbers will stabilize. In this window, you will see the probability for each student to be classified as excellent, average, or below average. In our data set, the first 50 rows were our new applicants. In the posterior prediction, those rows now have a prediction for each student.

For instance, the student in row 5 had an 69% probability of being an average student and a 31% probability of being an excellent student. This student also had a relative zero probability of being a below average student. While these probabilities are nice, I find that looking at how the posterior prediction is graphed will give you more context to that probability prediction. If we double click into student 5's "excellent" prediction of 31%, AMOS will show us more information about this prediction in a graphical form. See Figure 10.21. The graphic shows that the mean prediction is 31%, but if you examine the left-hand side of the graph, there is a large frequency of predictions that note this student has an even smaller probability of being an excellent student. The probability predictions are skewed to the left, or specifically, that there is a smaller likelihood of this student being classified as excellent at the end of the program. The graph gives us more context to the prediction and also lets us know what probability had the highest frequency. You can view a graph of any probability in posterior prediction by simply double clicking on the value. Ultimately, the probability derived from the Bayesian analysis is only as good as the training data. If your training data is biased or flawed, the posterior prediction will most certainly be flawed, too.

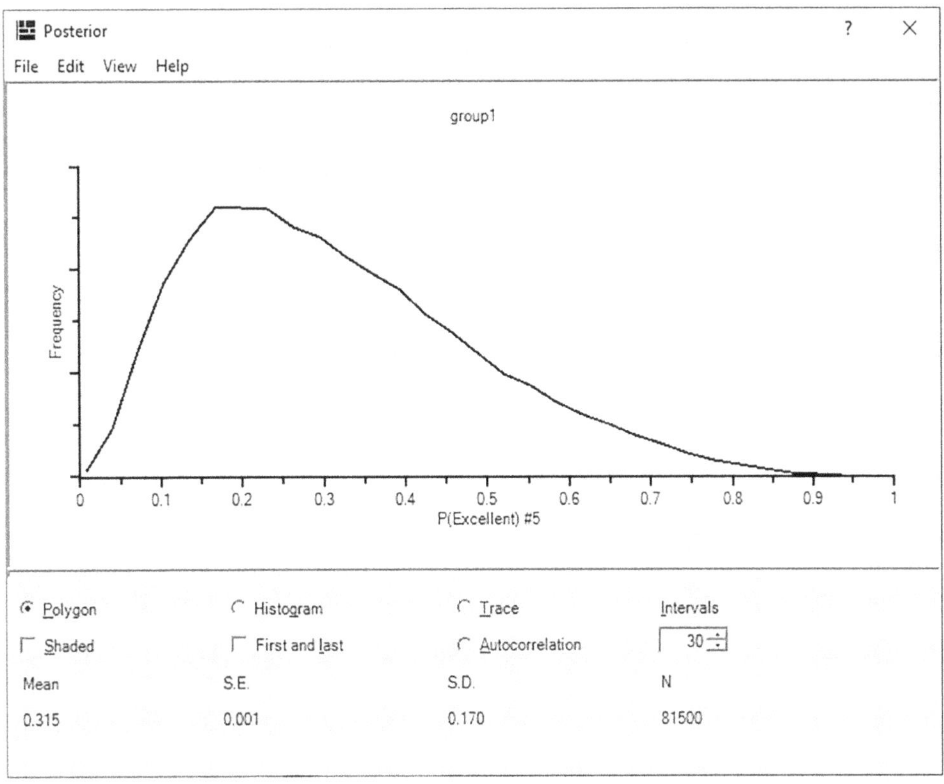

Figure 10.21 Graphical Representation of Posterior Prediction for Student Number 5

With mixture models, you can also let AMOS classify all the data (with no training data). In this example, you would set up three groups in AMOS. When you read in the data for each group, you will choose a specified classification column even though it is blank. In this example, let's choose the column "Studenttype" as in the previous example, except now there are no classifications in the column. AMOS will just list the values for this column as "cluster" and a number.

With no training data, AMOS will try to classify each student into a category/cluster based on the Bayesian analysis. In essence, AMOS is clustering the data into three groups.

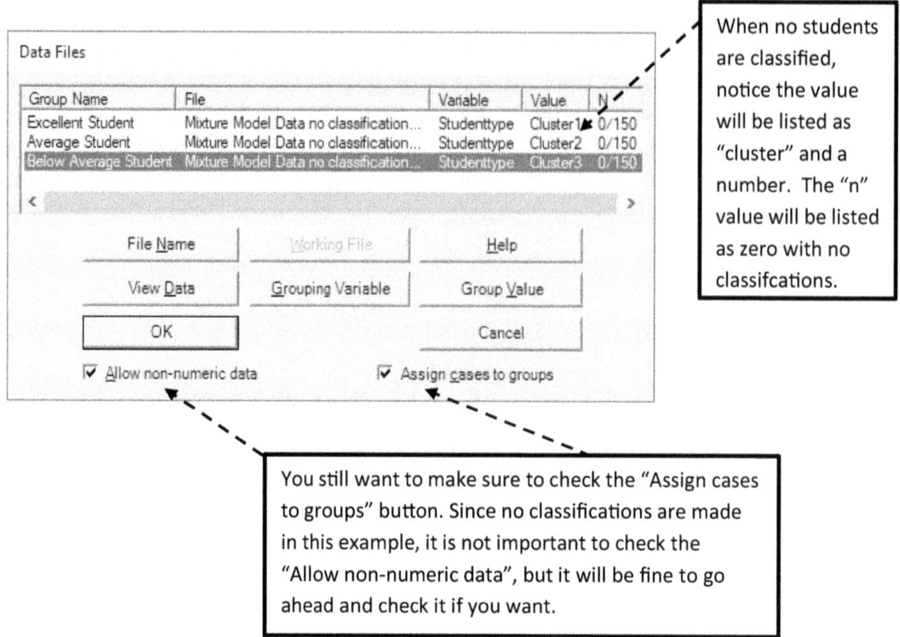
Data Files
Group Name | File | Variable | Value | N
Excellent Student | Mixture Model Data no classification... | Studenttype | Cluster1 | 0/150
Average Student | Mixture Model Data no classification... | Studenttype | Cluster2 | 0/150
Below Average Student | Mixture Model Data no classification... | Studenttype | Cluster3 | 0/150
File Name
Working File
Help
View Data
Grouping Variable
Group Value
OK
Cancel
Allow non-numeric data
Assign cases to groups
When no students are classified, notice the value will be listed as "cluster" and a number. The "n" value will be listed as zero with no classifcations.
You still want to make sure to check the "Assign cases to groups" button. Since no classifications are made in this example, it is not important to check the "Allow non-numeric data", but it will be fine to go ahead and check it if you want.

Figure 10.22 Reading in the Data File for Mixture Model With No Classifications in the Data

After you read in the data for each group, the analysis is exactly the same steps as the example when we used the training data. When you get to the posterior prediction, you will see three clusters and the probability of each candidate falling into a cluster. In Figure 10.23, I have included a posterior prediction that had training data and one that had no training data and how AMOS clustered the data into three groups. You can see that AMOS correctly predicted some students, but others are classified differently when there is no training data. For example, the student in row 13 is considered a 24% probability of being an Excellent student with the training data included and the same student is classified as a 4% probability of being in the Excellent group when no training data is included and AMOS assigns the groups. Ultimately, having training data will lead to better predictions in the end.

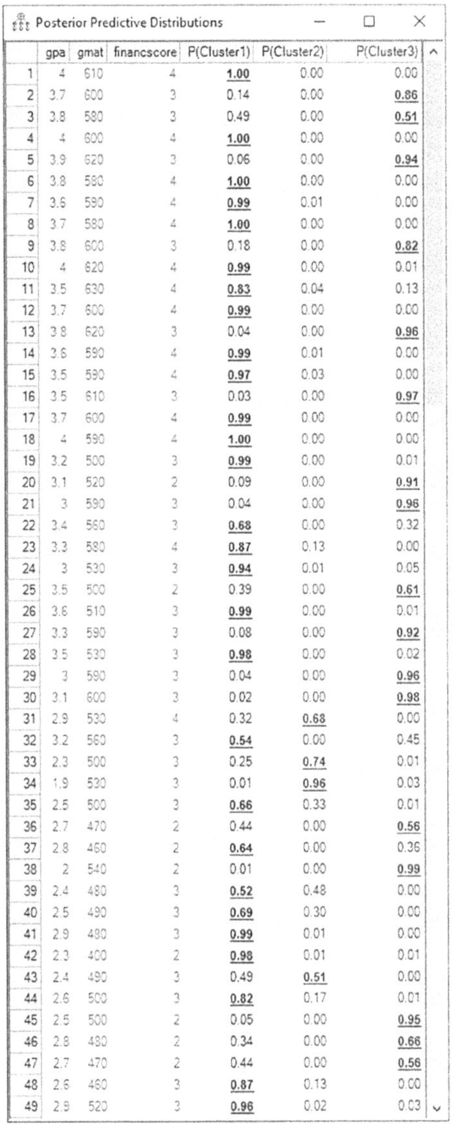

Posterior Predictive Distributions

	gpa	gmat	financscore	P(Cluster1)	P(Cluster2)	P(Cluster3)
1	4	610	4	**1.00**	0.00	0.00
2	3.7	600	3	0.14	0.00	**0.86**
3	3.8	580	3	0.49	0.00	**0.51**
4	4	600	4	**1.00**	0.00	0.00
5	3.9	620	3	0.06	0.00	**0.94**
6	3.8	580	4	**1.00**	0.00	0.00
7	3.6	590	4	**0.99**	0.01	0.00
8	3.7	580	4	**1.00**	0.00	0.00
9	3.8	600	3	0.18	0.00	**0.82**
10	4	620	4	**0.99**	0.00	0.01
11	3.5	630	4	**0.83**	0.04	0.13
12	3.7	600	4	**0.99**	0.00	0.00
13	3.8	620	3	0.04	0.00	**0.96**
14	3.6	590	4	**0.99**	0.01	0.00
15	3.5	590	4	**0.97**	0.03	0.00
16	3.5	610	3	0.03	0.00	**0.97**
17	3.7	600	4	**0.99**	0.00	0.00
18	4	590	4	**1.00**	0.00	0.00
19	3.2	500	3	**0.99**	0.00	0.01
20	3.1	520	2	0.09	0.00	**0.91**
21	3	590	3	0.04	0.00	**0.96**
22	3.4	560	3	**0.68**	0.00	0.32
23	3.3	580	4	**0.87**	0.13	0.00
24	3	530	3	**0.94**	0.01	0.05
25	3.5	500	2	0.39	0.00	**0.61**
26	3.6	510	3	**0.99**	0.00	0.01
27	3.3	590	3	0.08	0.00	**0.92**
28	3.5	530	3	**0.98**	0.00	0.02
29	3	590	3	0.04	0.00	**0.96**
30	3.1	600	3	0.02	0.00	**0.98**
31	2.9	530	4	0.32	**0.68**	0.00
32	3.2	560	3	**0.54**	0.00	0.45
33	2.3	500	3	0.25	**0.74**	0.01
34	1.9	530	3	0.01	**0.96**	0.03
35	2.5	500	3	**0.66**	0.33	0.01
36	2.7	470	2	0.44	0.00	**0.56**
37	2.8	460	2	**0.64**	0.00	0.36
38	2	540	2	0.01	0.00	**0.99**
39	2.4	480	3	**0.52**	0.48	0.00
40	2.5	490	3	**0.69**	0.30	0.00
41	2.9	480	3	**0.99**	0.01	0.00
42	2.3	400	2	**0.98**	0.01	0.01
43	2.4	490	3	0.49	**0.51**	0.00
44	2.6	500	3	**0.82**	0.17	0.01
45	2.5	500	2	0.05	0.00	**0.95**
46	2.8	480	2	0.34	0.00	**0.66**
47	2.7	470	2	0.44	0.00	**0.56**
48	2.6	460	3	**0.87**	0.13	0.00
49	2.9	520	3	**0.96**	0.02	0.03

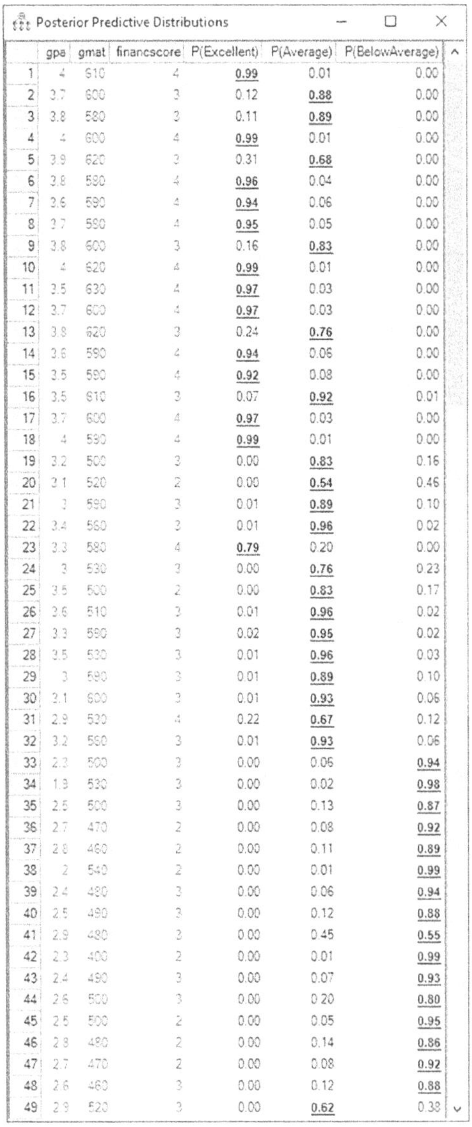

Posterior Predictions with no training data included and AMOS classifies students into groups.

Posterior Predictive Distributions

	gpa	gmat	financscore	P(Excellent)	P(Average)	P(BelowAverage)
1	4	610	4	**0.99**	0.01	0.00
2	3.7	600	3	0.12	**0.88**	0.00
3	3.8	580	3	0.11	**0.89**	0.00
4	4	600	4	**0.99**	0.01	0.00
5	3.9	620	3	0.31	**0.68**	0.00
6	3.8	580	4	**0.96**	0.04	0.00
7	3.6	590	4	**0.94**	0.06	0.00
8	3.7	580	4	**0.95**	0.05	0.00
9	3.8	600	3	0.16	**0.83**	0.00
10	4	620	4	**0.99**	0.01	0.00
11	3.5	630	4	**0.97**	0.03	0.00
12	3.7	600	4	**0.97**	0.03	0.00
13	3.8	620	3	0.24	**0.76**	0.00
14	3.6	590	4	**0.94**	0.06	0.00
15	3.5	590	4	**0.92**	0.08	0.00
16	3.5	610	3	0.07	**0.92**	0.01
17	3.7	600	4	**0.97**	0.03	0.00
18	4	590	4	**0.99**	0.01	0.00
19	3.2	500	3	0.00	**0.83**	0.16
20	3.1	520	2	0.00	**0.54**	0.46
21	3	590	3	0.01	**0.89**	0.10
22	3.4	560	3	0.01	**0.96**	0.02
23	3.3	580	4	**0.79**	0.20	0.00
24	3	530	3	0.00	**0.76**	0.23
25	3.5	500	2	0.00	**0.83**	0.17
26	3.6	510	3	0.01	**0.96**	0.02
27	3.3	590	3	0.02	**0.95**	0.02
28	3.5	530	3	0.01	**0.96**	0.03
29	3	590	3	0.01	**0.89**	0.10
30	3.1	600	3	0.01	**0.93**	0.06
31	2.9	530	4	0.22	**0.67**	0.12
32	3.2	560	3	0.01	**0.93**	0.06
33	2.3	500	3	0.00	0.06	**0.94**
34	1.9	530	3	0.00	0.02	**0.98**
35	2.5	500	3	0.00	0.13	**0.87**
36	2.7	470	2	0.00	0.08	**0.92**
37	2.8	460	2	0.00	0.11	**0.89**
38	2	540	2	0.00	0.01	**0.99**
39	2.4	480	3	0.00	0.06	**0.94**
40	2.5	490	3	0.00	0.12	**0.88**
41	2.9	480	3	0.00	0.45	**0.55**
42	2.3	400	2	0.00	0.01	**0.99**
43	2.4	490	3	0.00	0.07	**0.93**
44	2.6	500	3	0.00	0.20	**0.80**
45	2.5	500	2	0.00	0.05	**0.95**
46	2.8	480	2	0.00	0.14	**0.86**
47	2.7	470	2	0.00	0.08	**0.92**
48	2.6	460	3	0.00	0.12	**0.88**
49	2.9	520	3	0.00	**0.62**	0.38

Posterior Predictions with training data included to aid in classifications.

Figure 10.23 Comparison of Posterior Predictions With Training and No Training Data

With the Bayesian analysis, AMOS is using a stream of random numbers that depend on the "seed number". AMOS will change the seed number every time you run the analysis. Subsequently, when you run your analysis and then run it again, you might get slightly different answers because of those different seed numbers. To combat this so that you can get the same results even if you run the analysis again, you need to use the same seed number. To do this, you need to go to the "Tools" option on the menu bar at the top of AMOS, and then select "Seed Manager". A pop-up window will appear and show you the current seed and the seed number for the last four analyses run. The default in AMOS is for the "Increment the current seed by 1" option. If you change this option to "Always use the same seed", this will use the same seed so you can get the exact same results when you run the analysis again. Similarly, if another researcher wants to know what seed you used, you can go into this window and see the exact seed number used. If you want to specify the seed number, you can go to the "Current seed" option and hit the "Change" button and input a specific seed number. The seed number has no significance on what number you choose. It is just a starting point for AMOS to use in the Bayesian analysis.

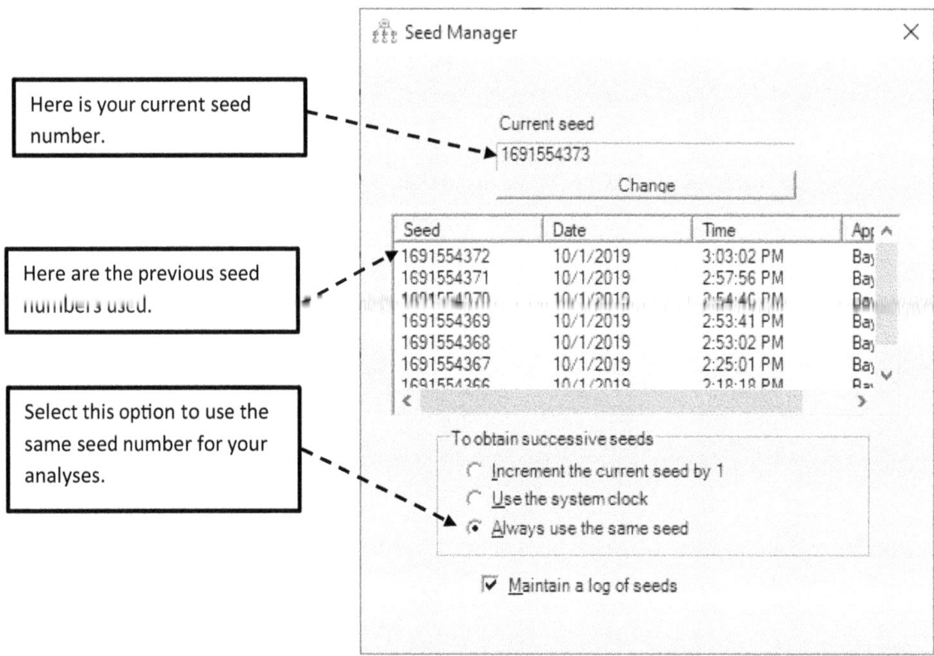

Figure 10.24 Seed Manager Window Along With List of Seeds Used

Analyzing Censored Data

Censored data occurs when the value of a measurement is only partially known. You will often see censored data in clinical trials where there is a drug trying to prevent patient death. With some of the patients, we have a definite birth and death date, but for patients who have not died, we still do not know how long each patient will live in the future. This same type of data can be used in the field of business where we are trying to understand customer defection. We may know when a customer started patronizing a business and when they left, but there are other patrons who have not yet left, and so their "customer lifetime" with a business is not known.

You typically have three different types of censoring. One type is left censoring, where the unknown value is below a certain point. Second, there is right censoring, where the unknown value is above a certain point. The last type of censoring is interval censoring, where the unknown value is between two known data points.

Let's look at an example to see how AMOS can help analyze censored data. We have a retailer that is trying to understand how long customers shop with them before defecting to another retailer. To understand this, the retailer has captured what year the customer initially started patronizing the retailer, frequency of purchases or the total number of purchases while they were a customer, and total sales or how much money was spent over the tenure of the customer. Lastly, the retailer has captured in days how long an individual was a customer of the retailer (noted in the Lifetime column). The retailer has also denoted if they are a current or former customer. Here is an example of data coded in SPSS in Figure 10.25.

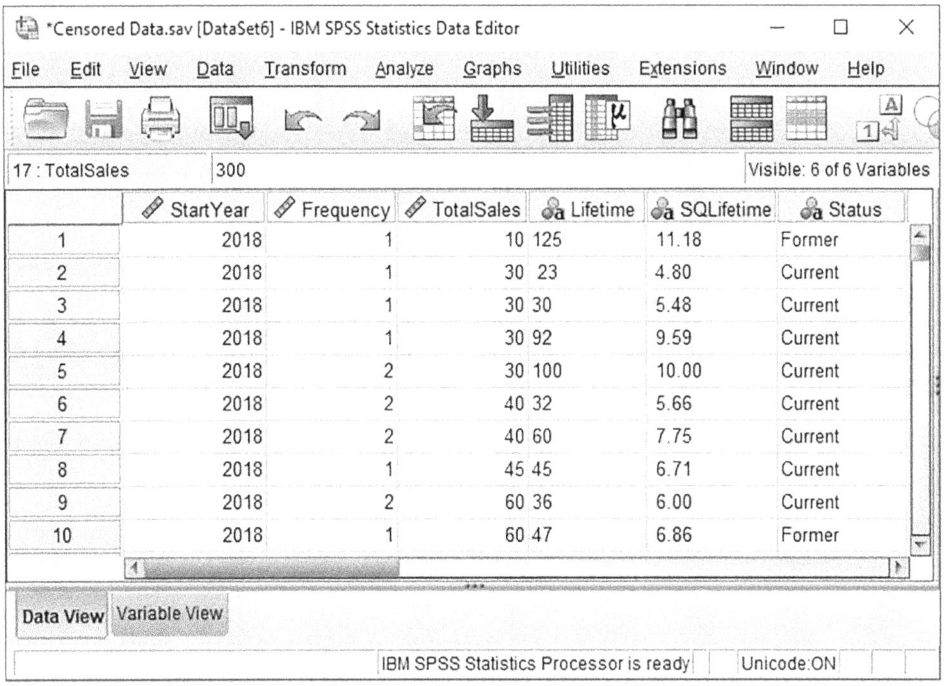

*Censored Data.sav [DataSet6] - IBM SPSS Statistics Data Editor

File Edit View Data Transform Analyze Graphs Utilities Extensions Window Help

17 : TotalSales 300 Visible: 6 of 6 Variables

	StartYear	Frequency	TotalSales	Lifetime	SQLifetime	Status
1	2018	1	10	125	11.18	Former
2	2018	1	30	23	4.80	Current
3	2018	1	30	30	5.48	Current
4	2018	1	30	92	9.59	Current
5	2018	2	30	100	10.00	Current
6	2018	2	40	32	5.66	Current
7	2018	2	40	60	7.75	Current
8	2018	1	45	45	6.71	Current
9	2018	2	60	36	6.00	Current
10	2018	1	60	47	6.86	Former

Data View Variable View

IBM SPSS Statistics Processor is ready Unicode:ON

Figure 10.25 Raw Data Coded in SPSS to Test a Censored Model

With classification of current and former customers, we are examining uncensored data with former customers and censored data with current customers. At this point, we do not know how much longer a customer will stay with the retailer. We are going to have to account for censored data in the lifetime column because we only partially know the value for current customers. You will also notice there is a column called SQLifetime. AMOS assumes censored data is normally distributed, and so to create a normal distribution with the data, we are going to take the square root of the lifetime column.

The data represents 132 respondents whose start year ranged from 1999 to 2018. With the former customers we have an exact lifetime in days, whereas with the current customers the lifetime cannot be determined yet. To use these unknown or censored data points, it has to be recoded in SPSS. For the current customers, the lifetime in days is going to be greater than the one presented in the data. We need to reflect this in the data, and so we will put a greater than symbol in front of the lifetime values and square root lifetime values for the current customers. To do this, you will need to convert the column in SPSS from numeric to string.

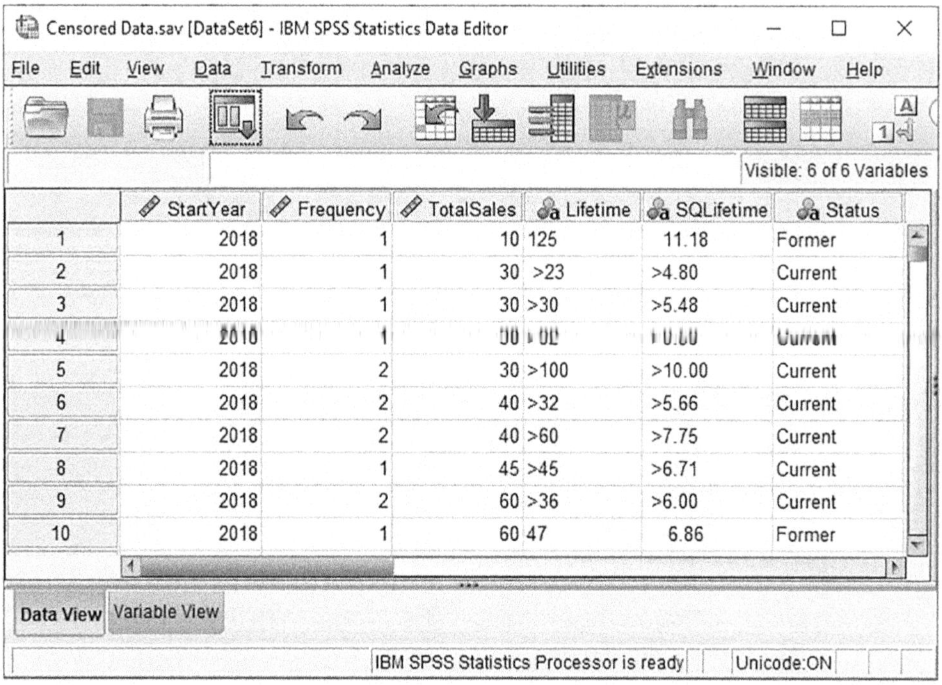

Censored Data.sav [DataSet6] - IBM SPSS Statistics Data Editor

File Edit View Data Transform Analyze Graphs Utilities Extensions Window Help

Visible: 6 of 6 Variables

	StartYear	Frequency	TotalSales	Lifetime	SQLifetime	Status
1	2018	1	10	125	11.18	Former
2	2018	1	30	>23	>4.80	Current
3	2018	1	30	>30	>5.48	Current
4	[illegible]	1	[illegible]	[illegible]	[illegible]	Current
5	2018	2	30	>100	>10.00	Current
6	2018	2	40	>32	>5.66	Current
7	2018	2	40	>60	>7.75	Current
8	2018	1	45	>45	>6.71	Current
9	2018	2	60	>36	>6.00	Current
10	2018	1	60	47	6.86	Former

Data View Variable View

IBM SPSS Statistics Processor is ready Unicode:ON

Figure 10.26 Data Coded for Unknown or Censored Points in SPSS

After altering all the current customers to reflect a greater than value for the lifetime of the customer, we are ready to save the data file and proceed to AMOS.

In AMOS, we are going to conceptualize a model that will help explain and project the lifetime of current customers by using the length of the time they have been a customer (StartYear), how many times they have purchased in the past (Frequency), and how much money they have spent (TotalSales). The first thing we need to do is read in the data to the AMOS program. Since we have a string variable in SPSS that has a greater than symbol in a field, we need to make sure to check the box that states, "Allow non-numeric data".

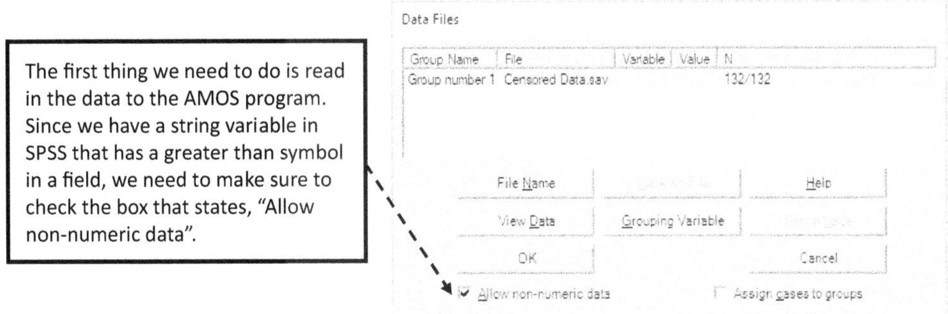

Figure 10.27 Allowing Non-Numeric Data With a Censored Model Test

After reading in the data, we are going to conceptualize the model just like a path diagram where StartYear, Frequency, and TotalSales have a direct relationship to the square root lifetime value.

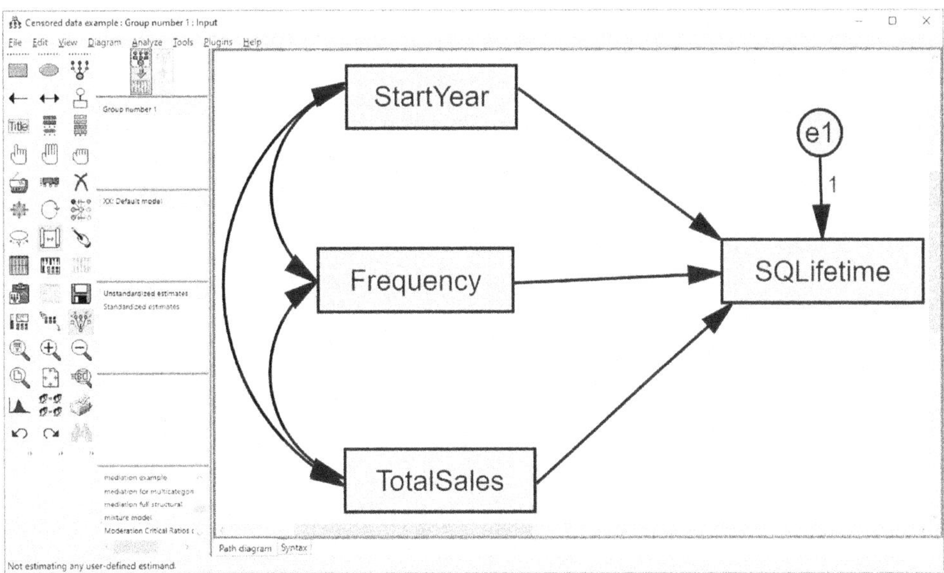

Figure 10.28 Censored Model in AMOS

Once the model is drawn, we are going to use the Bayesian Analysis option in AMOS . After clicking this button, you will see the Bayesian window pop up. The analysis will initially have a red frowny face, which means the analysis is not ready, and when that frowny face turns into a yellow smiley face, then you can interpret the data. The Bayesian window will initially give you a lot of descriptives. The first subheading is our regression weights and how each independent variable influences the square root value of the customer lifetime. Next, you will see the mean value for each construct along with variances, covariances, and intercept of the analysis.

Looking at the regression weights, you will see that with every increase of one year (Startyear), the square root value of the customer lifetime decreases by 3.75 (or 14 days). With every purchase made (frequency), the lifetime of the customer increases (0.12). Total sales in this example had relatively no impact on the lifetime of the customer.

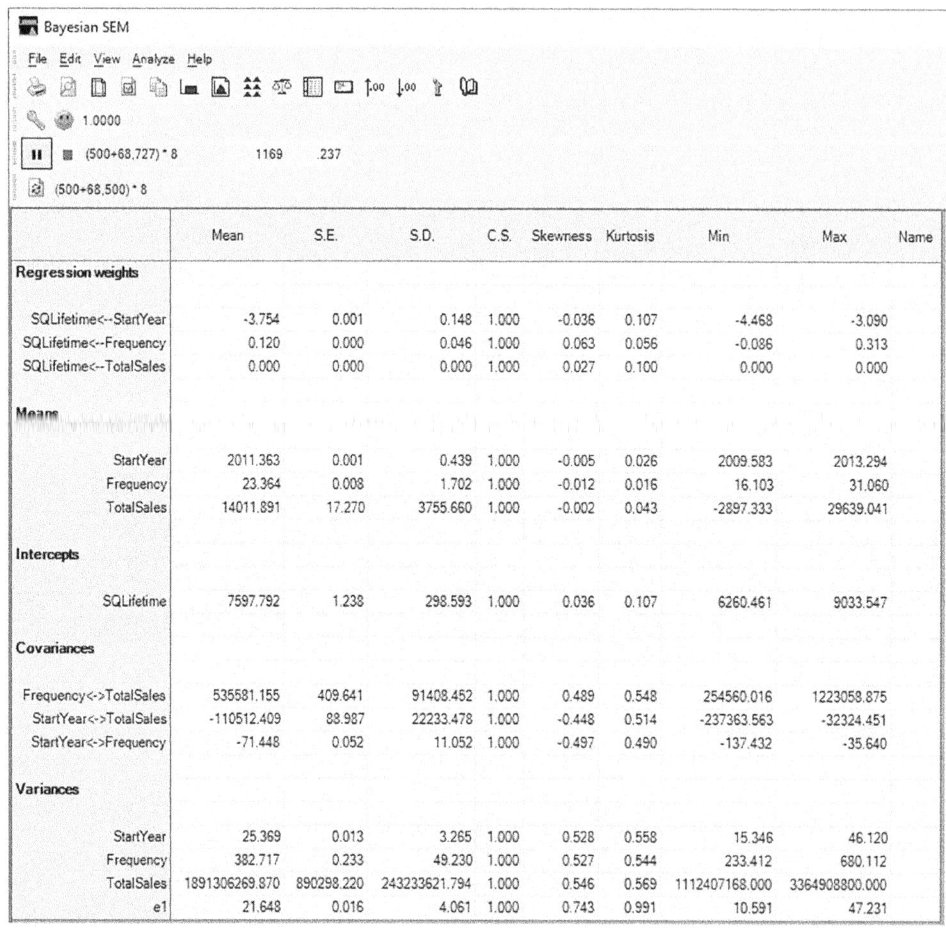

Bayesian SEM

File Edit View Analyze Help

1.0000

(500+68,727) * 8 1169 .237

(500+68,500) * 8

	Mean	S.E.	S.D.	C.S.	Skewness	Kurtosis	Min	Max	Name
Regression weights									
SQLifetime<--StartYear	-3.754	0.001	0.148	1.000	-0.036	0.107	-4.468	-3.090	
SQLifetime<--Frequency	0.120	0.000	0.046	1.000	0.063	0.056	-0.086	0.313	
SQLifetime<--TotalSales	0.000	0.000	0.000	1.000	0.027	0.100	0.000	0.000	
Means									
StartYear	2011.363	0.001	0.439	1.000	-0.005	0.026	2009.583	2013.294	
Frequency	23.364	0.008	1.702	1.000	-0.012	0.016	16.103	31.060	
TotalSales	14011.891	17.270	3755.660	1.000	-0.002	0.043	-2897.333	29639.041	
Intercepts									
SQLifetime	7597.792	1.238	298.593	1.000	0.036	0.107	6260.461	9033.547	
Covariances									
Frequency<->TotalSales	535581.155	409.641	91408.452	1.000	0.489	0.548	254560.016	1223058.875	
StartYear<->TotalSales	-110512.409	88.987	22233.478	1.000	-0.448	0.514	-237363.563	-32324.451	
StartYear<->Frequency	-71.448	0.052	11.052	1.000	-0.497	0.490	-137.432	-35.640	
Variances									
StartYear	25.369	0.013	3.265	1.000	0.528	0.558	15.346	46.120	
Frequency	382.717	0.233	49.230	1.000	0.527	0.544	233.412	680.112	
TotalSales	1891306269.870	890298.220	243233621.794	1.000	0.546	0.569	1112407168.000	3364908800.000	
e1	21.648	0.016	4.061	1.000	0.743	0.991	10.591	47.231	

Figure 10.29 Bayesian Estimation of Censored Dependent Variable

If you want to see the posterior distribution for one of the independent variables, you need to click/highlight the row of interest and then right click, which gives you an option to see the prior or posterior distribution. The posterior distribution will give you different options on how to view the data. See Figure 10.30.

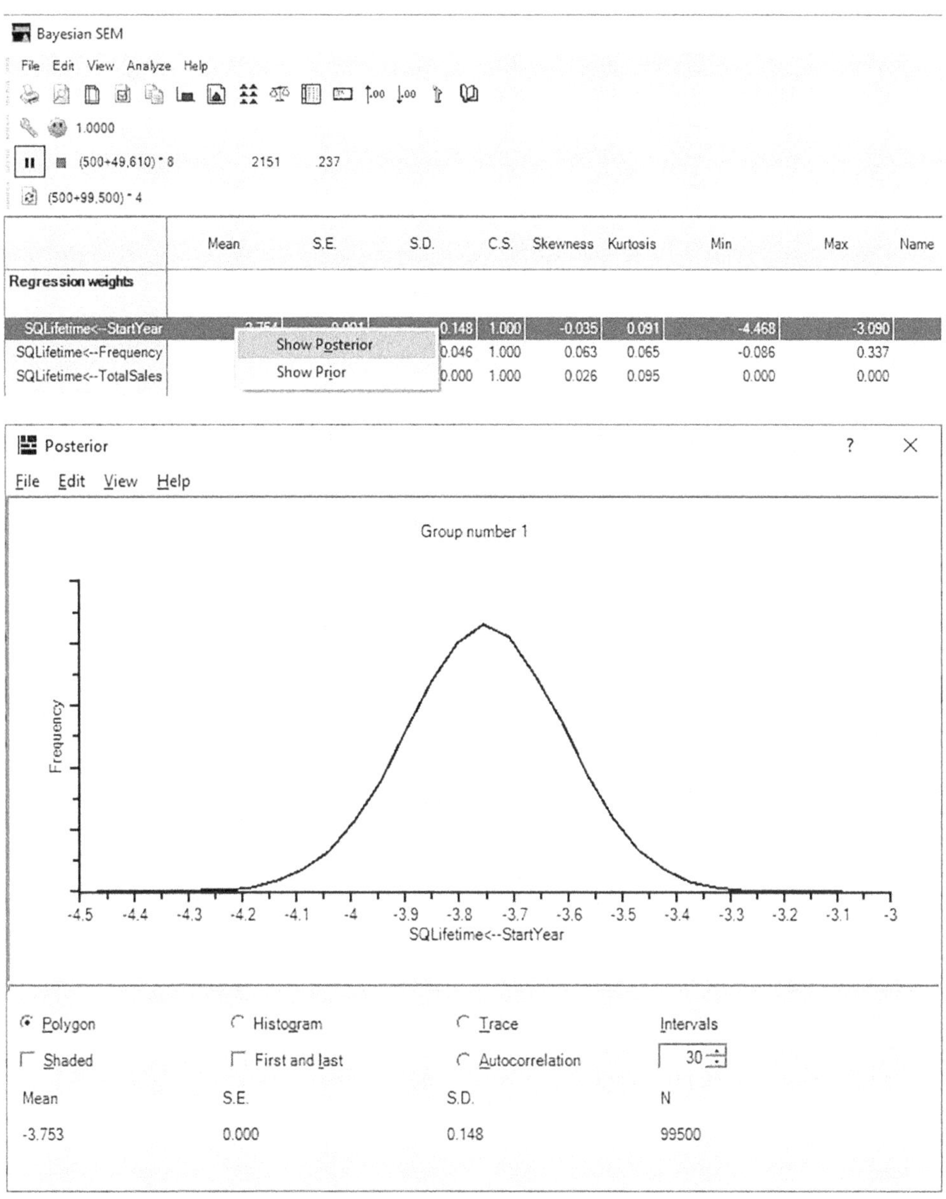

Figure 10.30 Show Posterior Prediction Graph of Relationship

So far, we have just examined the customer base as a whole, but what if we had a specific customer we wanted to examine and estimate how long the customer was going to be with the retailer? In the Bayesian window there is an icon at the top called posterior predictive . By clicking this button, you will see the posterior predictive distribution for every row in your data set. You will notice that the current customers do not have a value in the square root of the customer lifetime column. It simply has a greater than symbol. If you click on that greater than symbol, AMOS will create another pop-up window that will show you the predictive distribution for that specific case.

For instance, let's examine customer number 26, who has been with the retailer since 2015 and has made eight purchases that total $199. By clicking on that greater than symbol, we can see what is the expected lifetime (square root) as it pertains to days projected in the future to be with the retailer. See Figure 10.32 to view the predictive distribution for customer 26.

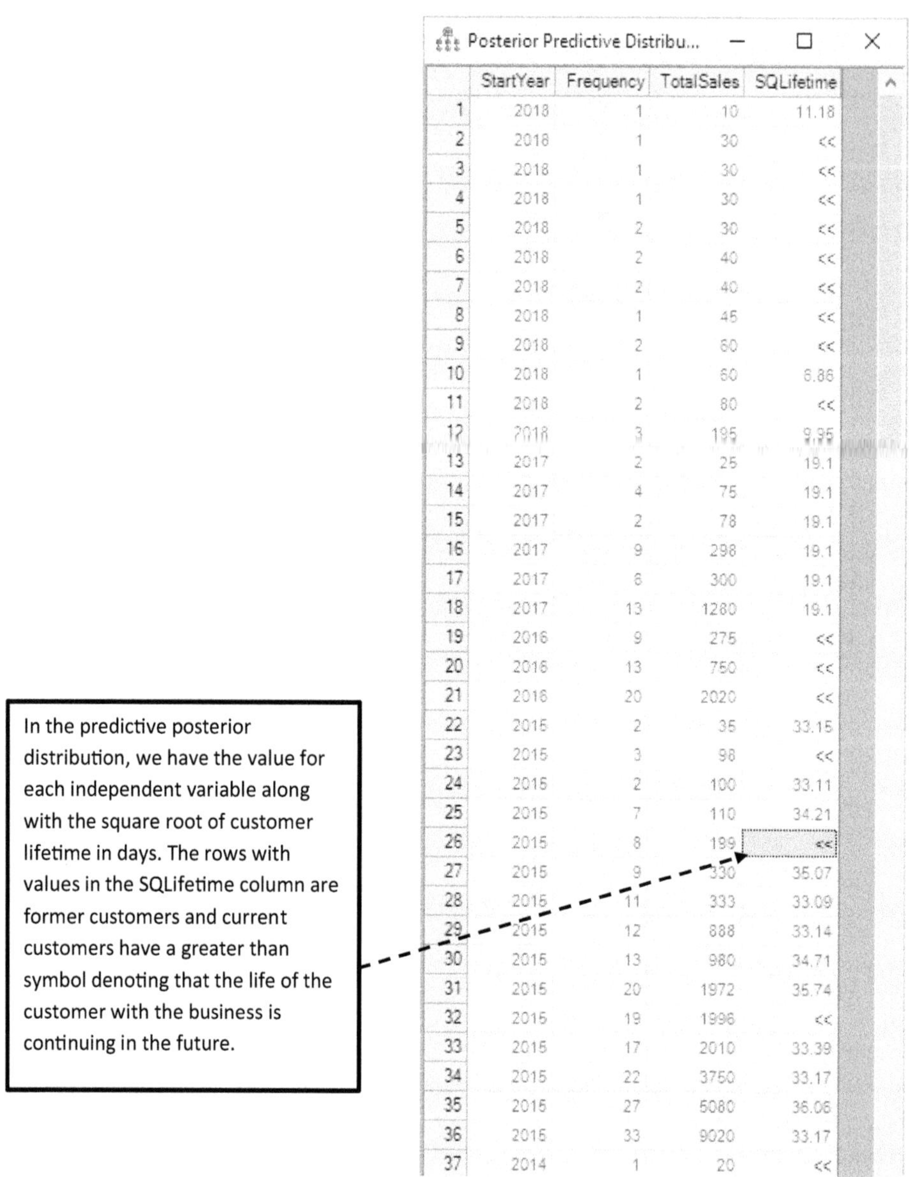
Posterior Predictive Distribu...
In the predictive posterior distribution, we have the value for each independent variable along with the square root of customer lifetime in days. The rows with values in the SQLifetime column are former customers and current customers have a greater than symbol denoting that the life of the customer with the business is continuing in the future.

	StartYear	Frequency	TotalSales	SQLifetime
1	2018	1	10	11.18
2	2018	1	30	<<
3	2018	1	30	<<
4	2018	1	30	<<
5	2018	2	30	<<
6	2018	2	40	<<
7	2018	2	40	<<
8	2018	1	45	<<
9	2018	2	60	<<
10	2018	1	60	6.86
11	2018	2	80	<<
12	2018	3	195	9.95
13	2017	2	25	19.1
14	2017	4	75	19.1
15	2017	2	78	19.1
16	2017	9	298	19.1
17	2017	8	300	19.1
18	2017	13	1280	19.1
19	2016	9	275	<<
20	2016	13	750	<<
21	2016	20	2020	<<
22	2015	2	35	33.15
23	2015	3	98	<<
24	2015	2	100	33.11
25	2015	7	110	34.21
26	2015	8	199	<<
27	2015	9	330	35.07
28	2015	11	333	33.09
29	2015	12	888	33.14
30	2015	13	980	34.71
31	2015	20	1972	35.74
32	2015	19	1996	<<
33	2015	17	2010	33.39
34	2015	22	3750	33.17
35	2015	27	5080	36.06
36	2015	33	9020	33.17
37	2014	1	20	<<

Figure 10.31 Individual Customer Predictions of Censored Data

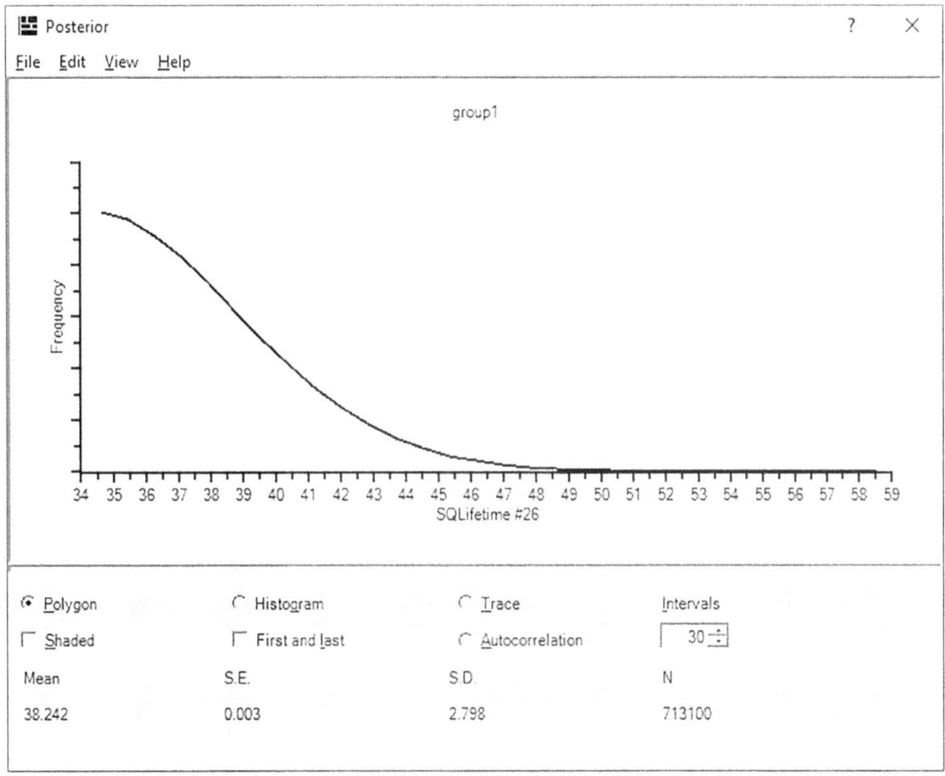

Figure 10.32 Graph of Posterior Prediction for Customer 26

The posterior distribution for customer 26 starts at 35, which means the customer has been with the retailer $(35)^2$, or a total of 1,225 days. If we look at the projections, customer 26 is projected to most certainly defect to another retailer by value 49 or by day 2,401. This means the customer is projected to leave the company in the next four years. This is the best-case scenario for the retailer. If you look at the mean value for this projection (38.242), this equates to the customer leaving at the 1,462-day mark or less than a year from the starting point of this analysis.

Examining the posterior prediction distributions will give you a better understanding on how each independent variable is influencing your dependent variable, which in this case was the customer lifetime in days. If you had a specific customer that you really valued, you can see the exact projections on how many days they are expected to be with the retailer. In this example, I used customer lifetime in days, but I could have just as easily used total sales as the dependent variable and examined what values promoted sales. Unknown or censored data can still be analyzed and projections made that can aide a researcher.

Non-Recursive Models (Feedback Loops)

A non-recursive model is a structural model where there is a feedback loop between two constructs. A recursive model is what we would consider a structural model where there are no reciprocal influences between constructs, or specifically, no feedback loops exist. The problem with feedback loops is you are creating an infinite loop in estimating the parameters between the feedback variables. Let's look at another example using the construct of Customer Delight to help understand the complexities of non-recursive modeling. In this example, Adaptive Behavior of the employee influences customers' feelings of delight but also a second construct called "Gratitude". Gratitude is the customers' feelings of appreciation or thankfulness to the employee. Customer Delight then influences the variable "Trust in the retailer", or "Trust" for short, which is the degree to which a customer believes a retailer has their best interest in mind. The construct of "Gratitude" influences a construct called "Confidence in the Retailer". Confidence in a Retailer is the belief in the ability of the retailer to perform a service. The constructs of Trust and Confidence in the Retailer have a reciprocal relationship where the more a customer trusts the retailer, the more confidence they have in them; and vice versa, the more confidence a customer has in the retailer, the more trust they will place with them. See Figure 10.33.

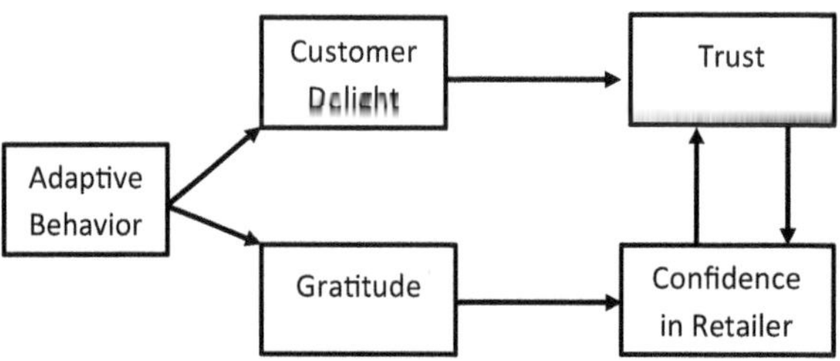

Figure 10.33 Structural Model With a Feedback Loop

The problem with non-recursive models is they tend to be under-identified. With a feedback loop included in the model, you need to make sure you have enough predictor variables included for each part of the feedback loop. In the example provided, both Trust and Confidence in the Retailer have a unique predictor. We could not have a relationship from Customer Delight to Confidence in the Retailer without the model being under-identified. The dependent variables in the feedback loop need to have what is called an "instrumental" variable. An instrumental variable is where a predictor will have a relationship with only one side of the feedback loop. Thus, the predictor will be "instrumental" in understanding the other side of the feedback loop. In our example, Gratitude is the instrumental variable for the construct of Trust, and Customer Delight is the instrumental variable for Confidence in the Retailer. If Customer Delight had a relationship to Trust and Confidence in the Retailer, then the construct of Confidence in the Retailer would not have an instrumental variable anymore. You would need an additional variable having a relationship only with Trust to have an instrumental variable for the Confidence in the Retailer construct. With most non-recursive models, you want to make sure you are providing enough predictor variables for each side of the feedback loop to be identified. Often you will find that only one half of the loop will be significant; the influence is not strong enough to close the loop. This is usually because you do not have enough unique predictors for each side of the feedback loop.

With non-recursive conceptualizations, model fit can be especially problematic if you are using a path model. You are better off to use a full structural model with measurement items and error terms included in order to help explain the structural relationships and feedback loop. Lastly, you also need to determine the stability of your parameter estimates in the feedback loop. Since you are creating an infinite loop with two regression weights, you need to determine if those weights are considered "stable"; or, put another way, the linear dependency in the feedback loop will provide a clearly defined relationship. AMOS will calculate a Stability Fit Index to help with this. If the stability index falls between −1 and +1, regression weights are considered stable. Saying that, let's look at the example in AMOS.

You can see that a full structural model is created and a feedback loop is drawn between the constructs of Trust and Confidence with the Retailer. One important component with a feedback loop is that the error terms for the unobservable constructs in the feedback loop need to be correlated. Since both constructs are influencing each other, it's advisable to correlate the error terms.

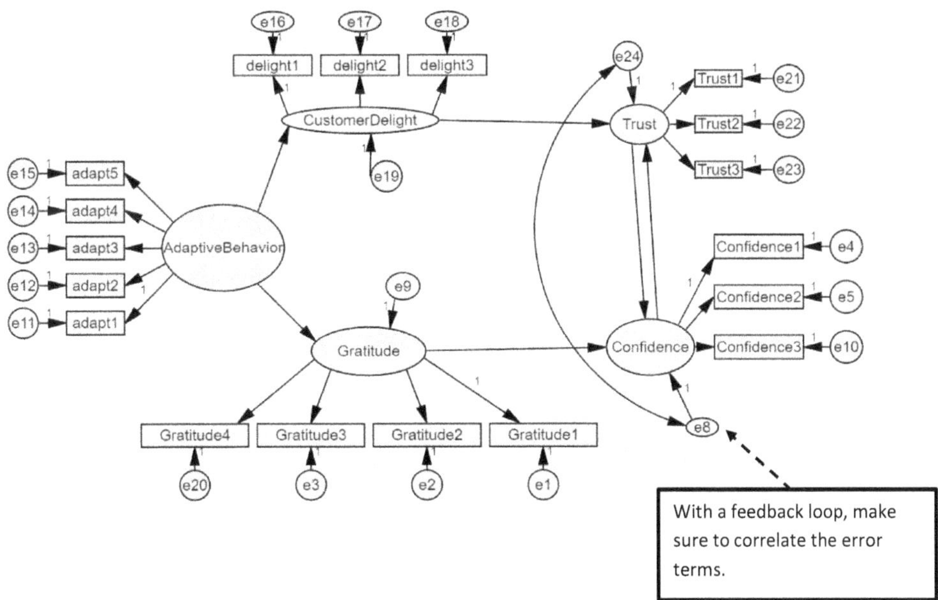

Figure 10.34 Trust and Confidence Feedback Loop Modeled in AMOS

Estimates (Group number 1 - Default model)

Scalar Estimates (Group number 1 - Default model)

Maximum Likelihood Estimates

Regression Weights: Group number 1

			Estimate	S.E.	C.R.	P	Label
CustomerDelight	<---	AdaptiveBehavior	.531	.033	16.152	***	
Gratitude	<---	AdaptiveBehavior	.275	.047	5.864	***	
Confidence	<---	Gratitude	.061	.023	2.621	.009	
Trust	<---	CustomerDelight	.459	.144	3.178	.001	
Gratitude2	<---	Gratitude	.961	.040	23.980	***	
Gratitude3	<---	Gratitude	1.012	.036	27.734	***	
Confidence2	<---	Confidence	1.077	.041	26.029	***	
Confidence3	<---	Confidence	1.096	.045	24.428	***	
adapt1	<---	AdaptiveBehavior	1.000				
adapt2	<---	AdaptiveBehavior	.977	.030	32.690	***	
adapt3	<---	AdaptiveBehavior	.998	.035	28.726	***	
adapt4	<---	AdaptiveBehavior	.996	.034	28.937	***	
adapt5	<---	AdaptiveBehavior	.931	.033	28.603	***	
delight1	<---	CustomerDelight	1.000				
delight2	<---	CustomerDelight	1.198	.044	27.384	***	
delight3	<---	CustomerDelight	1.177	.049	24.171	***	
Trust1	<---	Trust	1.000				
Trust2	<---	Trust	.917	.045	20.471	***	
Trust3	<---	Trust	.912	.045	20.303	***	
Gratitude4	<---	Gratitude	.908	.036	25.335	***	
Gratitude1	<---	Gratitude	1.000				
Confidence1	<---	Confidence	1.000				
Confidence	<---	Trust	.630	.047	13.368	***	
Trust	<---	Confidence	.632	.274	2.306	.021	

After drawing the model and running the analysis, let's look at the output in the Estimates link.

Our predictors of the feedback loop are significant.

You can see the feedback loop is positive and significant for both constructs. We have a significant feedback loop.

Standardized Regression Weights: Group number 1

			Estimate
CustomerDelight	<---	AdaptiveBehavior	.690
Gratitude	<---	AdaptiveBehavior	.275
Confidence	<---	Gratitude	.103
Trust	<---	CustomerDelight	.428
Gratitude2	<---	Gratitude	.824
Gratitude3	<---	Gratitude	.893
Confidence2	<---	Confidence	.890
Confidence3	<---	Confidence	.853
adapt1	<---	AdaptiveBehavior	.895
adapt2	<---	AdaptiveBehavior	.921
adapt3	<---	AdaptiveBehavior	.872
adapt4	<---	AdaptiveBehavior	.875
adapt5	<---	AdaptiveBehavior	.871
delight1	<---	CustomerDelight	.867
delight2	<---	CustomerDelight	.909
delight3	<---	CustomerDelight	.842
Trust1	<---	Trust	.776
Trust2	<---	Trust	.869
Trust3	<---	Trust	.862
Gratitude4	<---	Gratitude	.849
Gratitude1	<---	Gratitude	.883
Confidence1	<---	Confidence	.868
Confidence	<---	Trust	.868
Trust	<---	Confidence	.459

Figure 10.35 Estimate Output Showing Regression Weights for Direct Relationships and Feedback Loop

After initially finding a significant feedback loop, we need to check the stability of the relationships in the feedback loop. When AMOS detects that a non-recursive model is being analyzed, it will calculate the Stability index in the output. On the left-hand side, there is a tab called "Notes for Group/Model" that will show you the Stability index between Trust and Confidence in the Retailer. If you have multiple feedback loops, it will show you the index for all the proposed loops.

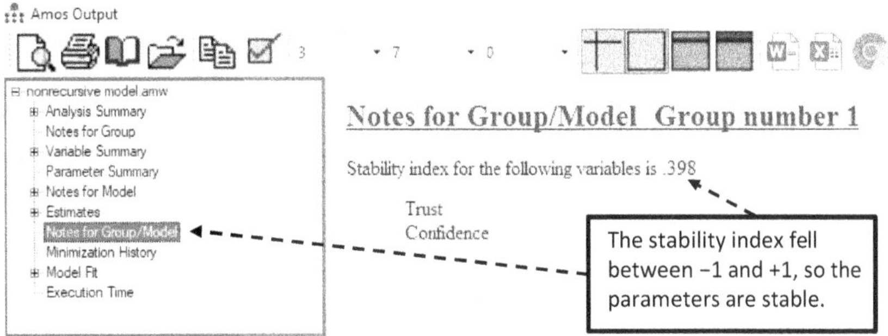

Figure 10.36 Stability Index for Trust and Confidence Variables

Next, let's check the model fit statistics. The results show that the model even with a feedback loop has an appropriate fit to the data. Thus, we can have confidence in our results with the inclusion of a feedback loop due to the significant regression weights, an acceptable stability index, and appropriate model fit.

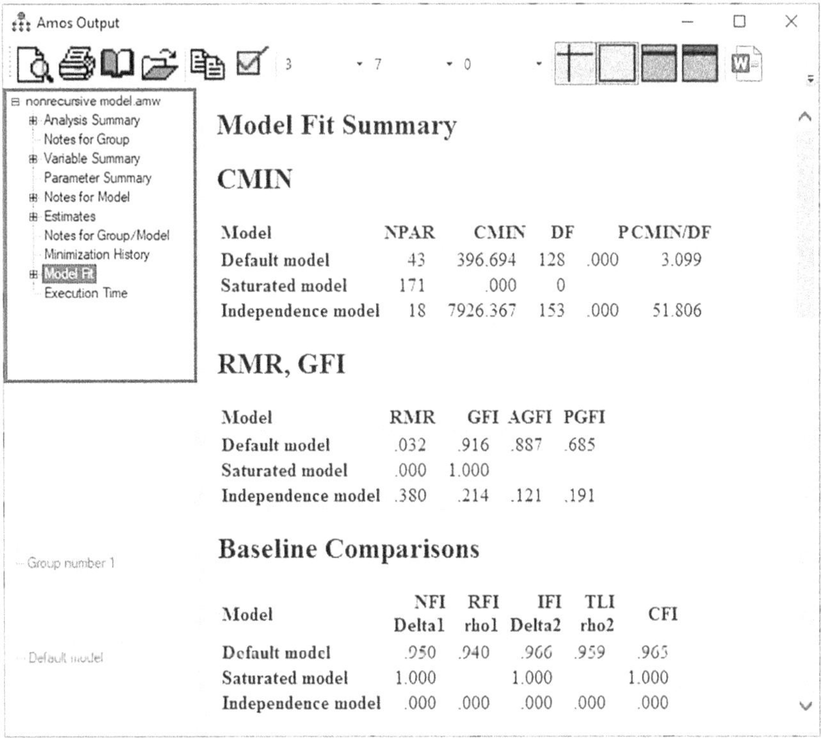

Model Fit Summary

CMIN

Model	NPAR	CMIN	DF	P	CMIN/DF
Default model	43	396.694	128	.000	3.099
Saturated model	171	.000	0		
Independence model	18	7926.367	153	.000	51.806

RMR, GFI

Model	RMR	GFI	AGFI	PGFI
Default model	.032	.916	.887	.685
Saturated model	.000	1.000		
Independence model	.380	.214	.121	.191

Baseline Comparisons

Model	NFI Delta1	RFI rho1	IFI Delta2	TLI rho2	CFI
Default model	.950	.940	.966	.959	.965
Saturated model	1.000		1.000		1.000
Independence model	.000	.000	.000	.000	.000

Figure 10.37 Model Fit Statistics of Feedback Loop Model

The example provided had just one feedback loop, but more complex models can have multiple feedback loops in a single model. Obviously, these models can be extremely complicated and often problematic in identification and stability. If you have multiple feedback loops in a model and one of the loops is considered "unstable", then the model as a whole is considered unstable even if the second loop has an acceptable stability index. Ultimately, many examples of reciprocal relationships can be modeled in SEM; the key is to make sure you have enough predictor variables to help explain the feedback loop.

Addressing Missing Data in AMOS

One of the nice perks of using AMOS is it uses a full information maximum likelihood method (FIML) to handle missing data. This method allows model parameters and standard errors to be estimated directly from the available data. With this method, the likelihood function is computed separately for variables that are not missing data, and a separate function is run for variables that are missing data. The two likelihood functions are then maximized together to find an estimate. Note this function is not an imputation but a method of computing maximum likelihood estimates of parameters.

If you have missing data, to use the full information maximum likelihood approach you need to go to the Analysis Properties and select "Estimate means and intercepts" under the "Estimation" tab at the top. This will allow AMOS to run your analysis via a FIML method.

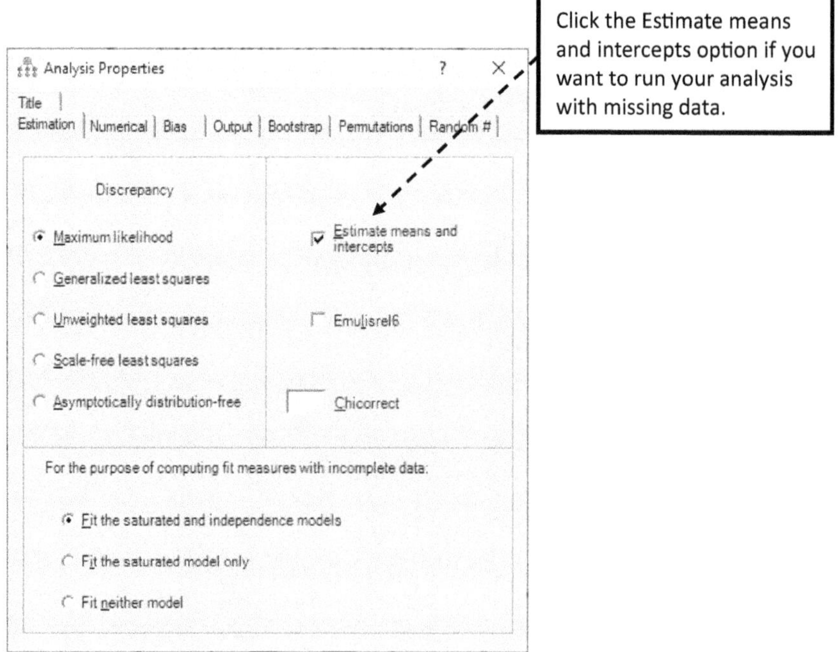

Figure 10.38 Using the Full Information Maximum Likelihood Method for Missing Data

Note that if you don't check the estimate means and intercepts option and have missing data, AMOS will prompt you with the following error message.

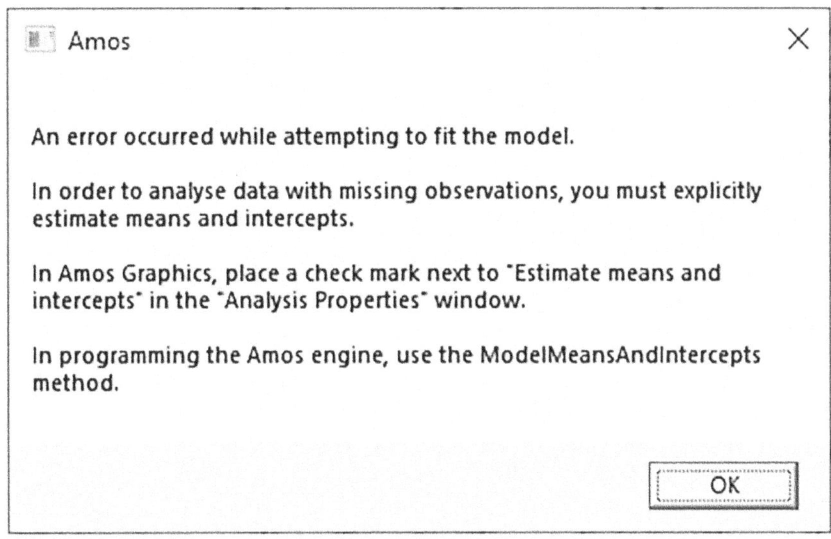

Figure 10.39 Error Message in AMOS if Missing Data Is Present

Once the estimate means and intercept option is chosen, AMOS will run the analysis for a measurement model or structural model and provide regression estimates for all estimated parameters.

One of the assumptions of SEM is that you have a complete data set that is not missing data. The FIML method will initially run your analysis with missing values, but if you want more advanced analysis options like bootstrapping or modification indices, AMOS will not perform these functions with missing data. In essence, you cannot run more complex functions with missing data that is addressed by FIML. This will require you to delete or impute the missing values. In Chapter 2, I talk about how to impute missing values in different ways (series mean and linear interpolation), but now we need to address imputation through regression imputation.

If you want to address imputing missing data via regression in AMOS, you will need to use the AMOS data imputation function . This is located under the Analyze tab at the top menu in AMOS. After clicking this function, a pop-up window will appear. You want to make sure "Regression imputation" is chosen in the pop-up window. AMOS wants you to rename your data file if an imputation is performed. If you do not specifically state a new file name, AMOS will alter the name to your existing file name and put "imputed" on the end of the name. See Figure 10.40.

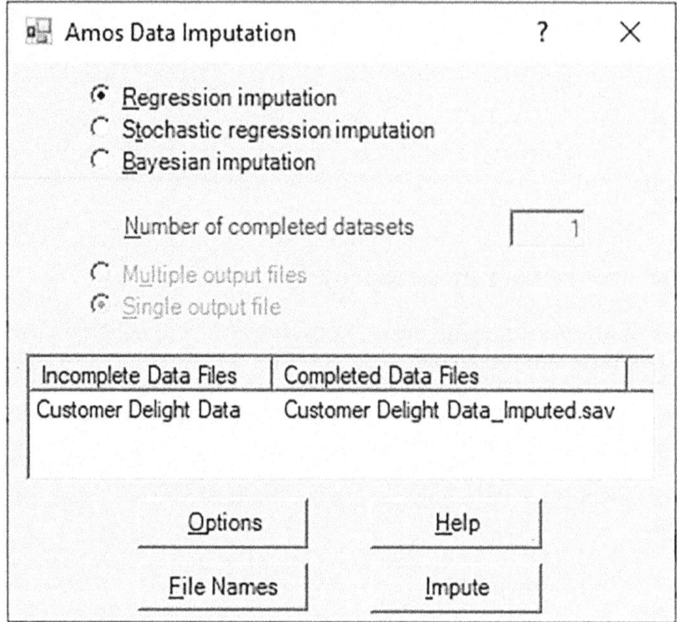

Figure 10.10 AMOS Imputation and Renaming of Data File

Once you have labeled your new data set and hit the "Impute" button at the bottom, AMOS will replace all missing values in all variables.

A word of caution needs to be given about using the AMOS imputation function. If you design a model in the AMOS graphics window with unobservable and observable constructs, and then decide to impute your data set, AMOS imputation will try to impute the values for the missing observable variables, but it will impute a score for the latent/unobservable variables as well. AMOS will create an imputed column which is the labeled name of your unobservable construct. You have two options to address this: (1) you can go into the new imputed file and delete all columns that are unobservable names; or (2) you can change the names of all the unobservables in your AMOS model. If you don't address this problem, AMOS will think your unobservable construct is an observable and will give you an error message. Obviously, a better option is to impute the data before you conceptualize your model with unobservable constructs. Lastly, to run your conceptual model, you will now need to read in the new file name and data that is imputed. AMOS does not automatically do this after an imputation. You need to make sure that AMOS is using the imputed data going forward.

The AMOS software can also use a Bayesian imputation to perform "multiple imputation". Multiple imputation is where the missing data is estimated multiple times. The Bayesian analysis estimates the missing value of the data multiple times based on the total variables of the study. This will produce numerous different completed data sets that include the different imputation of the missing data. The individual data sets are examined and then, ultimately, combined to form a single imputed data set. This method is labor intensive but has shown to be a valid method of handling missing data (Allison 2003).

Post-Hoc Power Analysis

A post-hoc or observed power analysis is a test of power after the sample has been collected. Using the existing sample size and effect size, you can determine the power of a specific relationship in your model. Using a post-hoc test for power assessment can often be misleading. These post-hoc power analyses can be (inappropriately) used as the reason or justification for non-significance. In essence, it was non-significant because the researcher did not achieve enough power from the estimated covariance matrix in predicting the relationship. More concerning is the relatively small sample size necessary to achieve acceptable power ratings in SEM. Taking our full structural model example used previously, if we wanted to calculate the post-hoc power for the Positive Word of Mouth estimates, we would need the number of predictors to Positive Word of Mouth (1), the squared multiple correlation of the construct (.254), the probability level (.05%), and the sample size (which was 500) in our example.

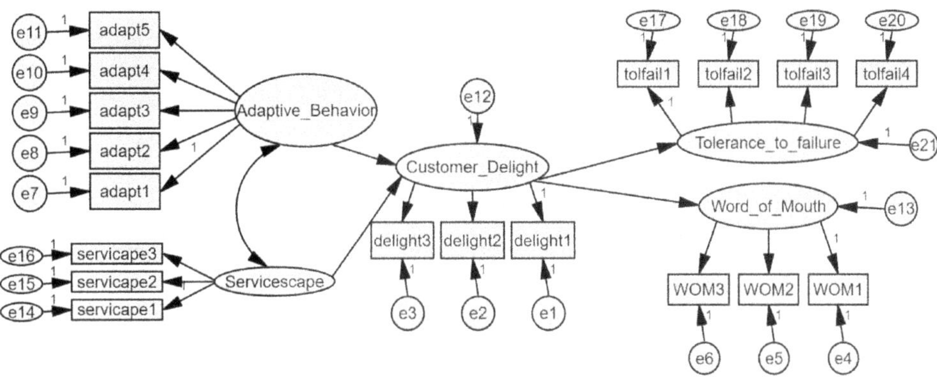

Figure 10.41 Full Structural Model to Test Post-Hoc Power

The post-hoc power analysis, based on this information, states that the power to assess the relationship of Positive Word of Mouth is $\pi = 1$, or a 100% chance of finding this result again if replicated. If I repeat this post-hoc power test and reduce the sample to 100, the power is $\pi = .99$. Again, this is almost a 100% chance of finding the same result, with a fifth of the sample. Let's take the sample down to 25 and run the calculation again. At a sample of 25, the power is $\pi = .81$, which is still considered an acceptable level of power to find an effect. To put it bluntly, post-hoc power analyses are not helpful and do not help to justify relationships found after the analysis. Power calculations are best suited in the design phase of research, not in the post-hoc analysis phase.

Using Specification Search to Perform Exploratory Factor Analysis

In Chapter 5, I explained how to use the specification search tool to trim a model. The specification search tool can also be used to perform an exploratory factor analysis (EFA). An EFA, as its name suggests, is an exploratory or investigative attempt to understand the factor structure of your constructs and if your indicators are loading on their appropriate factor. Unlike a confirmatory factor analysis (CFA), each construct/factor has a relationship to every indicator in the analysis. The goal of this test is to assure that your indicators are loading on their appropriate construct and not on another construct in the potential model.

With many of the examples in this book, we have talked about how customers' feelings of delight will lead to positive word of mouth about the experience. Let's say we wanted to perform an EFA on these two constructs. Both constructs had three observed indicators that were designed to measure the unobserved construct. The first step in testing this with the specification search function is to draw the constructs in the AMOS graphics window along with the indicators and error terms. We should have two unobserved constructs reflecting six indicators each. Both unobservable constructs will have a relationship to every indicator. Unlike a CFA, we do not need to set the metric, so no path from the unobservable construct to an indicator will be constrained to 1. All indicators are freely measured in this test. Saying that, we do have to set the variance for each unobservable construct to 1. This is done in order to estimate the potential different paths in the model. If we did not do this, the model would be considered under-identified. Lastly, we will still covary all unobservables in the model because they are considered independent variables. To see the standardized regression estimates, you need to go into the Analysis Properties window and select the standardized regression weight option. Do not select any other option in the Analysis Properties window, or it could create a conflict that will not display the factor loadings. See Figure 10.42 for a view of what the model should look like before using the specification search function.

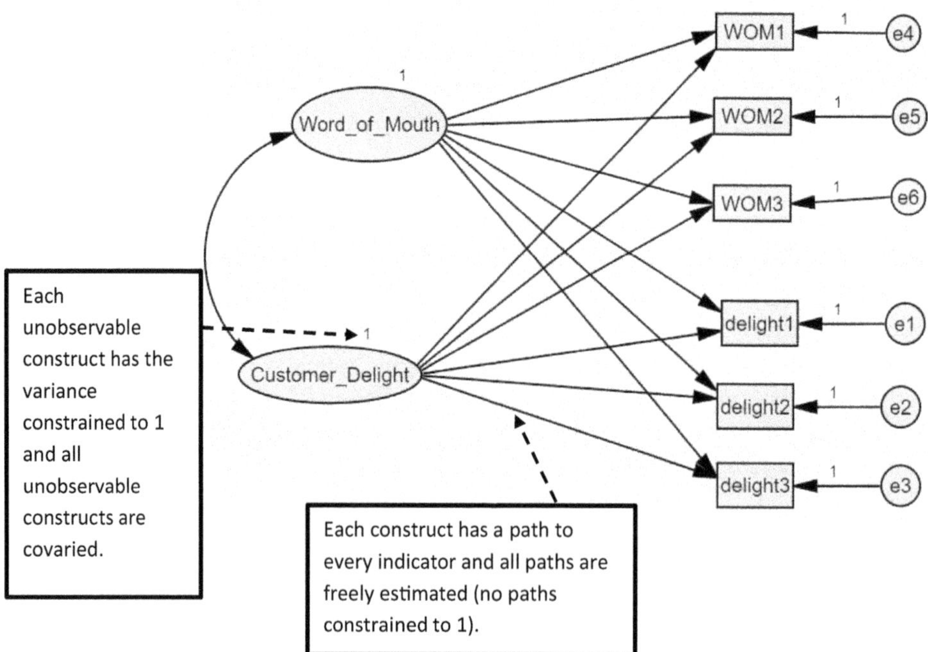

Figure 10.42 Exploratory Factor Analysis Model in AMOS

After forming the model, we are ready to use the specification search function. After, we click the specification search icon, the following window will appear (Figure 10.43).

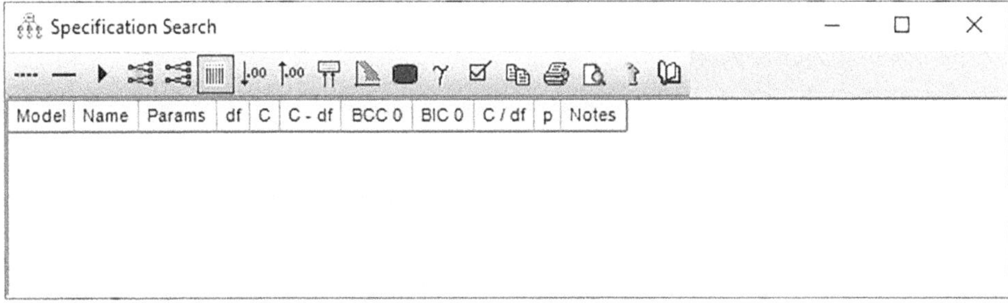

Figure 10.43 Specification Search Window in AMOS

The first icon in this window is the optional path function. Once you click this button, you can then choose which paths in the model are optional. The optional paths function means AMOS will run numerous possible models with and without the path included. With an EFA, we will select all paths to the indicators in the model and make them optional. We initially drew a path to every indicator from an unobservable construct, and now we will see which paths are statistically necessary or important in understanding the factor structure of our model. When you select each path or single headed arrow in the model, the color of the path will change. All optional paths will show up in the model as pink.

After selecting the optional paths in the model, you are ready to run the specification search analysis by pressing the triangle button. The specification search function will then start analyzing all possible combinations of the model with the optional relationships. The results will initially show you all the possible combinations. In this example, the specification search function produced 112 different possible models. Many of the models produced are inadmissible or unidentified. To find the best models produced from the analysis, you need to select the fit indices at the top. This will show you the best-fitting model first and then rank order the next best-fitting models. If I click on the chi-square/degrees of freedom heading (c/df), you can see that model 72 is listed as the best-fitting model (Figure 10.44). To see model 72, you just need to double click on the model number on the left-hand side. This will show you the paths that are included/removed in the model to produce this result.

The problem you can run into is that the fit indices might actually say different models are the "best" model. The chi-square/degrees of freedom note that model 72 is the best, whereas if you click on the BIC index, we see that model 52 is the best. So how do we know which model is the best one? Which model should we use when different fit indices are suggesting different options?

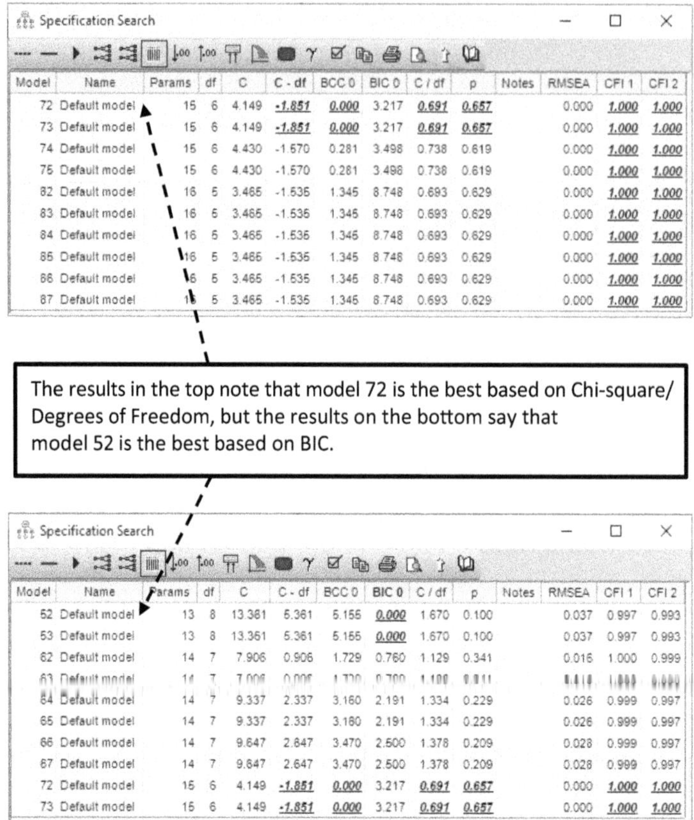

Model	Name	Params	df	C	C - df	BCC 0	BIC 0	C / df	p	Notes	RMSEA	CFI 1	CFI 2
72	Default model	15	6	4.149	***-1.851***	***0.000***	3.217	***0.691***	***0.657***		0.000	***1.000***	***1.000***
73	Default model	15	6	4.149	***-1.851***	***0.000***	3.217	***0.691***	***0.657***		0.000	***1.000***	***1.000***
74	Default model	15	6	4.430	-1.570	0.281	3.498	0.738	0.619		0.000	***1.000***	***1.000***
75	Default model	15	6	4.430	-1.570	0.281	3.498	0.738	0.619		0.000	***1.000***	***1.000***
82	Default model	16	5	3.465	-1.535	1.345	8.748	0.693	0.629		0.000	***1.000***	***1.000***
83	Default model	16	5	3.465	-1.535	1.345	8.748	0.693	0.629		0.000	***1.000***	***1.000***
84	Default model	16	5	3.465	-1.535	1.345	8.748	0.693	0.629		0.000	***1.000***	***1.000***
85	Default model	16	5	3.465	-1.535	1.345	8.748	0.693	0.629		0.000	***1.000***	***1.000***
86	Default model	[illegible]	5	3.465	-1.535	1.345	8.748	0.693	0.629		0.000	***1.000***	***1.000***
87	Default model	[illegible]	5	3.465	-1.535	1.345	8.748	0.693	0.629		0.000	***1.000***	***1.000***

Model	Name	Params	df	C	C - df	BCC 0	BIC 0	C / df	p	Notes	RMSEA	CFI 1	CFI 2
52	Default model	13	8	13.361	5.361	5.155	***0.000***	1.670	0.100		0.037	0.997	0.993
53	Default model	13	8	13.361	5.361	5.155	***0.000***	1.670	0.100		0.037	0.997	0.993
62	Default model	14	7	7.906	0.906	1.729	0.760	1.129	0.341		0.016	1.000	0.999
63	Default model	14	7	[illegible]	[illegible]	[illegible]	[illegible]	[illegible]	[illegible]		[illegible]	[illegible]	[illegible]
64	Default model	14	7	9.337	2.337	3.160	2.191	1.334	0.229		0.026	0.999	0.997
65	Default model	14	7	9.337	2.337	3.160	2.191	1.334	0.229		0.026	0.999	0.997
66	Default model	14	7	9.647	2.647	3.470	2.500	1.378	0.209		0.028	0.999	0.997
67	Default model	14	7	9.647	2.647	3.470	2.500	1.378	0.209		0.028	0.999	0.997
72	Default model	15	6	4.149	***-1.851***	***0.000***	3.217	***0.691***	***0.657***		0.000	***1.000***	***1.000***
73	Default model	15	6	4.149	***-1.851***	***0.000***	3.217	***0.691***	***0.657***		0.000	***1.000***	***1.000***

Figure 10.44 Comparison of Best-Fitting Model Across Different Indices

Let's look at both models in the AMOS graphics window to give us a better understanding on which one is more appropriate to use. Before we go into the AMOS graphics window, we need to see the parameter estimates for each model. To do this, we need to select the "Show Parameter" icon and then double click into the model we want to view. If we double click into model 72, we see that the Positive Word of Mouth and Customer Delight indicators are strongly loading on their respective construct, but we have two additional paths included. One path is from Word of Mouth to delight3, but the loading is very weak (.08) and is not considered an acceptable factor loading. We also have a path from Customer Delight to WOM2, but again, the path is loading at an unacceptable level (−.07). We see from this model that our indicators for each construct are strongly loading on their respective factor. There is some cross loading, but it appears to be rather weak and not a huge concern.

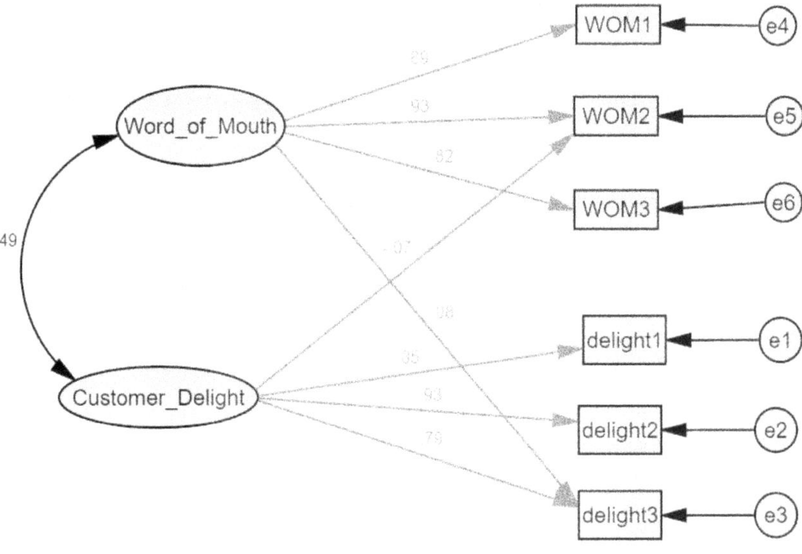

Figure 10.45 Model 72 From the Specification Search Window

Let's now look at model 52 and see if we get a similar or different pattern of results with our indicator loadings. See Figure 10.46.

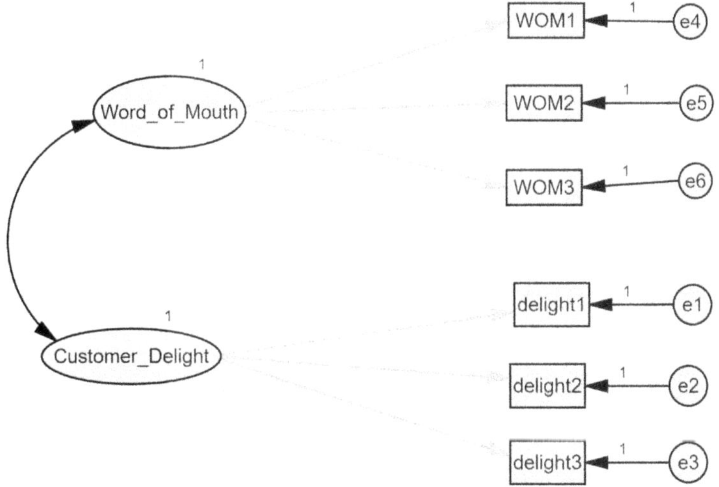

Figure 10.46 Model 52 From the Specification Search Window

With model 52, there are no cross loadings, and the only paths included in the model are from the construct of Customer Delight to its three indicators and from Positive Word of Mouth to its three indicators. The regression weights are all strong, giving initial support that all the construct's indicators are loading on their appropriate construct.

While we have initial confirmation that our indicators are loading on our constructs, AMOS will allow us to plot/graph these results in order to see what is the most appropriate number of optional relationships. In the icon window of the specification search window is the "Plot" option. Clicking on that button will pop up a second window with the results plotted. The plot window gives you the option of using a scree plot, a "Best fit" plot, and a scatter plot. It will also plot the results based on the different fit indices. The plots will show how much change took place on the y-axis compared to the number of different parameters estimated on the x-axis. The bottom of the screen will also show you fit values, but that information does not help in determining the appropriate model because different models will show very little difference in those values.

Of the plot model options, I find the scree plot to be most useful because it will give a clear picture on what is the optimal number of parameters to be estimated in a model. The scatter plot will give you the frequency of parameters chosen, but this is not that helpful. The "Best fit" plot method does not tell us much more than which model has the best model fit, which we can get without the plot. Let's look at the scree plot for the chi-square/degrees of freedom index.

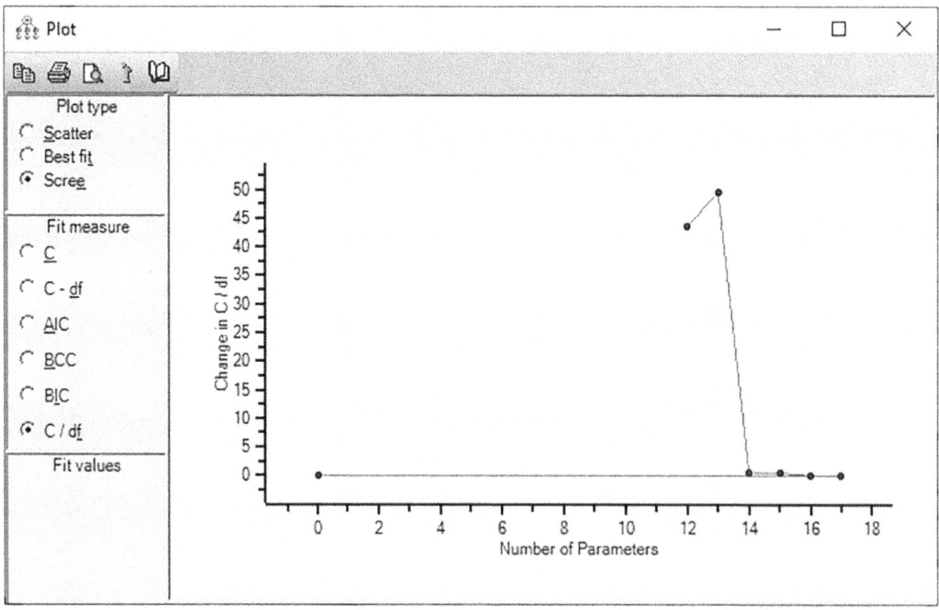

Figure 10.47 Scree Plot Based on Chi-Square/DF

The results show us that 13 parameters have the highest change in chi-square/degrees of freedom. When we move to a 14th parameter, the change in chi-square/degrees of freedom is substantial, and any additional parameters added are not really contributing to further explanation. If you click into the dot on the 13th parameter, it will give us the model number. In this example, the model number listed is model 52 that just had the three paths from Customer Delight to its indicators and the three paths from Positive Word of Mouth to its indicators. If we look at the results for the BIC index, we find similar results, where after the 13th parameter the line abruptly drops and then levels off in regards to how much is being explained with the addition of each parameter estimate.

Across all our analyses, it appears a 13-parameter estimate is the most appropriate, which corresponds to model 52. This EFA gives strong support that our indicators are loading on the appropriate constructs. One caveat with using the specification search function is that it will allow only 30 optional arrows. If you want to run an EFA with numerous constructs at once, other statistical options may be better suited.

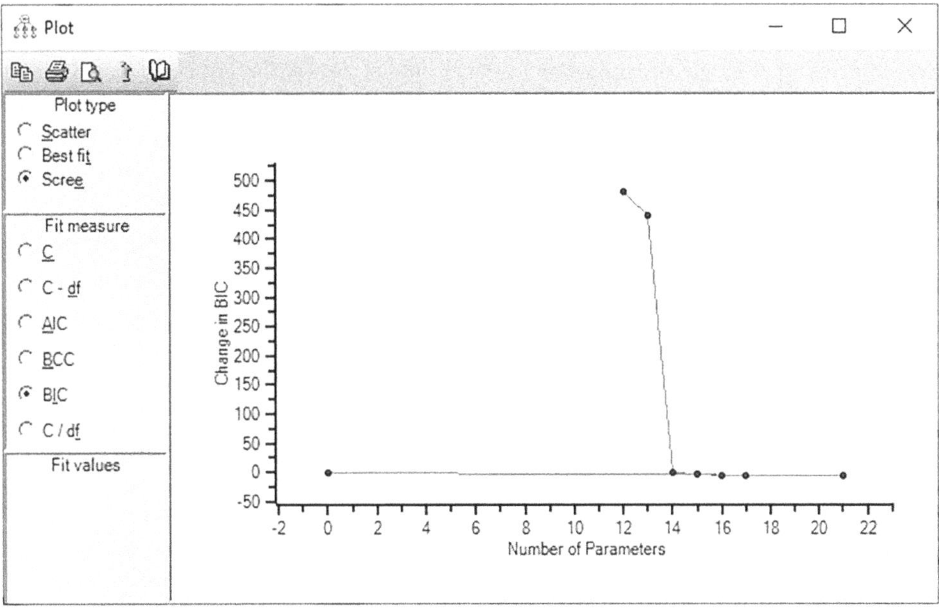

Figure 10.48 Scree Plot Based on BIC

How to Use Plugins to Create a Model Instead of Drawing a Model in AMOS

If you do not want to use the graphical interface to conceptualize your model, AMOS does have an option where you can use a syntax option to run your analysis. Numerous SEM programs in the past were solely syntax based, and if you feel more comfortable typing in the relationships than using the graphical interface, AMOS provides you with that option. This option is usually slower, but it does give you a nice documentation of the model and relationships when the coding is complete. As well, learning to code the data is a skill that is transferable to other statistical packages. Lastly, if you want to collaborate with other authors who only know how to use syntax, you can now speak a common language in the collaboration process. AMOS uses a form of Visual Basic that allows you to specify a model in text form.

AMOS uses "pd" functions that will represent an object in the graphics window. Here is a list of the five most prominent functions.

pd. Observed =	Denotes an observed object in a model
pd. Unobserved =	Denotes an unobserved object in the model
pd. Path =	Creates a path (structural or measurement) between specified objects in the model
pd. Cov =	Adds a covariance between specified objects in the model.
pd. Caption =	Adds a caption to the model

With each one of these functions, you need to make sure all data file names of variables and names of unobservable variables you created have a quotation mark at the beginning and ending of the name. AMOS will not know what variable you are trying to access without those quotation marks. A single program line in the coding format will equate to a single object added in the model or functions needed in the model.

Let's look at how we could use the Plugins function via syntax to run a confirmatory factor analysis. After this example, I will show you how to code a full structural model. The CFA example will be the same one we used in Chapter 4. We will start with a simple three construct factor analysis of the constructs of Adaptive Behavior, Customer Delight, and Positive Word of Mouth. We are going to model the observables for each construct along with all the error terms for each observable. To see what the model initially looked like in the graphics window, see Figure 10.49.

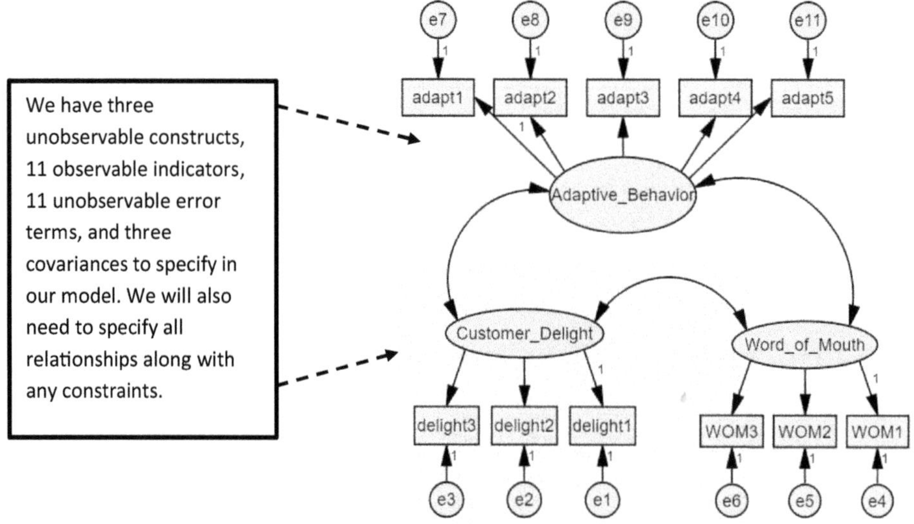

Figure 10.49 CFA Model From Chapter 4

There are two ways to code the data in AMOS. The first way is through the "program editor" software in AMOS. This not located in the graphics window. The program editor is a separate program that is solely code based (it will not draw a model). The second option is located in the graphics window and is located in the Plugins option at the top. The Plugins option will allow you to specify the model in a coding format, and then AMOS creates the model in the graphics window. I find this second option a little easier because you can still use the Analysis Properties button in the graphics window to specify different analysis options. I will show you both methods for coding the data, but let's first start with the "Plugins" option in the graphics window first.

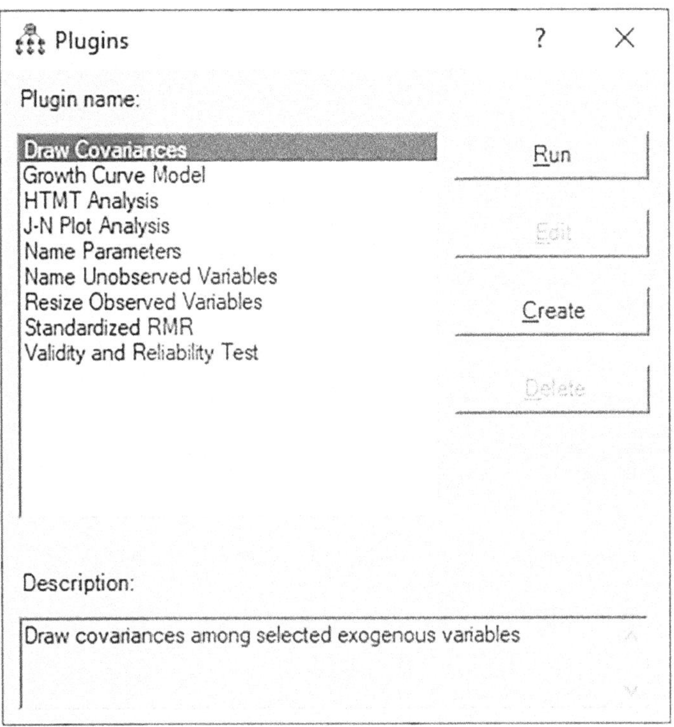

Figure 10.50 Plugins Window in AMOS

We first need to go to the AMOS graphics window and then select the "Plugins" option at the top right and then select "Plugins". A pop-up window will appear with the default plugins listed (see Figure 10.50). You can also hit ALT+F8, and it will take you directly to this pop-up window.

When the pop-up window appears, hit the "Create" button. This will bring up a program editor window with some default code already in the window. The first three functions will be "Name", which is the name you want to call this plugin; "Description", which is a brief description that can be entered about the model or file; and "Mainsub", which is the area where you will input the code that will tell AMOS what to turn into a graphic.

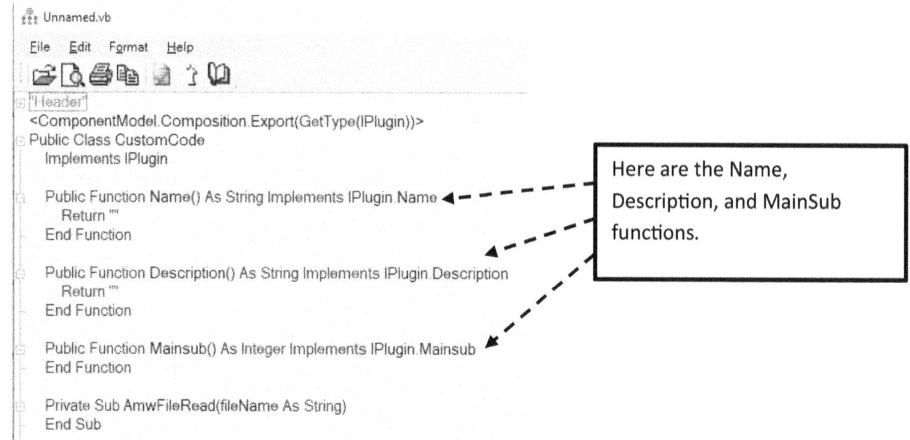

Figure 10.51 Plugins Window in AMOS

I am going to call this plugin "CFA Syntax", and I am going to include a description of the file as "CFA analysis using Syntax function".

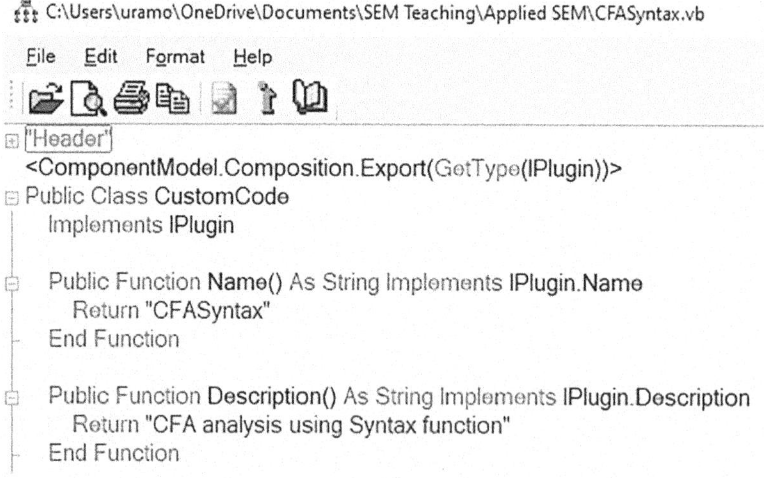

Figure 10.52 Name and Description Included in Plugin

Under the "Mainsub" function, we are initially going to enter all the unobservables and observables in the model. I am going to initially input all the indicators of the unobservable constructs. Adaptive Behavior had five indicators, while Positive Word of Mouth and Customer Delight had three indictors each. To input these observables, we are going to use the "pd. Observed" function. For the first Adaptive Behavior indicator (adapt1), we are going to let AMOS know this is an observable in the model by coding it:

pd. Observed ("adapt1")

Make sure you include the parenthesis and quotation marks in this line function. Next, we are going to include all the rest of the indicators. See Figure 10.53.

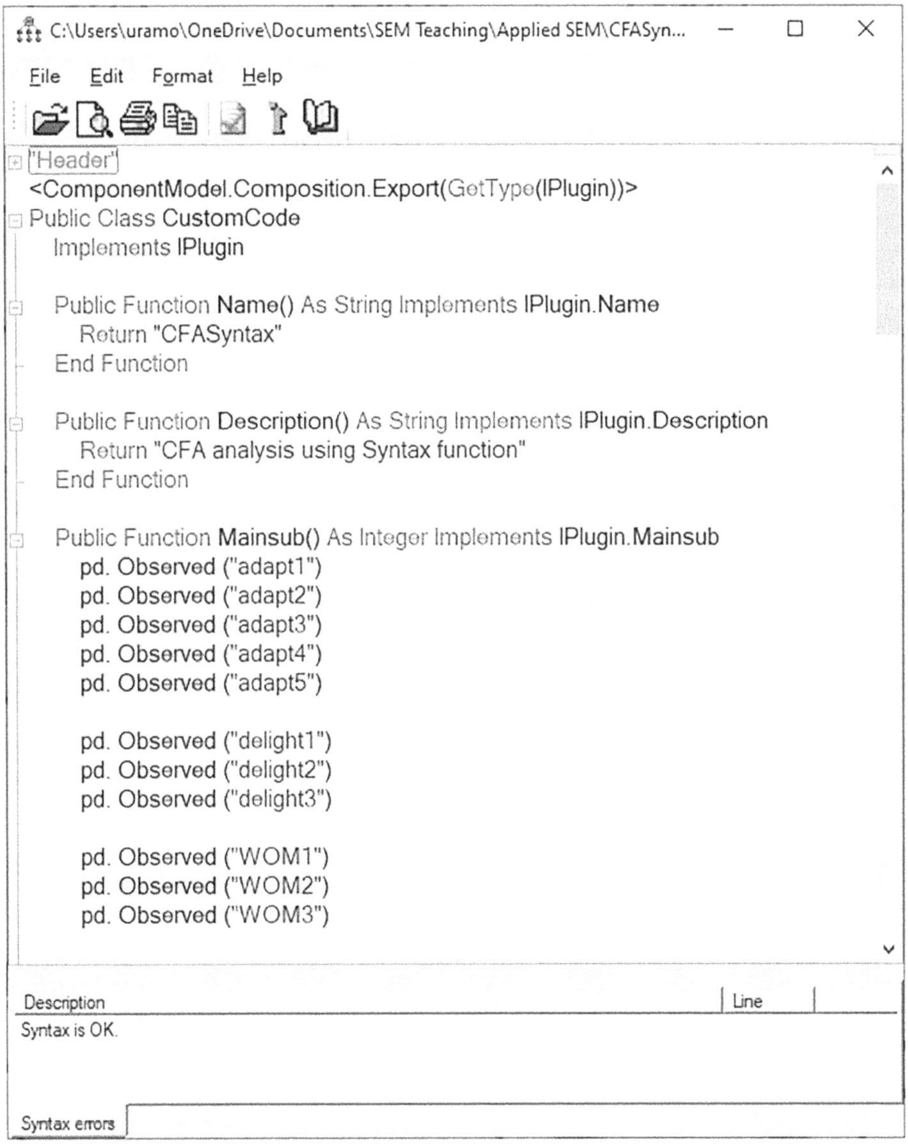

C:\Users\uramo\OneDrive\Documents\SEM Teaching\Applied SEM\CFASyn...

File Edit Format Help

```
"Header"
<ComponentModel.Composition.Export(GetType(IPlugin))>
Public Class CustomCode
   Implements IPlugin

   Public Function Name() As String Implements IPlugin.Name
      Return "CFASyntax"
   End Function

   Public Function Description() As String Implements IPlugin.Description
      Return "CFA analysis using Syntax function"
   End Function

   Public Function Mainsub() As Integer Implements IPlugin.Mainsub
      pd. Observed ("adapt1")
      pd. Observed ("adapt2")
      pd. Observed ("adapt3")
      pd. Observed ("adapt4")
      pd. Observed ("adapt5")

      pd. Observed ("delight1")
      pd. Observed ("delight2")
      pd. Observed ("delight3")

      pd. Observed ("WOM1")
      pd. Observed ("WOM2")
      pd. Observed ("WOM3")
```

Description	Line
Syntax is OK.	

Syntax errors

Figure 10.53 Observable Variables Coded in Plugin

Notice that I included a line space between the construct's indicators; this just helps to keep the code orderly instead of a huge list of indicators. You want to make sure you can easily see if you are missing an indicator for a construct.

Underneath the observables, we can start to include the unobservables. The unobservables will use the following function:

Pd. Unobserved ("construct name")

The first construct of Adaptive_Behavior is coded as: pd. Unobserved ("Adaptive_Behavior"). I will code the other unobservable constructs the same way.

The error terms in our model are also considered unobservables. Each indicator has an error term that needs to be coded as an unobservable. The "unobservable" error terms are coded the same way as the unobservable constructs. The first error term of "e1" is coded as:

pd. Unobserved ("e1")

We will code all the other error terms the exact same way. Again, it is okay to have a blank line between your coding in order to organize your coding into areas.

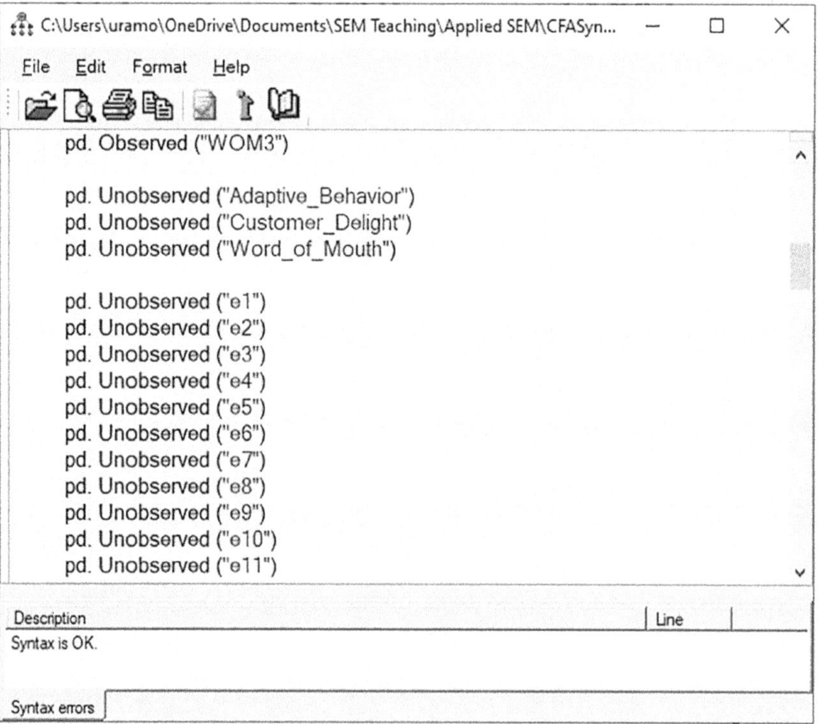
C:\Users\uramo\OneDrive\Documents\SEM Teaching\Applied SEM\CFASyn...
File Edit Format Help
pd. Observed ("WOM3")
pd. Unobserved ("Adaptive_Behavior")
pd. Unobserved ("Customer_Delight")
pd. Unobserved ("Word_of_Mouth")
pd. Unobserved ("e1")
pd. Unobserved ("e2")
pd. Unobserved ("e3")
pd. Unobserved ("e4")
pd. Unobserved ("e5")
pd. Unobserved ("e6")
pd. Unobserved ("e7")
pd. Unobserved ("e8")
pd. Unobserved ("e9")
pd. Unobserved ("e10")
pd. Unobserved ("e11")
Description
Line
Syntax is OK.
Syntax errors

Figure 10.54 Unobservable Variables Coded in Plugin

After telling AMOS what the unobservable and observable items are in the model, you can then add single headed or double headed arrow relationships in the model. You can also start to code any constraints that are in the model. Let's start with adding the single headed arrow relationships in the CFA. We are going to use the "pd. Path" function next. When using the path function, you have to denote where the arrow is pointing to and where it is pointing from in the code. You also have to denote if the relationship has a constraint. Here is how the function is set up:

pd. Path ("object where the arrow is pointing to", "object where the arrow is pointing from", constraint)

In the Adaptive Behavior construct, let's model the first indicator (adapt1). This indicator is also constrained to 1 because it is setting the metric for the construct. Here is how to code this relationship:

pd. Path ("adapt1", "Adaptive_Behavior", 1)

The unobserved Adaptive Behavior construct has a reflective path to its indicator of adapt1 and the path is constrained to 1. If we had no constraint in the path, then we would not include any value at the end of the line function. For instance, the next indicator to be coded for Adaptive Behavior would be: pd. Path ("adapt2", "Adaptive_Behavior"). You will need to code the relationship for each unobservable construct to its indicators. Make sure to code the constraint in each construct for the indicator that sets the metric.

After coding the paths from the unobservable construct to the indicators, you now need to code the error term relationships. The error terms are classified as unobservables, so they will be coded the same way as the unobservable constructs were just coded. One specific difference is that all error terms have a constraint of 1 in its relationship. When you are drawing your model using the graphics interface, AMOS will put this constraint in by default; but in the program editor window, you will have to specifically tell AMOS to put a constraint in the relationships from the error term to the indictors.

Let's now try to code the error term for the adapt1 indicator. The error number can be whatever number you choose, but to be consistent with the example from Chapter 4 where we drew the model in the graphics window, the error term is "e7". To code this relationship, it would be:

pd. Path ("adapt1", "e7", 1)

We would then need to code all the error terms for each indicator, making sure that every indicator had a constraint of 1 added.

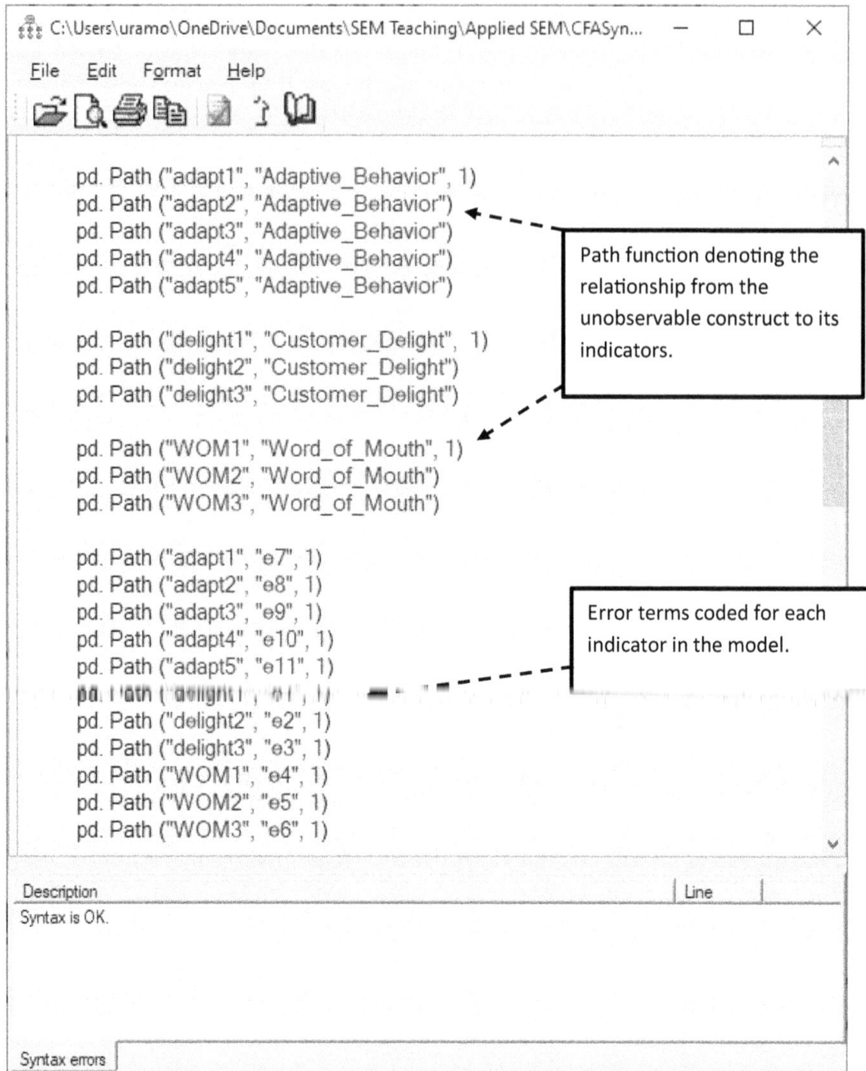
C:\Users\uramo\OneDrive\Documents\SEM Teaching\Applied SEM\CFASyn...
File Edit Format Help
pd. Path ("adapt1", "Adaptive_Behavior", 1)
pd. Path ("adapt2", "Adaptive_Behavior")
pd. Path ("adapt3", "Adaptive_Behavior")
pd. Path ("adapt4", "Adaptive_Behavior")
pd. Path ("adapt5", "Adaptive_Behavior")
pd. Path ("delight1", "Customer_Delight", 1)
pd. Path ("delight2", "Customer_Delight")
pd. Path ("delight3", "Customer_Delight")
pd. Path ("WOM1", "Word_of_Mouth", 1)
pd. Path ("WOM2", "Word_of_Mouth")
pd. Path ("WOM3", "Word_of_Mouth")
pd. Path ("adapt1", "e7", 1)
pd. Path ("adapt2", "e8", 1)
pd. Path ("adapt3", "e9", 1)
pd. Path ("adapt4", "e10", 1)
pd. Path ("adapt5", "e11", 1)
pd. Path ("delight2", "e2", 1)
pd. Path ("delight3", "e3", 1)
pd. Path ("WOM1", "e4", 1)
pd. Path ("WOM2", "e5", 1)
pd. Path ("WOM3", "e6", 1)
Path function denoting the relationship from the unobservable construct to its indicators.
Error terms coded for each indicator in the model.
Description
Line
Syntax is OK.
Syntax errors

Figure 10.55 Coding the Relationships to Indicators and Error Terms

With a CFA, all unobservable constructs are considered independent constructs. Thus, all independent constructs need to be covaried. To do this, we will use the covariance function of "pd. Cov". Here is an example of the covariance function:

pd. Cov ("Adaptive_Behavior, "Customer_Delight")

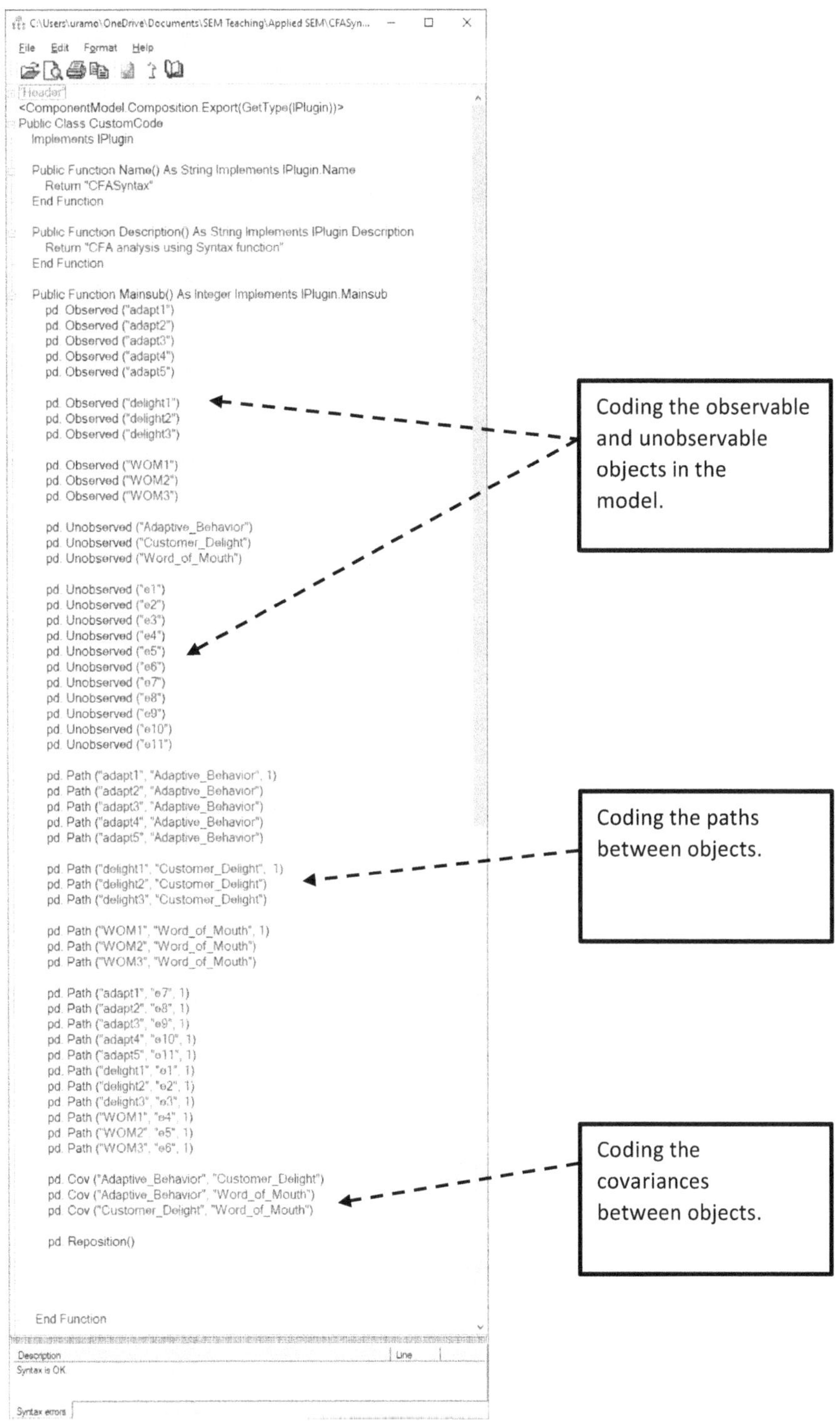

C:\Users\uramo\OneDrive\Documents\SEM Teaching\Applied SEM\CFASyn...
File Edit Format Help
'Header'
<ComponentModel.Composition.Export(GetType(IPlugin))>
Public Class CustomCode
Implements IPlugin
Public Function Name() As String Implements IPlugin.Name
Return "CFASyntax"
End Function
Public Function Description() As String Implements IPlugin.Description
Return "CFA analysis using Syntax function"
End Function
Public Function Mainsub() As Integer Implements IPlugin.Mainsub
pd. Observed ("adapt1")
pd. Observed ("adapt2")
pd. Observed ("adapt3")
pd. Observed ("adapt4")
pd. Observed ("adapt5")
pd. Observed ("delight1")
pd. Observed ("delight2")
pd. Observed ("delight3")
pd. Observed ("WOM1")
pd. Observed ("WOM2")
pd. Observed ("WOM3")
pd. Unobserved ("Adaptive_Behavior")
pd. Unobserved ("Customer_Delight")
pd. Unobserved ("Word_of_Mouth")
pd. Unobserved ("e1")
pd. Unobserved ("e2")
pd. Unobserved ("e3")
pd. Unobserved ("e4")
pd. Unobserved ("e5")
pd. Unobserved ("e6")
pd. Unobserved ("e7")
pd. Unobserved ("e8")
pd. Unobserved ("e9")
pd. Unobserved ("e10")
pd. Unobserved ("e11")
pd. Path ("adapt1", "Adaptive_Behavior", 1)
pd. Path ("adapt2", "Adaptive_Behavior")
pd. Path ("adapt3", "Adaptive_Behavior")
pd. Path ("adapt4", "Adaptive_Behavior")
pd. Path ("adapt5", "Adaptive_Behavior")
pd. Path ("delight1", "Customer_Delight", 1)
pd. Path ("delight2", "Customer_Delight")
pd. Path ("delight3", "Customer_Delight")
pd. Path ("WOM1", "Word_of_Mouth", 1)
pd. Path ("WOM2", "Word_of_Mouth")
pd. Path ("WOM3", "Word_of_Mouth")
pd. Path ("adapt1", "e7", 1)
pd. Path ("adapt2", "e8", 1)
pd. Path ("adapt3", "e9", 1)
pd. Path ("adapt4", "e10", 1)
pd. Path ("adapt5", "e11", 1)
pd. Path ("delight1", "e1", 1)
pd. Path ("delight2", "e2", 1)
pd. Path ("delight3", "e3", 1)
pd. Path ("WOM1", "e4", 1)
pd. Path ("WOM2", "e5", 1)
pd. Path ("WOM3", "e6", 1)
pd. Cov ("Adaptive_Behavior", "Customer_Delight")
pd. Cov ("Adaptive_Behavior", "Word_of_Mouth")
pd. Cov ("Customer_Delight", "Word_of_Mouth")
pd. Reposition()
End Function
Description
Line
Syntax is OK.
Syntax errors
Coding the observable and unobservable objects in the model.
Coding the paths between objects.
Coding the covariances between objects.

Figure 10.56 Total Code for the CFA Plugin

You will notice at the bottom of the Mainsub section I included a function that was listed as

pd. Reposition ()

This function will group the observable and error terms together with an unobservable construct when AMOS creates the model in the graphics window. If you don't specify this function, the model is going to have observables and unobservables just randomly placed on the graphics screen.

This is all the coding we need to enter into the Mainsub area. There is much more coding below this area, but it is fine to leave those blank at this point. Next, you need to check the syntax to make sure you do not have any errors. At the top of the screen are some icons.

Figure 10.37 Icons on Plugin Coding Screen

The icon with the checkmark on the page is the check syntax function. Once you have clicked this, you should get a "Syntax is Ok" message in the description section under the coding if no errors are present. If an error does occur, the error message will be displayed in the description section.

After checking your syntax, you need to save your coding. To run the coding in the AMOS graphics window, you need to save this file in the AMOS Plugins folder. If you do not save it in this folder, the graphics window will not be able to access and run the analysis. The location you need to save this file is typically:

C:\Users\username\Appdata\Local\AmosDevelopment\AMOS\26\Plugins

You can always hit the "Save As" button, and it should default into this location or the location that you specifically need to save the coding. Again, if it is not saved in the Plugins folder, AMOS can not run the analysis.

Once you save the file, you should see that Plugin is one of the default names when you click into the Plugin option on the graphics screen. You will also see at the bottom the description of the Plugin.

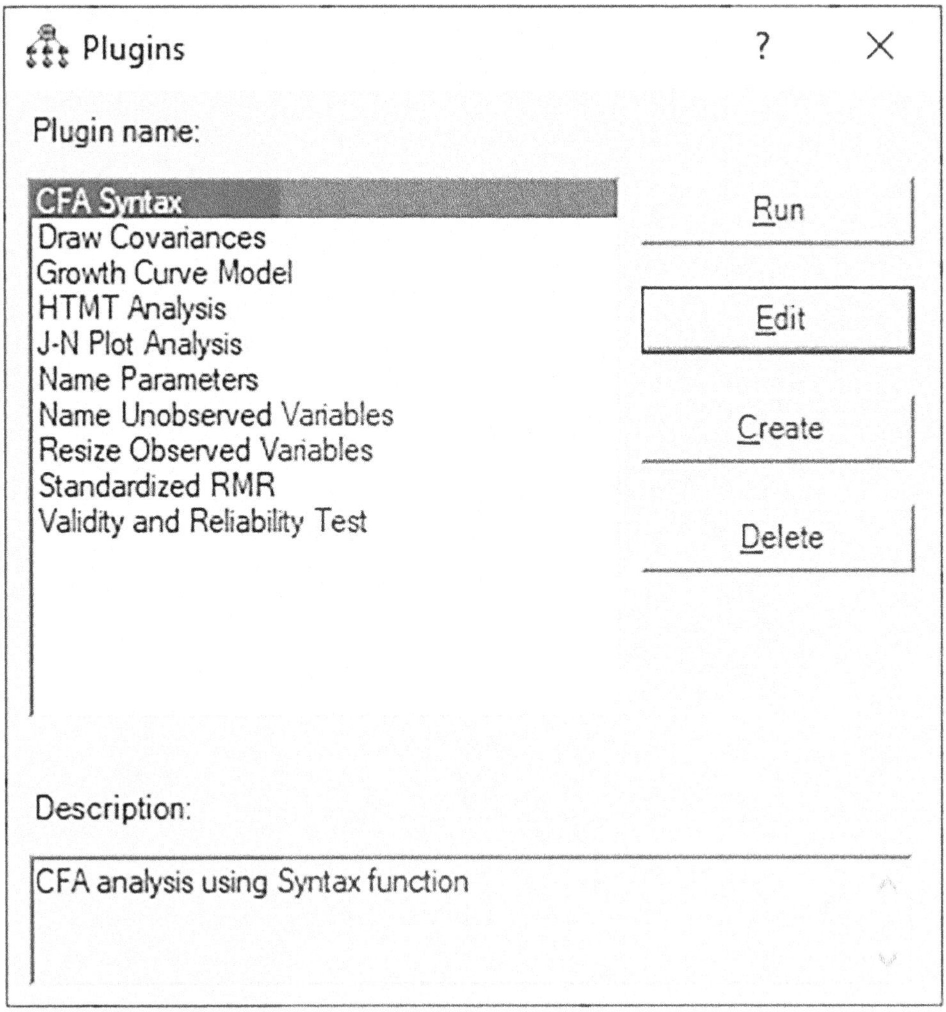

Plugins

Plugin name:

CFA Syntax
Draw Covariances
Growth Curve Model
HTMT Analysis
J-N Plot Analysis
Name Parameters
Name Unobserved Variables
Resize Observed Variables
Standardized RMR
Validity and Reliability Test

Run
Edit
Create
Delete

Description:

CFA analysis using Syntax function

Figure 10.58 CFA Syntax Listed in Plugin Window

To launch the Plugin, you need to create a new file in the AMOS graphics window and then read in the data file you want to use with the select data file icon  . Next, you will go to the Plugins option and then select your file, which was named CFA Syntax in this example. AMOS will conceptualize the model in the graphics window. Here is what the model looks like after running the Plugin:

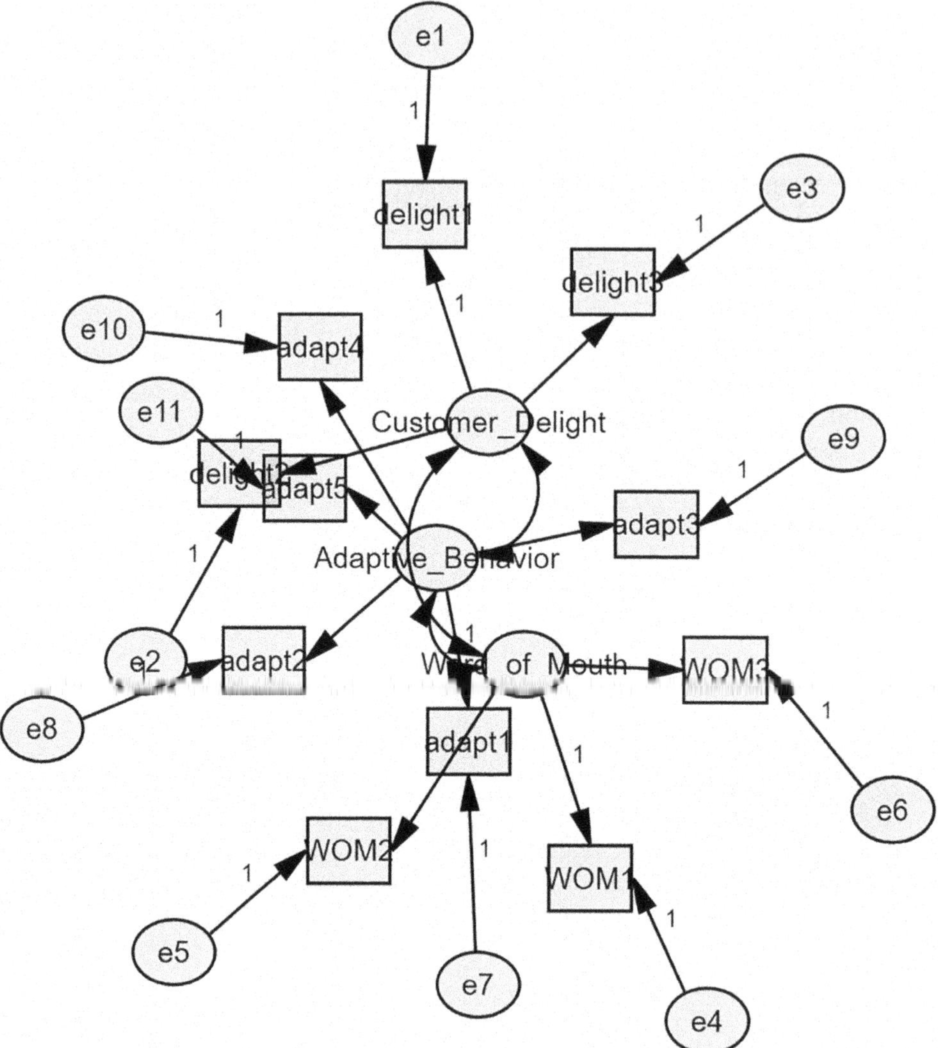

Figure 10.59 CFA Syntax Plugin Modeled in Graphics Window

I know that after looking at the model drawn by AMOS, many of you are thinking "Wow, this is a hot mess! I thought the reposition function we added was going to group the denoted objects around an unobservable construct". You are correct, the reposition function helps AMOS organize the model; this is the best AMOS can do without you specifically noting where you want each construct based on a pixel location, which is a very laborious process. Figure 10.60 shows you what the model looks like when the reposition function is not included in the coding.

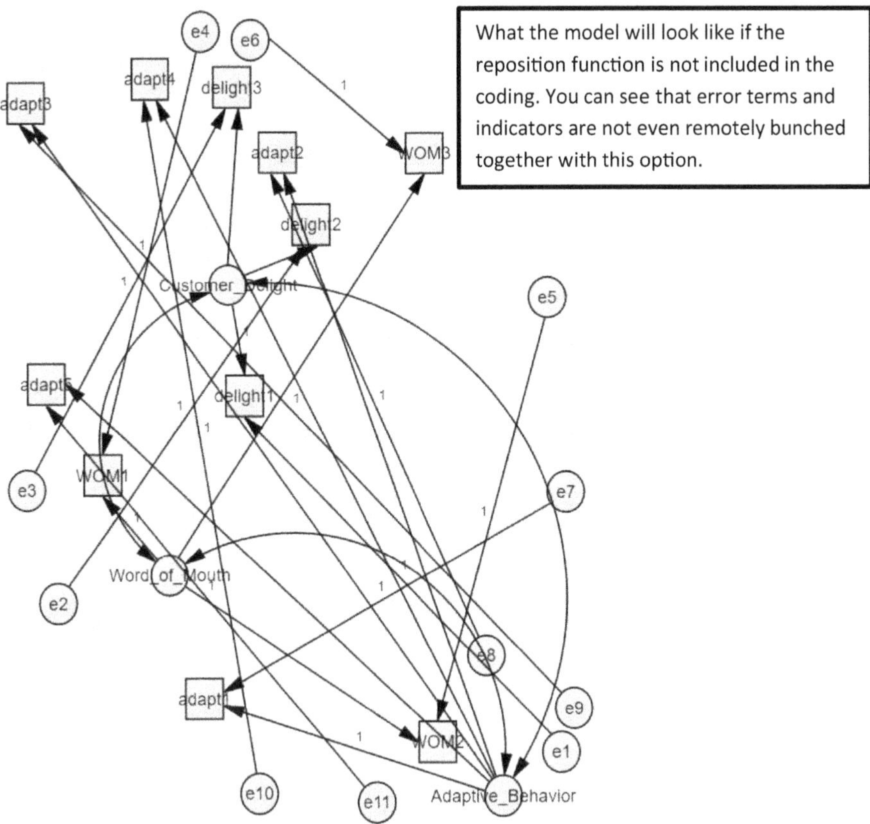

Figure 10.60 CFA Syntax Plugin with Reposition Code Removed

If you are using syntax in the Plugins function to draw the model in AMOS graphics, you probably do not really care what the model looks like; you are just concerned with the analysis. Once the model has been drawn, then you can use the calculate estimates button to run the analysis. The results of this analysis are the exact same as the test we performed in Chapter 4.

Using the syntax function with the Plugins function does have advantages and disadvantages. One of the disadvantages is you are going to see every model created listed in the Plugins function in the drop-down menu. I do not want to see every possible model I have created, because that could be a very long list. You can create the coding file and save it in another location and then simply copy it into the Plugins folder when you are ready to use it. By doing it this way, you see only the default plugins and then the file you just copied in. This is a work-around, but still a little bit of a hassle.

Another disadvantage is that the model that is created in the AMOS graphics window is hard to see and not very easy to interpret. You would almost need to go back into the coding to see the relationships or spend a lot of time fixing the model to make it graphically pleasing. The graphics window part is not that helpful with this function.

There are some advantages to using this function as well. While I do not prefer to code a whole model in this function, if you have a repetitive construct that you use continually, you can code the construct, its indicators, and error terms in the plugin for future use. For instance, if you consistently use an "Involvement" scale that was 13 items in the data set, you could code the unobservables and observables of the involvement construct and save it to the Plugins folder. When you were ready to include that construct in your model, you could use the plugin and save some time from creating a new 13-indicator construct every time. Additionally, if a construct-to-construct relationship is consistently being modeled, this Plugins function will save you some effort instead of creating the constructs in the model every time. You do need to make sure to call the specific observables the same name across your data sets if you use the Plugins function for this, or AMOS will not be able to anlayze the data because of the different observable's names listed in the data and in the model. The biggest advantage to coding the data this way is the flexibility it gives you in the analysis. You can code the unobservables and observables in the model along with relationships but can still use the analysis icons to select options and text viewing in an easy manner compared to coding all the requests in the program editor. It is kind of like the best of both worlds. You can use syntax code to conceptualize the model and then use the icon functions to denote options in the analysis. For functions like two group analysis and invariance testing, this option is substantially easier than the alternative of coding every analysis option needed in the program editor software.

Before examining how to use the dedicated program editor software, I want to give you one more example of plugin coding for a full structural model. In our example, we just examined the measurement model, but this time let's examine a full structural model where the measurement and the structural relationships are included.

I am going to call this plugin "StructuralTest", and it will include a simple description of a "full structural model test of Adaptive Behavior, Customer Delight, and Positive Word of Mouth". This model test will examine how Adaptive Behavior influences Customer Delight which influences Positive Word of Mouth. The initial coding of unobservables and observables will be exactly the same, but we are going to add error terms to the dependent variables and relationships between the constructs. We will also remove all the covariances between the constructs because now we only have one independent construct. See Figure 10.61 for the coding of the structural model test.

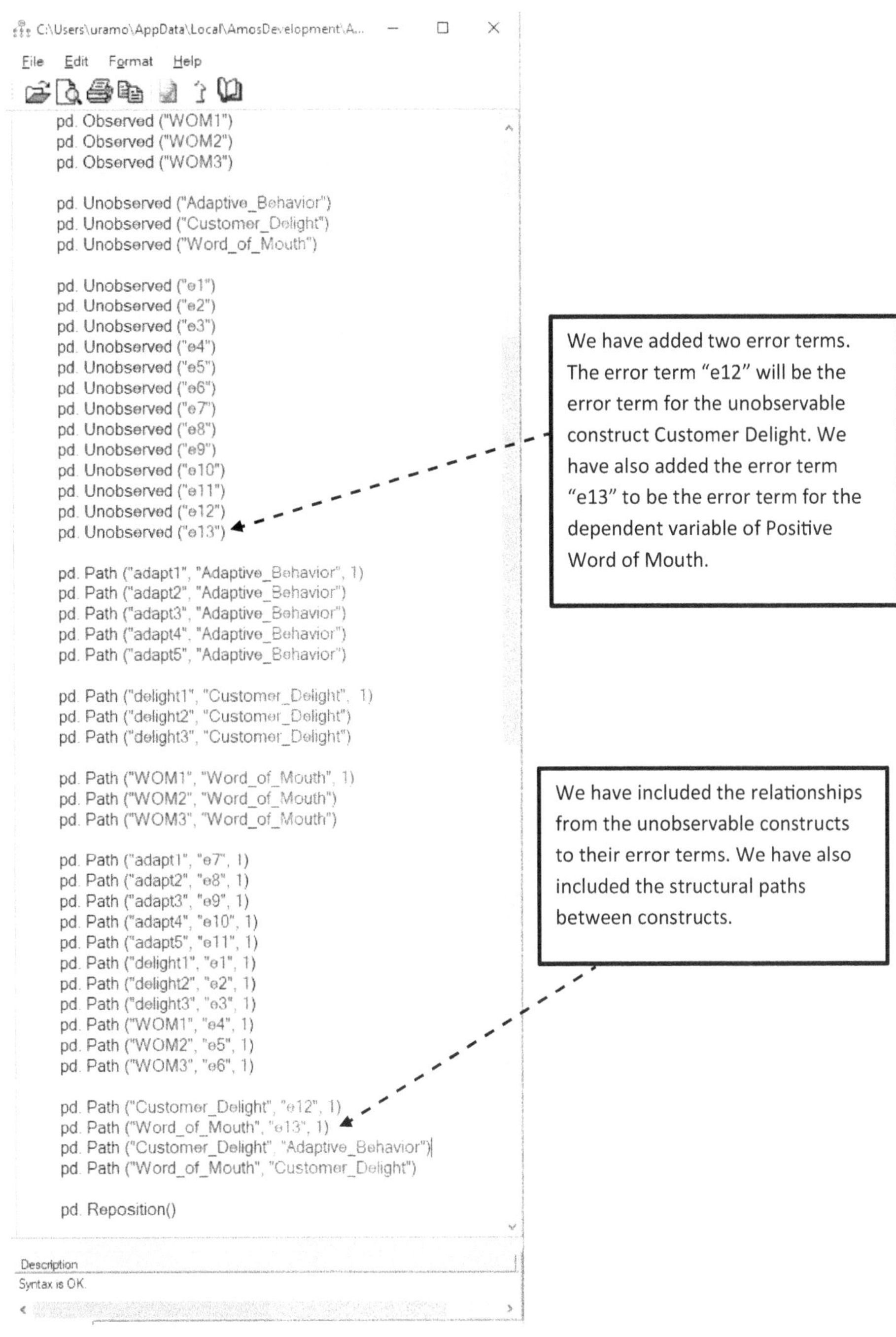
C:\Users\uramo\AppData\Local\AmosDevelopment\A...
File Edit Format Help
pd. Observed ("WOM1")
pd. Observed ("WOM2")
pd. Observed ("WOM3")
pd. Unobserved ("Adaptive_Behavior")
pd. Unobserved ("Customer_Delight")
pd. Unobserved ("Word_of_Mouth")
pd. Unobserved ("e1")
pd. Unobserved ("e2")
pd. Unobserved ("e3")
pd. Unobserved ("e4")
pd. Unobserved ("e5")
pd. Unobserved ("e6")
pd. Unobserved ("e7")
pd. Unobserved ("e8")
pd. Unobserved ("e9")
pd. Unobserved ("e10")
pd. Unobserved ("e11")
pd. Unobserved ("e12")
pd. Unobserved ("e13")
pd. Path ("adapt1", "Adaptive_Behavior", 1)
pd. Path ("adapt2", "Adaptive_Behavior")
pd. Path ("adapt3", "Adaptive_Behavior")
pd. Path ("adapt4", "Adaptive_Behavior")
pd. Path ("adapt5", "Adaptive_Behavior")
pd. Path ("delight1", "Customer_Delight", 1)
pd. Path ("delight2", "Customer_Delight")
pd. Path ("delight3", "Customer_Delight")
pd. Path ("WOM1", "Word_of_Mouth", 1)
pd. Path ("WOM2", "Word_of_Mouth")
pd. Path ("WOM3", "Word_of_Mouth")
pd. Path ("adapt1", "e7", 1)
pd. Path ("adapt2", "e8", 1)
pd. Path ("adapt3", "e9", 1)
pd. Path ("adapt4", "e10", 1)
pd. Path ("adapt5", "e11", 1)
pd. Path ("delight1", "e1", 1)
pd. Path ("delight2", "e2", 1)
pd. Path ("delight3", "e3", 1)
pd. Path ("WOM1", "e4", 1)
pd. Path ("WOM2", "e5", 1)
pd. Path ("WOM3", "e6", 1)
pd. Path ("Customer_Delight", "e12", 1)
pd. Path ("Word_of_Mouth", "e13", 1)
pd. Path ("Customer_Delight", "Adaptive_Behavior")
pd. Path ("Word_of_Mouth", "Customer_Delight")
pd. Reposition()
Description
Syntax is OK.
We have added two error terms. The error term "e12" will be the error term for the unobservable construct Customer Delight. We have also added the error term "e13" to be the error term for the dependent variable of Positive Word of Mouth.
We have included the relationships from the unobservable constructs to their error terms. We have also included the structural paths between constructs.

Figure 10.61 Plugin's Code for a Full Structural Model

How to Use the Program Editor to Conceptualize Your Model and Run the Analysis

The dedicated program editor software is included in the suite of AMOS programs when you install it on your computer. The program editor software allows you to fully code your model and request any analysis you need without using the AMOS graphics window. It has a slightly different coding structure from that of the previous example of conceptualizing a model through the Plugins function. This section is not going to be comprehensive in all the functions in the program editor. You could write another book just on understanding how to use all the functions possible in the program editor. I am going to give you some of the most basic functions to create and conceptualize models and also the ability to request different output options. If you would like more details on how to use syntax in AMOS, there are some great resources available (Arbuckle 2017).

When you open the program editor, the following window should appear.

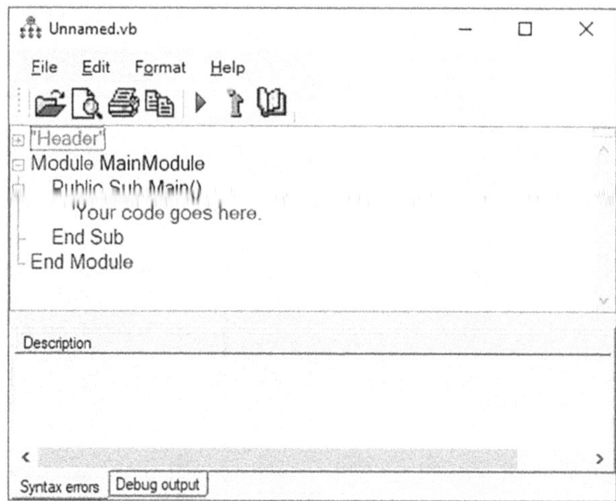

Figure 10.62 Opening Window of AMOS Program Editor

Under the "Module MainModule", you can type in a description of the model or description of the data being analyzed. It is just an area to give you greater clarity on the model you are working on. You do need to start each sentence with an apostrophe to let AMOS know this is just a description. Under the "Public Sub Main()" area is where you will place your code to request a model along with the output of the analysis.

Before we start coding syntax into the window, we need to tell AMOS what format we are going to use to anlayze the conceptual model. On the first line after the "Sub Main", you should enter:

Dim Sem as New AmosEngine

This will let us use the methods and properties of an object (denoted as Sem) to conceptualize a model. At the start, we also need to include the Try\Finally\Dispose\End Try function. This function allows us to use the AmosEngine in the analysis but will, in essence, release resources in order to run an analysis again. To use this function, we are going to put "Try" on the line right below Dim Sem as New AmosEngine, and then when we are finished coding the syntax for our conceptual model, we are going to include the following program lines:

```
Finally
Sem.Dispose ()
End Try
```

After the initial "Try" program line, we will start asking AMOS for the ability to see the output of our analysis. Here are some of the most popular requests:

Sem.TextOutput()	This line is necessary or you will see no output at all
Sem.Standardized()	This lets you see the standardized regression coefficients
Sem.Smc()	This lets you see the squared multiple correlation
Sem.Mods (4)	Requests modification indices showing only a chi-square of 4 or higher
Sem.TotalEffects()	Requests indirect, direct, and total effects
Sem.Bootstrap(5000)	Requests a bootstrap with 5,000 samples
Sem.ImpliedMoments()	Requests Implied Moments output
Sem.SampleMoments()	Requests Sample Moments output
Sem.Crdiff()	Requests the critical ratios for differences option
Sem.ModelMeansANDIntercepts()	Requests Estimate means and intercepts

Once we have listed the output we want, the next lines of program code will denote the relationships in the model. Unlike the coding with the Plugins, we are not required to note which objects are observable or unobservable. If the coding can not find a specific name in the data file, the coding will treat it as an unobservable. Before noting the relationships, we need to tell AMOS where the data file is. This is accomplished through the Sem.BeginGroup function. AMOS wants to know how many groups you have in your model. If there is only one group, AMOS wants to know where the data file is. You need to save your data file in a directory that AMOS can easily find. Here is the default location where AMOS will look:

C:\Users\username\Appdata\Local\AmosDevelopment\AMOS\VersionNumber(I am using 26)

Depending on how the program is installed, it might also be:

C:\Program Files\IBM\SPSS\AMOS\Version number (26)

I have saved my data in a folder called "AppliedSEM", and the data within that folder is called "Delight". To request that this data be used in the analysis, we need to use the following program statement:

```
Sem.BeginGroup(Sem.AmosDir & "AppliedSEM\Delight.sav")
```

To specify a relationship in the program editor, we need to use the Sem.Astructure function. This function will initially need to know where a single headed arrow is pointing to and then where it came from along with whether a constraint is placed on the relationship. Let's use the same CFA example we did in using the syntax function in the Plugins option. In that example, we have a three construct model of Adaptive Behavior, Customer Delight, and Positive Word of Mouth. Adaptive Behavior had five indicators, so let's address that construct first. To model adapt1 as a reflective observable of the Adaptive Behavior construct (unobservable), we need to use the following code:

```
Sem.AStructure("adapt1 = (1) Adaptive_Behavior + (1) e7)
```

In this program statement, adapt1 is where the arrow is pointing, Adaptive_Behavior construct is where the arrow is pointing from and you will notice at the front is a "(1)", which means the relationship has a constraint of one. Lastly, you will see that an error term is included for the adapt1 variable. With the inclusion of the "+" symbol, you can add another relationship going to adapt1. Notice that the error term is constrained to 1 as well. Here is what the code would look like for all the constructs in the CFA.

```
Sem.AStructure("adapt1 = (1) Adaptive_Behavior + (1) e7")
Sem.AStructure("adapt2 = Adaptive_Behavior + (1) e8")
Sem.AStructure("adapt3   Adaptive_Behavior + (1) e9")
Sem.AStructure("adapt4 = Adaptive_Behavior + (1) e10")
Sem.AStructure("adapt5 = Adaptive_Behavior + (1) e11")

Sem.AStructure("delight1 = (1)Customer_Delight + (1) e1")
Sem.AStructure("delight2 = Customer_Delight + (1) e2")
Sem.AStructure("delight3 = Customer_Delight + (1) e3")

Sem.AStructure("WOM1 = (1)Word_of_Mouth + (1) e4")
Sem.AStructure("WOM2 = Word_of_Mouth + (1) e5")
Sem.AStructure("WOM3 = Word_of_Mouth + (1) e6")
```

Once the relationships have been specified, we need to ask for model fit indices. This is usually done in the program statements after the relationships have been specified. To do this, we need to include the following line:

```
Sem.FitModel()
```

Note we did not request that covariances be included in the CFA analysis. All independent variables should be covaried, and in a CFA all variables are considered independent. With the AmosEngine function in AMOS, it will automatically covary those relationships for you. Unlike AMOS graphics, you do not have to denote that a covariance needs to be added between constructs. Let's take a look at what the final code should look like in Figure 10.63.

C:\Users\uramo\OneDrive\Documents\SEM Teaching\Applied SEM...

File Edit Format Help

```
['Header']
Module MainModule
  'CFA Analysis with three constructs
  'Adaptive_Behavior, Customer_Delight, and Word_of_Mouth
  Public Sub Main()
    Dim Sem As New AmosEngine
    Try
      Sem.TextOutput()
      Sem.Standardized()
      Sem.Smc()

      Sem.BeginGroup(Sem.AmosDir & "AppliedSEM\Delight.sav")
      Sem.AStructure("adapt1 = (1) Adaptive_Behavior + (1) e7")
      Sem.AStructure("adapt2 = Adaptive_Behavior + (1) e8")
      Sem.AStructure("adapt3 = Adaptive_Behavior + (1) e9")
      Sem.AStructure("adapt4 = Adaptive_Behavior + (1) e10")
      Sem.AStructure("adapt5 = Adaptive_Behavior + (1) e11")

      Sem.AStructure("delight1 = (1)Customer_Delight + (1) e1")
      Sem.AStructure("delight2 = Customer_Delight + (1) e2")
      Sem.AStructure("delight3 = Customer_Delight + (1) e3")

      Sem.AStructure("WOM1 = (1)Word_of_Mouth + (1) e4")
      Sem.AStructure("WOM2 = Word_of_Mouth + (1) e5")
      Sem.AStructure("WOM3 = Word_of_Mouth + (1) e6")


      Sem.FitModel()
    Finally
      Sem.Dispose ()
    End Try

  End Sub
End Module
```

Description | Line

Syntax errors | Debug output

Requesting Text output with standardized regression weights and Square multiple correlations.

Relationships from the unobservables to observables.

Request of model fit indices.

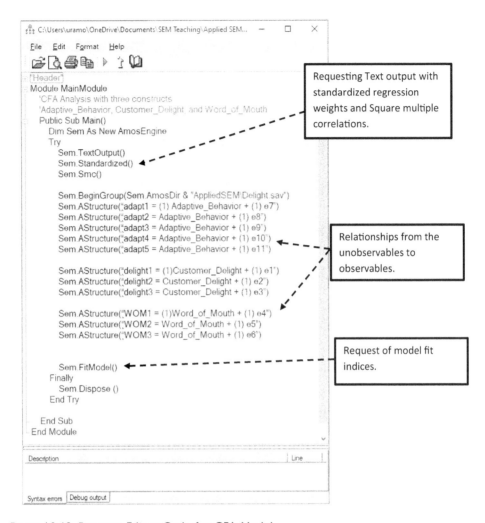

Figure 10.63 Program Editor Code for CFA Model

You need to make sure you save your file after you have finished coding. To run the analysis, you will need to hit the green arrow icon at the top of the screen.

If the analysis runs to completion, the text output should appear in a separate window. The text output will look exactly the same as it does using the graphics interface. See Figure 10.64.

Let's now extend our example to a full structural model where Adaptive Behavior leads to Customer Delight which leads to Positive Word of Mouth. We need to include a path

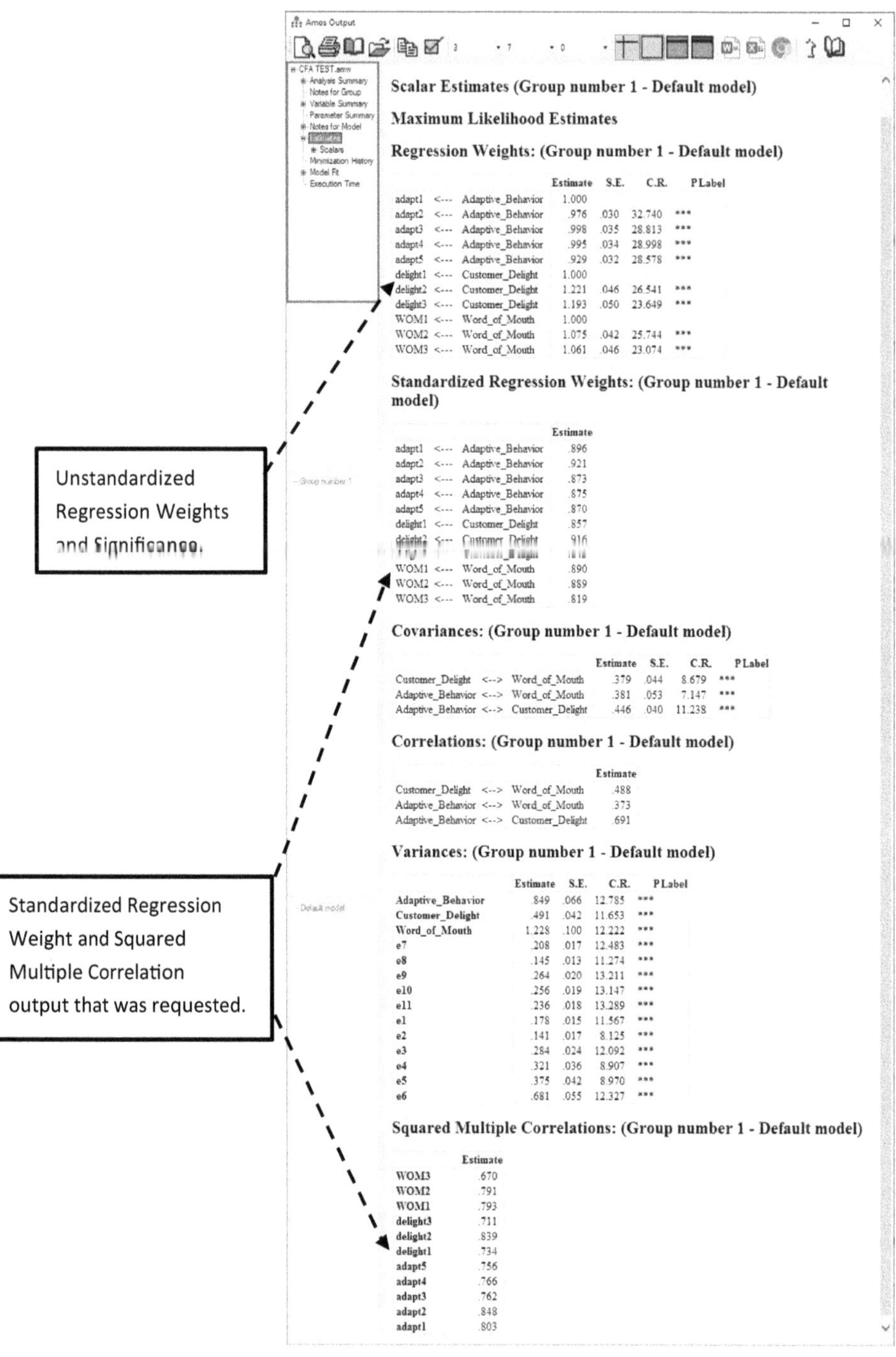

Scalar Estimates (Group number 1 - Default model)

Maximum Likelihood Estimates

Regression Weights: (Group number 1 - Default model)

			Estimate	S.E.	C.R.	P	Label
adapt1	<---	Adaptive_Behavior	1.000				
adapt2	<---	Adaptive_Behavior	.976	.030	32.740	***	
adapt3	<---	Adaptive_Behavior	.998	.035	28.813	***	
adapt4	<---	Adaptive_Behavior	.995	.034	28.998	***	
adapt5	<---	Adaptive_Behavior	.929	.032	28.578	***	
delight1	<---	Customer_Delight	1.000				
delight2	<---	Customer_Delight	1.221	.046	26.541	***	
delight3	<---	Customer_Delight	1.193	.050	23.649	***	
WOM1	<---	Word_of_Mouth	1.000				
WOM2	<---	Word_of_Mouth	1.075	.042	25.744	***	
WOM3	<---	Word_of_Mouth	1.061	.046	23.074	***	

Standardized Regression Weights: (Group number 1 - Default model)

			Estimate
adapt1	<---	Adaptive_Behavior	.896
adapt2	<---	Adaptive_Behavior	.921
adapt3	<---	Adaptive_Behavior	.873
adapt4	<---	Adaptive_Behavior	.875
adapt5	<---	Adaptive_Behavior	.870
delight1	<---	Customer_Delight	.857
delight2	<---	Customer_Delight	.916
[illegible]	[illegible]	[illegible]	[illegible]
WOM1	<---	Word_of_Mouth	.890
WOM2	<---	Word_of_Mouth	.889
WOM3	<---	Word_of_Mouth	.819

Covariances: (Group number 1 - Default model)

			Estimate	S.E.	C.R.	P	Label
Customer_Delight	<-->	Word_of_Mouth	.379	.044	8.679	***	
Adaptive_Behavior	<-->	Word_of_Mouth	.381	.053	7.147	***	
Adaptive_Behavior	<-->	Customer_Delight	.446	.040	11.238	***	

Correlations: (Group number 1 - Default model)

			Estimate
Customer_Delight	<-->	Word_of_Mouth	.488
Adaptive_Behavior	<-->	Word_of_Mouth	.373
Adaptive_Behavior	<-->	Customer_Delight	.691

Variances: (Group number 1 - Default model)

	Estimate	S.E.	C.R.	P	Label
Adaptive_Behavior	.849	.066	12.785	***	
Customer_Delight	.491	.042	11.653	***	
Word_of_Mouth	1.228	.100	12.222	***	
e7	.208	.017	12.483	***	
e8	.145	.013	11.274	***	
e9	.264	.020	13.211	***	
e10	.256	.019	13.147	***	
e11	.236	.018	13.289	***	
e1	.178	.015	11.567	***	
e2	.141	.017	8.125	***	
e3	.284	.024	12.092	***	
e4	.321	.036	8.907	***	
e5	.375	.042	8.970	***	
e6	.681	.055	12.327	***	

Squared Multiple Correlations: (Group number 1 - Default model)

	Estimate
WOM3	.670
WOM2	.791
WOM1	.793
delight3	.711
delight2	.839
delight1	.734
adapt5	.756
adapt4	.766
adapt3	.762
adapt2	.848
adapt1	.803

Figure 10.64 Output for Program Editor

relationship from construct to construct. In the program editor, we can use the relationship code <--, that is, the less than symbol and two dashes, resembling an arrow. If we want to include a relationship path from Adaptive Behavior to Customer Delight, we will add the following program line:

```
Sem.AStructure("Customer_Delight <-- Adaptive_Behavior")
```

Next, let's add the error terms for the unobservable dependent constructs. We can use this arrow symbol again to add error terms. Let's say I want to add the error term for the Customer Delight construct, and I will call it e12. Here is the program code to add that error term:

```
Sem.AStructure("Customer_Delight <-- (1) e12")
```

If we wanted to add a covariance, we could also use this arrow symbol. If I wanted to correlate the error terms for e1 and e2, I would use the following symbol <-->. This will denote a covariance in AMOS. Here is the program code:

```
Sem.AStructure("e1 <--> e2")
```

See Figure 10.6 to view the complete code for the full structural model.

To use the program editor option, you have to pay attention to detail. A missed parenthesis or a misspelled word will create an error message, but this message does not give you a lot of information on why the program is not running the analysis. At times, it can be quite frustrating, but this can be avoided by taking a methodical approach to writing your code and making sure each line is correct before moving on to the next one.

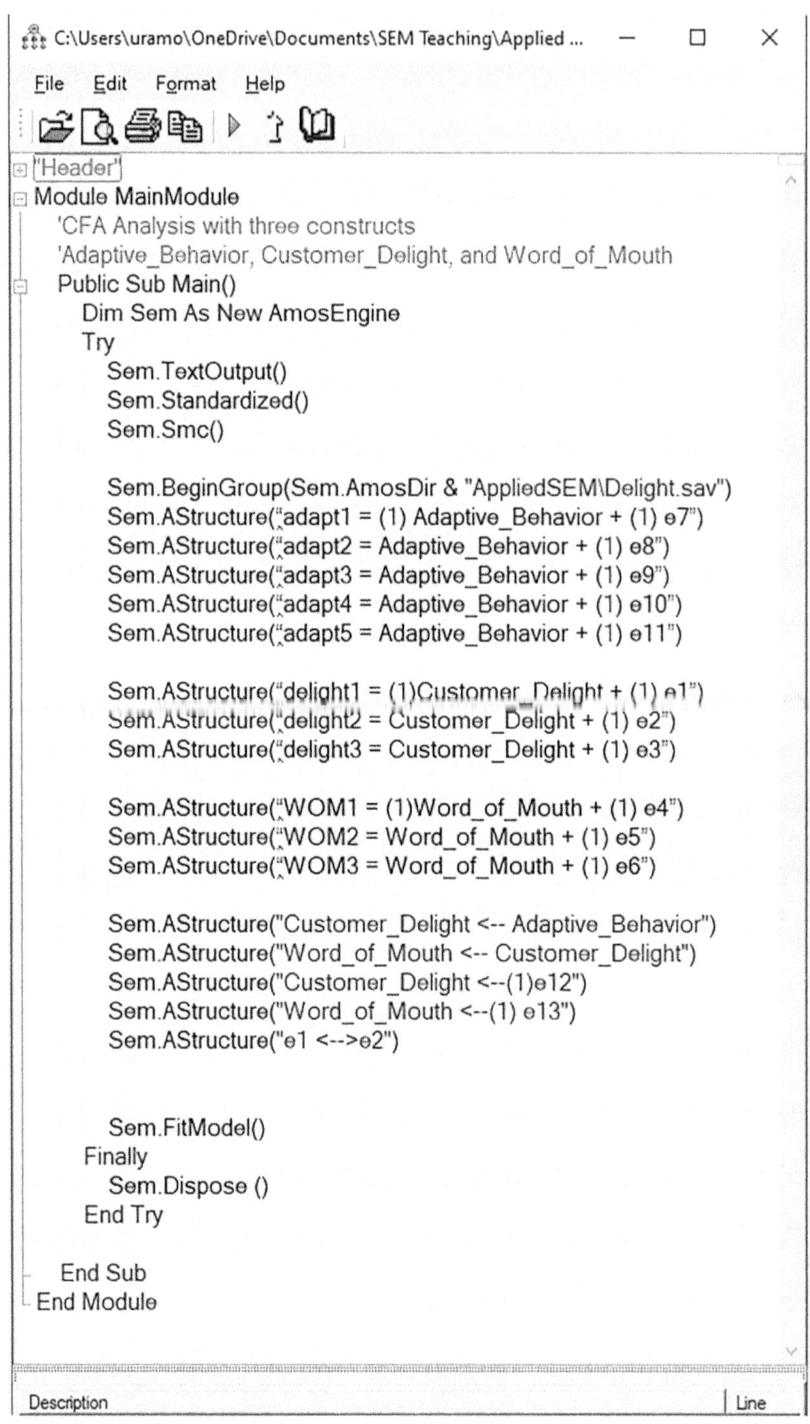

Figure 10.65 Program Editor Code for Full Structural Model

Definitions of Constructs Used in Examples for This Chapter:

Adaptive Behavior: customer's perception that an employee adapted/modified their normal job performance to meet their needs. This adaptation can be through verbal interaction, service performance, or meeting special requests. Construct was measured with a 7-point Likert scale of Strongly Disagree to Strongly Agree.

Customer Delight: customer's profoundly positive emotional state resulting from expectations being exceeded to a surprising degree. Construct was measured with a 7-point Likert scale of Strongly Disagree to Strongly Agree.

Positive Word of Mouth: customer's intention to spread positive information to others about a previous experience. Construct was measured with a 7-point Likert scale of Strongly Disagree to Strongly Agree.

Gratitude: customer's feelings of appreciation or thankfulness to the employee.

Trust in the Retailer: degree to which a customer believes a retailer has the customer's best interest in mind.

Confidence in the Retailer: the belief in the ability of the retailer to perform a service.

Mixture Modeling Discussion:

GPA: Grade point average in undergraduate degree. On a 4-point scale.

GMAT: Graduate program entrance exam. Ranges from 0 to 800.

Finance Score: Score in the undergraduate finance class. On a 4-point scale.

Student Type: Three classifications of student—Excellent, Average, and Below Average

Censored Data Discussion:

Start Year: The year the customer started patronizing the retailer.

Frequency of Purchases: Total number of purchases made while a customer is with a retailer.

Total Sales: Total dollar amount customer has spent with the retailer.

Lifetime: Number of days an individual has been a customer of the retailer.

Status: Current—is currently an active customer of the retailer. Former—customer is no longer patronizing the retailer.

Highlights of the Chapter:

1. When a portion of your sample underrepresents a population, you can use a weighted score in the analysis to give certain underrepresented groups greater influence in the analysis. You can weight scores in SPSS, but AMOS cannot read the weighted scores directly from the data. You need to weight the scores in SPSS and then create a covariance matrix that will be used as the input in AMOS.
2. If your data is non-normal, you can use a bootstrap option to address the non-normality. You need to use a maximum likelihood bootstrap to examine the structural relationships and examine if they fall within a 95% confidence interval. A Bollen-Stine test is also advisable to determine how well your model fits the bootstrap samples.

3. Mixture modeling is where predictions of group classification is made with Bayesian analysis. A "training" data set is often used to aid in predictions. With classification and prediction, AMOS must be allowed to access non-numeric data and also be able to assign cases to groups. The prediction of group assignments is located in the posterior predictions of the Bayesian analysis. Lastly, even with no training data, AMOS can try to assign groups based on the Bayesian analysis.
4. Censored data is where a value is unknown or partially known. This is usually because the value cannot be determined because it represents a future value. In AMOS, Bayesian analysis can be used to estimate the censored data. These future values (or censored) is represented by a greater than symbol in the data. Posterior predictions in the Bayesian analysis will give a probability of the future (censored) value.
5. Non-recursive models are structural models that have a feedback loop. With each construct in a feedback loop, you need to have dedicated predictor variables, also called instrumental variables. Additionally, you need to determine the stability of your feedback loop by examining AMOS's stability index test. Values within −1 to +1 are considered stable.
6. AMOS uses the full information maximum likelihood method to handle missing data. An imputation method is required to use more complex analyses like bootstrapping. AMOS can impute missing data via a regression imputation method. It can also use a Bayesian imputation to perform "multiple imputation".
7. Post-hoc power analysis is a test of power after the sample has been collected. In my opinion, they are not that helpful. Power calculations are best suited in the design phase of research, not in the post-hoc analysis phase.
8. You can perform an exploratory factor analysis with a specification search function in AMOS. The specification search will examine all possible combinations of indicators to unobservable constructs to see what has the best fit. The specification search function can also provide scree plots to show the optimal number of parameters to be estimated in verifying an exploratory factor analysis.
9. In the plugin functions, you can use syntax code to conceptualize and, ultimately, draw your model (or dedicated constructs) in the graphics window. These plugins can be saved and are handy when you have repetitive constructs that need to be added to different models. With the saved plugin, you can insert a model or construct conceptualization with a click of a button.
10. The dedicated program editor will allow you to use a syntax code to run all your analysis and avoid the graphical interface.

References

Allison, Paul D. (2003), "Missing Data Techniques for Structural Equation Modeling", *Journal of Abnormal Psychology*, 112 (4), 545–557.

Arbuckle, James L. (2017), *IBM SPSS AMOS 25 User's Guide*, IBM Corporation.

Appendix

Table of Chi-Square Statistics

Degrees of Freedom	*p = .10*	*p = .05*	*p = .01*	*p = .001*
1	2.71	3.84	6.64	10.83
2	4.60	5.99	9.21	13.82
3	6.25	7.82	11.35	16.27
4	7.78	9.49	13.28	18.47
5	9.24	11.07	15.09	20.52
6	10.64	12.59	16.81	22.46
7	12.01	14.07	18.48	24.32
8	13.36	15.51	20.09	26.13
9	14.68	16.92	21.67	27.88
10	15.98	18.31	23.21	29.59
11	17.27	19.68	24.73	31.26
12	18.54	21.03	26.22	32.91
13	19.81	22.36	27.69	34.53
14	21.06	23.69	29.14	36.12
15	22.30	25.00	30.58	37.70
16	23.54	26.30	32.00	39.25
17	24.76	27.59	33.41	40.79
18	25.99	28.87	34.81	42.31
19	27.20	30.14	36.19	43.82
20	28.41	31.41	37.57	45.32
21	29.61	32.67	38.93	46.79
22	30.81	33.92	40.28	48.26
23	32.00	35.17	41.63	49.72
24	33.19	36.41	42.98	51.17
25	34.38	37.62	44.31	52.62

Index

Note: Page numbers in italic indicate a figure and page numbers in **bold** indicate a table on the corresponding page.

Add an Error Term function 40–41, *59*
Allow non-numeric data option 295, 302, *300*, 304, *305*
alpha, Cronbach's: calculation of 26, 28–29, *28*; limitations of 87–88
alternative models approach 7
alternative structural models *8*, 146
Alt key shortcuts 61
AMOS (Analysis of Moment Structures): function [illegible] 61; graphics window 36–38, *37*; overview of 9; shortcut keys for 61; tips and guidelines for 53–59; *see also specific features*
AMOS Plugins folder 332
Analysis of Moment Structures *see* AMOS (Analysis of Moment Structures)
Analysis Properties function: capabilities of 49, *49*; confirmatory factor analysis with 74–76, *74–76*; Estimate means and intercepts option 265, 314, *314*; icon for *60*; iteration limits in 166; mediation testing with 173–181, *173–181*; Pairwise Parameter Comparison option 227–229; searching for multivariate outliers with 162, 165, *163–164*; shortcut keys for 61; *see also* bootstrapping
Analyze menu commands: Manage Groups 91; Scale 285; *see also* Descriptive Statistics
Assign cases to groups option 300, *300*
assumptions of SEM 8–9
average variance extracted (AVE) 83, 126

badness of fit measure 65–67
Bayesian Analysis 52, *60*; censored data in 305–309, *306–309*; imputation and 316; mixture modeling and 295–302; mixture modeling with *297–298*; shortcut keys for 61
beta 14
bias: bias-corrected confidence intervals 181; bias-corrected percentile method 175, *177*, 290; common method bias 62, 70, 102–109
Big TOE models 33
binary categorical variables 240–244, *240–243*, 259
Bollen-Stine bootstrap 290–293, *291*, *293*
Bootstrap ML option 287, *287*
bootstrapping: Bollen-Stine 290–293, *291*, *293*; mediation testing with 174–180, *174–180*, **180**; Monte Carlo 181, *181*; non-normal data and 166, 287–293, *287–293*; seed number in 194–195, *193–194*; *see also* estimands function
Bootstrap tab *see* bootstrapping
Browse Path Diagram command 55

Calculate Estimates function 49, *60*, 61, 335
categorical moderation: features of 223–229, *224–226*; moderated mediation with 234–231, *235–231*; pairwise parameter comparison and 227–229, *228–229*; treating continuous variables as 227
categorical variables, binary 240–244, *240–243*, 259; *see also* multicategorical independent variables
causation 6–7, **6**
censored data: analysis of 302–309, *303–309*; sample construct definitions for 345
centroid 163
CFA *see* confirmatory factor analysis (CFA)
CFA Syntax plugin 326–337, *326–328*, *330–335*
chain mediation *see* serial mediation
Change Shape function 44, *60*, 73
check syntax function 332
chi-square test: bootstrap distribution of 290–293, *292*; chi-square statistics, table of **347**; confirmatory factor analysis with 108–109, *108*; explanation of 65–67; scree plots based on 322–323, *322*; *see also* metric invariance
clipboard, copying models to 49
coefficient alpha 26
common method bias (CMB) 62, 70, 102–109
common method factors 104–108, *105–108*
Comparative Fit Index (CFI) 66

comparative statistics 66
competitive mediation 170
complementary mediation 170, *171*
composite reliability 28, 87–88
composite variables, in path analysis 128–130, *129*
Computation Summary window *37*
Compute Variable function 84–85, *84*, 199–202, *199*
conceptualization, theory leading to 8
configural invariance 90–93
confirmatory approach to SEM 7–8
confirmatory factor analysis (CFA): composite reliability of 87–88; convergent validity in 83–85; definition of 62–63; discriminant validity in 34, 83–85; error term correlation within constructs in 70, *69*; exploratory factor analysis compared to 63–64, *64*; factor loadings in 62, 64–65, 87–89; heterotrait-monotrait ratio of correlations 85–87; measurement model invariance across groups 90–98; metrics for 65; model fit statistics for 65–67; modification indices for 68; reporting results of 89–90, **89**, **90**; second-order 109–110, *109*; standardized residuals 82, *82*; three construct CFA analysis 71–82; two construct CFA analysis *63*; *see also* measurement model analysis
constrained parameters 98–102, *99–102*
constructs: correlation between 83–85; correlation of errors terms within 70, *69*; formative 115–121, *115–116*; labeling of 73; standardizing look of 57–58; *see also* variables
content validity 33–34
continuous moderators, moderated mediation with 229–234, *230–233*, **234**
continuous variables 227
control variables, adding to structural models 147, *148*
convergent validity 34, 83–85
Copy Model to Clipboard function 49, *60*, 61
correlation: calculation of 4–6, **5**, *5*; versus causation 6–7, **6**; between constructs 83–85; of error terms within construct 70, *69*; heterotrait 86; heterotrait-monotrait ratio of 85–87; monotrait 86–87
correlation matrices: as data input 133–137, *134–137*; mediation testing with 181, *181*
covariance: calculation of 2–4, **3**; covariance matrix 2–4, **3**; diagram symbols for 11; drawing with Draw a Covariance function 40, 56, *59*, 61, 74; Greek notation for 14; between independent variables 55–56; linear patterns in 2, *2*; in mixture modeling 295–296, *296*; model fit and 6; pd. Cov function for 330; in program editor code 341; rearranging 48; standardized residuals and 82, *82*; unmeasured 62–63
Create Dummy Variables command 245
Critical ratios for differences option 228
critical sample size 33
Cronbach's alpha: calculation of 26, *26–28*; limitations of 87–88
Ctrl key shortcuts 61
Current seed option (Seed Manager) 302, *302*

data files, selection of 48
Data Files window *71*, 300, *300*
data imputation 23–25, *24*, *61*, 315–316, *316*
Data Recode function *60*
data screening: impermissible values 19–21, *19–20*, **20–21**; missing data 21–25, *21–22*, **22**, *24–25*, 314–316, *314–316*; respondent issues 17–19, *18*
Define new Estimand function 250
degrees of freedom: calculation of 30–32, *31–32*, *60*; table of chi-square statistics **347**
Delete Objects function 43, *59*
deletion, listwise/pairwise 23–25
delta 14
dependent relationships 9–10, 115, *115–116*
dependent variables 11
Descriptive Statistics: Descriptives function 19–21, *19–20*, **20–21**, 200, 221; Frequencies function 21–25, *21–22*, **22**, *24–25*
Deselect All Objects function 42, *59*, 107
diagrams: browsing 55; examining with loupe 51; symbols in 9–11
direct path effect, diagram symbols for 11
discriminant validity 34, 83–85
distribution, non-normal 165–166
disturbance terms 10
domains, latent growth curve models across 277–281, *278–280*
Drag Properties function 51, *60*, 61, 106
Draw a Covariance function 40, 56, *59*, 61, 74
Draw Latent Variable function 71–72
Draw Observed Variable function 38, *59*, 61
Draw Parameter function *59*
Draw Path function 39–40, 61
Draw Unobservable Variable function 39, *59*, 61
D-Separation Preview function *61*
dummy code: binary categorical variables 240–241, *241*; multicategorical independent variables 244–247, *245*
Dummy Code function 244–247, *245*
Duplicate Objects function 44, *60*

EFA *see* exploratory factor analysis (EFA)
endogenous variables 11
epsilon 14
EQS 9
errors: adding to variables 40–41; correction within full structural model 162; correlation within construct 70, *69*; diagram symbols for 10; error variance invariance 98; in full structural model analysis 166; Greek notation for 14; labeling of 55; in latent growth curve models 270; in measurement model analysis 122–124; missing data 314–316, *315*; in structural model analysis 161; types of 62; for weighted scores *284*, 285

estimands function: for mediation testing with multiple mediators 182–188; for moderated mediation with categorical moderators 236–237, *236–237*; for moderated mediation with continuous moderators 230–233, *231–232*; for moderated mediation with multicategorical independent variables 253–256; for serial mediation *184–188*; serial mediation 188–192, *189–192*
Estimate means and intercepts option 265, 314, *314*
Estimates tab: in CFA sample model 78, *79*; Matrices option in 248; non-normal data and 288; Scalars option in 250, 255
eta 13
Examine Diagram with Loupe function 51, *60*, 61
Execution Time tab 78
exogenous variables 11
exploratory factor analysis (EFA): confirmatory factor analysis compared to 63–64, *64*; with specification search 317–323

F1–F12 shortcut keys 61
face validity 33
factor loadings: definition of 62; standardized 88–89; weak 87
factors: common method 104–108, *105–108*; definition of 62; factor loadings 64–65; factor variance invariance 96, loadings 62, 87, 88–89
feedback loops 310–314, *310–313*
Files in Current Directory window *37*
first order constructs 110
floodlight analysis 205–206, *206*
formative constructs: dependent relationships with 115–116, *115–116*; higher-order formative model for 116–121, *117–121*
formative indicators: definition of 62; identification problems with 111–114, *111–114*; reflective indicators compared to 110–111, *112–114*
freedom, degrees of: calculation of 30–32, *31–32*, *60*; table of chi-square statistics **347**
Frequencies function 21–25, *21–22*, **22**, *24–25*
full indicator interaction method 209–213, *209–212*, **218**
full information maximum likelihood (FIML) 23–25, 314–316, *314–316*
full mediation 170, *171*
full metric invariance *96*
full structural model analysis: control variables in 147–148, *148*; correlation of errors terms within 162; definition of 137; error messages in 161, 166; features of 137–142, *138–142*; moderation testing in 207–220; multiple group analysis in 149–161, *148–160*, 162, **162**; multivariate outliers in 162–164, *163–164*; non-normal distribution in 165–166; reporting results of 142, **143**, 162, **162**; specification search for 143–146, *143–146*; trimming and fit of 143–146, *143–146*

functions: listing by icon 38–53; quick reference of 59–61; shortcut keys for 61; *see also specific functions*

gamma 14, 31
Gaskin, James 87, 206
generalized least squares (GLS) 88
Goodness-of-Fit Index and Adjusted Goodness-of-Fit Index (GFI/AGFI) 66–67
graphics window 36–38, *37*, 41
Greek notation 13–15, **14**, *15*
grid lines, aligning objects with 58
Grouping Variable button 92, *92*
groups: creation of 91–92; measurement model invariance across 90–98; multiple group analysis of 149–161, *148–160*; parameter constraints across 98–102, *99–102*; parameter labels across 93–94, *94*
Groups Window *37*
Group Value button 92, *92*
Group Variable function 150

Harman's single factor test 102
heterotrait correlations 86
heterotrait-monotrait ratio of correlations (HTMT) 85–87
Heywood case 88
higher-order formative construct model 116–121, *117–121*
high level moderator tests 202, 217–219, *217*

icon ribbon: listing of functions in 36, 38–53, *38*; quick reference of 59–61; *see also specific functions*
identification: degrees of freedom 30–32, *31–32*; under-identification 32; just-identified models 29, 32–33; near identified models 32–33; over-identification 29–30
impermissible values, screening data for 19–21, *19–20*, **20–21**
imputation 23–25, *24*, *61*, 315–316, *316*
Incremental Fit Index (IFI) 66
independent variables: binary 240–244, *240–243*, 259; covariances between 55–56; definition of 11; multicategorical 244–259, *245–246*, *248–256*, **257–258**
index of moderated mediation 238–239
indicators: choosing 29; deleting 29; formative 62, 110–114, *112–114*; reflecting 47; reflective 110–111; resizing 56; rotation of 47, 56–57; single versus multiple 12, *12*
indices: model fit 66–67; modification 68, 74, 81, *81*
indirect effect calculations: with multiple mediators 182–188; with serial mediation 188–192
indirect only mediation 170, *171*
instrumental variables 310–311
interaction term method 197–206, *198–199*
interaction term method of moderation testing **200**, *200–206*

Interface Properties function *60*
invariance 90–98; configural 90–93; error variance 98; factor variance 98; metric 93–102, *96*; scalar 98
item measures, notation for 13
iteration limits 166

Johnson-Neyman point 205–206, *206*
just-identified models 29, 32–33

keyboard shortcuts 61
ksi 13
kurtosis 165

labels, error term 55
lambda 14
landscape orientation of AMOS page 53
latent common method factor 104–109
latent constructs, Greek notation for 13–14
latent growth curve models: across two domains 277–281, *278–280*; features of 260–269, *261–268*; with nonlinear patterns 273–277, *275–277*; predictors in 269–273, *270–273*; reporting results of 273, **274**; sample construct definitions for 281
linear interpolation 24–25, *25*
linear patterns 2, *2*
Link function *61*
LISREL 9
List Parameters function *61*
List Variables function 41–42, *59*
listwise/pairwise deletion 23
longitudinal data 260
loops, feedback 310–314, *310–313*
low level moderator tests 202, 217–219, *217*

Mahalanobis distance 163–164, *164*
Mainsub area (plugins) 325–332
Manage Groups window *60*, 91–92, *91*, 149
Manage Models window *60*, 101, 271–272, *271*
Manifest Variables 10
marker-variable technique 102–104
matched-pairs method 214–219, *214–217*, **218**
matrices: correlation 133–137, *134–137*, 181, *181*; covariance 2–4, **3**
Matrices option 248
"matrix not positive definite" error message 161
Matrix Representation function *61*
maximum likelihood estimation 8
mean, calculation of 198–199, *198*
mean centered variables 198–199, *199*, **200**, 221–223
mean splitting data 233
measurement errors: diagram symbols for 10; types of 62
measurement intercepts 98
measurement model analysis: common method bias in 102–109; definition of 12; dependent relationships with formative constructs 115–116, *115–116*; error messages in 122–124; exploratory factor analysis 63–64, *64*; formative indicators 110–111, *112–114*; full metric invariance 93–98, *96*; higher-order formative model 116–121, *117–121*; measurement model invariance 90–98; partial metric invariance 98–102; reflective indicators 110–111; sample construct definitions for 124–125; *see also* confirmatory factor analysis (CFA); exploratory factor analysis (EFA)
measurement model invariance 90–98; configural 90–93; error variance 98; factor variance 98; scalar 98
measurement residuals model comparison 98
measures: errors in 10; notation for 13; of unobserved constructs 11–13, *11–13*; validity of 33–34; *see also* measurement model analysis
mediation: with binary categorical independent variables 242–244, *242–243*; bootstrap seed number in 194–195, *193–194*; definition of 170; with multicategorical independent variables 247–251, *248–251*; with multiple mediators 182–188, *182–188*; sample construct definitions for 195–196; serial 188–192, *189–192*; testing for 172–181, *173–181*, **180**; types of 170–171, *171*; *see also* moderated mediation
method bias 62, 70, 102–109
metric invariance: full 93–98, *96*; partial 98–102
MIMIC (multiple indicator multiple cause model) 111–114
Minimization History tab 81
missing covariance error message 124, *124*
missing data: causes and assessment of 21–23, *21–22*, **22**; screening data for 23–25, *24–25*, 314–316, *314–316*
mixed model method 207–209, *207–208*, **218**
mixture modeling 293–302, *294–302*, 345
Model Comparison option 96–97, *97*, 155
model development approach 7
model fit: CFA sample model 81, *80*; definition of 6; feedback loop models 311, 314, *313*; latent growth curve models 265–269; multiple group analysis *160*, 161; non-normal data and 288, *291*; path analysis 131–133, *131*; specification search and 321–322; statistics for 65–68; structural models *143–146*
Modeling Lab *60*
models: conceptualizing with program editor 337–344, *337–338*, *341–344*; copying to clipboard 49; printing 52; repositioning of 51; resizing 51; saving current 50; *see also specific models*
Models and Computational summary window *75*
moderated mediation: with categorical moderators 234–238, *235–237*; with continuous moderators 229–234, *230–233*, **234**; with multicategorical independent variables 251–256, *252–256*, **257–258**; sample construct definitions for 259

moderation: definition of 197; in path models 197–206; *see also* moderation testing
moderation testing 234; categorical moderators in 223–229, *224–226*; full indicator interaction method of 209–213, *209–212*; interaction term method of 197–206, *198–199*, **200**, *200–206*; matched-pairs method of 214–219, *214–217*; mean center versus Z score in 221–223, *221–223*; mixed model method of 207–209, *207–208*; moderated mediation with categorical moderators 234–238, *235–237*; moderated mediation with continuous moderators 229–234, *230–233*, **234**; reporting results of 219, **218**, **220**; sample construct definitions for 238–239
modification indices 68, 74, 81, *81*
mole variable 103
monotrait correlations 86–87
Monte Carlo bootstraps 181, *181*
Move Objects function 43, *59*, 61
Move Parameter Values function 47–48, *60*
MPLUS 9
multicategorical independent variables 244–258; features of 244–247, *245–246*; mediation with 247–251, *248–251*; moderated mediation with 251–256, *252–256*, **257–258**; sample construct definitions for 259
multicollinearity 8, 34, 111, 161
Multiple Group Analysis 60
Multiple Group Analysis *60*; with full structural models 149–161, *148–160*, 162, **162**; with measurement models 92–93, *92–93*, *95*
multiple imputation 316
multiple indicators 12, *12–13*
multivariate outliers 162–164, *163–164*

names, variable 53–54
Name Unobserved Variables command 55
near identified models 32–33
negative linear patterns 2, *2*
noise, definition of 62
nonlinear patterns, in latent growth curve models 274–277, *275–277*
non-normal data: bootstrapping and 287–293, *287–293*; in full structural model analysis 165–166
Non-Normed Fit Index 66
non-positive matrix error message 161
non-recursive models 310–314, *310–313*
non-significant common method bias tests 109
Normed Fit Index (NFI) 66
"not an observed variable" error message 124, *124*
Notes for Model option 122, 313
null models 66
Nunnally, Jum C. 26, 33

Object Properties function 50, *60*; confirmatory factor analysis 73, *73*; measurement model analysis 106–108; shortcut keys for 61; variance labels in 295–296, *296*
objects: changing shape of 44; deletion of 43; deselection of 43; duplication of 44; moving 43; properties of 50; selection of 42–43; spacing of 58
observed power analysis 317, *317*
observed variables: diagram symbols for 10; drawing 38; entering into models 327, *327*; resizing 56; standardizing look of 57–58
optional path function 319
output, viewing 49, 58–59
overfitting 66
over-identification 29–30

pages: portrait versus landscape orientation of 53; zooming in/out 51
pairwise parameter comparison, categorical moderation and 227–229, *228–229*
parallel mediation 182
Parameter Constraints option 106
Parameter Format window *37*
parameter labels: across groups 93–94, *94*; moving 47–48; for multiple group analysis 152–153, *152*
parameters: constrained 98–102, *99–102*; definition of 13
Parameter Summary tab 30, 77, *78*
partial least squares SEM (PLS-SEM) 166–167
partial mediation 170, *171*
partial metric invariance 98–102
path analysis: correlation matrices as data input in 133–137, *134–137*; definition of 128; features of 128–133, *129–131*; model fit in 131–133, *131*; moderation testing for 197–206, **218**; pd. Path function 329, *330*
paths: constraints across groups 98–99, *99*; diagrams, browsing 55; drawing 39–40; rearranging 48; *see also* path analysis
pd. Caption function 324
pd. Cov function 324, 330
pd. Observed function 324, 327, *327*
pd. Path function 324, 329, *330*
pd. Reposition function 332
pd. Unobserved function 324, 328, *328*
Perform bootstrap option 287, *287*
phi 14
pick-a-point approach to moderation testing 202–206, *202–206*
PLS 9
plugins: CFA Syntax 326–337, *325–328*, *330–335*; creating models with 323–337, *325–328*, *330–335*; launching 333; names of 325
Plugins function: creating models with 323–337, *325–328*, *330–335*; shortcut keys for 61
Plugins menu commands *61*; Draw Covariances 56; Name Unobserved Variables 55; Resize Observed Variables 56
portrait orientation of AMOS page 53
positive definite error 161
positive linear patterns 2
Posterior Predictive Distributions 298–299, *298–299*

post-hoc power analysis 317, *317*
predictive validity 34
predictors, in latent growth curve models 269–273, *270–273*
Preserve Symmetries function 45–47, *60*
Print function 52, *60*, 61
probing the interaction 202–206
Proceed with the Analysis button 108
program editor: conceptualizing models with 337–344, *337–338*, *341–344*; features of 323–325

quadratic data 274–275

random error 62
Raykov's Rho 28
Read Data button 150
recursive model 77, 310
Redo Change function 52, *60*, 61
Reference Variables 10
Reflect Indicators function 47, *60*
reflective indicators 110–111
regions of significance 205–206
regression coefficient: of binary categorical variables 241, *241*; of multicategorical independent variables 246–247, *246*
Regression imputation option 315
Regression Weight field: bootstrapping and 290–293, *289–290*; in CFA sample model 73
regression weights 341–342, *342*
relative chi-square/df tests 133
Relative Fit Index (RFI) 66
relative indirect effects 242–244, *242–243*
reliability analysis 25–29, *26–28*; composite reliability 28, 87–88; Cronbach's alpha 26, *26–28*, 87–88; of weighted scores 286, *286*
Replace Missing Values option 24–25, *24–25*
replacing rule 147
Reposition Model function 51, *60*
Residual Moments option 82
residuals 10, 82, *82*
Resize Model function *60*
Resize Observed Variables command 56
Resize Whole Model function 51
respondent abandonment 17
respondent issues, screening data for *18*
respondent misconduct 17–19
result reporting: confirmatory factor analysis 89–90, **89**, **90**, **143**; full structural model analysis 142; higher-order formative model 121; latent curve growth models 273, **274**; mediation tests 180, **180**; moderated mediation with continuous moderators 234, **234**; moderation tests 219, **218**, **220**; multicategorical moderated mediation tests 256, **257** **258**; multiple group analysis 162, **162**
Rigdon, Edward E. 30
Root Mean Square Error of Approximation (RMSEA) 66–67, 133
Rotate Indicators function 47, 56–57, *60*

rule of ten 33
Run Analysis button 74

sample sizes 33
saturated models *see* just-identified models
Save Current Model function 50, *60*
Save function, shortcut keys for 61
Save Standardized Values as Variables option 221
scalar invariance 98
Scalars option 237; *see also* Define new Estimand function
scatter plots 322
Schreiber, James B. 33
scores, weighted: calculation of 282–286, *283–286*; error messages for *284*, 285; reliability analysis of *284*
scree plots 322–323, *322–323*
search *see* specification search
second-order confirmatory factor analysis model 109–110, *109*
Seed Manager *61*, 302, *302*
seed numbers 172; for Bayesian analysis 301, *302*; in bootstrapping *193–194*
Select All Objects function 42, *59*
Select Data File function 48, *60*, 61
Select One Object at Time function 42, *59*, 61
SEM *see* structural equation modeling (SEM)
Sem.AStructure() function 339–340, *340*, *344*
Sem.BeginGroup() function 339
Sem.Bootstrap() function 339
Sem.Crdiff() function 339
Sem.FitModel() function 340
Sem.ImpliedMoments() function 339
Sem.ModelMeansANDIntercepts() function 339
Sem.Mods() function 339
Sem.SampleMoments() function 339
Sem.Smc() function 339
Sem.Standardized() function 339
Sem.TextOutput() function 339
Sem.TotalEffects() function 339
serial mediation 188–192, *189–192*
series mean (SMEAN) 24
setting the metric 65
shared variance 84–86
shortcut keys 61
Show Whole Page function *60*
significance, regions of 205–206
significant common-bias method tests 108–109
single indicators 12, *12–13*
skew 165
SMARTPLS 9
Snap Spacing option 58
Sobel testing 172
Space Objects Horizontally function *61*
Space Objects Vertically function *61*
spacing 58
specification search: exploratory factor analysis with 319–323; structural models and 143–146, *143–146*

Specification Search function 52, *60*, 143–146, *143–146*
spotlight analysis 207
Stability Index 311–313
standard deviation 198–199, *198*
standardized factor loadings 88–89
standardized residuals 82, *82*
Standardized Root Mean Square Residual (SRMR) 66–67
standardized values, saving as variables 221
statistics, model fit 65–68
Statistics option 27, *26–27*
Stop Calculating Estimate function *61*
strictly confirmatory approach 7
structural equation modeling (SEM): advantages of 1; assumptions of 8–9; as causal modeling approach 6–7; conceptualization in 8; confirmatory approach to 7–8; covariance-based approach to 2–4, **3**; definition of 1; diagram symbols in 9–11; Greek notation in 13–15, **14**, *15*; identification with 29–32; software for 9
structural intercept comparison 272, *272*
structural models: alternative models for 146; measurement models compared to 12; non-recursive models 310–314, *310–313*; partial least squares SEM (PLS-SEM) 166–167; path analysis 128–137; sample construct definitions for 167; simple example of a variance based SEM (PLS-SEM) 166–167; *see also* full structural model analysis; moderation testing
structural relationships, Greek notation for 13
summary data, mediation testing with 181, *181*
symbols, diagram 9–11
symmetries, preservation of 45–47
"Syntax is Ok" message 332
systematic error 62

theory, conceptualization and 8
Title function 41, *59*
titles, graphics window 41
total effects 174
Touch Up function 48, *60*, 61
Transform menu: Compute Variable command 84–85, *84*, 199–201, *199*; Create Dummy Variables command 244; Replace Missing Values option 24–25, *24–25*
trimming of structural models *143–146*
troubleshooting *see* errors
Tucker Lewis Index (TLI) 66
two group analysis 149–161

under-identification 32
Undo Change function 52, *60*, 61
unidentified model errors 123–124, *123*
unidimensionality of a construct 9, 111
unique variance 62
unmeasured covariance 62–63
unobserved constructs: drawing 39, 71–72; entering into models 328, *328*; measurement of 11–13, *11–13*; standardizing look of 57–58
user-defined estimands 181–188, *184–188*

validity 33–34; convergent 83–85; discriminant 34, 83–85
variables: adding error terms to 40–41; composite 128–130, *129*; control 147–148, *148*; covariances between 55–56; dependent 11; independent 11; latent 9–10; listing 41–42; mean centered 198–199, *199*, **200**, 221–223; for measurement model examples 124, 167; name display for 53–54; resizing 56; saving standardized values as 221; standardizing look of 57–58; Z scores 221–223, *221–223*; *see also* binary categorical variables; multicategorical independent variables; observed variables; unobserved constructs
Variable Summary output 77, *77*
variance: calculation of 2; in mixture modeling 295–296, *296*; *see also* covariance
variance-based SEM (PLS-SEM) 166–167
View Interface Properties function 61
View Output function 49, 58–59, *60*, 61
View Text button 76

Weight Cases function 282–286, *283–286*
weighted scores: calculation of 282–286, *283–286*; error messages for *284*, 285; reliability analysis of *284*
Write a Program function *61*

yea-saying 17

zeta 14
Zoom-in function 50, *60*, 61
Zoom on Specific Area function 50
Zoom-out function 50, 61
Zoom Page function 51, 61
Z scores 221–223, *221–223*

For Product Safety Concerns and Information please contact our EU
representative GPSR@taylorandfrancis.com
Taylor & Francis Verlag GmbH, Kaufingerstraße 24, 80331 München, Germany

www.ingramcontent.com/pod-product-compliance
Ingram Content Group UK Ltd.
Pitfield, Milton Keynes, MK11 3LW, UK
UKHW031042080625
459435UK00013B/561

* 9 7 8 0 3 6 7 4 3 5 2 6 4 *